The Computer
and Literary Studies

THE COMPUTER
AND LITERARY STUDIES

edited by
A. J. AITKEN, R. W. BAILEY, AND
N. HAMILTON-SMITH

at the University Press, Edinburgh

© 1973
Edinburgh University Press
22 George Square, Edinburgh
ISBN 0 85224 232 8

North America
Aldine · Atherton, Inc.
529 South Wabash Avenue, Chicago

Library of Congress
Catalog Card Number 72-79287

Printed in Great Britain by
T. & A. Constable Ltd, Edinburgh

CONTENTS

Preface

The computer's principal attraction to the literary scholar lies in its ability to store, commonly in the physical form of magnetic tape, large tracts of text—corpuses of over one million words are now becoming common—and to search these at great speed and with super-human reliability for occurrences of specified words, word sets, alliterating syllables or whatever else the scholar chooses and can specify explicitly and unambiguously, and to isolate and count the significant occurrences. With its help, tasks which human beings have in the past carried out and often still do carry out with simpler aids but at great cost in time and tedium, can now be accomplished far less painfully, as some of the papers in the opening and closing sections of this book illustrate. Robinson's and Bailey's plan for a 'secondary index' (pp. 9-10), for example, illustrates one way in which the computer's retrieval facilities can be used to maximize the information contained in a limited body of data, overcoming the necessity for expensive and time-consuming multiple copying. Equally, we can now hope to accomplish projects so large, detailed and complex that only the computer's tireless capacity for manipulating and quantifying vast numbers of small details is equal to them, projects such as those described in Ott's paper on p. 199, and several other papers in the same or the preceding section. An additional motive for the application of the computer to literary problems, though it is seldom the sole one, is advanced in several papers in the central sections of this book: the computer's freedom from *parti pris*, from the natural human tendency unconsciously to doctor the data by overlooking contrary items of evidence so as to reach preconceived results.

This is not to say that the computer can relieve the human investigator from his own essential responsibilities—for the choice of the details the computer is to operate on and the operations it is to perform, for ensuring that these justify the human and computer effort applied to them, and for the evaluation of the results. Nor, for that matter, has the computer by any means removed all the tedium from lexicological, textual and metrical investigations. Frequently, as the papers by Bromwich, Fortier and McConnell, Dilligan and Bender, Waite, and Kliman remind us, these consist of a succession of steps in which a good deal of plodding human effort in checking and in entering new portions of information or settling uncertainties by human decision intervenes between the more repetitive and more extensive tasks handled by the computer. An important decision in any piece of literary computing is the allocation of labour between the literary scholar, the programmer (or the literary scholar acting as his own programmer) and the computer, the time of none of whom is free, so as to achieve the most economical overall balance.

Even if he should make the time to acquire for himself some knowledge of programming and of the relevant branches of mathematics, the beginner in literary computing will do well to enlist the collaboration of a friendly programmer and, for many of the kinds of study described in this book, a statistician. But before embarking on his project he will be well advised to pursue some research of his own to learn whether the text on which he wishes to pursue his investigation or some equally suitable text already exists in computer-readable form and whether programs to perform the same operations have already been written. This will call for a study of current and earlier issues of the journal *Computers and the Humanities*, which offers the completest lists of such information, and similar lists in other more specialized periodicals or newsletters such as *Calculi* (issued from the Kiewit Computation Centre, Dartmouth College), *Computers amd Medieval Data Processing* (from the Institut d'Études Médiévales of the University of Montreal), *Informatie Nederlandse Lexikologie* (from the Instituut voor Nederlandse Lexicologie, Leiden, Holland), and the University of Manchester Regional Computer Centre's valuable Literary and Linguistic Newsletter (now regrettably discontinued).

Having ascertained that the programs and texts in which he is interested do indeed exist, he may well discover, doubtless with expert help, that the difficulties of converting programs designed for one installation for use in another are formidable, though not necessarily insuperable, so that it will be an open question whether conversion or the writing of new programs on lines suggested by the existing ones is more economical. On the other hand, he may find that the conversion of bodies of text is less difficult, though probably not direct or instantaneous. He will also wish to consider, before he completes the negotiations to copy the text, whether the conventions of character set, punctuation and referencing it employs are adequate to his own purposes and how much editing of the text will be necessary before he can use it. In all these respects, no agreements leading to standardization, which could save vast numbers of hours of human and computer time, have yet been reached. Tallentire's timely plea (p. 39) for the provision of complete statistical appendices to concordances highlights one area where standardization of practice could avoid much frustration. For an attempt to overcome some of these limitations for one widely used program package, see the paper by Berry-Rogghe and Crawford on p. 309, and for advantages derivable from the availability of existing computer-readable texts, those of Waite and of Kliman.

Most local computing centres are likely to contain one or two computer scientists who can offer guidance in such matters. Best equipped of all to offer practical help, however, are those centres specializing in humanistic computing, of which, alas, too few as yet exist. For a description of the work carried out in one such centre, the reader should turn to the final two papers of this book. Other centres with similar activities can be found among the addresses of contributors listed on p. 345.

If, however, a new project demands the establishment of an independent body of data, those embarking on it would surely be helped by Schneider's account (p. 275) of the sorts of problems and considerations involved in this. And his 'best-buy' account of optical scanning and, in passing, other methods of data-input (p. 283) will repay careful consideration by anyone concerned with this stage of a project. Several papers include references to alternative methods of publication of output—as 'hard copy', by microfiche, by microfilm or simply by magnetic tape as a basis for further interrogation by computer (see especially the papers of Robinson and Bailey and of Kiss and his associates). A solution to the problem of output in exotic scripts is described by Hockey on p. 291.

One means which is open to anyone seeking guidance or cooperative help in any of these directions is to attend one of the increasingly frequent conferences on literary computing, notices of which normally appear in the periodicals mentioned above. The papers which make up this book are an outcome of one such conference. This was the Second Symposium on the Uses of Computers in Literary Research, held in the University of Edinburgh, 27th to 30th March 1972, under the auspices of that University's Institute for Advanced Studies in the Humanities. This symposium was a successor to a first symposium on the same subject held in Cambridge in March 1970, organized by Professor Roy Wisbey, then Director of the University of Cambridge's Literary and Linguistic Computing Centre, and Mr Michael Farringdon of the Department of Computer Science, the University College of Swansea. It is intended that a third symposium will follow in Cardiff in 1974. The Edinburgh symposium was organized by a committee, elected by the participants of the Cambridge symposium, consisting of Professor R. F. Churchhouse of the University College of Cardiff as chairman, Mr Farringdon, Mr Neil Hamilton-Smith of the Edinburgh Regional Computing Centre, and the undersigned; and, by later co-option, Professor Wisbey, and Professor John Lyons of the University of Edinburgh (representing the committee of Edinburgh's Institute for Advanced Studies). Most of the detailed management of the Symposium fell to Miss Jane Fingland, secretary of the Institute for Advanced Studies, and as well as attending to all that the organizing committee asked of her and much that it forgot, Miss Fingland also had a major hand in assisting the editors in assembling the contributions during the early stages of the compilation of this book.

Though the second symposium, like the first, was intended in the first instance as a means of meeting and exchange for scholars in this field from the British Isles, it was open to all and in the event not only attracted a somewhat larger total number of participants than did its Cambridge predecessor (100 as against 64) but included an even higher number from overseas. This finds its reflection in the list of contributors to this volume, no less than 23 of whom, out of 36, come from a range of European and of the Transatlantic nations. As with the Cambridge symposium, the Edinburgh one was intended to concern itself with 'literary' applications of computers, that is, those relating to literary language or based on the study of written texts, but in general leaving to other conferences other aspects of language study. The one paper which lies beyond these limits (that of Kiss and his associates, p. 153) was included as a valuable summing-up of a major local enterprise of research in linguistic computing. It also has implications for, as well as analogies with, literary studies of lexical co-occurrences and fits congruously enough alongside the papers on that subject within this volume.

To a limited extent this book may be regarded as a sequel to *The Computer in Literary and Linguistic Research* edited by Roy A. Wisbey (Cambridge University Press, 1971) which consists of a selection of revised versions of some of the papers read at the 1970 Cambridge symposium. Berry-Rogghe's paper on collocations (p. 103), Hockey's on output in Persian characters (p. 291), and perhaps all three of the papers on programming, can be regarded as carrying further themes already opened by the same contributors or others in the Cambridge volume. But only one other contributor is shared with that volume, and the two differ considerably in overall emphasis as well as, naturally, in detailed content, notably in the greater weight here of papers concerned with aspects of computational stylistics, collocations and textual and metrical problems.

Of the 34 short papers delivered at the Edinburgh symposium, several were either not submitted for publication or not submitted within the rather stringent time-limits imposed. A few papers, valuable enough in themselves, were excluded as inappropriate to the volume because, though the conclusions set out had indeed been reached with some computer help, the papers themselves were all but exclusively concerned with the literary problems rather than with the interaction of the investigator and his problem with the computer and its input and output ancillaries. In other words, the 26 papers printed here are chosen primarily as illustrating some of the ways the computer can help literary studies—generating dictionary citations, managing elaborate collections of data, producing lexical statistics, quantifying word frequencies or frequencies of occurrences of certain words in certain sentence positions, and so on—rather than as discussions of literary text or literature itself.

It is true that the book does include certain papers which offer illuminating and important statements on stylistics, literary lexicology, textual interrelationships and prosody, which students of these subjects will wish to examine. But its central value lies in the range and variety of proven techniques it describes for exploring and managing textual data with computer help. With some judicious skipping of the technical and statistical refinements, it should also be readable by literary scholars inexpert in computing or mathematics who wish to inform themselves how the computer's abilities to store, sort, retrieve, classify and count might be harnessed to their own research.

In producing the book, our task has been considerably eased by the authors' in general faithful compliance with the time limits imposed and the styles prescribed by the science editor of Edinburgh University Press, and by the speed and skill with which the Press dispatched a text that posed a large number of editorial and typographical problems.

A. J. Aitken
University of Edinburgh
November 1972

Applications to lexicography

J.L.ROBINSON,
R.W.BAILEY

Computer-produced microfilm in lexicography: toward a dictionary of early modern English

The plan for a series of regional and period dictionaries outlined by Sir William Craigie as early as 1919 has borne fruit in considerable lexicographical activity in the last fifty years. Of the dictionaries he envisaged, the *Dictionary of American English*—in large part the result of Craigie's immense energy—was the first to be completed, and the *Scottish National Dictionary* will soon follow, thanks to the unstinting efforts of David Murison. Fascicles of other dictionaries in Craigie's plan—the *Middle English Dictionary* and the *Dictionary of the Older Scottish Tongue*—continue to appear at regular intervals, and the promise of long-term support from the Canada Council suggests that we will eventually have a new dictionary of Old English under the editorship of C.J.E.Ball and Angus Cameron. An instalment of the new supplement to the *Oxford English Dictionary* will appear this year, though its scope is largely restricted to developments in English vocabulary in the twentieth century. One significant gap yet remains: the period from 1475 to the end of the nineteenth century, the portion of the English lexicon that Craigie assigned to two period dictionaries: an 'Early Modern English Dictionary' responsible for developments from 1475 to 1700, and a later dictionary giving a detailed treatment of vocabulary from 1700 to the present day.

When we began in 1966 to consider what contribution we might make toward filling the earlier half of the gap, we were faced with a variety of problems. First, we confronted a huge collection of citation slips for the Early Modern period that had grown under the editorship of the late Professor Charles C.Fries of the University of Michigan but had been allowed to run to weed, untended, for about thirty years. This uneven but still valuable resource consists of slips obtained from the Oxford editors at the end of the 1920s and a considerable body of additional slips collected through a substantial reading program supervised by Fries and his associates in the 1930s. Though some editorial work was carried out under Fries' direction, the work was indefinitely postponed in the early 1940s so that the limited resources for lexicography at the University of Michigan might be devoted entirely to the *Middle English Dictionary*, the chronologically earlier and more advanced project. In seeking to revive the project, our first endeavor was to analyze this collection and evaluate its present worth in order to determine what would have to be done before editorial work could resume. But at the same time we had to consider the limitations on financial support available for such work, since it would have been disingenuous if not foolhardy to assume that an adequate dictionary could be produced in the few years that governmental or private sources would be willing to budget.

Some earlier publications document our attempts to solve the problem of making existing materials available to the scholarly community in a useful form (*see* the references at the end of this paper). On this occasion, we give a more detailed account of the EMnE citation file than has hitherto been made public and outline some procedures we have adopted to maximize the value of the materials as they now exist. Although these procedures respond to the accident of inheriting a partially completed lexicographical file, nothing in our plan, we believe, is necessarily limited to the particular circumstances of our work with Early Modern English. We hope that others will find techniques similar to those we have developed useful in dealing with large bodies of linguistic data—not only lexicographical files, but also data obtained for linguistic atlases, historical grammars, and the like, in those instances where a long delay is anticipated between collection, sorting, and the completion of an edited work.

As it presently stands, the citation file for the 'Early Modern English Dictionary' (EMED) consists of a little over three million slips recording (in the usual way) an entry word, date of citation, illustrative text, and bibliographical information. In the summer of 1968, we examined 21,401 slips from the early entries for the letter G and believe that this sample, though it amounts to less than one per cent of the whole, fairly represents the character of the entire collection. A little more than half the slips (51·3 per cent) were used in the preparation of the *OED* and its 1933 *Supplement*. The remaining slips were collected by the EMED staff and a force of some 460 volunteer readers trained and supervised by Fries (a contribution amounting to 45·3 per cent of the present file). Further expansion was made through acquisition of slips prepared for Tilley's proverb dictionary, a collection of agricultural vocabulary made by F. R. Ray, and several similar bodies of specialized material.

The citations themselves are of two principal types: the majority are handwritten excerpts copied from EMnE texts and selected to illustrate particular usages. For the most part, these consist of complete sentences ranging from half a dozen to fifty words of text; they are unfortunately subject to the whims of human frailty and are sometimes legible only with difficulty. The second type derives from an intensive reading program undertaken by Fries in the Ann Arbor offices of the project; these slips consist of cuttings from multiply produced photocopies of fifty-seven texts specially prepared for the work. Editorial assistants marked up to 100 words from each page of each text and the cuttings were then distributed through the collection under the appropriate entry form. Titles were selected by Fries to supply two needs: to supplement technical and other vocabulary neglected by the Oxford editors, and to ensure adequate coverage of common usages in order to counterbalance the penchant of outside volunteers for the unusual. About 80 per cent of the present collection consists of handwritten slips, 20 per cent of photocopies and a few actual cuttings from EMnE books made by zealous volunteers in the days before books of the period became scarce.

During our examination of the citation file in 1968, we attempted to evaluate the range of new information to be found in the collection and the extent to which the total collection could be trusted to correct and augment the record for EMnE in the *OED*. One expected generalization was verified by our study: the material inherited from the *OED* is extensive and the new material added by Fries intensive. For example, some 209 titles are represented in the *OED* slips for the word 'grow' and only 64 from the work of Fries. The *OED* readers selected something less than two instances per title (338 slips of the total of 1857 for this word) while the contribution of Fries' reading program averages twenty-three instances per title (1505 of the total number of slips). While this example is not entirely representative of the whole collection—concentrated reading of two works on natural history yielded a large number of illustrations for 'grow'—it does suggest the differing and complementary aims of the two main sources of our material.

We also discovered that the distribution of slips is not evenly spread over the period but appears to be concentrated on the spectacular increase in English vocabulary in the late sixteenth century. Such a distribution shows a surprisingly good fit with the data provided in the *Chronological English Dictionary* (Finkenstaedt, Leisi, and Wolff 1970) to show the introduction of new vocabulary in the EMnE period. Table 1 shows a comparison of the distribution of slips in our sample from the letter G with the *CED*, though in neither case is the introduction of new senses for existing words taken into account. Nevertheless, we believe that the extensive additions to the file made by Fries and his associates add significant depth to the material already used by the editors of the *OED* and that this greater depth will yield new senses as well as allowing for more precise discriminations of meaning.

A companion study of selected technical vocabulary gave us a further glimpse into the character of the Michigan collection. We selected some fifty words with technical or specialized meanings and attempted to determine the adequacy of their treatment in the *OED* and in the citation file. Thirty-six of the words were selected from John Harris' *Lexicon Technicum* (1704) and fourteen from the *OED* itself; mainly they are specialized words in fields from anatomy to navigation but a few—such as *giblets* and *gleek* (a card game)—must have been in general currency. Two main words, two compounds, and six technical senses found in Harris are not recorded in the *OED* at all. Further study of thirty-two words showed that Fries' reading program had contributed additional citations for only half of them, and in only seven cases had Fries' readers collected more than one additional quotation. For these words, the files contain a total of 194 slips, 156 of which derive from the *OED* and only 38 from the

Dates	Number of slips in sample	Percentage of total	CED* (%)
before 1475	120	1	—
1476–1525	2114	10	8·7
1526–1575	3121	15	21·7
1576–1625	7560	35	36·0
1626–1675	4357	20	20·7
1676–1725	3210	15	13·1
after 1725	441	2	—
undated	478	2	—
	21,401		

* *A Chronological English Dictionary*. The percentages are based on 34,944 new words introduced in the period covered.

Table 1. Composition by date of the EMED citation file

subsequent reading program. We must conclude that in nearly doubling the size of the collection he obtained from the *OED*, Fries did not double the amount of information about the range of EMnE vocabulary, and one suspects that the Michigan collection repeats the literary bias of its predecessor.

As a result of our summer's work, we concluded that a variety of tasks would have to precede renewed editorial work. The following are among the most important of these.

1. Additional reading of scientific and technical works would have to be undertaken if significant additions to the coverage of the EMnE lexicon are to be made. Further support for this conclusion has come from our recent comparison of the files with the results of extracting usages from Robert Record's *The Vrinal of Physick* (1547), Ralph Lever's *The Art of Reason* (1573), and Claudio Corte's *The Art of Riding Reduced into English Discourses* (1584).

2. Certain neglected sources would have to be examined, particularly published and manuscript records to fill gaps in legal and commercial citations identified by our study, and a cursory glance at the list of works excerpted for the file. Diaries, letters, and personal papers also need examination for information about informal usage in the period, a need revealed by our examination of an extensive seventeenth-century letter collection.

3. Bibliographical work of an extensive sort would have to be undertaken to acknowledge modern scholarship. The extensive list of secondary works on various aspects of life in the period begun by Fries must be improved and supplemented with titles published since 1940. Modern

editions of EMnE texts must be selected as copy texts, a particularly pressing need given that some of our citations are now over a century old.
Finally, we must gather disparate notes on the vocabulary that have
appeared since the publication of the *OED Supplement* of 1933, a task
made easier by the recent appearance of the *Words and Phrases Index*
(Wall and Przebienda 1970).

4. Extensive sorting and pre-editing would be required to prepare the
file for efficient use by editors. The files contain extensive gatherings of
unfiled slips; specialized collections have not been distributed under
main headings; skeleton citations, mainly from concordances and dictionaries, need to be filled out. Superseded copy texts must be noted and
checked, and bibliographical information standardized.

5. A thorough examination of recently developed technical aids would
have to be undertaken to see the extent to which such techniques can aid
in hastening the production of a dictionary.

Although we managed to take some initial steps beyond evaluating the
original collection, contemplating the size of these essential tasks with no
hope of long-term financial support was not a pleasant exercise. Even
assuming that such tasks could be accomplished rapidly, we still faced the
costs of the editorial work itself. In estimating the expenditure of time
and money required for producing a completed dictionary, we have used
as a rule of thumb suggestions contained in A. J. Aitken's valuable paper
presented to the Cambridge conference that was the precursor of the
meeting which the present volume commemorates (Aitken 1971). Aitken
estimates that a well-trained editor can handle no more than 10,000 to
15,000 citation slips in a year of full-time work; hence the labor involved
in editing a dictionary from a collection of the size we now have—ignoring
the obvious necessity of considerable expansion—would thus amount to
something between two and three hundred 'lexicographer years'. In
other words, a staff of ten editors would need between twenty and thirty
years to finish the project; a budget of $3,000,000 for the entire task is
surely a conservative estimate. We need hardly underline the futility of
seeking foundation support for a project of this kind—its length and cost
make it a most unattractive candidate, particularly at a time of academic
recession when many foundations are transferring support to projects
more closely related to pressing social needs.

Fearing that the EMED project would once again lapse into long slumber
we have sought to reduce high priority preliminary tasks to manageable
and supportable size, applying the following general principles.

1. The project should be designed in stages, each of which would constitute a satisfying whole yet still approach the goal of a full dictionary of
Early Modern English; thus planning would need to remain flexible,
allowing a maximum range of options.

2. The project should, in so far as possible, give presently active scholars
immediate access to a useful portion of the information we have in the

collection. In this criterion, we memorialize the members of the Philological Society *circa* 1870 with pressing questions about words with initial Z.

3. The project should make maximum use of current technology and be designed in a form that anticipates projected technical developments. Whether our crystal ball is cloudy or not in this requirement we leave to your judgment and the future.

4. The project should facilitate widespread participation among scholars with interests in Early Modern vocabulary and, if possible, employ students in a way that contributes to their professional development.

As fundamentally optimistic men, we have excogitated a master plan. As custodians of our own funds, we have focussed our eyes on today, with wary glances at our bank balance. We prefer pipe dreams, but have had to act as plumbers.

Work begun early in 1970 derives from the four principles above and will lead to the first instalment in 1973 of the *Michigan Early Modern English Materials* (MEMEM, a collection of data drawn from the citation file and illustrating the use of selected modal auxiliaries. The auxiliaries selected for this initial instalment are listed in table 2; they will be illustrated by some 16,200 citations of EMnE usage (more than 11,000 had been entered into the system by March 1972) arranged chronologically under the entry words. (The approximate distribution of entries for the nine selected words treated in the initial instalment is shown in table 2.) Dissemination of the material will be in two forms: a collection of computer-generated microfiche and a magnetic tape; both will be inexpensive enough to be purchased by research libraries or computing centers, the former easily readable by means of widely available and inexpensive microfiche readers. It is hoped that the fiche collection will be of interest to scholars whose research interests take them beyond the data preselected for published dictionaries, the tape record useful to those interested in a large data base of EMnE for computer processing. A handbook describing the materials will be produced, including full bibliographical entries expanding the short forms that will appear on the fiche and the tape.

	Number of slips		Number of slips
can	2100	need	600
dare	500	ought	500
gin	50	shall	3375
may	2300	will	6000
must	775		
			Total 16,200

Table 2. Composition of 'Michigan Early Modern English Materials (1)'

Microfiche display has been chosen as the mode of dissemination for a variety of reasons, but central has been our wish to offer access to materials that would otherwise gather dust in our vaults for at least another thirty years. If funding extends beyond the end of 1972, as now appears possible, we expect to continue work by processing the materials for other auxiliaries and for such key verbs as *have*, *be*, and *do* as auxiliaries and as full verbs—perhaps to extend our coverage to additional grammatical words, prepositions, articles, pronouns, and the like. It will be possible to augment the initial materials both from texts already in machine-readable form and from isolated instances of particular interest that may come to light. Assuming continued financial support for the preparation of materials, the MEMEM can continue to grow in response to other requirements identified by the scholarly public. Because the costs of generating microfiche are relatively low, and because sets can be produced one at a time to respond to real rather than hypothetical demand, publication by microfiche is a potentially useful mode for distributing specialized collections of scholarly 'raw materials'.

Given adequate funds, augmentation of the collection we are establishing may come from several sources. Microfiche may be generated from texts already in machine-readable form (such as William Ingram's old-spelling version of Milton's poetical works), and we look forward to the fruition of efforts by members of the Modern Language Association of America to establish a computer 'archive' of textual materials. The lexicographical use of such an archive has already been pioneered by the *Dictionary of the Older Scottish Tongue* (*see* Aitken and Bratley 1967), though we still face the problem of selectivity that must be solved to prevent new materials in the archive from inundating the carefully chosen instances from our citation file. Anticipating the solution to that problem, we have designed our file-management system to allow for inexpensive addition and deletion of citations.

Entering our entire collection of more than three million slips into the system we have devised would doubtless be unjustifiably and prohibitively expensive. Direct photography is impracticable because of the poor legibility of the slips, and keyboarding costs are high whether the prepared copy is handed over to keypunch operators or designed for optical character reading (we are preparing costs estimates by trying both methods). Hence we have tried to devise a technique to optimize the value of the materials entered into the system, following in this as in other things the inspiration of Sir William Craigie. To reduce needless duplication of effort, Craigie devised a system to make multiple use of citations collected for the *Dictionary of the Older Scottish Tongue*. Particularly interesting quotations are marked not just for one entry word but for several; the slip is then filed under the first in alphabetical order of the three or four words selected by the reader. When an editor finishes the entry for that word, he refiles the slip under the next word marked on the slip and so passes the citation on to be used again and again.

In imitation of this procedure, we are preparing what we have designated a 'secondary index' to the citations already entered in the system. This index will contain references to all the words in the collection with the exception of a stop list of very high frequency words. For example, the following excerpt appears among our materials for 'can':

nothynge can helpe your lamentacyon.

The secondary index will give the user access to 'nothynge', 'helpe', and 'lamentacyon' even though the primary purpose of the citation is to illustrate a use of 'can'. 'Your' will be included in the stop list, but the linguist with a particular interest in this high frequency word can obtain a copious body of references by means of the magnetic tape that we will make available to him.

In the first instalment of MEMEM only the nine modal verbs listed in table 2 will appear in the primary alphabetical arrangement of the microfiche; through the secondary index, the user will have access to approximately 20,000 additional word types. As we continue to add materials to the primary alphabet of the collection, we can begin to compare what is already in MEMEM for a given word with the new material under consideration and hence avoid expensive duplication of information. As MEMEM continues to grow, we will be able to become more and more selective of new material to be added to the system. By such means we hope to maximize the value of each quotation and obviate the necessity of entering every slip from the citation file while still carrying out our mission of showing as much information as possible about the range of EMnE vocabulary.

There are difficulties and dangers, of course, in following such a procedure. It will demand more careful editorial work and thus better trained personnel than are required for standardizing and coding slips—tasks presently done very well by our student assistants. Nevertheless, we believe that the MEMEM resource can be made to contain nearly all the information in our present collection of three million slips by the judicious selection of about 100,000 citations, only six times the size of our pilot instalment. We should add, however, that these figures are based entirely on guesswork at the moment since we await completion of the first body of materials to produce the secondary index. By the end of 1972 we will be able to give a less speculative estimate of the overall scope of the project.

No matter what the value of MEMEM as an independent resource proves to be, however, constructing it has been worth while in helping to solve problems bequeathed us with the EMED collection. We have been forced to standardize entry forms, to recognize and correct bibliographical bobbles, to solve problems of cross-referencing. In these tasks, hard copy from the magnetic tape record has been invaluable, particularly in reconstructing the list of works actually and adequately read during past collecting stages. But beyond instructing us as lexicographers, developing our system has suggested other applications potentially valuable to a plan for producing a full 'Early Modern English Dictionary', especially if such a dictionary should be undertaken, as has been suggested, in a co-operative effort by more than one university.

Dissemination of the microfiche and secondary index makes it possible for scholars at several centers to involve themselves in the work of the dictionary; editors need not continue dictionary work beyond the limits of their enthusiasm and institutions can be protected from some of the difficulties in recruiting and maintaining a large staff of lexicographers. [*See* Bailey (forthcoming) for a discussion of this problem.] Furthermore, the scholar whose primary interests lie elsewhere can profit from the resources provided by MEMEM without the delays unfortunately so typical of lexicography.

As we noted in an earlier description of our work (Bailey and Robinson 1970), we have carried on some small experiments in computer-assisted editing. At the time of this work in 1969 we found that the cost of a cathode-ray terminal and the necessary supporting system amounted to between $7·00 and $10·00 per hour, an expenditure that would become prohibitive for long-term work on a dictionary of EMnE. Nevertheless, we found significant advantages in the computer-assisted procedure. It is possible for the lexicographer trained in traditional methods to operate such a system with no particular expertise in computer techniques since we have modelled the computer support system on the usual practices. With computer-assisted editing, moreover, publication is considerably facilitated, whether of a new or of a traditional sort. Once editorial work for a given entry is complete, the information added by the editor is immediately available through a computer network linking research centers or through the less visionary dissemination of magnetic tape in instalments. Further, computer-supported typesetting equipment can be linked to the system, and the production of error-free copy, time consuming and costly if undertaken in traditional ways, can be accomplished rapidly and efficiently.

We now believe that the obstacle presented by the expense of cathode-ray terminals has been overcome by the PLATO terminal developed at the University of Illinois for computer-assisted teaching (*see* Bitzer and Skaperdas 1969). This piece of equipment, now in production by Magnavox Corporation, is shown in figure 1. Cost of operation is considerably reduced by two features of this device: the transparent plasma panel on the face of the terminal and the microfiche projection system contained in the upper part. As we anticipate its use, the computer-generated microfiche we are now producing would be inserted into the terminal and a frame containing a desired citation projected from behind on to the plasma panel. In this respect, the operation of the terminal replicates the microfiche readers typically found in research libraries. After examining the citation, the editor composes a provisional definition on the keyboard and the text he creates appears on a portion of the panel we have designated the 'editorial workspace'. Once he has finished a provisional definition, he can enter a note on another portion of the screen—the 'scratch pad'—to remind himself of what he has done. As he continues to examine citations from the fiche, he can write a new definition, recall the full text of a previous definition from storage for refinement, or, using the keys he has established on the 'scratch pad', assign a new citation to a defining node previously established.

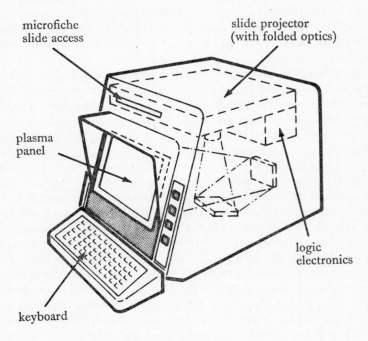

microfiche slide access

slide projector (with folded optics)

plasma panel

logic electronics

keyboard

Figure 1. Magnavox PLATO IV student terminal

The computer-editing technique allows for a variety of activities that traditional procedures make nearly impossible. An editorial staff can be established from scholars working at several institutions rather than at a single center since the terminals can be linked to a central processing unit through existing networks; such cooperation would obviate the difficulties presently facing many dictionary projects in the recruitment and continued support of a large, specialized staff. A larger cooperative effort is conceivable: an advisory board consisting of experts on various aspects of Renaissance life could, were they willing, be brought into more intimate participation in the work, both by contributions of new material to the system and by continuing involvement in the editorial work itself, since it would be possible for a scholar in virtually any part of the world to 'read over the shoulder' of the editor at work. Those who now make use of published dictionaries could have immediate access to the full range of materials and could signal the need for additional information as the work progresses.

But these are the stuffs that pipe dreams are made of, or idle conceptions of the perfect dictionary, though they are not beyond the reach of present technology. We believe that the project we have currently designed acknowledges the realities of current sources of support but at the same time anticipates extended uses of technological developments should money and manpower make those uses possible. Should the lack of either prevent the growth of a large-scale cooperative scheme for editing a dictionary of EMnE, we believe that the availability of MEMEM on microfiche alone will be a useful addition to resources available as aids to the study of Early Modern English and will save from certain oblivion the dedicated efforts of generations of collectors.

Acknowledgements
Since 1966, we have received support for our work from the Rackham School of Graduate Studies at the University of Michigan, from a grant for computer-oriented humanistic research supervised by the American Council of Learned Societies (1968), and from the National Endowment for the Humanities (1971-present). We also wish to record our thanks to the Institute for Advanced Studies in the Humanities, the University of Edinburgh, for fellowships (1971 and 1972) allowing the leisure to think about dictionary-making in an atmosphere where doing so is valuable and valued; to the American Council of Learned Societies for travel support. We add our gratitude to that of our predecessors on the EMED project for the substantial support given from 1929 to 1938 to Professor Fries, first by the General Education Board and later by the Rockefeller Foundation.

REFERENCES

Aitken, A. J. (1971) Historical dictionaries and the computer. *The Computer in Literary and Linguistic Research*, pp. 3-17 (ed. Wisbey, R. A.). Cambridge: Cambridge University Press.

Aitken, A. J. & Bratley, P. (1967) An archive of Older Scottish texts for scanning by computer. *English Studies*, **48**, 60-1.

Bailey, R. W. (forthcoming) Research Dictionaries. *American Speech*.

Bailey, R. W. & Robinson, J. L. (1968-69) The University of Michigan Early Modern English Dictionary project. *Shakespeare Research and Opportunities*, **4**, 120-1.

Bailey, R. W. & Robinson, J. L. (1970) Computers and dictionaries. *Computers and Old English Concordances*, pp. 94-102 (eds. Cameron, A., Frank, R. & Leyerle, J.). Toronto: University of Toronto Press.

Bailey, R. W. & Robinson, J. L. (in press) The computer in lexicography. *Hans Kurath Festschrift* (eds. Reidy, J. & Scholler, H.)

Bitzer, D. & Skaperdas, D. (1969) *The Design of an Economically Viable Large-Scale Computer Based Education System*. Urbana, Ill.: Computer-based Education Research Laboratory.

Finkenstaedt, T., Leisi, E., & Wolff, D. (1970) *A Chronological English Dictionary*. Heidelberg; Carl Winter.

Wall, C. E. & Przebienda, E. (1970) *Words and Phrases Index: A Guide to Antedatings, New Words, New Compounds, New Meanings, and Other Published Scholarship Supplementing the Oxford English Dictionary, Dictionary of Americanisms, Dictionary of American English and Other Major Dictionaries of the English Language*. 4 vols. Ann Arbor: Pierian Press.

A semasiological dictionary of the English language

In 1879 the readers for what became the *Oxford English Dictionary* were asked to:

> Make a quotation for *every* word that strikes you as rare, obsolete, old-fashioned, new, peculiar, or used in a peculiar way.
>
> Take special note of passages which show or imply that a word is either new or tentative, or needing explanation as obsolete or archaic, and which thus help to fix the date of its introduction or disuse.
>
> Make *as many* quotations *as you can* for ordinary words, especially when they are used significantly, and tend by the context to explain or suggest their own meaning. (Historical introduction, *OED*, p.xv.)

These instructions have a particular significance to me, as I have spent a great proportion of my working life making such excerpts. It is in the nature of this kind of work to be very interesting at the start of the reading process; with each new book the start can be equally stimulating. But once the work has become familiar the reader's standard of alertness diminishes, and it is in the recording of the more ordinary instances that faults of omission occur. Then the reader is jerked into alertness again by something outstanding and interesting, but it is always the unusual word which reawakens his interest.

So the raw material which reached the editors of the *Oxford English Dictionary* (*OED*) was weighted in favour of the earliest instances and the archaic, provincial, or metaphorical uses by untypical writers—at the expense of the ordinary phrases bearing the brunt of everyday expression. Nevertheless, the arranging of this massive material (amounting eventually to some six million citations) into orderly numbered paragraphs accompanied by definitions is a magnificent achievement which no one must disparage. In the case of the *OED*'s two distinguished successors now in progress, the *Dictionary of the Older Scottish Tongue* (*DOST*) at Edinburgh and the *Middle English Dictionary* (*MED*) at Ann Arbor, Michigan, the bulk of material is less voluminous and the quality of excerpting correspondingly better.

But we are left with the financial imponderable of what proportion of the whole can be printed. At Michigan the proportion has gone up since the dictionary's inception, and the usefulness of the dictionary for semantic analysis has correspondingly increased. But now with mechanized aids the order of magnitude of what can be excerpted and sorted has increased astronomically. Anyone visiting Pisa and Florence, for instance, must be left in breathless wonderment at the immense bulk of what is being prepared for the Academia della Crusca by the Centro Nazionale Universitario di Calcolo Elettronico.

In addition to the disadvantage of being able to print only an increasingly small proportion of the extracts which have been collected, we are also faced by the shortcomings of dictionaries that are arranged alphabetically.

My own approach avoids the haphazard switching from concept to concept caused by an alphabetical arrangement and the daunting bulk of the material which deters the collector. Arranged by concept and not by word, the material gains in interest as it increases in bulk. We can now call to our aid modern electronic equipment to sort dated citations in which appear

(a) obsolete or obsolescent words or phrases,

(b) the words or phrases now used in their place.

Having paired two citations (a) and (b) together, we can tag the significant words (A, B) or the significant members (A_1, A_2; B_1, B_2) of the phrases to numbered paragraphs in dictionaries, where we can find comparable dated citations arranged historically. From this body of material can be determined the period of time when both modes of expression were acceptable and fighting out their particular battle in the verbal struggle for existence. In the case of so mixed a language as English it is also necessary to tag the nationality of the contestants: this leads us to include certain etymological information, and the national origin of the phrased calques can also sometimes be inferred. Our modern machines can permute and combine these paired phrases in many different orders, whereas it would be much too expensive to set these out in conventional published form under all the different conceptual, historical, and alphabetical arrangements. What follows is a description of how a data bank is being constructed, from which concepts, words, and phrases can be drawn out, flexibly arranged to illustrate whatever aspect the individual scholar requires when investigating the life and death, the disease and health, of words in the context.

The raw materials used fall into three groups.

1. Modernized versions of earlier texts, the time-interval between the two being anything from 30 to 300 years. (Three centuries is really too long, but the *Revised Standard Version* is a specific revision of the *Authorized Version*, and I have made an exception in order to be able to use Thomas Nelson's magnificent machine-made concordance.)

2. Successive translations into English from the same foreign original, the time-interval being of the same order of magnitude as for (1), although I occasionally take comparative material from the two versions of the Wycliffite Bible.

3. Vernacular glosses of earlier vernacular texts appearing in medieval manuscripts and in copies of early printed books.

The last group has one advantage over the other two; it is that here we are certain of the text which confronted the modernizer. When we have to deal with a complex manuscript tradition it is sometimes very difficult to tell which variant version was in front of the scribe or maker of a modernized version in group (1). Also we must bear in mind in group (2) that the non-English texts (mainly Latin, Anglo-Norman, Medieval French, Hebrew, and *New Testament* Greek in my collections so far) may have been subject to scholarly revision and correction: consequently some of the changes in the late vernacular version will be reflecting, say, advances in *New Testament* scholarship rather than a change in taste for English words and phrases.

Our purpose is to study the birth, life, and death of a word or phrase used in a particular sense. Our two successive translations or versions give us an inkling of the sense without it being shackled to one particular word. In the case of translations we have the foreign word or phrase, the earlier native word or phrase, and the later native word or phrase, as three points from which to take our semantic bearings. One or more words differ between the earlier and later English versions, or our attention would not have been arrested by the passages in question. We begin, then, with a series of pairs of excerpts from successive versions such as the St John's and Harleian manuscript translations of Ranulph Higden's *Poly-chronicon*.

> (1450a Higd) Edengborouȝh is a cite in the londe of Pictes, betweene the water of Twide and the Scottes see, whiche was *callede* somme tyme the Castelle of Maidenes

and

> (1387a S. Joh.) Edynboruȝ is a citee in þe lond of Pictes bytwene þe ryuere of Twyde and þe Scottische see, and *heet* somtyme þe Castelle of Maydens, (vocabatur castrum puellarum)

From single pairs of excerpts such as these we proceed in the following way. We first consult the *OED* (A from 1882 to z from 1921) and the *MED* (A from 1956 to L from 1970) and then decide on the numbered paragraphs into which we would put the significantly differing words (shown in italics in the examples) of our excerpted passages. Let us take the simplest case, where the verbs of the two sentences differ, the rest of the context, spelling variants apart, remaining much the same.

In the later, more modern, version we have what I will call the *incoming* verb. When we have found its HEADWORD and paragraph number in the *OED* we can punch on paper tape 'HEADWORD (space) part of speech (space) paragraph number' in this form

CALL v. 11a   (1a)

Then, if the HEADWORD (or its first syllables) are spelt the same in the *MED* we can add another numbered paragraph:

CALL v. 11a *MED* 5a   (1b)

(In passing we may draw attention to the important fact that this double reference is to two definitions, one English and one American, and this

B

may have tightened our semantic definition—our fish may be passing or trying to pass through two nets of lessening size of mesh.)

Next, for the earlier translation we repeat the process of consulting first the *OED*:

HIGHT v. –1– 5   (2a)

Here the notation v. –1– shows that in the *OED* there were more than two verbs with the same HEADWORD and –1– is my notation for the *OED*'s superscript figure following the part of speech.

Another complication is that whereas the *OED* HEADWORDS reflect the most modern usage, the *MED* HEADWORDS are based on Chaucerian usage, and may have to be inserted thus:

HIGHT v. –1– 5 *MED* HOTEN –1– 2 ad   (2b)

While this process of consulting dictionaries is going on, the editor is consciously or unconsciously making a subjective judgment as to whether he would use either or both translators' versions, and if both, in what social context—in a lecture, in a public bar, in the pulpit, and so on.

If, as is frequently the case in the class of historical collections that I am making, the EARLIER word is obsolete and the LATER word is the one used today by educated people in writing normal prose, we make the judgment that the LATER is the incoming word or phrase and the EARLIER is the outgoing word or phrase.

Confining ourselves to the ideal single-word substitution already exemplified above we can rewrite (1b) and (2b) with limits of date (in brackets) culled from my own collections and such of the dated quotations in the dictionaries as seem to be close parallels to our context:

CALL v. 11a *MED* 5a (13c. on)   (1c)

showing a range from thirteenth-century quotations to modern, late twentieth-century, literary usage. Let us assume that our collected evidence points to our EARLIER verb becoming obsolete in its preterite tense in the fifteenth century:

HIGHT v. –1– 5 *MED* HOTEN –1– 2ad pret. (to 15c.)   (2c)

For clarity of thought it is dangerous to do so, but by this stage we have been labelling these words in our minds as:

INCOMER

CALL v. 11a *MED* 5a (13c. on)   (1d)

and

OUTGOER

HIGHT v. –1– 5 *MED* HOTEN –1– 2ad pret. (to 15c.)   (2d)

From this pair it is apparent that if all our extracts from our own collections and from those of the dictionaries came from the same geographical area and the same literary milieu, conflict between these words could have been taking place throughout the thirteenth, fourteenth, and fifteenth centuries. With these qualifications in mind, we can print 13 14 15 to the right of line (2d):

HIGHT v. –1– 5 *MED* HOTEN –1– 2ad pret. (to 15c.)   13 14 15   (2e)

The limits of the period of conflict are clear, the place of conflict depends on the certainty with which we can locate geographically and sociologically the last texts containing the OUTGOER and the first texts containing the INCOMER. The nationality of the INCOMER, whether loan-word or home-grown, sometimes comes to our rescue here, as in this result to which this part of the editing process has been tending:

CALL v. 11a *MED* 5a (13c. on) OD
    1450a Higd. Harl. I, c48, 6: Edengborouȝh is a cite in the londe of Pictes betweene the water of Twide and the Scottes see, whiche was callede somme tyme the Castelle of Maidenes.   (1f)
HIGHT v. –1– 5 *MED* HOTEN –1– 2ad pret. het (to 15c.) OE 13 14 15
    1387a Higd. S. Joh. I, c48, 6: Edynboruȝ is a citee in þe lond of Pictes bytwene þe ryuere of Twyde and þe Scottische see, and heet somtyme þe Castelle of Maydens, (vocabatur castrum puellarum)   (2f)

Here the HEADWORDS, their following strings of numerals, variant HEADWORDS, tenses, and date-limits in brackets are followed by nationalities (OD for the Danish language in England, OE for pre-Conquest English, OF for Norman or Continental French, L for Latin, and so on). On the lines below those starting with the HEADWORDS (CALL and HIGHT) and inset four spaces from the margin are the dates and references of the two texts excerpted; the dates, if approximate, being stated as cautiously as possible, with the four figures preceding the abbreviations *a* for ante, *c* for circa and *p* for post.

In brief, we can use machine-produced printout of two or more versions verse by verse with a convenient space where the editor can insert HEADWORDS in pairs, usually each pair being lightly pencilled in erasable coloured chalks. These HEADWORDS are then punched against a line-code for insertion into the data, and the whole can come back to the editor arranged alphabetically by OUTGOERS and/or INCOMERS. The editor can then use his big dictionaries volume by volume when adding paragraph numbers and the items following in the string.

At this stage, when many different pairs under (say) CALL v. and HIGHT v. –1– are brought together by machine and neatly typed one below another, the time is ripe for the editor to make his own final or near-final decision as to the meanings under which the citations are to be filed. Some of the CALL and NAME pairs neatly find a first general home in paragraph 564 in Peter Mark Roget's *Thesaurus of English Words and Phrases* (1852 onwards; a paperback edition having been published by Penguin Books in 1953). Here they can be joined by some sub-branches of the obsolete CLEPE and HIGHT v. –1– words; YCLEPT, as an archaic past participle, is part of Roget's 564 family of words under the heading of NOMENCLATURE (one wonders how usual it was in 1852 . . .).

A good translation is often the best commentary, and after some fifteen years of experimenting, I have found that to make one's own translation to fit both the paired extracts is the best and most foolproof solution. As much of this as is intelligible is then introduced in front of the number 564 within single quotation marks, as in the following examples:

```
12010 12010
   1                                    '(a place which is) called N'   564
   2  CALL v. 11a MED 5a (13c. on) OD
   3      1450a Higd. Harl. I, c48, 4: Also that same kynge made ij other
   4          nowble cites: oone was in Scottelande, whiche is callede
              Edenborouȝh,
   5  HIGHT v. –1– 5 MED HOTEN –1– 2ac pres. 3sg hatte (to 15c.) OE
                                                          13 14 15
   6      1387a Higd. S. Joh. I, c48, 4: He bulde also tweie opere noble citees,
   7          ((one)) in Scotlond þat hatte Edynborgh, (quæ dicitur
   8          Edenburgh) also 5 more exx in c48 translating dicitur
   9
12020 12020
   1  as 12011
   2  as 12012
   3      1450a Higd. Harl. I, c48, 5: that oper cite was in the costes of
   4          Englonde, towarde Scottelonde, which was callede Alcluid.
   5  as 12015
   6      1387a Higd. S. Joh. I, c48, 5: and anoper toward Scotlond, in þe
   7          endes of Engelond, þat hatte Alclud, (quæ dicitur Alcluid)
   8
   9
12030 12030
   1                              '(a place which once) was called M'   564
   2  CALL v. 11a MED 5a (13c. on) OD
   3      1450a Higd. Harl. I, c48, 6: Edenborouȝh is a cite in the londe of
   4          Pictes, betweene the water of Twide and the Scottes see,
   5          whiche was called somme tyme the Castelle of Maidenes,
   6  HIGHT v. –1– 5 MED HOTEN –1– 2ad pret. het (to 15c.) OE 13 14 15
   7      1387a Higd. S. Joh. I, c48, 6: Edynboruȝ is a citee in þe lond of
   8          Pictes bytwene þe ryuere of Twyde and þe Scottische see,
   9          and heet somtyme þe Castelle of Maydens, (vocabatur)
12040 12040
   1                              '( a place ) called ( after a person )'   564
   2  NAME v. –1– 1c/15c. on/ME
   3      1450a Higd. Harl. I, c48, 3: Ebrancus, the vthe kynge of Briteyne,
   4          made that cite of Yorke, whom he namede Caerbranc.
   5  CLEPE v. 3a MED 2ad. AFTER prep. 14b MED 10d (13-15c.) ME   15
   6      1387a Higd. S. Joh. I, c48, 3: Ebrankus þe fifte kyng of Britouns,
   7          bulde York, and cleped it after his owne name Caerbrank.
   8          (Hanc urbem construxit Ebrancus rex Britonum quintus, vocans
   9          eam ex nomine suo Caerbrank.)
```

The final outcome to which these operations have been directed is illustrated at the end of the paper. The paired quotations, arranged in reverse chronological order, are printed out in rectangles of 10 lines of 96 characters each. The left-hand column numbering each line, shown in the

immediately preceding illustration so that the means of inserting additions, corrections and substitutions can be seen, is omitted from this
final printout. I must here thank the tape-punching staff of Cambridge
University's Literary and Linguistic Computing Centre for their help in
perfecting this technique.

French loanwords in English and the stock-phrases in which they were
often embedded are best illustrated by quotations from Middle English
works of the fourteenth and fifteenth centuries; hence the importance of
using the *MED*. As only about half the alphabet has been compiled so
far for the *MED* information in the HEADWORD lines for words from the
second half of the alphabet is provisional: this is indicated by the use of
oblique strokes to enclose limits of date, as in the example line 12042
illustrated above:

NAME v. –1– 1c/15c. on/ ME   (3c)

But the word TEST in the semantic group 'test, people' 463 came into
use well after the Middle English period, so in line 3692 on page 22 it
appears as:

TEST v. –2– 2 (18c. on) NE   (4c)

However, it is in the nature of the collections that modern English
INCOMERS do not bulk large in the collections, so part of our editorial
work (and it is still a large part) must be regarded as provisional as long
as the *MED* is in progress. However much we may wish to put this
garner of information at the disposal of other scholars, it is the provisional
nature of each semantic group (*see* PROVE, TRY, and TEMPT on pages
22-3) which is so daunting. To print our present evidence part by part
would be possible, but each part would be subject to successive stages of
updating as the *MED* proceeds from letter to letter.

Provision of machine-readable material from the growing archive for
research purposes seems a greater possibility, provided that those applying for and receiving it are prepared for amendments and additions to
their earlier tapes arriving with their later batches. It would then be up
to them to correct their own archives from the mother archive.

In Cambridge we are now in the process of changing from Titan to the
IBM 370/165. However, it is not anticipated that these moves to more
modern equipment will hinder the flexibility of the general aim, which is
to be able to sort and print out either in order of INCOMERS, or in order of
OUTGOERS, or by semantic group or by national etymology, or by centuries
of conflict, or by all or several of the above groupings in varying logical
orders (giving at different times a remarkably different look and emphasis
to the same hard-won body of material).

When the *MED* is finished and the *Early Modern English Dictionary* is
well under way, computerized typesetting will surely be normal and the
University Presses of the world will be printing out as much (or as little)
of the Universities' treasures as the outside world requires. This paper
shows a foretaste of what this project may then provide.

62

/463.1/ 'test, people' 463

```
. . . . . . . . . . . . . . . . . . . . . . . . . . . . . . . . . . . . . .
1   1   1   1   1   1   1   1   1   1   2
0   1   2   3   4   5   6   7   8   9   0
0   0   0   0   0   0   0   0   0   0   0
0   0   0   0   0   0   0   0   0   0   0
```
. . . . . . TEST v. -2- 2

PROVE v. 1a   . . . .
ESSAY v. 1a, ASSAY 1a, 2a   . . . .
TRY v. 7a, 7b   . . . .
TEMPT v. 1a   . . . .
EXAMINE v. 2a, 2   . . . .
FRAIST v. 1, 1a   . . . .
FAND v. 1a, 1a   . . . .
AFOND v. 1a, 1a   . . . . .

3690

TEST v. -2- 2 (18c. on) NE   'test, people' 46?
    1961 N.E.B. Jn.6,6: This he said to test him;   18 19
PROVE v. 1a /13-19c./ OF
    1534 Tynd. Jn.6,6: This he sayde to prove him:

3440

TEST v. -2- 2 (18c. on) NE   'test, people' 46
    1952 R.S.V. Gen.22,1: After these things God tested Abraham,
TEMPT v. 1a /14-17c./ OF   17 00 1
    1611 A.V. Gen.22,1: After these things... God did tempt Abraham

3500

EXAMINE v. 2a MED 2 (14c. on) LOF examine oneself   'test, people' 46
    1611 A.V. 2Co.13,5: Examine yourselves whether ye be in the faith:
TRY v. 7a, 7b /16-17c./ OF   16 1
    1582 Rheims 2Co.13,5: Trie your ovvne selues if you be in the faith:

3450

PROVE v. 1a /13-19c./ OF   'test, people' 46
    1611 A.V. Ex.6,4: I will raine bread from heauen... that I may proue them,
ESSAY v. 1a, ASSAY v. 1a MED 2a (14-16c.,Arch.19c.) OF   14 15 16 .
    1395c Wyc.Pv. Ex.16,4: Y schal reyne to 3ou looues fro heuene... that Y asaie the puple,

3630

PROVE v. 1a /13-19c./ OF   'test, people' 46
    1534 Tynd. Jn.6,6: This he sayde to prove him:
TEMPT v. 1a /14-17c/ OF   14 15 16 1
    1395c Wyc.Pv.Hex. Jn.6,6: but he saide this thing: temptynge him

490

PROVE **v.** 1a /13-19c./ OF 'test, people' 463
1534 Tynd. 2Co.13,5: Prove youreselves whether ye are in the fayth or not
ASSAY **v.** 1a, ASSAY **v.** 1a MED 2a (14-16c.,Arch.19c.) OF 14 15 16 ..
1395c Wyc.Pv. 2Co.13,5: asaie ȝousilf if ȝe ben in the feith:

460

PROVE **v.** 1a /13-19c./ OF 'test, people' 463
1450a Higd.Harl. IV,77: ... prove ...
ASSAY **v.** 1a, ASSAY **v.** 1a MED 2a (14-16c.,Arch.19c.) OF 14 15 16 ..
1387a Higd.S.Joh. IV,77: Iosephus wolde assaye þe witte of his ȝonger sone.

470

ASSAY **v.** 1a, ASSAY **v.** 1a MED 2a (14-16c.,Arch.19c.) OF 'test, people' 463
1425c Glouc.Harl. 790n: ... asayed ...
FIND **v.** 1a MED FONDEN 1a (to 15c.) OE 14 15
1300c Glouc.Cal. 790: þe oþer doȝter þat he adde ifonded he ne' dorste to hire wende

480

ASSAY **v.** 1a, ASSAY **v.** 1a MED 2a (14-16c.,Arch.19c.) OF 'test, people' 463
1400a Curs.M.Trin. 3118: Hereþ of god al weldonde how he asayed his trewe seruonde
FIND **v.** 1a MED FONDEN 1a (to 15c.) OE 14 15
1325a Curs.M.Vesp. 3118: Herkens o godd þat all weldand, How he wald faand his lel seruand.

10

PROVE **v.** 1a /13-19c./ OF 'test, people' 463
1340c Rolle Ps.17,3(16,4): þou proued my hert... in fire þou examynd me and noght is funden
in me wickidnes.
FIND **v.** 1a MED FONDEN 1a (to 15c.) OE 13 14 15
1325c Horstm. Ps.17,3(16,4): þou fanded mi hert... with fire me fraisted, and in me nes
funden wickedhed.

20 ·

EXAMINE **v.** 2a MED 2 (14-17c.) LOF 'test, people' 463
1340c Rolle Ps.17,3(16,4): þou proued my hert... in fire þou examynd me and noght is funden
in me wickidnes.
FIST **v.** 1 MED 1a (14-15c.) OD 14 15
1325c Horstm. Ps.17,3(16,4): þou fanded mi hert... with fire me fraisted, and in me nes
funden wickedhed.

20

FIND **v.** 1a MED FONDEN 1a (to 15c.) OE 'test, people' 463
1325c Horstm. Ps.17,3(16,4): þou fanded mi hert... with fire me fraisted, and in me nes
funden wickedhed.
FIND **v.** 1a MED 1a (to 12c.) OE .. 12
950c Reg. Ps.17,3(16,3): ðu afandudest (_Probasti_) heortan mine... fyre ðu ameredest and
nys gemet on me unryhtwisnes

Going back to the first examples in this paper, I would like the reader to ponder two simple facts brought out by the quotations printed above: in the Northern Midland dialect area in the mid-fifteenth century, the Old English verbs *clypian* and *hātan* had yielded to their Anglo-Danish rival *kalla* their 'call, name' meanings. But from hasty consultation of the *OED* paragraphs (CLEPE v. 3a, YCLEPT pa.pple. and HIGHT v. –1– 5, crammed as they are with later archaisms from affected literary contexts) one might have no suspicion that this had been the case. This is my excuse for stubbornly continuing with my life-work, and here in Edinburgh publicly thanking a great Scots lexicographer, Sir William Craigie, for having encouraged me to start upon this idea of mine thirty-five years ago.

The problem of the context
in computer-aided lexicography

Once the input and output problems (Tollenaere 1972) facing us in connection with our work at the Institute of Dutch Lexicology in Leiden
were solved, our central problem became that of the context in computer-
aided lexicography. Although from the very beginning it has been my
intention to provide a fully automatic, flexible context on our continuous
cards, thus automating the first stage of dictionary making, I must humbly
confess that, during the last two years, I have faced the problem of the
computer-generated context in the same way as a cat faces a dish of hot
porridge.

The lexicography I have in view concerns only monolingual dictionaries dealing with the history of a given language. Dictionary making of
this kind requires a collection of slips with a headword in a sufficient
portion of context. This constitutes the lexical data, the lexicological
material. In traditional lexicology and lexicography—the problem of
the context concerns both—handmade slips have been provided either
by volunteers (*Oxford English Dictionary*) or by professional readers
(*Woordenboek der Nederlandsche Taal*, Leiden). In computer-assisted
lexicography, however, the quotation slips are no longer handmade but
consist of computer output. On dictionary slips, whether handmade or
computer-made, the headword is, as a rule, preceded and followed by a
sufficient portion of context. Handmade dictionary slips allow a context
with an optimum variability; words or even lines or sentences can easily
be omitted. No computer program, however, can fully automatically omit
words or unimportant subordinate clauses; this means that of necessity a
computer-made context will be less flexible.

If we ask what has already been done in the field of automatic contexting
of lexicological material, the answer is: quite a lot, both in theory and in
practice. Everybody who is acquainted with the publications of distinguished scholars such as Busa, Quemada, Wisbey, and Aitken, or with
the work going on in the lexicographical centres of Florence (Duro) and
Nancy (Imbs), will be well aware of this.

Much of what has been written and done, however, is nowadays of
purely historical interest. Speaking at the 'Colloque international sur la
mécanisation des recherches lexicologiques' in Besançon, June 1961, I
described a method of supplying a variable context by means of mechanical methods (punched-card equipment in conjunction with other mechanical ancillary machines: interclasseuse collator and reporteuse). This
method was applied to a bilingual text, the *Vocabulaire François &*

Flameng of Noël van Berlainmont (Antwerp 1536) with good results (Tollenaere 1961). It is, however, so complicated and time consuming, that now, only eleven years after it has been applied, I venture to call it a stone-age method. As a result we need not mention what has been done in the field of contexting by mechanical methods. It is, however, fair to state here that already during that 'stone-age' period of 1961, Professor Busa gave a sketchy but substantial outline of how a dictionary slip could be provided with a variable context by computer (Tollenaere 1961, pp. 109-10). Nor will the problem of a computer-generated context in a concordance (Quemada 1961; Busa and Zampolli 1968; Kamp 1969) be considered here.

In computer-generated context one can distinguish between a rigid and a flexible context.
The rigid context. Starting from a logical paragraph, a portion of text (for example, 100 words) determined by pre-editing, the computer will generate as many slips as there are words in the portion, and each individual dictionary word within a given block will have the same context. This means that the first word of the portion of text will have exactly the same context as the last word. Such a rigid context of a fixed length is made use of, at least as regards certain texts, for the dictionary of the Italian language to be published by the Accademia della Crusca in Florence (Duro 1968). I doubt, however, if such a context can always be considered a good substitute for the highly flexible context of our traditional handmade dictionary slips.

What we want is a *flexible context* that gets as near as possible to the flexibility of traditional handwork. I turn now to the question, to what extent and by what methods a computer-generated context can be made flexible.

A certain degree of flexibility can be obtained by what could be called *line-overlapping*. This method provides a fixed number of lines for each word, but with each word of a following line the context is a little different from the context given to each word of the previous line. A striking illustration of this method is provided by some dictionary slips made in the Literary and Linguistic Computing Centre (Cambridge). These constitute the material for a dictionary to the works of Wolfram von Eschenbach on which Professor Wisbey (1963, 1969) was collaborating with Professor Werner Schröder of Marburg. The lexicographical requirements of the project would, he said, apparently 'be met by providing a context of seven poetic lines for each word, normally the line in which the word occurs and three lines on either side' (Wisbey 1963). In doing this one gets a variable context of a fixed length. Professor Wisbey is right in assuming that such a context will meet the lexicographer's demands. We should, however, not forget that these computer-printed slips are confined to poetry only. They deal with short verses which, by definition, are to be considered much more a unity than the lines in prose writings.

A similar method of line-overlapping has been followed by Aitken and Bratley (1966). They speak about a program supplying 'excerpts for specified wordforms on 6″ × 4″ "slips" for dictionary use; each slip contains the key-word, a three-line context, the reference, and some other information, including, where applicable, rhyme-words'. From these last words, it seems clear that the Scottish texts on tape do not consist of poetry only.

With the Italian dictionary of the Florence Academy the line-overlapping method is applied to works with no pre-edited portions of context. The only difference is that Duro wants a bigger context, that is, ten or eleven lines (Duro 1968), instead of three (Aitken and Bratley 1966) or seven (Wisbey 1963). He does not explain, however, if in this connection he is considering only prose texts.

The contexts of the Nancy French dictionary (*Trésor de la Langue Française*) are of the same type but much bigger; in fact no less than eighteen lines are to be found on the slips (20 × 10·8 cm). But as these are in fact arranged in the order of the text (Sundqvist 1966) they cannot be considered as real lexicographical material. The editors at Nancy as a rule do not work with those slips, but with three-line concordances (Imbs 1967), in which the words are in alphabetical and chronological order.

If computer-generated dictionary slips are to be processed from prose texts, a program that should provide us with lexicographical material containing a prose line in which the headword occurs with a certain number of lines on either side of it, would, I think, not come up to the flexibility I have in mind.

The same applies to a variant of such a line-overlapping context, which Aitken suggested to the editors of the *Dictionary of Old English* and which he has permitted me to describe in his own words. 'Isolated in the middle of the slip would be a three-line context for first reading, preferably with the keyword placed at the end of the second line. Preceding this would be as much context as space and/or considerations of machine-time economy permitted (and at least four lines). Following would be only two lines. This is based on the assumption that the significant or "defining" context, in a great majority of cases, *precedes* rather than follows the keyword and that three lines beyond the keyword would in a large majority of cases complete the syntax. With such a slip the user could first pick out the immediate context, isolated in the middle of the slip, and only if this were inadequate need he look at the preceding or following context; the aim of this being to save waste of time in reading unnecessary context.'

This context has no more chance than the other ones of the same type of being a syntactic unit. A mechanically delimited portion of, for example, three times three lines of text seems, at least to me, too mechanical. The flexibility of such a context is, indeed, determined by lines, and a prose line is very seldom a syntactic unit. In my opinion, the flexibility of a context should not be based on lines, that is, rigid simply typographic units, but on variable, more or less syntactic, units.

The same line-overlapping or concordance principle has been used in the last few years for the Michigan period dictionary projects, most importantly for retrieving, from machine-readable texts of Sidney and Milton, slips of the Aitken–Bratley type for the Michigan Early Modern English Materials (Bailey and Robinson 1970, p. 98, note 13; Robinson and Bailey 1972).

I should not like to say that it would be impossible to make a dictionary on the basis of such material: it might even be a very good one. In the case of prose texts from the Middle Ages edited after the manuscripts in a diplomatic way, it is even possible that Mr Aitken's method would prove to be very practical. In any case, as a prose line is liable to be much less a unity than a line in poetry, an automatic prose context generated by the computer, using the method that I called line-overlapping, will necessarily be inferior in quality to a poetic context generated according to the same principle and with the same program.

I think, however, that we could, both for prose and verse texts, make a program that yields far better results than those achieved by mechanical line-overlapping. We should in this connection distinguish between two methods.

The first method makes use of pre-editing. With certain texts we are forced to pre-edit by the nature of the prose writing itself. This may be the case with, for example, documents containing treasurers' accounts from the Middle Ages. One could imagine pre-editing such a text by dividing it into rather small units of about the size of one or two lines, which one might call mini-contexts. The context on the dictionary slip might then consist of a central mini-context containing the headword with another peripheral mini-context on either side of it.

Whereas pre-editing is not a problem if it concerns a text that is not too voluminous, what if it has to be applied to, for example, five volumes of 800 pages each? I think that in such a case pre-editing would be so expensive as simply to prove impossible.

This means that in many cases, and more specifically with the very bulky material that we will have to process for our period-dictionary of early Middle Dutch (that is, before the year 1301), we will be forced to use a fully automatic contexting practice without any pre-editing at all. For these texts it will probably be wise to apply the Aitken–Bratley method in one way or another. Up till now we lack the necessary experience as regards this matter.

If however, we are dealing with modern texts with standard punctuation, it will be possible to apply to them a program focussed on formal properties of the text itself: number of characters or positions, punctuation and blanks. Such a program could, for example, instruct the computer to start from a portion of text of, say, 180 positions before the headword, and proceed to the right until a full stop, exclamation-mark, question-mark or semicolon (perhaps even a comma?) is reached within the next 60 positions (that is, before position 120), and if so, begin the context say at position 165; if not, search to the left from position 180 onwards until a full stop, and so on, is reached, for example, at position 190, and begin the context there. If no full stop, etc., is reached within the space of a second variable (to the left) of 180 positions, the program must stop at the last blank before position 180. A nearly similar procedure will be followed after the headword. This is shown diagramatically in figure 1.

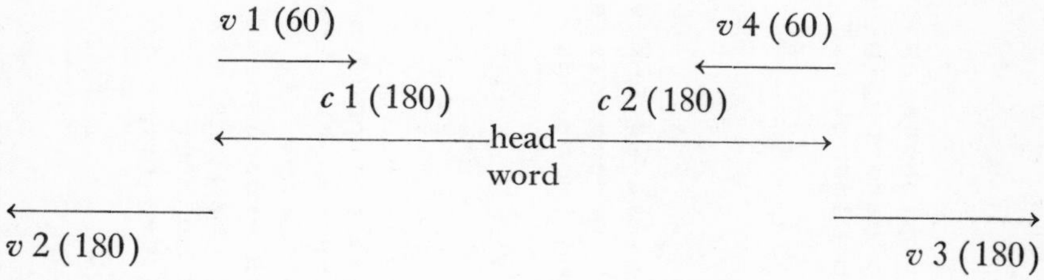

Figure 1

A special treatment must, of course, be given to the first words of a text; in as far as they are within the bounds of 180 positions their context will always start from position 1 onwards. In the same way the words at the end of the text, in as far as they are within the bounds of 180 positions, will always end with a full stop, a note of exclamation or interrogation. Examples are shown in figure 2.

The program of which I have given a rough draft provides us with a highly flexible context of approximatively six or seven lines, constituting a fair unity from a syntactic point of view. A context generated in this way could bear comparison with the manual context that is the result of traditional excerpting. The program could even be refined by building in a hierarchy in punctuation: 1. full stop, note of exclamation or interrogation ———→2. semicolon ———→3. colon ———→4. comma. This means that starting from position 180 before the headword and proceeding to the right the program would first look for a full stop, note of exclamation or interrogation before position 120, and, if no such punctuation mark should be present, then continue to the left searching in the second variable. If even there no such punctuation mark is met, then the program starts again from position 180 to the right searching for a semicolon, and so on. The context-generating program must be flexible, that is to say, it must be possible to make it fit the text. Both constants and variables will have to be adapted to the nature of the text.

But even with texts that have a normal punctuation, it should never be

sides

I have to thank several critics on both **sides** of the Atlantic, including some whose admiration for my play is most generously enthusiastic, for their heartfelt instructions as to how it can be improved.
B.SHAW, *Saint Joan* 82 [1924]

Atlantic

I have to thank several critics on both sides of the **Atlantic,** including some whose admiration for my play is most generously enthusiastic, for their heartfelt instructions as to how it can be improved.
B.SHAW, *Saint Joan* 82 [1924]

play

They point out that by the excision of the epilogue and all the references to such undramatic and tedious matters as the Church, the Feudal system, the Inquisition, the theory of heresy and so forth, all of which, they point out, would be ruthlessly blue pencilled by any experienced manager, the **play** could be considerably shortened. I think they are mistaken. The experienced knights of the blue pencil, having saved an hour and a half by disembowelling the play, would at once proceed to waste two hours in building elaborate scenery.
B.SHAW, *Saint Joan* 83 [1924]

Figure 2. Specimens of fully automatic contexts to Bernard Shaw's preface of *Saint Joan* produced by the program outlined in the text

think

They point out that by the excision of the epilogue and all the references to such undramatic and tedious matters as the Church, the feudal system, the Inquisition, the theory of heresy and so forth, all of which, they point out, would be ruthlessly blue pencilled by any experienced manager, the play could be considerably shortened. I **think** they are mistaken. The experienced knights of the blue pencil, having saved an hour and a half by disembowelling the play, would at once proceed to waste two hours in building elaborate scenery,
B.SHAW, *Saint Joan* 83 [1924]

audience

The intervals between the acts whilst these splendors were being built up and then demolished by the stage carpenters would seem eternal, to the great profit of the refreshment bars. And the weary and demoralized **audience** would lose their last trains and curse me for writing such inordinately long and intolerably dreary and meaningless plays.
B.SHAW, *Saint Joan* 83 [1924]

public

Nobody who knows the stage history of Shakespear will doubt that this is what would happen if I knew my business so little as to listen to these well intentioned but disastrous counsellors: indeed it probably will happen when I am no longer in control of the performing rights. So perhaps it will be as well for the **public** to see the play while I am still alive.
B.SHAW, *Saint Joan* 84 [1924]

forgotten that the computer-generated context must necessarily be more voluminous than the traditional one made by judgment of the lexicographer. From his experience he will be able to cut out from the text a context that is neither too long nor too short. As the computer has no judgment, the important thing is to get a context that makes it superfluous to go and look for the source. To abridge a context is less tedious than to be forced to lengthen it. I believe that abridging contexts will be a daily task for the lexicographer working with computer-generated dictionary slips.

Let me illustrate this by an example. If I should make a context in the traditional way for the word *necessary* in 'The Epilogue' to the 'Preface' of Bernard Shaw's *Saint Joan*, I could limit myself to the following eighteen words: 'It was *necessary* by hook or crook to shew the canonized Joan as well as the incinerated one'. A computer program proceeding from the headword *necessary* and taking no more than a minimum of 50 positions on either side until it meets a punctuation mark, would, however, yield the following result: 'I could hardly be expected to stultify myself by implying that Joan's history in the world ended unhappily with her execution, instead of beginning there. It was necessary by hook or crook to shew the canonized Joan as well as the incinerated one'. Such a context will no doubt meet the lexicographer's demands, but it is equally obvious that it will have to be abridged. A program taking at least 120 positions on either side until it meets a punctuation mark would have added to this context the following sentence: 'for many a woman has got herself burnt by carelessly whisking a muslin skirt into the drawing-room fireplace'.

It would, of course, be easy to get shorter contexts, but the danger is that too many of them should prove to be too short for the lexicographer's demands. A computer-generated file of two or five millions of dictionary slips with insufficient, inadequate context would simply mean a catastrophe and the bankruptcy of a method. Every lexicographer knows from his own experience that abridging a context to its lexicographical conciseness is only a matter of a few seconds. On the other hand, a context that proves too brief may cost minutes, in some cases even hours, to complete. The copiousness of the computer-generated context may truly be considered a drawback. But since this context presents so many advantages in comparison to the traditional one—an optimal legibility, a completeness rendering possible a quantitative approach, the possibility of unlimited repetition—the lexicographer will, I presume, be glad to take this little drawback into the bargain.

A method for generating a fully automatic context by computer, likewise on the basis of syntactic units, has been described by Stickel and Gräfe (1966). Starting from the headword the context contains in principle at least 25 words on either side, and ends with the punctuation mark that occurs before or after the headword. The program was developed by the German computing centre in Darmstadt for the Goethe-Wörterbuch of W. Schadewaldt. The program was applied to a juridical text (10,000 words) of Goethe.

A minor point concerning the computer-generated context on the dictionary slip has been the *position of the headword*. The question has sometimes been raised whether the headword should always have a fixed place on the dictionary card or slip, or if its position should be variable. If the place of the headword is a stable one, for example, always at the beginning of the central line, the card file will be easy to consult. But the same, or nearly the same result, that is, a clearly distinct place of the headword on a given line, can also be obtained by marking the headword with one or, if need be, two stars on either side, or/and by overprinting both the headword and the stars three times, creating something like boldface (Smith 1964).

As far as our work is concerned there is really no problem concerning the position of the headword. The bulk of the material to be printed by computer on our dictionary slips is on magnetic tape. That tape is similar to the tape used to print the corpus by cathode-ray tube output. I said similar and not identical, since our tape has been stripped of data necessary for the printing process but superfluous for our purpose. This means also that proofreading and correcting has been done beforehand. Since for obvious reasons (for example, avoiding breaking up words, needing two lines instead of one, keeping up the line numbering of the original document) it seems recommendable to preserve the lines of the text, such as they were ordered by computer for cathode-ray tube output in the printed document, it is clear that the headword will necessarily show up in a variable position. We do not consider this a drawback.

In this connection it might perhaps be useful to stress that each separate wordform can be a headword; we have, in fact, no lemmatizing at this phase of the work. I will not try to square the circle. Once we have a complete index of all word forms in the indexes which we make of our texts, lemmatizing might be done more easily and cheaply by hand at the pre-editing stage of the dictionary, resulting in a body of perfected lexicographical material.

A second minor point that does not properly concern the context is that we have decided not to make use of punched cards for our dictionary slips. In so far as poetical texts are concerned punched card size suits very well for dictionary slips. But even with prose texts it might be wise not to abandon the standard format of the punched card. We were, however, forced to do so, since the great bulk of the texts which we have to process consists of prose with line lengths of somewhere about 80 positions, and since, on the other hand, the original lineation should be preserved. So we thought it wise to adapt the computer-printed dictionary slips to our material, and not our material to the slips. Our cards, made of woodfree paper, will have a size of $9'' \times 3\frac{1}{2}''$, that is, about the same as a continuous punched card with unremoved side fringes and underfringe.

C

Abandoning the punched-card size means, moreover, that our diction- ary cards will not be punched. I consider this a gain, as punched output is at present to be considered less practical for our purpose. As a matter of fact punching would, no doubt, damage diacritical marks above and under the letters.

This paper was inspired chiefly by theoretical considerations of the feasi- bility of a flexible computer-generated context. I said in the beginning that, during the years gone by, I had faced this problem like a cat facing a dish of hot porridge. But we have at last been forced by our work, and also by the Edinburgh Symposium at which this paper was read, to begin eat- ing that porridge. Since the end of January, in close cooperation with Mr H. T. Wong, head of the programming section of our Institute, a context- generating computer program was started on the basis of a few fragments in Bernard Shaw's preface to *Saint Joan*. This program, operating on a non-pre-edited text, is of the fully automatic type, taking into considera- tion only formal properties of the text itself, without any human interven- tion. The aim of this pilot program was to find out what should be considered an optimum number of positions on either side of the head- word. It proved very useful. It made clear that decisions on printing computer-generated contexts on dictionary slips can never be a matter of theoretical considerations alone. It taught us not only that a comma is a rather poor context marker, but also that you need two sorts of variables: two short ones encroaching upon the space of both constants and two big ones of about the same size as the constants. Ultimately practical experi- ence with actual context-generating computer program operating on an actual text will settle what is the optimum solution. The proof of the pudding (or of the hot porridge) is in the eating.

Acknowledgements

I should like to thank Mr H. T. Wong and Mr A. J. Aitken for comments on a draft of this paper.

REFERENCES

Aitken, A. J. & Bratley, P. (1966) An archive of Older Scottish texts for scanning by computer. *English Studies*, **48**, 60-1.

Bailey, R. W. & Robinson, J. L. (1970) Computers and dictionaries. *Computers and Old English Concordances*, pp. 94-102 (eds. Cameron, A., Frank, R. & Leyerle, J.). Toronto: University of Toronto Press.

Busa, R. & Zampolli, A. (1968) Centre pour l'automation de l'analyse linguis- tique (C.A.A.L.), Gallarate. *Les Machines dans la linguistique*, pp. 25-37. Prague: Academia.

Duro, A. (1968) L'emploi des moyens électroniques pour la constitution du fichier lexicographique général par l'Academia della Crusca. *Les Machines dans la linguistique*, 201-20. Prague: Academia.

Imbs, P. (1967) *Centre de recherche pour un trésor de la langue Française*. Paris: Centre National de la Recherche Scientifique.

Kamp, H. (1969) Methoden zur Herstellung und Auswertung von Dialekt-Wörterbüchern mit Hilfe der elektronischen Datenverarbeitung. *NW*, **9**, 73-96.

Quemada, B. (1961) L'inventaire lexicographique en vue d'un Thesaurus national. *CahLex*, **3**, 119-31.

Robinson, J. L. & Bailey, R. W. (1972) Computer-produced microfilm in lexicography: toward a dictionary of early modern English. *The Computer and Literary Studies*, pp. 3-14 (eds. Aitken, A. J., Bailey, R. W. & Hamilton-Smith, N.). Edinburgh: Edinburgh University Press.

Smith, P. H. (1964) A computer program to generate a text concordance. *IBM Literary Data Processing Conference Proceedings 9-11 September 1964*, pp. 113-27. New York, NY: Modern Language Association.

Stickel, G. & Gräfe, M. (1966) Automatische Textzerlegung und Herstellung von Zettelregistern für das Goethe-Wörterbuch. *Sprache im technischen Zeitalter*, 247-57.

Sundqvist, A. (1966) Gammalt och nytt inom lexikografien. *NysvS*, **46**, 5-26.

Tollenaere, F. de (1961) La documentation lexicographique et ses propres besoins. *CahLex*, **3**, 101-15.

Tollenaere, F. de (1972) Encoding techniques in Dutch historical lexicography. *C.Hum.*, **6**, 147-52.

Wisbey, R. (1963) The analysis of Middle High German texts by computer—some lexicographical aspects. *Trans. philol. Soc.*, 28-48.

Wisbey, R. (1969) Ein computerlesbares Textarchiv des Frühmittelhoch-deutschen. *Jahrbuch für internationale Germanistik*, **1**, 37-46.

Stylistics and vocabulary studies

Towards an archive of lexical norms. A proposal

The analyst of literary style (among other scholars dependent upon concordances) has, in recent years, encountered a paradoxical situation. On the one hand he has found that the computer is spawning concordances at such a rate 'that, by the end of the century, we shall possess keys to the verbal usage of most major and many minor writers' (Wisbey 1971a, p. 22). On the other hand he has developed new requirements which are incompatible with what is currently offered. The analyst needs, but is rarely provided with, concordances so designed as to facilitate statistical comparison with relevant standard corpora. Laudable examples do appear, witness volumes 1 and 3 of the COMPENDIA series to medieval German texts (Wisbey 1968ff), but concordances to English works are rarely so thorough in their analytic apparatus.

Hastily conceived concordances to major literary figures appear each year with partial or total omissions even in basic lexical data, hence statistical investigation is rendered impractical if not impossible. In fact, computational analysts of style have come to dread the appearance of 'instant' concordances to writers in which they are particularly interested since the publication of a concordance in any format will pre-empt the market for some years—publishers being understandably reluctant to replace reference works which are adequate for many users. Of course, an author may be honoured by two or more computer-generated concordances, but only in unusual circumstances. The two recent Shakespeare concordances by Marvin Spevak (1968) and Trevor Howard-Hill (1969) are justifiable since each serves different scholarly needs. However, the fact that two rival concordances to G. M. Hopkins appeared within a year of each other suggests an accidental duplication of effort, a circumstance the more lamentable in that neither provides full frequencies for all of the poet's words, and the earlier of the pair (the Borello volume) is 'spavined from the start' by erroneous page and line references (Mariani 1971, p. 285). The pertinent fact here is this: because of the existence of two concordances having many excellent features in other respects, basic statistical data about a major poet will remain unavailable for many years.

A plea, therefore, for complete statistical data compatible with an analysis of standard corpora (Kučera and Francis 1967) seems to be called for, though it will seem futile to many. Since scholars are still groping toward efficient techniques in a discipline dependent on eclecticism, it is probably premature to expect a stable concordance format, though there are strong reasons for arriving at one soon. Paramount among them is the need to make comparisons between the lexical domains of various writers, a requirement possible only when concordance statistics can be directly related.

It is becoming obvious that advances in programming are not always accompanied by imaginative applications. The outputs from most concordance programs now include statistics vital to computational analysts of diverse interests, or are readily capable of doing so, but such data is often considered to be not worth printing by editors accustomed only to traditional uses of concordances. This wastage is deplorable, especially when one considers that inclusion would in no way incommode 'standard' concordance users—rather the addition of statistical data of the sort to be illustrated would extend the sphere of influence of a concordance far beyond the readership of the parent author. Nor need editors fear that the cost of publication would be increased significantly; a few pages of printout would suffice for all the statistics required.

A call for additional data in concordances necessitates some defence of the claim that statistical data is needed at all. To those who doubt that numerical analyses of vocabulary can further our notion of style, one could point to the fact that all statements about style are comparative and only as reliable as the data upon which the comparisons are based. Patrick Boyde's recent (1971) and succinct comment is appropriate here:

> *any interpretation of stylistic phenomena depends on comparison and contrast.* The facts about an author's style are to be sought in his work. The meaning of those facts is to be sought in the work of other authors (p. 18).

And, ever since Ferdinand de Saussure postulated that the language base common to all users (*la langue*) could theoretically be considered disjoint from the idiosyncratic usage of individuals (*la parole*), language analysts have sought ways to achieve the dichotomy in practice. In recent years, however, scholars have come to accept that 'style' and 'non-style' exhibit only an apparent duality, and that the difference lies in the relative frequencies of what is considered normal in specific contexts. Michael Riffaterre (1960) envisaged that analysts of the future would employ 'average readers' to detect stylistic devices, in the way that linguistic cartographers employ 'native informants'. However, for many of these 'devices' the detection could now be done by the more rigorous computer, since a comparison of relative frequencies is essentially a numerical operation. Furthermore, the problem of relying on human judgments is that neither 'informed' nor 'uninformed' readers are suitable for distinguishing stylistic features from contextually-normal ones, since, for example, in pieces of 'strict metrical form' from a 'remote period' and a 'homogeneous literary genre' (say a selection of Elizabethan sonnets) 'beginners will see nothing but "stylistic devices"; those with a little learning will see nothing but "context"' (Boyde 1971, p. 38).

It is the contention of the writer that well-ordered concordances offer the best hope for establishing what is normal in a given period and genre, and for isolating oddities peculiar to particular authors (at least as regards lexis, though syntactic insights would also be derived from parsed concordances). Evidence to support the primacy of concordances for stylistic functions is not hard to find. First, the basic statistical unit with which concordances deal is the word, which has demonstrable advantages over all other linguistic levels for stylistic investigation. As parameters of style, those units lower in linguistic rank than the word are inadequate, since they fail to discriminate even between radically different contexts under frequency analysis. Letter frequencies, for example, are stylistically insignificant, at least 'for a language as eccentrically written as English' (Hultzén, Allen, and Miron 1964, p.2). Indeed, it has even been convincingly argued that letter analysis is pointless in any area of linguistic investigation (Wilson 1954). Analysis of phonemes (and units of equivalent rank) has been similarly discouraged in stylistics since

> it has been abundantly established that phoneme distributions from even widely different texts, as far as subject matter is concerned, can be regarded as random samples from one basic distribution. Thus phoneme frequency does not appear to be style-conditioned. (Herdan 1960, p.119.)

However, as potential units for stylistic investigation increase in length, they increase in complexity also. All those more extensive than the word pose formidable difficulties for computational analysis. This fact is simply explained: as one seeks to quantify units of high linguistic rank (say syntactic structures) one increasingly enters the jungle of semantics, and the possibility of evolving an objective framework to *compare* the syntax of authors becomes remote. As Michael J. Gregory (1964) has pointed out, analysis at syntactic and higher levels usually reverts to lexical analysis when semantic problems are encountered: 'grammar cannot indicate why "he had a fear" differs from "he had a hope" . . . at least no grammar has yet done so. . . . So lexis takes over where the most delicate grammar ends'(pp. 72-3 and 82).

Therefore, the analyst reverts by default to the word. But, one may ask, what special qualities does it exhibit that are lacking in units higher and lower in the linguistic spectrum? To begin with, word frequency analysis has shown itself capable of resolving attribution problems, unlike that of letter and phoneme, hence the word must, by Herdan's criterion, be 'style conditioned'. Moreover, if different styles are seen as bas-reliefs foregrounded only slightly against flat areas of 'non-style', it is evident that a vast reserve of statistical data will be required to chart them. Only the word (via concordances, in conjunction with relevant standard corpora) can provide this comparative data. No potential parameter of style below or above that of the word is equally effective in establishing objective comparisons between authors and their common linguistic heritage. And the word is not only relatively unambiguously bounded for the computer (by the space and a small subset of orthographic symbols), but is small enough to ensure that even short genres such as poetry can meet the requirements for valid sample sizes upon which statistical investigations depend.

Editors of concordances can, then, provide data increasingly relevant to analysts of style, if they are made aware of their obligation to do so. Editors can no longer indulge themselves in experimental formats which later prove incompatible even with offerings of the same series, as has frequently happened. A case in point is the Yeats concordance (Parrish and Painter 1963), chosen as typical both of the Cornell concordance series and of concordances in general. This scholarly enterprise, excellent for traditional needs, has proved a most frustrating tool for the present writer's stylistic enquiries. The editors are not to blame—their format is still evolving and was not intended for the computational analyst. Still one regrets that essential counts inherent in the programs that generated this series were not printed. Objections might be raised at this point to any demand for data that would seem to clutter concordances with information of only specialist interest. After all, the relevant text from which each concordance was generated presumably remains in machine-readable form, hence information should be retrievable as needed. It was obviously Parrish's intention that the Cornell series should adopt this policy, seemingly a wise one considering the mutable demands of analysts. However, a useful object-lesson can be learned from his experience, since when requested to supply even such basic statistical data as the number of types and tokens for each author concordance, Parrish disclosed that

> we failed, for a number of reasons . . . to keep the promise once blithely made in print [in the introduction to the Yeats concordance] . . . that is, to keep on tapes copies of all the Cornell concordances (private correspondence of 3rd April 1971).

Yeats' poems presumably remain on tape, but recovery of the type and token counts from them directly is a needless expense, considering that the concordance contains (in somewhat scrambled form) the full word-frequency distribution. Still, significant lexical data about several major figures of the nineteenth and twentieth centuries will remain inaccessible until the Cornell texts are reprocessed, a task not likely to be recommended in our lifetimes.

Parrish has firmly resolved to 'keep on hand the tapes for future volumes', but reported no fundamental change in his policy for their preparation. Hence, no provision for *printed* statistical data has been made for projected concordances to plays by Yeats and Congreve, or to poems by Pope, Marvell, and Swift. This seems a great pity considering that 'as a cheap, handy, portable, reliable and essentially democratic random access device the printed book still has no rival' (Wisbey 1971, p.34).

Therefore, since editors are unlikely to provide elementary statistical data until petitioners become sufficiently vocal, it becomes the analysts' task to collect their own data, where possible, from existing concordances. To demonstrate that this is not an insuperable undertaking even where computer assistance is not available, I hand-compiled the basic data that appears as an appendix to this paper, intended as a supplement to the Cornell–Yeats concordance. It was later decided to confirm the compilation by computer. It is hoped that in future interested persons would announce their need for such data (in journals of computer applications) and their intention to supply the data if it were not forthcoming from others. In this way special concordances and statistical data might well come to light which would add to the existing archive of lexical norms. I now possess, for example, a concordance to all of the short stories of Virginia Woolf, as well as concomitant statistical data about these stories, and others by Katherine Mansfield.

As a pilot project, I offer to users of the Cornell Series the word-frequency distribution of Yeats' poetic canon. It presents statistical data embedded in the Cornell volume which is not retrievable without considerable effort. The principal reasons behind this compilation were to show that reconstitution of a partial bank was both possible and practical; to present a tool felt to be useful to other scholars; and to offer a set of statistics to the academic community, in the hope that the gesture will be reciprocated. The criterion for the inclusion of data is, foremost, availability. It is presented in a format like that employed by Kučera and Francis (1967) but with two additional data columns, a choice defended later in the paper.

I consider it axiomatic that any computer concordance should indicate the total number of words in its corpus, since most useful comparisons hinge upon this figure. This number is not provided for Yeats' poetry (the 'tokens') but figures for individual 'types' are either given or retrievable. However, type-frequencies for 'omitted words' are *not* provided for the Arnold and Byron volumes, so no synthesis of statistical appendices for those works could be attempted (at least by the method used with the Yeats corpus). Since the number of tokens in a concordance can be calculated by summing the product of each frequency of occurrence (X) times the number of types having this frequency (FX) this task was undertaken, initially by adding-machine, later by computer, which facilitated the presentation of data in a format compatible with that of Kučera and Francis. The percentage for each product of X times FX was also listed ($\%FX.X$), for reasons later explained.

Compilation of statistics for the Yeats corpus was complicated by several editorial policies common to each Cornell volume. First, frequencies for the words for which no contexts were provided by Parrish were listed, but these figures were given separate from the main concordance data. And, these 'omitted words' were listed alphabetically which meant hand sorting them into rank order for integration with the main list. Further, since omissions were made by the editor very arbitrarily, they ranged from single occurrences to the ubiquitous *the*, hence rank correlation over the entire lexical spectrum was necessary. This might still have been a relatively simple task (to interleave the 195 total and 3 partial omissions) had the number of types having a given frequency been listed. Since such figures, again, were absent, types had to be hand counted. The magnitude of this 'subroutine' will be appreciated by all those familiar with rank lists, since single occurrences alone for a corpus the size of Yeats' poetry comprise 4,698 entries, those 'twice occurring' 1,821, and so on. Again, the page-layout of the concordance complicated matters since one could not merely multiply the number of complete pages of, say, *hapax legomena*, by a fixed number of words per page, since randomly appearing hyphenated words occupied two lines and inflated the word count. Fortunately, since all hyphenated entries occupied two lines, and the second part of the compound was indented, it was possible to obtain individual FX counts by the simple expedient of subtracting the number of indentations from the total for each type. For mid-range words ordered in columns of random length, I found a 'word-ruler' to be most effective —a strip of paper graduated in units equal to the length of a column of ten words. The penultimate sorting procedure was to put the list of words 'not concorded' in rank order, matching each frequency of occurrence (X) with the types having this frequency (FX), then to interleave this data with that of the main list. Finally, with the knowledge that a type total should result by summing the 'FX' column, I checked the figure given by Parrish as the 'number of different words' in Yeats. Amazingly, our totals agreed—Yeats' poetic vocabulary seems to comprise 10,666 words. I had not expected an exact correspondence, since of the other two verifiable figures (the number of partial omissions and the number of total omissions) the latter, given by Parrish as 198, is wrong, the correct count being 195. There is no way to verify that my token count is correct, however, so I shall hedge and predict that Yeats' poetic canon comprises 'in the order of' 131,485 words.

The sceptic might wonder whether data assembled so laboriously justifies the effort. Its relevance to lexical analysts will be obvious, providing, at the most basic level, further evidence towards resolving the hypothesis that the 'bilogarithmic type/token ratio' is a linear relationship, hence a predictable and stable constant in lexical computations. Only when considerable data is made available for many other writers can the hypothesis be accepted as 'law', or ultimately rejected. Herdan, its proposer, has already dignified it with the pretentious status of a 'cybernetic law' (Herdan 1966, p.439).

More important than the type and token counts is the by-product generated by the summation—a *complete* ranking list of Yeats' lexis. Comparison of it with similar lists for related poets can reward even the casual observer. Ultimately, one hopes, comparison of many such lists will determine whether words in a given frequency range are principally

Author	Data	No. of 'Q-initial' hapax listed	No. of these 'Q-hapax' that also appear as hapax in one or more of remaining 6 authors
Arnold	Complete poems (20)	24	13
Blake	Complete poetry & prose (6)	13	12
Byron	*Don Juan* (8)	51	20
Dickinson	Complete poems (23)	22	14
Hopkins	Complete poems (1)	20	9
Joyce	*Ulysses* (9)	82	19
Yeats	Complete poems (21)	17	6

Table 1. A sample correlation of *hapax legomena* in
seven authors. Figures in parentheses denote sources
(*see* references)

'language-conditioned' or 'style-conditioned', and whether the effects
of syntax, genre, period, and subject predetermine a writer's lexis in a
definite sequence over definite frequency ranges. Table 2 compares the
highest frequency range of lexis for seven radically different writers, to
show that while most concur in 'preferring' a common vocabulary set of
highly-recurrent lexemes (no writer of the sample set shares fewer than
60 per cent of his upper quartile of tokens with the norm for twentieth-
century written English) the *order* of these words varies considerably.
When sufficient rank-lists are correlated, we might begin to plot the
points (if any exist and their order is consistent) at which the constraints
of syntax yield to those of genre, to period, to subject, and ultimately
to author. Because analysts suspect that the effects of an author can
be detected only when the above linguistic restraints are sufficiently
'damped', it has been proposed that examination begin at the opposite
end of the word distribution, which might be, perhaps, the 'author-
oriented' range of lexis. Parrish, in the introduction to Yeats, has encouraged this approach by noting that many of Yeats' most memorable
(and characteristic) words occur only once or twice in the entire canon. I
have elsewhere (Tallentire 1971) suggested some of the problems in this
approach, and offer table 1 to indicate the surprising degree of correlation
found even among *hapax legomena*. Only a small sample (those beginning
with the letter Q) have been compared. It would seem that far fewer words
than we would suspect are the exclusive patent of individual writers, even
those as supposedly eccentric as James Joyce.

From table 2 it may seem safe to conclude that syntax exerts so powerful an influence on lexis that for all writers of English, regardless of genre, period or subject, *the* will be the most frequently used word. Certainly the analysis of the million-word Brown Corpus revealed no deviants in this respect, among 500 samples representing 15 different genres. However, Dilligan and Ule (1971) in an investigation of an earlier period, the Elizabethan, point out that *the*, *and*, *I*, and *to* could at that time each occupy the first rank, and that *the* could even rank fourth, as it does in Marlowe's *Leir*. Nor is Marlowe particularly unorthodox for his time. Michael J. Preston has also confirmed (COMPENDIA, Vol. 4, 1972) that *the* ranked fourth in the songs of the Tudor Court. In fact, four words of that period and genre recurred more frequently than *the*: *I*, *and*, *my*, and *to* (the latter two sharing the third rank position with equal frequencies). It is fascinating to think that when sufficient data of this sort becomes available it might be possible (granting the myriad problems of orthographic variants and lexical peculiarities) to trace the literary history of each lexeme from its entry into the language and through its subsequent fluctuations to its present 'normal' use—to chart in fact the evolution of English vocabulary. We might also then examine Herdan's (1966, p. 295) frequent contention that English is gradually progressing towards 'monosyllabism'—a notion not rendered any less suspect by the very term itself.

Some of the above speculations may prove Utopian, but it is certain that stylistic studies would be much enriched by word frequency distributions for specific 'contexts' in conjunction with comparable data for specific authors. This follows from Riffaterre's premise that abnormal relative frequencies denote stylistic features of a work. It should be pointed out that this method of highlighting stylistic aberration is particularly promising for noting significantly *low* occurrences, since these are features hardly likely to be observed by the unaided eye. Of course, word frequency counts alone cannot illuminate all lexical idiosyncrasy. It must be admitted that words recognized as stylistically relevant in an author's canon might have identical relative frequencies in any list of norms, if the words appeared in unusual collocations. This fact has been recognized and projected stylistic tools such as Peggy Haskel's dictionary of collocations are in progress (Haskel 1971).

To return to table 2, a few observations might be made. First, since each of the Brown samples analysed by Kučera and Francis also revealed *the* to occupy rank 1, its prominence must be endemic to twentieth-century English in England and America. How long *the* will remain supreme, or when it achieved undisputed primacy, remains to be determined. Certainly no other word in twentieth-century English exhibits such stability. From table 2 it would also seem that, syntactically, the American Emily Dickinson is more English than the English, since her ten most frequent words are also the ten most frequent in the English norm, which correlates

English rank	Word (Norm (3))	American rank (15)	Blake (6)	Byron (8)	Dickinson (23)	Joyce (9)	Shakespeare (24)	Woolf*	Yeats (21)
1	the	1	1	1	1	1	1	1	1
2	of	2	2	4	5	2	5	3	3
3	and	3	5	2	4	3	2	2	2
4	to	4	4	5	3	5	4	6	8
5	a	5	6	3	2	4	6	4	4
6	in	6	3	6	9	6	10	7	7
7	that	7	12	12	7	9	9	11	5
8	it	12	21	23	8	12	15	10	22
9	is	8	8	21	10	19	11	—	16
10	I	20	7	11	6	10	3	15	6
Norms in author's first 10		8 of 10	8 of 10	6 of 10	10 of 10	8 of 10	8 of 10	7 of 10	8 of 10
11	for	11	15	10	12	15	14	16	13
12	be	17	22	—	16	—	—	—	—
13	was	9	—	13	23	13	24	9	—
14	as	14	23	8	11	24	7	18	21
15	you	33	10	—	—	16	—	—	11
16	with	13	11	14	19	11	21	14	19
17	he	10	14	6	25	7	—	12	14
18	on	16	—	—	—	14	23	20	17
19	have	28	24	—	—	—	—	—	—
20	by	19	17	—	—	22	12	25	—
21	not	23	—	17	—	—	—	17	—
22	at	18	—	25	—	21	19	—	—
23	this	21	20	—	—	—	—	—	—
24	are	24	—	—	—	—	—	—	—
25	we	41	—	—	21	—	—	—	—
Norms among author's first 25		22/25	19/25	17/25	17/25	19/25	17/25	17/25	16/25
Tokens		1,014,232	—	14,439	—	260,430	884,647	49,150*	131,485*
Types		50,406	—	—	—	29,899	29,066	6,578*	10,666
Types/Tokens		0·050	—	—	—	0·111*	0·033*	0·134*	0·081*
Log Types/Log Tokens		0·783	—	—	—	0·824*	0·751*	0·814*	0·787*

Table 2. Comparative ranking lists in the highest frequency range of lexis. Figures in parentheses denote sources (*see* references); asterisked data is my own

with only 80 per cent of the American 'top ten'. On the other hand, she is the most aberrant of the writers sampled in her relative dependency upon the indefinite article. I leave others to ponder the reasons why a sixteenth-century dramatist in his highest frequency range of lexis lies closer to the norms of 1923 than Virginia Woolf does (granted that my count derives from Spevak's modern spelling text of Shakespeare) but one supposes this is yet another manifestation of Shakespeare as a man for all centuries. In passing, Woolf's predilection for the past tense is also interesting. In the English and American norms *is* ranks ninth and eighth respectively, but in Woolf *was* usurps the role of most frequent verb, ranking ninth in her short stories. *Is* in the Woolf stories ranks a lowly 35th (hence the figure is not given in table 2 since it lies beyond the author's 'top 25' words). Of course this 'peculiarity' may well be 'normal' for twentieth-century short fiction, hence it is dangerous to assume that a stylistic feature peculiar to Mrs Woolf has been isolated.

The many blanks in my statistics for *tokens* and *types* indicate clearly that editors are not yet convinced of this data's relevance to concordance users. Still, four more mosaic pieces at least are offered toward the composite picture, now emerging, of the *actual* relationship patterning the 'differential' growth of vocabulary with text length.

What will be demanded of the concordances of the future can as yet scarcely be imagined, but it is certain that two practices employed in contemporary concordances, both the result of arbitrary editorial decisions, must cease. The first is that of determining the amount of context to be given the reader, and its format, by machine criteria rather than that supplied by the users. As programs become more sophisticated, and practical problems of syntax yield to mechanical resolution, we should of course escape from rigidly specified contexts generated from instructions such as 'print up to 40 characters either side of a centered headword'. The program used by Spevak for concording Shakespeare is a forerunner of future practices one hopes, since it is capable of adjusting the context 'threshold' to assume a syntactically well-formed frame for each key word. The second policy that must change is the dictatorial one of deleting words considered 'non-significant' by an editor. To provide a line of context for each occurrence of *the* or *and* (or even line references) is of course merely to reconstitute the text (though frequency counts at least are needed) but to delete infrequent words is fraught with hazards. It can, for example, render ineffective the most elementary function of a concordance, that of a finding list.

Consider the plight of a scholar who remembers the syncopated line from *The Waste Land* that reads

'O O O O that Shakespeherian Rag'

and hears an echo of Yeats in it. He decides to check his intuition that two modern poets have explored the same device. He would search in vain in the Parrish concordance since, in the line he sought

'O! O! O! O! But no, that is not it'
'all the words . . . are nonsignificant' (Parrish and Painter 1963, p. xi). It
is to the editor's credit that he cites this 'troublesome' line in his introduction, but this is little solace to one who skipped the introduction and
abandoned his quest—convinced he had a defective memory.

A few words about the format of the appended rank list are perhaps
called for. The criterion of compatibility with the analysis of the Brown
Corpus (regarded as our best contemporary English data base) is, alone,
sufficient justification for statistical purposes. *Any* deletions from the
Kučera and Francis format in statistics for authors writing in English must
rob the standard corpus of part of its potency for lexical comparisons.
And, since we cannot know the ultimate uses of such data, it is arrogant to
proscribe any part of it. However, the addition of further columns can
extend the stylistic uses somewhat.

In the past, the data contained in '$CUM \%$' columns of various analyses
(*see* appendix) have been useful mainly to language teachers interested
in determining how many specific words of a language make up a given
percentage of texts, so that all of the highest frequency 'function' words
might be included in language primers, with successively incremented
numbers of the most frequent 'content' words for different graded-
readers. However, a stylistic application was recently suggested by Dilligan
and Ule (1971). They propose

> a measure of vocabulary correspondence . . . that is not unduly in-
> fluenced by the preponderance of common words or the vagaries of
> once-words. It has the merit that it does not require a comparison of
> samples of equal size. For any two identical texts, the correspondence
> will be 100 per cent. The vocabulary correspondence is obtained by
> summing up for each word of vocabulary (in either text) the lower
> relative per cent frequencies with which the words occur in either of
> the two texts.

The input for this vocabulary matching program would, ideally, be an
alphabetical listing of the vocabularies of the authors concerned, with
the relative per cent frequencies given for each word. However, the same
data could be extracted from rank list distributions, provided that it was
possible to correlate each word with its rank, and its *individual* relative
per cent frequency. Adoption of the column headed $\% FX . X$ would make
correlation possible for different texts, though admittedly not easy, since
a search of the concordance proper would be necessary to equate a word
and its rank for low-frequency entries. It should be pointed out that my
cumulative type-total (the column headed '$SUM\ FX$') provides the
necessary ranks for the Yeats corpus, a particular 'rank range' being the
numerical difference between a listed type and the preceding type figure.
For example, the 4,698 different *hapax legomena* rank from 5,968 to
10,666 in this corpus.

While I could not include individual 'rank-lists by part of speech' in
D

my proposed appendix to the Yeats' poetic corpus, there are stylistic reasons why editors might undertake the requisite parsing during the inputting of their texts, especially for genres like poetry which frequently deploy lexis in peculiar syntactic roles. I offer one application (somewhat facetiously) to teachers interested in comparative approaches to poetry. We might generate lines of, say, 'the quintessential Yeats' by predetermining his dominant syntactic patterns—perhaps by a procedure like the one used by Milic (1968) for Swift—then filling the slots of the most frequent patterns with Yeats' most frequent lexemes, culled from the requisite parsed rank-lists. If the Yeats' stanza that occurred most frequently (hence the most characteristically) was an unrhymed quatrain having $x \pm a$ nouns, $y \pm b$ verbs, $z \pm c$ adjectives . . ., in syntactically specified patterns, the required lexemes could be skimmed from their respective rank-lists and pummelled into 'poetic' utterances by computer. Comparison of these computer-dictated (if humanly directed) fragments with actual stanzas by Yeats might well reveal insights into the process of poetic composition. Lest the reader consider this idea too fanciful for serious consideration, I submit that the poetry synthesized by Milic (1971) from stanzas by Dylan Thomas suggests that such procedures are not pointless.

Parsed frequency distributions might also be used to relate a given writer's vocabulary to what Josephine Miles (1967) calls the '260 main terms of poetry'. Miles correlates the nouns, verbs, and adjectives in the poetry and prose of five centuries, and her lists provide one of the few comprehensive sources of English lexical data. They must be approached with some reserve, however, since errors are frequent. The hazards inherent in purporting to supply any 'objective' statement about literature are of course known to us all—witness the example of the 'Zipf law'. This measure (once accepted as a fact) underwent successive, but debilitating modifications, and its current status is better subsumed in the 'Zip flaw'. (The fact that the two designations are equal phonetically serves to reinforce my earlier views on the unsuitability of the phoneme in stylistic analysis.) Miles' errors, however, are more elementary than Zipf's. And, since her lists are often used as a lexical base even for languages other than English in lieu of 'native' norms (*cf.* Boyde 1971) it behoves me to defend my charges of inaccuracy. Consider just one statement. 'Of the 260 main terms for poetry, about 50 are disyllabic: *golden, silver,* . . ., *hearty,* . . ., *eternal,* . . ., *heavy,* . . ., *superior,* . . ., *various,* . . ., *memory.*' It is obvious from my truncated list that 'polysyllabic' was meant instead of 'disyllabic', but that in itself is trivial. There are, however, in addition to the four non-disyllables listed, four omissions from Miles' list of 50 words (*lady, holy, bosom,* and *woman*); two transcription errors (*hearty* for *beauty* and *heavy* for *heaven*); and one addition not among the original 260 terms (*memory*). Hence, of 50 entries, fully one-fifth are in some way erroneous. Still, for comparative data over an extensive period Miles remains our only source, a fact which should lend support for the accumulation of computer-assembled norms.

Before concluding any appeal for the acquisition of diverse lexical data it should be admitted that the cumulation of lexical norms will be neither simple nor fully computable. Even with common high-frequency types (like *in*) one might be dealing with a Latin phrase in some contexts (*in loco parentis*, for example), hence one must be careful to match like with like in any lexical comparison. In texts from early periods and genres, problems of comparison will be myriad, involving ambiguous contractions (like *o'* for *of*) and spelling variants. These problems can be largely overcome by programs which group words designated as 'paradigms' by an editor, but further difficulties lie in wait. The fact that homographs can be different parts of speech and have vastly different meanings is not the least of these (consider *mean* as a verb, adjective, and noun). Still, even if an analyst groups such ambiguous forms together, he has still adhered to the standard practice of lexicographers, and useful comparisons can be made if equivalent lists for other authors are available.

Lest the principal point in this somewhat meandering 'preamble to an appendix' be forgotten, let me sum up. Statistical appendices to author concordances in a form compatible with analyses of some definitive corpus are not luxuries to abet esoteric investigations. Rather, they will increasingly be needed by scholars in most areas of literary and linguistic research. Further, the problems inherent in reconstituting partial data oblige editors to supply full counts—especially since existing concordance programs readily produce them. Finally, the call for, and dissemination of, such data as is here appended should serve several purposes. It cannot fail to make an academic community aware of individual needs, no less of new research possibilities. It will convince compilers of future concordances that statistical users comprise a significant cartel. But more important, the steady accumulation of *comparable* data with each new concordance will enable us gradually to chart the tidal currents in the lexis of our language. For, just as a navigator must account for 'set' (his ship's lateral movement due to current) before 'drift' (wind effects) can be resolved, so too must the analyst of style determine the set of language before the drift of particular authors can be appreciated.

REFERENCES

Borello, A. (1969) ed. *A Concordance to the Poetry in English of Gerard Manley Hopkins*. New Jersey: Scarecrow Press. [1]
Boyde, P. (1971) *Dante's Style in his Lyric Poetry*. Cambridge: Cambridge University Press. [2]
Dewey, G. (1923) *Relativ[e] Frequency of English Speech Sounds*. Cambridge, Mass.: Harvard University Press. [3]
Dilligan, R. J. & Bender, T. K. (1970) eds. *A Concordance to the English Poetry of Gerard Manley Hopkins*. Madison: University of Wisconsin Press. [4]
Dilligan, R. J. & Ule, L. (1971) Reply to Tallentire (1971) in *TLS* (22.10.71) 1336. [5]

Erdman, D.V. (1967) ed. *A Concordance to the Writings of William Blake*. Ithaca: Cornell University Press. [6]

Gregory, M.J. (1964) An approach to the study of style. *Linguistics and Style* (eds. Enkvist, N., Spencer, J. & Gregory, M.J.) London: Oxford University Press. [7]

Hagelman, C.W. (1967) ed. *A Concordance to Byron's Don Juan*. Ithaca: Cornell University Press. [8]

Hanley, M.L. *et al.* (1962) *Word Index to James Joyce's Ulysses*. Madison: University of Wisconsin Press. [9]

Haskel, P.I. (1971) Collocations as a measure of stylistic variety. *The Computer in Literary and Linguistic Research*, pp. 159-68 (ed. Wisbey, R.A.). Cambridge: Cambridge University Press. [10]

Herdan, G. (1960) *Type-Token Mathematics*. 'S-Gravenhage: Mouton. [11]

Herdan, G. (1966) *The Advanced Theory of Language as Choice and Chance*. New York: Springer-Verlag. [12]

Howard-Hill, T.H. (1969) ed. *Oxford Shakespeare Concordance*. London: Oxford Univerity Press. [13]

Hultzén, L.S., Allen Jr., J.H.D. & Miron, M.S. (1964) eds. *Tables of Transitional Frequencies of English Phonemes*. Urbana: University of Illinois. [14]

Kučera, H. & Francis, W.N. (1967) *Computational Analysis of Present-Day American English*. Providence: Brown University Press. [15]

Mariani, P. (1971) Hopkinssong Wordspawn. Review of Borello (1969) & Dilligan & Bender (1970). *C.Hum.* 285-9. [16]

Miles, J. (1967) *Style and Proportion*. Boston: Little Brown & Co. [17]

Milic, L.T. (1968) *A Quantitative Approach to the Style of Jonathan Swift*. The Hague: Mouton. [18]

Milic, L.T. (1971) The possible usefulness of poetry generation. *The Computer in Literary and Linguistic Research*, pp. 169-82 (ed. Wisbey, R.A.). Cambridge: Cambridge University Press. [19]

Parrish, S.M. (1959) ed. *A Concordance to the Poems of Matthew Arnold*. Ithaca: Cornell University Press. [20]

Parrish, S.M. & Painter, J.A. (1963) eds. *A Concordance to the poems of W.B. Yeats*. Ithaca: Cornell University Press. [21]

Riffaterre, M. (1960) Stylistic context. *Word*, **16**, 207-18. [22]

Rosenbaum, S.P. (1964) ed. *A Concordance to the Poems of Emily Dickinson*. Ithaca: Cornell University Press. [23]

Spevak, M. (1968) ed. *A Complete and Systematic Concordance to the Works of Shakespeare*. 6 vols. Hildesheim: Georg Ulms Verlagsbuchhandlung. [24]

Tallentire, D.R. (1971) The mathematics of style. *TLS* (13.8.71) 973-4. [25]

Wilson, K. (1954) Psycholinguistics. Memoir 10, *Publications in Anthropology and Linguistics*. Bloomington: Indiana University Press. [26]

Wisbey, R.A. (1968ff) COMPENDIA (Computer Generated Aids to Literary and Linguistic Research). Leeds: W.S.Maney & Son Ltd. [27]

Wisbey, R.A. (1971) Publications from an archive of computer-readable literary texts. *The Computer in Literary and Linguistic Research*, pp. 19-34 (ed. Wisbey, R.A.). Cambridge: Cambridge University Press. [28]

Wisbey, R.A. (1971a) The Computer and Literary Studies. *Symposium on Printing*, pp. 9-26 (ed. Reed, R.). Leeds Philosophical and Literary Society. [29]

APPENDIX : WORD-FREQUENCY DISTRIBUTION TO THE CORNELL YEATS CONCORDANCE

SYMBOLS USED IN APPENDIX
as found in Kučera and Francis, p.299, except those marked

X	Frequency of occurrence
$FX=f_x$	Number of types of frequency X
$*\%FX$	The ratio of each FX figure over the type total (10,666) as a percentage
$SUM\ FX=\underset{x}{\Sigma}f_x$	Sum of types due to frequency X and preceding values of X
$CUM\ \%FX=\%\underset{x}{\Sigma}f_x$	Per cent of types due to frequency X and preceding value of X
$FX.X=f_xX$	Number of tokens accounted for by types of frequency X
$SUM\ FX.X=\underset{x}{\Sigma}f_xX$	Sum of tokens due to frequency X and preceding values of X
$*\%FX.X$	The relative per cent frequency of tokens
$CUM\ \%FX.X=\%\underset{x}{\Sigma}f_xX$	Per cent of tokens due to frequency X and preceding values of X

X	FX	%FX	SUM FX	CUM%FX	FX.X	SUM FX.X	%FX.X	CUM%FX.X
8436	1	0.0094	1	0.0094	8436	8436	6.4159	6.4159
6023	1	0.0094	2	0.0188	6023	14459	4.5808	10.9967
3320	1	0.0094	3	0.0281	3320	17779	2.5250	13.5217
2841	1	0.0094	4	0.0375	2841	20620	2.1607	15.6824
2357	1	0.0094	5	0.0469	2357	22977	1.7926	17.4750
2132	1	0.0094	6	0.0563	2132	25109	1.6215	19.0965
2088	1	0.0094	7	0.0656	2088	27197	1.5880	20.6845
1751	1	0.0094	8	0.0750	1751	28948	1.3317	22.0162
1118	1	0.0094	9	0.0844	1118	30066	0.8503	22.8665
1081	1	0.0094	10	0.0938	1081	31147	0.8221	23.6886
1079	1	0.0094	11	0.1031	1079	32226	0.8206	24.5093
1019	1	0.0094	12	0.1125	1019	33245	0.7750	25.2843
1007	1	0.0094	13	0.1219	1007	34252	0.7659	26.0501
992	1	0.0094	14	0.1313	992	35244	0.7545	26.8046
974	1	0.0094	15	0.1406	974	36218	0.7408	27.5453
922	1	0.0094	16	0.1500	922	37140	0.7012	28.2466
850	1	0.0094	17	0.1594	850	37990	0.6465	28.8930
799	1	0.0094	18	0.1688	799	38789	0.6077	29.5007
789	1	0.0094	19	0.1781	789	39578	0.6001	30.1008
737	1	0.0094	20	0.1875	737	40315	0.5605	30.6613
716	1	0.0094	21	0.1969	716	41031	0.5445	31.2058
713	1	0.0094	22	0.2063	713	41744	0.5423	31.7481
665	1	0.0094	23	0.2156	665	42409	0.5058	32.2539
633	1	0.0094	24	0.2250	633	43042	0.4814	32.7353
610	1	0.0094	25	0.2344	610	43652	0.4639	33.1992
590	1	0.0094	26	0.2438	590	44242	0.4487	33.6479
589	1	0.0094	27	0.2531	589	44831	0.4480	34.0959
575	1	0.0094	28	0.2625	575	45406	0.4373	34.5332
567	1	0.0094	29	0.2719	567	45973	0.4312	34.9644
556	1	0.0094	30	0.2813	556	46529	0.4229	35.3873
540	1	0.0094	31	0.2906	540	47069	0.4107	35.7980
526	1	0.0094	32	0.3000	526	47595	0.4000	36.1980
514	1	0.0094	33	0.3094	514	48109	0.3909	36.5890
508	1	0.0094	34	0.3188	508	48617	0.3864	36.9753

38.0941	0.3673	50088	483	0.3469	37	0.0094	1	483
38.4508	0.3567	50557	469	0.3563	38	0.0094	1	469
38.8067	0.3559	51025	468	0.3656	39	0.0094	1	468
39.1596	0.3529	51489	464	0.3750	40	0.0094	1	464
39.5087	0.3491	51948	459	0.3844	41	0.0094	1	459
39.8555	0.3468	52404	456	0.3938	42	0.0094	1	456
40.1947	0.3392	52850	446	0.4032	43	0.0094	1	446
40.4715	0.2768	53214	364	0.4125	44	0.0094	1	364
40.7469	0.2753	53576	362	0.4219	45	0.0094	1	362
41.0214	0.2746	53937	361	0.4313	46	0.0094	1	361
41.2899	0.2685	54290	353	0.4407	47	0.0094	1	353
41.5515	0.2616	54634	344	0.4500	48	0.0094	1	344
41.8093	0.2578	54973	339	0.4594	49	0.0094	1	339
42.0656	0.2563	55310	337	0.4688	50	0.0094	1	337
42.3212	0.2555	55646	336	0.4782	51	0.0094	1	336
42.5722	0.2510	55976	330	0.4875	52	0.0094	1	330
43.0559	0.4837	56612	636	0.5063	54	0.0188	2	318
43.2886	0.2327	56918	306	0.5157	55	0.0094	1	306
43.5168	0.2282	57218	300	0.5250	56	0.0094	1	300
43.7404	0.2236	57512	294	0.5344	57	0.0094	1	294
43.9632	0.2228	57805	293	0.5438	58	0.0094	1	293
44.4028	0.4396	58383	578	0.5625	60	0.0188	2	289
44.8302	0.4274	58945	562	0.5813	62	0.0188	2	281
45.0371	0.2069	59217	272	0.5907	63	0.0094	1	272
45.2401	0.2031	59484	267	0.6000	64	0.0094	1	267
45.4402	0.2000	59747	263	0.6094	65	0.0094	1	263
45.6379	0.1977	60007	260	0.6188	66	0.0094	1	260
45.8242	0.1863	60252	245	0.6282	67	0.0094	1	245
46.0098	0.1856	60496	244	0.6375	68	0.0094	1	244
46.1939	0.1841	60738	242	0.6469	69	0.0094	1	242
46.3764	0.1825	60978	240	0.6563	70	0.0094	1	240
46.5574	0.1810	61216	238	0.6657	71	0.0094	1	238
46.7316	0.1742	61445	229	0.6750	72	0.0094	1	229
46.8996	0.1681	61666	221	0.6844	73	0.0094	1	221
47.0662	0.1666	61885	219	0.6938	74	0.0094	1	219
47.2320	0.1658	62103	218	0.7032	75	0.0094	1	218

X	FX	%FX	SUM FX	CUM%FX	FX.X	SUM FX.X	%FX.X	CUM%FX.X
213	1	0.0094	76	0.7125	213	62316	0.1620	47.3940
209	1	0.0094	77	0.7219	209	62525	0.1590	47.5530
208	1	0.0094	78	0.7313	208	62733	0.1582	47.7111
204	1	0.0094	79	0.7407	204	62937	0.1552	47.8663
197	1	0.0094	80	0.7500	197	63134	0.1498	48.0161
196	1	0.0094	81	0.7594	196	63330	0.1491	48.1652
194	1	0.0094	82	0.7688	194	63524	0.1475	48.3127
188	1	0.0094	83	0.7782	188	63712	0.1430	48.4557
187	1	0.0094	84	0.7875	187	63899	0.1422	48.5979
184	1	0.0094	85	0.7969	184	64083	0.1399	48.7379
183	1	0.0094	86	0.8063	183	64266	0.1392	48.8771
182	1	0.0094	87	0.8157	182	64448	0.1384	49.0155
179	1	0.0094	88	0.8251	179	64627	0.1361	49.1516
177	2	0.0188	90	0.8438	354	64981	0.2692	49.4208
176	1	0.0094	91	0.8532	176	65157	0.1339	49.5547
174	2	0.0188	93	0.8719	348	65505	0.2647	49.8194
170	2	0.0188	95	0.8907	340	65845	0.2586	50.0780
168	1	0.0094	96	0.9001	168	66013	0.1278	50.2057
167	1	0.0094	97	0.9094	167	66180	0.1270	50.3327
166	2	0.0188	99	0.9282	332	66512	0.2525	50.5852
165	2	0.0188	101	0.9469	330	66842	0.2510	50.8362
163	1	0.0094	102	0.9563	163	67005	0.1240	50.9602
162	1	0.0094	103	0.9657	162	67167	0.1232	51.0834
161	1	0.0094	104	0.9751	161	67328	0.1224	51.2058
158	2	0.0188	106	0.9938	316	67644	0.2403	51.4462
156	1	0.0094	107	1.0032	156	67800	0.1186	51.5648
154	2	0.0188	109	1.0219	308	68108	0.2342	51.7991
150	1	0.0094	110	1.0313	150	68258	0.1141	51.9131
148	1	0.0094	111	1.0407	148	68406	0.1126	52.0257
145	2	0.0188	113	1.0594	290	68696	0.2206	52.2463
144	1	0.0094	114	1.0688	144	68840	0.1095	52.3558
142	2	0.0188	116	1.0876	284	69124	0.2160	52.5718
138	2	0.0188	118	1.1063	276	69400	0.2099	52.7817
137	1	0.0094	119	1.1157	137	69537	0.1042	52.8859

53.1939	0.1019	69942	134	1.1438	122	0.0094	1	134
53.4928	0.2989	70335	393	1.1719	125	0.0281	3	131
53.5917	0.0989	70465	130	1.1813	126	0.0094	1	130
53.6898	0.0981	70594	129	1.1907	127	0.0094	1	129
53.8845	0.1947	70850	256	1.2095	129	0.0188	2	128
53.9803	0.0958	70976	126	1.2188	130	0.0094	1	126
54.0754	0.0951	71101	125	1.2282	131	0.0094	1	125
54.1697	0.0943	71225	124	1.2376	132	0.0094	1	124
54.4503	0.2806	71594	369	1.2657	135	0.0281	3	123
54.6359	0.1856	71838	244	1.2845	137	0.0188	2	122
54.7279	0.0920	71959	121	1.2938	138	0.0094	1	121
54.8161	0.0882	72075	116	1.3032	139	0.0094	1	116
54.9036	0.0875	72190	115	1.3126	140	0.0094	1	115
54.9903	0.0867	72304	114	1.3220	141	0.0094	1	114
55.0762	0.0859	72417	113	1.3313	142	0.0094	1	113
55.4139	0.3377	72861	444	1.3688	146	0.0375	4	111
55.4976	0.0837	72971	110	1.3782	147	0.0094	1	110
55.8292	0.3316	73407	436	1.4157	151	0.0375	4	109
55.9113	0.0821	73515	108	1.4251	152	0.0094	1	108
55.9927	0.0814	73622	107	1.4345	153	0.0094	1	107
56.0733	0.0806	73728	106	1.4438	154	0.0094	1	106
56.1532	0.0799	73833	105	1.4532	155	0.0094	1	105
56.3114	0.1582	74041	208	1.4720	157	0.0188	2	104
56.4680	0.1567	74247	206	1.4907	159	0.0188	2	103
56.7783	0.3103	74655	408	1.5282	163	0.0375	4	102
56.9320	0.1536	74857	202	1.5470	165	0.0188	2	101
57.0841	0.1521	75057	200	1.5657	167	0.0188	2	100
57.3100	0.2259	75354	297	1.5938	170	0.0281	3	99
57.4590	0.1491	75550	196	1.6126	172	0.0188	2	98
57.5328	0.0738	75647	97	1.6407	173	0.0094	1	97
57.6773	0.1445	75837	190	1.6689	175	0.0188	2	95
57.8918	0.2145	76119	282	1.6970	178	0.0281	3	94
58.1040	0.2122	76398	279	1.7251	181	0.0281	3	93
58.3139	0.2099	76674	276	1.7251	184	0.0281	3	92
58.6599	0.3460	77129	455	1.7720	189	0.0469	5	91
58.7284	0.0684	77219	90	1.7814	190	0.0094	1	90

X	FX	%FX	SUM FX	CUM%FX	FX.X	SUM FX.X	%FX.X	CUM%FX.X
89	1	0.0094	191	1.7907	89	77308	0.0677	58.7961
88	5	0.0469	196	1.8376	440	77748	0.3346	59.1307
86	3	0.0281	199	1.8657	258	78006	0.1962	59.3269
85	1	0.0094	200	1.8751	85	78091	0.0646	59.3916
84	1	0.0094	201	1.8845	84	78175	0.0639	59.4555
83	2	0.0188	203	1.9032	166	78341	0.1263	59.5817
82	4	0.0375	207	1.9407	328	78669	0.2495	59.8312
81	4	0.0375	211	1.9782	324	78993	0.2464	60.0776
80	3	0.0281	214	2.0064	240	79233	0.1825	60.2601
79	6	0.0563	220	2.0626	474	79707	0.3605	60.6206
78	2	0.0188	222	2.0814	156	79863	0.1186	60.7392
77	3	0.0281	225	2.1095	231	80094	0.1757	60.9149
76	6	0.0563	231	2.1658	456	80550	0.3468	61.2617
75	2	0.0188	233	2.1845	150	80700	0.1141	61.3758
74	2	0.0188	235	2.2033	148	80848	0.1126	61.4884
73	1	0.0094	236	2.2126	73	80921	0.0555	61.5439
72	1	0.0094	237	2.2220	72	80993	0.0548	61.5987
69	4	0.0375	241	2.2595	276	81269	0.2099	61.8086
68	4	0.0375	245	2.2970	272	81541	0.2069	62.0154
67	5	0.0469	250	2.3439	335	81876	0.2548	62.2702
66	6	0.0563	256	2.4002	396	82272	0.3012	62.5714
65	9	0.0844	265	2.4845	585	82857	0.4449	63.0163
64	5	0.0469	270	2.5314	320	83177	0.2434	63.2597
63	3	0.0281	273	2.5595	189	83366	0.1437	63.4034
62	2	0.0188	275	2.5783	124	83490	0.0943	63.4977
61	6	0.0563	281	2.6345	366	83856	0.2784	63.7761
60	5	0.0469	286	2.6814	300	84156	0.2282	64.0043
59	4	0.0375	290	2.7189	236	84392	0.1795	64.1837
58	7	0.0656	297	2.7845	406	84798	0.3088	64.4925
57	4	0.0375	301	2.8221	228	85026	0.1734	64.6659
56	7	0.0656	308	2.8877	392	85418	0.2981	64.9641
55	3	0.0281	311	2.9158	165	85583	0.1255	65.0896
54	5	0.0469	316	2.9627	270	85853	0.2053	65.2949
53	4	0.0375	320	3.0002	212	86065	0.1612	65.4561

66.0767	0.1521	86881	200	3.1502	336	0.0375	4	50
66.3003	0.2236	87175	294	3.2065	342	0.0563	6	49
66.5559	0.2555	87511	336	3.2721	349	0.0656	7	48
66.8061	0.2502	87840	329	3.3377	356	0.0656	7	47
67.1210	0.3149	82254	414	3.4221	365	0.0844	9	46
67.4632	0.3422	88704	450	3.5158	375	0.0938	10	45
67.8313	0.3681	89188	484	3.6190	386	0.1031	11	44
68.1256	0.2943	89575	387	3.7034	395	0.0844	9	43
68.6048	0.4791	90205	630	3.8440	410	0.1406	15	42
68.8854	0.2806	90574	369	3.9284	419	0.0844	9	41
69.2201	0.3346	91014	440	4.0315	430	0.1031	11	40
69.4870	0.2670	91365	351	4.1159	439	0.0844	9	39
69.7760	0.2890	91745	380	4.2096	449	0.0938	10	38
70.1137	0.2397	92189	444	4.3221	461	0.1125	12	37
70.3601	0.2464	92513	324	4.4065	470	0.0844	9	36
70.7062	0.3460	92968	455	4.5284	483	0.1219	13	35
71.0682	0.3620	93444	476	4.6597	497	0.1313	14	34
71.4948	0.4267	94005	561	4.8191	514	0.1594	17	33
71.9086	0.4137	94549	544	4.9784	531	0.1594	17	32
72.3801	0.4715	95169	620	5.1659	551	0.1875	20	31
72.6767	0.2966	95559	390	5.2878	564	0.1219	13	30
73.0076	0.3308	95994	435	5.4285	579	0.1406	15	29
73.4122	0.4046	96526	532	5.6066	598	0.1781	19	28
73.8434	0.4312	97093	567	5.8035	619	0.1969	21	27
74.2587	0.4153	97639	546	6.0004	640	0.1969	21	26
74.7150	0.4563	98239	600	6.2254	664	0.2250	24	25
75.0983	0.3833	98743	504	6.4223	685	0.1969	21	24
75.5356	0.4373	99318	575	6.6567	710	0.2344	25	23
75.9204	0.3848	99824	506	6.8723	733	0.2156	23	22
76.5114	0.5909	100601	777	7.2192	770	0.3469	37	21
77.0742	0.5628	101341	740	7.5661	807	0.3469	37	20
77.5366	0.4624	101949	608	7.8661	839	0.3000	32	19
78.0157	0.4791	102579	630	8.1943	874	0.3281	35	18
78.8432	0.8275	103667	1088	8.7943	938	0.6000	64	17
79.4760	0.6328	104499	832	9.2818	990	0.4875	52	16
80.1947	0.7187	105444	945	9.8725	1053	0.5907	63	15

X	FX	%FX	SUM FX	CUM%FX	FX.X	SUM FX.X	%FX.X	CUM%FX.X
14	67	0.6282	1120	10.5007	938	106382	0.7134	80.9081
13	73	0.6844	1193	11.1851	949	107331	0.7218	81.6298
12	89	0.8344	1282	12.0195	1068	108399	0.8123	82.4421
11	96	0.9001	1378	12.9196	1056	109455	0.8031	83.2452
10	114	1.0688	1492	13.9884	1140	110595	0.8670	84.1123
9	122	1.1438	1614	15.1322	1098	111693	0.8351	84.9473
8	154	1.4438	1768	16.5760	1232	112925	0.9370	85.8843
7	207	1.9407	1975	18.5168	1449	114374	1.1020	86.9863
6	298	2.7939	2273	21.3107	1788	116162	1.3599	88.3462
5	391	3.6659	2664	24.9766	1955	118117	1.4869	89.8331
4	579	5.4285	3243	30.4050	2316	120433	1.7614	91.5945
3	904	8.4755	4147	38.8806	2712	123145	2.0626	93.6571
2	1821	17.0729	5968	55.9535	3642	126787	2.7699	96.4270
1	4698	44.0465	10666	100.0000	4698	131485	3.5730	100.0000

Some quantitative vocabulary aspects
of a Dutch poem

The title of this paper, it will no doubt be noticed, formulates several restrictions: its subject matter is not poetry in general, but just *one Dutch poem*; no full account of this poem will be given, only *a few aspects* mentioned, and these aspects are limited in range since they lie on the *vocabulary* level only; the vocabulary itself is taken in a very restrictive sense, namely, the *quantitative* one. Yet I think that it is possible, even from the rather limited basis taken for this research, to throw some little light on the 'use of computers in literary research' in general.

However, before going straight to the topic, I think it may be useful to say a few words about the object of investigation, the text itself. The poem in question is a long lyrical epic called *May* (Dutch: *Mei*) containing 32,235 words. It is a description in three songs of the life of May, who arrives from the sea while her sister April is dying. She wanders through Holland, happy in the achievement of so much sensitive beauty. After a while, however, she tries to go beyond mere aesthetics and reach something or someone (represented by the god Balder) who is durable and everlasting. She will soon come to realize that her aim does not lie within the reach of human beings. Disappointed and sad she dies, to be succeeded by her sister June.

This is a very brief summary of the story and meaning of the poem. In the Netherlands and Flanders, *May* is considered a classic, and it is still read in nearly all Dutch secondary schools.

It was written in 1889 by the young Dutch poet Herman Gorter and is regarded as one of the masterpieces of Dutch impressionism. As to its verbal style, and especially its vocabulary, two features are striking at first sight: there is the richness, the abundant use of words on the one hand, and the creativity, the power of Gorter to coin a great many 'new words', on the other. It is precisely with aspects of those two features that we will deal.

THE DISTRIBUTION OF 'NEW WORDS' IN 'MAY'

Elsewhere (Martin 1971a) we have discussed the concept of 'new words' at some length. For clarity's sake we repeat very briefly our basic ideas: 'new words' are words formerly not existing in the word stock though perhaps possible, that is, they are not yet fixed in the word stock. These word stock fixations can be approximated by a representative thesaurus (in our case, a set of 12 dictionaries and/or word lists) with a margin of error that does not exceed 10 per cent [8 per cent being the highest number of omissions found in our sources for the most extensive Dutch dictionary, the *WNT* (*Woordenboek der Nederlandse Taal*—the Dutch equivalent of the *Oxford English Dictionary*), after the first screening]. According to this method *jongensloos* (boyless) would be a 'new word' in Dutch, in contrast to *kinderloos* (childless), although the former is perfectly possible—both the elements and the (surface and deep structure) rules needed to generate the wordstring exist in Dutch—and thus virtually in existence. It will be clear then that 'new words' are to be distinguished from 'neologisms', the latter being, in our opinion, words formerly not possible in the language. 'New words' were detected by having the computer compare the text with the thesaurus. As a result 460 'new words' were discovered in *May*. For further technical information we refer to our earlier publication (Martin 1971a). Of course nobody will claim that the creation of new words is the poet's monopoly, every language-user having this creative power at his disposal. In general, however, it is accepted that a poet makes more use of this dynamic language freedom and in our case especially there were good reasons to believe so [the n(new words)/V(types) ratio being 8 per cent for Gorter, as against 2 per cent or less for Dutch novels].

We consequently took it as a working hypothesis that the number of new words was a typical stylistic feature of Gorter's *May*, and turned our attention to the distribution of this feature throughout the poem, bearing in mind that: 'Numerical data may in some cases reveal a striking anomaly in the *distribution* of stylistic elements, and may thus raise important problems of aesthetic interpretation' (Ullmann 1966).

In the case of new words two alternatives were possible, distributionally speaking: either the number of new words was evenly spread throughout the whole work, in which case we were dealing with a constant or stationary stylistic feature; or their number was not evenly spread, in which case the question arose of what form the distribution took and why.

One of the (quantitative) characteristics of the new words we detected was that, of the 460 words which fell into this class, only 16 had a frequency higher than 1 (14 with $f=2$, and 2 with $f=3$). A stationary or constant distribution of the new word-types would consequently follow a relatively simple model, the number of new words appearing in a fragment being dependent on the *size* of that fragment only, not on the *place* of the fragment in the text. On the other hand, if we divide a text into a number of (say 10) fragments of equal size the proportion of word-types belonging to a frequency class greater than 1 (for example, with $f=10$) will become smaller and smaller the nearer we reach to the end of the text, and so should be greater, for example, in fragment 9 than in fragment 10.

In other words, a stationary distribution of words with $f=10$ should for fragments of equal size yield the same number of word-tokens, but not the same number of types. In the case of the *hapax legomena* (and more than 95 per cent of our new words were hapaxes), types and tokens fall together so the distribution of word-types is not different from that of word-tokens, and in this case fragments of equal size will yield the same number of types. We divided our text into 10 parts of 3,000 occurrences each (taking into account both the length of our text and the total number of new words) and consequently expected for the first 30,000 occurrences of the text:

$$(460 - 13)/10 = 44 \cdot 70 \text{ new words with a } sd \text{ of } 6 \cdot 32$$
$$[sd = \sqrt{Npq} = \sqrt{(447 \times 0 \cdot 90 \times 0 \cdot 10)}].$$

The number of new words per fragment for $p = 0 \cdot 05$ should thus lie between 32 and 57. The observed values are shown in table 1. The most striking deviations were those in the fourth and fifth segment ($N = 9,000$–15,000).

N	n	
1–3,000	30	–
3,001–6,000	30	–
6,001–9,000	48	
9,001–12,000	69	+
12,001–15,000	69	+
15,001–18,000	54	
18,001–21,000	56	
21,001–24,000	31	–
24,001–27,000	27	–
27,001–30,000	33	
30,001–32,235	13	

Table 1. N = text-fragment, n = number of new words,
+ or – = positive or negative significant difference
with the expected values

When examining this part of the text we found that the poet introduced Balder's song at the end of the fourth fragment and the beginning of the fifth ($N = 11,848$–12,102 and 12,199–12,732). The song of the young god Balder occupies a special place in Gorter's poem: the rhyme-scheme alone shows this already: there is a change from binary rhyming pairs into stanzas of 5 or 6 lines. Counting the number of new words in this part it was found that the 789 words included 42 new ones, whereas only 44·70 were expected in 3,000 word occurrences. The deviation was clear enough then. We thereupon divided the poem again into 10 parts of 3,000 occurrences each, leaving out Balder's song. We obtained the distribution shown in table 2.

The expectation per segment now was $(460 - (9 + 42))/10 = 40 \cdot 90$ new words. As the standard deviation was 6·08, significant deviations (for $p = 0 \cdot 05$) would be values higher than or equal to 52·80 and less than or equal to 29·10. So even disregarding Balder's song, the number of new words was not distributed evenly throughout the poem: there were only

N	n	
1–3,000	30	
3,001–6,000	30	
6,001–9,000	48	
9,001–11,847⎫		
12,103–12,198⎬	60	+
12,733–12,789⎭		
12,790–15,789	51	
15,790–18,789	57	+
18,790–21,789	42	
21,790–24,789	34	
24,790–27,789	25	−
27,790–30,789	32	
30,790–32,235	9	

Table 2

3 significant deviations instead of 6, but there remained a significant surplus in the middle of the work and a significant deficit at the end.

To test this further we divided the poem into 3 parts following the author's own division into songs (tables 3 and 4). Here again N stands for the text-length, n_0 is the observed number of new words, n_e is the expected number (that is, n total × per cent text length), d is the difference between n_0 and n_e. The χ-square test showed that in both tables 3 and 4 model and observation differed significantly, resulting from the differences of the second and third song.

What conclusions can be drawn now from the above calculations? We think we can advance the following interpretation of the non-stationary distribution of new words in the poem: First of all we find a significant surplus of new words in Balder's song: it accentuates the special character of this part of the work and makes it more exuberant than the rest. This fits perfectly with Balder's divine character, giving him a greater creative (language) power. Secondly the distribution of new words reflects the classical structure of the work (this becomes most apparent when we leave out Balder's song): the first part has a slight non-significant deficit, the second has a significant surplus, the third a significant deficit: in the first part the poet is not yet so exuberant as in the second song but is moving in that direction, the summit is reached in this second song, and the mood falls away again in the third and last song.

RICHNESS OF VOCABULARY IN 'MAY'

Another striking feature of Gorter's style in *May* is the richness of vocabulary, his copious use of different words. Expressed in quantitative terms this means *inter alia* that $\bar{f}$, the average frequency of the vocabulary, is rather low in this poem: for a total of 32,235 tokens or word-occurrences there are 5,665 different words or types, that is, $\bar{f} = 5 \cdot 69$.

N	n_0	n_e	% text length	d
1–9,914	116	142	(30·75)	−26
9,915–26,342	295	234	(50·96)	+61
26,343–32,235	49	84	(18·27)	−35
	460	460		

Table 3 (Balder's song included)

N	n_0	n_e	% text length	d
1–9,914	116	132	(31·53)	−16
9,915–26,342	253	209	(49·73)	+44
(−Balder's song = 732 words)				
26,343–32,235	49	78	(18·72)	−29
	418	418		

Table 4 (without Balder's song)

It must of course be kept in mind that the number of types (V) here is based on word-forms and not on lemmatized words, which makes V higher and $\bar{f}$ consequently lower. However, compared to other Dutch works of approximately the same length, and also on the basis of 'word-form' types, we observe that $\bar{f}$ does in fact show a great deviation; $\bar{f}$ in *May* is 5·69, while in two Dutch novels of similar length ($\pm$ 33,000 word-occurrences) we found $\bar{f}$ to be 8·81 and 8·23 respectively (Martin 1970).

This finding is in line with the general view of Gorter's vocabulary in *May* as highly diversified, a typical example of the descriptive, abundant impressionism of that time. What we were interested in was the influence of rhyme words on the vocabulary extension, in other words, if the text were not written in binary rhymes would we find the same number of types? To answer this question we used a vocabulary reduction based on the binomial model. This method has already been explained by Muller (1964) and Evrard (1967). We will briefly summarize the argument. Suppose we have a fragment T' from a text T. T has V types, T' has V' types, this being a smaller number as there are certain words which do not appear in T'. We call these words $V'0$. How can we calculate $V'0$?

The proportion between the text-lengths, T'/T, we call p, p always being < 1; q is the complement of p, that is, $1 - p$ or $1 - T'/T$. With words of frequency 1 in T there are 2 possibilities in T': either they do not appear ($= V'0$) or they appear ($= V'1$). The chance of their not occurring in $T' = q$, the chance of their occurring $= p$. Thus $pV1$ denotes $V'1$, whereas some words having $f = 1$ in T will have $f = 0$ in T'. This will be $qV1 = V'0$. The same calculation can be made for the $V2$-words: they will be spread

E

over 3 classes in T', namely, $f=2, f=1$, and $f=0$. The chances for each of these possibilities can be expressed as $p^2+2pq+q^2$, being an application of the binomial $(p+q)^2$. We will not repeat the whole reasoning here but simply state that a frequency class x of a text T is divided into $x+1$ sub-frequency classes in T' which we call y, y having values distributed from x to 0, the number of the latter being $q^i Vi$.

In this way $V'0$ equals the sum of $q^1 V1 + q^2 V2 + \ldots q^n Vn$ or $\sum_{i=1}^{n} q^i Vi$ and so $V' = V - \sum_{i=1}^{n} q^i Vi$.

Let us return to our text. N was equal to 32,235; V to 5,665. Deducting the rhyme word from each verse, we got a text of 32,235–4,384 (= the number of verses or rhyme words) = 27,851 word tokens. Since N was brought down to 27,851 words we expected V to be reduced by 520 word-types, as is shown in table 5.

May (original)	*May* (reduced)
$N = 32,235$	$N = 27,851$
	$p = 27,851 / 32,235 = 0.864$
	$q = 1 - 0.864 = 0.136$
$V1 = 3,657$	$q^1 V1 = 0.136 \times 3,657 = 497.35$
$V2 = 724$	$q^2 V2 = (0.136)^2 \times 724 = 13.94$
$V3 = 319$	$q^3 V3 = (0.136)^3 \times 319 = 7.97$
$V4 = 193$	$q^4 V4 = (0.136)^4 \times 193 = 0.66$
$V5 = 120$	$q^5 V5 = (0.136)^5 \times 120 = 0.05$
$V6 = 89$ etc.	
	$V'0 = 520.07$
$V = 5,665$	$V' = 5,665 - 520 = 5,145$

Table 5

To test that this model fits our text we left out the words appearing in second place in each verse, which would apparently have no special stylistic function. We consequently expected 520 word-types to disappear if we discounted the word tokens (4,384) appearing in second place. There was in fact a loss of 547 types, and this is in good agreement with our model (the *sd* being 26). However, when we discounted the last word in each verse, V was reduced by 1,349 word-types; as shown above, we would expect a decrease only of approximately 520.

That means that the rhyme words give a V-surplus of 829 types to our model. It was noticed, moreover, that 1,099 of these 1,349 word-types in rhyme position had $f=1$, which could account for the high relative frequency (64.56) for the hapaxes as word-types. Furthermore the second rhyme word in particular showed new types (659 hapaxes for the second rhyme word, 440 for the first).

What conclusions can be drawn from this second investigation? We think we might say that the extensive vocabulary Gorter uses in *May* can partly be explained by the form in which the text is written: rhyme words yielding a much higher number of types than is expected on the base of an even distribution of types throughout the text.

In this process it is the second rhyme word which plays the most decisive role. However, the high V-score cannot solely be explained by the rhyme-factor. Discounting the rhyme surplus, V is 4,836 whereas other Dutch texts of the same length yield $V = 3,800$ and 4,083 respectively (Martin 1970). If the latter texts can be taken as a yardstick, we may say that half of the great variety of types Gorter uses in *May* can be explained by the fact he wrote a binary rhyming text.

CONCLUSION

As to concrete results we can summarize ours in a few lines (though we may wonder whether the length of formulation has any relation to their relevance). The findings are:

1. In using new words in his poem *May*, Gorter laid some special stress on Balder, giving him a greater creative (language) power than the other (human) personages in the poem.

Secondly, the distribution of these words reflects the classical structure of the poem: a rise—summit—fall movement.

Thirdly, Gorter used a very extensive vocabulary in his poem; this is sensed on a first reading. But at least half of this surplus of types is concentrated in the rhyming words, especially the second rhyme, which indicates that much of this vocabulary 'richness' was in fact due to rhyme-force.

2. More generally speaking we hope we have proved that, with regard to style, a quantitative approach to a work of literature is as meaningful as the more traditional qualitative approach. Quantitative here is to be taken as a synonym for statistical. In other words, this paper considers a few aspects of the probability structure of language, more particularly of vocabulary. Consequently we have assumed that (at least some) elements which we can abstract from speech, in this case the distribution of new words and the extension of V, behave as statistical or random variables, that is, they have a definite probability of occurrence. To put it more plainly; there is a measurable order in art just as in every human work, and for this reason we think it meaningful to look for the 'Quantität', and not just for the 'Quidität' and the 'Qualität' (Fucks 1968).

3. It is in this respect that we would add a few words about the role of the computer in a work of this kind. In this study, of course, we made use of the computer as an administrative and calculating machine: comparing text and thesaurus, making indices and rhyming vocabularies, comparing the latter with the alphabetical word list, calculating the reduction of the vocabulary and so on.

In a quantitative approach, however, we believe the computer becomes much more a control machine and testing device, verifying certain results (testing their significance) or evaluating certain hypotheses. This opens up the possibility of what we would call 'experimental stylistics'. Here the investigator, thanks to the rapid intervention of the computer, can evaluate non-stylistic (for example, statistical) or incompletely worked out literary hypotheses. The alternative we formulated for the distribution of 'new words' in our text, for instance, was not a stylistic or textual hypothesis but simply the statistical null hypothesis.

This can lead us perhaps to style investigations which do not necessarily rest on textual hypotheses (Martin 1971b). In other words the experiment as such is not so foolish as it may look at first sight. Columbus 'knew' that the earth was round and therefore he sailed out to discover India; if he had gone without a reason he would perhaps have discovered America as well. Of course experimental investigations now carry fewer risks as we have much better aids. This is true for literary research too. Thanks to the computer an experiment can be carried out rapidly and efficiently. It remains true, however, that the problem of interpretation is not solved by this method. In other words, the distance between observation and interpretation still exists, although in our opinion there is a fundamental distinction between traditional and computer style studies. Traditional research usually starts from a conclusion which has to be proved. Computer studies, on the contrary, often generate these proofs experimentally without having to use a completely worked-out textual hypothesis. The latter can be drawn much more easily *a posteriori* from the computer evidence. In this way quantitative and computer approaches can open, in our opinion, new horizons for literary research.

REFERENCES

Evrard, E. (1967) Deux programmes d'ordinateur pour l'étude quantitative du vocabulaire. *Revue*, **3**, 81-95.

Fucks, W. (1968) *Nach allen Regeln der Kunst*. Stuttgart: Deutsche Verlags-anstalt.

Martin, W. (1970) *Analyse van een Vocabularium met Behulp van een Computer*. Brussels: Aimav.

Martin, W. (1971a) Distributie van 'nieuwe woorden' in *Mei* van Herman Gorter. *De nieuwe Taalgids*, **64**, 163-76.

Martin, W. (1971b) Stijlonderzoek per computer: enkele beschouwingen. *Nieuw Vlaams Tijdschrift*, **24**, 268-85.

Muller, Ch. (1964) Calcul des probabilités et calcul d'un vocabulaire. *Travaux de Linguistique et de Littérature*, **2**, 235-44.

Ullmann, S. (1966) *Language and Style*. Oxford: Blackwell.

S.MICHAELSON,
A.Q.MORTON

Positional stylometry

Stylometry may be defined as the use of numerical methods for the solution of literary problems. The problems are usually problems of authorship, of integrity, and of chronology. The numerical methods range from the simple counting of features thought to be, or assumed to be, significant and relevant to the problem to multivariate statistical analyses of the general characteristics of language and of composition.

Stylometry is a tool to be used when external evidence is lacking and the solution to the problem must come from the study of the texts which present the problem. Stylometry is therefore particularly useful in classical studies, especially for Greek texts which were written and reproduced by hand in an era when the rights of authors were limited, and practices which by our contemporary standards are quite criminally irresponsible were generally employed and accepted. A writer anxious either to attract attention for his views, or to escape responsibility for them, would attach to them some illustrious name likely to achieve his object. The disciples of some master who had not written on some problem which arose after his death would supply a text to provide his guidance in the new situation. Libraries anxious to fill gaps in their collections would be offered texts designed to complete their collections.

Before anyone expresses shock at such widespread immorality it should be recalled that when the great furniture-maker Chippendale was at work, England contained about 2,000 rooms which could have contained his pieces and it must be unlikely that he filled every room in every house whose owner had the means to purchase his works. Yet it has been calculated that there are over 6,000 Chippendale pieces in the United States at this moment. This suggests that in purchasing antiques or judging Greek texts it is unwise to rely on trade descriptions; any attribution should be accepted or rejected after a critical examination.

In Greek texts, as indeed in antique furniture, integrity is a problem. In both fields new works include parts of old works. Josephus, for example, felt that he could not do justice to battle scenes and borrowed from Thucydides, thus marring the integrity of his text at the moment of its creation.

Stylometry was not much employed by serious scholars until the end of the Second World War. The reason for their reluctance was the lack of method in the subject. Where differences between texts were large and obvious, where a method was least required, stylometry could pile up illustrative data to justify the conclusion, but where the differences between texts were slight or seemed to be contradictory, where a method was most to be desired, the simple counting of features was found to be least effective.

In Greek studies the birth of modern stylometry dates from the work of W.C.Wake (1946, 1956), who established the first indicator of authorship for Greek prose writers. In Wake's work there can be seen, clearly laid out, the three principles which distinguish modern stylometry from its predecessors. The material studied is the frequent occurrence of an event independent of subject matter; the occurrence is examined in a wide range of texts to establish general conclusions about all writers in a group and the comparison of counts is made by using modern small sample statistics. Wake turned away from the enticing study of rare words and features peculiar to individual writers to concentrate on frequent events found in all writers of Greek prose, because all writers of Greek have much more in common with each other (the words, the grammar, and the structure of the language) than they can have peculiar to themselves. Wake was soon able to show that what is most characteristic of an author is not his few personal idiosyncracies but the rates at which he performs the operations which he shares with all his colleagues.

Wake was, and is, a professional scientist. Attempting a solution of the problem of the authorship of the *Corpus Hippocraticum* he did not approach the problem as would a literary critic whose inclination would be to treat it as a unique problem to be dealt with in isolation. Wake saw the problem as typical of a set of similar problems and looked for a solution which would be the particular application of a general theory, a theory which would present solutions to all problems of this type. His conclusions would apply to all writers of Greek prose.

Wake's third contribution to modern stylometry was to set out the pattern of argument which must be followed. He took a wide range of samples from a variety of authors. He then compared them in sets to isolate any possible influence; to determine what difference a change of subject matter made, he compared works written about the same time by the same author but on contrasting subjects. If the differences between samples could be explained as chance variation, they were ignored; if the differences were too great to be explained by chance variation, then an alternative explanation was required. Wake used the cross-comparison of sets of samples to demonstrate that the differences in sentence length distributions were due to a difference of authorship and not to any other cause.

This pattern of argument is fundamental to stylometry. A habit is measured by recording some occurrence. Only a wide-ranging examination can establish a test of authorship: an occurrence for which differences within a text (or between texts) are only random sampling differences (that is, differences for which chance variation is an acceptable explanation); whereas the differences between separate authors' texts can be statistically significant, because these differences are too large for them to be explained

No of words in sentences	No of sentences in text
1-5	100
6-10	190
11-15	126
16-20	73
21-25	32
26-30	15
31-35	7
36-40	5
41-45	1
46-50	4
51-55	2
56-60	1

Total 556

Table 1. A typical sentence-length distribution of a Greek writer. The First Epistle to the Corinthians in the Greek text of Aland, Black, Metzger and Wikgren, London 1968. Mean 12·155; variance 2·897; standard deviation 1·703. The statistics of the distribution are: mean 12·16; standard error 0·36; median 9·69; standard error 0·31; first quartile 6·03; standard error 0·27; third quartile 15·07; standard error 0·71; ninth decile 21·84; standard error 1·14. The statistics of the distribution as log normal are: log mean 0·982; log standard deviation 0·295; log standard error 0·013

as happening by chance. A test of chronology will have the same pattern: differences between texts written within a period will be negligible; differences between periods will be too great to be explained by chance variation.

Wake's work is not only the historical foundation of Greek stylometry, it is the logical foundation for the positional studies with which this paper deals. Table 1 and figure 1 illustrate a typical sentence-length distribution of a Greek prose writer, namely the sentence-length distribution of the First Epistle to the Corinthians from the Greek *New Testament*. Such distributions are generally described by their mean, their median, their first and third quartiles, and their ninth decile. Some of the distributions, including this example, can be fitted to a log-normal distribution by a suitable transformation.

The authors began their studies by an examination of vocabulary. The conception of vocabulary contains some potentially misleading elements. For example, there are over one million named species of insect. If vocabulary is defined as the number of words used by a writer, then a descriptive entomologist will have a vocabulary of over one million words, unless it is admitted that the vocabulary belongs to the subject as much as to the writer on it. Another aspect of vocabulary that has caused some difficulties

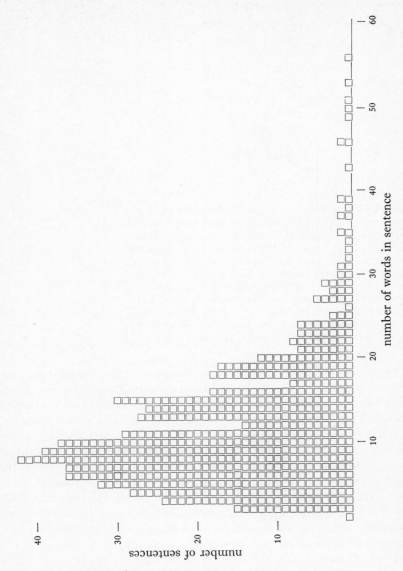

Figure 1. A typical sentence-length distribution of a
Greek author, the First Epistle to the Corinthians in
The New Testament

is the treatment of low-frequency words, especially the group of once-occurring words. It is true that in any text when the words are arranged by frequency of occurrence, the largest group is of the words which occur once. It is also true that this group of rare words illustrates the writer's skill, his general culture, and his special interests; however, the mathematical difficulties of handling this group have not yet been overcome.

The authors turned from low-frequency vocabulary in the hope that high-frequency vocabulary would be more tractable. In a series of papers they have looked at aspects of high-frequency vocabulary. It was soon clear that high-frequency vocabulary in Greek writing, defined to be words which occur more often than does the most-frequent noun in the text, has marked positional bias. High-frequency particles and connectives are most often to be found among the first three words of Greek sentences. High-frequency words such as the particles and connectives only rarely, and in some cases never, occur as the last word of Greek sentences. Thus Greek sentences come in three parts. Among the first three words there is a high proportion of high-frequency words; in the last two places these are absent and, in between, the particles occur at rates generally much lower than the rates at which they occur in the first three positions.

Having often lamented the absence of any unifying theory of stylometry which alone can give rise to rapid progress, the authors decided to look at word position and its attendant feature, word mobility. A potential advantage of such studies is that the mean position of a word or other occurrence in a sentence is independent of the number of occurrences of the word or other feature. Another advantage is that the whole set of positions which a word, or other occurrence, can occupy is summarised by its mobility. A word which is found in all positions in sentences, from first word to last, and shows no preference for any particular position would be completely mobile. A word found only in one position in sentences would be completely bound.

To simplify the following exposition only word positions will be referred to, but the reader should understand that other features than words can be examined, if need be in units other than sentences.

Word position and word mobility can be measured in a number of ways, but in view of the information already available on sentence-length distributions it seems sensible to adopt similar conventions and to define position by counting the ordinal position of a word as the first, second, third word, and so on, measuring from the start and end of a sentence, and to measure mobility in terms of *isotropy*. Sentence-length distributions are *isotropic*; it matters not at all if they are counted from the first word of the sentence to the last or from the last to the first. If a word is completely mobile it will occupy all positions in sentences from the first word to the last and its mean position will therefore be the mid-point of the sentence. The mid-point of a sentence is an isotropic position; it is the same distance from both beginning and end. Thus a mobile word can be defined as one for which the forward and backward statistics, those measured by counting from the first and from the last word, show only random sampling differences.

If a word is bound, that is, if it occurs in a range of preferred positions, then it will show *anisotropy* in its statistics. For example, the particle *de* occurs most often as the second word in sentences. In the forward count the majority of occurrences are recorded as of word 2; in the backward count the record resembles the parent sentence length distribution with the last word of the sentence excised. The mean of the forward statistics is not much over 2; the mean for the backward statistics is not much under the mean sentence length less one word.

It is true that there are circumstances in which isotropic statistics would be produced by bound words, for example, a word which occurred only as first or last word in sentences, but these conditions are not met with in the study of Greek writers.

In practice there are two kinds and three classes of words which are encountered in Greek studies. The first kind is those with *isotropic statistics*. Many of the words in this group do not ever occur as the last word of sentences, but the expected number of such occurrences is small and the difference made to the statistics by their inclusion or exclusion is so much less than the relevant standard errors of the statistics that the departure from precise isotropy is negligible.

There are two classes of anisotropic words. The first is of words which are mildly anisotropic. A mild degree of anisotropy is defined as one which disappears when grouped data is used but is visible with ungrouped data. The most frequent examples of words in this class are conjunctions used to introduce sentences and prepositions used to introduce the last word, or the last two words of sentences. The second class is of words clearly anisotropic even with the data grouped in the usual convention for sentence-length distributions. The most obvious frequent characteristic of such words is that their occurrence is independent of sentence length.

Isotropic Distributions
The convention which has been adopted for recording occurrences of words within sentences means that any sentence with no occurrence of the count-word is discarded, while a sentence with one occurrence of the count-word is divided into two parts, one part from the first word up to and including the count-word and the other from the last word back to, and again including, the count-word. This means that the sum of the two positions, the forward and backward counts, is always one more than the number of words in the sentence. A sentence with N occurrences of the count-word is recorded N times; it is divided into $2N$ parts and one part is allocated to each set of positional statistics. As a result the occurrences

of a word are recorded in a selection of sentences from the parent sentence-length distribution, a selection which is related to the parent distribution but not in any simple way.

If a word occurred at random in sentences of all lengths and occurred no more often than once per sentence, then the sentences in which it appeared would be a random selection from the sentences of the parent distribution and the statistics of the positional distribution would show this to be the case. It is interesting to note that, in all the instances so far recorded, the mean length of sentence in the selected sentence-length distribution is significantly higher than the mean of the parent distribution, suggesting that the vocabulary of short sentences, sentences with around six words or fewer, is quite different from the vocabulary of longer sentences.

The most remarkable feature of positional distributions is their comparatively constant variance. The range of positions to be occupied is from the first word of any sentence up to the last word of the longest sentence, which means that a positional distribution will have a mean of about half that of the mean of the selected sentence-length distribution in which the occurrences are recorded but the variance will be near to the variance of the parent sentence-length distribution. This has important consequences which can be simply illustrated. For the sentence-length distribution of the First Epistle to the Corinthians, previously tabulated, the variance is 2·897. The conjunction *kai* occurs 278 times in the 556 sentences and the variance of the positional distribution is 2·986. The standard error of the mean of the parent sentence-length distribution is 0·36. If the variances of the parent sentence-length distribution and of the positional distribution of *kai* were identical, then the standard error of the mean for the positional distribution would be in the proportion of $1/\sqrt{2}$, that is, $0·36/0·71 = 0·51$. The variance of the positional distribution is 0·52. The negative particle *ou* occurs 72 times in the epistle, one-quarter as often as the conjunction *kai* and so the standard error of its positional distribution would be, on the hypothesis of a constant variance, twice the standard error of the mean of the positional distribution of *kai*, that is, 1·02; it is in fact 1·00.

The stability of the variance of positional distributions means that when the rate of occurrence of a count-word is less than once per sentence, then the standard errors of the statistics of the positional distribution, which depend directly on the variance and inversely on the square root of the number of occurrences, will always be greater than the corresponding standard errors of the statistics of the sentence-length distributions in which the occurrences have been recorded. It follows that, for samples which are above the minimum sample size for sentence-length distributions, the positional distributions of all isotropic words which occur often enough to enable the positional distribution and its isotropy to be demonstrated will provide tests of authorship. Such tests of authorship will not be independent of sentence length, indeed they will only illuminate certain aspects of the parent sentence-length distribution, but they are not without their uses.

Two such uses can be briefly illustrated. The first is from Plato's dialogues, a type of text which caused Wake some trouble. The dialogue exchanges contain a high proportion of very short sentences; sentences with five words or fewer. The continuous prose has a low proportion of such sentences. Samples from the dialogues showed statistically significant differences within works depending on the ratio of dialogue exchange to continuous prose within the samples. The exclusion from the samples of all sentences with five words or fewer would not recommend itself to scholars as anything but an arbitrary change of rules to escape from a difficulty and also leave truncated distributions to be wrestled with.

Within the dialogues the conjunction *kai* occurs frequently, but not often in very short sentences. If the positional distributions for *kai* are chosen, then all the short sentences are excluded and the statistically significant differences vanish with them. Table 2 shows the positional distributions of the occurrences of the conjunction *kai* in two samples chosen from the *Laws* to give the extreme contrast of dialogue exchange and of continuous prose. The first sample, from *Laws* book 3 cap. 676-81a, has 100 occurrences of *kai* in 113 sentences. The second, *Laws* book 5 cap. 726-32b has 100 occurrences in 81 sentences. The sentence-length distributions of the two samples show large significant differences but the forward and backward positional distributions of *kai* have χ^2 4·04 and 3·60 for four degrees of freedom, representing differences which are not statistically significant. When the *two*, both forward and backward positional distributions, are added to give a mean positional distribution, χ^2 is 5·24 for the comparison of the two *Laws* samples. The significant difference of the sentence-length distributions has been removed. There is no great loss of sensitivity in the making of comparisons with other writers, for the third sample is of the central section of Plato's *Seventh Epistle*, a section which has been shown to be an insertion (Levison, Morton, and Winspear 1966). When the third sample is compared with the sum of the first two, χ^2 is 14·07 for four degrees of freedom and the difference is significant at the 1 per cent level. This shows that the occurrence of a word can be used as a tracer to select certain types of sentence without ambiguity.

The second use of mobile words to supplement sentence-length distribution is the converse of the last example. A mobile word occurs in certain types of sentence and the type is characterized by length. The mean position of such a word is dependent on the mean length of sentences in which it occurs. Therefore the mean length of sentence in which occurrences are recorded will be a useful unit in which to record the occurrences of a mobile word. For example, the word *Christos* is a nominal

Position in sentences	No of occurrences in		
	Laws Bk 3	Laws Bk 5	Epistle 7
1-5	49	28	19
6-10	47	45	41
11-15	30	49	13
16-20	25	28	24
21+	49	50	47
Totals	200	200	144

Table 2. The positional distributions of the conjunction *kai* in samples from Plato's *Laws* and from the interpolation in Epistle Seven

adjective and occurs frequently in some limited parts of texts and is missing from most parts of texts; this pattern of occurrence is not surprising as it is part of the subject matter of certain passages. Any attempt to characterize its use or occurrence by frequency counting fails. But the mean position of occurrences, and so the mean length of sentence in which they occur, is independent of the number of occurrences recorded, and the use of the word can be characterized by mean length of the sentences in which it is used. For example, table 3 shows the occurrences of *Christos* in three epistles of the New Testament.

	1st Corinthians	Galatians	Ephesians
No of words in Epistle	6735	2211	1918
No of sentences in Epistle	556	166	80
Mean length of sentence (in no of words)	12·16	13·78	30·31
St. error of mean	0·36	0·77	3·21
Occs of CHRISTOS	58	38	45
Mean length of sentence with occurrences	20·59	19·45	61·11
St. error of mean	1·78	2·18	6·59

Table 3. The mean length of sentence in which the mobile word CHRISTOS occurs illustrated from three *New Testament* Epistles. Sentences with *N* occurrences are counted *N* times

It is clear that both the writers of these epistles put *Christos* into long sentences. But the increase in both Pauline epistles is of about 50 per cent of the mean sentence length, in Ephesians it is just about 100 per cent of the mean sentence length. It appears that a number of high-frequency words which have been difficult to treat because of their intimate connection with the subject matter of the text can be used to discriminate between authors.

Another use of isotropic distributions is to display the periodicity of a number of occurrences. Figure 2 illustrates the forward distribution of the conjunction *kai* in the First Epistle to the Corinthians. The peaking at intervals of six words, at positions 1, 7, 13, and 19, is readily shown to be statistically significant (Whittaker and Robinson 1925, chapter 13). The figure illustrates a previous demonstration that this writer extends his sentences by a unit of six words, one of which is the introductory occurrence of the conjunction *kai* (Levison, Morton, and Wake 1966).

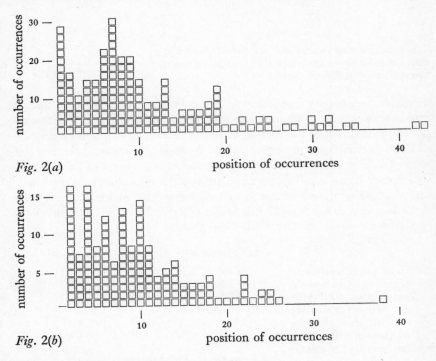

Fig. 2(*a*)   position of occurrences

Fig. 2(*b*)   position of occurrences

Figure 2. Periodic effects in isotropic distributions.
(*a*) In the forward count of the occurrence of the conjunction *kai* in the text of First Corinthians. The peaks at 1, 7, 13, 19, and 25 words are statistically significant. (*b*) In the backward count of the occurrence of the neuter article *to* in the Fourth Gospel. The tendency to finish the sentence with 1 or 3 or 5 or 7 words following the article is marked

Isotropic distributions can also demonstrate heterogeneity in a text. If a text is amended by the insertion of a passage, then the interpolation can be detected if the occurrence of some frequent isotropic word is affected by it. For example, the positional distribution of the conjunction *kai* is known to be isotropic in the writing of the Apostle Paul but in the two epistles which are known to have been revised, in Romans and in Second Corinthians, the result is to separate the forward and backward distributions. The separation is due to the occurrences in the anomalous passages

Epistle	Log mean position	St. error of log mean
Romans		
F	0·987	0·025
B	1·104	0·027
1st Cor.		
F	0·889	0·022
B	0·894	0·024
2nd Cor.		
F	1·012	0·029
B	0·967	0·033
Galatians		
F	0·917	0·058
B	0·939	0·074

Table 4. An illustration of how interpolation and revision lead to the separation of the Forward and Backward statistics of a mobile word occurring in the text. The occurrence of the conjunction *kai* in the four Pauline epistles. Romans, which has had a new first chapter added and has been revised, shows statistically significant differences between *F* and *B* distributions and in comparison with First Corinthians. Second Corinthians, which has been less altered, shows no significant difference between *F* and *B* distributions but with a significant difference for the comparison of the *F* distribution with that of First Corinthians

being too near the start, or too near the end of the sentences to pass as Pauline, and the consequence is a shift in the positional distributions. Table 4 shows the forward and backward positional distributions of the conjunction *kai* in all four Pauline epistles of *The New Testament*. In First Corinthians and in Galatians, shown in every test to be homogeneous, the forward and backward distributions, which are log-normal, do not differ by any statistically significant amount, but Romans and Second Corinthians, shown by previous tests to differ, to have been edited and revised (Michaelson and Morton 1972a), show statistically significant differences between the forward and backward distributions.

These illustrations do not exhaust the possible uses of isotropic positional distributions but show only the immediate uses to which they have been put.

ANISOTROPIC DISTRIBUTIONS

In strict logic it is impossible to defend the classification of anisotropic distributions into the two classes of those which are mildly anisotropic and those which are acutely anisotropic, but in practice, at least for Greek writers, the distinction is readily made and has a practical purpose.

Fig. 3(*a*)   position of occurrences

Fig. 3(*b*)   position of occurrences

Fig. 3(*c*)   position of occurrences

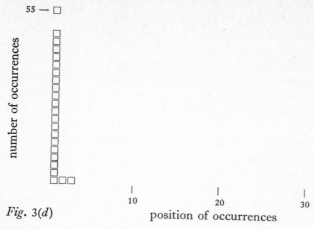

Fig. 3(*d*)   position of occurrences

Figure 3. Typical anisotropic distributions. (*a*) The
occurrence of the conjunction *kai* in the sentences of
First Corinthians. Forward count. (*b*) The forward
record of the occurrence of the preposition *eis* in the
Fourth Gospel. (*c*) The occurrence of the particle *de*
in the First Epistle to the Corinthians. Forward
count. (*d*) The occurrence of the verb *apekrithe* in
the Fourth Gospel. Forward count

The difference between the two classes of anisotropic distribution are
shown in figure 3, which shows the distribution of the conjunction *kai* in
the First Epistle to the Corinthians: of the preposition *eis* in the Fourth
Gospel: of the particle *de* in First Corinthians, and of the verb *apekrithe*
in the Fourth Gospel.

The distinction between the two types of distribution is clear, in the
first two cases there is a preference for a position which involves a small
proportion of the total number of occurrences, and if the data is grouped
into cells of five words, as is the usual convention in recording sentence-
length distributions, the differences between the forward and backward
distributions are obscured. In the second pair of illustrations, a large proportion of the occurrences are recorded in a preferred position and the
remainder of the occurrences look like a random scatter in all the other
positions. The forward and backward distributions are quite markedly
different. What both classes of words have in common is that the division
of the occurrences into those in the preferred position and those in all
other positions makes a test of authorship, except in the case of verbs, and
the occurrences in the preferred position are independent of sentence
length.

Where they differ is in the efficient treatment of the occurrences as a test
of authorship. Mildly anisotropic words show relatively few occurrences
in the preferred position compared to the number of sentences in which
these are recorded. For example, we have 28 occurrences of *kai* as the first

F

word in 556 sentences of First Corinthians and 43 occurrences of *eis* as the second last word in 1171 sentences of the Fourth Gospel. This means that only simple comparisons can be made by treating the whole text, or large sections of it, as block samples. The frequency of occurrence of most of the acutely anisotropic words is high enough for them to occur in more than 10 per cent of the sentences of the text and so make possible the use of cumulative sum charts for the complete inspection of the text (Michaelson and Morton 1972c).

As was already noted, the partial exception to this rule is that verbs, for example, *apekrithe* (he replied), *legei* (he said), *aspasontai* (give my regards), show a marked preference to occur as the first words of sentences in those sections of the text, direct speech and final greetings, which are their natural setting. The cumulative sum chart of such words, however, is a series of square waves, the rates of occurrence are zero or well above zero, and a distinction between writers is possible by comparison of the means of the non-zero sections of the text.

By the use of positional distributions and cumulative sum charts a detailed inspection of a text and an assessment of its integrity and authorship is possible in a way not previously practicable. The machine-readable text is prepared and a concordance of the text is made from it. All the words which occur often enough to enable tests of significance to be employed are then selected and their positional distributions examined. The isotropic distributions reveal some special features of the writer's craft: the anisotropic distributions furnish a set of cumulative sum charts which enable the authorship and integrity of the text to be analyzed in full detail (Michaelson and Morton 1972c).

Normally the examination of positions is made in sentences so that the conclusions can be related to sentence structure, and to grammatical rules and linguistic principles, for example the manner in which a writer extends a sentence or completes it. But if there is any serious doubt about the punctuation of the text then positions can be recorded in the intervals between some frequent conjunctions and particles. If the occurrence of the mark-word is mobile, then the distribution of the intervals between occurrences is negative exponential; if the mark-word is anisotropic in its positional distribution then the distribution of the intervals is often log-normal.

The particle *de* occurs most often near the beginning of sentences and so the intervals between occurrences is not random, which would result in a negative exponential distribution, but shows too many intervals of an average length of a complete sentence and too few of much less than one sentence. The resultant distribution is log-normal.

CHRONOLOGY

At the present time no indicator of chronology has been established for Greek writers. It has been shown that chronological differences between texts do exist (Morton 1965; Thomson 1966), but these were assays and not proposals for the mining and reduction of ores. With the introduction of positional statistics it is now possible to isolate, by a choice of tracer words, the features of the texts which are responsible for the chronological differences. A large-scale investigation into the changes produced by intervals of time in an author's career has now begun in Edinburgh.

CONCLUSION

Stylometry began to progress when a series of questions was posed, all questions of the type—How often has this event occurred? To this fundamental question has now been added two more. One—Where does this event occur? Two—How often does this event occur in this position? The range of stylometry has been correspondingly increased.

REFERENCES

Aland, K., Black, M., Metzger, B.M. & Wikgren, A. (1968) *The Greek New Testament*. London: Wikgren.

Hainsworth, J.B., Michaelson, S. & Morton, A.Q. (1972) The authorship and integrity of the poems of Hesiod. *J. roy. phil. Soc.*, **1**.

Levison, M., Morton, A.Q. & Winspear, A.D. (1966) Plato's Seventh Letter. *MIND*, **40**.

Michaelson, S. & Morton, A.Q. (1971a) *Forgar, Science in Archaeology*, **4**.

Michaelson, S. & Morton, A.Q. (1971b) Last Words. *New Testament Studies*, **18**.

Michaelson, S. & Morton, A.Q. (1972a) The spaces in between. *L.A.S.L.A. Revue*, **1**.

Michaelson, S. & Morton, A.Q. (1972b) The new stylometry. *Classical Quarterly*, May.

Michaelson, S. & Morton, A.Q. (1972c) The authorship and integrity of the Athenaion Politeia. *J. roy. Soc. Edin.*

Michaelson, S., Morton, A.Q. & Winspear, A.D. (1972) *Computer Calepraxis*. Universities of Calgary and Edinburgh, May.

Morton, A.Q. (1965) The authorship of Greek Prose. *J. roy. statist. Soc.*, **128**.

Morton, A.Q. & Winspear, A.D. (1971) It's Greek to the Computer. Montreal.

Thomson, N.D. (1966) The Chronology of Xenophon. *B.Litt. Thesis*. University of St Andrews.

Wake, W.C. (1946) The authorship of *Corpus Hippocraticum*. *Ph.D. Thesis*. University of London.

Wake W.C. (1956) Sentence length distributions of Greek authors. *J. roy. statist. Soc.*, **120**.

Whittaker, E.T. & Robinson, G. (1925) *The Calculus of Observations*. London: Blackie.

Beyond the concordance : algorithms for description of English clauses and phrases

In general the fruits of computer study of literary style have proved disappointing, especially to those unfamiliar with the details of either linguistics or computing machinery. Concordances produced automatically have been as useful as those done by exhaustive human effort, and are perhaps more reliable. Published statistical studies of literary texts have not often involved computers, yet it is clear that the counting, averaging, and correlation of data for large bodies of literature are more suitable to a computer's memory and accuracy than a person's impatience and limited capacity for boredom. Starting late in 1969, a series of algorithms for description of stylistic features called EYEBALL was planned by Robert Rasche and myself; this sought to make better use of the computer's abilities. We wished to produce a consistently reliable description of selected components of the language of literary texts, and to make the descriptions available for a wide range of interpretations and evaluations. Among the components we decided to include were word lengths, sentence and clause lengths, vocabulary-frequency statistics, word-class distributions, and analysis of other syntactic elements based on a reasonably intricate parsing of sentences (*see* Ross and Rasche 1972a, 1972b).

The computer programs had to meet specifications which literary scholars interested in a description of style rightly demanded. First, input must be only the text itself. If extensive marking is required during the preparation of a text for computer reading, there are significant disadvantages and added time on the part of both the keypuncher and the researcher. Texts especially prepared and edited for a limited purpose, such as a concordance, could not be used for further analysis, and future stages of technology, such as the possible development of efficient optical scanning, could never be exploited.

The scholars, of course, demanded that results be quite reliable. Description of literary style often entails work with relatively infrequent portions of a text, for example, the percentage of adverbs in Dickens as against that in Thackeray, and there is not much margin for error. Efforts by researchers in the 1950s and 1960s to solve the problems of machine translation convinced us that a totally automated parsing algorithm has little chance of being more than 50 per cent accurate. Since we did not feel that such a 'one-pass' procedure was possible, even with the storage of a large dictionary and the use of many syntactic rules, we moved immediately to a design which required human intervention at two points to process the partially analyzed text. Reliability was maintained by making every decision of the machine liable to check and correction, if needed.

Another reasonable expectation was that operations be kept simple enough to be used by those scholars with limited expertise and experience in either computer programming or linguistics. The various steps in both the initial preparation of the text and the intermediate analysis had to be clearly defined, and easy to perform. Finally, programs must be written in the FORTRAN language which is supported at most installations, so as to be readily available to a spectrum of potential users.

In the development of the programs it became clear that some parsing could be done automatically, as long as the ability to review machine decisions was preserved. With this motivation, additional procedures were designed in 1971–72, under the general title of GUESS. This algorithm involves rather simple logic operations, and so does not increase machine time appreciably. Its structure should be of interest to scholars outside the field of stylistics, since it may suggest something about the way a person understands English syntax. One might profitably compare the rules of this algorithm, especially those for clause parsing, with the recent paper by Bever and Langendoen (1971) in which the existence of 'perceptual strategies which directly map external strings on to their internal structures' is postulated. They find that segmentation of clauses is based in part on strategies which anticipate where nominal phrases end, and they show that the 'first "Nominal Verbal" sequence' is nearly always taken to be the subject and predicate until contradictory lexical evidence forces a re-interpretation. The GUESS algorithm may be said to simulate rules of this sort.

BACKGROUND

The main purpose of this paper is to describe the new approaches that have been developed, but a general idea of the nature of EYEBALL is a necessary prelude. The input of the first phase of the program is the text itself, in computer-readable form, with punctuation, but with no other precoding. Each word is isolated and stored in an array that in the course of analysis receives these additional pieces of information:

1. location in the text;
2. numerical indicator of the word's place in the text concordance;
3. word length in syllables;
4. syntactic category (noun, verb, determiner, pronoun, etc.);
5. syntactic function (subject, predicate, complement, adjunct);
6. phrase-clause code which shows if the word ends a syntactic unit;
7. the word (in machine representation); and
8. punctuation, if any, which follows the word.

Contractions which compress two words into one ('I'm') are expanded to allow syntactic marking. The GUESS algorithm supplies many categorical and functional labels (4 and 5) and provides some phrase endings (6).

One part of the operation of the program which has been tested extensively is the premarking of the categories and of some functions of frequent 'function words' (that is, pronouns, determiners, conjunctions, auxiliary verbs, and the like). A dictionary of about 200 words, arranged in eleven classes, is built in. When a function word belongs to more than one syntactic category (such as 'for' which can be either a preposition or conjunction), a hierarchy has been established which first marks prepositions, and then subordinators, since these classes are treated during the first intermediate syntactic processing. If there are other kinds of ambiguity, for example 'is', which can be either an auxiliary or a main verb, the premarking decision is easily overridden in later stages of analysis. Words not found in the function-word dictionary are 'content words'; their function and category are not determined during this phase of the procedure.

During the initial analysis of the text, words of three categories are flagged for attention in the first intermediate stage—prepositions, subordinators (relative pronouns, conjunctions, and adverbs), and special markers ('to' for infinitives, and the expletives 'there' and 'here'). The purpose of the GUESS algorithm is to determine locations of the main elements of phrases and subordinated clauses automatically. Their initial design was an effort to implement the suggestions of Ellegård (1963) and Brodda and Karlgren (1964), who showed that certain sequences of word-categories, called by Ellegård 'paradigmatic frames', are either very frequent or mandatory in English. One clearly-defined example assumes that prepositional phrases do not include verbs. If the first word of a sequence is a preposition, and the third a verb (for example, 'is'), then the phrase cannot be more than two words long. There are some rather reliable ways to detect the ends of prepositional phrases, and to classify the words they contain. Since most phrases and many clauses are relatively short, and their structures easy to predict, automatic description is possible. Prepositional phrases of considerable length, and clauses with numerous content words, especially in unbroken series, are not amenable to automatic description.

The strategy of the GUESS algorithm is different from that which Ellegård employed. Ellegård's approach was to use the 'experience' of analyzing the words in one frame to store the category of a given content word (noun, adjective, verb, or adverb) in an expanding dictionary; the analysis was recursive. Thus, words which fell between a determiner and another function word ('the *red* could', 'a *man* of') were called nouns. The nouns thus marked, plus nouns from other tests, were used as the key to the determination of adjectives, since the adjective category was defined as those words framed by a determiner and a noun ('the *bright* red', 'a *healthy* man'). The difficulty which arises when a word has multiple categories (and which appears in 'the *red* man') was recognized by Ellegård as an inevitable problem which he had not solved. The GUESS algorithm does not retain information about the labels for other instances of particular words. Instead it marks only the words under focus, and each new phrase or clause is treated in isolation from the others. Another important difference between EYEBALL and other computing procedures for stylistic analysis is the inclusion of the functional labels, which makes the syntactic description considerably more complete than is possible with only categorical labels.

Rules in an algorithm of this sort are bound to rehearse what is usual and familiar, since they are designed to identify and mark components of relatively short and regular phrases and clauses. Thus the lists given by Milic (1967) of the most frequently encountered three-word sequences of categories (a list which starts with preposition + determiner + noun) are for the most part accounted for in the algorithm. Obviously each rule will suggest a variety of exceptions, some of relatively high frequency, others quite exotic and dependent on usage of a particular lexical item. It should be recalled that the function of this set of programs is to reduce the amount of intermediate processing; any mistakes are easy to correct.

PARSING OF PREPOSITIONAL PHRASES

The model used when the first version of the prepositional phrase analyzer was designed was the left-to-right process a person uses when reading (or listening to) a phrase. For each word, these questions were asked:

1. Is there terminal punctuation (period, exclamation, or question)?
2. If the word is a function word, what is its category?
3. Could this be of a category which comes outside of or after the phrase?

If either the first or the third question were answered 'yes', then an assessment of the most likely categories within the phrase was made. If the phrase seemed to be long, then certain words were marked provisionally as being part of the phrase in the hope that a clearly-defined ending would turn up. Thus, a determiner or an intensifying adverb in the second position led to the assumption that the phrase was at least three words long, and a noun was searched for. The program as presently designed is based on a quite different model.

The computer now scans the *entire* set of words for terminal punctuation and then for inadmissible word classes; a determination is made of the likely ending *before* the left-to-right marking starts. If the preposition is 'to', tests determine if 'to' is likely to signal an infinitive. For situations where the preposition is followed by a definite ending ('He stayed in.'), the preposition is marked as a particle, and as part of the predicate. A preposition followed by another preposition ('out of sight'), or one followed by a coordinator and another preposition ('to and from school'), is flagged, and the second preposition is treated as if it were the start of the phrase.

If these procedures do not eliminate the item, an effort is made to label the words between the preposition and the end of the phrase. In effect there is a division between categories unlikely to appear in a phrase, and those which can appear. The first inadmissible word is assumed temporarily to be the first word after the end of the phrase. Categories which indicate a probable ending are:

auxiliary verb, 'not'	part of a verbal phrase
clause marker, subordinator	signals start of another clause
preposition	start of another prepositional phrase
interjection	

Categories which can be included in a prepositional phrase are:

content word	potential noun or adjective
pronoun	potential head of phrase
coordinator	
determiner, intensifier	noun modifiers

Once the ending is determined, separate parts of the program treat phrases of 2, 3, and 4 words. A summary of the section for four-word phrases should illustrate the kinds of rules which are used.

1. When the second word is a determiner, followed by two content words in a row, the first content word is an adjective, and the second a noun. If the third is a content word and fourth any function word, the content word is a noun, and the phrase is assumed to be three words long. If the third is a determiner or intensifier, the fourth is a noun if it is a content word; otherwise, automatic parsing of the phrase is abandoned. (Similar rules are used for nominal phrases which start with a determiner.)

2. If the second word is a content word, the third also a content word, and the fourth a function word, then the second is marked as an adjective, the third as a noun, and the phrase is assumed to be three words long. If three content words follow the preposition, no guess as to the length or syntax is possible.

3. If the second word is a pronoun, the search is for other pronouns in the third or fourth positions, as part of a series. If a pair of pronouns, joined by a coordinator in the third place, is found, the phrase is marked.

4. An intensifier in the second position leads to an adjective + noun combination if followed by two content words, and a noun alone if followed by one content word.

A summary of rules for longer phrases follows:

1. If there are three or more content words in a row, marking is abandoned. The difficulty here is that there is no way to tell if the three words are a pair of adjectives and a noun ('on big fat horses'), or are part of two different structures ('from big houses eat some dinner').

2. For similar reasons, marking is abandoned if there is more than one coordinator among the seven words after the preposition.

3. After the exclusions, the phrase is marked. Single content words, that is, ones framed by function words, are marked as nouns; content-word pairs are marked as adjective + noun combinations.

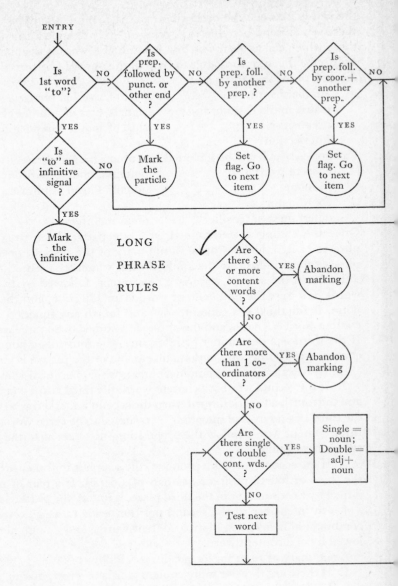

Figure 1
Prepositional phrases

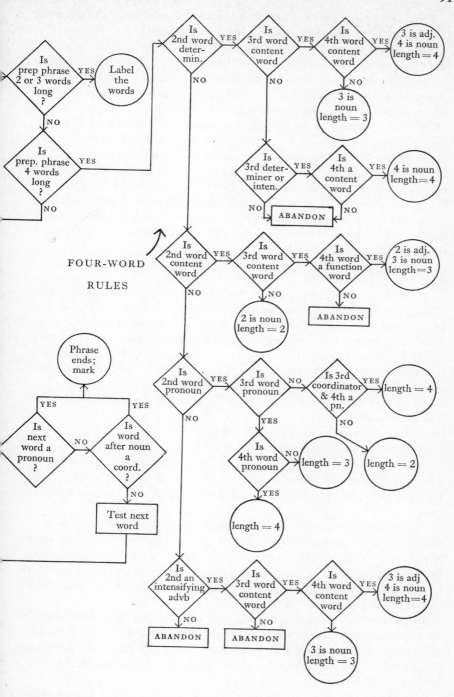

FOUR-WORD

RULES

4. If a pronoun follows what has been marked as a noun, the phrase is terminated after the noun, and the pronoun is excluded.

5. If a function word which could start another nominal phrase occurs in a group of words which has no coordinator, the phrase is considered as ending after the first apparent noun or the first pronoun. Thus, the series 'for the man the suit fit very well' will end after 'man', while 'behind the dog and the cat was an elephant' will end after 'cat'.

To return briefly to the conceptual model: the reader of a phrase presumably does not have information about the most likely ending of a series of words when he finds a preposition; he must discover it during the process of reading (or listening). There may be cues in the stress and intonation patterns of the spoken language which indicate the approach of a phrase ending; it is remotely possible that the combination of terminal punctuation and the conventional double space is noticed unconsciously on the printed page, but the human cannot anticipate these facts, while the computer can.

PARSING OF CLAUSES

The subordinated clause program first separates very short, punctuated clauses of two or three words from the longer ones. A colon, semi-colon, or terminal punctuation are the only reliable signals that a clause ends. Therefore, even when all categories and functions have been accurately marked, designating which is the last word of the clause will be necessary during the intermediate processing. The short-clause section considers all reasonably frequent possibilities and inserts appropriate labels. The subordinated clause in 'He liked what he ate.' has these labels from the initial processing:

what = subordinator, function unknown;
he   = pronoun, function unknown;
ate = content word (that is, category and function unknown).

The GUESS program adds the functional labels of subject to 'he', complement to 'what', and labels 'ate' as a verb which functions as a predicate.

The program treats the words of longer clauses as if all were part of the same clause; it stops when it gets to punctuation or to the tenth word after the subordinator. If a determiner, an auxiliary verb, or a pronoun is found, labeling is done by special parts of the program. Prepositional phrases falling within the clause are marked according to the procedure just discussed.

The determiner routine finds the length of a nominal phrase introduced by a determiner and locates the noun head and possible adjectives. Its rules more or less duplicate those for prepositional phrases which have a determiner in the second position. Functions of these phrases are inserted later in the procedure.

The auxiliary-verb routine tries first to discover if the pre-marked auxiliary is actually the main verb of the clause, as occurs when it is followed immediately by a determiner ('the man is the hero') or a preposition ('the man was from Nebraska'). The algorithm does not assume periodic construction of verbal phrases; it will mismark such items as 'the man is the hero desired'. The researcher is reminded of the computer's decision in the output, and he can correct its errors. If the auxiliary is followed by a content word, the program searches for an indication of a nominal or prepositional phrase which comes right after the content word. If either is found, the content word is labeled as a main verb (category) and predicate (function).

The pronoun routine scans a list of subject and object forms ('I' and 'he'; 'me' and 'him'; and so on). Pronouns in prepositional phrases are blocked from consideration. A word not on the list, whose function is ambiguous ('you' and 'it'), is merely flagged within the routine, but there is an effort to determine function by the pronoun's position in the clause.

The category of the word immediately after the subordinator seems to have particular importance in the determination of the functions of several words in the clause. The subordinators are initially divided: ones which cannot become main clause-elements comprise one group, while words which can be relative pronouns, that is, function as the subject or complement, are the other. The following 'second-word' rules have been implemented, and their reliability seems quite high.

These rules obtain if the subordinator can be a relative pronoun ('who', 'which', and so on). If the second word is a preposition or an auxiliary verb, the relative pronoun functions as a subject. If the second element is a nominal phrase (a pronoun, or a phrase beginning with a determiner), the nominal phrase functions as the subject, and the relative pronoun as the complement. If the subordinator cannot be a relative pronoun ('when', 'however', and so on) and the second word is a pronoun or determiner, the first nominal phrase is the subject, as in 'when the man is eaten', or 'when you are home'. There is, of course, no change in the marking of the subordinator. This rule is part of a more general one that the first nominal phrase before a verb is likely to be the subject and to precede the complement. The GUESS program assumes a subject-predicate-complement, or 'SVO' sequence of main clause-elements. As a result it contains instructions which check certain nominal phrases (personal pronouns and those initiated by a determiner) in order to assign labels. If the clause already has an identified subject and complement, either because of marking in the pronoun routine or by the 'second-word' rules, then no further marking is tried. If either a subject or a complement has been found, then the relative pronoun or the first unmarked nominal phrase is assigned the opposite function. If there is no nominal phrase with a known function, then the first one is labeled subject and the second, complement.

Another section of the program, also based on the assumption of 'SVO'

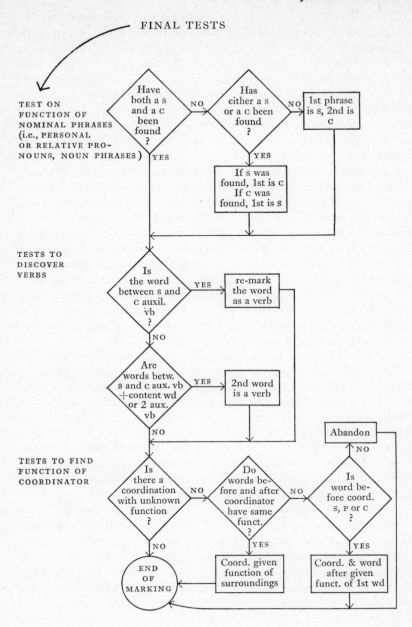

FINAL TESTS

TEST ON
FUNCTION OF
NOMINAL PHRASES
(i.e., PERSONAL
OR RELATIVE PRO-
NOUNS, NOUN PHRASES)

Have both a s and a c been found ?

Has either a s or a c been found ?

1st phrase is s, 2nd is c

If s was found, 1st is c
If c was found, 1st is s

TESTS TO
DISCOVER
VERBS

Is the word between s and c auxil. vb ?

re-mark the word as a verb

Are words betw. s and c aux. vb +content wd or 2 aux. vb

2nd word is a verb

TESTS TO FIND
FUNCTION OF
COORDINATOR

Is there a coordination with unknown function ?

Do words before and after coordinator have same funct. ?

Abandon

Is word before coord. s, P or c ?

END OF MARKING

Coord. given function of surroundings

Coord. & word after given funct. of 1st wd

s = subject,
c = complement,
P = predicate

Figure 2
Subordinated clauses

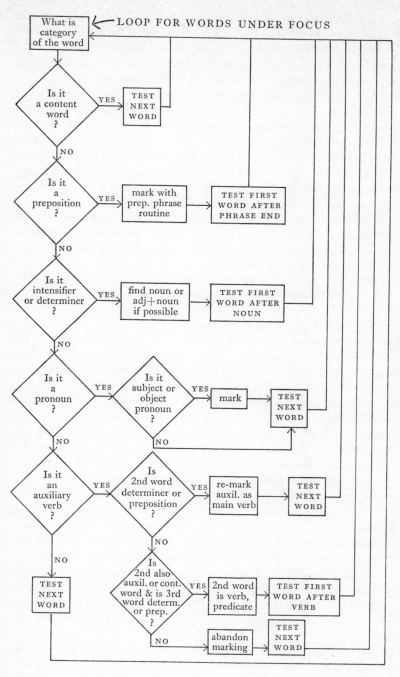

order, marks as predicate certain words framed by identified subjects and complements. If there is a single content word, or single auxiliary verb, then it is marked as the main verb. If two words are present, the first of which is a pre-marked auxiliary, and the second either another auxiliary or a content word, the latter is labeled as the main verb.

A final set of instructions allows for the marking of the functions of some coordinators. When a coordinator is surrounded by two words which have the same function, the coordinator is assumed to have the same function as its neighbors. An effort is made to use other coordinators as a bridge between a word of known function and one whose function has not been determined. If the word before the coordinator is part of a subject, predicate, or complement, then the coordinator and the word following it are assumed to have the same function.

The algorithm for analyzing independent clauses is conceptually the same as the one for subordinated clauses, except that the capital letter is the only formal signal of where the clause starts. Although no tests have yet been made on independent clauses using the GUESS algorithm, it seems reasonable to assume that the program will prove equally reliable, even if the 'second-word' rules cannot be used.

PROBLEMS AND FURTHER WORK

Possible ways for sophisticating the operations of the GUESS algorithm have been considered, but none has been specifically designed or tested. The program now marks from left to right along a limited number of words. As noted, there does not seem to be a reliable indicator of clause ending other than punctuation. It would be pointless to direct the computer to continue until it found a clear indication of the presence of another clause, say a subject pronoun or punctuation mark. This process could automatically mis-mark hundreds of words and waste computer time. Therefore, it seems likely that only ten or so words can be marked at a time. The algorithm is designed to avoid series of three or more content words, and this is a major limitation on its usefulness. It is not at all difficult to think of rather long clauses which are composed entirely of such items, and which are unmarkable: 'if strong men need especially powerful vitamin capsules, they get them'. Even though such combinations exist, clauses with a scattering of function words seem to be far more frequent in English. This suggests, incidentally, the possible definition of a stylistic characteristic, since a text with a relatively large proportion of 'unmarkable' phrases and clauses will be quite dissimilar in style from another where nearly every item can be automatically marked by this algorithm.

In the design of the GUESS algorithm, the rules include the premarking of function words; the labeling of content words depends almost entirely on their location *vis à vis* the function words and punctuation. A possible way of overcoming this limitation might be to include a limited scanning for suffixes, which reveal categories, such as those found in 'reg*al* good*ness* deserv*ed* praise', where '-al' designates an adjective, '-ness' a noun, and '-ed' a verb. However, a plan to mark words which end with '-ly' as adverbs was abandoned because the list of exceptions is quite long ('ally', 'belly', and so on), and because the categories of '-ly' words often vary ('he dressed neatly' would be marked accurately, but 'a likely story' would not). Another problem is that most words do not have clearly defined morphological markers: only in government documents [sic] and other non-literary media are frequencies high enough to merit serious consideration. Most content words, especially those of high frequency in English, are not marked for category.

Expanding the dictionary to include a couple of hundred of the most frequent content words has been considered. Aside from the extra storage in the computer, one disadvantage with a larger dictionary is that every word in a text must be subjected to a comparison test with the entire list until a match is found; the longer the dictionary, the more tests, and the greater the expenditure of computer time. If the input text had a rather fixed vocabulary, for example, if one wished to survey the style of official weather bureau reports, then the use of such a lexicon might be feasible. For literary works, though, there is probably no dictionary large enough to include all possible words: one can cite Blake's peculiar 'Tyger' with the 'y' or think of the chaos which would result if dialect passages in *Wuthering Heights* were to be studied.

One attractive possibility in this line would be to expand the dictionary by the hundred or so most frequently encountered verb forms. If the main verb can be located, then the functions of many nominal phrases can be determined, and some of the problems caused by successions of content words might be reduced. The flagging of such verbs presents another advantage in that many of the forms of 'strong' verbs in English are unambiguous. Unlike nominal phrases, verbal phrases are liable to interruption, by single words ('he *is* perhaps *not* fully *clothed*'), by prepositional phrases ('he *is* of all our lapdogs *loved* the best'), or by clauses ('he *is* when he eats *talking* obscurely'). If the verbs were known, more complete parsing would be possible.

SYNTACTIC DESCRIPTION AND LITERARY STYLE

An adequate description of style seeks to generalize about all the words in a text, as well as to provide a basis for isolating unusual or idiosyncratic components. It tries not only to account for the variety of syntactic, lexical, or compositional components, but also to describe the extent to which variety is (or is not) a noticeable property of the work of literature. The description of style, as distinguished from its explanation (*see* Weitz 1966), takes no responsibility for accounting for the origin (or 'generation') of the text, if by origin we mean the peculiarity of the author's psyche, or notions about intellectual history or literary conventions which

G

might govern the production of works of art at a certain time. It seems a sufficiently demanding task, for the present at least, to describe the styles of individual works, and to build a basis upon which some generalizations of a wider range might ultimately be founded.

Assembling accurate descriptions based on a consistently applied methodology from an author's entire body of writings is a prelude to a description of his style; an analogous case obtains if a corpus is defined by a genre or historical era. It is possible to reduce the amount of material which must be described if proper sampling is used, but, even so, the number of texts and the ultimate size of a representative sample soon become so large that only with computer help can the counting and analysis be done. Recall that the most thorough effort to put literature in computer-readable form has been for the preparation of concordances, and that, unfortunately, very little use has been made of this body of material beyond the concordances themselves.

In our effort to move beyond studies of vocabulary, the syntactic description produced by EYEBALL is essentially an account of the features of surface structure. This decision was made, in part, because such features seem to be what most readers mean by style. Studies of literature which have employed the full range of transformational grammar, and of the apparent relationships between surface and deep structures [most notably those of Ohmann (1959, 1964, 1966) and Levin (1964)] have dealt almost exclusively with very detailed analyses of short passages. Whether this limitation is a result of choice or inherent in the complexity of transformational grammar is not clear. Although the GUESS algorithm in particular, and EYEBALL in general are based on structural grammar, the presence of both a categorical and a functional label for each word makes the fully marked text amenable to interpretation by more than one grammar. Some preliminary tests indicate that the way the marked text is 'read' by the computer and interpreted can be modified so that the various transformations which are present are categorized and counted.

A modest effort has been made to test this methodology on small prose selections by Emerson and Thoreau (Ross 1972a) and two poems by Yeats (Ross 1972b). These studies combined close analysis of short passages with statistical generalizations based on a manually-calculated simulation of the EYEBALL computer program. Aside from the illumination that was cast on particular literary problems, the use of stylistic descriptions which were consistent for all the texts allowed for a wide range of comparisons based on explicitly defined terms. The addition of computer aid to stylistic descriptions soon will open large bodies of literature to careful and exact analysis and criticism.

Acknowledgements
Support by the computer centers of the University of Pennsylvania (1969–71) and the University of Minnesota (1971–72) is gratefully

acknowledged, as is the travel grant by the University of Minnesota which allowed this paper to be presented at the 1972 Edinburgh Symposium on the Uses of Computers in Literary Research. The aid of Robert Rasche of the Economics Department, Michigan State University, especially in all programming matters, has proven to be invaluable. The EYEBALL programs in IBM or CDC FORTRAN are available from the author.

REFERENCES

Bever, T. & Langendoen, D. (1971) A dynamic model of the evolution of language. *Linguistic Inquiry*, **2**, 433-64.

Brodda, B. & Karlgren, H. (1964) Relative positions of elements in linguistic strings. *SMIL*, **3**, 49-101.

Ellegård, A. (1963) Design for a mechanical distribution analysis of English word classes. *Structures and Quanta : Three Essays on Linguistic Description*. New York: Humanities Press.

Levin, S. (1964) *Linguistic Structures in Poetry*. The Hague: Mouton.

Milic, L. (1967) *A Quantitative Approach to the Style of Jonathan Swift*. The Hague: Mouton.

Ohmann, R. (1959) Prolegomena to the analysis of prose style. *Style in Prose Fiction: English Institute Essays 1958* (ed. Martin, H.C.). New York: Columbia University Press.

Ohmann, R. (1964) Generative Grammars and the Concept of Literary Style. *Word*, **20**, 423-39.

Ohmann, R. (1966) Literature as sentences. *CE*, **27**, 261-7.

Ross, D. & Rasche, R. (1972a) Description and user's manual for EYEBALL. Univ. of Minnesota Department of English, mimeograph.

Ross, D. & Rasche, R. (1972b) EYEBALL: A computer program for description of style. *C.Hum.*, **6**, 213-21.

Ross, D. (1972a) Emerson and Thoreau: A comparison of prose styles. *Lang. S*, forthcoming.

Ross, D. (1972b) Stylistic contrasts in Yeats' Byzantium poems. *Lang. S*, forthcoming.

Weitz, M. (1966) *Hamlet and the Philosophy of Literary Criticism*. Cleveland: World.

Word association and thematic analysis

The computation of collocations and their relevance in lexical studies

The terms 'collocation' and 'collocability' were first introduced by J.R. Firth in his paper 'Modes of Meaning' published in 1951 (*see* Firth 1957, 1968). Firth does not give any explicit definition of 'collocation' but he rather illustrates the notion by way of such examples as: 'One of the meanings of *ass* is its habitual collocation with an immediately preceding *you silly* . . .'. Although some of his other contributions to linguistic and stylistic analysis (such as 'prosodic features') have had a considerable impact, his notion of 'collocation' has not been seriously considered until the last decade. The reasons for this neglect are probably twofold: on the one hand, the rather vague terms in which he described the notion (*cf.* Haskel 1971) and, on the other hand, the practical restrictions imposed by the prohibitive scale of a textual study of collocability. The latter drawback has been remedied by the introduction of the digital computer in textual analysis. As to the former, several recent attempts have been made by scholars at defining the notion 'collocation' more precisely within the framework of modern linguistic theory. For relevant theoretical discussions on this topic, the reader is referred to the bibliography (Haas 1966; Halliday 1961, 1966; Lyons 1966; McIntosh 1966; Sinclair 1966; van Buren 1967). The applicability of these theories was investigated extensively in the OSTI sponsored 'Lexis Research Project' directed by Sinclair (Sinclair, Jones, and Daley 1970).

The present paper reports on a pilot study attempting to make explicit the notion of 'collocation' in statistical and computational terms. Firth himself stressed that collocation was not to be equated with mere co-occurrence of lexical items but he always used the phrase 'habitual' or 'usual' collocation implying a gradation in collocability among the set of words which are found to occur in the environment of a particular item. As a technically more workable definition of 'collocation' we borrowed the one formulated by Halliday (1961) as:

> the syntagmatic association of lexical items, quantifiable, textually, as the probability that there will occur at n removes (a distance of n lexical items) from an item x, the items a, b, c . . .

In other words, the aim is to compile a list of those syntagmatic items ('collocates') significantly co-occurring with a given lexical item ('node') within a specified linear distance ('span'). 'Significant collocation' can be defined in statistical terms as the probability of the item x co-occurring with the items $a, b, c, \ldots$ being greater than might be expected from pure chance. Consider the following statistical data as being given:

Z : total number of words in the text
A : a given node occurring in the text Fn times
B : a collocate of A occurring in the text Fc times
K : number of co-occurrences of B and A
S : span size, that is, the number of items on either side of the node considered as its environment.

First must be computed the probability of B co-occurring K times with A, if B were distributed randomly in the text. Next, the difference between the expected number of co-occurrences and the observed number of co-occurrences must be evaluated. The probability of B occurring at any place where A does not occur is expressed by:

$$p = Fc/(Z - Fn)$$

The expected number of co-occurrences is given by:

$$E = p.Fn.S$$

The problem is to decide whether the difference between observed and expected frequencies is statistically significant. This can be done by means of computation of the 'z-score' as a normal approximation to the binomial distribution (Hoel 1962) using the formula:

$$z = (K - E)/\sqrt{Eq} \qquad (q = 1 - p).$$

This formula has proved highly satisfactory in that it yielded a gradation among collocates which largely corresponded with our semantic intuitions. It is, however, by no means proposed as the ultimate one. Further studies on a larger scale than the present one and possibly embodying a greater variety of texts might well require modifications to it. Thus, for some nodes a Poisson distribution would be more appropriate than a binomial one. Another flaw in the formula is that it does not account for the possibility of a node co-occurring with itself within the specified span. This possibility was temporarily dismissed on account of its relative rarity. But other studies with a stylistic rather than a lexical inclination might find such aspects highly relevant. It is nevertheless hoped that the subsequent illustrations of the application of the formula will prove its relative validity. But first a few words must be said about the nature of the data.

In order to obtain a fairly comprehensive picture of the collocational relations of lexical items a very large corpus would have to be processed. Halliday (1966) quotes the figures of some 20 million running words! It is obviously not feasible even with our largest computers to process a corpus of this size. (Even the Brown University corpus of American English has a limit of one million words.) The number of running words processed in the present pilot study amounted to 71,595. This figure is of course far off the 20 million mark, but it proved sufficient for an initial methodological investigation. The data consisted of a nineteenth-century prose work and two modern plays, namely *A Christmas Carol* by Charles Dickens (1922), *Each his own Wilderness* by Doris Lessing (1959) and *Everything in the Garden* by Giles Cooper (1963). The choice of these texts was motivated by their availability in machine-readable form rather than by any stylistic considerations. Prior to the analysis a concordance and statistical information on each text (such as a frequency profile, average sentence length, and so on) were obtained. But the three texts were subsequently conflated as the size of each separately did not warrant results of any statistical significance. Thus, the aim of the study was not in the first place stylistic, but rather methodological, being concerned with answering such questions as 'what is the optimal span size?', 'should grammatical items be ignored?', and so on. For computational purposes, the lexical unit was defined as the 'graphic word', that is, a sequence of characters delimited by specified word boundary markers such as 'space' and the punctuation marks, thus adopting the same conventions used in the statistical analysis of American English at Brown University (Kučera and Francis 1967).

The texts were processed on the Atlas computers at Manchester and Chilton. The initial stages of the program—written in Atlas Autocode—are similar to an ordinary concordance program where the context is limited to the specified span. A particular keyword being selected as node, all items occurring within the span are conflated into an alphabetical list and their number of co-occurrences with the node is counted. This list is then tested against a previously compiled 'dictionary' consisting of an alphabetic word-frequency table for the entire text. The total number of occurrences of each collocate is subsequently recorded, after which the z-scores are computed. As initial node the item *house* was chosen, partly because the word count had shown it to occur with relatively high frequency (83 instances), and partly because our intuitions about the syntagmatic bonds of this item are fairly clear, thus providing a valuable touchstone for an automatic analysis. The initial 'collocational set' consisted of all graphic words occurring within a span of three items on either side of the node *house*, regardless of intervening sentence boundaries. The small size of the textual sample compelled us to discard all collocates co-occurring with *house* only once. This decision caused some valuable collocations to be lost (such as *four-roomed house*) but, conversely the inclusion of the item *Amazons* (occurring in the context: 'This house is full of Amazons . . .') was avoided. Table 1 contains a listing, in order of absolute frequency of co-occurrence, of all items collocating at least twice with *house*, including indications of their total frequency in the data (Fc), their observed (K) and expected frequency of co-occurrence (E), and the respective z-scores. As might have been expected, those items co-occurring most frequently with *house* are grammatical. Table 2 is a re-ordering of table 1 in terms of relative collocational significance. Due to the limitations of the sample the order established is obviously not fully representative of the collocational behaviour of *house* in the English language as a whole. It is, for example, highly likely that in a larger sample *sold* would occur more frequently in other environments than *house* and that *Commons* would stand out more clearly as forming part of the idiom *House of Commons*.

Collocate	K	Fc	E	z-score
THE	35	2368	20·6315	3·2978
THIS	22	252	2·1955	13·3937
A	15	1358	11·5661	0·9316
OF	13	1163	10·1327	0·9096
I	12	1674	14·5849	−0·6865
IN	12	843	7·3447	1·7299
IT	9	1193	10·3941	−0·4368
MY	8	271	2·3611	3·6780
IS	7	362	3·1539	2·1721
HAVE	7	403	3·5111	1·8682
TO	7	1482	12·9121	−1·6660
SOLD	6	7	0·0609	24·0500
YOU	5	1711	14·9073	−2·6034
AND	4	1568	13·6614	−2·6488
BUT	4	383	3·3369	0·3641
COMMONS	4	4	0·0385	21·2416
FOR	4	502	4·3737	−0·1794
HIS	4	468	4·0775	−0·0385
INTO	4	92	0·8015	3·5792
NOT	4	413	3·5983	0·3221
ONE	4	244	2·1258	1·2879
'RE	4	147	1·2807	2·5999
WELL	4	254	2·2130	−0·1209
ALL	3	366	3·1888	−0·1060
COULD	3	116	1·4462	1·9887
DECORATE	3	3	0·0261	19·9000
EMPTY	3	7	0·0609	11·9020
HAS	3	67	0·5837	2·9359
OUT	3	181	1·5769	1·1348
WAS	3	572	4·9836	−0·0890
BE	2	363	3·1626	−0·6557
BEEN	2	134	1·1674	0·7713
BEFORE	2	67	0·5837	1·6451
LIKE	2	188	1·6379	0·2833
EVERY	2	59	0·5140	2·0736
ABOUT	2	168	1·3522	0·5363
BUYING	2	4	0·0348	10·5970
DID	2	146	1·2729	0·6462
DO	2	374	3·2585	−0·6993
FAMILY	2	20	0·1742	4·3744
FULL	2	25	0·2178	3·8209
GET	2	101	0·8799	1·1949
GHOST	2	89	0·7754	1·3916
IF	2	268	2·3349	−0·2197
KNOW	2	247	2·1520	−0·1038
LIVED	2	13	0·1132	5·6067
LOVES	2	10	0·0871	6·4811

Table 1 (contd)

Collocate	K	Fc	E	z-score
MORE	2	90	0·7841	1·3740
MOTHER	2	129	1·1239	0·8558
MUCH	2	93	0·8102	1·3227
MYRA	2	73	0·6360	1·7232
NICE	2	54	0·4704	2·3908
ONLY	2	60	0·5227	2·0441
OTHER	2	74	0·6447	1·6889
OPPOSITE	2	6	0·0522	8·5192
OUTSIDE	2	12	0·1045	5·8626
PAINTING	2	4	0·0348	10·5970
PEOPLE	2	121	1·0542	0·9220
UP	2	201	1·7512	1·8829
REMEMBER	2	26	0·0226	3·9425
SEE	2	127	1·1065	0·8503
SOMETHING	2	67	0·5837	1·9026
THAT	2	758	6·6041	−1·8030
THEY	2	327	2·8490	−0·5175
TONY	2	86	0·7492	1·4459
THERE	2	95	0·9877	1·2896
WITH	2	431	4·0012	−0·9090
YEARS	2	50	0·4252	2·3712
YES	2	345	3·0900	−0·5818

Table 1. Collocates of 'house' in order of frequency of
co-occurrence. Span = 3 items on either side of the
node

Where the 'significance limit' should be drawn is in the last resort
subject to the judgment of the individual investigator and to the purpose
of his study. At the 0·1 per cent level of significance statistical tables put
this limit at a 2·576 z-score (Spiegel 1961). This figure was adopted as a
workable hypothesis for the present study but is by no means applicable
to other types of data and corpus sizes. By drawing this particular limit
we run the risk of excluding from consideration 'unusual' but 'creative'
collocations (an example of which being Dickens's use of the adjective
young with *house*) alongside with obviously irrelevant ones. Similarly,
those items with a negative z-score are excluded, although they might
possibly be deemed to be of a particular stylistic interest as they seem to
'repel' the node. However, it is our view that 'unusual' collocation needs
to be explained with reference to an explicit definition of 'usual' collocation. The present study is an attempt to investigate how the latter can be
best established.

The next question to be considered is how adequate the chosen span
size was. Table 3 shows how an increase of the span size from 3 to 6
affects the sets of statistically significant collocates. All newly introduced
collocates are in italics. Some of these, such as *enter, rooms, fronts, garden,*

SOLD	24·0500	ONLY	2·0441	DID	0·6462
COMMONS	21·2416	COULD	1·9887	ABOUT	0·5363
DECORATE	19·9000	SOMETHING	1·9026	BUT	0·3641
THIS	13·3937	UP	1·8829	NOT	0·3221
EMPTY	11·9090	HAVE	1·8682	LIKE	0·2833
BUYING	10·5970	IN	1·7299	HIS	−0·0385
PAINTING	10·5970	MYRA	1·7232	WAS	−0·0890
OPPOSITE	8·5192	OTHER	1·6889	KNOW	−0·1038
LOVES	6·4811	BEFORE	1·6451	ALL	−0·1060
OUTSIDE	5·8626	TONY	1·4459	WELL	−0·1209
LIVED	5·6067	GHOST	1·3916	FOR	−0·1794
FAMILY	4·3744	MORE	1·3740	IF	−0·2197
REMEMBER	3·9425	MUCH	1·3227	IT	−0·4368
FULL	3·8209	WHERE	1·2896	THEY	−0·5175
MY	3·6780	ONE	1·2879	YES	−0·5818
INTO	3·5792	GET	1·1949	BE	−0·6557
THE	3·2978	OUT	1·1348	I	−0·6865
HAS	2·9359	OR	0·9316	DO	−0·6993
'RE	2·5999	PEOPLE	0·9220	WITH	−0·9090
NICE	2·3908	OF	0·9096	TO	−1·6660
YEARS	2·3712	MOTHER	0·8558	THAT	−1·8030
IS	2·1721	SEE	0·8503	YOU	−2·6034
EVERY	2·0736	BEEN	0·7713	AND	−2·6488

Table 2. Collocates of 'house' in decreasing order of significance

. . ., seem indeed highly relevant, whereas others, such as *God, Bernard, stop*, are to be considered 'intruders'. An investigation at this point of the respective concordances and statistical data on each text showed that the stylistic nature of the corpus is highly relevant in defining the optimal span size. Increasing the span size resulted in effect in introducing 'desirable' collocates from *A Christmas Carol* but undesirable ones from the plays. The obvious explanation lies in the marked difference between the mean sentence length which amounts to 14·03 in *A Christmas Carol* but only to 6·7 in the modern plays. Although by no means all significant collocates occur solely within the sentence boundaries, the majority nevertheless do. However, a general policy concerning the span size to be adopted in this pilot study could not be based upon observations of the behaviour of a single node. Other items of medium frequency were similarly tested, including verbs, adverbs, and adjectives. As it proved that the majority of significant collocates do appear in the immediate vicinity of their nodes, it seemed appropriate to provisionally adopt a span of four for both types of data and for all nodes which were non-grammatical items, except in the case of adjectives where a span of only two seemed indicated.

Much more could be said at this point about further stylistic differences between the two types of data as well as about the collocational relevance of 'grammatical' items. A case might be put forward for considering as

potential collocates only those items which stand in a grammatical relation to the node. Generally speaking, this would have the effect of including only relevant items. However, unless a very sophisticated grammatical
analysis which takes into account anaphoric reference is applied, a great
many important collocates might be lost. Consider, for example, the
following quote from *A Christmas Carol*. It is hard to envisage at the
moment a grammatical model which would be powerful enough to relate
to the node *face* all italicized items which we felt to be semantically
related to it:

> Marley's face. It was not in as impenetrable a shadow as the other
> objects in the yard were, but had a *dismal light* about it, like a bad
> lobster in a dark cellar. It was not *angry* or *ferocious*, but *looked at*
> Scrooge as Marley used to look with ghostly *spectacles* turned up on
> its ghostly *forehead*. The *hair* was curiously stirred, as if by breath
> or hot air; and, although the *eyes* were wide open, they were perfectly
> motionless. That, and its *livid* colour, made it *horrible*, but its *horror*
> seemed to be in spite of the face and beyond control, rather than part
> of its own *expression*.

Span=3				Span=4			
Collocate	K	Fc	*z-score*	*Collocate*	K	Fc	*z-score*
sold	6	7	24·0500	sold	6	7	20·7566
commons	4	4	21·2416	commons	4	4	18·3415
decorate	2	3	19·9000	decorate	3	3	15·8837
this	22	252	13·3937	this	22	252	10·7863
empty	3	7	11·9090	empty	3	7	10·2360
buying	2	4	10·5970	buying	2	4	9·0697
painting	2	4	10·5970	painting	2	4	9·0697
opposite	2	6	8·5192	opposite	2	6	7·5951
loves	2	10	6·4811	loves	2	10	5·5975
outside	2	12	5·8626	*entered*	2	10	5·5975
lived	2	13	5·6067	*near*	2	11	5·2373
family	2	20	4·3744	outside	2	12	4·9038
remember	2	26	3·9425	lived	2	13	4·7583
full	2	25	3·8209	remember	3	26	4·9102
my	8	271	3·6780	*rooms*	2	15	4·3255
into	3	92	3·5792	*flat*	2	18	3·8170
the	35	2368	3·2978	*big*	2	19	3·7878
has	2	50	2·9359	*Bernard*	2	20	3·6876
				family	2	20	3·6676
				my	9	271	3·3055
				full	2	23	3·2845
				into	3	92	2·8326
				the	42	2368	2·3182
				every	3	59	2·7971
				Mrs	2	29	2·6713

Table 3. Significant collocates of 'house'

Table 3 (contd)

	Span=5				Span=6		
Collocate	K	Fc	z-score	Collocate	K	Fc	z-score
sold	7	7	21·6383	sold	8	7	22·5581
commons	4	4	16·3571	commons	4	4	14·8871
decorate	3	3	14·1356	decorate	3	3	13·8456
fronts	2	2	11·5635	fronts	2	2	10·5971
this	22	252	9·6080	*cracks*	2	2	10·5971
empty	3	7	9·0914	this	22	252	8·4908
buying	2	4	8·0577	empty	3	7	8·2410
painting	2	4	8·0577	buying	2	4	7·3117
opposite	2	6	6·1350	painting	2	4	7·3117
loves	2	10	4·8677	opposite	2	6	5·8695
entered	2	10	4·8677	loves	2	10	4·3741
near	2	11	4·6050	entered	2	10	4·3741
outside	2	12	4·6050	black	2	12	3·9168
black	2	12	4·3742	near	2	11	4·1308
remember	3	26	4·2689	outside	2	12	4·1308
lived	2	13	4·1691	remember	2	26	3·7847
rooms	2	15	3·9122	lived	2	13	3·7118
garden	2	17	3·5230	rooms	2	15	3·6698
flat	2	18	3·4019	God	5	64	3·6806
big	2	19	3·2829	*stop*	3	27	3·2550
into	5	92	3·2795	garden	2	17	3·1308
God	4	64	3·1869	flat	2	18	3·0115
family	2	20	3·1728	every	4	59	2·9325
Bernard	2	20	3·1728	big	2	19	2·9009
my	9	271	2·8011	my	11	271	2·8854
full	2	25	2·7980	into	5	92	2·8849
				family	2	20	2·7310
				Bernard	2	20	2·7310
				whole	2	23	2·6771

Table 3. Significant collocates of 'house'

As such a sophisticated computerized syntactic analysis is not yet available, a purely linear span seems presently to be the best solution. Greater flexibility of the span size relative to the grammatical structure of the context can be obtained by excluding as collocates a number of 'grammatical' items or 'functors' which have only minimal semantic content. A proposed 'exclusion list' would contain such items as *and*, *but*, *it*, *its*, *nor*, *or*, *that*, *what*, *whether*, *which*, *who*, and all forms of the auxiliaries *be*, *do*, and *have*. This would in some cases effectively increase the span from 4 to 6 or 7 items, thus including some collocates which are semantically related to the node but occur at greater distances from it.

Finally, we should like to anticipate the next stage in our study of collocation. The eventual aim of a collocational analysis is not just to establish sets of syntagmatically related items but to extend these to include paradigmatically related items so that eventually a 'semantic

	house	room	office	home	place	flat	hall	chamber	hut	cellar	warehouse	grocer's	world
live in/at	*	*		*	*	*		*	*				*
leave	*	*		*	*		*						
door	*	*					*			*	*		
empty	*	*									*		
window	*		*						*				
close			*		*							*	
dark		*						*		*			
garden	*					*							
move				*	*								
let out			*	*									
furnished			*	*									
stay in/at				*	*								
wall			*					*					
pass		*										*	
enter	*					*							
full	*												*

Table 4. The structure of the semantic field of 'habitation terms'

field' might be established. A program is being designed which will take as input the set of collocates of a given node and examine their collocational relations with other items, thus forming a network of semantically related items. Starting with the node *house*, a preliminary attempt was made to simulate manually such an automatic scan, by making use of available collocational sets and concordances. The results, which are plotted in table 4, embody a provisional 'semantic field of habitation terms'. Considering that this 'field' emerged from as small a sample as some 72,000 running English words it seems, apart from some obvious gaps, intuitively quite acceptable. The methods outlined in this paper when applied to a corpus of considerable size could lead to the establishment of a 'thesaurus' of English, based on an objective and consistent analysis of how words are actually used rather than on subjective intuitions. Other stylistic applications to the analysis of the vocabulary (or even 'conceptual world') of an individual author are easy to envisage. How in more general terms collocational studies can contribute to computer-aided stylistic analysis is discussed, among others, by Sedelow and Sedelow (1966, 1967).

REFERENCES
Cooper, Giles (1963) Everything in the garden. *New English Dramatists—7*, pp. 141-221. London: Penguin.

Dickens, Charles (1922) *A Christmas Carol*. London: Macmillan.

Firth, J.R. (1957) Modes of meaning. *Papers in Linguistics 1934–51*, pp.190-215. London: Oxford University Press.

Firth, J.R. (1968) A synopsis of linguistic theory 1930–55. *Selected Papers of J.R. Firth 1952–59* (ed. Palmer, F.R.). London: Longman.

Haas, W. (1966) Linguistic relevance. *In Memory of J.R. Firth*, pp. 116-48 (ed. Bazell, C.E., *et al.*). London: Longman.

Halliday, M.A.K. (1961) Categories of the theory of grammar. *Word*, **17**, 241-292.

Halliday, M.A.K. (1966) Lexis as a linguistic level. *In Memory of J.R. Firth*, pp.148-63 (ed. Bazell, C.E., *et al.*). London: Longman.

Haskel, Peggy (1971) Collocations as a measure of stylistic variety. *The Computer in Literary and Linguistic Research*, pp.159-69 (ed. Wisbey, R.A.). Cambridge: Cambridge University Press.

Hoel, P.G. (1962) *Introduction to Mathematical Statistics*. New York: Wiley.

Kučera, H. & Francis, W.N. (1967) *Computational Analysis of present-day American English*. Brown University Press.

Lessing, Doris (1959) Each his own wilderness. *New English Dramatists—1*, pp.11-97. London: Penguin.

Lyons, J. (1966) Firth's theory of meaning. *In Memory of J.R. Firth*, pp.288-302 (ed. Bazell, C.E., *et al.*). London: Longman.

McIntosh, A. (1966) Patterns and ranges. *Papers in General, Descriptive and Applied Linguistics*, pp.183-99. London: Longman.

Sedelow, S.Y. & Sedelow, W.A., Jr. (1966) A preface to computational stylistics. *The Computer and Literary Style*, pp.1-13 (ed. Leed, J.). Kent, Ohio: Kent State University Press.

Sedelow, S.Y. & Sedelow, W.A., Jr. (1967) Stylistic analysis. *Automated Language Processing*, pp.181-213 (ed. Borko, H.). New York: Wiley.

Sinclair, J.McH. (1966) Beginning the study of lexis. *In Memory of J.R. Firth*, pp.410-31 (ed. Bazell, C.E., *et al.*). London: Longman.

Sinclair, J.McH., Jones, S., & Daley, R. (1970) *English Lexical Studies*. OSTI Report. Department of English, The University of Birmingham.

Spiegel, M.H. (1961) *Theory and Problems of Statistics*. London: Schaum.

van Buren, P. (1967) Preliminary aspects of mechanisation in lexis. *CahLex*, **11**, 89-112; **12**, 71-84.

Lexicometric analysis of co-occurrences

FROM TEXT TO CONNEXIONS: FORMALIZATIONS

FROM SIGNS TO ITEMS

A text read horizontally is defined as a succession of signs belonging to entities of various kinds contributing to its overall meaning. In the experiment we describe in this paper (but it is only one variant of other possible experiments based on different definitions), formal entities are taken to four increasingly homogeneous levels of significance.

Level A. The most extensive unit consists of two corpora of texts selected on a sample basis: tracts distributed in Paris in May 1968 both from overtly extreme left-wing groups (these organizations are national rather than local) and Action Committees whose political standpoint is less clearly defined (these are 'spontaneous' grass root organizations). In our paper these will be referred to as GP (Groupes Politiques) and CA (Comités d'Action).

Level B. Within these two corpora, sample texts represent fifteen collective writers represented as equally as possible (nine GP and six CA) and three periods (1-13 May, 14-30 May, and 31 May-16 June). We shall only be discussing here some examples taken from the fifteen writers (representing the Action Committees and the Groups).

Level C. Within each of these subsections the maximal meaningful unit scanned by the computer at any one time is the sentence defined by strong punctuation marks (full stop and end of tract).

Level D. Within the sentence the unit to be included in the lexicological table is defined by the graphic segment between two delimiters. We call this an *item*, that is, an instance of a minimal form (*ERA* 56, 1970a). The two corpora we have analyzed contain a total of 60,755 items.

Apart from these choices, the linguist does not interfere with the text other than by establishing a glossary of functional forms with a view to partly 'degrammaticalizing' the sentences; a program will remove all the frequently occurring grammatical function words and forms of 'être' and 'avoir', which account for 50 per cent of the items. We do not therefore hold the original text in the memory store but instead an utterance condensed for experimental purposes; this consists of a succession of graphical items enclosed within their delimiters and by separators which indicate precisely where the higher level groupings may be located.

FROM ITEMS TO COLLOCATES

The linguist adds another datum to the sequence of compartmentalized items: the pole (*P*) of statistical structure (*ERA* 56, 1970b, 1971a, 1971b).

H

It consists of a lexical form of a certain frequency occurrence around which the computer will search for all the sentence contexts in the previously defined text. This polarization results in not one but two searches: searches to the *left* of the pole and searches to the *right*. This produces two distinct files and it is important in French to retain the order, that is to say, before and after the lexical form which constitutes the pole. In both files the items identified in this way are added together in the case of identical items and are automatically sorted in alphabetical order. This accounts for a double matrix of collocates, in which each collocate is followed by a number of indices: the first index measures the co-frequency observed (cfo) between the collocate F and its pole P within previously defined limits; the second measures the sum and mean of the proximities defined as $1/d$ (d being the distance or number of items interspersed between the pole and each collocated item); the third combines the parameters we have defined earlier (co-frequency and proximity) in a formula which gives a comparative value to the different collocations; the coefficient C chosen here to represent each form may be written:

$$C = \frac{cfo(F, P)\sqrt{\Sigma(1/d)}}{f(P)} \quad .$$

In fact, what is being searched for and handled by the computer is no longer the experimental and still linear text, but a pile of sentence-based contexts situated to the left and right of a formal axis, a sort of *archi-text* consisting of various spans which merge into each other. Each lexical form which occurs in the neighbourhood of the pole is present depending upon the triple status of its positioning, its frequency of occurrence in the pole sentences, and of all the distances between it and the pole. Let us consider, for example, the two following sentences taken from a CA tract and their two forms 'travailleurs' ($f=2$) and 'étudiants' ($f=2$):

    'Avec les flics,

            1   0

    les *travailleurs* et les *étudiants* savent s'y prendre'

    'On vit de jeunes

        4   3   2   1   0

    travailleurs commencer à venir se battre avec les *étudiants*'

'Travailleurs' appears in these left side spans of 'étudiants' with the coefficient:

$$C = (2/2)\sqrt{(1/1 + 1/4)} = 1 \cdot 07 \quad .$$

In relation to the size of the computer on which we run the programs written by P. Lafon at Saint-Cloud (an IBM 1130 with a memory of 8 K-words and one disk), the memories are soon working to capacity. This is particularly the case if the basis of the inventory is level A (GP corpus and CA corpus) and if frequently occurring poles are chosen as exploratory axes ('travailleurs', 'étudiants', 'lutte', . . .). We must make a selection of the most relevant collocations. How does the computer go about it?

FROM COLLOCATES TO CO-OCCURRENTS

Each pole will project a system of different affinities for the forms which occur with it in the same sentences. The pole would appear to have a marked preference for certain forms, whereas it remains neutral towards other forms and even seems to reject them from its spans. This phenomenon can be observed and measured.

Lexical forms in a text have a relative frequency (fr) which is the relationship between their occurrences and the sum total of items; sentences in which the pole is present form a sample of this text. If we accept then that an ensemble is the statistical norm of its parts, we would expect that a form F in a given place in the text would indicate a certain likelihood of occurrence corresponding to its relative frequency. In a sample of n items identified to the left and right of a pole P, there is a probability occurrence at each item in the spans; this probability occurrence for the entire sample may be represented:

$$n \times fr(F)$$

We call this the *theoretical co-frequency* (*cft*) of F. When we compare this theoretical index with the co-frequency observed for this form in the neighbourhood of P, we shall know if the pole P really does attract the form F, and to what degree it is possible to affirm this. We arrive at a deviation $\delta = cfo - cft$.

A z test (at $\alpha = 0.01$) will then show which among the many collocations of P are: those which are very clearly attracted statistically by the pole, ultra-positive co-occurrents which exceed the upper significance threshold; those which are not so clearly attracted by the pole and which may occur by chance, being more or less neutral forms; those which the pole seems to reject, collocations whose frequency occurrence is lower than their probability occurrence (this list is not a faithful and accurate one, because the real lexical taboos do not in fact appear in the lists).

In this study we are only concerned with the first category which we shall call *co-occurrents* in the narrow sense of collocations which are statistically positive and extremely relevant. It only remains now to classify these privileged forms according to the criteria of their observed co-frequency and proximity, that is to say, in the present program, by using the coefficient of co-occurrence C.

The new files set up in the computer enable us to draw an initial type of graph of statistical attraction called *flat lexicograph* ('lexicogramme plat') or one level statistical attraction graph (see figures 2 to 5). Using this graph as a basis we can develop an analysis relying on the direct and one way link which relates the closest co-occurrents to a pole according to a certain preferential order. This analysis applies to the contextual functioning of identical forms used in two different texts as well as to the functioning of different forms encountered in a single text.

FROM CO-OCCURRENTS TO CONNEXIONS

The calculations carried out for a pole can in turn be made for each of the selected co-occurrents. Recurrence has its own specific laws and products. Its laws may be subject to infinite modulation whether the intention is to highlight a restricted graph of priority nodes and mean paths or to determine in detail the network of the attraction ramifications, until the entire lexicon has been examined (except of course the hapax). In the examples given, the exigency of the rules has affected the absolute frequency of the co-occurrent in the text and the value of the correlation coefficients. In level A of the corpora, for instance, we have only allowed the graphs to continue where $f > 20$ for the GP and where $f > 10$ for the CA and where $C > 5$ in both cases (the primitive value of C is multiplied by 100); in level B of the writers, we had to make $f > 5$ and $C > 2$. These *itineration rules* select the principal connexions from which the graph goes off in the direction of other co-occurrents which in turn could be used as connexions.

This method of establishing co-occurrences in chain form gives rise to a complex product which we call a *multi-storey lexicograph* ('lexico-gramme étagé') of many levels (see figures 8 to 14). It would become a tree structure developed progressively if at every new level the attraction relations called upon new connexions. In fact, this is not the case; instead we have cycles, loops and impasses as well as paths. The configuration of the graphs is already instructive in itself; redundancy characteristics of the writers are apparent throughout. However, above all it is the detailed analysis of the nodes, branches and circuits which draws attention to the stereotypes and sorts them according to their degree of usage; in this way the *textual* trends can be observed. And subsequently this suggests it would be possible to discover the presence of relations at a second degree, simply by the interference of various patterns, which would be the result of an *archi-textual* reading.

But when we speak of contextual functioning of surface stereotypes, of deep relations, are we not getting back to the meaning and imposing an interpretation of the content on the statistical description of attractions?

COLLOCATES, CO-OCCURRENTS, CONNEXIONS: SOME INTERPRETATIONS

COLLOCATES: AMPLITUDES AND POSITIONS

The computer issues matrixes which have to be linguistically and even politically interpreted. We will restrain ourselves to a few examples (for a detailed study, see *ERA* 56, 1973).

Several on-going researches are at present dealing with collocations. To put it briefly, they are concerned with the *amplitude* of collocates (A) (that is, the mean collocative span:

$$A = \frac{n \text{ collocated items}}{f(P)})\quad .$$

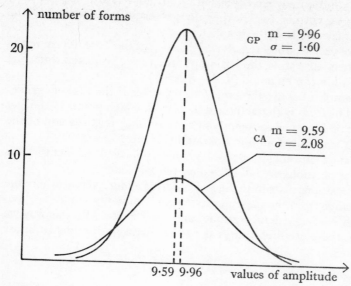

Figure 1

The distribution of amplitudes follows a Gaussian curve. Consequently every text can be characterized with the curve of its lexical amplitudes summing up its individual use of lexicon. Here follow the profiles built from a sample of 129 lexical forms taken as poles from the two corpora (41 and 88 respectively).

The curves have the same characteristics. The mean is almost identical in both cases. However, a Snedecor test applied to both standard deviations brings out a significant score:

$$F = \frac{4 \cdot 33}{2 \cdot 56} = 1 \cdot 69 \quad .$$

At $\alpha = 0 \cdot 05$, the tables show $1 \cdot 61$ as a critical value. The CA curve is significantly broader than for the GP and shows a larger percentage of lexical forms at both extremities. On the left side of the CA curve, there is a system of forms functioning for the most part in short sentence units which is essentially the one used in slogans, vivats, appeals, headings and signatures; on the right, there is a system of vocabulary functioning in long sentence units, which is essentially the one used in comments or vindications and in lists of demands with only the weakest punctuation marks. *Interpretation*: on the CA curve we find a prevalence of *micro-units of speech* having opposite characteristics; the tracts are divided into two types of speech: imperative and didactic. Conversely the GP use a common set of forms characterized by a higher degree of homogeneity.

But the case could arise when the specific vocabularies are more particularized in the GP corpus, so that they do not reach the threshold of the major frequencies we base the graphs on.

It is also possible to study the *average position* of the lexical form in the sentence. When separating the left amplitude (LA) from the right one (RA), a deviation can be noted ($LA - RA = \delta$):

Either both amplitudes are the same ($\delta \simeq 0$)—this is the case of 'greve' and 'lutte'. The form is characterized as central, which points to the fact that it might be found as frequently at the begining as at the end of the sentence or it is usually found in the middle of the sentence.

Or a discrepancy appears ($\delta > 0$; $\delta < 0$), which points to the fact that the most frequent positions are lateralized on the same side.

These basic positions distribute the lexical forms along a vector where the values of δ range from the most negative (e.g. 'militants' and 'vive') to the most positive (e.g. 'démocratique' and 'capitaliste'). In this way we discover that there are such things as predominant positioning in linear distribution.

	<—		—»	
pouvoir	1		1	étudiants
revendications	2		2	grève
lutte	3	travailleurs	3	lutte
jeunes	4	196	4	immigrés
millions	5		5	français
unité	6		6	syndiqués
solidarité	7	in CA	7	RATP
ensemble	8		8	paysans
arme	9		9	syndicales
briser	10		10	entreprises
seule	11		11	continuent
étrangers	12		12	obtenir
vive	13		13	intellectuels
isoler	14		14	forces
soutenons	15		15	Citroën
	<—		—»	

Figure 2.

N.B. In figures 2-14, the numbers shown under
the lexical forms represent absolute frequencies (f);
those which sometimes appear with the arrows
represent the value of the C coefficient multiplied by
100. A numerical notation sets the co-occurrents in
order on the basis of those values. The relation <—
means 'attracts preferentially on its left'; the
relation —» means 'attracts preferentially on its right'.

action	1		1	étudiants
comités	2		2	occupent
usines	3	ouvriers	3	usines
CA	4	47	4	base
deux	5		5	employés
face	6		6	victimes
ensemble	7	in CA	7	Flins
solidarité	8		8	Sochaux
continue	9		9	Renault
hier	10		10	grands
Flins	11		11	Sorbonne
intentions	12		12	Aviation
dire	13		13	magasins
4	14		14	voie
aujourdhui	15		15	usine

Figure 3

étudiants	1		1	étudiants
jeunes	2		2	jeunes
millions	3	travailleurs	3	lutte
revendications	4	312	4	grève
luttes	5		5	militants
appelle	6		6	revendications
service	7	in GP	7	entreprises
dix	8		8	travail
appel	9		9	quartier
500000	10		10	usines
lycéens	11		11	intellectuels
solidarité	12		12	latin
soutien	13		13	doivent
grande	14		14	manuels
exploitation	15		15	lycéens

Figure 4

étudiants	1		1	étudiants
jeunes	2		2	Flins
comités	3	ouvriers	3	lutte
usines	4	127	4	Caen
syndicats	5		5	paysans
unir	6		6	Redon
militants	7	in GP	7	combat
conseils	8		8	jeunes
fils	9		9	Le-Mans
organisation	10		10	force
vive	11		11	compris
solidarité	12		12	progressistes
usine	13		13	direction
commune	14		14	refusent
lycéens	15		15	apprentis

Figure 5

CO-OCCURRENTS: HOMOGRAPHS AND SYNONYMS

The study of co-occurrents produced by a pole at the first level enables us to define major semantic areas beyond the spectrum of the lexical forms statistically attracted. In doing so, we may compare one pole to another.

Figures 2-5 represent the four lexicographs produced by 'travailleurs' and 'ouvriers' in the two sets of tracts. We would have expected greater similarity between the four lexicographs. It is almost impossible to consider that 'ouvriers' in the GP corpus and 'ouvriers' in the CA corpus belong to the same homograph, since the spectra are so different. And if moreover we consider the extremely limited number of identical co-occurents, we can hardly say that 'ouvriers' and 'travailleurs' are synonymous; however, these lexical forms have formal areas of co-occurrence in common.

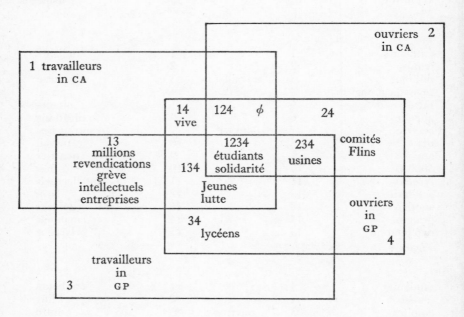

Figure 6. Overlapping areas of 'travailleurs' and 'ouvriers'.

Figure 6 shows that the areas concerning the homographs do not overlap to any greater extent than those concerning the synonyms. However, 'travailleurs' in CA more closely resembles 'travailleurs' in GP than do all the other binary comparisons.

The next point worthy of note is the fundamental *core* of co-occurrence, this common area (see 1234 in figure 6) in which 'étudiants' and 'solidarité' are to be found. This core translates the urge for junction which

was common to the students and members of the working class, according
to most writers of tracts. This political interpretation is strengthened by
the presence of various forms which may be considered as being part and
parcel of a specific semantic field, that of solidarity. See the left sets of
co-occurrents below (the number in brackets specifies the rank of the
co-occurrent):

commune (7), unir (6), ensemble (7), ⎤
larges (26), solidarité (8; 12)   ⎦   ◁——   ouvriers
                                                   CA+GP

appelle (6), appel (9), ensemble (8),   ⎤
soutenons (15), soutien (13), service (7),   │
unité (6), millions (3; 5),   │
500000 (10), communes (18), unir (16),   │
jonction (19; 28),   │   ◁——   travailleurs
solidarité (7; 12), rejoint (34),   │   CA+GP
coude (22), solidaires (36),   │
regroupe (55), nombre (21; 30),   │
(aux) côtés (17), (partie) intégrante (37). ⎦

Another remarkable area of attraction is found on the right of 'ouvriers',
namely places where strikes occurred. This is represented below:

ouvriers   ⎡ Flins (2; 7), Caen (4), Redon (6), Le Mans
CA+GP   ——≫   │ (9), poste (21), Mulhouse (29), Rhodiacéta
                          │ (30), Rhodia (37), usines (36), Sochaux (8),
                          │ Renault (9), Sorbonne (11), grands magasins
                          ⎣ (10 and 13), Sud-Aviation (12), usine (15).

(The spectrum of 'travailleurs', although it is the head-form in the
frequency index, is much poorer in this field.)
    There is also a correlative set of concrete actions and names of allies:

ouvriers   ⎡ lutte (3), combat (7), occupent (2), refusent
CA+GP   ——≫   │ (14), battre (19), résistance (20), descend-
                          │ ent (22), manifesté (25), manifester (26),
                          │ battent (27), sauver (31), unir (36), etc. . . .
                          │ étudiants progressistes (1, 12), base (4),
                          │ employés (5), paysans (5), victimes (6),
                          │ jeunes (8), apprentis (15), larges (masses)
                          ⎣ (39), etc. . . .

On the contrary, 'travailleurs' elicits a large number of abstract terms
particularly in the GP lexicograph. We will not mention all of them, with
the exception of the derived forms ending in '-tion':

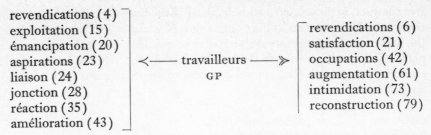

revendications (4)
exploitation (15)
émancipation (20)
aspirations (23)   <——— travailleurs ———»
liaison (24)   GP
jonction (28)
réaction (35)
amélioration (43)

revendications (6)
satisfaction (21)
occupations (42)
augmentation (61)
intimidation (73)
reconstruction (79)

(As for the attraction system of 'ouvriers' in the GP corpus, it produces only three derived forms of this kind: 'organisation', 'direction', 'directions'.)

If we now consider how the writers reflect the general patterns, we find they do it irregularly in fact. The best example is provided by 'ouvriers' as used by the group called in May 1968 Mouvement du 22 Mars (see figure 7).

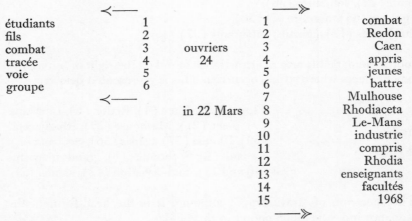

	<——			—»	
étudiants	1		1		combat
fils	2		2		Redon
combat	3	ouvriers	3		Caen
tracée	4	24	4		appris
voie	5		5		jeunes
groupe	6		6		battre
	<——		7		Mulhouse
		in 22 Mars	8		Rhodiaceta
			9		Le-Mans
			10		industrie
			11		compris
			12		Rhodia
			13		enseignants
			14		facultés
			15		1968
			—»		

Figure 7

Two basic ideas may be derived from this manipulation of homographs and pseudo-synonyms. The first one comes from the wide range of possible usages. For some producers of tracts (the three trotskyist groups, the C.A. d'Entreprises, for instance), 'ouvriers' is an occasional substitute for 'travailleurs'; elsewhere in other producers (22 Mars, the maoïsts of the U.J.C.M.L., the C.A. de Quartiers and the socialists of the P.S.U.), 'ouvriers' has specific co-occurrents showing original usages. The fact that two writers use one identical term is hardly more incidental than the fact that the same writer uses two pseudo-synonyms. Meaning and lexical usage are interdependent but they do not identify with each other.

The second conclusion concerns the different impact of each writer on the general patterns. The more important writer (that is to say the one whose marked stereotyped sequences reach the highest rates) often carries heavier weight on the lexicograph of a pole, which explains its unbalanced character. So we must be very careful when interpreting it. The occurrences should be balanced as far as possible by adding many writers of the same importance. Only then common characteristics may appear. This is the case with 'travailleurs' and, to a lesser degree, 'ouvriers'. In conditions of this kind, sum-total of particularities gives rise to general trends.

CONNEXIONS: BRANCHING TREES

Let us now step down from the graph origin to its immediate co-occurrents which in turn will be considered as the origins of further graphs. These *connexions* can then be studied in a number of different ways only three of which will be retained here.

Paths and Cycles. Figure 8 stems from the lexical form 'lutte' (the reason for choosing this form as an origin lies in the even distribution of 'lutte' through the different texts and periods. This graph and the others are built from itineration rules which are specified in each case). It seems only natural at first sight that graph 8 (CA) should be less extensive than the GP graph built according to the same rules, and so wide and complex that we could not represent it in this text: our GP corpus is twice the size of the CA.

But if we compare the Restricted Graphs (figures 9 and 10), then we do get a reverse result. At the very start of the GP graph three lexical forms are seen to generate one another very closely into a co-occurrence node acting as the centre of attraction of the unrepresentable GP graph. This is not quite the case with the CA node whose restricted graph looks more extended (see figure 10).

In the restricted graph of figure 9, a common lexical structure of the texts, due to the fact that they are 'political', prevails over the discrepancies arising from their diverging ideological stands. And yet what a difference there is between the Communist Party and the anarchist-maoïsts!

In fact these ideological divergences already appear in the GP graph. We can detect some regions of this graph which act as poles of attraction and interference that are common to several texts, and some other regions which are more exclusively representative of one highly repetitive writer. The different aspects in the spread of the lexical forms reflect unequal frequency loads. However, it is interesting to focus on a particular region.

Chains. Let us consider the lexical form 'revendications' in both CA and GP graphs and follow the major connecting paths and cycles. The result is given by the chains of figures 11 and 12, and that leads us to the following interpretations. On comparing the two graphs we find a startling dissimilarity of pattern: in the GP graph (figure 12) the right side chain of 'revendications' splits into two branches at the first connecting link leading up to a whole network of political and organizational trade-unionist

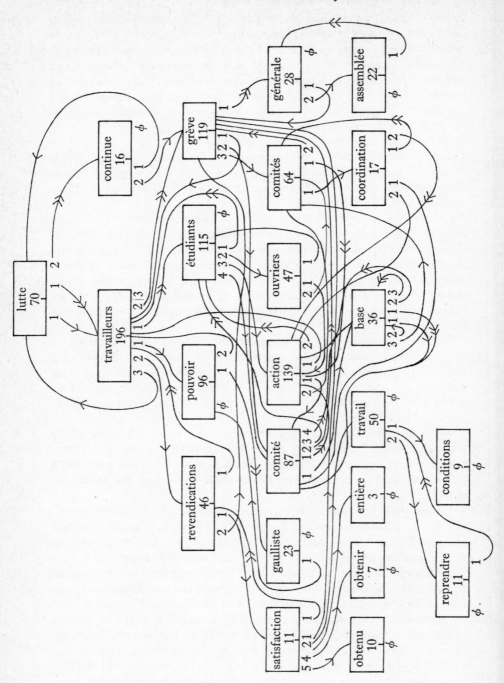

Figure 8. CA graph. Itineration rules: $f > 10$, $c > 2$.

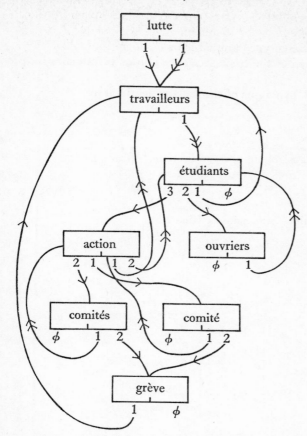

Figure 9. CA restricted graph. Itineration rules: $f > 20$, $c > 5$.

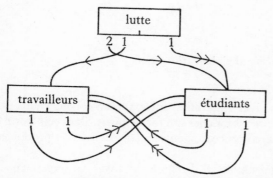

Figure 10. GP restricted graph. Itineration rules: $f > 20$, $c > 5$.

vocabulary. The upper link between 'ouvrières' and 'revendications' attracts three different connected systems:

first, the communist stereotype (union forces démocratiques);

next, a duplicated form of the basic sequence (luttes travailleurs lutte/ grève);

lastly, 'organizational' syntagms of the most general nature.

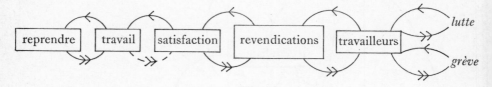

Figure 11. 'Revendications' CA chaining. Itineration rules: $f > 10$, $c > 2$.

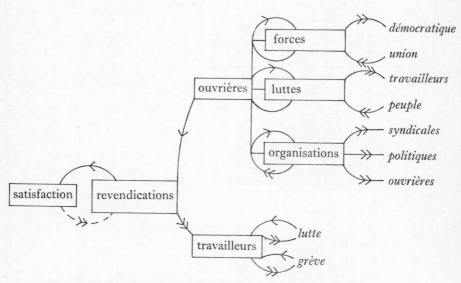

Figure 12. 'Revendications' GP chaining. Itineration rules: $f > 20$, $c > 2$.

At the threshold of the given itineration rules, the CA corpus yields no such results since these annex branches are far below it. Between 'lutte' and 'satisfaction' only the reference to agents and direct motives produces the chaining (see figure 11).

In this way through the statistical dissimilarities we can trace lexical differences, which in turn help us to detect deep political divergence.

Circuits. In the multi-storey lexicographs, some connexions have a special significance. When a form A is a left co-occurrent of B, and B a right co-occurent of A, they are linked to form a *circuit*. We can characterize a circuit by adding the coefficients related to each co-occurrence arrow, which gives us the following formula:

$$A \overset{\longleftarrow}{\underset{\longrightarrow}{}} B \qquad C(AB) = C(B, A) + C(A, B)$$

$$= cfo\sqrt{(\Sigma 1/d)} \left(\frac{1}{f(A)} + \frac{1}{f(B)} \right) \ .$$

We find, for instance, in the 'Coordination des comités d'action':

$$\text{travailleurs} \overset{\longleftarrow}{\underset{\longrightarrow}{}} \text{étudiants}$$
$$f = 35 \qquad 10 \cdot 6 \quad f = 26$$

with 14·2 above.

Several circuits may be linked together, and may also be reinforced by additional arrows. E.g. the three-form chain in P.C.F.:

$$\begin{array}{ccc} 66 \cdot 1 & 38 \cdot 1 & 53 \cdot 4 \\ \text{parti} \overset{\longleftarrow}{\underset{\longrightarrow}{}} \text{communiste} \overset{\longleftarrow}{\underset{\longrightarrow}{}} \text{français} \\ 61 \cdot 9 & 65 \cdot 8 & 41 \cdot 5 \end{array}$$

Of course the repetitive writers are richer in circuits, but this kind of lexical pairs is found even in texts showing a great lexical variety. If the plain arrow of co-occurrence is by itself a sign of redundancy in a text (B being partially predictable when A appears), the double arrow in a circuit makes those chains particularly poor in information. For the fifteen writers of level B, we have grouped the circuits with the highest coefficients (at least one of the arrows must have a coefficient $C > 10$). Let us see first the strongest circuit of each writer. For seven of them (4 CA and 3 GP), the major circuits link two or three forms which compose the name of the group. This is not only because of the signature at the bottom of each tract, but it reveals as well a self-reference phenomenon throughout the text. The circuits are as follows:

$$\text{comité} \overset{\longleftarrow}{\underset{\longrightarrow}{}} \text{action}$$

$$\text{comité} \overset{\longleftarrow}{\underset{\longrightarrow}{}} \text{action} \overset{\longleftarrow}{\underset{\longrightarrow}{}} \text{lycéen}$$

$$\text{mouvement} \overset{\longleftarrow}{\underset{\longrightarrow}{}} 22 \overset{\longleftarrow}{\underset{\longrightarrow}{}} \text{mars}$$

For the eight other writers, such self-referent circuits are either lower in the list, or even are not repetitive enough to pass the frequency threshold (a form must appear more than five times in a text to be used as a pole). We can then consider that the major circuit takes the place of a signature, and stands as a relevant characterization for the writer, allowing the reader to identify him. For example:

grève ⇄ générale   in F.E.R.

classe ⇄ ouvrière   in J.C.R. and U.J.C.M.L.

comités ⇄ action   in P.S.U. (this is a signature circuit, but curiously enough the Unified Socialist Party refers to a political structure that is not his own).

pouvoir ⇄ conseils ⇄ ouvriers   in Situationnistes

gestion ⇄ directe   in Anarchistes

Let us see now, not only the first circuit, but the four or five major circuits for each writer (as the three repetitive writers F.E.R., U.J.C.M.L., P.C.F. have more than twenty circuits, we will only take the first five into account). Our material of about fifty pairs may be grouped in three semantic families which correspond to the different protagonists, settings and places of May 68 in France.

1. The names of organizations (~ 20 circuits) referred to above.
2. The main protagonists of the class struggle (~ 15 circuits).

The core of these chains is the pair

travailleurs ⇄ étudiants

these two forms being the most frequent in our corpus: $f = 510$ for 'travailleurs', $f = 460$ for 'étudiants', out of 60,750 items. This circuit links—at least in language—the student rebellion and the workers' strike. It is found as such in five of our fifteen writers, but it may be enriched with additional forms:

jeunes ⇄ travailleurs ⇄ étudiants   in C.A. de quartier, F.E.R

travailleurs ⇄ étudiants ⇄ paysans   in C.A. ouvriers-étudiant

Elsewhere some circuits are built on one form only:

étudiants ⇄ enseignants   in P.S.U.

travailleurs ⇄ manuels ⇄ intellectuels   in P.C.F.

The circuit classe ⇄ ouvrière, found in five writers, may be added to this survey of 'good heroes'.

Circuits naming the enemies are far less numerous in our texts:

pouvoir ⇄ gaulliste   in C.A. Lycéens, P.C.F.

état ⇄ policier   in Mouvement du 22 Mars

régime ⇄ chômage ⇄ misère   in U.J.C.M.L.

3. Places and dates

manifestation ⇄ lundi ⇄ 6   in Mouvement du 22 Mars

13 ⇄ Mai ⇄ 1968   in Voix Ouvrière

quartier ⇄ latin   in F.E.R.

ouvriers ⇄ Flins   in U.J.C.M.L.

round off the May setting in France.

Figures 13 and 14 show the multi-storey lexicographs drawn from 'lutte' in U.J.C.M.L. and P.C.F. We only picked up the first co-occurrent right and left of the poles, to show clearly the main circuits. The two graphs contain twenty forms each, but, except for the initial pole, they have only one form, 'travailleurs', in common. However, the discrepancy between the respective contents must not mask the similarity between the structures: out of the (20 × 2) 40 arrows, more than a half (22 in U.J.C.M.L., 26 in P.C.F.) enter into circuits, either single or chained. U.J.C.M.L. shows two single circuits, one of three forms, one of four. P.C.F. shows one of two forms, one of three, one of five, and gives us the longest chain in our corpus, when unwinding as a litany the six-circuit chain which sums up the Communist Party line, in May 68 as well as before and after May:

programme ⇄ commun ⇄ gouvernement ⇄ populaire ⇄

union ⇄ forces ⇄ démocratiques

Graphs of this kind tend to give us a somewhat caricatural picture of our texts, but they bring out the weight of repetition and redundancy phenomena in political speech. The linguistic necessity of covering 'noise' in communication and the pedagogical need for repetition seem to invade the whole speech, and this is perhaps detrimental to content and information.

CRITICISM AND FURTHER DEVELOPMENT

The main difficulty in treating statistically the syntagmatic line comes from the great diversity of the linguistic forms. Markovian processes, which are very efficient in the study of phonemic series, become useless in the present case: the variety of forms used in a text gives any combination whatever a very low degree of probability occurrence. From this point of view speech is a series of nearly impossible events. Even more so, the binomial hypothesis does not cover syntactic constraints which reduce the field of possible combinations, and introduction of grammatical

I

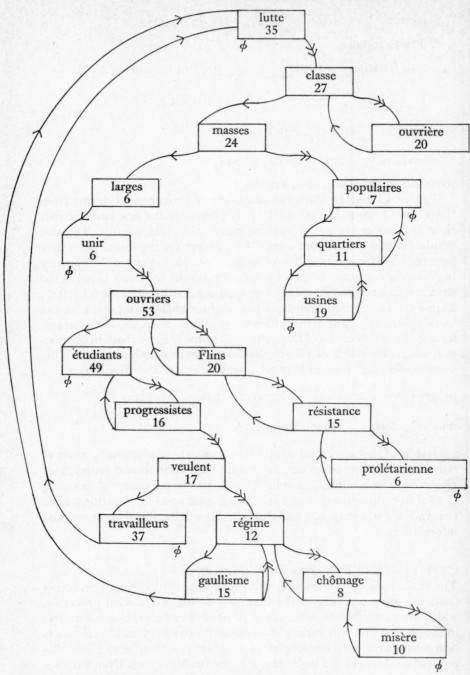

Figure 13. Graph of 'lutte' in U.J.C.M.L. Itineration
rules: $f > 5$; c, the first on each side.

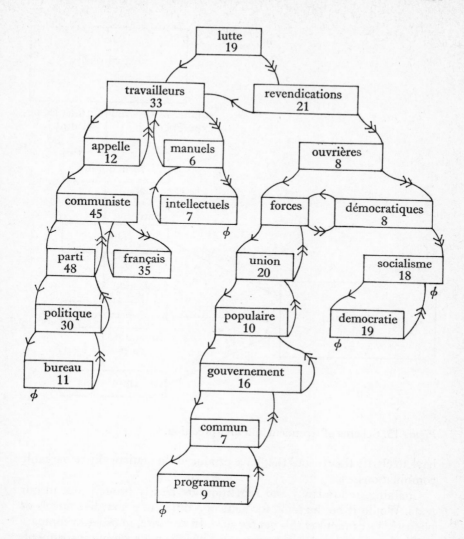

Figure 14. Graph of 'lutte' in P.C.F. Itineration rules:
$f > 5$; c, the first on each side.

categories in distribution hypothesis is an extremely complex problem that we have not yet considered.

The second difficulty comes from the fact that proximity of two forms is due to different causes: it may be related to syntactic order, or to semantic facts, or even to some chance effect. The two forms appear in the same sentence and this is the only thing the computer can detect without preliminary linguistic analysis. It is when interpreting that we

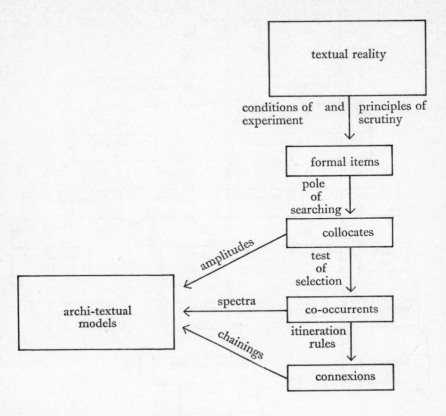

Figure 15. Schema of treatment and interpretation.

have to clarify the reasons that have produced the statistically remarkable combinations.

Chaining, redundancy and repetition are clearly brought out in our texts. Would it be the same for texts of a different genre, like novels or poetry? We cannot say this yet for sure. In any case, in order to compare texts of varying length and nature, we need some accurate instrument. Perhaps we should at first take apart each parameter (proximity and co-frequency), as coefficient C now merges two ill-controlled indices into one formula. This is so because their variations do not follow the same laws. (Roughly speaking, we could say that proximity accounts for syntactic facts, while co-frequency accounts for semantic facts.) In $\Sigma 1/d$, the co-frequency parameter interferes with the proximity parameter; the use of the mean instead of the sum would be preferable. Cfo and $f(P)$ should be converted into relative frequencies, to allow further comparisons. As for cft, which we have used so far in the selection test only, it could perhaps be introduced in the C coefficient itself.

At any rate, the aim of our project is to attempt a synthesis of all the relationships between forms within the syntagmatic line; therefore we will go as far as working out a single coefficient. However, we shall do so at a further stage, setting separate thresholds for each parameter in order to have a better control over the limits of each.

But one could work out a very different way of giving the complete description of the main syntagmatic links in a text. This could be done by putting together all the forms of a text which occur with sufficient frequency. We could then tabulate their respective positions with references to their co-frequencies and proximities. It would be possible to use factorial analysis of correspondences in this tabulation, producing a complete projection of collocates in the linear chain of speech.

In fact, whatever the products and the way they are obtained, we work on piled up sentences. We call that an *archi-text* (see figure 15). Beyond a pure linear reading (that of the immediate context), two other readings appear possible. First, the paradigmatic reality can be brought out of the syntagmatic reality, by cumulating all that has been written in the same text to the left and right of a formal axis. Secondly, out of this material we can get a new syntagmatic model where each lexical form is loaded with all its uses within the text.

REFERENCES

ERA 56 (1970a) *Traitement automatique des textes*, 1: *La perforation*. Ecole Normale Supérieure de Saint-Cloud.

ERA 56 (1970b) Approches d'une définition statistique des co-occurrences du vocabulaire. *Struktur und Funktion des Sozialen Wortschatzes in der Franzosischen Literatur*, pp. 49-54. Halle R.D.A. Martin-Luther Universität n° 3 / 4.

ERA 56 (1971a) Analyse lexicométrique des co-occurrences et formalisation. *Les applications de l'information aux textes philosophiques*, pp. 8-23. Paris: C.N.R.S.

ERA 56 (1971b) Quelques groupes politiques en Mai 68: recherches lexico-métriques. *Les partis politiques* pp. 64-79 (ed. J. Charlot). Paris: Armand Colin.

ERA 56 (1973) *E.R.A.* 56 and M. Demonet, J. Gouazé, M. Mouillaud. *Des tracts en Mai 68. Mesures de vocabulaire et de contenu*. Paris: Armand Colin.

(*ERA* 56: Equipe de Recherche Associée au C.N.R.S. no. 56, Ecole Normale Supérieure de Saint-Cloud.)

Students and workers in May 68 student tracts
A study of three French Student Organizations :
Fédération des Etudiants Révolutionnaires
Mouvement du 22 Mars
Union des Etudiants Communistes

The present study concerns the analysis of the context of the word 'lutte' as used in political tracts of three left-wing student organizations in Paris in May and June 1968. These organizations are the Fédération des Etudiants Révolutionnaires, the Mouvement du 22 Mars and the Union des Etudiants Communistes.

The word 'lutte', which we studied in both substantival and verbal form, was chosen in the first place because we considered it one of the main characteristics of the 'May movement'. Indeed, this was above all a movement of revolt, of opposition, of struggle against '*le pouvoir*', whether this term designated 'power', authority, government, etc. We preferred 'lutte' to the word 'combat' for two main reasons. First, the 'significance-span' of 'lutte' is much larger than that of 'combat', and, above all, 'lutte' can be used very specifically in an expression like 'la lutte des classes'. Secondly, 'lutte' was shown to be one of the most frequently used words in the May 68 tracts (it came in the third position after 'étudiants' and 'travailleurs' in the frequency ranking made by Geffroy, Lafon, and Tournier (1971). The term 'combat' came only eighteeenth.

We assumed that the collocations of the words 'lutte' and 'lutter' would allow us to show an aspect of the political perspectives and strategies of the three organizations, in so far as these perspectives and strategies are verbalized. In other words: who are the principal actors, and which are the important objectives mentioned by the three organizations? Or, who carries on the struggle, with whom, against whom or what? How? For what end and/or for whom?

We chose to analyze tracts, since in May and June 1968 they represented one of the privileged modes of communication, together with posters or graffiti. The tracts marked the political events; they responded to one another. The temporal aspect is very important: very often, tracts are written in relation to a specific, temporally and sometimes spatially restricted situation. This is the main difference between tracts and other texts containing a collective standpoint, such as manifestos, programmes, etc.

Tracts differ also from newspapers because they are not issued regularly and their readers do not pay for them. Moreover, the information and political analyses in tracts are always rather schematic. A tract should be able to be read quickly, hence the style is generally condensed. It only reproduces the themes from the authors' ideology which are relevant to the particular political situation.

This condensation is of particular interest as far as the comparison between organizations is concerned, but it is not without some methodological complications. In fact, a rigorous analysis would have demanded a day-by-day comparison, or at least a comparison over very short periods. The May and June movement could indeed be divided into at least four phases:

1. from 3 to 12 May (closing of the Sorbonne and street fighting),
2. from the 13 May demonstration up to General de Gaulle's second speech (30 May),
3. from 31 May to 12 June, when the 'gauchistes' groups were dissolved by the government,
4. from 13 June up to the elections of 30 June.

It was impossible to make a comparison along these lines, because the organizations we chose to study did not always issue their tracts at the same time; moreover, the samples would have been too small to allow any comparison, in view of our methodological requirements, which will be described later. For this reason we regrouped the tracts produced between 3 May and 30 June.

We assumed that if the positions of each of our three organizations were slightly different from one phase to another, the differences should not be so noticeable as to make impossible any transversal comparison during this historical period. (This consideration is only relevant to the three organizations concerned in the present study, since another organization, the *Union des Jeunesses Communistes (marxiste-léniniste)* underwent profound changes in May and June 1968, which led to its disintegration.) We shall now outline the characteristics of the three organizations: the Fédération des Etudiants Révolutionnaires (F.E.R.), the Mouvement du 22 Mars (22M), and the Union des Etudiants Communistes (U.E.C.).

We chose these student organizations because they were set up independently of one another. As student organizations, they have no common historical past, since they were not set up as a result of scissions in a common political movement. The political divergencies which exist between the U.E.C. and the F.E.R. are due to a previous split in the international communist movement, which took place before these two organizations came into being.

The U.E.C. was set up in 1956, during the 14th Congress of the French Communist Party (P.C.F.) and although it is not officially a student wing of this party, it has—and it had in 1968—strong theoretical and political links with the Party. Among the three organizations we have studied, the U.E.C. is the only one backed by a strong party and, what is more, a party which claims to be the party of the working class.

The F.E.R. is one of the student trotskyist organizations. It was set up in April 1968 and was a re-alignment of the former trotskyist groups called Revolution and C.L.E.R. (Liaison Committees of Revolutionary Students). The latter was formed by student members of the O.C.I. (International Communist Organization for the Reconstruction of the IVth International).

The 22M, as its name indicates, was formed on the 22nd of March 1968, on the campus of Nanterre, when students occupied the administrative building to protest against the arrest of student members of the National Vietnam Committee. The 22M differs from the two previous organizations in that it does not consider itself marxist-leninist; it may even be opposed to marxism-leninism, particularly with regard to organizational problems.

The method which was applied (AAD, for *Analyse Automatique du Discours*) is based upon the following hypotheses (Pêcheux 1969):

If a set of discourse sequences is dominated by identical *conditions of production* (which we explain below), the corpus constituted by this set of sequences will present *specific characteristics* which represent the *trace* of discourse processes related to the considered conditions (typically these characteristics will be commutations in relation to an invariant context).

This procedure, which consists of analyzing the corpus in reference to itself, without any reference to a dictionary or to a set of *a priori* equivalence classes, is not far from Harris's procedure (1969).

However, we need to give the following additional information:

1. The corpus is constituted on the basis of a dominant *condition of production*; its determination is a theoretical, extra-linguistic decision: in our case, the decision is based upon historical knowledge. Subsequently our hypothesis was the following: the presence of the word 'lutte' or 'lutter' in any sequence of our material induces a process of lexical selections and combinations within syntactic structures; and this process will be distinct for the three organizations we have studied. In other words we assumed that the three sets of sentences including 'lutte' were really three corpora, each of them being dominated by a specific *condition of production*.

2. Unlike Harris's decomposition of the sequence into kernel sentences, the AAD procedure retains the marks of connexion (coordinations, subordinations) between the elements (elementary utterances) resulting from this decomposition.

3. The AAD method excludes the comparison of a discourse with itself (by self-superposition), which is the case in Harris's work.

At this point, we should like to give a brief description of the AAD system:

The computer analysis requires a preliminary analysis, which at the moment is manual. (For the present study, it was carried out by

Cl. Haroche and N. Bourdin.) However, linguists are trying to automate this phase of the work, at least in part.

The preliminary phase consists of transforming each discourse sequence of the corpus into objects which can be compared by a systematic procedure. (In other words, and according to Harris's point of view, we consider that the direct comparison between surface structures is impossible.) Those objects, into which the discourse sequences are transformed, are connex graphs, in the mathematical meaning of the term. This transformation is purely linguistic (no interpretation is made). Each graph, corresponding to each sequence of the corpus, has the following properties:

1. The *nodes* of the graph are elementary utterances, including the position of the subject, verb, possible preposition and complement (in fact 8 morpho-syntactic categories).

2. The *arrows* connecting the nodes mark the relations between the utterances; these are essentially:

Coordination: England and France are western countries.

Subordination: There are troubles in France because France is dominated by the bourgeoisie.

Determination: The bourgeoisie, which dominates France, has difficulties.

The form taken by the automatic treatment itself is as follows. The corpus is introduced into the computer as a *data set* consisting of two lists: the lists of the utterances and the list of the binary relations, with the mark of their connector. The programme (FORTRAN IV, IBM 360) compares each graph to each other in the following way:

1. Given a binary relation $Em \overset{\phi x}{\to} En$, belonging to graph 1, we try to find in other graphs binary relations with the *same* connector ϕx.

For instance: $Ep \overset{\phi x}{\to} Eq$, belonging to the graph i. The group of utterances Em, En, Ep, Eq is then transmitted to a subroutine, which assesses the proximity between Em and Ep on the one hand, and En and Eq on the other.

Briefly, the way of computing this proximity is as follows: As we stated earlier, each utterance is constituted by the same succession of morpho-syntactic categories. In this way it is possible to compare automatically the lexical content of each category (subject, verb . . .) in Em and Ep, and En and Eq, and the proximity relation is measured by the number of identity relations. A weighting system is introduced with the data set so that the importance of the identity depends on the kind of morpho-syntactic category in which it occurs. In this way, we obtain an arithmetic value, expressing the proximity between both binary relations.

If this value is equal or greater than a *fixed value* (introduced with the data set, and characterizing the proximity-level considered acceptable), then the group of the four utterances or quadruplets is kept in the memory in the following form:

$Em, Ep, En, Eq, \phi x.$

2. Given the list of the quadruplets, we form chains by right-adjunction of a quadruplet to another quadruplet. For example:

$Em, Ep, En, Eq, \phi x$ Em En Er

$En, Eq, Er, Es, \phi y$

ϕx ϕy

$\longrightarrow$ $\longrightarrow$

Ep Eq Es graph 1

3. When all chains have been formed, we superimpose the chains which have the same connector. For example:

Em En Er

ϕx ϕy

$\longrightarrow$ $\longrightarrow$

Ep Eq Es

Ep Eq Er

ϕx ϕy

$\longrightarrow$ $\longrightarrow$

Et Ev Ew graph 2

The result of this superposition (based upon a supposed transitivity relation) constitutes what is called a 'semantic area':

ϕx ϕy

Em En Er

Ep Eq Es

Et Ev Ew graph 3

4. Finally, certain semantic areas are regrouped into 'hyper-domains', by considering the left-utterance in each area.

The relations between commuting sequences within an area are indicated by lines and arrows. *Lines* are used to characterize symmetric relations (equivalence or contextual synonymy). *Arrows* stand for non-symmetric relations (for example, relations of implications between two terms or syntagms).

From a methodological point of view, we need to stress that *certain decisions concerning the program could be modified*. For instance, the rule inducing the comparison only between binary relations which have the same connections could be avoided. The transitivity rule used for building up the semantic area could be discarded. The procedure for the assessment of the proximity between binary relations could be modified (the arithmetic measure is certainly too approximate).

All the student organizations involved in the May-June 68 movement issued specific objectives, slogans and political tracts, on which the results of this study throw further light. We shall now present and comment on our results in order to outline, for each of the three organizations, the features of the specificity mentioned above.

We shall begin with a general remark: the student movement is not an autonomous political phenomenon, restricted to the world of intellectuals

and their university training; the concrete forms the movement took in
France depended on an element which is in a way exterior to the student
movement itself (we will comment further on what we mean by 'exterior'),
but at the same time has a specific influence on it, and *produces a series of
effects*. This element is the antagonistic struggle carried on, in the structure of French society, between the proletariat and the capitalist bourgeoisie. In fact, in the three corpora we find references to the working-class
struggle, stating explicitly the students' support for the workers' struggles
and the workers' class interests:

HD 1   22 M
Vive la lutte │ des étudiants   │
              │ des travailleurs │

HD 1   U.E.C.
Vive la lutte │ des syndicats │
              │ des ouvriers │
              │ des étudiants │

HD 2   F.E.R.
la lutte des │ doit faire │   │ des masses   │
   étudiants │ fait   │ partie intégrante de la lutte │ de classe   │
             │   │   │ du prolétariat │

However, merely mentioning the reference to the working-class movement, which could be found nowadays in many student movements in
capitalist countries, is not sufficient to pinpoint the specific features of
the French May 1968 Movement. By observing only their immediately
visible characteristics (street fights, student and police behaviour . . .),
other student movements could, from an empirical standpoint, be considered similar to the French movement, but as distinct from others, this
movement was chronologically followed by a wave of workers' strikes.
This does not mean that the student movement *caused* the strikes, but it
does mean that it is *absolutely impossible* to take one's bearings in the 1968
French student movement without analyzing its actual relation to the
struggle of the French working class. Indeed, this movement is to be
viewed in a situation in which struggle is dominant and in which the
proletariat played the most important rôle.

So our first consideration is how the three student organizations refer
to the workers' struggle (adversary, objectives, means of action).

With regard to the U.E.C., whose links with the P.C.F. are as determina-
tive as obvious for the other student organizations, it expresses the
objectives of the working-class movement, the nature of the adversary
and the means of action in very similar terms to the P.C.F., that is to say
in terms of seizing political power (state power). The *political* objective
is made very explicit:

D 7

| Régime | de démocratie véritable
| Pouvoir |

HD 2

Gouvernement populaire (à participation . . .) ouvrant la voie au social-
isme.

D 13

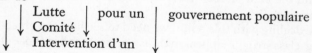

D 18

Gouvernement d'union démocratique

This objective is related in an antagonistic way to the description of the
political adversary:

D 14

↑ Politique du pouvoir Gaulliste ↑
↓ Période du pouvoir populaire ↓

Finally, the struggle *for* this objective (i.e. political victory over this
adversary) is expressed in relation to the means by which they will realise
this objective:

HD 5

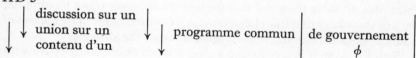

D 28

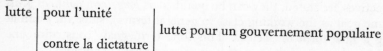

These themes are explicitly mentioned in the way the communist students
described the struggle:

HD 3

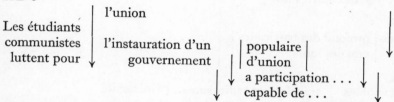

It would appear that the U.E.C. plays the rôle of representing the P.C.F.
among the students, of whom none or few are of working-class origin.

So the question: 'How does the U.E.C. justify its speaking in the name of the P.C.F.?' leads to another question, which may not be formulated in the same terms by the proletariat, since the P.C.F. is very strong among the masses of the workers and exerts a considerable influence on them.

The second question is: how does the P.C.F. justify its claims of being *the conscious and organized political representative of the proletariat*? We will see this later when we consider how this question is put by the F.E.R. on the one hand and the 22M on the other, and also the different consequences of this question.

However, before dealing with this point, we need to see how the objectives of the working-class struggle appear in the F.E.R. tracts and in those of the 22M.

The results of the analysis of the F.E.R. tracts show that for this organization the struggle is mainly directed against certain consequences of capitalism. It is essentially a defensive action, aimed at preventing a worsening of the situation (e.g. unemployment):

D 2

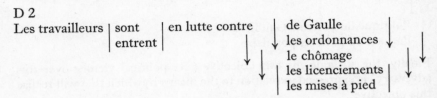

Les travailleurs | sont | en lutte contre | de Gaulle
| entrent | | les ordonnances
| | | le chômage
| | | les licenciements
| | | les mises à pied

Let us emphasize for the moment the rather unpolitical character of these objectives, in the sense that the seizure of power is not mentioned; we will show later that this characteristic is counterbalanced by a series of political slogans referring to the organization of the struggle.

With the 22M, it is rare to find a clear statement of its objectives with reference to the working class in the context of the word 'lutte'. When the objectives are stated, they can be qualified as *long-term political goals* (the same goal as the working class in general terms), since they aim at creating a new form of society. This long-term goal 'construire une société' is to be brought about by immediate action (barricades):

D 18
le sens | de la lutte
| des barricades

D 13
le sens | profond des barricades
| vrai des mots

D 21
nous voulons | transformer radicalement l'Université
| construire une société (qui) . . .

To comment briefly on this first series of results, we note that the objectives of the F.E.R. do not go, politically speaking, as far as those of the U.E.C., while the 22 M aims directly at the working class and is not pre-occupied with the seizure of power, since its problems lie *beyond or outside* this particular objective.

We examined the different consequences of the proletarian struggle against the capitalist bourgeoisie in the discourse of the three student organizations. Now we will move on to consider the different ways in which the organizations view themselves as 'students' supporting the working-class struggle. Indeed, we stated earlier that very few students are of proletarian origin, so that the proletariat can be considered as being actually absent from the university, today as in 1968. (One could argue that the proletariat *is* present in the universities . . . as service employees; but this remark might be considered unintentionally funny, since it highlights the fact that, under the given political circumstances, the proletariat could not, imaginably, occupy any other place in the university.) We will show how this absence determines the very forms of the reference made to the working class.

We will start with the 22 M, where the question of being exterior does not seem to arise. As a matter of fact, the 22 M results show that 'les étudiants' (like 'les lycéens', 'les enseignants', etc.) belong to an equivalence class which also includes 'les travailleurs':

D 7

les étudiants	
les lycéens	ont lutté pendant plusieurs heures
les enseignants	
les travailleurs	

It would seem that the groups mentioned in the above example are described as having a common *class position* (to use marxist terms), which means at the same time both their internal homogeneity and the similarity of the positions they occupy. In the same way that class solidarity unites the workers, another kind of solidarity (which will be defined below) welds together students, secondary school pupils and teachers, and unites them at the same time with the working class.

In other words, the differences arising from what marxism-leninism calls *class situation* (that is, differences arising from the position in the economic structure) are as it were cancelled out by this new kind of solidarity that binds different social groups struggling, be it for different reasons (repression, exploitation), against a common oppressor, the bourgeoisie, or its representatives.

This new kind of solidarity, which seems to fill the gap between different class situations will be commented upon below; first, we will show the quite different standpoint of the U.E.C. on this problem.

Apart from the adjectivation referred to above:

HD 3
les étudiants communistes luttent pour . . .

we observe formulations of the following kind:

HD 6

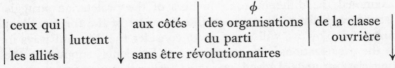

So it appears that certain participants in the political situation of May 1968 seem not be identified by their class situation (unlike 'les travailleurs' or 'la bourgeoisie') but, for the U.E.C. as well as for the 22M, by the political attitudes they adopt. Contrary to the 22M, however, the U.E.C. considers that adopting those attitudes implies solidarity in the struggle for political power ('ceux qui'='les alliés'), and not the kind of solidarity which cancels out class differentiation.

In tracts of the F.E.R., we have the ambiguous notion of the student struggle which *is and at the same time is not* a part of the workers' struggle.

HD 2

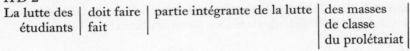

D 6

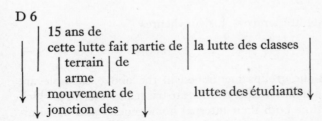

The commutation between syntagms (such as 'cette lutte fait partie'/ 'doit faire partie'; 'jonction des luttes') does not provide directly the relations between these syntagms. Nevertheless, we can comment on results by referring to our knowledge of the F.E.R. ideology (and we may assume that, when the tracts were distributed, those who were to read them also possessed this knowledge): if, at the same time, the student struggle is and is not an integral part of the proletarian struggle, this means that the state of integration could be actualized only by means of the 'junction' between both struggles . . . that is to say, by correctly organizing them, as we will see later on.

On further interpreting these results, we may assume that each of the three organizations is concerned with the working-class struggle in a specific way; this in turn determines *how* the student movement can be integrated with the workers' struggle. In other words, for each organization there exists *a crucial element*, specifying the objective and subjective conditions by which the relative exteriority of the student movement in regard to the workers' struggle could eventually be reduced or even could vanish altogether.

We now proceed to consider this crucial element more fully. Let us take another look at the U.E.C. result quoted above:

HD 6

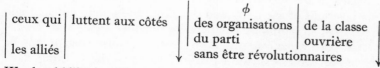

| ceux qui | luttent aux côtés | φ des organisations du parti sans être révolutionnaires | de la classe ouvrière |
| les alliés | | | |

We should like to make two comments about this result: First, among the students, some come to belong to the political category of their working-class allies by the mere fact that they are up against the same problems, although they do not consider themselves to be revolutionaries. Secondly, the political representatives of the working class are its organizations and its party; supporting the working class necessarily means supporting the working-class organizations. This is the condition *sine qua non*, the crucial element, which determines the link to the working class.

As regards the first point, we can see that the objective basis of the alliance we mentioned, taking into account the necessary stages, consists not only of struggling for a political transformation ('lutte pour un gouvernement populaire'), but also, and most important, of putting forward shared immediate demands:

HD 1

| vive la lutte des travailler | syndicats ouvriers étudiants | pour une université | φ réellement | démocratique |

D 11

| mise en avant satisfaction | des revendications | concrètes pressantes |

D 22

intérêt des étudiants et intérêts des travailleurs

D 24

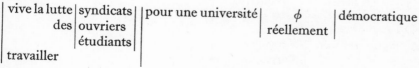

| Ceux qui luttent l'union | pour la satisfaction des revendications | pressantes des étudiants des travailleurs |

This implies that the political alliance proposed by (the party of) the working class is directed to *those who* ('ceux qui'), within and outside the

K

university, have—like the working class—concrete and urgent demands, because they are likely to become workers themselves and find themselves unemployed. These possible allies, the students being the most obvious, belong to the strata and class categories of the petty bourgeoisie, recently engaged in a process of destructuration-restructuration which brings them closer to the proletariat, although at the same time they are submitted to political and ideological contradictions (one can quote, for example, the typical case of a shopkeeper's son who graduated in engineering and who remains unemployed).

With regard to the second comment above, we will outline to what extent the positions of the F.E.R. and the 22M can be differentiated and considered; in other words we will describe what we called the 'crucial element' for both organizations. Both protest against what might be called *the metonymic rôle* of the P.C.F. in relation to the working class, against its claim of speaking in the name of the working class.

Consequently, we can identify a critical standpoint in the F.E.R. and 22M tracts which is not directly aimed at the communists as such (as we might find in reactionary or fascist organizations fighting '*the* communists' or '*the* marxists'), but at those who assume leadership or organizational responsibilities in the P.C.F., and who are blamed for being traitors to the working-class interests. Once more, it is not an *organization* that is blamed, but a mode of *behaviour*. For example:

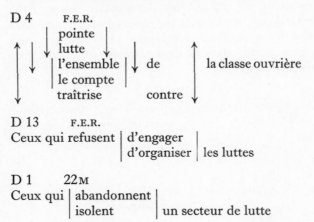

D 4   F.E.R.
           pointe
           lutte
           l'ensemble   de   la classe ouvrière
           le compte
           traîtrise   contre

D 13   F.E.R.
Ceux qui refusent | d'engager
                  | d'organiser | les luttes

D 1   22M
Ceux qui | abandonnent |
         | isolent | un secteur de lutte

So one could say that, for the F.E.R. as much as for the 22M, the struggle of the working class is 'too serious a matter' to be left to the party, *if there is any*, which may claim the label of 'the working-class party'. The main difference, as will be shown below, between the F.E.R. and the 22M, is that the F.E.R. considers that the working-class struggle needs a party; since in the eyes of the F.E.R., this party does not yet exist, it has to be built up. On the contrary, for the 22M, the working-class struggle does not need a party at all, whatever the leadership.

This now allows us to state explicitly the crucial element in the F.E.R. and 22M results.

In the F.E.R. discourse, the decisive term of 'organisation' remains always very close to the nominalization of the verb 'organiser'. When used as a substantive, this term is preceded by an equivalent nominalization derived from the verb 'construire'. For example:

HD 1

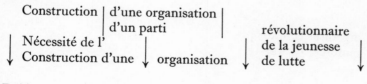

D 11

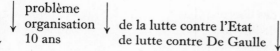

It is also possible to recognize the objective criteria for the regrouping of workers and students, as proposed by the F.E.R. (by means of organizing young people, including particularly the students). This emphasis on the rôle of the young people may be explained by reference to the ideology of the F.E.R. From their point of view, the bourgeoisie will seek to strengthen its dictatorship by increasing unemployment, amongst other means; in this event, it is the young people, including the students, who are the most vulnerable.

D 7

D 15

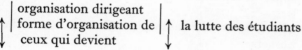

For the F.E.R., this regrouping constitutes the means to reduce and nullify the 'exteriority of the student movement'. We have already mentioned the theme of the 'junction' of the struggles. We can see now that, in order to actualize this 'junction', student struggle needs organization and leadership, according to the F.E.R.; hence a struggle is carried on by this movement in order to organize and lead the student movement.

D 1

D 5
| il faut
| les étudiants constituent | un facteur d'ordre

D 13
| emprise sur |
| lutte de | le mouvement étudiant

D 14
il faut | organiser la lutte |
| renforcer l'UNEF |
and

D 3
| des libertés |
lutte pour la défense | de l'UNEF |
| du marxisme |

Like the U.E.C., the F.E.R. considers students as representing a large category within the university, but unlike the U.E.C. positions this is less an economic and political category than a historical bloc consisting of 'the young people'. Consequently, this category corresponds less to a political ally than to support for the (re-)building of the workers' movement; by this means the F.E.R. (as a branch of the O.C.I.) could at last set up on its own account, politically speaking—that is to say, it could contest for the leadership of the struggle.

In the 22M tracts, the crucial element is totally different from those we described in the two other organizations. Indeed, the 22M conceives the relation between the student movement and the working-class movement neither in terms of a political alliance nor in terms of a possible 'junction'. We showed earlier that the exteriority problem seems to be, in some way, solved in the policy of the 22M, this policy consisting of a new kind of 'binding' solidarity. Now we have to examine how the 22M achieves this solidarity of the student movement with the working class:

D 4
| côtés |
| intéret | de la classe ouvrière

dans
D 10
la lutte contre l'exploitation capitaliste

The result below clearly shows the mechanism of the solidarity between students and workers:

HD 4

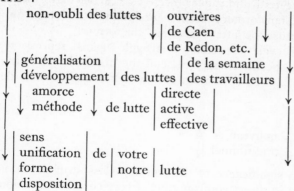

```
non-oubli des luttes | ouvrières
                     | de Caen
                     | de Redon, etc.

généralisation  |               | de la semaine
développement   | des luttes    | des travailleurs

amorce          |               | directe
méthode         | de lutte      | active
                                | effective

sens
unification     | de | votre  |
forme               |    | notre  | lutte
disposition
```

We can now see the main characteristics of the struggles as viewed by the 22 M: this movement is not preoccupied with any organizational problem, in the way this term is used either by the U.E.C. or the F.E.R. Struggle is defined by its significance and the locally and conjuncturally determined forms of the relationship that exists between the actors 'vous' and 'nous', who play complementary or even interchangeable rôles in the unification of the struggle. Hence, for the 22 M, the crucial element is the *concrete situation in which the struggle takes place,* in so far as 'the actual significance of the struggle' is revealed by this situation *hic et nunc,* and by the actual conditions of the struggle (place, duration, physical intensity):

HD 2

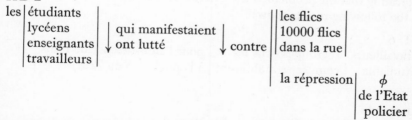

```
les | étudiants   |                  |        | les flics
    | lycéens     | qui manifestaient|        | 10000 flics
    | enseignants | ont lutté        | contre | dans la rue
    | travailleurs|                  |
                                              | la répression |  φ
                                                              | de l'Etat
                                                              | policier
```

Clearly, the struggle against the police ('contre la répression de l'Etat policier' or 'bourgeois') stands for the struggle against capitalist exploitation (that is, the kernel of the working-class struggle):

HD 3

```
la police      |    | l'exploitation |
la repression  | de | la police      |

lutte | est      |        | l'Etat         || policier
      | se mène  | contre | la répression  || bourgeois
```

HD 5

```
la lutte contre | la répression |                    | l'Etat policier
                | l'Etat        | est la lutte contre| l'exploitation
```

So the struggle for long-term and vague objectives is carried on by means of immediate action ('transformer radicalement l'université', 'construire une société . . .'), because the latter 'actualize' the former.

In this context the cycle 'repression—struggle against repression' should be noted. The specific characteristic of the 'méthode nouvelle', implemented by the 22M in opposition to the 'types traditionnels de lutte':

D 15

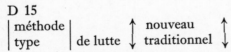

is to reveal the deep significance of the working-class struggle, as is immediately apparent in direct confrontation. Every concrete situation of this kind is a dynamic element, strengthening the solidarity, where and whenever the struggle takes place, in contrast to what, in the eyes of the 22M, leads to the fragmentation, and the bureaucratic, electorialist isolationism of the old form of struggle:

D 23

la lutte se mène dans la rue et

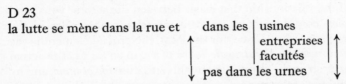

Nevertheless, symptomatic traces are to be found in the 22M discourse, indicating that the problem of the exteriority has not been totally solved, as the following results show:

HD 6

| travailleurs | regroupés dans les | pour l'auto-défense de Flins |
| étudiants | comités se mobilisent | à l'appel . . . (du 22M) |

D 16

| demande | | Flins |
| appel | des travailleurs de | chez Renault |

CONCLUSION

To sum up: the different contexts in which the term 'lutte' occurred in the tracts of our three groups revealed specific uses of this term, which we could consider as homonyms.

1. The F.E.R. is engaging in a day-to-day struggle to bring about the 'junction' between students and workers, a union which had not yet been realized; this will be achieved by young people acting as intermediaries.

2. The U.E.C. is conducting a day-to-day struggle alongside the working class organizations to bring about an alliance (or union) which in turn will lead to a new democratic régime.

3. The 22nd of March movement is carrying on a day-to-day struggle in order to bring about a total change of society, which could only happen in the future.

Acknowledgements

We are very grateful to N. Bourdin and Cl. Haroche for preparing the material for computer analysis, and to G. Seidel, whose critical remarks on the content, as well as the translation, helped us greatly.

REFERENCES

Geffroy, A., Lafon, P. & Tournier, M. (1971) *A la Recherche du particulier et du général dans le vocabulaire des tracts de Mai 1968*. Paris: École Normale Supérieure de Saint-Cloud.
Harris, Z. (1969) Analyse du discours. *Langages*, **13**, 8-45.
Pêcheux, M. (1969) *Analyse automatique du discours*. Paris: Dunod.

An associative thesaurus of English and its computer analysis

Ever since Kent and Rosanoff, two clinical psychologists, collected word association responses to one hundred words from a large sample of people early in this century, tabulations of such data have continued to exercise the imagination of experimental and clinical psychologists. Although our understanding of the processes which generate the impressive regularities in this kind of data has not progressed very far since that time, there has been a steady accumulation of descriptive and experimental information. In fact, the literature on word association phenomena is now extremely large. The field has been surveyed very ably in a recent book by Cramer (1968). Interesting relationships have been demonstrated between word association data and a number of psychological processes at various levels of complexity. These include studies of memory, learning, problem solving, concept formation, and verbal behaviour.

We shall not attempt here even a brief review of the philosophical origins of interest in associations, or of the early work of the psychologist Wundt and of the psychiatrist Jung on word associations. Such reviews can be found in Woodworth and Schlosberg (1955), and in Deese (1965). We shall confine ourselves to pointing out that it has always been and remains to be a general belief that associative processes are a basic component of thought and cognitive processes in general. It has been the hope of many investigators that the regularities of associative responses will yield some insight into the structure of the human mind. This belief underlies the several recent attempts at applying structural methods of analysis to word association data. The work reported in this paper is also an outcome of this approach.

WORD ASSOCIATION DATA

The traditional method of obtaining word association 'norms' (so called, because of the early hopes of using this data as a norm against which abnormalities can be detected and measured) is to show or say a word to several people and ask them to say the word which first comes to their minds upon perceiving the stimulus. When this procedure is followed with say 100 persons, data of the kind shown in table 1 is obtained. This table shows the frequencies with which various responses are given by this sample of people. Notice the highly skewed form of the frequency distribution, and the considerable agreement among the people as to the most popular response.

Many tabulations of such norms have been collected during the last decade or two (see, for example, Palermo and Jenkins 1964; Postman and

Frequency	Responses
15	moth
9	cabbage; net
6	insect; wing; wings
4	caterpillar; summer; yellow
2	ant; beauty; cabbage-white; chrysalis; flower; flowers; flutterby; flutter; opera
1	bat; bird; bliss; calm; colour; colours; dead; elusive; fragile; grace; heat; insects; meander; rugby; song; stomach; worm

Table 1. Word association responses to *butterfly*

Keppel 1970). Recently it has been increasingly realized that it is better to regard associations between words as forming a network, rather than just to concentrate on the list of responses to any given stimulus (Deese 1965; Pollio 1966; Kiss 1968, 1969). Deese introduced the idea of using factor analysis on a matrix of correlations between a set of stimulus words, where the correlations are based on a comparison of the corresponding response distributions. Pollio (1966) and Kiss (1968) then attempted the application of graph theory to word association networks. These approaches give rise to a point of view according to which words are embedded in a multidimensional associative space, whose dimensions can be discovered by factor analysis and multidimensional scaling, while the proximity relations can be studied by numerical taxonomy and clustering methods.

It has been the hope of most investigators in this area that the analysis of such an associative space will yield some insight into the organization of the subjective lexicon. It must be emphasized that such associative organization is but one particular facet of the subjective lexicon and that others, for example those relating to the nature of relational organization, will need different methods of study. However, the extensive experimental literature supports a view claiming that associative organization is an aspect of many if not all cognitive processes involving the subjective lexicon.

WORD ASSOCIATION NETWORKS

The background to an application of graph theory to word associations is given in another paper (Kiss 1968). We shall confine ourselves to a brief presentation of the main ideas here.

A word association network is a directed linear graph with labelled arcs (links). The nodes of the graph are words (or verbal units), and the arcs represent estimates of stimulus–response associative probabilities. The labels of the arcs are the conditional probabilities of words being given as responses to the specified stimuli. Figure 1 shows an example of an association network in the environment of the word *butterfly*.

In such a graph a path is a sequence of arcs. The length of a path is just the number of arcs in it. A circuit is a closed path. A loop is a closed path of length one. If we start from a node and find all the nodes which can be reached by following paths of lengths 1, 2, ..., n, we obtain what we shall call the n-step environment of a node. The number of arcs going into a node is called the indegree, and the number of arcs coming out of a node the outdegree of a node.

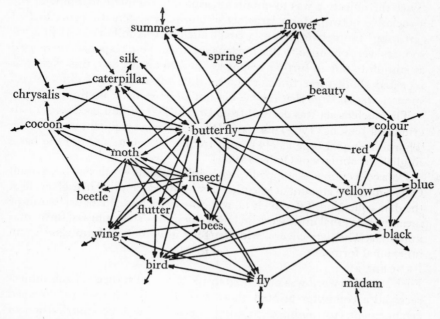

Figure 1. Part of the association network around *butterfly*

It is often useful to regard such a graph as a network in which signals are passed from node to node. Imagine that each node is a 'repeater' station which sums the incoming signals and transmits the sum along the outgoing arcs. Such an interpretation is called a signal flow graph. It is now possible to define the transmittance between a node A and a node B as the total signal strength reaching B if a unit signal is injected at A, via all possible pathways in the network. If we limit the path lengths to n, then we obtain the n-step transmittance. The basic rules for calculating transmittances are that the resultant value for two series-connected arcs is the product of their values, while the resultant for parallel-connected arcs is the sum of the values. [For further details see Kiss (1968).]

An Associative Thesaurus of English

The usefulness of word association data in experimental psychology and the hope of obtaining information for a study of the associative organization of the lexicon prompted us to initiate a project aimed at the collection and analysis of associative data for a sizeable segment of the lexicon. It was felt that such a collection of data would be of interest also in clinical psychology, education, linguistics, and for computer interpretation of natural language. We shall now turn to the description of the procedures followed in the data collection.

THE STIMULUS WORDS

Since the objective was to obtain a reasonably complete mapping of the associative network for a large set of words, a systematic procedure of 'growing' the network from a small nucleus was followed. At first responses were obtained to this nucleus set, then these responses were used as stimuli to obtain further responses, and so on. In fact, this cycle was repeated about three times, since by then the number of different responses was so large that they could not all be re-used as stimuli.

The nucleus set was derived from (a) the 200 stimuli used in the Palermo and Jenkins (1964) norms, (b) the 1,000 most frequent words of the Thorndike and Lorge (1944) word frequency count, and (c) the basic English vocabulary of Ogden (1954).

Data collection was stopped when 8,400 stimulus words had been used. Only a minimal amount of selection of stimuli was applied in each cycle of the data collection. Effectively all responses which were English words or meaningful verbal units were included, including some phrasal forms and numerals. The data cover a wide range of grammatical form classes and inflexional forms.

PROCEDURE

Each stimulus word was presented to 100 different subjects. Each subject received a computer-printed sheet with 100 stimuli in a randomized arrangement (to minimize priming effects). The total contribution of each subject was thus 100 responses. The verbal environment of each word for each subject was different.

The instructions asked the subject to write down against each stimulus the first word it made him think of, working as quickly as possible. The total time spent on this task was measured, and most subjects completed the sheet in five to ten minutes.

Most of the data was collected in a classroom setting under supervision. Sheets which had more than 25 per cent blank responses were rejected and fresh data was collected.

SUBJECTS

A stratified sampling procedure was adopted, with the aim of making the sample representative of the British undergraduate student population. The student population was chosen because of its easy accessibility and because of its widespread use in psychological experimentation. It also ensures that most subjects have a reasonably large vocabulary.

Two factors were controlled in the sampling: (a) the region of Great Britain in which the subject had spent most of his/her life, and (b) the faculty of study. The distribution of geographical origin was based on

Government statistics and was controlled by carrying out the data collection at many different universities in Great Britain. Predictions were derived from the known composition of student intake of each university, and final adjustments were made by rejecting and re-collecting data if discrepancies were apparent in the sample composition. Similarly, the data collection was organized in various faculties to reflect the known distribution of students according to subject of study.

The age range of the subjects was 17 to 22, with a mode of 19. The sex distribution was 64 per cent male and 36 per cent female. The majority of subjects were undergraduate students.

The Thesaurus data

The Thesaurus currently exists in three different forms. It is being published on microfilm; it exists on 9-track IBM-compatible magnetic tape; and there are a few line-printer hard copies. Owing to the rather great bulk of this data, the hard copy form is very laborious to use: the material occupies some six volumes of closely printed line-printer paper. We are hoping to be able to accommodate all of the data on a single reel of special thin-based microfilm in a Bell and Howell casette. This form is just being published (Kiss, Armstrong, and Milroy 1972) at the time of writing this paper. The film contains two sections, one listing for all 8,400 stimuli both the incoming and outgoing connections in order of frequency, and the other listing the incoming connections for all words which occur only as responses. There are a total of 55,732 nodes in the Thesaurus network. In its present form the data is an accurate representation of the subjects' responses, including spelling mistakes and variant forms. The data was proof read in segments by four different persons, and a great deal of automated checking was also employed during various stages of the computer processing. The microfilm has been produced directly from the computer magnetic tapes.

A number of descriptive statistics have now been derived about the total data and these will be presented in a forthcoming paper. We shall just mention here a few interesting features. The distributions of the node indegrees and of the total frequency of occurrence of response words are both very close to a lognormal distribution at the lower frequency range, with a systematic deviation at the high-frequency end. This is also true of the frequency distribution of any particular response word in itself. It also appears that for high-frequency response words the dispersion parameter of the lognormal portion is much the same for all words and only the means are different.

The general picture which emerges so far is that the Thesaurus forms a network which is very densely connected near its 'central' (high-frequency) area, with a progressive thinning out of links towards the 'peripheral' parts. For example, some of the largest indegrees are those of man (1,071), money (750), and sex (847). On the other hand, about 60 per cent of the nodes have an indegree of only one.

The outdegree distribution is of course less variable, since there is an upper limit of 100 imposed by the fact that 100 responses were obtained to each stimulus, and, on the other hand, an outdegree of one would require a complete agreement among the 100 subjects on a single word as the only possible response. This never happens. The range of the outdegree distribution is in fact from 7 to 82.

A COMPUTER-BASED THESAURUS

We have recognized from the outset of this project that manual examination of hypotheses relating to such a large collection of data will be difficult if not impossible, and for this reason planned for a computer data-base with an associated suite of programs to facilitate its interrogation in various ways. In this section we shall mention three different programs of this kind. The first of these has been implemented in COBOL and is running on the IBM 360/50 at Edinburgh, the second exists in POP-2 for the ICL 4130 and PDP 10 computers. The third is under development in POP-2.

The first interrogation program is designed for the extraction of an n-step environment around any word. The program can derive environments based either on a stimulus–response or on a response–stimulus direction of the links. Input parameters can define both n, and a threshold value for any link to become part of the extracted data. The output consists of an alphabetically sorted listing of node names, each with its associated list of incoming or outgoing links. Each link is represented by a word and a numeric value (the percentage response frequency).

The second program derives the value of the total transmittance existing between a pair of nodes through pathways of lengths up to n. Again, input parameters define n and a threshold. This program can also be used for the calculation of a complete transmittance matrix among a designated set of words and has been found useful in applying cluster analysis techniques to the data, as will be described below.

The third program, or rather set of programs, is intended for interactive conversational use from an on-line console. Its purpose is to make possible fast associative searches for any particular region or item in the Thesaurus. These programs make the Thesaurus accessible as an on-line, computer-based dictionary of the thesaurus type. An example of the type of associative search process with which we are going to experiment is the iterative extraction of sets of 10—20 words to which the user can assign weights, thereby determining the next set to be displayed on the console. The strategies which can be used in selecting the next set can be flexible, but one example is to use a cumulative convergence of 'activation' on words from links originating from words that have been given high positive weights by the user during the search. This kind of search enables one to 'home in' on a desired region or item very rapidly. Searches of this kind could then easily be linked to an interrogation of a coupled conventional dictionary for the provision of detailed lexicographical information. Computer readable forms of some large dictionaries already exist (Olney, Revard, and Ziff 1968).

COMPUTER ANALYSIS OF SEMANTIC STRUCTURE

One of the primary reasons for the Thesaurus project was our conviction that the word association experiment provides a workable approach to the large-scale semantic analysis of the lexicon. We hasten to acknowledge that associative structure is but one aspect of semantic structure, and that it must be complemented by a 'relational' analysis.

The theoretical orientation which underlies our thinking in this area can be summarized briefly as follows. We use the ideas of words (or larger verbal units) which can have one or more word senses, which are in turn mapped one-to-one on to concepts. Two different kinds of relations can be introduced over a set of words. One is the relation of relevance, which reflects, roughly speaking, 'what goes with what' in the world or in our minds. The relevance relation is reflected in the connections which are found in the word association data. The other relation is similarity, which reflects the degree to which two words have overlapping relevance distributions. The similarity relation is reflected in a similarity coefficient computed from the distributions of relevance connections attached to each word.

Two different approaches to the semantic structuring of the Thesaurus data can now be distinguished. One is aimed at the discovery of semantic components for a word (covering all its word senses). The other is aimed at the discovery of groups of words which are relevant to each other because the concepts they label go together (although may not be similar to each other). The analysis of semantic components for a word is a local operation, confined to the n-step environment of the word. It consists in attempting to find clusters of words in that environment, such that members of a cluster have similar relevance link distributions. These clusters presumably reflect some particular facet of a concept labelled by the word. Such a 'componential' analysis involves the introduction of a specific 'point of view', determined by the word being analyzed. This is discussed in more detail below.

The discovery of groups of relevant words, on the other hand, is a global operation on the whole Thesaurus. We would like to call such groups 'semantic fields', because of the relation of this idea to the linguistic notion of semantic fields. Because of the size of the data, and the expected large overlapping between such groups, this approach presents formidable computational problems which we have not so far tackled.

COMPUTING SEMANTIC COMPONENTS

Consider now the local approach to clustering, where one attempts to find semantic components in an n-step environment of a word. Our approach here can be contrasted with that of Deese (1965) who used factor analysis to discover the main dimensions of such environments. The factor analysis was performed on a matrix of 'overlap coefficients' [which can be shown to be one minus the so-called Canberra non-metric dissimilarity coefficient of Lance and Williams (1966) under the usual conditions]. The coordinates for the calculation of the overlap coefficients are provided by the total set of words occurring as responses to the words in the environment. Instead of this method, it is possible to use the set of stimulus words which elicit some or all of the words in the environment, as coordinates. This method is usually avoided since it introduces a bias: the original set of stimulus words are chosen by the experimenter and thus limit the choice of any subset which might be chosen for clustering purposes. However, when clustering a set of words which are all in the same environment of one particular word, and so are likely to be semantically related to that word, a biassed set of coordinates may actually be useful in introducing a 'point of view', by preventing some of the meanings of multiple-meaning words from intruding into the clustering, and thus upsetting it. For instance, if the words *fly* and *wings* occur as responses to the word *insect*, the fact that both are responses to *aeroplane* is not really relevant.

In the method which we are investigating at present, the set W of words to be clustered is obtained as the 3-step environment of a word. In order to reduce the size of this set, we usually apply a threshold of 2 to all links which do not originate directly from the word analyzed. The first-level responses are then regarded as a set C of coordinate words (these are the words which are directly linked to the word analyzed). Let us call the total transmittance from $c \in C$ to $w \in W$, $t(c, w)$, using paths of length up to n. Then the coordinate of w corresponding to c' is

$$\frac{t(c', w)}{\sum\limits_{c \in C} t(c, w)}$$

that is, we make the normalizing assumption that the total inflow to a word w from the set C should be unity (this ensures that, if two words w and w' have links to each word in the network in constant ratio, though not necessarily with identical values, as might conceivably occur with ideal synonyms, then they will have exactly the same coordinate values).

Having obtained the coordinates in this way, a dissimilarity matrix is calculated for the set of words, using the Canberra dissimilarity coefficient (DC), and clustering is performed on this matrix. In actual practice, the coordinates are calculated on an ICL 4130 in the POP-2 language. The DC calculation and clustering is done by the CLUSTAN 1A package (Wishart 1969a) on the IBM 360/50. We intend to rewrite the POP-2 algorithms in a language suitable for running on the 360/50, possibly COBOL, when these algorithms have reached a satisfactory state of development.

At present, we use the 'average linkage' clustering algorithm. Despite the faults in its mathematical properties (Jardine, Jardine, and Sibson 1967), this method does produce clusters which are intuitively meaningful, and from which an easily interpretable dendrogram may be drawn to present the results. While *Bk* methods would seem to be ideal for this work from a theoretical point of view (Jardine and Sibson 1971), they have two main drawbacks: first, they are not computationally practicable for the size of data set which we are considering, and, secondly, there is no simple manner for presenting the results of a *Bk* clustering of large data sets. *K*-dendrograms are neither easy to draw nor to read.

RESULTS

So far, we have clustered on thresholded data sets only, and the results we have obtained must be regarded as preliminary. Figure 2 is part of the dendrogram obtained for the 3-step environment of *butterfly*, the corresponding results for the *friend* environment are shown in figure 3. We have not drawn the complete dendrograms as we believe that obtaining very large numbers of very small clusters is not particularly useful, as clusters of this sort do not satisfy the minimum criteria of internal coherence coupled with isolation from other clusters. In fact, even the number of clusters which we do show is probably somewhat more than the true number of distinct modes present in the data (*see* Wishart 1969 for a discussion of this point).

SUMMARY

We have described what is, to our knowledge, the largest collection of systematic information about the associative habits of speakers of the English language. As such, the Associative Thesaurus constitutes one particular kind of 'cognitive map' of this population of people. It contains information which is of interest both from the linguistic and from the psychological points of view.

The theoretical background to the data collection was provided by an approach to structural analysis through word association networks. In such networks the connecting arcs indicate relevance, while measures based on the distributions of relevance links indicate similarity. Within this approach the whole repertoire of graph theory becomes available for structural analysis.

The data was collected by systematically 'growing' an association network from a relatively small nucleus of about 1,000 words. The data now contains nearly 56,000 distinct items. A stratified sampling of the subjects was used, in which geographical origin and faculty of study was controlled for the undergraduate students taking part in the project. Biases from individual subjects were controlled by a randomized stimulus presentation and by keeping the total contribution of each subject low.

The Thesaurus exists in microfilm publication and as a computer database. In the latter form it is augmented by a suite of programs which facilitate its examination for research purposes.

L

clustering strength: 0·7   0·8   0·9   1·0

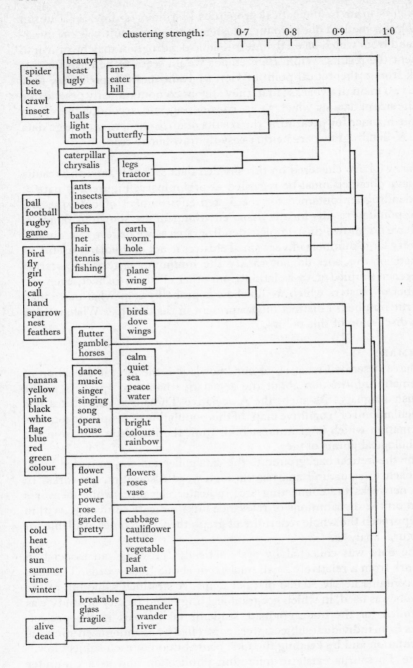

Figure 2

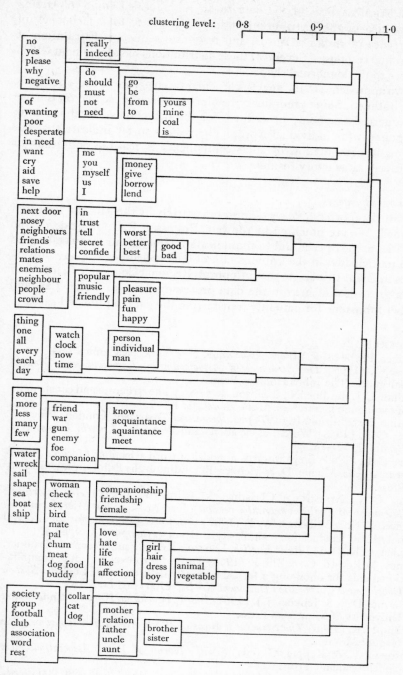

Figure 3

Statistical analysis of the data so far has revealed some interesting regularities in the distribution of node indegrees, total frequency of occurrence of response words, and response frequency distribution of individual responses. Several of these distributions have a segment which is close to the lognormal shape.

Two approaches to the analysis of semantic structure in the Thesaurus were outlined. Some preliminary results have been presented on the use of numerical taxonomy procedures for the detection of local semantic components for individual words. The results so far indicate that the automatic computation of such components is feasible and leads to intuitively satisfactory results.

Acknowledgements
The work reported here was supported entirely by the Medical Research Council. We are indebted to the late Professor R.C.Oldfield for the facilities at the Speech and Communication Unit; to our many colleagues who participated in the arduous task of data collection at many universities in Great Britain; to the Edinburgh Regional Computer Centre staff for a great deal of help in the data processing; and to Eileen Law and Isobel Johnstone for patiently transferring the data to punched cards.

REFERENCES

Cramer, Phebe (1968) *Word Association*. New York: Academic Press.

Deese, J. (1965) *The Structure of Associations in Language and Thought*. Baltimore: The Johns Hopkins Press.

Jardine, C.J., Jardine, N., & Sibson, R. (1967) The structure and construction of taxonomic hierarchies. *Math. Biosci.*, **1**, 173-9.

Jardine, N. & Sibson, R. (1971) *Mathematical Taxonomy*. London: Wiley.

Kiss, G.R. (1968) Words, associations and networks. *J. verb. Learn. verb. Behav.*, **7**, 707-13.

Kiss, G.R. (1969) Steps towards a model of word selection. *Machine Intelligence 4* (eds. Michie, D. & Meltzer, B.). Edinburgh: Edinburgh University Press.

Kiss, G.R., Armstrong, Christine, & Milroy, R. (1972) *An Associative Thesaurus of English (microfilm version)*. East Ardsley: EP Microform Ltd.

Lance, G.N. & Williams, W.T. (1966) Computer programs for hierarchical polythetic classification ('similarity analyses'). *Computer J.*, **9**, 60-4.

Ogden, C.K. (1954) *Basic English*. London: Kegan Paul, Trench & Trubner.

Olney, J., Revard, C., & Ziff, P. (1968) Toward the development of computational aids for obtaining a formal semantic description of English. *System Development Corporation Document No. SP-2766 / 001 / 00*.

Palermo, D.S. & Jenkins, J.J. (1964) *Word Association Norms*. Minneapolis: University of Minnesota Press.

Pollio, H.R. (1966) *The Structural Basis of Word Association Behavior*. The Hague: Mouton.

Postman, L. & Keppel, G. (eds) (1970) *Norms of Word Association*. New York: Academic Press.

Thorndike, E.L. & Lorge, I. (1944) *The Teacher's Word Book of 30,000 Words*. New York: Columbia University Press.

Wishart, D. (1969) Mode analysis: A generalisation of nearest neighbour which reduces chaining effects. *Numerical Taxonomy* (ed. Cole, A.J.). London: Academic Press.

Wishart, D. (1969a) *CLUSTAN 1A*. St Andrews: The Computing Laboratory, University of St Andrews.

Woodworth, R.S. & Schlosberg, H. (1955) *Experimental Psychology*. New York: Holt.

P.A.FORTIER,
J.C.McCONNELL

Computer-aided thematic analysis
of French prose fiction

The main problem confronting the scholar who studies thematic structures is impressionism. He may feel that the development of a certain theme, or the interrelation of several themes, is crucial for understanding a text, and that this can provide the basis for a new interpretation of it. But this interpretation is all too frequently founded on shifting sand, because when he tests his original hypothesis the scholar usually rereads the text in question. And the natural tendency—even positing no distractions—is to highlight details which support the original insight or feeling and to overlook things which contradict it, or call for further refinement. A not infrequent result is that when the new interpretation is presented to the community of scholars, the basic insight on which it is founded is called into question. The scholar with the new interpretation cannot demonstrate the correctness of his underlying insight; he has his impressions. His questioners cannot disprove the insight; they have different impressions. Intellectual exchange at this point is stymied.

With this problem in mind, we are constructing a system for computeraided thematic analysis. We say 'computer-aided' because our system makes extensive use of human intervention. We are dealing with both the syntactic and semantic aspects of language, and work with automatic translation has revealed severe limitations in the machine's ability to handle such complex and imprecise entities. Thus in our system the machine facilitates and handles the 'busy-work' of tagging words by basic form and part of speech, but a human operator decides what basic form and part of speech should be attached to each keyword. Similarly, synonym dictionaries provide everything from entirely equivalent terms to words associated to a concept in a remote or metaphorical way. Here again we felt that human control at the creation of the theme lists would avoid grief further along.

Our programs are written in PL/1 for the IBM 360/65 at the University of Manitoba, and take for granted the existence of that university's monitor system for remote terminals, or a similar one, such as IBM's ATS. The frequency and distribution of single words, specified themes, groups of themes, and even grammatical classes of words can be analysed by our system. Bar graphs will show their frequency and distribution throughout the text or in any portion of the text. These graphs will provide supporting or detracting evidence for the scholar's impressions. Specialized concordances, or distribution tables can also be produced.

The major task in our system is the preparation of data for the programs which produce these analyses. Two sub-systems handle this: one produces, from literary texts, complete lists of words from which rapid and efficient searches can be made: another creates lists of words evoking themes.

The literary text is recorded on card images, with embedded coding for accents, capitalization, etc. After the text has been proofread and corrected, the accent and capitalization codes are moved to the end of each word for easier sorting, and a keyword concordance, from which no words are excluded, is produced, proofread and re-corrected. We call this machine-readable concordance the vertical list. It is in alphabetical order by keyword, and contains as many fixed-length records as there are words in the text; each record contains the keyword, its frequency, identification of its position, and one hundred bytes of context.

The next step is to add grammatical information, such as part of speech and basic form, to each record, so that searches can be done on the basic form rather than on the inflected forms of words, thus avoiding the problem of multiple forms and homographs (see figure 1).

This process begins with GRM10, a program which uses the vertical list and a master form file as input, and outputs a file containing three types of card images. The header card shows that information follows for a new keyword, that is to say a group of letters which may in fact be several different words in the true sense. The grammar cards provide sets of grammatical information required for this keyword. One grammar card is made up for each true word. These grammar cards are taken by the program from the master form file, if they are in it. The sequence cards record all the positions of this keyword, and leave a space for entering a number that shows which grammar card matches each occurrence of the word. The concordance corresponding to the vertical list is available to aid in categorizing. If only one grammar card corresponds to all occurrences of the keyword, a flag in this card makes it unnecessary to enter codes in the sequence cards. The data output by this program is put into many small files, because the terminal system at the University of Manitoba permits files of no more than 936 card images. Our files contain about 700 records on generation, to allow ample room for expansion when data is added.

Once the codes have been placed in the sequence cards, and any grammar cards which may have been lacking in the master form file have been added, the file is submitted to GRM20, which tests the format of each card, and also checks that each entry on the cards is matched in the vertical list. Any card which does not meet specifications is written on to a reject file, along with associated cards if necessary. A message describing the error is printed, and the rest of the file is checked. When the errors have been corrected, the reworked file is submitted to GRM20 and re-examined. Eventually the file becomes perfect.

Two options exist in this program. The cards can be tested to make

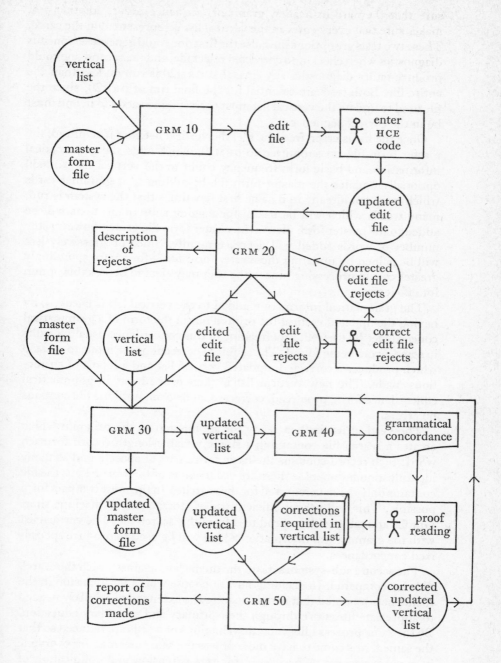

Figure 1. System for addition of grammatical information to vertical lists

sure that they are in header, grammar, sequence order. Another test makes sure that every entry in the vertical list is represented in the cards. These two tests are optional because the first one could generate erroneous diagnostics when checking a corrected reject file, and the second one could produce faulty diagnostics any time that GRM20 is run on less than the entire file. Both tests are essential for the final run of GRM20, since the file used to update the vertical list must correspond exactly to it, and must be in the correct sequence.

Once the file is error-free, the file, the vertical list, and if required, the master form file are submitted to GRM30, which adds the grammatical information and basic form frequency count to the vertical list. GRM30 optionally updates the master form file by adding to it grammar cards which were not already in it. The first few times that the system is run, many words which will be useful for tagging subsequent texts will be added to the master form file. As the master form file grows, however, the number of words added will decrease rapidly. Since progressively less will be gained by updating the master form file—for a correspondingly greater cost in processing time—the user may elect to bypass this option for efficiency.

The grammatical information added to the vertical list is checked, by having the updated vertical list printed out in the form of a grammatical concordance by GRM40. Proofreading of this concordance usually results in some errors being found. The required corrections are input to GRM50 which produces a corrected, updated vertical list and a report of corrections made. The new vertical list is then printed out in grammatical concordance form, proofread, corrected, and so on, until the file contains no errors.

The vertical list is then ready for submission to the program which creates a search file containing a single variable-length record for each word; each record contains the basic form, part of speech, and as many identification numbers as there are occurrences of the word. Thus the file contains only the data required for the searches, in the most compact form possible. This will permit efficient use of storage and of machine time. Graphs and tables will be produced from this search file. The vertical list with the grammatical information added will be used to produce specialized concordances.

The second sub-system sets up the theme lists against which the search files are compared. In deciding how to choose words for inclusion in the theme lists we noted that people acquire the extended vocabulary needed to appreciate literature through their primary and secondary education. By the same process idiosyncratic valuations of words are reduced so that the same terms come to have more or less the same meaning for everyone in a given society. A basic tool for this extension and codification of vocabulary is the synonym dictionary. There are ten such dictionaries for French, each drawn up from a different point of view, but all having in

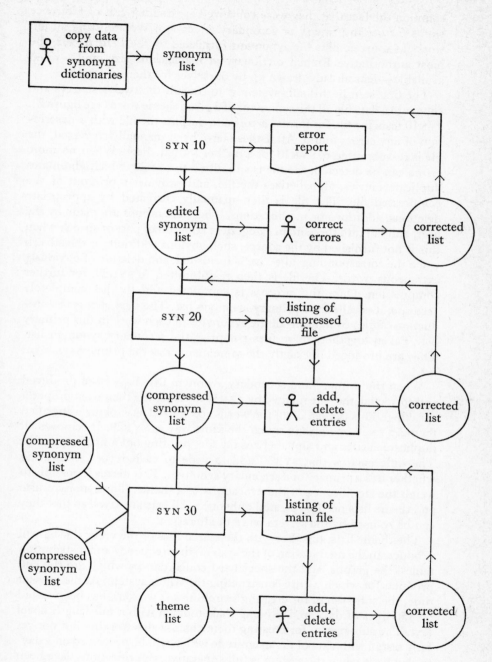

Figure 2. System for creation of theme lists

common the fact that they were conceived as teaching aids or reference works for use in primary or secondary education. We are using all ten works as sources, plus the synonyms furnished by the *Petit Robert*, the most authoritative French dictionary of manageable size, and—when available—lists already drawn up by ourselves for thematic study.

The first step in this sub-system is to consult the twelve sources and copy into a data file all the synonyms of a given theme word (see figure 2). SYN10 tests the file for format errors and outputs the file with a description of any errors found. After these have been manually corrected, the file is re-submitted to SYN10 for a further format check. When no more errors can be detected, the file is submitted to SYN20, which eliminates duplicate entries, alphabetizes the file, and provides a printout of the compressed file. The file is then manually corrected by appropriate deletions, additions or modifications. These alterations are made by the user, and fall into three main categories: addition of part of speech when this is not furnished by the source, such obvious additions as the adverb when the corresponding adjective is furnished, and deletion of obviously extraneous words. The file is then re-submitted to SYN20, for further compression. Once this process is completed and the list completely accurate, it is called the primary synonym list. The next step is the production of files containing all the synonyms of each work in this primary list. Taken together, these files comprise the secondary synonym list. They are produced in exactly the same manner as the primary synonym list.

When the primary and secondary synonym lists have been produced and corrected, they are merged by SYN30 to create the theme list properly speaking. This is a list of all the words recognized as evoking a specified theme. SYN30 operates in much the same way as SYN20. It removes all duplicate entries and alphabetizes the file, printing out a final copy of it. The difference is that SYN30 adds a code to each record, indicating whether it is a primary or a secondary synonym. This makes it possible to weigh the significance of the evocations of a theme. The synonym lists and theme lists need be created only once. All lists are saved so that they can be re-used by the system without alteration.

The theme lists, together with the search files or the vertical lists, will produce, in the final section of the system, the frequency and distribution tables, the graphs, and the specialized concordances which are the end products for which we are constructing the whole system. At the present time, the sub-system for creating search files is written, has been tested on 150 lines of data, and is being shaken down with a full-length novel text. The sub-system for creating theme lists is also working but not yet fully tested with data of the magnitude which will be processed on a day-to-day basis when the system is fully operative. Specifications have been drawn up for the final sub-system to produce usable output and strategies mapped out. We have delayed writing this sub-system until the programs which provide data to it have been completely shaken down.

We are confident that our system's output will permit more thorough and objective analysis of French texts than has hitherto been possible. Once a good number of such analyses have been carried out on many different works of literature, it should be possible to determine thresholds of frequency beyond which a theme can automatically be considered to be important. It is also possible that Professor Gunnel Engwall's (1971) work on the vocabulary of the French novel in the 1960s will contribute to the establishment of such thresholds. At that point it could become feasible to use statistics in determining the importance of a theme.

It may not be clear why our system is limited to French texts. Part of this is based on practical considerations. English, for instance, has considerably fewer inflected endings than French. Salton (1968) and Sedelow (1965) have demonstrated that a complex system like ours is not necessary to study this language. A program which strips off inflected endings, after comparison with an exclusion list to prevent false matches, is quite sufficient. German, with its long un-hyphenated compound words and its separable prefixes, probably requires a more sophisticated system than the one we have set up.

Our system has grown out of a number of thematic studies using hand counts, word lists and concordances. The tediousness of using these primitive research tools showed the necessity for a more advanced system. This earlier work did have the advantage of supplying us with concrete examples of what we expect our system to produce and of promoting a theoretical justification of our work in terms of symbolist literary theory. Since the examples and justification are all in the realm of French literature, we felt it prudent not to claim any wider application.

In France, the symbolist approach to literature can be traced to Baudelaire's translations of Poe's works. Poe's theory of artistic creation is announced in the second paragraph of 'The Philosophy of Composition' (1927):

> Nothing is more clear than that every plot, worth the name, must be elaborated to its *dénouement* before anything is attempted with the pen. It is only with the *dénouement* constantly in view that we can give a plot its indispensable air of consequence, or causation, by making the incidents, and especially the tone at all points, tend to the development of the intention.

Although Poe wrote these lines in jest, Baudelaire and his successors took them seriously. In fact, Baudelaire (1933) improved on Poe, saying that every single word must be subordinate to the grand design of the work. This concept of the ideal work of art as a unified whole, in which every aspect must be calculated to produce the final effect, together with a stress on words or language in literature, forms the basis of symbolist literary criticism.

Paul Valéry—the major exponent of symbolist criticism—wrote much more extensively on the subject than Baudelaire. Valéry's esthetics are a convenient theoretical base for computer-aided study of prose fiction, because Valéry, who wrote no novels, died in 1945. Thus he cannot be accused of justifying a certain type of novel, nor of distorting literary theory to permit computerized study. Scattered throughout the thousands of pages in which Valéry reflects on literature, can be found the elements of a coherent theory of the novel. His general concept of art leads to his definition of literature, and these considerations provide a basis for understanding his theory of the novel.

Valéry (1957c) defines art in terms of its intention, which is to produce an esthetic effect on the beholder. Literature is distinguished by the fact that it uses language to do this (1957a). Valéry (1957f, i, 1960) frequently repeated Mallarmé's saying: 'Ce n'est pas avec des idées qu'on fait des vers, c'est avec des mots'. He stresses the necessity for a thorough understanding of the medium which literature uses to achieve its effects. He notes that language usually has the pragmatic function of conveying a precise meaning; the artist's problem is to use it for the non-utilitarian goal of producing an entity with an inner coherence, capable of touching the reader's emotions (Valéry 1957g). To achieve this goal, the author sets up a series of relations which do not mirror the external world, which are independent even of grammar (Valéry 1957e). The author creates his effect by exploiting the evocative power of the words he uses, through an appeal to the memory and to the associative capacity of his reader (Valéry 1957b). In poetry, it seems that this evocative effect is produced by a dense concentration of emotionally charged elements. If the same effect is to operate in longer texts like novels, Valéry (1957d) recognizes that it must be achieved by a high frequency of elements which create a certain state of mind in the reader. This use of language is not, of course, the only tool at the novelist's disposal. Valéry (1957d) recognizes two others: plot and characterization. In doing so, he notes a distinction which most critics have overlooked. He does not say that plot, characterization and atmosphere imitate reality. He rather points out that they are fictions, to which the author gives a veneer of truth by introducing details drawn from real life.

Valéry (1957j) alludes to 'The Philosophy of Composition', and paraphrases in his own name Poe's declaration that all the elements in a work must combine to produce the final effect. He defines the novelist's goal as production of the suspension of disbelief (Valéry 1957h). He recognizes three means of achieving it: the evocative power of words, the fictitious structures of plot, characterization and atmosphere, and the introduction of true-to-life details. Thus the three means must work together for a common aim. This leads to the theoretical justification for our system.

In prose fiction, the evocative power which Valéry recognizes is, of necessity, created through frequent use of a single key word, or of words related to a single concept, that is to say a theme. Once the most frequent words or themes can be identified, the theme, or themes, can be related to the rest of the work in such a way as to shed light on the fictional structures of plot, characterization and atmosphere, and to show why the author chose to incorporate certain aspects of reality, rather than certain others, into his work. By providing factual information about themes, our system can lay solid foundations for interpretations of works of prose fiction.

eau	37	clapotis	3	bateau	1
coq	50	dériver	3	brouillard	1
fleuve	30	détremper	3	crues	1
humide	12	flaque	3	déborder	1
rive	12	flot	3	dégoutter	1
glisser	10	nager	3	dissoudre	1
pluie	10	pont	3	île	1
frais	9	sueur	3	inondation	1
mer	8	aborder	2	jaillir	1
boueux	7	estuaire	2	liquéfier	1
radeau	7	fontaine	2	marée	1
à bord	5	larme	2	mousse	1
bac	5	laver	2	noyer	1
brume	5	mouiller	2	océan	1
couler	5	navigation	2	pêcheur	1
embarcadère	5	port	2	pétrolier	1
flotter	5	salive	2	pleurer	1
digue	4	amarre	1	rivière	1
marine	4	amont	1	ruisseler	1
boire	3	au large	1	sécher	1
canots	3	aval	1		

Total: 302

Table 1. Words evoking water in 'La Pierre qui pousse'. Source: *Index des mots de Camus, L'Exil et le Royaume*, produced by the Centre d'Etude du Vocabulaire Français at the University of Besançon

Some examples can illustrate how this works. In 'La Pierre qui pousse', a short story by Camus, the theme of water is important: it is evoked 302 times in this 30-page text (see table 1). The water theme characterizes all the descriptions of the décor; it is linked to death, to solitude and to stone. The 'growing stone' mentioned in the title is produced by deposits left by the water of a spring; stone thus becomes a sort of quintessence of the entire décor and is related to solitude and to death. The picture of stones used to anchor slum hovels in place attaches to the theme of stone the concept of privation. Finally, a secondary character vowed to carry a 110-pound stone in a religious procession. When he can no longer continue, the main character takes it, and carries it, not to the church, but to the man's own house in the slums. Because of the thematic network including stone, misery, water, solitude, death and the décor, this gesture, quite clearly, has transcendent, or mythical, import; Camus is creating a secular myth of fraternal cooperation. This also explains in passing why the author chose constantly to stress the rain and the humidity of the décor.

Beckett's play, *En attendant Godot*, poses a problem because the characters' activity seems to be gratuitously incoherent. A concordance shows that the theme of doubt is evoked 76 times by the speeches of the two main characters, Vladimir and Estragon, and 329 times through hesitation required by the stage directions (see table 2). The author also introduced several insoluble contradictions into his text. Thus the theme of doubt is not a product, whose origins have to be traced in explaining the play, but a basic characteristic of the atmosphere. Vladimir and Estragon state that they find the atmosphere of doubt unbearable. Although Godot's identity and his very existence are problematic, every allusion to Godot presents him as capable of giving fixed form to the two main characters. Godot, it seems, could save them from the doubt which poisons their existence. Two minor characters, Pozzo and Lucky, embody a savage caricature of human society, one which applies equally to liberal and to communist society. This shows why Vladimir and Estragon do not give a form to their life by integrating themselves into society. The structures of the play explain the domination of doubt: this theme reflects black despair about all forms of human society. This type of pessimism was rampant among European intellectuals in the immediate post-war era, when Beckett was writing his play.

A. Expressions of doubt by Vladimir and Estragon

ne pas savoir	51	se demander	8	douter	3
oublier	8	le doute	6		

B. Hesitation required by stage directions

silence	117	hésiter	14	se recueillir	2
un temps	90	fouiller	13	repos	1
s'arrêter	62	chercher	12	se reprendre	1
réfléchir	17				

Total: 405

Table 2. Evocations of doubt in *En attendant Godot*.
Source: Computer-generated concordance to the play produced at the University of Saskatchewan, Regina Campus

Céline's first novel, *Voyage au bout de la nuit*, opens with the First World War; the protagonist then moves on, to Africa and to the United States, before settling down as a doctor in a Parisian slum. *Voyage au bout de la nuit* is considered to be one of the most pessimistic and depressing novels ever written in the French language. Some discoveries about the theme of violence show one means used to achieve this effect. Although war necessarily implies violence, analysis of the violence theme shows that it appears most frequently, not in the war section, but in the African section of the novel, where everything and everyone is dominated by biological forces (see table 3). Furthermore, the origins of the war are not mentioned; the text simply notes that 'it came out of the depths' (Céline 1962). The first description of the biological forces dominating in Africa is also presented as a revelation of the depths. The parallel inherent in the fact that violence, a concomitant of war, is most heavily concentrated where biological forces dominate—together with the common origin of war and of biological forces in the depths—makes war a biological phenomenon in *Voyage au bout de la nuit*. Since man is usually more sanguine about his ability to influence politics than about his control over biological forces, the extended comparison of war to a biological entity—like a sickness—is clearly one means used by Céline to create a pessimistic and depressing aura about his novel.

word	Tot	Gu	Af	EU	Ra	In	Vi
violence	4		1				3
violent	14	1		3	3	2	5
coup	186	34	23	14	46	27	42
balle	26	19	1		1		5
hurler	24	2	4		12		6
casser	22	5	1	5	3	3	5
torturer	15	5	2	3	2	2	1
brutal	14	5	2	1	2	1	3
haine	14	2	4	4	3		1
rage	14	6	2	1		3	2
éclater	13	3	4	2	2	1	1
brusquement	12	2	3	2	2	1	2
cogner	12	3		2	3	1	3
secouer	12	4	3		2		3
enrager	11	3	2		2		4
sauvage	11	1	8		2		
agressif	10	1	6		2		1
catastrophe	10		1	2	2	2	3
arracher	9	3		1	4		1
hostile	9	1		3	4		1
pétard	9				9		
furieux	8		1	3	2		2
tonnerre	8	2	4	1	1		
trique	8	2	6				
assaut	7	1	1	1	1	2	1
colère	7				2		5
gifle	7		1		2		4
brutalité	6	1	2	2	1		
fureur	6				3	1	2
rafale	6	1	2		1	1	1
rageur	6	2	2	1		1	

M

word	Tot	Gu	Af	EU	Ra	In	Vi
chicotte	5		4	1			
claquer	5	1			3		1
fracas	5	1	1	1	1		1
haineux	5	4			1		
haïr	5	2	1			2	
bombe	4			4			
bousculer	4	1			2		1
éclat	4	2		1	1		
étrangler	4	1			3		
étriper	4	3		1			
éventrer	4	2			2		
fracasser	4		2	2			
révolution	4			2	1		1
secousse	4			2	1		1
trombe	4		1	3			
viol	4		1	2			1
assaillir	3	1	1		1		
avalanche	3			1	1		1
brusque	3			2			1
chahuter	3				1		2
escrimer	3	2			1		
hostilité	3	1	2				
massacre	3	2	1				
massacrer	3	2				1	
trépigner	3	2	1				
bousiller	2	1	1				
brute	2	1					1
carnage	2		2				
effraction	2	1		1			
forcené	2		1				1
foudre	2			1	1		
gifler	2		2				
martinet	2				2		
riposter	2				2		
saccager	2	1			1		
sauvagement	2	1			1		
supplice	2			1	1		
torgnole	2				2		
virulent	2		1		1		
agresser	1		1				
agression	1	1					
agressivité	1		1				
assomer	1				1		
bagarre	1	1					
bourrasque	1						1
brandir	1		1				
brusquer	1	1					
cabosser	1						1
catastrophique	1			1			
choc	1			1			
collision	1						1
démolir	1				1		

word	Tot	Gu	Af	EU	Ra	In	Vi
estourbir	1				1		
étripade	1		1				
étripailler	1	1					
exploser	1				1		
explosif	1		1				
explosion	1	1					
fouet	1					1	
fouetter	1		1				
fracasseur	1	1					
hacher	1			1			
irruption	1				1		
lacérer	1		1				
massue	1				1		
néronien	1		1				
pilonner	1				1		
raclée	1				1		
regifler	1						1
sadisme	1	1					
s'engouffrer	1			1			
triquer	1			1			
violer	1	1					
vulnérer	1			1			
Grand total	679	148	117	82	157	52	123
Average	1·4	1·5	1·7	1·5	1·5	·9	1·3

Table 3. Words evoking violence in *Voyage au bout de la nuit*. Source: Computer-generated concordance to the novel produced at the University of Wisconsin, Madison. The six divisions of the table correspond to the six main sections of the novel, and are identified according to the following code:

Tot—total number of occurrences in the Pléiade Edition, 489 pp.

Gu—the war section, 100 pp. in the Pléiade Edition

Af—the African section, 70 pp. in the Pléiade Edition

EU—the American section, 56 pp. in the Pléiade Edition

Ra—the Rancy section, 107 pp. in the Pléiade Edition

In—the Intermediary section, 60 pp. in the Pléiade Edition

Vi—the Vigny section, 96 pp. in the Pléiade Edition

Average—the number of evocations divided by the number of pages

Although these studies were elaborated without the help of our system, they can stand as examples of how we intend to use it. We definitely are not interested in making broad extrapolations on the sole basis of the frequency of a given word or theme. We are much less interested in setting up computerized stylistics as an arcane pseudo-science, from the point of view of our more traditionally minded colleagues in literature departments. Our system will provide semi-processed material, to which the critic will apply his trained sensitivity and interpretative power. He will relate the data concerning themes to the other elements of the text, and formulate an interpretation which will account for much more than the frequency and distribution of words. Our system should, and must, lead to results justifiable in terms of an accepted theory of literature and capable of standing on their own merits as literary criticism.

Acknowledgements
The authors wish to thank the Canada Council for its continuing generous support of the work reported in this paper. They are also grateful to many persons for help and encouragement, particularly Michael Day, Queens University (Kingston), David Eaket, University of Saskatchewan (Regina), Francis Pardo (New York), and William Reid, University of Manitoba (Winnipeg).

REFERENCES
Baudelaire, C. (1933) Notes nouvelles sur E.A.Poe. *Nouvelles Histoires Extraordinaires*, pp. v-xxiii (ed. Crépet, J.) Paris: Conard.
Céline, L.-F. (1962) *Romans*. Paris: Gallimard.
Engwall, G. (1971) Etude sur la fréquence des mots dans quelques romans français (1962–1968), communication read at the XIIIth International Congress on Linguistics and Romance Philology. Québec, 25 Aug.–5 Sept.
Poe, E.A. (1927) The philosophy of composition. *The Poems and Three Essays on Poetry*, pp. 189-202 (ed. Johnson, R.B.). Oxford: Oxford University Press.
Salton, G. (1968) *Automatic Information Organization and Retrieval*. New York: McGraw-Hill.
Sedelow, S.Y. (1965) *Stylistic Analysis: Report on the First Year of Research*. Santa Monica: System Development Corp.
Valéry, P. (1957a) Discours au PEN Club. *Œuvres I*, pp. 1359-61 (ed. Hytier, J.). Paris: Gallimard.
Valéry, P. (1957b) L'Enseignement de la poétique. *Œuvres I*, pp. 1438-43 (ed. Hytier, J.). Paris: Gallimard.
Valéry, P. (1957c) Fragments des mémoires d'un poème. *Œuvres I*, pp. 1464-1491 (ed. Hytier, J.). Paris: Gallimard.
Valéry, P. (1957d) Hommage à Marcel Proust. *Œuvres I*, pp. 769-74 (ed. Hytier, J.). Paris: Gallimard.
Valéry, P. (1957e) L'Invention esthétique. *Œuvres I*, pp. 1412-15 (ed. Hytier, J.). Paris: Gallimard.
Valéry, P. (1957f) Poésie et pensée abstraite. *Œuvres I*, pp. 1314-39 (ed. Hytier, J.). Paris: Gallimard.
Valéry, P. (1957g) Poésie pure. *Œuvres I*, pp. 1456-63 (ed. Hytier, J.). Paris: Gallimard.

Valéry, P. (1957h) Propos sur la poésie. *Œuvres I*, pp. 1361-78 (ed. Hytier, J.). Paris: Gallimard.

Valéry, P. (1957i) Souvenirs littéraires. *Œuvres I*, pp. 774-84 (ed. Hytier, J.). Paris: Gallimard.

Valéry, P. (1957j) Sur la technique littéraire. *Œuvres I*, pp. 1786-8 (ed. Hytier, J.). Paris: Gallimard.

Valéry, P. (1960) Degas et le sonnet. *Œuvres II*, pp. 1207-9 (ed. Hytier, J.). Paris: Gallimard.

A project for computer-assisted analysis of French prose fiction, 1751–1800

Students of francophone literature are generally aware that prose fiction experienced intensive growth during the eighteenth century. Indeed, when one compares the number of titles written in the seventeenth century (Williams 1931) with the production during the first half of the eighteenth century (Jones 1939), approximately 1,000 titles are encountered in each period. The average annual rate of production, then, has doubled. A list of French prose fiction generated between 1751 and 1800 is presently being compiled by Professor Angus Martin (Macquarie University, New South Wales), Professor Vivienne Mylne (University of Kent at Canterbury) and myself. According to data which will be included in the forthcoming *Bibliographie du genre romanesque français*, it appears that the pattern of accelerating production continues to the end of the century, approximately 2,000 separate titles having so far been identified within the fifty-year period.

In view of this escalation, it would be useful to establish parameters capable of measuring the behavior of external and internal elements. For example, do descriptors such as titles and stated places of publication undergo significant change when two periods of production are compared? Again, in the case of the 1751–1800 list in which internal descriptors, when known, are included, do we find significant changes within a fifty-year span: for example, in preference of narrative locale, in the names and social station of characters? Thirdly, are there suggestions of cofrequency between internal and external parameters? Answers, even partial answers, to these questions may provide insight into authorial and public taste as evidenced in the appearance of francophone prose fiction during later years of the Enlightenment.

As a preliminary modus operandi, two five-year segments of the *Bibliographie du genre romanesque français* have been processed by an IBM 360/67, using the Computerized Language Analysis System (CLAS) written in PL/1, developed by Professor George Borden of the Pennsylvania State University (1971). Two pilot samplings embrace the novels and tales first published from 1751 through 1755, plus a second five-year period, 1771–75. Fiction first appearing in periodicals or collections has not been considered. Although separated by an interval of fifteen years, which witnessed the appearance of two landmarks in French prose fiction—Voltaire's *Candide* in 1759 and Rousseau's *La Nouvelle Héloïse* in 1761—the two populations are remarkably similar in raw quantity: 196 titles observed in the 1751–55 group; 200 titles in the

1771–75 group. Title word types exhibit a similar stability: 749 title word types in the 1750 group; 759 title word types in the 1770 group. In addition, there are 1,861 title word tokens in the 1750 group and 2,038 of the same in the 1770 lists.

This material when prepared for input was coded with the following parsing descriptors: nouns, proper nouns and names, adjectives, determiners (articles, possessive pronouns), pronouns, verbs (including participles used adjectivally), adverbs, prepositions, interjections, conjunctions (between similar parts of speech), connectives (in compound titles), plus symbols for omissions and subtitles. French diacritics were also retained.

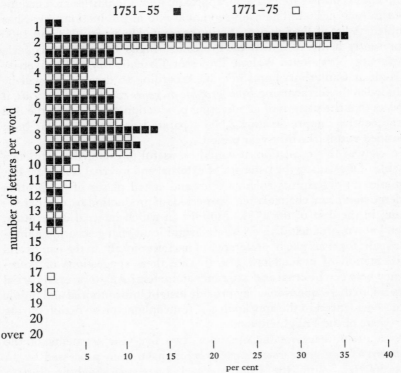

Figure 1. Title word lengths

For the present study basic output of the CLAS program provided (1) a profile of word lengths, (2) a concordance in ascending alphabetical order, (3) a word list of decreasing frequencies. The three types of output were generated for titles, stated places of publication, and for names of characters and locales of narrative action. A preliminary description of the computer-assisted analysis is presented herewith.

Beginning with word length of title vocabulary, the two populations 1751–55 and 1771–75 appear virtually identical (figure 1). Two-letter words account for about 33 per cent of both totals, with eight-letter words registering a second peak of about 12 per cent in both groups. The 1770 group, however, shows a higher incidence of length types, two of which run to seventeen/eighteen letters. Upon examination, these turned out to be, invariably, names of characters, usually coupled with a noble or religious tag: for example, *Le Chapelain Goodman*.

Title lengths within each period have been manually classified into three groups: titles of fifteen or more words; titles containing between six and fourteen words; titles of five words or less (table 1). The moderate 6-14 word groups appear most popular in both populations. A shift in popularity, however, is evidenced in the extremes, the 50s tending to prefer shorter titles, the 70s longer ones. The greater title length of the 70s parallels the trend to greater title word length. Application of a chi square test to title lengths within each period did not produce a level of significant difference on a ·05 scale. However, a chi square application to both title populations did indicate significant change (table 2). In brief, the 1770 title population is statistically distinct from the 1750 population in terms of anticipated rates of word occurrence.

	total	15+ words no/%	−6 words no/%	6-14 words no/%
1751	41	4/10	9/22	28/68
1752	44	4/09	7/16	33/75
1753	34	4/11	10/29	20/60
1754	35	4/11	3/08	28/81
1755	42	6/14	9/21	27/65
	196	22/11 /9%-14%/ ±5%	38/19 /08%-29%/ ±21%	136/69 /60%-81%/ ±21%
1771	49	5/10	7/14	37/76
1772	36	7/19	5/14	24/67
1773	36	7/19	5/14	24/67
1774	33	6/18	7/21	20/61
1775	46	12/25	1/02	33/73
	200	37/18 /10%-25%/ ±15%	24/12 /02%-21%/ ±19%	139/69 /61%-76%/ ±15%

Table 1. Title lengths

Compound titles (for example, *Louise ou le pouvoir de la vertu*) and multiple titles (that is, titles with more than one narrative or with subtitles) display higher variance in the 50s than in the 70s (table 3). Between 1751 and 1755 compound titles range between 16 and 42 per cent of the annual production. Between 1771 and 1775, on the contrary, the rate is more stable: 30 to 40 per cent of the annual production. Again, the

	+15 words	−6 words	6-14 words
1751	4	9	28
1752	4	7	33
1753	4	10	20
1754	4	3	28
1755	6	9	22
	observed $\chi^2=6\cdot5$		
1771	5	7	37
1772	7	5	24
1773	7	4	25
1774	6	7	20
1775	12	1	33
	observed $\chi^2=10\cdot4$		
totals			
1751–55	22	38	136
1771–75	37	22	139
	observed $\chi^2=7$		

Table 2. Chi square test of title lengths

	total	compound titles *with* ou no / %	multiple titles (*also subtitles—* et, suivi de) no / %
1751	41	14/34	3/07
1752	44	7/16	6/13
1753	34	9/26	4/10
1754	35	15/42	2/06
1755	42	15/35	1/02
	196	60/30 /16%-42%/	16/08 /02%-13%/
1771	49	20/40	12/24
1772	36	15/41	6/16
1773	36	13/36	3/08
1774	33	10/30	6/18
1775	46	18/39	8/19
	200	76/38 /30%-40%/	35/17 /08%-24%/

Table 3. Compound and multiple titles

multiple title group has a frequency range in the 50s between 2 and 19 per cent. In the 70s we note an annual fluctuation between a low of 8 per cent and high of 24 per cent. Obviously, both compound and multiple title forms are rising in popularity in the 1771–75 period and the two title

1751	1752	1753	1754	1755
3/03	3/06	4/03	2/04	3/05
3/12	1/02	4/27	5/04	7/04
3/15	2/03	3/09	3/03	3/08
3/04	4/05	8/05	3/05	10/06
5/06	1/03	4/05	1/06	2/12
3/05	3/04	3/09	2/05	3/05
4/03	3/08	4/05	4/07	5/05
3/04	17/31	6/06	1/06	7/05
1/03	48 total	1/04	3/13	1/03
3/15	6·8 aver.	37/73	4/04	3/01
3/05		110 total	5/05	5/06
2/05		12 aver.	4/19	3/06
3/04			3/>39 part omitted	3/09
7/03			2/09	3/04
52/90			1/10	3/09
142 total			43/139	61/88
10 aver.			182 total	149 total
			12 aver.	9·9 aver.

1771	1772	1773	1774	1775
3/04	1/09	2/04	3/02	5/05
3/14	4/18	1/09	3/03	2/03
4/05	1/05	5/06	3/10	6/08
2/15	2/20	3/03	2/05	3/04
2/08	1/03	4/07	4/16	1/06
4/03	5/11	11/10	4/05	4/16
4/06	4/02	4/05	3/14	7/05
2/06	1/04	2/04	3/07	3/19
2/05	4/05	3/05	3/05	7/01
5/11	4/29	4/05	4/12	1/02
1/05	2/02	3/03	35/79	1/06
4/03	7/04	2/04	114 total	4/01
2/05	3/07	4/04	11 aver.	1/05
2/11	3/03	48/69		4/03
6/04	3/05	117 total		1/06
6/08	45/127	9 aver.		1/02
4/19	172 total			6/13
1/03	11 aver.			3/05
1/07				60/110
3/03				170 total
61/50				9 aver.
211 total				
10 aver.				

Table 4. Compound titles containing *ou*. Comparison of 1st and 2nd parts. N.B. Phrases such as *conte allégorique* or *traduit de l'anglais*, which apply to both parts of the compound, have not been included in the above word counts

types would appear to account for much of the quantitative success of longer titles in the early 1770s.

The number of words occurring in each part of a compound title offers provocative behavior. Normally the second half of a compound title has the greater number of words (table 4). Seven exceptions, however, are observed in the early 50s and eight in the early 70s. When a chi square test is applied to the word counts in the first part of compound titles, no significance is noted between the 50s and the 70s (table 5). In the second half of compounds a chi square equal to 16·1 is noted, indicating a significant difference between the two populations. Comparison of the two compound groups taken in their entirety does not demonstrate significant difference between the two periods according to another chi square test. In raw occurrences as well, this class appears to have a stable frequency. Given the decrease in annual variance between the percentage of compound titles and non-compounds noted in the 70s, the compound title group would seem to be evolving toward more stereotyped applications, including satires.

First part	1	2	3	4	5 or more
1751–55	9	6	26	9	11
1771–75	14	13	17	19	12

The observed $\chi^2 = 7\cdot8$ appears barely significant at the ·1 level. The data suggest little or no difference between the two periods.

Second Part	less than 4	4	5	6 or more
1751–55	11	10	14	24
1771–75	18	9	17	32

The observed $\chi^2 = 16\cdot1$, a significant difference at the ·005 level.

Table 5. Length of compound titles containing *ou*

From the CLAS printout of decreasing frequencies, single title words and lemmas have been extracted manually according to frequency and also stability of frequency between the two periods. In this study 'high' frequency has been defined as no less than two occurrences. Stability was measured as a difference of no more than two between the two chronological populations (tables 6, 7, 8). Lemmas (shown in italics in the tables) are composed of words having morphological variants such as plurals, feminine or irregular endings, as well as words representing a common core of meaning (for example, vengeance, venger). Among the high-frequency words which are stable in both lists, twelve nouns comprise the largest syntactic group: auteur, *aventure*, *femme*, *isle*, monde, manu-

	1751–55	1771–75		1751–55	1771–75
à	35	36	monde	4	3
amusant	3	5	manuscrit	3	2
auteur	6	5	nouveau (adj.)	11	10
avec	7	5	œuvres	4	3
aventure	11	11	ou	3	2
contenant	3	2	par	18	16
dans	8	7	petit	2	3
dit	3	2	pièces	3	2
etc.	3	3	roi	3	2
femme	8	10	roman	4	6
galant	4	3	sur	5	4
grec	4	2	tiré	3	5
heureux	2	3	un	26	28
imité	3	4	véritable	3	5
isle	3	2	vie	3	4
italien	4	2	voyage	8	7
luimême	3	3		213	207

Table 6. High-frequency stable title vocabulary

High-frequency title vocabulary which increases in 1770s			High-frequency title vocabulary which decreases in 1770s		
	1751–55	1771–75		1751–55	1771–75
ami	4	7	ellemême	3	1
amour	8	17	fait	4	2
anecdote	6	26	fille	6	3
anglais	19	25	folie	4	2
conte	14	22	histoire	61	45
de	268	275	indien	5	2
en	12	16	oriental	4	2
et	61	70	ouvrage	10	6
français	6	13	on	18	7
homme	3	10	servir	7	4
le	235	254		$\chi^2 = 2{\cdot}8$	
lettre	14	23			
nouvelle	3	19			
ou	64	77			
Paris	2	5			
philosophe	5	11			
que	3	7			
sentiment	2	8			
traduction	25	40			
	$\chi^2 = 38{\cdot}2$				

Table 7

scrit, œuvres, pièces, roi, roman, vie, *voyage*. Eleven adjectival types follow closely: *amusant*, contenant, *galant*, *grec*, *heureux*, *imité*, *italien*, *nouveau*, *petit*, *tiré*, *véritable*. Next in type frequency are eight so-called function words: *à*, avec, dans, etc., ou, par, sur, *un*. Verbal forms (excluding verbal adjectives) are, predictably, low in frequency. The highest token frequencies occur among the function words. The most popular noun token frequencies are found in *aventure* (11), *femme* (8/10) and *voyage* (8/7). As a group, adjectives have the lowest token frequencies.

High-frequency title words used in 1750s only		High-frequency title words used in 1770s only	
23 types / 126 tokens		*30 types / 153 tokens*	
cabriolet	3	allemand	14
célèbre	3	beauté	3
chevalier	11	choix	6
Cythère	3	comique	3
comtesse	4	curieux	4
dédié	3	dames	3
délices	3	elle	4
docteur	3	école	3
écrit	4	écrit	4
est	3	effets	3
faux	3	édition	3
grâces	3	*époux*	3
heure	3	*épreuve*	8
jour	4	gaules	3
madame	6	jeune	10
mademoiselle	5	jolie	4
marquis	7	langue	3
monsieur	10	libre	3
mémoires	30	Londres	3
plaisir	4	leur	3
siècle	4	*moral*	18
vengeance	3	*poésies*	9
vraisemblance	4	*prince*	4
		propre	3
		Rosalie	3
		sans	4
		suivi de	6
		tableaux	4
		triomphe	4
		vertu	8

Table 8

If the stable high-frequency words give us a sense of continuity of public taste and authorial preference, the same is not true for words which increase or decrease in frequency between the two periods sampled. Nineteen words increase in frequency versus only ten whose popularity declines in the 70s (table 7). Four function words (en, et, ou, que) appear in the rising group in contrast with only one (*son*) in the descending frequency table. Application of a chi square test to the rising frequency population in table 7 indicates a significantly altered rate of collective use ($\chi^2 = 38\cdot2$). In the decreasing frequency group, the chi square rate is a mere 2·8.

As a general comment one is tempted to describe the list of rising frequency words in table 7 as cosmopolitan and sentimental: words such as *anglais, français, philosophe* and *traduction*, as well as sharp increases in *ami, amour* and *sentiment*. Also, increases in generic literary terminology such as *anecdote, conte, lettre* and *nouvelle* should be mentioned. The declining frequency list shows such words as *fille, folie, histoire, oriental* and *ouvrage* dropping in raw popularity. These words, in comparison with the rising frequency list, can be categorized as more imaginative, if not fanciful in connotation.

	1751–55	1771–75
France		
Paris	11	40
Paris–another town	23	90
Provinces	13	14
	47	144
Western European		
Dutch Provinces	62	57
Belgian Provinces	3	6
Swiss Cantons	5	12
German Provinces	15	11
Italian Provinces	4	3
Great Britain	43	41
	132	120
Non-Western European		
Orient and Africa	11	2
Fanciful	7	3
Central European	2	3
No Place	23	9
	43	17
Grand Totals	222	281

Table 9. Stated places of publication

Also of interest are the high-frequency words which occur only in one of the two periods. The 50s generate but 24 non-recurring types with 129 tokens. On the other hand the 70s display 30 unique types and 153 tokens. The highest raw frequencies in the 50s are found in the words chevalier (11), monsieur (10), *marquis* (7), *madame* (6) and mademoiselle (5), all terms of address or titles, plus mémoires (30). In the 70s the highest raw frequencies are *allemand* (14) and *moral* (18).

If one were to attempt to qualify briefly, at this point, the quantitative behavior of the words used in titles of prose fiction during the two periods surveyed, the 70s appear, without question, to be richer in high frequencies, more dynamic and more complex, despite a novelistic production numerically identical to the 50s.

A final category of external data has been derived from the stated places of publication for each title (table 9). In the three rubrics—France, Other Western European, Non-European—we note a trebling of stated places of publication in France, that is Paris, or Paris and another town. In the Other Western European group one observes a slight decrease in the 70s occasioned especially by minor declines in the Dutch provinces. More significant declines are registered throughout the Non-European group. Such shifts point not only to changes in taste, but also to censorship policies and to political and economic considerations: for example, the Seven Years War. Without question francophone fiction is more frequently claimed to be printed wholly or partially in France, especially Paris, in the 70s. The dramatic increase in tokens in the 70s indicating places of publication iterates the more avowedly cosmopolitan quality of this period, and the growing acceptability of the novel as a genre.

If we pass, briefly, to some internal data, names of characters and locales of narrative action, more differences than similarities would seem to be the order of the day. But first, a word of caution. Of the 196 titles recorded in the 50s, 32 items have not yet been located. In the present study contents are likewise unknown for 54 of the 200 titles listed in the 70s.

Some 208 character types and 569 character tokens have been processed during the 1750 period. In the 70s 231 character types and 565 tokens have so far been noted. A profile of the two populations (figure 2) shows that the 70s tend to longer names, a phenomenon which parallels the profiles of title word length in figure 1.

Among the most popular single names of heroines 'Julie' is the front-runner in the 50s (5 occurrences), followed closely by 'Rosalie' and 'Sophie' (4 occurrences each). In the 70s 'Sophie' takes a commanding lead (10 occurrences), followed by 'Adélaide' and 'Henriette' (5 occurrences each). 'Julie' occurs only four times in the later list. High-frequency masculine names in both printouts appear to be wrapped in titles of nobility. Most popular in the 50s is 'comte' (18 occurrences) and 'chevalier' (14 occurrences), closely followed by 'monsieur' (13); 'marquis' is noted 8 times. It should be pointed out that titles of nobility are in most instances accompanied by a surname. In the 70s the masculine order is somewhat altered: 'comte' occurs with about the same frequency as do 'marquis' and 'monsieur'; but the title of 'chevalier' is definitely less popular now. On the other hand, 'baron' is rising. Female titles of nobility remain relatively stable in frequency, unlike the names of heroines just noted. Of interest is the decline in types and tokens pertaining to noble titles. There are fewer mentions of titles of nobility, male and

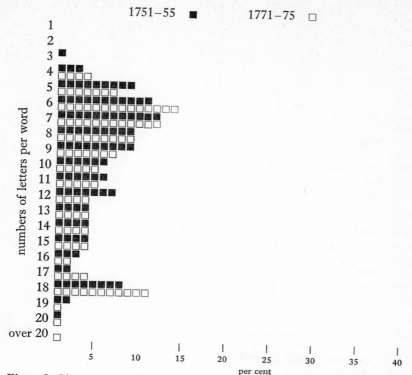

Figure 2. Character word lengths

female, in the 70s. A similar attrition can be observed in foreign (non-French) titles. The data suggest that characters in novels of the 70s are increasingly described as individuals rather than as social stereotypes, a development which predicates a rise in more realistic and sentimental types of fiction.

The locale of narrative action undergoes a number of shifts according to the contents surveyed to date. For example, one finds a rise in provincial attributions and a decline in Paris as a setting (table 10). In Other Western European locales, only Italy appears to change appreciably between the two periods (a rise from 6 to 11). In Non-European locales, there is a decline in oriental/African locales, and an incisive drop in fanciful locations. A chi square test comparing locales of action in the 50s with those in the 70s produces a significant level of difference: $\chi^2 = 9 \cdot 4$ with a significance level of $\cdot 01$.

Finally, one can attempt correlations between the external and internal data. We have already noted the parallel behavior of title word lengths and character word lengths. But does there appear to be a statistical likeness between stated places of publication and locale? A chi square test applied to the stated locales of narrative action and putative places of

N

	1751–55	1771–75
France		
Paris	42	24
Provinces	33	22
General	16	29
	—	—
	91	75
Western European		
Dutch Provinces	4	1
Belgian Provinces	3	1
Swiss Cantons	2	0
German Provinces	8	8
Italian Provinces	6	11
British Isles	20	24
	—	—
	43	45
Non-Western European		
Orient and Africa	35	22
Fanciful	45	15
East Europe	10	5
Americas	4	9
	—	—
	94	51

Table 10. Locales of narrative action. N.B. Of the 196 titles identified between 1751–55 and 200 between 1771–75 contents of only 165 and 139 respectively are surveyed herewith

publication in the 50s does not generate a significant difference ($\chi^2 = 3 \cdot 16$). The correlation of rates of occurrence, then, is close—another clue to the more homogeneous profile of the 1750 material. On the other hand, the relationship between place of publication and narrative locale in the 70s generates a high level of difference ($\chi^2 = 35$). This confirms the growing divergence between Paris as a preferred place of publication and the rising style of provincial locales for action.

   In conclusion, the quantification of external and internal data taken from the *Bibliographie du genre romanesque français* suggests a fruitful direction for further research. From the evidence presented herewith one begins to acquire a greater awareness of the parameters within which a specific work of fiction can be appreciated. As such, a novel appearing in the early 1750s may appear to be perfectly typical of the behavioral preferences of the day. Or again, the work may stand out as a maverick or strikingly original piece of literature. Taking again the two well-known examples of French fiction produced midway between the periods under analysis, Voltaire's *Candide* and Rousseau's *Héloïse*, both would appear to be closer to the norms of the 1770s than to those observed in the early 50s, although certain features of *Candide* (title length, locales and character types, for example) hark back to earlier preferences.

By way of a final comment, the quantitative similarity of the two populations in the 50s and 70s does not reflect the anticipated rate of increase in production during the second half of the eighteenth century. The observed production of new titles in the 70s appears particularly depressed by comparison with a projected output. In view of this depression the shifts from the habits and preferences of the 50s become even more significant, if we can conjecture that a more propitious politico-economic climate would have stimulated the production of fiction with a subsequent increase in the kinds of changes already noted. When the entire half-century has been machine-processed we will have a sensitive source of measurement that will lend itself to many applications, both within the literary domain and without. The comparisons and correlations presented in this communication, then, are but a hint of information which remains to be gleaned.

Acknowledgements
Input preparation and most manual classifications of output were supervised by Mrs Geoffrey Wilson, State College, Pa. Professor Thomas Hettmansperger, Department of Statistics, The Pennsylvania State University, performed all chi square tests. Funds for input preparation were provided by an in-house grant from funds allocated by the National Science Foundation.

REFERENCES
Borden, G. (1971) A computerized language analysis system. *Computers and the Humanities*, **5.3**, 129-41.
Jones, S.P. (1939) *A list of French prose fiction from 1700 to 1750*. New York: H.W. Wilson.
Martin, A., Mylne, V. & Frautschi, R. (in press) *Bibliographie du genre romanesque français*. London: Mansell.
Williams, R.C. (1931) *Bibliography of the Seventeenth-Century novel*. New York: Century.

Textual and metrical studies

Computer applications in textual criticism

The title of this paper and the fact that it is opening this section may have raised hopes that it contains an analysis of all possible computer aids in editing texts. This is not so; not only because the space available is too short for this, but mainly because I think that it conforms better to the aims of this collection to discuss experiences and results of practical work than to give a study of possible methods.

Therefore I want to make a double restriction to the title: (*a*) I will concentrate, after some preliminaries, on only one of the five steps necessary for textual editing, and (*b*) I will do this against the background of a single project, namely a large new critical edition of the Greek New Testament, of which the Epistle of St James is planned to appear about 1975.

Roughly speaking, one can distinguish five steps in the preparation of a critical edition (apart from such prerequisites as the collection of witnesses, etc.):

1. The *collation* of the manuscripts and other witnesses
2. the evaluation of step 1, that is, the *characterization* of the witnesses, the statement of their interrelationship
3. the constitution or *reconstruction of the text* to be edited
4. the *compilation of the apparatus criticus*
5. the *printing* of both text and apparatus

A critical edition aims at the results of step 3, namely a text which is as similar to the original as possible, and of step 4, the apparatus, which reflects the history of its transmission and represents the basis on which the edited text has been reconstructed by the editor. Step 5, the printing of text and apparatus, is only the means by which the results of steps 3 and 4 are fixed and disseminated, as it is for other kinds of publication.

Nevertheless, this last step has more weight for critical editions than for other publications: the best preparation of text and apparatus may be made almost worthless by such ugly things as misprints. Therefore, when the final publication is prepared in the traditional way, a great amount of time and accuracy is necessary for this last (and least interesting) phase. A whole series of new collations, similar to that of step 1, have to be made: first, the errors in the manuscript which goes to the printer must be eliminated; then, when the manuscript has been 'copied' by the compositor, the galleys must be collated against the manuscript—a work which is as necessary as tedious and time-consuming.

Recently it has become a truism that automatic photo-composition can help here to save much time and effort, and can guarantee correct and error-free reproduction of the manuscript, provided that it has been prepared in machine-readable format. Therefore it almost goes without saying that this will be the method of printing the New Testament edition.

A consistent application of photo-composition in textual editing does, however, not start with the transcription of the completely prepared text and apparatus on to paper tape or another data carrier. Consequently, when editing the N.T., we hope to be able to compile the apparatus automatically. Since the apparatus will be very extensive (about one page for one line or less of text), I think that this is the only means to provide error-free, complete and consistent data from the several hundred witnesses which will be represented there.

To compile the apparatus automatically will be possible when:

(*a*) all the readings of all the witnesses have been classified and stored in the computer, and when

(*b*) the text has been established, that is, when one reading from each set of variant readings (including the conjectures of the editor) has been adopted for the printed text.

This is quite simple in theory, but tends to become somewhat complicated in practice, especially when a large number of witnesses and variant readings must be handled. I would maintain that there is nowadays no other means than electronic data processing to guarantee the exactness, completeness and consistency legitimately required of a modern edition.

Electronic data processing allows us to handle larger masses of data with higher exactness than is possible by traditional methods. Of course, this automatic data manipulation cannot replace philological skills and decisions. The judgment of the truth or falsity of the readings, the restoration of the text, and the reconstruction of the history of its transmission remain the proper task of the textual critic; but the computer can guarantee consistent and error-free execution of the more mechanical part of the work which follows the philological one (steps 4 and 5, compilation of the apparatus, and final printing), and of the more mathematical part of the work which precedes the philological one, namely the classification of the witnesses and the definition of the relationship between them (step 2).

When done by computer, these classifications and definitions can be made on the basis of all existing readings of the manuscripts, and irrespective of whether these readings are true or false. There is no doubt that this is a firmer basis for philological judgment than could be supplied by traditional methods which rely on selected 'common errors' in the construction of a stemma, and which in practice run a double risk of argument in a circle: one, because a selection of 'significant errors' does seldom correspond to the rules imposed by statistics; the other circle consists in the very concept of 'common *errors*' which presupposes the knowledge of the correct text.

To sum up: by means of this new tool, which we have in electronic data processing, new and higher standards are imposed not only on the results of other sciences, but also on critical editions—standards which can scarcely be satisfied by traditional methods. This is, in my view, the main reason why electronic data processing should be employed in the preparation of critical editions, especially in large and complex projects. The question whether it is possible or not to save time and/or money by these methods is only of secondary importance. The expenses necessary for future critical editions may possibly be even higher than they have been in the past when these tools were not yet available.

For the rest of this paper I want to show how we try to cope with the large and complex tradition of the N.T. text. There exist about 5000 Greek manuscripts of the N.T., including the lectionaries, apart from other witnesses such as the translations and the quotations by Greek and Latin Fathers of the Church. It is obvious that no edition and no apparatus can specify all those witnesses completely. However, all the papyri and all the majuscule manuscripts will be represented with all their readings, but only a part of the 2768 known minuscule manuscripts can be specified.

In order to ascertain how many and which ones are to be chosen, all the manuscripts have been collated for 1000 selected passages of the N.T. Starting from this material, we try to get a preliminary classification of the manuscripts and definition of their mutual relations as a basis for deciding which of them shall appear in the apparatus. Some sample pages of computer output may help to clarify the procedure. The input data for these lists were the readings of 243 manuscripts at 30 selected passages out of the two Epistles of St Peter. However, the same or slightly modified programs will later process the complete text as contained in all the manuscripts selected for the edition.

For the 1000 test passages, one card was punched for each variant reading. This card contains a number identifying the passage (which represents a single word or a whole phrase), followed by the text of the reading and, on as many continuation cards as necessary, the Gregory numbers of the manuscripts which have this reading. For convenience of the transcription, these numbers may be typed in any order: they are checked and rearranged by the input program. (For the rest of the work, a paper tape equipment with Latin and Greek character font, including accents and breathings, will be used, thereby obviating the transcription of Greek characters which was necessary on the punched cards.)

It should, however, be noted that the classification programs which I am discussing are independent of the language of the text to be edited; they may be used also for other, non-Greek texts which have a large and complex tradition.

The first output of the program, after an unchanged listing of the input (and eventually error messages where some inconsistency in the input cards has been detected), is a list of all the witnesses which occurred on the input cards or paper tape. In this list, corrected manuscripts are listed as two separate witnesses; they have identical readings, except for the corrected passages. So, the 243 witnesses which occur in our 30 passages are physically only 209 manuscripts, of which 32 have corrections and/or marginal readings and therefore are treated as two or three witnesses.

The next list (see table 1) which is generated from the input data may be regarded as a preliminary critical edition with complete positive apparatus. For each passage, which is identified by its number as on the input card, first the reference and the context are printed as the heading line. Then follow the readings, which are numbered and sorted alphabetically (except the first one, which for convenience is that given by the largest number of manuscripts—in the New Testament, the KOINE-text). Then follow for each reading the Gregory numbers of the manuscripts which support the single readings.

The final 'Novi Testamenti Graeci Editio Maior Critica', a sample page of which appears in an article on this project by Aland (1969), will show a somewhat similar disposition. In the heading line, which contains the text, the single words and the spaces between them are numbered, as the passages are in our test material. The existing divergent readings will be printed immediately below this heading line, and will be identified by the letters b, c, d . . . besides the word-numbers. This method allows a quick view of the existing variant readings for each passage, and allows a simple and clear reference to the rest of the page, containing the apparatus, where the witnesses for each reading will be listed. More details may be found in the articles by Aland (1969) and Fischer (1970).

The next list (see table 2) gives a very concise synopsis of what was printed before in full (table 1). It shows, in the heading lines, the numbers of the passages and, below the passage-number, numbers indicating how many manuscripts have readings for the single passages, that is, how many manuscripts do not omit them for any reason, including damage to the document. On the left margin, there are printed a current numbering and the Gregory numbers of the manuscripts. Within the table itself are printed the numbers of the readings which the single manuscripts support at each passage. These numbers are identical to the numbers by which the variant readings are identified in the full list previously printed (table 1). So, for example, P 72 has for passage 26 the reading no. 3 (namely 'SINE ADD.', as can be seen by inspecting the list of table 1). Points behind the numbers appear in lines where corrected manuscripts are listed and mark those readings which are identical in the original manuscript and in the corrected one. The list which is reproduced here as table 2 is the second of two similar lists, namely the print-out of the program after the automatic elimination of the fragmentary witnesses (like P 74), and the witnesses which at all the passages have identical readings to one of the other witnesses. These witnesses (for the 30 passages of 1.2 Pt, consisting of 6 fragments, and 18 manuscripts identical to other witnesses) are listed separately and do not appear in the rest of the lists.

The next list (table 3) presents the material under a different aspect: it shows not the number of the reading which each manuscript has for each passage, but the size of the group of manuscripts which have the same reading for the specified passage. So, for example, the reading which P 72 has for passage 26 is supported by a total of 41 manuscripts. From this diagram, one may see at a glance where the single witnesses have a unique reading, not supported by any other manuscript (for example, P 72 for passages 29.39.40.53, or the corrector of the Codex Sinaiticus (01 C) for passage 27. Also cases like 01 and 01 C at passage 30 are to be noted here; this is a unique reading of 01 which has not been corrected by 01 C, as can be seen by inspecting the list of table 2).

This list gives a fairly good picture of the behaviour of the single witnesses: some have almost exclusively a series of high numbers behind them, as 020 or 025, etc. This means that those manuscripts are part of the KOINE-group which is represented by the mass of the minuscule manuscripts. Other manuscripts show both small and large numbers, for example, 01 or 03. These are manuscripts which are not part of the KOINE-group; the large numbers which occur there are caused by readings which they have in common with the KOINE-test. Inspecting this list not from left to right, but vertically, we get further information: we see by how many manuscripts the majority text is represented at the single passages. For passage 32, for example, there exist two nearly equivalent groups of 100 and 105 manuscripts; here the majority text is split into two.

The three lists which we have just discussed merely present the material as it results from the collation under different aspects and in different degrees of abstraction: table 1, which we called the 'preliminary edition', shows, in full text, the context of the examined passages and the existing variant readings with the witnesses supporting them. Table 2 abstracts the variant readings from the text and shows only the witnesses that support at the single passages identical readings, irrespective of how these readings differ from other readings. One must make use of list 1 to be able to decide this question. This abstraction permits, on the other hand, a much better synopsis of the material as regards the relationship between the single witnesses; in the single columns, identical numbers indicate identical readings supported by the manuscripts listed at the left margin. Table 3, showing the size of the groups of manuscripts that support the same reading, abstracts even from this aspect; to find out whether or not two manuscripts, for which in this list identical numbers are printed, support the same reading is possible only by means of list 2 (except of course for the number 1 and for large numbers). What all these three lists have in common is the fact that for each passage and for each of the witnesses a single characteristic is shown: in list 1, the text of a variant reading which it supports; in list 2, coincidence or divergence with other manuscripts at the single passages; in list 3, the number of other witnesses supporting the same reading for the single passages.

The next list (table 4), resembling a mileage chart such as one finds in motoring handbooks, goes only one step farther in that it abstracts from the single passages as well; it represents a similarity matrix, indicating how often (at how many passages) the two manuscripts listed above the columns and in front of the rows have the same reading. (Table 4 shows only the upper left corner of this matrix, containing the similarities of 25 manuscripts; the whole matrix produced for the 30 passages of 1.2 Pt has 219 rows and columns, namely for 243 manuscripts minus 6 fragments and 18 identical manuscripts, and occupies 23 printed pages. The programs can handle up to 2000 manuscripts.) Inspecting this matrix, one may, for example, state that 04 and 04C2 have 25 readings in common. However, these absolute values are not very practical for computing, since some manuscripts (as the 04) may have lacunae, and because those matrices may be compared with each other only when the numbers are in the same range, irrespective of how many passages have been checked. So a further list (not reproduced here) shows the same matrix, but the numbers no longer indicate the absolute number of coincidences, but the average ('percentage') values, that is the number of coincidences divided by the number of passages on which both manuscripts are present. High numbers in this matrix stand for close relationship of two manuscripts, low numbers indicate high dissimilarity.

Dom Quentin (1922) called these 'listes de concordance . . . l'un des plus utiles et des plus sûrs instruments de classement préliminaire'. But when they are compiled for as many witnesses as in our case, they become very bulky, and their usefulness is rather limited. Therefore, one must look for some computer aids for the evaluation of these large matrices, that is for the classification of the witnesses on the basis of the similarities listed there. For this purpose, a further list is compiled, showing for each manuscript the degrees of relationship or similarity to all the other witnesses; it brings together on to one page all the information for one manuscript which in the matrix is spread over several pages. Table 5 shows the page containing the percentages of coincidence of P 72 with the other manuscripts. These percentages are arranged in decreasing order, with the Gregory numbers of the witnesses listed behind the respective percentage values. So, we find, for example, a coincidence of exactly 60 per cent = at 18 of 30 passages between P 72 and the two manuscripts 03 (= Codex Vaticanus) and 1739. The second half of this list printed for each manuscript shows these relations graphically. The two diagrams display the distribution of the single manuscripts into 20 classes of relationship of 5, 10, 15, . . ., 95, 100 per cent. The numbers of manuscripts falling into the single classes are plotted in a linear (left curve) and a logarithmic scale (right curve). The exact numbers of manuscripts in the single classes and the cumulative totals are printed below the graphs. For P 72 we find, for example, that the largest group of 78 manuscripts is in the class 15-20 per cent, that is: 78 manuscripts agree with P 72 at 15-20 per cent of the 30 passages; the mean degree of relationship of P 72 to the other manuscripts is 26·37 per cent, with a standard deviation of 9·56. These curves and values are to some degree characteristic of the single manuscripts, as may be seen from table 6a, showing the graphs for 020, a majuscule manuscript of the KOINE-group: here, the maximum of 63 manuscripts is at the level of 75-80 per cent of coincidence, the mean being 72·57, the standard deviation 16·06, which is very similar to that of the minuscule manuscript 1521 with a mean of 72·47 and a standard deviation of 16·70 (table 6b).

When we now arrange the manuscripts in increasing order of these mean values of relationship, as is shown in table 7, this brings together those manuscripts with similar degrees of relationship to the rest of the witnesses. This has a similar effect to the construction of a 'spectrum line' by the taxonomic method which, as far as I know, J.G. Griffith (1969) was the first to apply to the classification of manuscripts. He starts directly from the similarity matrix and rearranges it by trial-and-error methods so that the high totals are located at the top left and bottom right-hand corner and along the diagonal line, and the low totals in the top right-hand corner. As a test shows, the order achieved by this method is similar, yet not identical, to that established by sorting the manuscripts according to the mean values of relationship to the other manuscripts. One of the main advantages of the latter method is that it needs much less computer time than the taxonomic one. In the right-hand part of table 7, the 'distances' between the ordered manuscripts (that is, the difference between the mean values of the similarities of two adjacent manuscripts) are calculated and plotted in a linear (left half of the graph) and a log-arithmic scale (right half). This can perhaps help to detect the 'clusters' of manuscripts which show the least differences.

We have not yet had enough experience to see how far statistical methods can help here. Therefore I have tried a further method to reveal the mutual relations of the manuscripts and to detect those groups of manuscripts which perhaps form a family. This program starts from the groups of manuscripts which at the single passages have a common reading. Table 8 shows a part of the output of this program. To each of the groups, a group identification consisting of three numbers is given; the first number indicates the size of the group, the second number is the current number of the first manuscript of the group, and the third number distinguishes, if necessary, group-identifications of groups with identical size and first manuscript. The groups are then listed in ascending order of size. The next step is to check if such a group occurs also as a part of a larger group of manuscripts occurring at another passage (in mathematical terms, if it is a sub-set of a larger set of manuscripts). A further step could be to try to detect also the 'hidden' groups or sub-sets, that is those groups of manuscripts which are common to two or more larger groups, but do not coincide at any passage. But this demands an immense amount of com-puter time, and my attempts to reduce computer time and, above all, the output of this program to a reasonable size are still too far from giving convincing results to be discussed here.

In conclusion, I need not emphasize that my attempts to use the computer to help with the problems of textual editing are very far from automatic textual criticism or textual editing in its philological phase. There are tasks in textual editing which should be wholly left to computers, such as the final printing. For the rest, the best that can be done to help the textual critic is to supply him with a firm basis for his work.

REFERENCES

Aland, K. (1969) Novi Testamenti Graeci Editio Maior Critica. Der gegenwärtige Stand der Arbeit an einer neuen großen kritischen Ausgabe des Neuen Testaments. *New Test. Stud.*, **16**, 163-77.

Fischer, B. (1970) The use of computers in New Testament studies, with special reference to textual criticism. *JThSt*, N.S. XXI. 297-308.

Griffith, J.G. (1968) A taxonomic study of the manuscript tradition of Juvenal. *Mus. Helv.* **15**, 101-38.

Quentin, H. (1922) *Mémoire sur l'établissement du texte de la Vulgate*. Rome and Paris: Desclée and Gabalda.

APPENDIX : TABLES

UEBERSICHT UEBER DIE BEZEUGUNG (ERGAENZT)
----

26   1.PT 1,22(1) EN TH YPAKOH THS ALHTHEIAS *ADD.* EIS PHILADELPH

       1 (193 ZEUGEN):   ADD.DIA PNEYMATOS

018	020	025	049	049C	056	0142	
61	61C	61MG	69	88	88C	93	
181	189	206	254	254C	255	296	3
330	363	378	393	398	398C	421	42
452	453	456	459	464	464C	465	46
617	619	619C	621	623	623MG	630	6
794	808	832	876	901	901C	901MG	9
1102	1175	1240	1240C	1245	1270	1292	12
1505	1509	1521	1524	1597	1599	1609	16
1678	1717	1719	1729	1734	1735	1736	17
1837	1838	1840	1842	1848	1849	1849C	18
1890	1890C	1895	2086	2100	2127	2130	21
2242	2243	2243C	2298	2356	2401	2412	24

       2 (1 ZEUGE):   ADD.DIA PNEYMATOS AGIOY

1104

       3 (41 ZEUGEN):   SINE ADD.

P72	01	01C	02	03	04	04C2	0
436	615	629	629C	945	1067	1241	12
1739	1739C	1845	1845C	1850	1852	1881	23

       4 (5 ZEUGEN):   LACUNA

P81	093	0206	631	1066

27   1.PT 1,22(2) EK *ADD.* KARDIAS ALLHLOYS AGAPHSATE

       1 (231 ZEUGEN):   ADD.KATHARAS

P72	01*	04	04C2	018	020	025	0
33	36	38	38MG	43	43C	61	
94	102	103	104	131	133	142	1
296	307	307C	309	312	321	322	3
393	398	398C	421	424	424C	426	4
456	459	464	464C	465	467	468	4
619	619C	621	623	623MG	629	629C	6
720C	794	808	832	876	901	901C	9
996	999	1067	1102	1104	1175	1240	12
1359	1360	1367	1398	1404	1409	1448	14
1563	1597	1599	1609	1610	1611	1611C	16
1719	1729	1734	1735	1736	1736C	1739	17
1837	1838	1840	1842	1845	1845C	1848	18
1882	1885	1886	1889	1890	1890C	1895	20
2147	2186	2197	2200	2242	2243	2243C	22
2495	2541	2544	2652	2674	2696		

       2 (1 ZEUGE):   ADD.*ALHTHINHS* SED POST *KARDIAS*

01C

Table 1

5	6	36	38	38MG	43	43C
2	103	104	131	133	142	180
7C	309	312	321	326	326C	326MG
4C	426	429	431	440	442	451
8	479	491	522	606	608	614
1	642	643	656	665	720	720C
4	915	918	927	959	996	999
5	1360	1367	1398	1404	1448C	1501
1	1611C	1643	1643C	1649	1661	1661C
1	1758	1765	1785	1827	1831	1832
5	1877	1877C	1882	1885	1886	1889
8	2143	2143C	2147	2186	2197	2200
5	2544	2652	2674	2696		

3	62	81	218	322	323	365
9	1409	1448#	1495	1495C	1563	1718
4	2492	2541				

9	049C	056	0142	4	5	6
MG	62	69	81	88	88C	93
	189	206	218	254	254C	255
	326C	326MG	330	363	365	378
	436	440	442	451	452	453
	522	606	608	614	615	617
	641	642	643	656	665	720
	914	915	918	927	945	959
	1243	1245	1270	1292	1297	1315
C	1495C	1501	1505	1509	1521	1524
	1649	1661	1661C	1678	1717	1718
	1758	1765	1785	1827	1831	1832
C	1850	1874	1875	1877	1877C	1881
	2127	2130	2131	2138	2143	2143C
	2374	2401	2412	2464	2492	2494

O

BEZEUGUNGSLISTE (ZAHLEN GEBEN NUMMER DER VARIANTE ZUR BE

		26	27	28	29	30	31	32	33	34	35	36	37
VORH.	ZEUGEN:	217	217	217	217	218	218	218	219	216	215	217	211
	GRGNR												
1:	P72	3	1	4	3	7	1	4	4	1	4	2	1
2:	01	3	1	4	1	2	4	4	4	3	9	3	5
3:	01C	3.	2	4.	1.	2.	1	4.	4.	3.	1	2	6
4:	02	3	3	4	1	3	4	4	4	3	1	2	4
5:	03	3	3	4	1	7	4	4	4	1	4	2	1
6:	04	3	1	4	1	7	1	4	4	3	4	1	
7:	04C2	3.	1.	4.	1.	7.	1.	4.	4.	3.	4.	1.	
8:	018	1	1	1	1	1	1	1	4	3	1	1	1
9:	020	1	1	1	1	1	1	2	1	10	1	1	1
10:	025	1	1	1	1	1	1	1	1	3	1	1	4
11:	044	3	1	4	2	3	1	4	4	1	4	2	1
12:	049	1	1	1	1	1	1	1	1	3	2	1	1
13:	049C	1.	1.	1.	1.	1.	1.	1.	1.	3.	3	1.	1.
14:	056	1	1	1	1	1	1	4	1	10	1	1	4
15:	0142	1	1	1	1	1	1	4	1	10	1	1	4
16:	4	1	1	2	1	5	1	4	1	10	1	3	1
17:	5	1	1	2	1	3	1	4	1	3	1	1	4
18:	6	1	1	1	1	5	1	1	1	10	1	1	4
19:	33	3.	1	4	1	1	1	4	4.	3			4
20:	36	1	1	1	1	5	2	1	1	10	1	1	4
21:	38	1	1	1	1	3	1	1	1	10	1	3	1
22:	43C	1.	1.	1.	1.	1	1.	1.	1.	3	2	3.	1.
23:	61	1	1	1	1	1.	1	4	3	11	9	3	1
24:	61C	1.	1.	1.	1.	1.	1.	4.	3.	11.	9.	1	1.
25:	61MG	1.	1.	1.	1.	1.	1.	4.	1	11.	9.	1.	1.
26:	62	3	1	1	1	1	1	1	4	10	6	2	1
27:	69	1	1	1	1	3	1	1	1	10	9	3	1
28:	81	3	1	4	1	7	4	4	4	3	1	2	4
29:	88	1	1	1	1	1	1	1	1	10	1	3	4
30:	88C	1.	1.	1.	1.	1.	1.	1.	1.	10.	1.	3.	4.
31:	93	1	1	1	1	1	1	1	1	3	1	3	1
32:	94	1	1	1	1	5	2	1	1	10	1	1	3
33:	102	1	1	1	1	5	1	1	1	10	1	3	4
34:	103	1	1	1	1	1	1	4	1	10	1	3	4
35:	104	1	1	3	1	1	1	4	1	10	1	3	4
36:	131	1	1	1	1	1	1	1	1	3	2	1	1
37:	133	1	1	1	1	5	1	1	1	10	1	1	1
38:	142	1	1	1	1	7	1	4	1	10	9	3	1
39:	180	1	1	1	1	5	2	1	1	10	1	1	4
40:	181	1	1	2	1	1	1	3	1	10	1	1	1
41:	189	1	1	1	1	5	1	1	1	10	1	1	4
42:	206	1	1	1	1	1	1	4	1	1	1	3	4
43:	218	3	1	1	1	5	1	4	1	3	1	3	4
44:	254	1	1	1	1	1	1	4	1	10	1	3	4
45:	254C	1.	1.	1.	1.	1.	1.	4.	1.	10.	1.	3.	4.
46:	255	1	1	1	1	1	1	1	1	1	1	1	1
47:	296	1	1	1	1	5	1	1	1	10	1	1	1
48:	307	1	1	1	1	1	1	1	4	10	1	3	4
49:	307C	1.	1.	1.	1.	1.	1.	4	4.	10.	1.	3.	4.
50:	309	1	1	1	1	1	1	1	1	3	1	1	1
51:	312	1	1	1	1	3	1	1	4	10	1	1	1
52:	321	1	1	1	1	1	1	1	1	10	1	3	1
53:	322	3	1	4	1	1	1	4	4	10	4	2	4
54:	323	3	1	4	1	1	1	4	4	10	4	2	4
55:	326	1	1	1	1	1	1	4	4	10	1	1	1
56:	326C	1.	1.	1.	1.	1.	1.	4.	4.	10.	1.	1.	4
57:	326MG	1.	1.	1.	1.	1.	1.	4.	1	10.	1.	1.	4.
58:	330	1	1	1	1	1	1	1	1	3	2	3	1
59:	363	1	1	1	1	3	1	4	1	3	1	3	1
60:	365	3	1	1	1	1	1	1	4	10	5	2	1

Table 2

(STSTELLE AN)

9	40	41	42	43	44	45	46	47	48	49	50	51	52	53	54	55
5	215	214	214	218	217	218	215	215	216	216	217	218	215	217	217	217
7	5	14	2	2	2	9	2	1	7	3	6	2	3	11	2	1
2	1	1	3	1	1	1	2	3	7	3	3	2	3	1	1	1
2.	1.	1.	3.	1.	1.	1.	1	1	7.	3.	3.	2.	3.	1.	1.	1.
2	6	7	3	1	1	5	1	1	4	3	3	2	1		2	1
2	6	15	3	2	2	9	2	4	7	1	6	2	3	9	2	2
		6	3	1	2	8	1	1	4	3	6	1	2	3	2	1
		6.	3.	1.	1	8.	1.	1.	4.	3.	6.	1.	2.	3.	2.	1.
4	1	1	1	1	1	1	1	1		2	1	1	3	1	1	1
1	1	1	1	1	1	1	1	1	1	2	1	1	1	1	1	1
1	6	3	5	1	9	2	1	9	3	6	2	3	3	1	1
6	8	2	1	1	1	2	1	7	3	3	2		1	2	1
4	1	1	1	1	1	1	1	1	1	1	1	1	1	1	1
4.	1.	1.	1.	1.	1.	1.	1.	1.	1.	1.	1.	1.	1.	1.	1.
4	1	1	1	1	1	1	1	1	3	1	1	1	2	1	1
4	1	1	6	1	1	1	1	1	1	1	1	1	2	1	1
1	1	1	1	1	1	1	1	1	5	1	1	1	1	1	1
7	6	1	1	1	1	1	1	1	7	3	1	6	4	2	1
4	14	1	1	2	1	1	1	15		3	2	1	1	2	1
7		1	2	1		15				3	2	1	1	1	1
1	6	1	1	1	1	1	1	7	1	6	1	1	1	1	1
4	1	1	1	1	1	1	1	1	4	1	1	1	1	3	1
4.	1.	1.	1.	1.	1.	1.	6	1.	1.	1.	1.	1.	1.	1.	1.
1.	1.	1.	1.	1.	1.	1.	1.	1.	1.	1.	1.	1.	1.	1.	1.
1.	1.	1.	1.	1.	1.	1.	1.	1.	1.	1.	1.	1.	1.	1.	1.
4	1	1	1	1	1	1	1	1	1	1	1	1	1	1	1
7	6	1	1	1	1	1	1	8	1	1	1	1	8	1	1
7	6	1	1	1	3	1	1	5	3	3	1	6	7	1	1
1	7	1	1	1	1	1	1	3	1	1	2	1	1	1	1
1.	7.	1.	1.	1.	1.	1.	4	3.	1.	1.	2.	1.	1.	1.	1.
4	1	1	1	1	1	1	1	1	1	1	1	1	1	1	1
4	1	1	1	1	1	5	1	1	7	5	6	1	1	1	1
1	1	1	1	1	1	1	1	1	1	3	1	1	1	1	1
1	6	1	1	1	1	1	1	11	5	3	2	1	2	1	1
4	13	1	1	1	1	2	1	1	1	1	1	1	1	1	1
4	1	1	1	1	10	1	1	1	1	1	1	1	1	1	1
1	1	1	1	1	1	1	1	1	1	1	1	1	1	1	1
1	1	1	1	1	1	1	1	4	1	1	2	1	1	1	1
4	1	1	1	1	1	9	1	1	1	1	1	1	1	1	1
7	15	1	1	1	9	1	1	1	3	4	1	1	10	1	1
1	6	1	1	1	6	1	1	8	3	1	1	1	9	1	1
1	15	1	1	1	6	1	1	8	3	5	1	1	9	1	1
1.	15.	1.	1.	1.	6.	1.	1.	2	3.	5.	1.	1.	9.	1.	1.
1	1	1	1	1	1	1	1	6	2	2	1	1	1	1	1
1	1	1	1	10	1	1	1	6	5	3	2	1	1	1	1
1	6	1	1	1	1	1	1	7	1	6	1	1	1	1	1
1.	6.	1.	1.	1.	1.	1.	1.	7.	1.	6.	1.	1.	1.	1.	1.
4	1	1	1	1	1	1	1	7	4	1	1	1	1	1	1
4	1	1	1	1	1	1	1	1	3	6	1	1	1	1	1
1	1	1	1	1	1	9	1	7	1	6	1	1	1	1	1
7	3	3	1	1	1	9	1	4	3	6	2	3	9	1	1
7	3	3	1	1	1	9	1	7	3	6	1	3	9	1	1
1			1	1	1	1	1	1	1	1	1	1	1	1	1
1.			1.	1.	1.	1.	1.	1.	1.	3	1.	1.	1.	1.	1.
1.			1.	1.	1.	1.	1.	1.	1.	3.	1.	1.	1.	1.	1.
4	1	1	1	1	1	1	1	1	5	1	1	1	1	1	1
1	1	1	1	1	11	1	1	1	1	1	1	1	1	1	1
4	1	1	1	1	1	1	1	1	1	1	1	1	1	1	1

BEZEUGUNGSLISTE KUMULATIV (ZAHLENANGABEN BETREFFEN GROESS...

GRGNR		TESTST. 26	27	28	29	30	31	32	33	34	35	36	37
	VORH. ZEUGEN:	217	217	217	217	218	218	218	219	216	215	217	211
1:	P72	41	213	31	1	28	209	105	45	34	13	52	110
2:	01	41	213	31	213	2	4	105	45	49	20	75	1
3:	01C	41	1	31	213	2	209	105	45	49	155	52	2
4:	02	41	3	31	213	19	4	105	45	49	155	52	96
5:	03	41	3	31	213	28	4	105	45	34	13	52	110
6:	04	41	213	31	213	28	209	105	45	49	13	90	
7:	04C2	41	213	31	213	28	209	105	45	49	13	90	
8:	018	175	213	170	213	111	209	100	45	49	155	90	110
9:	020	175	213	170	213	111	209	11	169	120	155	90	110
10:	025	175	213	170	213	111	209	100	169	49	155	90	96
11:	044	41	213	31	3	19	209	105	45	34	13	52	110
12:	049	175	213	170	213	111	209	100	169	49	6	90	110
13:	049C	175	213	170	213	111	209	100	169	49	1	90	110
14:	056	175	213	170	213	111	209	105	169	120	155	90	96
15:	0142	175	213	170	213	111	209	105	169	120	155	90	96
16:	4	175	213	11	213	50	209	105	169	120	155	75	110
17:	5	175	213	11	213	19	209	105	169	49	155	90	96
18:	6	175	213	170	213	50	209	100	169	120	155	90	110
19:	33	41	213	31	213	111	209	105	45	49			96
20:	36	175	213	170	213	50	3	100	169	120	155	90	96
21:	38	175	213	170	213	19	209	100	169	120	155	75	110
22:	43C	175	213	170	213	111	209	100	169	49	6	75	110
23:	61	175	213	170	213	111	209	105	3	3	20	75	110
24:	61C	175	213	170	213	111	209	105	3	3	20	90	110
25:	61MG	175	213	170	213	111	209	105	169	3	20	90	110
26:	62	41	213	170	213	111	209	100	45	120	1	52	110
27:	69	175	213	170	213	19	209	100	169	120	20	75	110
28:	81	41	213	31	213	28	4	105	45	49	155	52	96
29:	88	175	213	170	213	111	209	100	169	120	155	75	96
30:	88C	175	213	170	213	111	209	100	169	120	155	75	96
31:	93	175	213	170	213	111	209	100	169	49	155	75	110
32:	94	175	213	170	213	50	3	100	169	120	155	90	1
33:	102	175	213	170	213	50	209	100	169	120	155	75	96
34:	103	175	213	170	213	111	209	105	169	120	155	75	96
35:	104	175	213	5	213	111	209	105	169	120	155	75	96
36:	131	175	213	170	213	111	209	100	169	49	6	90	110
37:	133	175	213	170	213	50	209	100	169	120	155	90	110
38:	142	175	213	170	213	28	209	105	169	120	20	75	110
39:	180	175	213	170	213	50	3	100	169	120	155	90	96
40:	181	175	213	11	213	111	209	1	169	120	155	90	110
41:	189	175	213	170	213	50	209	100	169	120	155	90	96
42:	206	175	213	170	213	111	209	105	169	34	155	75	96
43:	218	41	213	170	213	50	209	105	169	49	155	52	110
44:	254	175	213	170	213	111	209	105	169	120	155	75	96
45:	254C	175	213	170	213	111	209	105	169	120	155	75	96
46:	255	175	213	170	213	111	209	100	169	34	155	90	110
47:	296	175	213	170	213	50	209	105	169	120	155	90	110
48:	307	175	213	170	213	111	209	100	45	120	155	75	96
49:	307C	175	213	170	213	111	209	105	45	120	155	75	96
50:	309	175	213	170	213	111	209	100	169	49	155	90	110
51:	312	175	213	170	213	19	209	100	45	120	155	90	110
52:	321	175	213	170	213	111	209	100	169	120	155	75	110
53:	322	41	213	31	213	111	209	105	45	120	13	52	96
54:	323	41	213	31	213	111	209	105	45	120	13	52	96
55:	326	175	213	170	213	111	209	105	45	120	155	90	110
56:	326C	175	213	170	213	111	209	105	45	120	155	90	96
57:	326MG	175	213	170	213	111	209	105	169	120	155	90	96
58:	330	175	213	170	213	111	209	100	169	49	6	75	110
59:	363	175	213	170	213	19	209	105	169	49	155	75	110
60:	365	41	213	170	213	111	209	100	45	120	9	52	110

Table 3

R MSS-GRUPPE MIT GLEICHER VARIANTE)

40	41	42	43	44	45	46	47	48	49	50	51	52	53	54	55
215	214	214	218	217	218	215	215	216	216	217	218	215	217	217	217
1	2	2	2	11	25	8	197	26	71	26	48	19	1	14	207
109	113	14	209	206	162	8	1	26	71	23	48	19	158	202	207
109	113	14	209	206	162	207	197	26	71	23	48	19	158	202	207
3	5	14	209	206	10	207	197	23	71	23	48	178		14	207
3	29	14	2	11	25	8	3	26	113	26	48	19	25	14	10
	36	14	209	11	5	207	197	23	71	26	170	2	3	14	207
	36	14	209	206	5	207	197	23	71	26	170	2	3	14	207
60	113	194	209	206	162	207	197		113	141	170	19	158	202	207
109	113	194	209	206	162	207		142	7	141	170	178	158	202	207
109	36	14	2	206	25	8	197	3	71	26	48	19	3	202	207
3	2	2	209	206	162	8	197	26	71	23	48		158	14	207
60	113	194	209	206	162	207	197	142	113	141	170	178	158	202	207
60	113	194	209	206	162	207	197	142	113	141	170	178	158	202	207
60	113	194	209	206	162	207	197	142	71	141	170	178	10	202	207
60	113	194	1	206	162	207	197	142	71	141	170	178	10	202	207
109	113	194	209	206	162	207	197	142	18	141	170	178	158	202	207
37	36	194	209	206	162	207	197	26	71	23	170	13	10	14	207
60	2	194	209	206	162	207	197	142	4	141	170	178	158	202	207
37			209	11	162			1		23	48	178	158	14	207
109	36	194	209	206	162	207	197	26	113	26	170	178	158	202	207
60	113	194	209	206	162	207	197	142	4	141	170	178	158	1	207
60	113	194	209	206	162	207	1	142	113	141	170	178	158	202	207
109	113	194	209	206	162	207	197	142	113	141	170	178	158	202	207
109	113	194	209	206	162	207	197	142	113	141	170	178	158	202	207
109	113	194	209	206	162	207	197	142	113	141	170	178	158	202	207
60	113	194	209	206	162	207	197	142	113	141	170	178	158	202	207
37	36	194	209	206	162	207	197	3	113	141	170	178	1	202	207
37	36	194	209	206	2	207	197	3	71	23	170	13	2	202	207
109	5	194	209	206	162	207	197	2	113	141	48	178	158	202	207
109	5	194	209	206	162	207	3	2	113	141	48	178	158	202	207
60	113	194	209	206	162	207	197	142	113	141	170	178	158	202	207
109	113	194	209	206	10	207	197	26	18	26	170	178	158	202	207
60	113	194	209	206	162	207	197	142	113	141	170	178	158	202	207
109	113	194	209	206	162	207	197	142	71	141	170	178	10	202	207
109	36	194	209	206	162	207	197	3	18	23	48	178	158	202	207
60	3	194	209	206	3	207	197	142	113	141	170	178	158	202	207
60	113	194	209	206	3	207	197	142	113	141	170	178	158	202	207
109	113	194	209	206	162	207	197	142	113	141	170	178	158	202	207
60	113	194	209	206	162	207	197	142	4	141	170	178	158	202	207
109	113	194	209	206	162	207	197	23	113	141	48	178	158	202	207
37	29	194	209	206	25	207	197	142	71	13	170	178	3	202	207
109	36	194	209	206	162	207	197	142	71	141	170	178	158	202	207
109	29	194	209	206	3	207	197	3	71	10	170	178	25	202	207
109	29	194	209	206	3	207	197	5	71	10	170	178	25	202	207
109	113	194	209	206	162	207	197	1	113	1	170	178	158	202	207
109	113	194	209	206	3	207	197	142	18	23	48	178	158	202	207
109	36	194	209	206	162	207	197	26	113	26	170	178	158	202	207
109	36	194	209	206	162	207	197	26	113	26	170	178	158	202	207
60	113	194	209	206	162	207	9	142	4	141	170	178	158	202	207
60	113	194	209	206	162	207	197	142	71	141	170	178	158	202	207
109	113	194	209	206	162	207	9	23	113	26	170	178	158	202	207
37	4	14	209	206	25	207	197	23	71	26	48	19	25	202	207
37	4	14	209	206	25	207	197	26	71	26	170	19	25	202	207
109			209	206	162	207	197	142	113	141	170	178	158	202	207
109			209	206	162	207	197	142	113	23	170	178	158	202	207
109			209	206	162	207	197	142	113	23	170	178	158	202	207
60	113	194	209	206	162	207	197	142	18	141	170	178	158	202	207
109	113	194	209	206	1	207	197	142	113	141	170	178	158	202	207
60	113	194	209	206	162	207	197	142	113	141	170	178	158	202	207

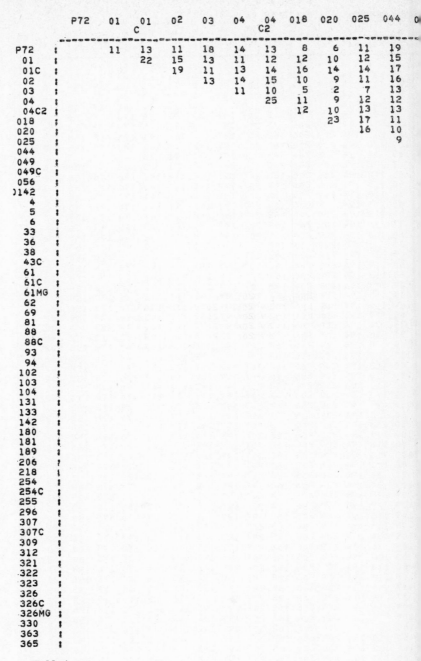

	P72	01	01C	02	03	04	04C2	018	020	025	044	0
P72		11	13	11	18	14	13	8	6	11	19	
01			22	15	13	11	12	12	10	12	15	
01C				19	11	13	14	16	14	14	17	
02					13	14	15	10	9	11	16	
03						11	10	5	2	7	13	
04							25	11	9	12	12	
04C2								12	10	13	13	
018									23	17	11	
020										16	10	
025											9	
044												
049												
049C												
056												
)142												
4												
5												
6												
33												
36												
38												
43C												
61												
61C												
61MG												
62												
69												
81												
88												
88C												
93												
94												
102												
103												
104												
131												
133												
142												
180												
181												
189												
206												
218												
254												
254C												
255												
296												
307												
307C												
309												
312												
321												
322												
323												
326												
326C												
326MG												
330												
363												
365												

Table 4

49	056	0142	4	5	6	33	36	38	43 C	61	61 C	61 MG
6	7	7	7	9	7	11	6	6	5	7	7	7
10	10	9	12	11	8	14	10	9	11	13	12	12
13	14	13	15	15	12	15	13	12	12	14	14	14
9	12	11	10	15	9	15	10	10	8	9	9	9
3	2	2	3	4	2	9	4	2	3	4	4	4
10	11	10	9	14	9	12	10	8	8	9	10	10
11	12	11	10	15	10	11	11	9	9	9	10	11
26	22	21	20	17	23	11	20	22	24	22	23	23
25	25	24	25	17	25	10	22	24	23	24	25	26
16	17	17	13	16	15	9	18	13	14	13	14	15
10	10	9	11	14	10	14	9	11	9	11	11	11
29	24	23	22	17	25	11	21	24	28	24	25	26
	24	23	22	17	25	11	21	24	27	24	25	26
		29	23	20	24	11	21	23	22	22	23	24
			22	19	23	10	20	22	21	21	22	23
				18	24	10	21	24	22	24	23	24
					17	13	19	17	15	15	16	17
						9	23	26	23	21	22	23
							9	9	11	11	11	11
								20	19	19	20	21
									24	22	21	22
										24	23	24
											29	28
												29

```
P72    ( 30 TESTSTELLEN, DAVON  4 SINGULAER = 13.33%,

65.52%= 19/ 29  044
63.33%= 19/ 30 1739C
60.00%= 18/ 30   03      1739
53.85%= 14/ 26   04
53.33%= 16/ 30 1243      1852      1881
50.00%= 15/ 30  322       323       945      1241
50.00%= 13/ 26  04C2
47.83%= 11/ 23   33
46.43%= 13/ 28 2464
43.33%= 13/ 30  01C      1448      1735
37.93%= 11/ 29   02       629
36.67%= 11/ 30   01       025        81       424C      1175      1448C
               1505      2138      2541
34.48%= 10/ 29 2495
33.33%= 10/ 30  218       623      1067      1359      1409      1563
               1718      2298      2374      2412
32.00%=  8/ 25 1875
30.00%=  9/ 30    5        62       307C       365       398       398C
                431       436       614        621       623MG     629C
                642       876      1661       1765      1845      1850
               1895      2200      2492
28.57%=  8/ 28  326
27.59%=  8/ 29  018       808      1611
26.67%=  8/ 30  142       206       296        307       312        426
                442       522       606        630       832        996
               1495      1495C    1611C      1661C      1831      1838
               1890      2147      2243
25.00%=  7/ 28 326C
24.14%=  7/ 29  467       619      1270   .   1785
24.00%=  6/ 25 1066


                    110
                    100
                     90
                     80    ⋮
                     70    ☰
                     60    ☰
                     50    ☰☰.
                     40    ☰☰☰
                     30    ☰☰☰
                     20    ☰☰☰
                     10    ☰☰☰☰☰  ..
                         --==+==--+-==-+-==-+

P72              0     0    2    78   51   46   12   11    3
SUMMEN           0     0    2    80  131  177  189  200  203   2
UEBEREINST.(%) 5.0  10.0 15.0 20.0 25.0 30.0 35.0 40.0 45.0  5
```

Table 5

EHRHEITSTEXT = 23.33%)

```
23.33%=  7/ 30   056    0142        4        6       61      61C
                 61MG    104      181      254     254C      255
                 363     378      393      452      456      459
                 615     641      643      901      914      915
                 918    1292     1315     1367     1501     1524
                1609    1717     1729     1837     1840     1842
                1845C   1874     1889     1890C    2401
21.43%=  6/ 28   326MG  2127
20.69%=  6/ 29   619C   1297
20.00%=  6/ 30   020     049      049C      36       38       69
                  88      93       94      103      131      133
                 321     330      421      453      464      464C
                 465     479      491      608      617      636
                 656     720      794      901C     901MG    913
                 927     999     1104     1240     1240C    1245
                1404    1521     1678     1719     1734     1751
                1827    1848     1877     1877C    1882     1886
                2131    2143     2143C    2242     2544     2652
20.00%=  5/ 25  2696
19.05%=  4/ 21   665
18.18%=  4/ 22   631
17.86%=  5/ 28  1736    1736C
17.39%=  4/ 23  2130
17.24%=  5/ 29  1360
16.67%=  5/ 30   43C      88C     102      189      309      440
                 468     720C     959     1509     1643     1643C
                1649    1849C    1885     2086     2356
13.79%=  4/ 29  2674
13.33%=  4/ 30   180
```

```
     *
   ***
   ***
   *****
   ***** **
   *********
   **********
----+----+----+----+ MITTELW. = 26.37, STREUUNG =  9.56
4    2     1    1     0     0     0     0     0     0
4   216   217  218   218   218   218   218   218
.0 60.0  65.0 70.0  75.0  80.0  85.0  90.0  95.0 100.0
```

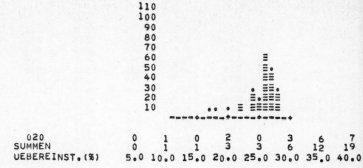

Table 6a

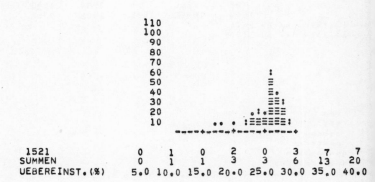

Table 6b

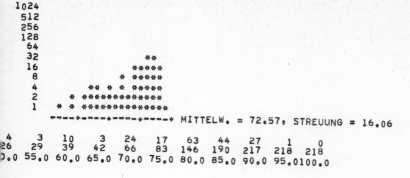

```
1024
 512
 256
 128
  64
  32                      **
  16                      *****
   8              *      *****
   4        ** **  *  *  *****
   2     *  **************
   1   *  *  ******************
    ----+-----+-----+-----+  MITTELW. = 72.57, STREUUNG = 16.06

  4     3    10     3    24    17    63    44    27     1     0
 26    29    39    42    66    83   146   190   217   218   218
).0 55.0 60.0 65.0 70.0 75.0 80.0 85.0 90.0 95.0100.0
```

```
1024
 512
 256
 128
  64
  32                   **
  16                   *****
   8              *******
   4        ** *  ********
   2     *  **************
   1   *  *  ******************
    ----+-----+-----+-----+  MITTELW. = 72.47, STREUUNG = 16.70

  5     2     9    14    18    16    58    36    28     8     1
  8    30    39    53    71    87   145   181   209   217   218
 .0 55.0 60.0 65.0 70.0 75.0 80.0 85.0 90.0 95.0100.0
```

HANDSCHRIFTEN GEORDNET NACH AUFSTEIGENDEM MITTELW.

1	5	03	MITTELW. =	16.24,	STREUUNG =	11.1
2	1	P72	MITTELW. =	26.37,	STREUUNG =	9.5
3	183	1852	MITTELW. =	29.93,	STREUUNG =	10.5
4	125	1175	MITTELW. =	31.05,	STREUUNG =	7.7
5	2	01	MITTELW. =	36.70,	STREUUNG =	6.9
6	129	1243	MITTELW. =	37.40,	STREUUNG =	9.7
7	11	044	MITTELW. =	38.02,	STREUUNG =	7.3
8	4	02	MITTELW. =	38.56,	STREUUNG =	8.5
9	6	04	MITTELW. =	39.35,	STREUUNG =	8.5
10	167	1739	MITTELW. =	40.48,	STREUUNG =	12.0
11	128	1241	MITTELW. =	40.71,	STREUUNG =	9.6
12	53	322	MITTELW. =	42.77,	STREUUNG =	10.4
13	7	04C2	MITTELW. =	42.82,	STREUUNG =	8.2
14	145	1505	MITTELW. =	43.49,	STREUUNG =	9.3
15	214	2495	MITTELW. =	43.52,	STREUUNG =	8.7
16	168	1739C	MITTELW. =	43.54,	STREUUNG =	11.5
17	54	323	MITTELW. =	44.70,	STREUUNG =	9.8
18	63	398	MITTELW. =	46.03,	STREUUNG =	6.6
19	188	1881	MITTELW. =	46.07,	STREUUNG =	8.6
20	28	81	MITTELW. =	46.27,	STREUUNG =	7.9
21	19	33	MITTELW. =	47.29,	STREUUNG =	7.9
22	3	01C	MITTELW. =	47.31,	STREUUNG =	7.3
23	118	945	MITTELW. =	48.81,	STREUUNG =	8.8
24	64	398C	MITTELW. =	49.90,	STREUUNG =	7.0
25	212	2464	MITTELW. =	49.93,	STREUUNG =	9.2
26	10	025	MITTELW. =	50.55,	STREUUNG =	7.2
27	200	2138	MITTELW. =	51.48,	STREUUNG =	8.5
28	92	623	MITTELW. =	53.62,	STREUUNG =	8.2
29	207	2298	MITTELW. =	55.65,	STREUUNG =	7.5
30	151	1611	MITTELW. =	55.95,	STREUUNG =	9.4
31	94	629	MITTELW. =	56.02,	STREUUNG =	8.5
32	17	5	MITTELW. =	56.14,	STREUUNG =	8.0
33	86	614	MITTELW. =	56.68,	STREUUNG =	8.8
34	93	623MG	MITTELW. =	56.73,	STREUUNG =	9.0
35	96	630	MITTELW. =	57.06,	STREUUNG =	9.1
36	217	2652	MITTELW. =	57.15,	STREUUNG =	9.7
37	211	2412	MITTELW. =	57.16,	STREUUNG =	8.5
38	83	522	MITTELW. =	57.30,	STREUUNG =	9.5
39	95	629C	MITTELW. =	57.70,	STREUUNG =	9.7
40	164	1735	MITTELW. =	59.12,	STREUUNG =	7.0
41	61	378	MITTELW. =	59.36,	STREUUNG =	9.8
42	152	1611C	MITTELW. =	60.21,	STREUUNG =	9.6
43	203	2147	MITTELW. =	60.67,	STREUUNG =	8.7
44	140	1448	MITTELW. =	60.87,	STREUUNG =	7.2
45	177	1842	MITTELW. =	61.16,	STREUUNG =	10.1
46	132	1292	MITTELW. =	61.23,	STREUUNG =	9.6
47	42	206	MITTELW. =	61.65,	STREUUNG =	10.0
48	204	2200	MITTELW. =	61.93,	STREUUNG =	9.6
49	148	1524	MITTELW. =	62.00,	STREUUNG =	10.4
50	175	1838	MITTELW. =	62.25,	STREUUNG =	10.5
51	32	94	MITTELW. =	62.36,	STREUUNG =	12.7
52	71	442	MITTELW. =	62.82,	STREUUNG =	9.2
53	66	424C	MITTELW. =	63.11,	STREUUNG =	11.2
54	218	2674	MITTELW. =	63.27,	STREUUNG =	15.6
55	213	2492	MITTELW. =	63.65,	STREUUNG =	11.0
56	30	88C	MITTELW. =	63.66,	STREUUNG =	12.9
57	75	459	MITTELW. =	63.96,	STREUUNG =	11.0
58	91	621	MITTELW. =	63.96,	STREUUNG =	8.6
59	115	915	MITTELW. =	64.11,	STREUUNG =	10.9
60	35	104	MITTELW. =	64.13,	STREUUNG =	11.3
61	193	1890	MITTELW. =	64.50,	STREUUNG =	10.0
62	44	254	MITTELW. =	64.52,	STREUUNG =	10.5
63	45	254C	MITTELW. =	64.55,	STREUUNG =	10.5

Table 7

S VERWANDTSCHAFTSPROFILS   * = 0.1%, LINEAR   *=0.01% LOG

```
TTELW.-ABST =  10.13********************************************** **********
TTELW.-ABST =   3.56      *********************************************** *********
TTELW.-ABST =   1.12                               *********** *******
TTELW.-ABST =   5.65********************************************** **********
TTELW.-ABST =   0.69                               ****** *******
TTELW.-ABST =   0.62                               ****** ******
TTELW.-ABST =   0.55                               ***** ******
TTELW.-ABST =   0.78                               ******* *******
TTELW.-ABST =   1.14                             ********** *******
TTELW.-ABST =   0.23                                 ** *****
TTELW.-ABST =   2.06           ********************** ********
TTELW.-ABST =   0.05                                 * ***
TTELW.-ABST =   0.67                               ******* *******
TTELW.-ABST =   0.03                                  **
TTELW.-ABST =   0.02                                  **
TTELW.-ABST =   1.16                           ********** *******
TTELW.-ABST =   1.33                         *********** ********
TTELW.-ABST =   0.04                                  **
TTELW.-ABST =   0.20                               ** *****
TTELW.-ABST =   1.03                          ********** *******
TTELW.-ABST =   0.01                                  *
TTELW.-ABST =   1.51                      ************** ********
TTELW.-ABST =   1.08                        *********** *******
TTELW.-ABST =   0.04                                  **
TTELW.-ABST =   0.62                               ****** ******
TTELW.-ABST =   0.92                          ********* *******
TTELW.-ABST =   2.15          *********************** ********
TTELW.-ABST =   2.03          *********************** ********
TTELW.-ABST =   0.30                               *** *****
TTELW.-ABST =   0.06                                 * ***
TTELW.-ABST =   0.12                                 * ****
TTELW.-ABST =   0.54                               ***** ******
TTELW.-ABST =   0.05                                 * ***
TTELW.-ABST =   0.34                               *** ******
TTELW.-ABST =   0.09                                 * ***
TTELW.-ABST =   0.01                                  *
TTELW.-ABST =   0.14                                 * ****
TTELW.-ABST =   0.40                               **** ******
TTELW.-ABST =   1.42                     ************** ********
TTELW.-ABST =   0.24                               ** *****
TTELW.-ABST =   0.86                          ********* *******
TTELW.-ABST =   0.45                               ***** ******
TTELW.-ABST =   0.20                               ** *****
TTELW.-ABST =   0.29                               *** *****
TTELW.-ABST =   0.07                                 * ***
TTELW.-ABST =   0.42                               **** ******
TTELW.-ABST =   0.28                               *** *****
TTELW.-ABST =   0.07                                 * ***
TTELW.-ABST =   0.25                               *** *****
TTELW.-ABST =   0.11                                 * ****
TTELW.-ABST =   0.46                               ***** ******
TTELW.-ABST =   0.28                               *** *****
TTELW.-ABST =   0.17                               ** *****
TTELW.-ABST =   0.37                               **** ******
TTELW.-ABST =   0.02                                  *
TTELW.-ABST =   0.30                               *** *****
TTELW.-ABST =   0.01                                  *
TTELW.-ABST =   0.15                                ** ****
TTELW.-ABST =   0.02                                  *
TTELW.-ABST =   0.37                               **** ******
TTELW.-ABST =   0.02                                  *
TTELW.-ABST =   0.03                                  **
TELW.-ABST =   0.11                                 * ****
```

20/2/1   (126. GRUPPE)

```
.X.. .... .... .... ....    ..XX X.X.. .... .... .X..   .... .... .... ..
.... .... .... .... ....    .... .... .... .X.. .X..   .X.. X... .X.. ..
.... ...X ... .X.. .X.
     01     61     61C    61MG    69    142      440      1315     140
   1882    1889    2356    2495    2674
   1 MAL KOMMT DIESE HSS-GRUPPIERUNG VOR, UND ZWAR IN (TESTST./VARIANTE):
35/ 9
   3 WEITERE BELEGE FINDEN SICH BEI FOLGENDEN GRUPPEN-NUMMERN:
   172      178       179
```

23/4/1   (127. GRUPPE)

```
...X .XX. .... .... ....    .... .... .... .... ...X   .... .... ...X X.
...X .... ..XX .X..    ..X.. .... .... .... ....   .... ...X .... X.
.... ..X. .... .... X..
     02     04     04C2    181     321      322      378      436      44
    918     945    1067    1524    1643    1678    2298    2652
   1 MAL KOMMT DIESE HSS-GRUPPIERUNG VOR, UND ZWAR IN (TESTST./VARIANTE):
48/ 4
   3 WEITERE BELEGE FINDEN SICH BEI FOLGENDEN GRUPPEN-NUMMERN:
   174      176       178
```

23/2/1   (128. GRUPPE)

```
.XXX .... ..X. .... X.X.    .... ...X .... ..X. ....   .... ..X. .... ..
.... .X.. .... .... ....    .... .... .... .... ....   .... .X.. .... ..
.... ...X. .... ..
     01     01C     02     044      5       33      81     104     29
   623MG    794    1509    1735    1838    1842    1848    2464
   1 MAL KOMMT DIESE HSS-GRUPPIERUNG VOR, UND ZWAR IN (TESTST./VARIANTE)
50/ 3
   1 WEITERER BELEG FINDET SICH BEI FOLGENDER GRUPPEN-NUMMER:
   175
```

25/5/1   (129. GRUPPE)

```
.... X... .... .... ....    .... .... .... .... ....   ...X X... .... X:
.... .... .... .... .X..    .... ...X ...X .... ....   ...X X..X ..XX ..
...X ..X. .... .X.. ...
     03     254    254C    322     323      398    398C     614      6:
   1611    1611C    1739    1739C    1852    1881    2138    2200    22
   1 MAL KOMMT DIESE HSS-GRUPPIERUNG VOR, UND ZWAR IN (TESTST./VARIANTE)
53/ 9
   ALS UNTERGRUPPE EINER GROESSEREN HSS-GRUPPE KOMMT DIESE HSS-KOMBINA
```

25/1/1   (130. GRUPPE)

```
X... X... .X.. .... ....    .... .... .... .... ....   .X.. .... .... X:
.... .... .... .... .X..    .... X..X X... .... ....   .... X... .... .
...X ..X. ..X. XX.. ...
     P72     03     025    206     322      323      522      614      6
   1739    1739C    1852    1881    2138    2200    2298    2412    24
   1 MAL KOMMT DIESE HSS-GRUPPIERUNG VOR, UND ZWAR IN (TESTST./VARIANTE)
45/ 9
   ALS UNTERGRUPPE EINER GROESSEREN HSS-GRUPPE KOMMT DIESE HSS-KOMBINA
```

Table 8

```
•••  ••••  ••••  •X••  ••••  ••••     ••••  ••••  •••  ••••  ••••
•••  •X••  XX••  ••••  ••••  ••••     ••••  ••••  X••X  ••••  ••••
1495      1505      1609      1729    1736      1736C
```

```
••  X•••  ••••  X•X•  X•••  ••••     ••••  •X••  •••X  X•••  ••••
••  ••••  ••••  ••••  ••••  ••••     ••••  ••••  ••••  ••••  ••••
453       614       623       623MG  720       915
```

```
••  ••••  •••X  ••••  ••X•  ••X•     ••••  ••••  •••X  X•••  ••••
••  •••X  ••••  ••••  ••X•  X••X     ••••  ••••  ••••  ••••  ••••
326C      326MG    431       459     467       623
```

```
••  ••XX  ••••  ••••  ••••  ••••     ••••  •X••  ••••  •••X  ••••
••  ••••  ••XX  ••••  ••••  ••••     ••X•  •••X  ••••  ••••  •••X
945       1241     1292      1501    1505      1524
495
```

CHT VOR

```
•   ••••  ••••  ••••  ••••  ••••     ••X•  •X••  ••X•  •••X  ••••
•   ••••  ••XX  ••••  ••••  ••••     ••X•  •••X  ••••  ••••  •••X
630       945       1175     1241    1243      1505
495
```

CHT VOR

Algorithms, *stemmata codicum*
and the theories of Dom H. Quentin

In recent years considerable effort has been directed toward putting the
humanities on a more rigorous and rational basis. Scholars have frequently
been criticized by those who find the classical procedures logically insufficient and who propose to rectify these deficiencies by the use of new
logical or mathematical techniques.

It must be admitted that it is not unusual to find examples of papers
whose conclusions are meaningless, either because an arbitrary interpretation has been added to a simple description of raw data, or because
although a procedure claimed to be scientific has been used, this procedure
has nowhere been described in any detail and so, in effect, remains completely subjective (Laurier 1971).

In my opinion, however, the charge of lack of rigour has often been
exaggerated and unduly sweeping. As regards textual criticism, the fundamental methodological problems have long been fully recognized
by scholars in the field, and the various methods of reconstituting texts
were analyzed in depth long before the current wave of methodological
criticism arose (Quentin 1926; Bédier 1928; Dain 1932; Pasquali 1952).

I do not believe, therefore, that one can expect quick solutions to old
problems by the use of new techniques in textual criticism, nor indeed in
the humanities generally. On the other hand, it would be foolish to ignore
the contributions which such new methods can make within certain
limits. They oblige philologists to maintain a high standard of rigour,
while freeing them from tedious mechanical operations of the *collatio
codicum* type. They may help to clarify certain as yet unsettled aspects of
the methodology of textual criticism, for example, the precise functions
of *stemmata codicum*, the concept of archetype, and the problem of
'bifides' and 'multifides' *stemmata*.

Within these limits, it seems to me that, initially at least, the use of
experimental computer algorithms in textual criticism will be more useful
than attempts to construct mathematical theories. In the entire field of
the humanities only the first steps have been taken in the search of general
laws, so that opportunities for the use of mathematics are limited (Hockett
1968; Gardin 1971).

We can define an algorithm as a fixed sequence of specified steps which
leads in an unambiguous way from given data to well-defined results
(Markov 1962; Marcus, Nicolau and Stati 1971). Thus to formulate
a research procedure as an algorithm does not require mathematical
theory, but it does require that all the concepts involved be made explicit

P

and precise, and that the algorithm itself be defined clearly and comprehensively. This does not necessarily involve using a computer. In fact, the first experiments using algorithmic procedures with non-numerical data were performed before the computer era.

On the other hand a computer can function *only* when controlled by an algorithm. Thus it can be used only when the procedure it is to carry out has been specified with the precision indicated above. Using a computer permits us to put the concept of an algorithm to the maximum use: any illogicality or ambiguity will be detected since it will give rise to erroneous or nonsensical results.

This is, in my opinion, the most important motivation for the use of computers in textual criticism: the computer offers principally a contribution to clarification, at least in the sense of a distinction between what may be specified in the form of an unambiguous and repeatable procedure, and what may be left to the critical intuition and experience of each scholar.

THE 'PRO' AND 'CONTRA' OF THE DOM QUENTIN METHOD

In the spirit of the preceding paragraphs, my work during the last few years has been chiefly directed towards an algorithmic specification of the *recensio* method of Dom H. Quentin (Quentin 1922, 1926). From the theoretical point of view this choice does not involve real limitations, since the fundamental problems of *recensio* (the selection of basic elements for the *stemma* construction, interpolation and polygenesis, likelihood of 'planes hautes', and so on) are almost the same in any methodology.

From the practical point of view, however, Quentin's method is the only one which deals in a regular manner with interpolation phenomena, keeping track of them during the very construction of *stemma*. It seems to me that this advantage is particularly valuable, because of the interest of being able to treat automatically the most confused, thus most interpolated, textual histories.

Quentin's original procedure is open to three fundamental criticisms. The first concerns the discrimination between 'variants' and 'errors'. His procedure does not permit any such distinction to be drawn, with the result that it is impossible to distinguish between 'concurrence in innovation', which is the only kind of agreement significant for the formation of families, and 'concurrence in conservation'. Typically, this leads to an erroneous multiplication of subarchetypes in order to justify the agreement of correct readings, the reality being an independent derivation of certain manuscripts from the archetype (Zarri 1969).

Consider the following *ad hoc* example. Suppose we find the famous 'arma virumque' in four manuscripts A, B, C, D, in the two last of which 'arma' has been transformed into 'asma', which is obviously an error. For Quentin the two readings 'arma' and 'asma' form two equivalent variants, and the linkage of the four manuscripts in one *stemma* must therefore be as shown in figure 1, in which the subarchetypes α and β have been introduced respectively to justify the agreement of *A* and *B* on 'arma', and *C* and *D* on 'asma'. But the 'concurrence in conservation' on 'arma' has no value, and the real situation is shown in figure 2, where *A* and *B* derive quite independently the correct reading 'arma' from the archetype *x*.

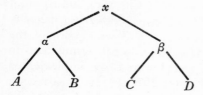

Figure 1

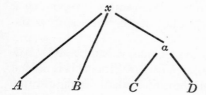

Figure 2

This is a defect which is at the heart of the method, and is thus impossible to correct during its practical use. It is worth noting that this defect is shared by all the methods based solely upon 'variants'; consequently the recent suggestion of Froger (Froger 1968), who proposes an *a posteriori* critical study of Lachmannian type, is valuable also in our case.

The other two criticisms are concerned more with the logical formulation of the method than with fundamentals. They have been previously formulated by Dain in his paper for the Nîmes Congress of 1932 (Dain 1932), and recently confirmed by the author in experimental computer work (Zarri 1969). The first relates to the basic operation of Dom Quentin's method which is the elimination of the 'nonsignificant variants', suspected to have entered the different manuscripts independently (proper noun variants, systematic errors of dictation and copying, and so on). Quentin fails to specify exhaustively the criteria for this selection, which is thus liable to become somewhat arbitrary and subjective. Interestingly, this subjectivity is very like that inherent in the Lachmannian choice of 'characteristic errors', which Dom Quentin severely criticizes.

Furthermore, according to Quentin, 'significant variants' only are to be considered in the search for 'characteristic zeros', that is to say in the construction of 'elementary *stemmata*'. But he does not specify in an unambiguous way the criteria for linking these 'elementary *stemmata*' together to obtain a single stemmatic structure. This disadvantage is obviously the most important from a practical point of view, because it prevents the systematic use of the method and its careful validation in concrete cases.

Up to now I have been principally concerned with the elimination of this last defect in Quentin's strategy, and so I have modified it principally in the stage following the finding of 'characteristic zeros'. Briefly, the *collatio codicum* operation is retained as in the original formulation, in order to keep a 'positive' apparatus. In recent years I have implemented several *collatio* algorithms (Zarri 1968, 1969, 1971a). The most recent, which has reached an adequate degree of generality, keeps track of the 'shifts' concerning any number of items (words or punctuation marks, in the case of 'word for word' *collatio*) without excessively increasing the computation time. A 'shift' occurs when two texts have to be moved to one another in the core store in order to put them into correspondence after an *addidit* or *omisit* (Zarri 1971a). The 'degree' of a shift is the number of items involved.

The next step, the choice of 'significant variants', is hampered by lack of precision in the selection rules as indicated earlier. Since this is indeed an operation more suitable for philological intuition than for algorithmic formulation, my procedure is for the moment an interactive one. This entails the philologist's evaluation of the results obtained with a certain criterion of choice, the modification of this choice leading to new stemmatic constructions, a new evaluation, and so on.

The search for 'characteristic zeros' and 'intermediate' manuscripts also follows the original formulation. According to this, a manuscript is 'intermediate' between two others only if, from the examination of 'significant variants', the latter *never* ('characteristic zero') agree with each other in discordance with the former. In Quentin's view the aim is the construction of 'elementary *stemmata*', in order to overcome the lack of orientation inherent in the 'intermediate' concept. He does this by producing four geometrical figures which can be associated with each triplet of manuscripts marked by a 'zero' (Quentin 1926).

I have abandoned this approach because of the above mentioned ambiguity concerning the role of 'elementary *stemmata*' in the final synthesis. Furthermore, the constructions indicated by Quentin do not take into account all the possible orientations which may be linked to a 'characteristic zero' (Zarri 1971a). I have therefore preferred a strategy which leads to an undirected final *stemma* without any attempt at orientation during the construction. This position does not entail an important loss of generality, and is undoubtedly more consistent with the fundamental decision to use the 'variants' rather than 'errors' (see in this connection the analogous position of Froger (Froger 1968)).

I shall now briefly describe my proposals for transforming also the last part of Quentin's method into algorithmic procedure.

'Chains' and 'Stemmata'

My first algorithm for the use of 'intermediate' relations obtained during the search for 'zeros' was based on a very simple observation. I had noticed that certain 'linear' sequences of manuscripts $A-B-C-D-...$ established from the 'zeros' using simple transitive properties like 'B is intermediate between A and C, and C between B and D' happened sometimes to converge on some manuscripts, giving rise to phenomena which can be interpreted either in terms of interpolation, or of archetype or subarchetype derivation.

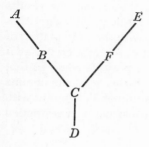

Figure 3

This is a quite trivial remark: for example, if it is possible from the study of 'zeros', to establish independently of one another two 'chains', $A-B-C-D$ and $E-F-C-D$, we can reasonably assemble them into a structure like that shown in figure 3. The real stemmatic construction can be of the inverted type, that is, D can act as an archetype (my aim is to obtain, as mentioned above, undirected *stemmata*). But undoubtedly these intersections give rise to embryos of *stemmata*.

Then by forming all the chains compatible with the 'zeros' distribution for a certain set of manuscripts, we can hope to reach, using their interrelations, one or more complete stemmatic structures. The algorithm for the construction of the chains is as follows. First we assemble all the triplets which it is possible to form from the n manuscripts under consideration, and then isolate those characterized by a 'zero'. We now examine all the combinations formed by *four* manuscripts. Each of these can be split into four triplets, possibly characterized by a 'zero'. It is now easy to decide if the four manuscripts form a chain: for example, in the case of the set $ABCD$, where we suppose A 'intermediate' between C

and *D*, *B* between *A* and *D*, and also *B* between *C* and *D*, while the triplet *ACD* has no 'zero', we will have

$$
\begin{array}{llll}
A & B & C & D \\
ABC &   & C & A & B \\
ABD &   &   & A & B & D \\
ACD &   & \emptyset \\
BCD &   & C &   & B & D \\
\hline
    &   & C & A & B & D
\end{array}
$$

Hence the result here is the chain *CABD*, keeping in mind that the real 'origin' can be either *C* or *D*.

Once every group of four manuscripts has been examined, and all the possible chains obtained, each subset of size five is considered, split into the five subsets each of four manuscripts and checked, by using the preceding results, to see if the linearity hypothesis is verified. The algorithm proceeds then to the examination of the subsets of size six, seven, and so on, using at each step, for the construction of the chains, the results obtained from the subsets analyzed in the previous step. The algorithm terminates in one of two ways: either it can stop with the examination of the subset which coincides with the original set of *n* manuscripts, or if none of the subsets of a certain size have given a positive result so that there is no way of continuing the construction. Either way one obtains all the chains of the size at which the algorithm terminated, together with possible chains of smaller size whose progressive construction was stopped earlier.

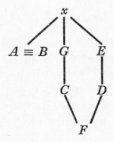

Figure 4

For example, an application of this algorithm to the 'zeros' distribution proposed by Quentin for the 'Lai de l'Ombre' (Quentin 1926, pp. 147-164) gave an undirected construction which, 'hanging' from the hypothetical lost manuscript *x*, had a shape, as shown in figure 4, not very different from Quentin's *stemma* (figure 5), except for the *codex descriptus* characterization assumed by the *C* and *D* manuscripts in front of *G* and *E* (Zarri 1971a).

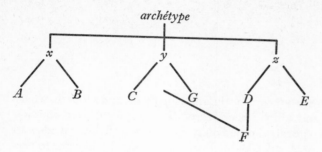

Figure 5

This agreement is not all that significant, as the 'tripartite' appearance does not derive in any way directly from the algorithm, which merely suggests an 'undirected' construction without determining specifically the 'hanging' point to obtain the real *stemma*. Moreover, I have used Quentin's data for my construction, checking only that there is consistency between the distribution of 'zeros' and positive apparatus, but without in any way checking this latter. My aim was only a practical verification of the logical coherence of the algorithm, and from this point of view the experiment was successful.

THE 'NON-LINEAR' STRUCTURES

It should be clear that this algorithm cannot consider *all* the relations which contribute to the forming of a *stemma*. It can only make clear the linking 'linear' paths, and recognize the ramifications which appear from the crossing of the various chains. All the different manuscript combinations which cannot furnish a chain are immediately discarded. Consider again the fictitious example of the last section. If we discover, when we consider the ABD triplet, that A is 'intermediate' between B and D, then the fact that we cannot now construct a 'linear' chain means that we consider the group no further.

This is a loss of information which can seriously distort the relationships we discover between the manuscripts. This is particularly unfortunate when we recall that one of the most important problems in *stemmata* construction is the recovery of at least some of the lost manuscripts. Such a task obviously requires us to use all the information which is available.

I therefore modified the algorithm (Zarri 1971b), in order to obtain useful information also from the manuscript groups where the 'zeros' distribution cannot give rise to a linear chain. So far, however, I consider only those 'non-linear' structures connected with the subsets of size four. I will now explain briefly their properties.

Let us suppose the case

A	B	C	D			
ABC				A	B	C
ABD				A	B	D
ACD				$\emptyset$		
BCD				C	B	D

that is, three triplets with B constantly 'intermediate', and a fourth, where B does not appear, and which has no 'zero'. The graphical interpretation shown in figure 6 appears immediately and was well known also to Quentin (Quentin 1922, pp. 223-5). For convenience I will refer to this structure as $1BACD$, where '1' is the identification number, and the first letter following this figure is the symbol of the mid-star manuscript.

If we have

A	B	C	D			
ABC				A	B	C
ABD				A	B	D
ACD				$\emptyset$		
BCD				$\emptyset$		

similar to the former case but with only two 'intermediate' relations, we can interpret it as in figure 7, where x is a lost manuscript, which explains the lack of a 'zero' in the BCD triplet. However, the reliability is not so great as for '1'; a construction such as is shown in figure 8 equally satisfies the lack of an 'intermediate' relation in the BCD triplet (the link between C and D ensures that the two manuscripts 'agree' sometimes 'against' B). The x hypothesis requires independent supporting evidence or, at least, it must not conflict with other results.

This structure will be marked with '2', and described as $2ABCD$, where the first two letters represent the 'linear' side of the *stemma*, and the last two the diverging manuscripts.

With a 'zeros' distribution such as

A	B	C	D			
ABC				$\emptyset$		
ABD				A	B	D
ACD				A	C	D
BCD				$\emptyset$		

the interpretation is very simple. The linking of the four manuscripts must be as shown in figure 9. We notice that the absence of the 'zero' in the ABC and BCD triplets can easily suggest a modification such as that of figure 10. The existence of the 'lost' manuscripts is here much more problematic than in '2', because the circular form of this structure easily allows some transmission of readings to prevent the 'zero' in A and D. If we consider the first of the two suggested structures as a directed one, with A acting as an archetype or subarchetype, the unaffected transmission of a certain reading from A to B and C, in opposition to an 'innovation' of D, causes an 'agreement' of B and C 'against' D. This 'agreement against' suffices to prevent a 'zero' in the BCD triplet without introducing other manuscripts except the original four.

Consequently I have decided to retain the simplest graphical resolution, without additional manuscripts. This structure will be described as $3ABCD$, where the two middle manuscripts represent the alternative paths to pass from A to D. Naturally, if during the final synthesis operation some x manuscript is introduced into this structure as a consequence of some other structure, then the new result will be supported by its agreement with the original 'zeros' distribution.

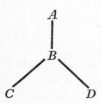

Figure 6

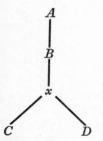

Figure 7

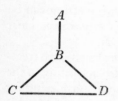

Figure 8

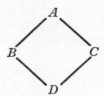

Figure 9

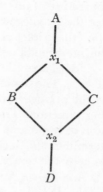

Figure 10

Of the four 'non-linear' structures which I have as yet studied, that remaining is perhaps, with '1', the most interesting from a philological point of view. Let us consider the case in which, during the examination of a group of manuscripts of size four, we find it impossible to construct a single chain and are obliged to construct two 'linear' structures simultaneously if we are to take into account all the relationships in the triplets. For example,

$$
\begin{array}{llll}
A & B & C & D \\
ABC & & A \quad B \quad C \\
ABD & \emptyset & & \emptyset \\
ACD & & & A \quad D \quad C \\
BCD & \underline{\quad B \quad C \quad D} & \underline{\quad D \quad C \quad B} \\
& A \quad B \quad C \quad D & A \quad D \quad C \quad B
\end{array}
$$

There is no contradiction in writing at the same time BCD and DCB, since the elementary chains obtained from the triplets are not directed. We have now a manuscript (A) in a fixed, privileged position, such that each end of the string formed by the remaining manuscripts is linked to it. The graphical resolution is shown in figure 11, where the arrows indicate that, starting at A, the other manuscripts can be traversed in either direction.

Figure 11   *Figure* 12

A constant feature of this structure is the lack of a 'zero' in the triplet which relates the privileged manuscript to the two extremities of the 'linear' chain (the triplet ABD in our example). We could consider, therefore, the interpretation shown in figure 12; but the arguments offered in the case of '3' against the systematic introduction, *a priori*, of x are equally valid here. The structure will be described as $4ABCD$, where the first letter is the privileged manuscript, and the following string can be read in either direction. The philological interest of '4' is in the clear discrimination of two manuscript families, A and BCD.

We can terminate this section with an example, the algorithmic treatment of a song by the troubadour Peire Vidal (the sixth according to the edition by D'Arco Silvio Avalle (Vidal 1960)). Without considering for the moment the R and K manuscripts (since a succession of 'double zeros' clearly shows they coincide respectively with C and I), we obtain from the algorithm the following structures

'chains'
CHD^aNQS
IHD^aNQS
CHD^aI
NHD^aI
'non-linear structures'
$1D^aCIN$
$1HCIN$
$2D^aHCS$
$2CD^aIQ$
$2CHIQ$
$3CD^aSQ$
$3CHSQ$
$4CNQS$

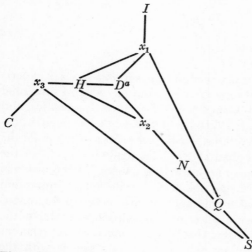

Figure 13

The synthesis of these structures is shown graphically in figure 13, where x_1, x_2 and x_3 represent hypothetical lost manuscripts. It is easy to verify, for example, that H and D^a are really inserted in two 'stars' where C, I and N are the 'rays', according to the '1' relations, and also that it is possible to run from C along the string NQS in both directions. Adding K and R, the hypothetical x_4 and x_5 to represent the 'singular variants' which would prevent N and H from having a 'zero', and with a 'hanging' point between x_3 and H, we at last obtain the directed *stemma* shown in figure 14, which is quite consistent with the 'significant variants' retained from the 'positive apparatus' (Zarri 1971b, pp. 7-8).

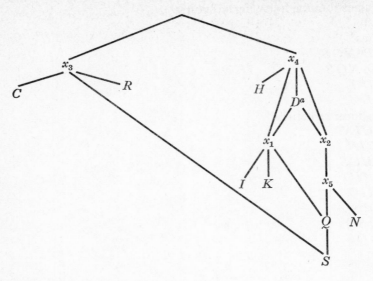

Figure 14

CONCLUSIONS

The illustrative example of the last section comes from a series of experiments concerning Peire Vidal's manuscript tradition, which I presented at the XIIIth International Congress of Romance Linguistics and Philology, Québec 1971 (Zarri 1971b). For that work I defined a provisional means of *stemmata* synthesis, which took as its starting point the results of the algorithm described above. This made use firstly of the chains, and afterwards of the 'non-linear' structures (in the order in which they have been described), and used a criterion of 'minimum complexity' which minimized the number of links between the manuscripts, and the number of lost manuscripts. In addition, each step of the construction was checked to ensure that no new 'intermediate' relations were introduced at the junctions which were inconsistent with the original 'zeros'.

The experiments gave unambiguous results only when the number of 'linear' and 'non-linear' elements did not exceed twenty. They gave results which are at least somewhat ambiguous for higher numbers of elements. This should not be regarded as discouraging. It is a direct consequence of the fact that, in certain cases, the basic data obtained with Quentin's method furnish different *stemmata* solutions, between which the philologist must choose according to his own critical experience.

To complete the synthesis algorithm, it will be necessary to examine the origins of this final uncertainty by studying the 'zeros' distributions to which the phenomenon is related, that is to say, by studying the relationship between this ambiguity and the initial philological evidence.

If this final problem can be resolved, the translation of the essential core of Quentin's method into precise algorithm terms will have been completed, at least as far as practical work is concerned. Then and only then, as I indicated in my initial remarks, will it be time to study the mathematical properties of the method in its algorithmic form—specifically its relationship to Graph Theory. The aim then would be to arrive at a mathematical description of the method sufficient for all its properties to be derived by deductive reasoning.

For the moment, the primary need is for substantial practical experimentation on a large number of manuscript traditions.

REFERENCES

Bédier, J. (1928) La tradition manuscrite du Lai de l'Ombre. *Romania*, **54**, 161-96, 321-56.
Dain, A. (1932) Edition des textes classiques. Théories et méthodes. *Actes du Congrès de Nîmes (30 Mars-2 Avril 1932)*, pp. 61-88. Paris: Les Belles Lettres.
Froger, J. (1968) *La critique des textes et son automatisation*. Paris: Dunod.
Gardin, J.C. (1971) Archéologie et calculateurs: nouvelles perspectives. *Rev. int. Sc. soc.*, **23**, 204-18.
Hockett, C.F. (1968) *The State of the Art*. 'S-Gravenhage: Mouton.
Laurier, A. (1971) Problèmes posés par la formalisation et l'automatisation des démarches déductives dans la Critique Textuelle et l'Analyse de Contenu. *Problèmes posés par la formalisation et l'automatisation des méthodes d'analyse de transmission du discours écrit ou oral (Rap. 30/CNRS/CADA/1971)*, pp. 52-87 (eds. Laurier, A. & Virbel, J.). Marseille: Centre d'Analyse Documentaire pour l'Archéologie.
Marcus, S., Nicolau, E. & Stati, S. (1971) *Introduzione alla linguistica matematica* (Ital. trans. by F. Franciosi). Bologna: Pàtron.
Markov, A.A. (1962) *Theory of algorithms* (Eng. trans. by Schorr-Kon, J.J. & PST Staff). Jerusalem: Program for Scientific Translation Ltd.
Pasquali, G. (1952) *Storia della tradizione e critica del testo* (2nd ed.). Firenze: Le Monnier.
Quentin, H. (1922) *Mémoire sur l'établissement du texte de la Vulgate (1ère partie—Octateuque)*. Roma: Desclée et Cie; Paris: J. Gabalda.
Quentin, H. (1926) *Essais de critique textuelle*. Paris: Librairie A. Picard.
Vidal, P. (1960) *Poesie* (critical edition by D'Arco Silvio Avalle). Milano-Napoli: Riccardo Ricciardi.
Zarri, G.P. (1968) Linguistica algoritmica e meccanizzazione della 'collatio codicum'. *Lingua e stile*, **3**, 21-40.
Zarri, G.P. (1969) Il metodo per la 'recensio' di Dom H. Quentin esaminato criticamente mediante la sua traduzione in un algoritmo per elaboratore elettronico. *Lingua e stile*, **4**, 161-82.
Zarri, G.P. (1971a) L'automazione delle procedure di Critica Testuale, problemi e prospettive. *Lingua e stile*, **6**, 397-414.
Zarri, G.P. (1971b) *Primi risultati nell'applicazione dei calcolatori ai problemi di Critica Testuale, costruzione degli 'stemmata codicum' (Com. 48/CNRS/CADA/1971)*. Marseille: Centre d'Analyse Documentaire pour l'Archéologie.

R.J.DILLIGAN,
T.K.BENDER

The lapses of time: a computer-assisted investigation of English prosody

The problem the literary scholar faces in using a computer always reminds us of the problem the poet Lucretius faced when he tried to explain Greek science to his dull-witted patron, Memmius:

I am well aware how very hard it is
To bring to light by means of Latin verse
The dark discoveries of the Greeks. I know
New terms must be invented, since our tongue
Is poor, and this material is new.

The poverty of Memmius's vocabulary, however, is nothing to the poverty of the computer's vocabulary. To a literary scholar, words are the signs of things. They exist not as discrete, determined objects but as the focus of grammatical, emotive, cultural, and semantic resonances. To the computer, words have no connotations and very little meaning. They are simply numbers stored in memory. To give a simple example; if a computer were programed to recognize rhyme patterns and were set to work on Yeats's 'Sailing to Byzantium', it could note that in the first three stanzas there were lines that did not rhyme while in the fourth stanza all lines rhymed. It would be the problem of the literary scholar to explain why the two words that do not rhyme in stanza one are 'young' and 'dies', and how the world of perfect artifice portrayed in stanza four demands, at the very least, a perfect rhyme scheme. The computer is not about to displace the literary scholar and there is no need to respond to the increasing use of computers as aids to literary scholarship by going into future shock. The computer can be of use to the literary scholar mainly when, before he concerns himself with the interpretation of words, he must concern himself with the patterns of their recurrence in very large texts. A computer will not tell him anything about the rhyme or meter of a single short lyric that he cannot find out for himself by reading it; but when he wishes to study a whole collection of lyrics of, say, 154 sonnets, the computer may provide him with some useful primary information arranged in a way that will facilitate his enquiry.

One advantage of computer studies of prosody is that there are a large number of things that are important in the determination of meter which the computer can be programed to recognize. Indeed, the sheer bulk of detail involved in thorough discussions of prosody demands some supplementation of the prosodist's hand and ear. In any syllable of an iambic pentameter line, one needs to keep a record of stress, ictus, assonance, alliteration, and elision. For each line one wishes to keep track of the patterns of stress, ictus, assonance and alliteration in relation to each other and the metrical pattern, as well as the number of words, the syllable count for each word, the actual and possible elisions, the number of syllables, the number and position of function words, enjambment, end stopping, caesura, and weak ending. Conservatively there are at least fifty such things to be noted for a single line. In a Shakespearean play of 2,200 lines, there are easily over 100,000, none of which, taken singly, is likely to have a great deal of importance but which, cumulatively, are of great relevance to the prosodic style of the play. And once one had such information for a single play, one would of course want to compare it with similar information for other plays, Shakespearean and non-Shakespearean. There are in fact a number of questions about the history of English prosody that are amenable to computational enquiry—the development of blank verse from Milton to Wordsworth, the heroic couplet in Dryden and Pope to give just two. What the computer offers the prosodist is the ability to follow his own interests and inclinations in studying any particular poet but at the same time to produce results in a form that others could use in comparative and syncretic studies.

Our own particular interest is in nineteenth-century British poetry and we would like to describe the methodology of a computer analysis of the iambic verse of Gerard Manley Hopkins as an illustration of the possibilities of computational prosody. The computer used in this enquiry is an IBM 370/155 and all programs were written in PL/I. [An earlier version of these programs was written in FORTRAN V for a Univac 1108 and we will be happy to forward documentation on either version to interested scholars. Hardware requirements for the PL/I programs include 380K core, 3 IBM 2400 tape drives, and one IBM 2314 disk drive.] The description of iambic pentameter that is the basis of these programs was proposed by Morris Halle and Samuel Jay Keyser (1971). Their description of the iambic pentameter (pp. 165-77) regards it as a sequence of ten positions in which syllables receiving primary stress occupy even numbered positions. Two optional unstressed syllables are permitted at the end of the line, and position one may be unoccupied. Schematically this can be represented as

$$(w) \; swswswsws(x)(x)$$

where s represents a position with primary stress, w a position with any level of stress less than primary, x an unstressed syllable, and parenthesized positions are optional. A position may be composed of a single syllable or at most two vowels immediately adjoining or separated by a single sonorant consonant. There are three possible conditions which constitute a metrical line:

1. Fully stressed syllables occur in s positions only and in all s positions.
2. Fully stressed syllables occur in s positions only but not in all s positions.
3. Stress maxima occur in s positions only but not in all s positions.

A stress maximum is defined as a fully stressed syllable occurring between two unstressed syllables in the same syntactic constituent in a line of verse (Halle-Keyser, p. 169).

To scan a line according to this theory, one assigns syllables or sonorant sequences to positions numbered one through ten omitting from the numbering extra-metrical syllables in verse final and verse medial positions. If the third condition is violated and stress maxima occur in odd numbered positions, the line is judged unmetrical. The number of exceptions to conditions 1 and 2 contained in the line determine the degree of metrical complexity of a line. The line

> Splendid with phantasies ariel

is unmetrical since stress maximum occurs in position 7. (If we assume the line's first position is vacant—the line after all only has 9 syllables— we would then have stress maximum in position 5.) The complexity of the line

> Which the tides cover in their overflow

is specified as 5 because it contains five exceptions to conditions 1 and 2. (Position three, 'tides', violates both 1 and 2 so is counted twice.)

The algorithm we use in scanning verse differs somewhat from that proposed by Halle-Keyser, although it is based upon their idea that lines are judged unmetrical or metrical by virtue of the occurrence of stress maximum in certain positions. There are eight steps to the scanning algorithm:

1. Number syllables in the line from left to right.

2. If number of syllables is greater than the permitted number, check for an extra-metrical syllable in verse final position.

3. If the number of syllables equals the permitted number and the final position is occupied by an unstressed syllable, consider the possibility that position one is vacant.

4. If the number does not equal the permitted number, list every possible assignment of extra-metrical syllables and sonorant sequences that reduce or increase the number of syllables to the permitted one.

5. If it is impossible to adjust the number of positions to the permitted number the line is unmetrical.

6. Evaluate all possible assignments for degree of complexity against conditions one and two.

7. Test for metricality against the occurrence of stress maxima.

8. A line is metrical if there is at least one possible assignment of syllables to the permitted number which passes the test for metricality in step 7.

The principle difference between this algorithm and the procedure suggested by Halle-Keyser is that it is very explicit about the method of assigning syllables to positions. Halle-Keyser's procedure does not take account of the fact that there are many lines of verse in which there are more than the required number of sonorant sequences, lines like

Q

> Where the eye fixed, fled the encrimsoning spot
> Clustering entrancingly in beril lakes
> Like an Assyrian Prince, with buds unsheathed.

In each of these lines, there is only one assignment of syllables to positions which will produce a metrical line, though there are two or three sonorant sequences. Step four of the algorithm will generate each of the possibilities and step eight will choose the correct one. The line

> A glorious wanton; — all the wrecks in showers

has two possible assignments that will pass the test for metricality in step seven; either 'glorious' is taken as trisyllabic and the final syllable of 'wanton' is taken as extra-metrical, or 'glorious' is taken as bisyllabic and the last syllable of 'wanton' is counted as position five. In this case the algorithm will take the latter possibility which has a complexity of zero as contrasted with the former which has a complexity of three. Step three of the algorithm will accommodate lines such as

> Thou that on sin's wages starvest

which has both a missing syllable and an extra-metrical one. In assigning a numerical complexity to these lines, the scanning program adds the number of rejected possibilities to the complexity of the selected scansion. Thus the line

> A glorious wanton; — all the wrecks in showers

is ultimately assigned a complexity of one to reflect the fact that there is an alternate possible scansion to it as contrasted with a line like

> When chiefs and monarchs came their gifts to lay

in which there is only one possible scansion and the complexity is zero. What this algorithm does, then, is simulate the actual experience of scanning a line where one is aware of actual and potential scansions.

The application of the scanning algorithm to a text of poetry occurs in the third phase of a four-phase process by which the prosody of a text is analysed. These phases are, in order of application, a concordance phase, a transcription phase, a scanning phase, and a cataloguing phase. The concordance phase requires no comment since concordance programs are available 'off the shelf' at virtually any university computing center, and the basic methodology of the production of concordances is widely understood. We will simply point out that there are a large number of computer concordances already in existence so prosodists will in many cases be able to build on existing work rather than begin from scratch. The transcription, scanning, and cataloguing phases however, require some description.

The transcription phase requires the existence of a machine-readable concordance of the text to be analysed, because the first step in the phonemic transcription of verse by computer is to have the computer punch out the lexicon of the text on hollerith cards, one word to a card. These cards are then encoded with the phonemic transcription of the word which is then keypunched on each card. For Hopkins, the transcriptions were taken from Daniel Jones's *English Pronouncing Dictionary* (1924) and, where Jones did not contain a word, the *Oxford English Dictionary*. Should the *O.E.D.* ever be available in machine-readable form, and we can't imagine that one day it won't be, this encoding will be almost completely eliminated. But as it stands now, it can be turned over to relatively unskilled assistants with the investigator concerning himself only with the accuracy of their work. A twenty thousand word text will produce a lexicon of between 4,500 and 6,500 words so it would be fair to say that this method reduces the effort involved in hand transcription by between 2/3 and 3/4. Further, the encoding performed for one poet can be used for another since it is a simple task to have the computer compare the lexicons of two texts and produce a list of words from one not found in the other.

The print-out of the machine-readable concordance is used to identify homographs and function words which need to be marked in the machine-readable text before transcription. At this point one distinguishes prepositions from particles, the use of 'have' as main verb from its use as an auxiliary, the present from the past tense of 'read', and the like. In general, this is done by adding numerical suffixes to the orthographic text, so that one has READ where the present tense occurs, and READ1 where the past tense, etc., and entries reflecting this marking are encoded in the lexicon. The pre-marked orthographic text and the encoded lexicon are then used as input for a transcription program which looks up each word from the orthographic text in the lexicon and substitutes for it the phonemic representation. The third and fourth lines of figure 1 show typical output of this program.

The scanning phase of the analysis uses this transcription as its input. It is principally concerned with metrical pattern, elision, assonance, and alliteration and its scope in testing for these features is a single line. The scanning routine does some pre-processing before testing for these features. It determines the positions of stressed vowels and punctuation, counts the number of syllables in the line, and generates separate lists of the vowels and initial consonant clusters, in order to test the metrical pattern, possible elisions, assonance and alliteration respectively. The occurrences of stress and punctuation are recorded as bit strings in which line positions correspond to bits from right to left; that is, the rightmost bit represents position one, the next rightmost position two, etc.

A line such as

From crown to tail-fin floating, fringed the spine,

which has primary stress in positions two, four, six, eight, and ten would be recorded as

1010101010.

The punctuation between positions seven and eight and after ten would be recorded as

11011000000.

```
LINE  1012 CONTAINS  5 ELIDABLE SYLLABLES. THERE ARE 10 POSSIBLE ASSIGNMENTS
OF SYLLABLES TO POSITIONS

THANNE LONGEN FOLK TO GOON ON PILGRIMAGES.                        001 00 001
)A+NC LO+#G>N FO+LK TO GO+N |N PI+LGRIM|/+DQ>S.
  X       XXXXX              X      XXX    X

)A+N_ LO+#G_N FO+LK TO GO+N |N PI+LGRIM|/+DQ>S.
  X       X

)A+N_ LO+#G>N FO+LK TO GO+N _N PI+LGRIM|/+?Q>S.
  X                         X

)A+N_ LO+#G>N FO+LK TO GO+N |N PI+LGR_M|/+DQ>S.
  X                               X

)A+N_ LO+#G>N FO+LK TO GO+N |N PI+LGRIM|/+DQ_S.
  X                                      X

)A+NC LO+#G_N FO+LK TO GO+N _N PI+LGRIM|/+DQ>S.
          X                 X

)A+NC .LO+#G_N FO+LK TO GO+N |N PI+LGR_M|/+DQ>S.
          X                        X

)A+NC LO+#G_N FO+LK TO GO+N |N PI+LGRIM|/+DQ_S.
          X                              X

)A+NC LO+#G>N FO+LK TO GO+N _N PI+LGR_M|/+DQ>S.
                            X      X

)A+NC LO+#G>N FO+LK TO GO+N _N PI+LGRIM|/+DQ_S.
                            X            X

)A+NC LO+#G>N FO+LK TO GO+N |N PI+LGR_M|/+DQ_S.
                                   X         X
```

Figure 1. Output from elision file of scanning
program showing phonemic transcription and syllable
assignments for Chaucerian verse.

Vowels are recorded as integers with each vowel phoneme being assigned
a unique integer. The vowels in this line would be stored as an array of
values in which the positions in the array correspond to the positions in
the line. For this line the array would contain
        28 42 26 38 2 54 4 2 28 44.
The initial consonants would be stored as character code:
        FR KR T T - FL - FR) S.
Recorded in this way, the information in the transcription is easily
evaluated for different patterns. Assonance patterns are recognized, for
example, by the fact that each occurrence of a vowel phoneme will generate the same number. The pattern can then be recorded as a bit string
with the same conventions as for stress. Assonance in the line would be
recorded as
        0010010000.
Alliteration similarly would be recorded as
        0000001100 (T)
and
        0010010000 (F)
If we wished to know all positions in a line that contained alliteration, we
could combine the separate bit strings with a boolean OR operation:
        0000001100
     OR 0010100000
        0010101100.

If we wished to know in what positions assonance and alliteration coincided we would combine the assonance and alliteration strings with a boolean AND:

$$0010010000$$
$$\text{AND } 0010101100$$
$$\overline{0010000000.}$$

This result indicates that assonance and illiteration coincide at position eight, as in fact they do.

The tests for stress maximum and metricality, though a bit more involved, are similar to the tests just described. To test for stress maximum the computer examines the bit string record of stress and creates a new bit string identifying the location of all 1 bits preceded and followed by 0 bits. In our sample line it turns out that all the stress bits are such so that the generated string is identical with the stress string.

$$1010101010.$$

By definition, the last positions in a line can never be a stress maximum position. As it was generating the different bit strings and arrays, the computer was also counting the number of vowels in the line. Since the number of vowels in the line is ten it now generates a bit string of a 1 bit followed by nine 0 bits.

$$1000000000.$$

It then performs a boolean operation with this string and the string generated from the stress string which specifies that 1 and 1 yield 0, 0 and 0 yield 0, 1 and 0 yield 0, and 0 and 1 yield 1:

$$1000000000$$
$$\text{BOOL } 1010101010$$
$$\overline{0010101010.}$$

It now performs the same boolean operation on the result and the punctuation string.

$$1011000000$$
$$\text{BOOL } 0010101010$$
$$\overline{0000101010.}$$

This specifies that stress maxima occur in positions two, four, and six of the line. To determine whether or not the line is iambic, the computer performs a boolean AND operation on the string containing the positions of stress maxima and a string in which bits representing odd numbered positions are set to 1 and even numbered positions are 0.

$$0000101010$$
$$\text{AND } 0101010101$$
$$\overline{0000000000.}$$

Since the result of this operation is zero, we know that stress maxima occur in this line only in even positions. Had the position string been zero, we would have known that stress maxima did not occur in the line. If we wished to test for trochaic meter, we would have performed our

AND operation with the position string and a string in which bits representing even positions were set to one, 1010101010. The result of this operation would have been 0000101010 and since it would not be zero, the line could not be trochaic. Other tests are also carried out on these bit patterns. For example, iambic pentameter lines with weak endings are identified by the fact that the bit for position ten is zero in the stress string. The total number of stress maxima in a line is obtained by counting the 1 bits in the stress maximum string and the total number of occurrences of stress maximum in a given position is obtained by keeping track of the position of 1 bits. Identical counting is done for assonance, alliteration, and their coincidence.

Not all the information generated by the scanning program is recorded in bit strings. Records of each assonating vowel and alliterating consonant are kept as integers and character code respectively. The line numbers of lines which require elision, iambic lines, trochaic lines, iambic pentameter lines with weak endings, lines without stress maximum, lines whose complexity exceeds a limit specified for each poem, unmetrical lines, and lines containing syllables in which assonance and alliteration coincide are all stored in arrays set aside for that purpose. The current limit for these lists of line numbers for any given feature is 30,000 occurrences, but an updated version of this program will soon allow this limit to be in the neighbourhood of 300,000 occurrences. The orthographic and phonemic representations of each line are stored on a random access file which gives the investigator the option of not merely obtaining lists of line numbers but of following those lists with a printout of the actual lines and their transcription. Figure 2 shows listing of the thirty-eight variables for which the scanning program keeps running totals for each poem and for the entire corpus. A table of the percentages is also kept and printed out after the totals for the entire corpus. The scanning program draws histographs of the location by position of stress, stress maximum, punctuation, assonance, alliteration, coincidence of assonance and alliteration, as well as histographs of the distribution of sentence length in words, sentence length in syllables, distribution of monosyllabic, bisyllabic, trisyllabic, etc., words. These graphs are very useful in developing ideas about the position of caesura, end stopping, stress distribution and the statistics they reflect may be used in clustering studies (Dilligan and Ule 1971). But the over-all design of the output of the scanning program is such that it provides information in a format that is immediately usable by scholars who have no familiarity with a computer and no desire to work up a knowledge of statistical linguistics.

Besides printing out information, the scanning phase also keeps a record of the result of the scansion of each line on a magnetic tape. This magnetic tape is the input for the cataloguing phase of the analysis. In this phase, the ability of the computer to sort large files of information is utilized to obtain information about the frequency and location of

```
NUMBER OF SYLLABLES . . . . . . . . . . . . . . . . . . . .    321
NUMBER OF STRESS MAXIMA . . . . . . . . . . . . . . . .        95
PERCENTAGE OF STRESS MAXIMA . . . . . . . . . . . . . .        29
NUMBER OF LINES . . . . . . . . . . . . . . . . . . . .        31
PERCENTAGE OF STRESS MAXIMA LINES . . . . . . . . . .          100
NUMBER OF LINES WITHOUT STRESS MAXIMUM. . . . . . . .          0
NUMBER OF IAMBIC LINES. . . . . . . . . . . . . . . .          30
PERCENTAGE OF IAMBIC LINES. . . . . . . . . . . . . .          96
NUMBER OF TROCHAIC LINES. . . . . . . . . . . . . . .          0
PERCENTAGE OF TROCHAIC LINES. . . . . . . . . . . . .          0
NUMBER OF IRREGULAR LINES . . . . . . . . . . . . . .          0
PERCENTAGE OF IRREGULAR LINES . . . . . . . . . . . .          0
NUMBER OF AMBIGUOUS LINES . . . . . . . . . . . . . .          0
PERCENTAGE OF AMBIGUOUS LINES . . . . . . . . . . . .          0
NUMBER OF HR LINES. . . . . . . . . . . . . . . . . .          0
NUMBER OF MR LINES. . . . . . . . . . . . . . . . . .          0
NUMBER OF LR LINES. . . . . . . . . . . . . . . . . .          0
NUMBER OF ASSONATING SYLLABLES. . . . . . . . . . . .          159
PERCENTAGE OF ASSONATING SYLLABLES. . . . . . . . . .          49
NUMBER OF ASSONATING LINES. . . . . . . . . . . . . .          28
PERCENTAGE OF ASSONATING LINES. . . . . . . . . . . .          90
NUMBER OF ASSONATING PATTERNS . . . . . . . . . . . .          46
NUMBER OF ALLITERATING SYLLABLES. . . . . . . . . . .          45
PERCENTAGE OF ALLITERATING SYLLABLES. . . . . . . . .          14
NUMBER OF ALLITERATING LINES. . . . . . . . . . . . .          16
PERCENTAGE OF ALLITERATING LINES. . . . . . . . . . .          51
NUMBER OF ALLITERATING PATTERNS . . . . . . . . . . .          19
NUMBER OF LINES WITH COINCIDENT ASSON & ALLIT . . . . .        8
PERCNT OF LINES WITH COINCIDENT ASSON & ALLIT . . . . .        25
NUMBER OF SYLLABLES WITH COINCIDENT ASSON & ALLIT . . .        12
PERCNT OF SYLLABLES WITH COINCIDENT ASSON & ALLIT . . .        3
NUMBER OF LINES EXCEEDING SPECIFIED COMPLEXITY. . . . .        3
PERCNT OF LINES EXCEEDING SPECIFIED COMPLEXITY. . . . .        0
AVERAGE COMPLEXITY. . . . . . . . . . . . . . . . . . .        0
NUMBER OF AMETRICAL LINES . . . . . . . . . . . . . . .        1
PERCNT OF AMETRICAL LINES . . . . . . . . . . . . . . .        3
NUMBER OF LINES TO BE ELIDED. . . . . . . . . . . . . .        24
NUMBER OF LINES SHORTER THAN SPECIFIED LENGTH . . . . .        0
```

Figure 2. Listing of variables from scanning program.

individual patterns. For example, every line with stress maxima in positions two, six, and eight will generate a bit pattern as follows:
        0010100010.
Using IBM's SORT/MERGE program we can sort the records of the scanning using the stress maximum position bits and line numbers as a sort key. This will arrange the text so that the lines with stress maximum in positions two, six, and eight will be grouped together. If we use three sort keys and sort on the number of stress maxima in a line, their position, and identifier, we can arrange the lines with stress maximum in two, six, and eight so that they come in sequence with all other lines containing three maxima. If we add a fourth sort key, complexity, between the position and identifier key, the lines would be grouped so that lines with stress maxima in the same position would be arranged in the order of their complexity. By selecting the proper number and sequence of sort keys, an investigator can index the results of the scanning program in an infinite variety of ways to facilitate his analysis.

While the cataloguing phase of analysis is in many ways the most powerful, there are several problems associated with it that must be mentioned. The first of these is expense. It takes about 6 minutes of machine time on a 370/155 to analyse 1,000 lines of poetry, including the time it takes to generate a KWOC concordance for the text. Multiple field sorting of large records, however, can easily double or triple the total machine time. In fact, it is fair to say that there is no theoretical upper limit to the amount of computer time one could spend trying different combinations and sequences of sort fields. This consideration leads to the second problem. The use of the SORT/MERGE routine, though not overly complicated, does require a fair amount of computer experience, if it is to be used with the greatest economy and flexibility. For unlike the programs used in the first three phases, the indexing phase cannot be easily reduced to a single program with user specified options. Different sequences of sorting require very different Job Control Language specifications and the alteration of calling parameters within programs. Finally, the amount of output generated by this sorting can be formidable. A complete listing of a single sort takes roughly 50 pages and if a number of sorts are performed and listed one has very quickly generated reams of paper. Only scholarly prudence and a firm grasp of the potentialities of the SORT/MERGE can keep this cataloguing phase under control; but used sensibly, the cataloguing can be a great help to analysis.

The methodology we have been describing has been used to analyse a broad historical sample of English verse from Chaucer to Hopkins. The type of results that it produces may be illustrated by a brief discussion of some of the more interesting results obtained from an analysis of Hopkins's verse. We will limit our remarks to the poems Hopkins wrote before 1876 (Poems 1 to 27 in the Gardner and Mackenzie edition (1970)), and within those poems to the 840 lines of iambic verse they contain out of of a total of 1,005 lines.

Since Hopkins's later verse is replete with every kind of metrical licence, it is interesting to note that only five unmetrical lines occur in these poems.

> Splendid with phantasies aerial (1.8.2)
> Some carried the seafan; some round the head (2.58)
> For us was gathered the first-fruits (6.3)
> None besides me this bye-way's beauty try (12.ii.9)
> And I'll love my distinction; near or far (14.ii.12).

The last two of these lines contain a pronoun '*me*', and possessive adjective, '*my*', which need to be taken as receiving primary lexical stress if the lines are to be taken as metrical; in both lines, there is a good rhetorical justification for such a stress. Since these two lines are the only exceptions to the general rule that such function words don't receive primary stress, what they point to, we think, is the way different aspects of verse design, to use Jakobson's term, may interact. The general propositions that function words do not receive primary stress and that semantically important do are both aspects of English phonology that need to be a part of verse design for stressed verse. In particular verse instances, the second proposition may override the first. For Hopkins, this happens quite rarely. It could well turn out that for another poet this is a much more frequent occurrence and therefore more premarking of function words would be required before transcription. The first two lines in the list of unmetrical lines are simply that: exceptions to the metrical norm for which there is no justification. (In the second line,

> Some carried the seafan; some round the head

one could, in the context of traditional prosody, claim it is metrical by eliding 'the' and claiming that the third foot was catalectic; to do this, however, seems to us to turn prosody into a shell game: now you see it, now you don't.) Line 6.3,

> For us was gathered the first-fruits

has a textual history that has some bearing on its meter. When it was first printed in *The Union Review* in 1863, 'first-fruits' was unhyphenated. The editors of the fourth edition of Hopkins's poems prefer a manuscript reading with the hyphen. With the hyphen, the line contains three primary stresses and stress maximum occurs in position seven; without the hyphen, there are four primary stresses and the additional stress in position eight prevents stress maximum from occurring in position seven. Hopkins's problems with editors who wished to regularize his verse began very early indeed.

The regularity of the metrical pattern of the early verse is also seen in the distribution of stress, stress maximum, assonance, and alliteration. In the 'Author's Preface' to his poems (Gardner and Mackenzie, p. 46), Hopkins remarks that the second foot in an iambic line was particularly sensitive and almost always regular, the exceptions occurring when the poet wanted some special effect. Whether this is true of iambic verse in general only an extended enquiry could reveal; but it is certainly true that in the poems Hopkins wrote before 1876, the fourth position (the ictal position of the second foot in traditional terminology) is the most likely to receive stress maximum. The following table (figure 3) shows the frequency of stress maximum in ictal positions for Hopkins's early iambic verse.

position	number of stress maxima
2	478
4	531
6	449
8	274

Figure 3. Table of occurrence of stress maximum in ictal positions in poems 1-27 of Gerard Manley Hopkins.

There are no pentameter poems in which stress maximum occurs less frequently in position four than in any other. In four octosyllabic poems, 'The Alchemist in the City', 'My Prayers must meet a brazen heaven', 'The Habit of Perfection', and 'Nondum', the fourth position is not the one containing the most stress maxima. The reason for this is that in octosyllabic verse, caesura tends to occur between positions four and five when there is a syntactic break in the line. By and large in Hopkins's octosyllabics, the verse is end stopped with rare internal pauses. In pentameter lines, however, there is much more internal punctuation though it tends to occur after positions five, six or seven. In all iambic verse, both assonance and alliteration occur much more frequently in even than in odd positions as the following histographs (figures 4 and 5) illustrate.

It is in his use of elisions that we begin to get some sense of Hopkins straining against metrical convention. In the 746 iambic pentameter and octosyllabic lines of the early poems, 116 require elision and in 64 of these 116 there is more than one possible sequence that could be elided:

> To crosses meant for Jesu's; you whom the East (11.5)
> Or if they try it, I am happier then: (12.24)
> But now I am so tired I soon shall send (14.36).

And there are a number of lines in which the demands of syllable count are in direct conflict with assonance and internal rhyme:

> My heaven is brass and iron my earth
> Yea iron is mingled with my clay. (18.9-10)

These lines anticipate the opening lines of 'The Windhover' where tmesis is used to preserve syllable count in line one but the opening two syllables of the second line must be taken as elided to preserve the iambic pattern that line one insists upon

> (. . . mornings minion, king- / dom of daylight's dauphin . . .)

ASSONANCE DISTRIBUTION IN IAMBIC LINES. GERARD.MANLEY HOPKINS, POEMS 1 - 27
MAXIMUM VALUE: 173
SCALE 1:   4

POSITION
```
  1        127     XXXXXXXXXXXXXXXXXXXXXXXX.XXXXXXXX
  2        165     XXXXXXXXXXXXXXXXXXXXXXXXXXXXXXXXXXXXXXXXXX
  3         65     XXXXXXXXXXXXXXXXX
  4        173     XXXXXXXXXXXXXXXXXXXXXXXXXXXXXXXXXXXXXXXXXXXXX
  5         65     XXXXXXXXXXXXXXXX
  6        136     XXXXXXXXXXXXXXXXXXXXXXXXXXXXXXXXXXX
  7         90     XXXXXXXXXXXXXXXXXXXXXX
  8        142     XXXXXXXXXXXXXXXXXXXXXXXXXXXXXXXXXXXXX
  9         51     XXXXXXXXXXXX
 10         89     XXXXXXXXXXXXXXXXXXXXXXX
```

Figure 4. Histograph of positions in which assonance
occurs in poems 1-27 of Gerard Manley Hopkins.

ALLITERATION DISTRIBUTION IN IAMBIC LINES. GERARD MANLEY HOPKINS, POEMS 1 - 27
MAXIMUM VALUE: 218
SCALE 1:   5

POSITION
```
  1        131     XXXXXXXXXXXXXXXXXXXXXXXXXXX
  2        188     XXXXXXXXXXXXXXXXXXXXXXXXXXXXXXXXXXXXXXX
  3         85     XXXXXXXXXXXXXXXXX
  4        218     XXXXXXXXXXXXXXXXXXXXXXXXXXXXXXXXXXXXXXXXXXXXXX
  5         78     XXXXXXXXXXXXXXXX
  6        180     XXXXXXXXXXXXXXXXXXXXXXXXXXXXXXXXXXXXX
  7         88     XXXXXXXXXXXXXXXXX
  8        179     XXXXXXXXXXXXXXXXXXXXXXXXXXXXXXXXXXXXX
  9         64     XXXXXXXXXXXX
 10        120     XXXXXXXXXXXXXXXXXXXXXXXX
```

Figure 5. Histograph of positions in which alliteration
occurs in poems 1-27 of Gerard Manley Hopkins.

We can set these exceptions against a very conventional usual practice.
Thirty-two lines require elision of adjacent vowels, twenty-eight lines
have an extra-metrical syllable in verse final position, twenty-four require
elision of a sequence containing a single sonorant between two vowels.
More rare, but likewise quite conventional, are the six alexandrines that
occur in pentameter, and three lines which have extra-metrical syllables
in verse medial positions. There are, finally, eight lines in which an elision
must be made in sequences containing fricatives rather than sonorants:
>With the dainty-delicate fretted of fingers (2.64)
>The field is sopp'd with merciful dew. (8.3)
>He hath put a new song in my mouth, (8.4)
>Which should ere now have led my feet to the field (17.9)
>It is the waste done in unreticent youth (17.10)
>I have found my music in a common word, (19.5)
>I have found the dominant of my range and state— (19.13)
>Oh! till thou givest that sense beyond, (23.43)

That Hopkins was conscious of something unusual in these lines is pointed to by the fact that six of these eight examples are paired within single poems. And the complicated effect of line 2.64 with its filigree of assonance and alliteration and the unique elision of vowels separated by two consonants is an uncanny anticipation of Hopkins's later manner.

A full discussion of the results obtained from the analysis of these early poems would in fact have to include a discussion of them in the light of the later poems. One ought, we suppose, to offer with them a kind of recursive definition of sprung rhythm as the specific differences noted between the conventional and sprung rhythm poems. Such a definition would not be a complete one of sprung rhythm of course, but it would at least clear the ground for a rigorous one. What we have tried to suggest is the uses to which the results of the methodology we have been describing might be put.

We began with Lucretius; we would like to conclude with him as well. After explaining to Memmius the difficulty of the task at hand, Lucretius goes on to assure him of his willingness

> To keep watch through the night, seeking the words,
> The song, by which to bring into your mind that splendid light
> By which you may see darkly hidden things.

The computer is willing to keep watch through the night seeking the words but the literary scholar's mind must provide that splendid light whereby you may see darkly hidden things.

Acknowledgements

We would like to express our gratitude to the Graduate School of the University of Southern California and the Leo S. Bing Fund for their support of this investigation.

REFERENCES

Dilligan, R. J. & Ule, L. J. (1971) The mathematics of style. *T.L.S.* 22 October 1971.

Gardner, W. H. & Mackenzie, N. H., eds (1970) *The Poems of Gerard Manley Hopkins*, 4th edition, revised and enlarged. London: Oxford University Press.

Halle, M. & Keyser, S. J. (1971) *English Stress: Its Form, Its Growth, and Its Role in Verse*. New York: Harper & Row, Publishers, Inc.

Jones, D. (1924) *English Pronouncing Dictionary*. New York: E.P. Dutton & Co., Inc.

Approaches to metrical research in Plautus

A poet, especially a dramatic poet, can use the metrical pattern of his lines as one way of producing an impact on his audience; the effect may be particularly great when the writer departs from his usual standards. At the same time, understanding the metrical conventions of a language can contribute to the knowledge of the development of that language. Information about a writer's metrical preferences is therefore sought frequently by literary and linguistic scholars. This presentation concentrates on the methods used in a study of Plautus' metrics which has received support from the American Council of Learned Societies under its program of Awards for Computer-Oriented Research in the Humanities; variations of these methods may well be applicable to a variety of other studies.

The use of computers to assist in metrical studies is already well established, at least for work in Latin. As in many other applications of computers, the assistance of these machines may hasten completion of a project and certainly will render the results more complete and accurate, provided that appropriate care has been taken. For several works by classical Latin authors, complete lists of scansions have been prepared, with full information about the occurrences of words of different metrical shapes in various positions within a line (Ott 1970; Waite 1970b).

The most common meter in classical Latin, dactylic hexameter, is based not on patterns of stress accents as modern English meter is, but on patterns of long and short syllables, which are grouped together in a repetitive system to form feet and lines. The dactylic hexameter is the meter of writers to Latin epics, such as Vergil; its form is

$$-../-../-../-../-../-.$$

where a long syllable is indicated by - (hyphen), a short syllable by . (point) instead of ∪, and breaks between feet are marked by / (slash). A spondee (--) may be substituted for any of the dactyls, although this replacement is very rare in the fifth foot. In the sixth foot, which is lacking one syllable of the full dactyl, either a long or a short syllable may be in the final position. If this last position of the line is disregarded, there are only 32 scansions possible, a fact which is of great assistance in preparing computer programs to automate the scansion of poetry written in this meter. Further, for many syllables in a word, it is possible to ascertain the syllable length by simple rules which depend only on the spelling of the word; for instance, any vowel which is followed by two consonants, except a mute before a liquid, must be in a long syllable. When this and similar rules are applied with due regard for possible elision of final syllables in words, the quantity, or length, of a large enough number of syllables is decided so that only one of the 32 patterns remains possible for more than 90 per cent of the lines. Further, the number of lines which are erroneously scanned is extremely small (Greenberg 1967; Ott 1970).

For Plautus' writings, the situation is quite different. This dramatic poet lived from approximately 251 to 184 BC, nearly 175 years before Vergil; he is the earliest writer of Latin verse whose works remain extant in any substantial quantity. Because of his early date, there is a considerable controversy about whether his meter is based on syllabic length, as is that of the classical authors, or whether it is partially or completely dependent on the stress accent of the individual words. It is therefore necessary to be able to test both possibilities separately and in combination; the data must be considered in several different fashions. Since the accent of an individual word is normally taken as depending directly on the length of the syllables in that word, providing information about syllabic lengths allows testing both forms of scansion with nearly equal ease; different computer programs can be applied to the same specially prepared text. On the assumption that meter should be fairly regular, indication of which method of scansion produces more uniform results can contribute to our knowledge of the development of the Latin language as well as to our understanding of Plautus' works.

Even if syllabic length is taken as the basis of Plautine metrics, the nature of his lines is far more complex than that of the classical dactylic hexameters. One of the most common of the many meters which Plautus uses is the iambic senarius; for instance, in the *Truculentus*, which will be used as a sample play, 296 out of 968 lines, over 30 per cent, are in this meter. The fundamental metrical unit is an iamb (.-), and it is repeated six times. Again, the last syllable of the line is anceps, either long or short. Further, the next-to-last syllable must be short. Of more concern is the fact that in the first five feet of the line, the following patterns may be substituted for an iamb with no immediately obvious restrictions: a spondee (--), an anapest (..-), a dactyl (-..), a tribrach (...), or a proceleusmatic (....). Perhaps it would be easier to summarize by saying that a trochee (-.) is impossible in an iambic line. Because there are theoretically 6^5 or 7776 scansions possible, when the final syllable is treated as anceps, the methods applied in scanning classical dactylic hexameters by computer are impractical; therefore, a totally different approach was devised, involving the marking of the length of each syllable prior to determining the scansion for any line.

As with nearly every computer project in literature, an initial requirement for this work was a text in a form which a computer could use. Fortunately, Plautus is the subject of a continuing lexical study by Albert Maniet at the Université Laval in Québec and, with the co-operation of Louis Delatte, it was possible to obtain from the Laboratoire d'Analyse Statistique des Langues Anciennes in Liège a magnetic tape copy of the text of the *Amphitruo*, *Asinaria*, *Aulularia*, *Bacchides*, and *Captivi*, the first five plays in Lindsay's Oxford Classical Text. For these plays obtained through Delatte, comparatively little editing was required to convert the texts into the form chosen as a standard for this project.

Subsequently, the *Rudens*, *Stichus*, *Trinummus*, and *Truculentus*, the last four of the twenty complete plays in Lindsay's edition, were put into machine-readable form. Experience in preparing the texts on the Dartmouth Time-Sharing System using a Honeywell 635 computer with 160K words of core has suggested that it is best to type the text directly into disc files twice, preferably from different kinds of terminals so that mistakes in special characters like punctuation are less likely to result in identical errors; IBM 2741 or Novar terminals, with upper- and lower-case characters, and model 33 teletypes, with only upper-case characters, have been used. This method of direct input is practical because up to 133 interactive terminals have simultaneously accessed the Dartmouth system, which depends on software developed entirely at the college. After the number of lines in each version of the input text has been verified as correct, the two are collated by a simple program. The errors which are found are corrected in both copies of the text, and the collating and correcting are repeated until the two texts are identical. Careful proof-reading against the printed text at this point uncovers about one error in every 100 lines of the computerized text; how many mistakes remain undetected is, of course, unknown.

Once a text has been prepared accurately in machine-readable form, it is now a comparatively routine matter to compile a forward and a reverse concordance for each play as a working tool for later consultation. For metrical studies, where the exact metrical form of a word is often influenced by the following words, the form of concordance in which words are sorted by context seems preferable; such an arrangement facilitates finding instances where a word beginning with a vowel or *h* causes the elision of the final syllable of a word ending in a vowel or *m*. Since it is uncertain when these working concordances will be consulted or for what words they will be used, each one is printed on a line printer and kept available for eventual use.

At approximately the same stage in the work, a frequency list is compiled. Like other authors, Plautus tends to use a comparatively few words very often and many of the forms in a given play only once in that play. Unlike most Latin authors for whom material is available, *et*, the conjunction *and*, is not the most frequently used word; rather, *est*, the word for *is*, usually occurs most often, and *et* is several places down the list. The preceding compilations are produced under batch-processing with programs in FORTRAN and a minimal number of assembly-language subroutines coupled with a standard SORT-MERGE package; all the other work is done under time-sharing in the BASIC language, with the use of another SORT-MERGE package where appropriate.

The compilations which have been described are preliminary by-

products and working tools in the process of preparing the text for
scansion. This preparation entails marking the length of each syllable in
the play; then the metrical pattern can be determined directly, if syllabic
length is chosen as the governing factor, or the location of the word
accents and their pattern can be discovered, if stress accent is considered
instead of quantity. Obviously, one way of marking the lengths of syllables
would be doing so during the preparation of the text itself, but there are
many disadvantages to this approach which are readily apparent. For
instance, it is frequently advisable to consult a printed dictionary such
as Lewis and Short, *A Latin Dictionary*, which has been taken as a standard for this project; words in texts, however, rarely occur in alphabetized
order, so that much page-turning would be required as the dictionary
was consulted. Much more important is the fact that no advantage would
be taken of the multiple occurrence of many forms, which should be
marked consistently and which ideally should be treated only once rather
than many times.

Therefore, instead of tagging manually the syllables of each word in a
play during the initial preparation of the text or at a later stage, a totally
different approach is used. A simple alphabetized word list is prepared
for each play; this list merely provides evidence that a form occurs,
without indicating where or even how many times it is found. Once the
word list has been compiled, each word is inspected, and the length of
the syllables in it is entered with an interactive program which also
provides some simple checks, primarily to ascertain that the correct
number of syllables has been indicated. Even though this procedure
takes advantage of the alphabetical order of the words to simplify consulting a dictionary and also puts together successive forms of the same
root, which are quite likely to have the same scansion as the root itself,
there was considerable tedium involved in preparing the dictionary for
the initial play; for subsequent plays, words found in the earlier versions
of the dictionary can be used directly. A short sample of the dictionary
for the *Truculentus* is given in figure 1, it makes clear that each vowel
in a word is marked. The spelling with *j* and *v* has been preferred
over the one with consonantal *i* and *u*.

There are, unfortunately, many forms in Latin which can have more
than one scansion, if spelling alone is considered. Most obvious are
nouns in the nominative or ablative singular of the first declension, but
there is also confusion between the present and perfect tenses in the form
venit, and there are words which are homonymous in the standard,
lexical sense. Since the correct scansion for these words can almost
always be derived from the semantic context of the word, those words
which can have two or more scansions are included in the dictionary but
are marked with the arbitrary sign *W* to indicate their status. Additionally, there are some words for which no scansion is found in Lewis and
Short's dictionary or for which the scansion depends on the emphasis

```
VOCATUS;W
VOLAM,11
VOLEBAS,122
VOLGO,22
VOLNUS,21
VOLO,12
VOLT,2
VOLTIS,21
VOLTURII,2112
VOLUMUS,111
VOLUNT,12
VOLUP,11
VOLUPTAS,122
VOLUPTATEM,1221
VORAT,15
VORTERUNT,222
VORTIT,W
VOS,2
VOSMET,21
VOSTRA,W
VOSTRAE,292
VOSTRAM,21
VOSTRAS,22
VOSTRIS,22
VOSTRO,22
VOSTRUM,21
VOTAT,15
VOTO,W
ZONA,W
ZONAM,21
```

Figure 1. Sample of the dictionary for the *Truculentus*

demanded by the context. The questionable syllables in these words are marked by a *3*, since the correct syllable length will be determined later from metrical considerations, where possible, rather than from semantic information. All words are included in the dictionary, however, so that it will not be necessary to make repeatedly the determination that the same word is of indefinite scansion as dictionaries for subsequent plays are prepared.

After each word in the dictionary has been marked, various checks are made to detect impossible scansions, such as a vowel marked as short in a syllable followed by two consonants which make the syllable long. Another program prints out all the pairs of words which are spelled identically up to some particular vowel but have preceding vowels which are marked differently; the rationale for this test is the fact that such words probably, but not necessarily, come from the same root and therefore should usually be marked in the same way for that root. At any time that an error is detected, interactive editing facilities allow the possibility of immediately making corrections in the dictionary or in the text itself.

Once the dictionary is in a satisfactory condition, the play is temporarily divided up into 100-line segments. For each segment, a word list is prepared, and, on the basis of this list, a small dictionary is extracted from the larger one for the full play. This segmentation makes it possible, at the cost of a few extra steps, for the next program to work faster and to operate easily within the 16k words of core normally available to an individual user on the Dartmouth system; more important, the short

R

length of text being processed also helps avoid human errors caused by fatigue. The next program goes through the segment of text word by word, looking up each word in the short dictionary. If, by some mischance, a word is not found, or if a word is found to be marked with a *W* indicating that the scansion is dependent on the context, the line containing the word is printed on a terminal, unless it has already been given, and then the word itself is printed. The scansion is immediately entered directly by the person using the program. On the basis of the information which has been put in or of the coding found in the dictionary, indications of syllable length are inserted after each vowel in the text. About half an hour of a person's time is required for this processing of 100 lines of text. At this stage, the text itself looks like the sample of the first 10 lines of the *Truculentus* given in figure 2; the line-numbering is by tens to allow easy inclusion of text added or rearranged by editors after the numbering scheme had become fixed. The results shown here are kept to be used as the data for all future analyses, and any errors in marking which are discovered later are corrected in this file.

```
 10  %PRO% PE2RPA2RVA1M PA2RTE1M PO2STU1LA5T #PLA9U2TU1S LO1CI2
 20  DE2 VO2STRI2S MA2GNI2S A2TQU8E1 A1MO9E2NI2S MO9E2NI1BU1S,
 30  #A1THE2NA2S QU8O2 SI1NE1 A2RCHI1TE2CTI2S CO2NFE1RA5T.
 40  QU8L1D NU2NC? DA1TU2RI2=N E2STI1S A1N NO2N? A2DNU1O2NT
 50  +ME1LI1O5R ME2 QU8I1DE4M VO23I2S+ ME2\ A28LA2TU2RU1M SI1NE1 MO1RA2;
 60  QU8I1D SI2 DE2 VO2STRO2 QU8I2PPI1A1M O2RE1M\? A28NU1O2NT.
 70  E9U2\ HE2RCLE1! I1N VO28I2S RE1SI1DE2NT MO2RE2S PRI2STI1NI2,
 80  A1D DE2NE1GA2NDU1M U1T CE1LE1RI2 LI2NGU8A2 U2TA2MI1NI2.
 90  SE1D HO2C A1GA2MU1S QU8O2JA2 HU2C VE2NTU1M'ST GRA2TI1A2.
100  #A1THE2NI2S +TRA2CTO2\+ I1TA1 U1T HO2C E2ST PRO2SCA9E2NI1U1M
```

Figure 2. Marked text of the beginning of the *Truculentus*

Up to this point, the words in the play have been treated by the computer only as discrete entities totally independent of their context in a line; this approach has been taken despite the fact that the length of the final syllable in a word is very often modified by the nature of the beginning of the next word in the line. The next routine treats each line as a unit; like most computer programs for scanning Latin, it works through the line from the end to the beginning, an approach which greatly simplifies the treatment of the final syllables in words. In particular, elision, or loss of a final syllable ending in *m* or a vowel, is assumed whenever the succeeding word begins with *h* or a vowel. Lengthening of a short final syllable ending in a consonant is also assumed whenever the next word begins with a consonant other than *h*.

The results of this scanning program are given in two forms. Figure 3, again for the first 10 lines of the *Truculentus*, shows the form which is used by a person to check and verify the results of the scansion whenever there is any question about them. Word endings are indicated by *I*, elision by *]*, and hiatus, or the lack of elision where it could occur, by *[*; since elision is normally assumed, a special indicator for hiatus must be

```
PLMETERQ  04/24/71  12:28


      %        -    - I -   - I -   . - I      - - I . -
   10 %PRO% PERPARVAM PARTEM POSTULAT #PLAUTUS LOCI

      -I -    - I -   - I-    ]. - - I    - . .
   20 DE VOSTRIS MAGNIS ATQUE. AMOENIS MOENIBUS,

      .   - - I  -I . .  ]-    . - - I -   . =
   30 #ATHENAS QUO SINE. ARCHITECTIS CONFERAT.

      -  I -    I . - -   I-   . I - I -   I- .-
   40 QUID NUNC? DATURI=N ESTIS AN NON? ADNUONT

      . .- I -I   . : I - -   I -[-   - - - I . .I . -
   50 +MELIOR ME QUIDEM VOBIS+ ME ABLATURUM SINE MORA;

      - I -I -I -    -I -   .  ]- . [-   .-
   60 QUID SI DE VOSTRO QUIPPIAM OREM? ABNUONT.

      -[ -     ]- I - - I . . - I - - I -   . -
   70 EU HERCLE! IN VOBIS RESIDENT MORES PRISTINI,

      - I - . -     ]- I . . -I -   ]- - - .-
   80 AD DENEGANDUM UT CELERI LINGUA UTAMINI.

      . I - I. - - I -   ]- I -   I  - .-
   90 SED HOC AGAMUS QUOJA HUC VENTUM'ST GRATIA.

      .  - - I   - - [. ]. I - I-  I -   - ..
  100 #ATHENIS +TRACTO+ ITA UT HOC EST PROSCAENIUM
```

Figure 3. Results of scanning the first 10 lines of the *Truculentus*

put into the text where it occurs, and \ (reverse slash) has been chosen as the sign. The scansion also is kept in a condensed form, with indications of changes of speakers, as data for other computer programs to use.

The most important of the next series of programs is one which checks iambic senarii, septenarii, and octonarii, and trochaic septenarii and octonarii for regularity; these are the meters most used by Plautus, and dialogue passages are normally written in one of them. The sections of the play in each meter must be treated separately, and the data file is therefore divided into individual files for each meter, with Lindsay's suggestions at the back of the Oxford Classical Text as an initial guide. Each line is checked to be certain that it contains exactly the requisite number of feet and that there are no illegal feet, such as trochees in iambic lines. In some lines, particularly where there is a long series of short syllables, two scansions may be possible, and these verses are indicated.

Initially, a number of lines are noted as impossible to scan. Inspection often indicates that such lines contain hiatus, which must be marked in the text so that the programs will not assume elision. Another frequent occurrence is synizesis, the merging of two syllables into one within a word; this phenomenon is found particularly often in possessive adjectives like *meo*, which is either one or two syllables depending apparently on the emphasis which the word is to be given. A special program also

checks to be certain that the penultimate syllable in iambic and trochaic
lines is really short where it is required to be so; trochaic septenarii lack
the final syllable of the last trochee, so that the penultimate syllable of
the line can in fact be short. As corrections are found to be necessary,
they are entered in the marked text, and the scanning and checking are
repeated as many times as necessary; several repetitions are easily feasible
within a single day. An analogous program checks anapestic lines, which
tend to be in clusters of varying numbers of feet.

At this point, one special check is made. As mentioned previously, for
some words the scansion is uncertain in Lewis and Short's dictionary;
the scansion can vary for others, such as the dative case of the personal
and reflexive pronouns *mihi*, *tibi*, and *sibi* (.. or .-). These questionable
syllables have been marked specially to indicate that the length of the
syllable is unknown and cannot be determined directly by the semantic
context. A variant of the program which checks scansion is now used to
try all these questionable syllables as first long and then short; whenever
a line cannot be scanned with one option and can with the other, the
length of the syllable has been determined by the process of elimination
and can be entered in the marked text. At the same time, the amount of
emphasis which the word should receive is suggested.

Ultimately, there do remain some lines which do not scan, often because
of a textual corruption acknowledged by editors. For the lines which
admit two scansions, a choice must be made; where syllables of questionable length are involved, they are arbitrarily treated as long. There are
also a few lines, primarily those containing a long series of short syllables,
for which two scansions would often be admissible; for these, the scansion
is entered directly from a terminal, with consideration of the conditions
of word endings.

```
10 .%--F-I-F-I-F.-FI--FI.-
20 .-I-F-I-F-I-F].-F-I-F..
30 ..-F-I-FI.]-F.-F-I-F.=
40 .-I-FI.-F-I-F.I-FI-I-F.-
50 .X
60 .-I-F]-I-F-I-F.]-F.[-F.-
70 .-[-F]-I-F-I..F-I-F-I-F.-
80 .-I-F.-F]-I..F.-I-F]--F.-
90 ..I-FI.-F-I-F]-I-F-I-F.-
100 ..-F-I-F-.[.].FI-I-FI--F..
```

Figure 4. Data file of scansions with feet marked for
the first 10 lines of the *Truculentus*

The results of these steps are shown in figure 4; the data are used far
more easily by a computer than by a person, but the important thing to
note is the fact that indications of the boundaries of feet have been added
and are indicated by *F*. It now becomes possible to ask specific questions,
such as the number of times a word-end coincides with a foot boundary

at a given position in the line. For the most part, it seems preferable to provide the answers to such questions as they are asked rather than to attempt to think up all the likely questions in advance and then to print out the appropriate tables.

TYPE	1		2		3		4		5		TOTAL	
·⁻	43	15%	105	35%	52	18%	118	40%	33	11%	351	24%
⁻⁻	147	50%	122	41%	171	58%	125	42%	216	73%	781	53%
··⁻	53	18%	18	6%	7	2%	7	2%	33	11%	118	8%
⁻··	42	14%	36	12%	54	18%	29	10%	13	4%	174	12%
···	6	2%	13	4%	12	4%	15	5%	1	0%	47	3%
····	5	2%	2	1%	0	0%	2	1%	0	0%	9	1%
TOTAL	296		296		296		296		296		1480	

POSITION 6

·⁻	175	59%
··	121	41%
TOTAL	296	

Figure 5. Table summarizing the meter of the iambic senarii in the *Truculentus*

There are exceptions, however, and tables of some kinds have been constructed. The one in figure 5 gives a summary of the results for all the 296 lines in the iambic senarius meter in the *Truculentus*. For each type of foot, the absolute number of lines out of 296 and percentage with this pattern are given for each of the first five feet. In the right-hand column, the summaries across the different feet in a line are provided. The sixth foot, because of the special restrictions placed on it, is treated separately. It is interesting to observe that in a so-called iambic meter, iambs predominate only in the last foot, while in most positions, spondees are the most common metrical form; this situation may be a reflection of the apparent preponderance of long syllables in the Latin language (Waite 1970a, p. 106). It also appears that iambs do occur somewhat more often in even-numbered feet. Since there is therefore some reason to think that feet should be treated in pairs, the results have been summarized in this form; the tables are somewhat more complex because of the increased number of possibilities, although by no means all of the 36 possible combinations do in fact occur. Similar tables are easily prepared for the other standard meters.

Very preliminary comparisons of data from the *Asinaria, Aulularia,* and *Truculentus* have suggested an extremely high degree of similarity between the metrics of the different plays. Since they were presumably written by the same author, these results are encouraging but not surprising. There are many other questions whose answers await further analysis. In particular, the whole relationship of word accent and meter has not yet been treated; with the marked texts available, it should be comparatively easy to devise the computer programs required to prepare various kinds of tables, since word accent and the length of the syllables in words are interrelated. Other questions of special interest to metricians, such as the conditions governing the occurrence of tribrachs (...) could be posed; answers might be suggested by collecting and sorting appropriately the lines containing this metrical pattern. Others might find it more relevant to inspect the lines where rare metrical patterns are found to determine if the meter was perhaps being used to emphasize a special dramatic effect.

Many such questions can be posed, but perhaps the method of the study which has been described is as important as its potential effects on the knowledge of Latin metrics. Information which can be assigned to a word definitely in advance has been done so; that which is dependent on the context has been entered as it is necessary to provide it, using the context itself as a guide. Metrical patterns have been treated, but the same means of entering data could be applied equally well to various lexical, morphological, and grammatical analyses and to a wide range of other possibilities. Finding the appropriate balance between a computer's ability to handle large quantities of repetitive data and a person's ability to make decisions on the basis of very complex rules is an important part of using a computer effectively. Perhaps the approach taken in studying Plautus' metrics offers one reasonable approximation of this balance and may be useful to others in the future.

REFERENCES

Greenberg, Nathan A. (1967) Scansion purement automatique de l'hexamètre dactylique. *Revue* of the Laboratoire d'Analyse Statistique des Langues Anciennes, **3**, 1-30.

Ott, Wilhelm (1970) *Metrische Analysen zur Ars Poetica des Horaz*. Göppingen; Alfred Kümmerle.

Waite, Stephen V.F. (1970a) Approaches to the analysis of Latin prose, applied to Cato, Sallust and Livy. *Revue* of the Laboratoire d'Analyse Statistique des Langues Anciennes, **2**, 91-120.

Waite, Stephen V.F. (1970b) Metrical indices to Statius' *Achilleid. Hephaistos*, **I, 1**, 28-70.

Alliteration in Barbour's *Bruce*:
A study using SNAP programming

The Bruce, a Scots poem of roughly 13,500 lines by John Barbour, presents rewarding possibilities for studying the manipulation of alliteration in a poem. My hypothesis is that as a prosodic device, alliterations rise and fall in harmony with the effect of the work—that is, where Barbour makes an especially forceful statement, where he is describing battle and where the emotional thrust is especially great, *there* is alliteration. The work, relating the struggle for independence in the early fourteenth century and written during the flowering of the alliterative revival later in that century, is not uniformly alliterative as are the *Wars of Alexander, Gawain and the Green Knight* and, to cite a later Scots poem, the *Tua Mariit Wemen and the Wedo* (*c.*1500). Rather, Barbour writes in octosyllabic couplets with alliteration either an alternate means of driving the rhythm of the line or, more often, an ornament to it.

These lines, for example, from the *Tua Mariit Wemen and the Wedo* show alliteration used as the structural frame of the line. That is, every line contains two, three or more words that alliterate and there is no other structural device, such as rime or regular meter:

> Apon the Midsummer evin, mirriest of nichtis,
> I muvit furth allane, neir as midnicht wes past,
> Besyd ane gudlie grein garth, full of gay flouris,
> Hegeit, of ane huge hicht, with hawthorne treis;
> Quhairon ane bird, on ane bransche, so birst out hir notis
> That never ane blythfullar bird was on the beuche hard . . .
> (lines 1-6).

Dunbar's poem, though late, is a good example because having consciously chosen the then archaic alliterative meter as a demonstration of his virtuosity he is very consistent (Mackenzie 1932).

In contrast Barbour's lines are structured by rime and meter, mainly iambic, as for example in these lines from Book I (Skeat 1894), where Barbour makes a low-keyed comment on the Scots' naïveté:

> ʒe traistyt in lawte,
> As sympile folk but mawyte;
> And wyst nocht quhat suld eftir tyd.
> For in this warld, that is sa wyde,
> Is nane determynatly that sall
> Knaw thingis that ar for to fall;
> But god, that is off maist poweste,
> Reserwyt till his maieste

> For to knaw, in his prescience,
> Off alkyn tyme the mowence. (lines 125-34)

Here there is little alliteration. In the following passage on battle, however, although octosyllabic couplets continue, alliteration seems to be the
shaping force, in the third, seventh and ninth lines especially:

> On athir syd thus war thai yhar,
> And till assemble all redy war.
> Thai strucht thar speris, on athir syd,
> And swa ruydly gan samyn ryd,
> That speris all to-fruschyt war,
> And feyle men dede, and woundyt sar;
> The blud owt at thar byrnys brest.
> For the best, and the worthiest,
> That wilfull war to wyn honour,
> Plungyt in the stalwart stour,
> And rowtis ruyd about thaim dang. (II, 346-56)

Since Barbour's work links the poems of the alliterative revival and
French-inspired poems in octosyllabic couplets, studying where and
how he uses alliteration seems to be a worthwhile endeavor. I believe that
he heightens some passages by a deliberate use of the alliterative meter.

A study that would either support or refute this hypothesis seemed, for
two reasons, to require a computer. First, it can deal with the tedious
chore of finding the lines with alliteration, without missing any because
of fatigue or momentary inattention—not that every example of alliteration in the text is necessary to establish a fairly precise idea of how
Barbour uses it. Secondly, the computer would not be subjective in its
decisions, that is, notice the alliteration only where it would be interesting
to find it. A further strong inducement to doing the study at all was that
an orthographic text (prepared by Dr J. A. C. Stevenson, Deputy Editor of
the *Dictionary of the Older Scottish Tongue*) was already available in
computer-readable form in the *Older Scottish Textual Archive* (see
Aitken 1971). By courtesy of both A. J. Aitken, Senior Editor of the
Dictionary of the Older Scottish Tongue, and Queens College in New York,
the computer tape was made available. Here is an example of the benefits
to be derived from a standardized literary archive, such as the one that the
editors of the *DOST* have assembled. It would hardly be worth the time
and money required to key-punch all of Barbour's *Bruce* merely to study
alliteration. But as part of an archive of Older Scottish texts, *The Bruce* is
available for any kind of study (Aitken 1971).

I chose SNAP as my programming language because I could do it
(Barnett 1969). After taking a course in FORTRAN the summer before
I learned SNAP, I could understand it and do all the problems in the text,
but I could not devise any new programs of my own or adapt any of the
textbook's programs to my problems. FORTRAN, of course, is the first
and the most widespread of all the computer languages. As such, it has

been thoroughly debugged. And there is no doubt that someone who can grasp it can certainly use it for this sort of data collection. SNAP in fact is based on FORTRAN and a SNAP program is translated into FORTRAN in the SNAP processor. Because it is a new language, SNAP is not yet thoroughly debugged, but most of the operations are in good working order and Dr Barnett is improving it constantly.

Within a few weeks of my introduction to SNAP, even before I finished the course, I developed three programs. It is these that I have been refining and modifying. My plan is eventually to combine these and other programs to provide me with the data for a stylistic analysis. In other words, the computer does not do the literary criticism—I do. But the computer helps by providing the data.

The first program counts words in a line. I have had to learn to restrain myself from doing operations simply because they could be done, such as counting the number of characters in a word, but counting words was an easy exercise for me to start with, and perhaps it needs no further justification. Also it might be interesting to know the ratio of alliterating to non-alliterating words in a line. The effect, for example, of 'Defoullyt foully wndre fete' where three of four words alliterate—all the content words in fact—is different from 'Yar mony a fey fell wndre fete' where three of seven alliterate.

The program prints final totals of lines containing nine, eight, etc., words and also prints lines containing fewer than four and more than eight words (table 1). It was interesting to discover that so many lines (84.2 per cent) had six, seven or eight words in eight syllables—an indication, perhaps, that Barbour relies mainly on words of native rather than foreign origin.

Interestingly enough, once I could write a program in SNAP, it was fairly simple to translate it into FORTRAN—with the help of a programmer—in this case my husband, a computer engineer. A comparison of the two programs shows that SNAP is much closer to natural language. It is very wordy, but for this reason it is comfortable for people who are more used to words than numbers. It is also easy to go back to a program written months before and still understand it. No format statements are required, simplifying all print procedures. It is also easy to insert what I call 'keyholes'—print commands that enable one to see into the operation when there is a problem. Operations are identified by name rather than by number, making comment cards unnecessary. Finally, all values are integers and it is easy to look at one character of a record at a time. These advantages compensate for SNAP's wordiness and its inability to handle, at present, do-loops.

The second program prints every line that contains initial alliteration—that is, it does not note internal alliteration as in the line 'Wndyr hors feyt defoulyt yar'. Perhaps I should pause here to explain my criteria for determining alliteration. In Old English, alliteration occurs only on

SET THE NINE COUNT TO 0.
SET THE EIGHT COUNT TO 0.
.
.   [etc. to one count]*
SET THE ONE COUNT TO 0.
(INPUT ACTION) READ A RECORD. SET N TO 1.
IF THE N-TH CHARACTER OF THE RECORD IS " " REPEAT FROM INPUT
ACTION.
IF THE N-TH CHARACTER OF THE RECORD IS " < " REPEAT FROM INPUT
ACTION.
IF THE N-TH CHARACTER OF THE RECORD IS "?" REPEAT FROM FINAL
ACTION.
SET THE BLANK COUNT TO 0.
(LOOP START) INCREASE N BY 1.
IF THE N-TH CHARACTER OF THE RECORD IS " " CONTINUE WITH
BLANK CHECK, OTHERWISE REPEAT FROM LOOP START.
(BLANK CHECK) INCREASE N BY 1.
IF THE N-TH CHARACTER OF THE RECORD IS " " CONTINUE WITH
OUTPUT ACTION, OTHERWISE INCREASE THE BLANK COUNT BY 1.
REPEAT FROM LOOP START.
(OUTPUT ACTION) INCREASE THE BLANK COUNT BY 1.
IF THE BLANK COUNT IS EQUAL TO NINE INCREASE THE NINE COUNT
BY 1, PRINT THE RECORD, CONTINUE WITH INPUT ACTION.
IF THE BLANK COUNT IS EQUAL TO EIGHT INCREASE THE EIGHT
COUNT BY 1, CONTINUE WITH INPUT ACTION.
.
.   [etc. to one count, printing only lines < 4 and > 8.]
(FINAL ACTION) PRINT "//TOTALS//".
PRINT "THE NINE COUNT IS   " THEN THE NINE COUNT.
PRINT "THE EIGHT COUNT IS " THEN THE EIGHT COUNT.
.
.   [etc. to one count]

EXECUTE.

Results with 181 records (nine blanks)

ON SARACENYS WARRAYAND   00001660
                                        [the only record with < 4]

                                        [Totals for the whole tape:
TOTALS
THE NINE COUNT IS   0   30
THE EIGHT COUNT IS   23   2,119
THE SEVEN COUNT IS   57   5,055
THE SIX COUNT IS   56   4,224
THE FIVE COUNT IS   31   1,720
THE FOUR COUNT IS   4   359
THE THREE COUNT IS   1   30
THE TWO COUNT IS   0   2⎫
THE ONE COUNT IS   0   3⎬ defective lines
                                         _____
                                         13,542]

* Comments not in the program appear in brackets.

Table 1. SNAP word count.

stressed syllables, but later, alliteration, which can become decorative,
is on unstressed syllables also. Therefore, I am not at this stage taking
stress into account. In Old English, two or three words alliterate in a line
that contains eight to ten syllables. In Middle English and Older Scots
there are often more alliterating words and also more syllables, but I
consider two occurrences of alliteration to be a valid minimum for each
line. In Old English it is common to find that all vowels alliterate with
each other; this is less common in Scots. For example, *Beowulf* has 15·5

per cent vocalic alliteration while Dunbar's poem has only 2·5 per cent
(Oakden 1930). Therefore, I decided to treat each vowel as alliterating
only with itself. In English but not in Scots, *h* and vowels alliterate
together. Thus in Barbour *h* is a separate phoneme. In Old English *sp, sc*
[ʃ], *st* are the only groups that alliterate only with identical groups, but
later there were many licenses—in both directions: the creation of new
groups and the elimination of groups. For example, Dunbar adds the
group *sm* and also allows all *s*'s to alliterate together. Thus *sch* [ʃ] and *s*
alliterate. Elimination of groups is the standard I chose for Barbour. I
also consider that *wr* alliterates not only with *w* but also on occasion with
r, as in the line 'Quhethir it wes through wrang or richt'.

Because there are so many function words that alliterate but do not
contribute to the actual effect of alliteration, I had to find a way to discount
them, at least temporarily. These are the conjunctions, auxiliaries, noun-
determiners, interrogatives and some miscellaneous words usually unstressed in the line. Many function words begin with a thorn, a *y* in the
MSS and on the computer tape. When I devised a program that printed
out these 'thorn' words from a sample data deck, I verified that *most* were
function words. Then I combined this '*y*-list' program with the alliteration program to get alliteration without thorns. Later I may try to re-
consider them, because while a line like 'Yis child yat clemys zour man to
be' does not seem to have the effect of alliteration on the two function
words, 'yis' and 'yat', a line like 'Yat yai and yairis had yaim wrocht'
certainly seems to be alliterating on the pronouns. Quite often, however,
the more important words beginning with the thorn sound begin with *th*
rather than *y*. Still another problem with *y*-words is that some words
on the tape begin with *y*'s that are not thorns but 'real' *y*'s, vowel or
consonant: for example, 'ythanly', meaning assiduously, and 'yemanry';
fortunately, however, 'real' consonant *y* is almost always represented by
yok ('ȝ') in the MS, and *z* on the tape.

The program (table 2) prints the alliterating letter, then the record
and finally the line number. As soon as any alliteration is found the record
is printed, so as yet there is no indication in this program of double
alliteration on two letters or triple alliteration on one letter.

Other function words can be eliminated by inserting in the alliteration
program a function word test or a stop list. There are some forty function
words in Barbour. In this program (table 3) only the word 'and' is
eliminated, but the same procedure may be followed to discount the
others.

Another problem is that phonemes are not always consistently represented by the same letter. An editing program is necessary, but first I
wanted simply to count the occurrences of some letters that might need
editing to see the extent of the problem and thus determine the best way
to deal with it. The letters concerned are *q, th, c, w*, and *v*. *Quh*, for example, is [xw] or perhaps [hw] and alliterates in Dunbar with *w* (lines

```
SET THE LINE NO TO 0.
(INPUT) READ A RECORD. SET N TO 1.
IF THE N-TH CHARACTER OF THE RECORD IS "  " REPEAT FROM
INPUT.
IF THE N-TH CHARACTER OF THE RECORD IS "‹" REPEAT FROM
INPUT.
INCREASE THE LINE NO BY 1.
SET L TO N.
IF THE N-TH CHARACTER OF THE RECORD IS "Y" CONTINUE WITH
RE-TRY.
(LOOP START) INCREASE N BY 1.
IF THE N-TH CHARACTER OF THE RECORD IS "  " INCREASE N BY 1,
OTHERWISE REPEAT FROM LOOP START.
IF THE N-TH CHARACTER OF THE RECORD IS "  " CONTINUE WITH
RE-TRY.
IF THE N-TH CHARACTER OF THE RECORD IS "Y" CONTINUE WITH
LOOP START, OTHERWISE CONTINUE WITH ALLITERATION CHECK.
(ALLITERATION CHECK)
IF THE N-TH CHARACTER OF THE RECORD IS THE SAME AS THE L-TH
CHARACTER OF THE RECORD CONTINUE WITH OUTPUT ACTION,
OTHERWISE REPEAT FROM LOOP START.
(OUTPUT ACTION)
PRINT THE N-TH CHARACTER OF THE RECORD THEN "    " THEN THE
RECORD THEN "    " THEN THE LINE NO. REPEAT FROM INPUT.
(RE-TRY) INCREASE L BY 1.
IF THE L-TH CHARACTER OF THE RECORD IS "  " INCREASE L BY 1,
OTHERWISE REPEAT FROM RE-TRY.
IF THE L-TH CHARACTER OF THE RECORD IS "  " CONTINUE WITH
INPUT.
IF THE L-TH CHARACTER OF THE RECORD IS "Y" REPEAT FROM
RE-TRY, OTHERWISE SET N TO L. REPEAT FROM LOOP START.
EXECUTE.
```

Results through the 15th line*

B	SUPPOS YAT YAI BE NOCHT BOT FABILL	00000210	2
S	YAN SULD STORYS YAT SUTHFAST WER	00000220	3
H	HAWE DOUBILL PLESANCE IN HERYING	00000240	5
T	THAT SCHAWYS YE THING RYCHT AS IT WES	00000270	8
A	AND SUTH THINGIS YAT AR LIKAND	00000280	9
W	YARFOR I WALD FAYNE SET MY WILL	00000300	11
M	GIFF MY WYT MYCHT SUFFICE YARTILL	00000310	12
S	TO PUT IN WRYT A SUTHFAST STORY	00000320	13
I	YAT IT LEST AY FURTH IN MEMORY	00000330	14
L	SWA YAT NA TYME OF LENTH IT LET	00000340	15

* The last eight characters of the record are the
record no. Excess spaces between the end of the line
and the record no. are omitted.

Table 2. Alliteration program without thorns.

[This program is similar to the one in table 2. Between the INPUT and the
LOOP START insert the following:]

```
(1-ST FWORD TEST)
IF THE L-TH AND SUBSEQUENT CHARACTERS OF THE RECORD ARE
NOT "AND" CONTINUE WITH LOOP START, OTHERWISE CONTINUE
WITH RE-TRY.
```

[At the ALLITERATION CHECK operation, change CONTINUE WITH OUTPUT
ACTION to CONTINUE WITH FUNCTION WORD TEST. This operation follows:]

```
(FUNCTION WORD TEST)
IF THE N-TH AND SUBSEQUENT CHARACTERS OF THE RECORD ARE
NOT "AND" CONTINUE WITH OUTPUT ACTION, OTHERWISE CONTINUE
WITH LOOP START.
```

[At the end of the RE-TRY operation, change REPEAT FROM LOOP START to
REPEAT FROM 1-ST FWORD TEST.]
Results: Same as in table 2 except line 9 eliminated.

Table 3. Alliteration program, function word AND eliminated.

195, 336), which in turn alliterates with *wr* (line 529). *Qu*, on the other hand, is [kw] and thus alliterates with [k], spelt sometimes with a *c*, sometimes with a *k*.

There is a two-fold problem with these letters. On the one hand, lines that look like alliterating lines really are not: '& *ch*aungyt *c*ontenance & late'. On the other hand, lines that actually do alliterate are not noted by the alliteration program: 'Bot men *s*ayis it wes *c*ertane thing'.

[This program is the same as the one in tables 2 and 3 except for the OUTPUT ACTION.]

(OUTPUT ACTION)
PRINT "/" THEN THE N-TH CHARACTER OF THE RECORD THEN "   "
THEN THE RECORD THEN "   " THEN THE LINE NO.
IF THE N-TH CHARACTER OF THE RECORD IS "Q" CONTINUE WITH ASTERISK.
IF THE N-TH CHARACTER OF THE RECORD IS "T" INCREASE N BY 1, OTHERWISE CONTINUE WITH C.
IF THE N-TH CHARACTER OF THE RECORD IS "H" CONTINUE WITH ASTERISK.
(C) IF THE N-TH CHARACTER OF THE RECORD IS "C" CONTINUE WITH ASTERISK.
IF THE N-TH CHARACTER OF THE RECORD IS "W" CONTINUE WITH ASTERISK.
IF THE N-TH CHARACTER OF THE RECORD IS "V" CONTINUE WITH ASTERISK, OTHERWISE REPEAT FROM INPUT.
(ASTERISK)
PRINT "**".*
REPEAT FROM INPUT.

Results

B	SUPPOS YAT YAI BE NOCHT BOT FABILL	00000210	2
S	YAN SULD STORYS YAT SUTHFAST WER	00000220	3
H	HAWE DOUBILL PLESANCE IN HERYING	00000240	5
T	THAT SCHAWYS YE THING RYCHT AS IT WES	00000270	8
************************************			
W	YARFOR I WALD FAYNE SET MY WILL	00000300	11
************************************			
M	GIFF MY WYT MYCHT SUFFICE YARTILL	00000310	12
S	TO PUT IN WRYT A SUTHFAST STORY	00000320	13
I	YAT IT LEST AY FURTH IN MEMORY	00000330	14
L	SWA YAT NA TYME OF LENTH IT LET	00000340	15

* Only half this number of asterisks are actually printed.

Table 4. Alliteration program with asterisks.

The first problem can be solved simply by adding an asterisk print operation to the alliteration program, underlining with a row of asterisks all lines with alliteration on the problem letters (table 4). These lines I can then examine myself and discard where necessary. This is an example of using the computer to do a partial job. In my judgement it is easier to do part of this job myself than write the rather complicated program that would enable the computer to make the decision about the alliteration.

An advantage of doing my own programming is that where a programmer might try to work out every last detail with the computer, I can easily decide which aspects of the job I am willing to do myself.

The second problem, the missed alliteration, is more complex. Here, too, I decided that part of it could better be done in conjunction with the computer rather than by the computer alone. Since, as the 'Phoneme Count Program' had determined, problem *c*'s occur only 297 times in tens of thousands of words, problem *w*'s only 362 times and *v*'s only 76 times, I decided to examine these myself. I simply added a command to that program to print out any lines containing problem *c*'s and *w*'s, and *v*'s (table 5).

WR WORD	TO PUT IN WRYT A SUTHFAST STORY	00000320
CE WORD	AND CERTIS YAI SULD WEILL HAWE PRYS	00000410
CH WORD	WAN GRET PRICE OFF CHEWALRY	00000450
V WORD	YE LAND VJ ZER AND MAYR PERFAY	00000590
CH WORD	TO CHEYS A KING YAR LAND TO STER	00000640
WM WORD	HAID YE WMBETHOCHT ZOW ENKRELY	00001150
WR WORD	ZE HAD NOCHT WROCHT ON YAT MANER	00001170
V WORD	AND HAD CONSIDERYT HIS VSAGE	00001390
CH WORD	HAIFF CHOSYN ZOW A KING YAT MYCHT	00001420
V WORD	HAVE HALDYN VEYLE YE LAND IN RYCHT	00001430
CH WORD	YAT BE OYIR HIM CHASTY	00001470
CH WORD	AND FRA HE WYST QUHAT CHARGE YAI HAD	00001680
WR WORD	IN ALL THING AS YAI WRAYT HIM TO	00001750
CH WORD	GYFF YOU WILL HALD IN CHEYFF OFF ME	00001810
WR WORD	YE TOYIR WREYTH HIM AND SWAR	00001930
WR WORD	AND TURNYT HIM IN WRETH AWAY	00001905

TOTALS		[Totals for the whole tape:
THE NO OF WN WORDS IS	0	89
THE NO OF WM WORDS IS	1	21
THE NO OF WR WORDS IS	5	50
THE NO OF WP WORDS IS	0	86
THE NO OF WS WORDS IS	0	99
THE NO OF WT WORDS IS	0	17
THE NO OF CE WORDS IS	1	42
THE NO OF CI WORDS IS	0	12
THE NO OF CH WORDS IS	6	243
QUH WORDS *****10		1,154
QU WORDS	0	53
TH WORDS	27	949
THE NO OF V WORDS IS	3	76]

Table 5. Results with 181 records.

That leaves lines containing *q* and *th*. These can be treated by the over-write in SNAP, which is available but which I have not yet programmed. This program when complete will deal only with lines in which no alliteration was found previously. *Quh* will be temporarily changed to *w*, *qu* to *k* and *th* to *x*. Eventually a tape will be produced that will contain only the lines with true alliteration.

Then I shall begin to answer questions about alliteration. The most important one is: how often do lines that alliterate cluster together and when there is this clustering, how does alliteration contribute to the effect of the passage in question? Another interesting problem connected to the larger one of prosody is: what is the rhythm of alliteration? Are alliterating words next to each other; separated by a function word; in a formula or tag; in the same phrase or different phrases within the line? Is there any double alliteration in a line? Each variety has a different rhythm. Other interesting things to know about alliteration are: how often does an alliter-ative letter continue into the next line? This is a common practice in Older Scots alliterating poems. How many sets of two lines, three lines or four lines alliterate on the same letter? What is the function of eye alliteration, increasingly used in the later Middle Ages. How can the program deal with internal alliteration? Do function words play some role? It would also be interesting to test the program on medieval literature that is generally held to be non-alliterative. But the most important project is to correlate the presence or absence of alliteration to the effect of passages. This of course cannot be done by computer.

In conclusion, SNAP programming has made it possible for me to write my own programs and to look forward to extending their use until I can answer all of these interesting questions, not only about Barbour but also about other medieval verse, such as the drama cycles, which, I think, use alliteration to indicate stylistic level. But that is another problem.

Acknowledgements

A. J. Aitken, Senior Editor, *Dictionary of the Older Scottish Tongue.* Professor Joseph Raben, Editor, *Computers and the Humanities.* Queens College Computer Center Personnel. Dr Michael Barnett, Wilson Company, NYC. COMNET, Washington, DC.

REFERENCES

Aitken, A. J. (1971) Historical dictionaries and the computer. *The Computer in Literary and Linguistic Research.* pp. 3-17 (ed. Wisbey, R. A.). Cambridge: Cambridge University Press.

Barnett, M. P. (1969) *Computer Programming in English.* New York: Harcourt, Brace & World.

Mackenzie, W. M. (1932) *The Poems of William Dunbar.* London: Faber and Faber.

Oakden, J. P. (1930) *Alliterative Poetry in Middle English.* Repr. 1968. New York: Archon Press.

Skeat, W. W. (1894) *The Bruce.* Edinburgh and London: Blackwood.

Problems of input and output

Analysis of a data base for information retrieval:
The London Stage 1660–1800

By *analysis* I mean here the process by which one arrives at the total strategy required to secure a desired conclusion to a computer project. The focus of any such process is a set of input specifications describing in exact detail how the data will be presented to the machine. But no such set of specifications can be derived in isolation from several factors having little or nothing to do with the character of the input text itself: the method of input, one's computing and programming facilities, and the use to which the data is to be put. Analysis consists of untangling the conflicting demands of these three variables and of the relatively fixed factor of the data source itself.

In our case, the source was at least a constant: *The London Stage, 1600–1800*, 'A calendar of Plays, entertainments and afterpieces, together with casts, box receipts, and contemporary comment, compiled from the playbills, newspapers, and theatrical diaries of the period', eleven volumes, 8,000 pages, 21,000,000 characters. The structure of this work was of course all-important, but perhaps its sheer length had more effect on our eventual strategy than any other feature. A small change in procedure could have a very large effect on the expected frequency of error or cost in time or money.

It soon became clear that typing for scanning by an optical character recognition device would be our method of input. Since we were able to use a character set that quite adequately expressed the typographic features of our text, the typing process was the main strategic factor arising out of our choice of input method.

Since the project had a full-time programmer and our academic computing facility would provide us with plenty of time at little cost, it was clear that we should use the computer whenever we could to accommodate the demands of the other factors. Programming would have the twofold function of lightening the typists' load and of providing our potential users with a retrieval service suited to their needs.

By studying bibliographies in eighteenth-century theatre research we were able to determine that most users would want information about performances of plays and about the careers of the actors, actresses, managers, and others associated with the stage. Moreover, the nature of the data base itself could tell us much about how it would be used. I shall illustrate my remarks on the source by reference to a sample page (figure 1). A typical entry begins at line 46. It consists principally of the casts of a play and of an afterpiece. You will notice that most of the other entries

COMMENT. Mainpiece: Reduc'd to two acts. After which (being particularly   *Wednesday 17*
desired) will be performed the *New Serenata*, composed by Dr Arne in honour   DL
of the late Royal Nuptials.

JUDAS MACCHABAEUS. As 5 March.   CG   **5**
    MUSIC. As 26 Feb.
       COMMENT. By Command of their Majesties.

TANCRED AND SIGISMUNDA. As 24 Sept. 1761, but Tancred – Garrick;   *Thursday 18*
Sigismunda – Mrs Cibber; Officers: Scrase, Castle, &c. Also HIGH LIFE   DL   **10**
BELOW STAIRS. As 8 Sept. 1761.
    SINGING. *Hearts of Oak*. [No cast listed, but see 9 Feb.]
       COMMENT. Benefit for Mrs Cibber. No Building on Stage. Part of Pit laid
into Boxes. Ladies send servants by 3 o'clock.

       15

KING HENRY IV, Part 2. As 18 Jan. Also THE CORONATION. As 13 Nov.   CG
1761.
    DANCING. III: *The Pleasures of Spring*, as 12 Feb.
       COMMENT. Last time of performing *The Coronation* till Easter Monday.

       20

SAMSON. As 10 March.   *Friday 19*
    MUSIC. As 5 March.   DL
       COMMENT. Oratorio By Desire. "Mrs Pritchard's great demand for places
tomorrow night, obliges her to request the Ladies will send their Servants early
to prevent any mistakes in placing them."

       25

SEMELE. *Cast not listed.* Parts were: Jupiter, Cadmus (King of Thebes), Athamas   CG
(Prince of Boeotia, in love with Semele); Somnus, Apollo, Cupid, Juno, Iris,
Semele (Daughter of Cadmus); Ino; Chorus of Priests and Augurs; Chorus of
Loves and Zephyrs; Chorus of Nymphs and Swains; Attendants (Larpent MS 43).   **30**
    MUSIC. As 26 Feb.
       COMMENT. This day publish'd *Semele* set to Music by Mr Handel. Price 1s.
As it is performed this evening at the Theatre Royal in Covent Garden. Printed
for J. & R. Tonson in the Strand.

       35

THE MISTAKE. Principal characters by: Garrick, King, Palmer, Yates, Bransby,   *Saturday 20*
Philips, Burton, Blakes, Mrs Clive, Mrs Davies, Mrs Bennet, and Mrs Pritchard.   DL
[See parts assigned 22 April.] Also THE OLD MAID. As 14 Nov. 1761, but
Harlow, Heartwell, Servant, Trifle omitted.
    DANCING. End of Play: By Particular Desire of several persons of Quality a *Minuet*   **40**
by Noverre and Mrs Palmer.
    ENTERTAINMENT. A New Interlude, call'd the *Farmer's Return from London*.
Farmer – Garrick; Farmer's Wife – Mrs Bradshaw.
       COMMENT. Benefit for Mrs Pritchard. Part of Pit laid into Boxes.

       45

THE JEALOUS WIFE. Oakly – Ross; Major Oakly – Shuter; Charles – Clarke;   CG
Lord Trinket – Dyer; Sir Harry Beagle – Bennet; Capt. O'Cutter – Barrington;
Russet – Dunstall; Paris – Holtom; Tom – R. Smith; Harriet – Mrs Lessingham;
Lady Freelove – Mrs Vincent; Mrs Oakly – Mrs Ward. Also FLORIZEL AND
PERDITA. Florizel (with new songs in character) – Mattocks; Autolicus (with   **50**
songs in character) – Shuter; King – Hull; Shepherd - Gibson; Perdita (with
new songs in character) – Miss Brent. The Music composed by Dr Arne, with
a *Dance* incident to the Pastoral by Granier, Mrs Granier, &c.
    DANCING. *The Pleasures of Spring*, as 12 Feb.
       COMMENT. Benefit for Ross. Mainpiece: Never acted there. Afterpiece: **55**
Not acted this season. No Building on Stage. Tickets and Places to be had of
Mr Ross in the Little Piazza, Covent Garden; and of Mr Sarjant, at the Stage Door.

Figure 1

on this page, *Judas Macchabaeus*, *Tancred and Sigismunda*, *King Henry IV*, and *Samson*, actually consist of casts as well, except that the casts are referred to instead of listed. As this page shows, information about casts of plays, actors, and roles is the most important kind of information to be found in this data base. Comment sections also pertain to the people of the stage and the works they produced. Our top priority, we decided, was an index to cast lists; not an index by page, but an index by date, by theatre, by play, by role, and by actor to each whole record of an actor playing a role at a theatre on a date. This would mean that by selection and hierarchical sorting one could abstract an actor's whole career, giving the facts of every one of his performances; or a play history, showing exactly how its roles moved from actor to actor, as it moved from theatre to theatre and epoch to epoch. Our first task in presenting the text to the machine, then, was to make sure that the computer would be able to identify all items in a cast list, and preserve the context in time, place, and work of art in which they were embedded. Secondly, to make possible a comprehensive printed index to *The London Stage*, we must capture all proper names of persons and places and all titles of works of art in material parenthetical to those items both in and out of the *Comment* sections. Our third priority was to classify and index all recurrent references in the parenthetical text to company business, like 'Mainpiece, reduced to two acts' (line 1), 'By Command of their Majesties' (line 7), and 'Benefit for Mrs Cibber' (line 13).

The only way to free the typist from distracting detail so that she could concentrate on the difficult enough task of simply giving us an exact copy of the text was to reduce coding of the data to an absolute minimum and to use any natural keys to content in the text as it stands as a basis for programs enabling the computer to interpret the text and tag the items we wanted to identify. We would try to do automatically after data entry much of the interpreting, abstracting, and labelling usually done at data entry.

There were two kinds of information that the computer needed in order to perform its analysis of the data: field delimiters and structural signals. A field delimiter tells, for instance, where an actor's name begins and ends, and a structural signal announces the beginning of a regular syntactical pattern like a cast list. We discovered that natural delimiters and structural signals did abound but that there were a great many variations in the forms they took. Under the circumstances the best strategy would be to use the most common natural delimiters and signals as a sort of standard grammar by which to correct all minor variations and ambiguities. Either the typist could correct the aberrant variations herself, or an editor could revise the text beforehand and she could follow the copy thus revised, or we could revise the text by computer methods after the entry was complete. In practice the typist was asked to make some simple and basic changes by herself, she followed editorial marks for some changes requiring special knowledge, and we reserved for a second course of editing after entry, rearrangements of the text so elaborate that it was very difficult to crowd the editorial instructions on the page or for a typist to follow them. It now remains for me to describe what evolved as the text's standard syntax and to show how the typist achieved it with editorial assistance and a set of input specifications. Again I shall resort to illustrations from the sample page (figure 1).

One of the first things that Adam did was to name the animals, and one can well understand his motives. It's thus one begins to understand the universe in which one lives. We named the basic unit of *The London Stage* a 'Performance entry'. It contains everything that happened at a theatre on a date. A typical 'performance entry' begins at line 46. It contains four 'sections': a 'mainpiece section', the cast of (*The Jealous Wife*); an 'afterpiece section', the cast of (*Florizel and Perdita*); a 'dance section'; and a 'comment section'. The mainpiece and afterpiece sections each contain a 'play' consisting of a title of a play, and a 'cast list' for that play. The cast list consists of 'parts' and 'performers' of those parts. The dance section contains a 'dance', *The Pleasures of Spring*, and a 'reference' to a cast list, 'as 12 Feb.'. In the performance entry above, we see (line 38) a reference, 'As 14 November' followed by an 'update', 'but Harlow, Heartwell, Servant, Trifle omitted'.

Each performance entry is headed by information concerning the time and place of the performance. *The Mistake* (line 36) has a 'date', '20', and a 'theatre', 'DL'. Date and theatre comprise the 'performance header'. The dance section (line 18) gives us the place on the program or 'time' of the dance performance: act 'III'.

We call anything in the class of roles, dances, and songs a 'part', and anything in the class of actors, dancers, and singers a 'performer'. The sentence in the afterpiece section (line 53) describing a musical and dancing interlude contains two parts, 'music composed by Dr Arne' and 'a *Dance*', and two performers of the dance, 'Granier, Mrs Granier'. By our standards, however, it is a very ungrammatical sentence. The comment section (line 56) contains 'index items' like 'Mr Ross' and 'little Piazza' which are 'names'; an index item may also be a 'title' like '*Semele*' in line 32. Index items occur only in 'parenthetical text' or 'noise', which may be defined as any kind of textual unit that I have not previously named. Comments except for index items are noise. The extra words in the sentence on lines 52 and 53 are noise. The phrase 'By particular desire of several persons of quality' in line 40 is noise. I use the term 'noise' to convey the fact that our grammar has no way to describe the way words relate in these character strings.

To sum up: Everything in a performance entry is either a date, a theatre, a section, a play, a cast list, a part, a performer, a time, a reference, an update, an index item, or it is noise. To enable automatic identification of these categories they must be expressed in a rigid syntax. The syntax we arrived at for expressing *The London Stage* is described in figure 2. It provides structural signals and delimiters for every item I have named.

1) *performance header*: '*pdd mm yy ttttt play. '
2.1) *play section*: '*xplay.   cast list. '
2.2) *cast list section*: '*xcast list. '
2.21) *cast list*: 'cast group; cast group; cast group. '
2.211) *cast group*: 'part-performer; '
'part-performer, performer; '
'performer, performer; '
'part, part-performer; '
'part, part-; '
'"as" reference'
'"as" reference, update'
'"see" reference'
'"see" reference, update'
2.212) *time*: 'time: cast group; '
2.3) *comment section*: '*cnoise index-item noise '
2.31) *index-item*: ' $name= '
' +title= '
3) *noise*: '(noise)'
'[noise]'
'[noise% '
'*cnoise*x '

Notes. Spacing is an element of syntax. Single quotation marks enclose items of syntax but are not part of syntax. Numbers indicate degree of subordination.
1) '*' precedes the structural signal; structure is indicated by letter immediately following. 'p' indicates performance entry and therefore whole structure described above. 'd' is number of day, 'm' is number of month, 'y' is number of year, and 't' is a letter of the *London Stage* abbreviation of the theatre.
2.1) 'x' is a letter signifying the kind of section that follows (performance, song, dance, music, etc.). It also conveys the structure of the section.
2.21) A series of cast groups may be as long as necessary.
2.211) A series of parts or performers may be as long as necessary. Any combination of cast groups in any order is allowed, except that only one type of reference is allowed in a play section and it must come first in the cast list.
3) Noise may precede or follow any item in a performance entry. It is a character string of indeterminate length. Noise of any sort may contain index items.

Figure 2. Syntax required for input of *The London Stage*

Most of this syntax is natural; that is, it is the syntax that the text itself uses most of the time to express the items it contains. But the format of the text is in some ways more elaborate than our system requires. So the typist converts the date-theatre information into the simplified foramt called for in the header, giving only the numbers that change as the text does. She indicates italicized character strings by putting a plus in front of them and an equal sign after. She also abbreviates 'cast not listed' to 'cnl' and drops the redundant '&c' that often appears at the end of cast lists (line 54). She abbreviates the title of dancing, singing, and entertainment sections to '*d', '*s', '*e', saving keystrokes while she enters structural signals. Her only other care is to follow copy as edited.

Editors have to know something about the theatre in the eighteenth century and about how the programs work in order to perform their task properly. I will illustrate both the editing system and our syntax by editing the sample page. To eliminate the need for marginal instructions and make their wishes easier to understand and simpler to apply, the editors used three coloured pencils. By virtue of being coloured, the pencil at one stroke marks the place and tells the typist what to do.

Beginning at the top, in line 2, the editor underlines 'Dr Arne' in blue, thus instructing the typist to insert the delimiters for a name, giving us '$Dr Arne='. No mark has to be made under 'New Serenata' because the typist has a standing order to delimit all italicized items by a plus in front and an equal sign after, our code for titles as well. The next two sections (lines 5-6) need no editing because the syntax for a reference to a previous cast is correct as it stands, and it will cause the computer to bring forward the casts referred to and list them in place of the references. The title 'Judas Macchabaeus' is naturally delimited by the theatre abbreviation before it and the full stop plus two spaces after it. 'As 5 March' is a logical cast group because it follows a play section and is followed by a period and a new section. It is recognized as a reference because it contains the word 'as'. '*m' will introduce the music section; this code will tell the computer to expect a simple cast list structure, not a cast list proceeded by a play title. In line 7, the name 'Their Majesties' is underlined in blue as an index item. In the next entry, the cast of the mainpiece will be found and updated if the typist simply copies the text as it stands.

When a cast group such as that beginning 'Tancred–Garrick' (line 9) follows an 'as' reference, the computer will recognize it as an update instruction, find 'Tancred' in the previous cast and put Garrick in the role when it brings the cast forward. With one exception, the parts in this section are naturally distinguishable from the performers because the parts are followed by hyphens and the performers are followed by a semicolon or the end of a section. The exception is the last group, in which the colon should be a hyphen. Since neither editing nor typing rules cover this egregious bad grammar it will not be corrected until after entry. The entries of two items following a role, separated by commas, and ending a section will identify them as performers playing the same role. That is, each will be recorded as playing a part named 'Officers'. The plural will be helpful when the records are separated by sorting, showing in any context that at least one other performer also played the part. The typist's standing order eliminates the '&c' at the end of the cast list.

The 'see' reference to a previous cast in the singing section on line 12 will be ignored by our programs as it now stands because the brackets around it delimit it as noise. Since a 'see' reference is uncertain anyhow, the brackets are overcautious and our editor will strike them out with a red pencil, meaning to delete, as well as the redundant 'no cast listed'. Because the keyword 'see' occurs in this reference, all performers' names in the list brought forward will automatically be tagged with a question mark that will follow them wherever they go.

The next two entries are correct as they stand except that 'Easter Monday' in the comment section of the first must be underlined in blue and delimited as a name.

Because the casting information concerning *Semele* is so exceptionally expressed as not to be covered by editing rules, the editor will convert it to noise temporarily by enclosing it in red parentheses, a signal for the typist to use the special delimiters for noise that are editorially inserted, a bracket before and a percentage sign after. After entry, in the second course of editing, a hyphen will be inserted after each part to delimit it as a part and the redundant 'Parts were' will be stricken out. 'Larpent MS' will be preserved from the noise category by delimiters for a title, a plus before and equal after. In the comments section the title, *Semele*, will be delimited as a title by virtue of the typist's standing order to indicate strings in italics by a plus before and an equal after.

The syntax following *The Mistake* in the next entry is so common an aberration from the norm that we correct it by a special editing scheme. The editor crosses out the word 'by' in the cast list with a yellow pencil, calling into play another typists' standing order, to convert any 'by's' crossed out in yellow to hyphens. He strikes out the colon with a red mark. Now 'Principal characters' becomes a part played by Garrick, King, Palmer, and so forth. The 'and' in front of 'Mrs Pritchard' at the end of the series will also have to be stricken out, to prevent that actress's name from going into the file as 'and Mrs Pritchard'. The bracketed information following this cast list cannot become a 'see reference' because our programs do not recognize references to the future. This reference is therefore doomed to the noise category, where its natural brackets will send it anyway without editorial help. In the same entry, the updated reference to *The Old Maid* will not work without special coding too complicated for the data entry phase, and it will wait for editing at a future time. The dancing section in this entry can be brought into line by putting red parentheses delimiting noise around the phrase 'by particular Desire of several persons of quality', and yellow marks on 'by' and 'and', causing the typist to act upon her standing orders that 'by' become a hyphen and 'and' a comma. The entertainment section is actually a small play and will be treated as such once the noise preliminary to the title is set off. The final performance entry on the page fits our required syntax exactly, and like most of *The London Stage*, it can be interpreted automatically as it stands.

What is the fate of the noise? It is not relegated to the waste basket, but saved for a filtering process in which words and phrases referring to recurrent kinds of company business will be classified and indexed. Each item's locus as modifier of a theatre, play, part, or performer will be retained, and a tag indicating its class of noise will be atttached to the item it modifies. Some sort of concordance of the noise will help in the process of classifying, and eventually we hope to be able to retrieve any class of thing in *The London Stage* that we can give a name to.

Acknowledgement
I am indebted to Will Daland, the programmer-analyst of *The London Stage* project, for many of the ideas in this paper.

Optical scanning as a method of input: the experience of *The London Stage* project

As an input problem *The London Stage*, consisting of everything that is known about performances in London from 1660 to 1800, perhaps presents a special case because of its length and because of its destined use. Because it is 21,000,000 characters long, economy was imperative. A saving of a few farthings per page justified more drastic measures than would be practical for a smaller text. Also, because the text was to be used as a base for information retrieval, a method had to be chosen that captured all textual keys to categories of content and allowed for some tagging of items during the input process. I make these reservations at the outset because scanning may not be the best way to convert a small text destined for a less demanding analysis, even though it has proved successful for *The London Stage*.

Furthermore, I will not discuss the technical triumphs claimed by the various manufacturers of scanning equipment. I assume that since none of us here is going to buy scanners for £100,000 and up, we are not interested in what they *can* do, but in what they *do* do when installed on the floors of service bureaux which can provide us with scanning at a rate that comes within our means. My experience suggests that there is a wide gap indeed between what scanners can and do do. One manufacturer produces a scanner that *can* read simultaneously a set of 360 discrete characters, but to my knowledge only one of the dozens in service bureaux using his scanner in the United States does read even as many as the 88 found on an ordinary typewriter, and the rest are for the most part reading only the numbers on cheques for banks. Nor does it matter how fast a machine actually is if the bureau using it delivers to us the highest quality of output at the lowest cost. The best bureau for our purposes may not be the one that uses the best machine.

THE CASE FOR OCR

As I have suggested elsewhere (Schneider 1971), there are roughly ten ways of converting a text to tape. My study of the feasibility of these for *The London Stage* led to the conclusion that optical scanning excelled keypunching on technical as well as economic grounds and that it excelled all other keyed input methods on economic grounds while holding its own technically. We could not use the machine-readable tape by which the printer had cast the type for the original text.

An efficient system of keyboard entry ought to have a good character repertoire and a simple way to correct mistakes during and after keying. The system should also be cheap. The keypunch, besides having an inadequate character set for the expression of literary text and lacking a good way of correcting mistakes during keying, also calls for elaborate precautions to keep track of the thousands of cards it produces. On top of this, keypunch operators require more money than typists. The Magnetic Tape Selectric Typewriter (MTST) and some other key to tape devices handle these technical problems better but cost twice as much as the keypunch. From my point of view, much better hardware at the price, I believe, is the Cathode Ray Terminal (CRT) designed for data entry. This answer to any text handler's prayer uses a TV-type screen for a page and a computer (its own or yours) to carry out revisions on the screen instantly upon commands from the keyboard. Not until the page is exactly as desired is it entered. But besides being expensive, CRT's are new and uncommon. Under the circumstances scanning copy from an ordinary IBM Selectric typewriter, costing one-tenth of a keypunch and one-twentieth of an MTST and found in offices everywhere, is the best solution. This device becomes a computer input device by a simple flick of the wrist that attaches a typing element with a scanning font. Anyone who can type can operate it anywhere. The cost of scanning is not negligible, but it is made up for by the low cost of keying with a machine that any housewife can use at home in her spare time.

SCANNING DEVICES

At present scanners are designed to read specific sets of characters in particular type fonts. Some read several sets at once, some one set at a time, some only one, and some only part of a set or one part of a set at a time. Scanners are marketed by IBM, Control Data, ICL, Farringdon, National Cash Register, Recognition Equipment, Compuscan, Scan-Optics, Scandata and several other companies. Only those made by Recognition Equipment, Compuscan, Scan-Optics and Scandata can read pages of text in upper and lower case. The Scandata machine reads several typed and printed fonts, the Compuscan machine reads several typed fonts, and the Recognition Equipment machine, as I have found it, reads one typed font. The only machines we could find in Britain that read upper and lower case text as a service to the general public are the Scan-Optics and the Scandata readers.

There are two ways in which scanners identify characters: The mask method and the feature analysis method. The first systematically applies a mask of each character in the font until it secures a match to the unknown character while the second identifies characters by their curves, straight lines, crosses, angles, open and closed spaces. While the masking method may be faster for one font, the feature analysis method works for any normal font and is also more tolerant of variations in spacing and quality of impression in a given font. Recognition Equipment's machine uses the masking technique and Scandata's the feature analysis technique. Compuscan's machine uses a combination of the two methods.

Scanners, contrary to what one might expect, are more, rather than less, sensitive to details than human eyes, and consequently they are more easily confused by slight amounts of dirt on the page, little specks in the paper, small irregularities in spacing, faulty impressions, and slight variations in contrast. While the eye and brain together do a marvellous job of ignoring extraneous detail, the scanner has to include every visible irregularity in its analysis of the character before it, with the result that it often fails to recognize characters having flaws so minute that one needs a magnifying glass to detect them with the human eye. REI scanners when faced with a nonrecognized character automatically insert a special symbol instead of the character. Compuscan, Scan-Optics, and Scandata machines stop and flash the guilty character, highlighted in context, on a screen, so that a human operator can decide what it is supposed to be and insert it. It is quite difficult to talk about error rates of scanners because it must be established, for every error, whether the reader or the typing was at fault, and how much the machine is expected to compensate for typing. The scanner with the best record for less than perfect typing might be preferable to a scanner that was perfect for perfect typing but could not tolerate imperfection. In my experience an expectation of one mistake in 20,000 characters in scanner output is realistic.

SCANNING SERVICES

Over a year ago, in December 1970, I first began to seek bids for scanning *The London Stage*. My first bid, from Dissly Systems in Easton, Pennsylvania, was for direct scanning of the text from the pages of the printed book itself, and this bid was so high that one could retype and scan the whole text for much less. Dissly is a Scandata bureau whose total energy is devoted to programming and engineering that will enable their readers to scan any printed text using the Roman alphabet, however many different fonts that text may use. Their hope is to cut drastically the cost for printing new editions of existing books. Dissly is to be commended for their forward-looking attitude, but in order to scan the multifont *London Stage*, I take it, they were going to read text in each font separately, merge the fragments thus obtained, proof read, and correct the merged text. They could thus guarantee an extremely high rate of accuracy along with their high price. In the process they could also automatically flag font changes and format features in such a way as to locate our main categories of content. But they could not tag all proper names and titles, which could be done by pre-editing if we entered the data by keying, nor could they locate parenthetical noise in cast lists that would prevent our programs from interpreting the data. Direct scanning, then, besides costing more than typing and scanning, would leave us with quite a bit of work still to do when the scanning was finished. Dissly's price for scanning typed pages was also out of the question.

The alternative to direct scanning of the printed page was scanning of the same text retyped in a font suitable for scanning. Bureaux reading typed fonts from which we received bids were Compuscan in Leonia,

New Jersey, Corporation S in Dallas, Texas, Information Control Incorporated in Kansas City, and Computer Services Centre, Wembley, England.

Compuscan's bid was the highest and there were other disadvantages from our point of view. Although they advertised a capacity to read several fonts, they discouraged the use of all but IBM's Prestige Elite 72, on the ground that the others were not good for character-recognition machines. To use the Prestige Elite font, however, they had to chisel off part of the number one to distinguish it from the small '1' and chop a hole in the zero to distinguish it from the capital 'O'. The principal deficiency for us, though, was simply the lack of square brackets in the character set. Our text was riddled with square brackets, and we would have to teach our typists to put an American cent sign in place of every left bracket and a plus-minus sign in place of every right bracket. When a hundred thousand brackets are at stake, shopping may be well worth the trouble.

Corporation S in Dallas, I found, used a Recognition Equipment scanner fitted with a font that had square brackets and they also bid lower than Compuscan. Their font had been designed for OCR by a book publisher in Florida named Perry, who also gives his name to the font. The Perry font, like most early OCR fonts, is ugly and hard for humans to read. The small 'g', 'p', 'q', 'j', and 'y' stand on top of the line instead of dipping their tails below in the familiar way, and the tail of the small 'g' goes the wrong way so that to the human eye it looks very like a small 'e'. Copy typed in this font, we found, had a maddening way of looking wrong when it was right and right when it was wrong. This would not facilitate proofreading. We also discovered that Corporation S's machine would not acknowledge two spaces after a period at the end of a sentence. However many spaces one input to this scanner one space was output. We were counting on these two spaces as natural delimiters of certain kinds of data, and our programs were already developed on the assumption of two spaces after periods at the end of sentences. Our typists would have to use a special code to indicate the ends of sentences. Nor were there any single or double quotes. Our typists could substitute a half slash for the one and a square, or 'lozenge' as they called it, for the other.

Our next bid was from Information Control Incorporated (ICI), who were using a Scandata machine that could read either OCRB in the IBM Selectric version or IBM Courier 72. The OCRB typing element had both parentheses and brackets, single and double quotes, and a 'one' clearly distinguishable from a small '1'. The Scandata machine could preserve our double space after a period and ICI's was the lowest bid of all, so we decided to scan *The London Stage* on this machine. Before production in Kansas City was well started, however, my long-scheduled sabbatical leave in London intervened, and the work was transferred to a Scandata bureau in Wembley, called Computer Services Centre. I shall give a **generalized version of experiences at Kansas City and Wembley.**

Our troubles were not over with the discovery of the Scandata machine. We were still to experience several of those totally unpredictable difficulties that seem inevitably to occur when machines are set to work on jobs normally performed by humans, often subconsciously. Instead of quoting us a price per thousand characters, which is standard practice, ICI quoted us a price per page. This meant that to get the lowest price per character, we must pack each page to the maximum allowable limit. Since our programming would treat the whole text as one continuous line, we didn't want to hyphenate any words, but if typists kept all words intact many lines would fall far short of the optimum 75 characters per line. Our solution was to ignore line endings altogether, typing right up to position 75, returning the carriage to position one and continuing as if the carriage return were not there. This way the typist would not have to bother about whether the next word would fit into the line. She merely typed until her keyboard jammed, hit the carriage return, and carried on typing. Since no spaces were assumed at the end of a line, inserted spaces would show. We could use a code to show space at the beginning of a line if necessary. This was fine, but the scanner had been built to expect text turned out in the conventional style and, although I have never been conscious of it, it is an unbreakable rule of conventional text that a line never begins with punctuation. But with our system there was punctuation at the beginning of a line two or three times on every page. The scanner ignored much of the punctuation in the initial position, leaving the unused space at the *end* of the line where it broke words in two, nine times out of ten. Surprisingly and greatly to their credit, the technicians found a way to program the scanner so that it would pick up punctuation in the initial position, and it was thus that the Scandata machine proved to us at once the truth and the value of its vaunted flexibility.

We next noticed that our computer was reading zero and capital 'O' as the same code in scanner output. The scanner had been designed on the assumption, probably derived from Hollerith card technology, that zero would be known because it resided in a number field and 'O' because it resided in a letter field. Either we had to insert delimiters before and after every number field in our text, or we had to physically modify the capital 'O' on all of our eight type balls. This we succeeded in doing without destroying more than one type ball. Another bug was caused, with tragic irony, by the scanner's finest characteristic, its power to find and read a character regardless of its size or spatial position. It therefore 'saw' every double quote as if it were two apostrophes occupying two ems of space. We solved this problem by putting a routine into our input program that converted any two consecutive apostrophes to one double quote. This expedient worked most of the time, but of course failed on those occasions when an apostrophe in the text was followed by a double quote or a single quote.

QUALITY CONTROL

Strictly speaking, we cannot say that any character in our original text has been converted to computer tape until we have visual proof of that fact on a printout made by the computer on which the data is ultimately to be processed. Moreover, the only way to be sure that the tape produced by one's scanning service is mechanically, electronically, and logically compatible with one's own system is to put it on and list it.

Actually, the scanning process involves four distinct texts: A. the original printed text; B. the text as typed for OCR; C. the text as coded on the scanner's output tape; D. the text as listed by the line printer of one's local system. The point of the game is to get as much of A on to D as possible. This means that the character set of the local print chain is another limiting condition of the quality of ultimate output. A legible and complete copy of the final text is essential, for the easier it is to check quality, the easier it is to obtain it. Since scanners, like people, can have good days as well as bad, it is probably well to agree in advance with a scanning service on an acceptable standard of accuracy. Possibly the most concrete way of defining that standard while at the same time ironing out incompatibilities between texts A, B, C, and D is to run a sample batch, large enough to be truly representative, through the whole system a sufficient number of times to produce the measure of quality desired.

Even though a scanner makes only a small number of errors, the errors it does make can be disastrous. It is important to know, before it is too late, whether the more frequent types of errors will have a crucial effect on the usefulness of the output. The Scandata machine, for example, had a proclivity for reading our modified capital 'O' as a small 'g'. Since the month name 'October' recurred incessantly in our data and since a basic program keyed on month names, we could not tolerate this error and the machine's O-recognizing circuit had to be rewired to eliminate the confusion. Please note: a service bureau having its own staff of programmers and engineers is much to be preferred to one that does not.

SUMMARY

Scanning is preferable to other methods of input because typing is cheaper, while being technically competitive with other keyboard methods. Scanners recognize characters either by matching a mask to the character or by analyzing its distinctive features. Recognition Equipment, Compuscan, Scan-Optics, and Scandata make scanners suitable for the conversion of text. They use different techniques, but methods and efficiency of machines are not important to the user; prices, character sets, fonts, format-handling capacity, design limitations, and quality are. These depend more on the setup of individual service bureaux than on machines used. The best way to settle incompatibilities between the original text, the typing element used, the scanner, and one's local system, while at the same time establishing a level of accuracy for use as a measure of quality for the rest of the job, is to process a representative sample as many times as it takes to reach the desired end product.

Acknowledgement

I am indebted to Will Daland, programmer-analyst of the *London Stage* project, for many of the ideas in this paper.

REFERENCE

Schneider, B. R. (1971) The production of machine-readable text. *C. Hum.*, 6, 39-47.

T

A concordance to the poems of Hafiz with output in Persian characters

Hafiz, the best known of the Persian lyric poets, was born in the city of Shiraz in about 1320 and lived for approximately seventy years. Four hundred and ninety-five of his lyric poems or *ghazals* survive, most of which consist of between 7 and 10 couplets, although the longest, poem 329, has 25. Until recently no concordance of his works existed but the development of the COCOA program at the Atlas Laboratory has now allowed this need to be met.

PREPARATION OF THE TEXT

The first problem encountered was that of putting some 10,000 lines of Persian into machine-readable form. Initially an alphabet was devised which gave a simple transliteration system for the Persian letters. As there are more than twenty-six letters in the Persian form of the Arabic alphabet, we had to resort to characters such as $ (or π as it comes out on the lineprinter), =, *, & and even α or $_{10}$ for some of the rarer letters. In the original script each letter has up to four forms (initial, medial, final, and independent), used in different positions in a word, but in our transliteration system each letter has only one equivalent. Table 1 shows the Persian alphabet and its equivalents in transliteration.

Several other characters were incorporated into the text in order to reproduce features of the Arabic script which are not properly speaking letters of the alphabet, but nevertheless require to be distinguished. (was used for ﺯ and ' for ﺀ to distinguish them from w and y and these characters were placed in the alphabet after w and y respectively. A colon was used for *shadda*, which in Arabic script denotes doubling of the consonant over which it is written. In our transliteration this was placed after the letter to which it refers. The Arabic *alif madde* (ā in an initial position) was transliterated by | A, as against A for simple *alif*, although the distinction is ignored for the purposes of alphabetic order.

Another problem occurred in compound words in which the first part ends with *hē*, o in our transliteration. In a compound word *hē* appearing in the middle should be either a medial form or an initial one if it occurs after one of the eight letters which do not join on to the following one. However, it is written as a final form or an independent form if it comes after a letter which does not join. In order that these words should be written correctly in the final concordance, a comma was inserted before the o in the transliteration. Thus the word سیاه‌نامه‌تر which is in fact a compound of three words, سیاه SYAO, نامه NAMO and تر TR is trans-literated SYA, ONAM, OTR.

alif	ا	A	sad	ص	I
be	ب	B	zad	ض	α
pe	پ	P	ta	ط	V
te	ت	T	za	ظ	&
se	ث	=	'ain	ع	E
jim	ج	J	ghain	غ	U
chim	چ	C	fe	ف	F
he	ح	H	qaf	ق	Q
khe	خ	X	kaf	ك	K
dal	د	D	gaf	گ	G
zal	ذ	*	lam	ل	L
re	ر	R	mim	م	M
ze	ز	Z	nun	ن	N
zhe	ژ	)	vav	و	W
sin	س	S	hē	ه	O
shin	ش	$	ye	ی	Y

Table 1

One feature of Persian grammar, the *ezāfe*, caused particular problems. The *ezāfe* is a short vowel added to a noun to indicate a genitive relation-ship between that and the following noun, for example, *manzele jānān* 'the house of life', which, since short vowels are not written in Persian, is not normally reproduced in writing or in our transliteration (MNZL JANAN). However, when the first noun ends in a vowel or a silent *hē*, the *ezāfe* suffix becomes -*ye*, which is reproduced in writing as ه or ی (for example, افتادة *aftāde ye*, ابروی *abrū-ye*, استغنای *esteghnā-ye*). If such words had been transliterated by our normal system, they would have been listed separately in the concordance, not with the same words without *ezāfe*. In order to avoid this but at the same time to preserve the distinction in writing, we inserted ? before the O or transliterated Y as ?. The ? was declared as a padding letter or character of type 1 in the COCOA program and thus had no influence on the sorting.

A hyphen was used as a word separator to divide the various suffixes and prefixes of Persian from the word to which they are attached. This ensures that a word such as جهانرا JOAN-RA is listed under JOAN and under RA, not under JOANRA, even though it is written as one word in Persian. The hyphen was used in a similar manner to separate the parts of those compound words which it was felt should be listed under their separate parts, not as an individual entry, e.g. مردمافكن MRDM-AFKN would be listed under مردم MRDM and افكن AFKN. It would not be listed as MRDMAFKN.

Although it was felt that a concordance is not a dictionary and that words should be identified by their spelling only, not by their meaning, nevertheless in three cases it was found necessary to separate identical spellings. MY- is a prefix in Persian and was thus separated from the rest of the word by -. However, MY is also a Persian word meaning 'wine', and as it occurs several times with a suffix, for example, MY-ST, it becomes indistinguishable from the prefix MY-. As we had decided not to include separate entries for the suffixes and prefixes in the final concordance, some means had to be found of retaining MY 'wine'. We inserted a plus between the M and Y of MY 'wine' in all occurrences. A plus was then inserted in the alphabet between O and Y. This ensured that M+Y was listed as a separate word between MOYMNA and MYARYD. A similar means was adopted for distinguishing the infix -AY- from the vocative particle AY meaning 'O'. In this case we inserted a plus in the word to be omitted so that DQYQ, O-AY-ST becomes DQYQ, O-A+Y-ST.

Essentially the same problem was encountered with the two words B and B-. B- is a verbal prefix and should be omitted as such. B is a preposition and should therefore be included. We had to choose a different character to distinguish between these two as a plus would have meant that B+ would be listed between BOYN and BY instead of at the beginning of the entries for the letter B. Instead, a full stop was placed between B and - for the verbal prefix so that, for example, بكند was transliterated as B.-KND. The full stop was placed at the very beginning of the alphabet so that B.- was listed after B and before BA

All these insertions to the text meant that we had an alphabet of

.ABPT=JCHXD*RZ)S$Iαv&EUFQKGLMNW(O+Y'

We had also included the characters :?|, to denote peculiarities of the script and - as a word separator for the concordancing.

INPUT AND CORRECTION OF THE TEXT
The text was input to the multi-access files of the Chilton Atlas using a remote console in St Cross College, Oxford. The multi-access system is organized by an RXDS Sigma 2 computer which provides extensive editing facilities without using Atlas. Each poem was numbered at the beginning and each couplet referenced as a separate verse using the angle brackets required by the COCOA program to denote references. Thus the input for a typical poem, number 117, was as follows:

```
⟨N 117⟩
⟨V 01⟩
DL MA B DWR RWT-T Z CMN FRAU DARD
KO CW SRW PAY-BND-ST W CW LALO DAU DARD
⟨V 02⟩
SR MA FRW NYAYD B KMAN ABRW? KS
KO DRWN GW$O GYRAN Z JOAN FRAU DARD
```

GROATS number	GROATS input	Persian character	GROATS number	GROATS input	Persian character
1	space	space	36	D	ـد
8	(	ؤ	37	E	ـع
9	)	ژ	38	F	ـف
11	$	ش	39	G	ـگ
12	?	ـ	40	H	ـح
13	&	ظ	41	I	ـص
14	*	ذ	42	J	ـج
15	/	ض	43	K	ـک
16	0	.	44	L	ـل
17	1	۱	45	M	ـم
18	2	۲	46	N	ـن
19	3	۳	47	O	ـہ
20	4	٤	48	P	ـپ
21	5	٥	49	Q	ـق
22	6	٦	50	R	ـر
23	7	٧	51	S	ـس
24	8	٨	52	T	ـت
25	9	٩	53	U	ـغ
28	=	ـث	54	V	ـط
32	'	ـأ	55	W	ـو
33	A	ل	56	X	ـخ
34	B	ـب	57	Y	ـي
35	C	ـچ	58	Z	ـز

Table 2. Persian font with GROATS input characters.
(1) Medial forms and numerals

⟨V 03⟩
Z BNF$O TAB DARM KO Z ZLF AW ZND DM
TW SYAO KM BOA BYN KO CO DR DMAU DARD
⟨V 04⟩
B CMN XRAM W B.-NGR BR TXT GL KO LALO
B NDYM $AO MAND KO B KF AYAU DARD
⟨V 05⟩
$S &LMT W BYABAN B KJA TWAN RSYDN
MGR |ANKO $ME RWY-T B RO-M CRAU DARD
⟨V 06⟩
MN W $ME IBHGAOY SZD AR B OM B.-GRY'YM
KO B.-SWXTYM W AZ MA BT MA FRAU DARD
⟨V 07⟩
SZD-M CW ABR BOMN KO BR-YN CMN B.-GRYM
VRB |A$YAN BLBL B.-NGR KO ZAU DARD
⟨V 08⟩
SR DRS E$Q DARD DL DRDMND HAF&
KO NO XAVR TMA$A NO OWA? BAU DARD

GROATS number	GROATS input	Persian character	GROATS number	GROATS input	Persian character
72	(	ؤ	106	J	ﺟ
73	)	ژ	107	K	ﻚ
75	$	ﺶ	108	L	ﻞ
77	&	ﻆ	109	M	ﻢ
78	*	ﺬ	110	N	ﻦ
79	/	ﺾ	111	O	ﻪ
92	=	ﺚ	112	P	ﭗ
96	'	ﺌ	113	Q	ﻖ
97	A	ﻞ	114	R	ﺮ
98	B	ﺐ	115	S	ﺲ
99	C	ﺟ	116	T	ﺖ
100	D	ﺪ	117	U	ﻎ
101	E	ﺢ	118	V	ﻂ
102	F	ﻒ	119	W	ﻮ
103	G	ﮒ	120	X	ﺦ
104	H	ﺢ	121	Y	ﻰ
105	I	ﺺ	122	Z	ﺰ

Table 2 (contd.). (2) Final forms accessed by shift characters + and −

A concordance was run of each individual poem as soon as it was input. This was a very effective way of finding typing errors. A concordance of one poem took two to three seconds on Atlas and the output was sent back to the multi-access files so that it could be listed on the console and corrections made at once using Sigma 2's editor.

When the complete text had been input, the poems were linked up into one file which occupied 113 blocks (1 block =4,096 characters) on the Data Products Disc and was 13,072 lines long.

The next stage in our proof-reading was to generate a complete word-count using that option in the COCOA program. In seven minutes Atlas produced a list in alphabetical order, reverse alphabetical order and order of frequency as well as a frequency profile. As a complete concordance was too big to run as a single job on Atlas, a separate concordance was done for each letter of the alphabet. Whilst this took more time, it left the output in a far more manageable form. The output from the word-count gave us some idea how many lines each letter would generate. The first concordance runs, which included all prefixes, infixes, and suffixes, were used simply as a basis for more corrections to the text. It was mainly inconsistencies that came to light at this stage and these were corrected using the editor on Sigma 2.

GROATS number	GROATS input	Persian character	GROATS number	GROATS input	Persian character
136	(	ؤ	170	J	ﺟ
137	)	ﮋ	171	K	ﻙ
139	$	ﺸ	172	L	ﻝ
141	&	ﻇ	173	M	ﻣ
142	*	ﺬ	174	N	ﻧ
143	/	ﻀ	175	O	ﻫ
145	1	آ	176	P	ﭘ
156	=	ﺛ	177	Q	ﻗ
160	'	ﺌ	178	R	ﺭ
161	A	١	179	S	ﺳ
162	B	ﺑ	180	T	ﺗ
163	C	ﭼ	181	U	ﻏ
164	D	ﺩ	182	V	ﻃ
165	E	ﻋ	183	W	ﻭ
166	F	ﻓ	184	X	ﺧ
167	G	ﮔ	185	Y	ﻳ
168	H	ﺣ	186	Z	ﺯ
169	I	ﺻ			

Table 2 (contd.). (3) Initial forms accessed by shift characters ⟨ and ⟩

DEFINITION OF THE PERSIAN CHARACTERS AND DEVELOPMENT OF THE CHARACTER TYPING PROGRAM

Whilst the text of Hafiz was being prepared in Oxford, programs were being developed at the Atlas Laboratory to enable the concordance to be output in Persian characters on an SC 4020 microfilm recorder using the Atlas Algol Graphic Output package GROATS. The first stage of this work was to define a font of Persian characters. GROATS allows up to four fonts, each of 256 characters, to be accessed in one program, but one font was sufficient for our purpose. Four forms of every letter of our alphabet were defined, one each for initial, medial, final, and independent forms as well as a set of numerals. For a more detailed description of the character definition procedures see Churchhouse and Hockey (1971). Each character is assigned a GROATS number as it is defined and the font is stored on the disc occupying four blocks. The font of 256 characters was theoretically divided into four tables each of 64 characters, the first containing the medial forms as they are most frequent, the second containing final forms, the third initial and fourth independent forms. Table 2 shows the complete Persian font.

GROATS number	GROATS input	Persian character	GROATS number	GROATS input	Persian character
200	(	ؤ	234	J	ج
201	)	ژ	235	K	ك
203	$	ش	236	L	ل
205	&	ظ	237	M	م
206	*	ذ	238	N	ن
207	/	ض	239	O	ه
220	=	ث	240	P	پ
224	'	ة	241	Q	ق
225	A	ا	242	R	ر
226	B	ب	243	S	س
227	C	چ	244	T	ت
228	D	د	245	U	غ
229	E	ع	246	V	ط
230	F	ف	247	W	و
231	G	گ	248	X	خ
232	H	ح	249	Y	ى
233	I	ص	250	Z	ز

Table 2 (contd.). (4) Independent forms accessed by shift characters , and .

In order to access a character the appropriate font must first be called. A non-standard font such as ours is called by giving its disc area a logical number of 123 in the program's job description. If a job description contains the statement:

DISC 123 R124 PERSIAN FONT

any call to a font in the program will read the font definitions from this disc area instead of the standard fonts available with the GROATS package. A call in the program of:

font (1);

will make available font 1 on this disc area and all subsequent character typing in the GROATS program will use this font until another is called. An ALGOL string is used to access an individual character or characters in the font and the input characters are read into an array by the procedure:

readstring (CHARARRAY, M, N, STR);

where

1. CHARARRAY is an integer array.

2. M is the address of the first element in the array into which a character is to be read (normally 1).

3. N is initially set to the maximum element number and the routine thus checks that the input does not overflow the array. On exit from the routine, N is reset to the address of the first available element.

4. STR is a string which may consist of one or two characters or be a null string. If it is two characters only input characters between these two characters will be read into CHARARRAY. If it is one character input between this character and the next new line is read into CHARARRAY. If it is a null string, a record, that is, the characters between two new lines, is read.

Thus the procedure **readstring** will read successive records of text, if it is called in a loop with STR as a null string.

Characters are typed by the procedure:

typestring (addr (CHARARRAY, M));

This simply types the characters which are stored in the array CHARARRAY beginning at the element numbered M until the string is exhausted, using the font which is currently called. The character actually typed is the one whose GROATS number corresponds to the internal code of the character in the string. Thus, if the Persian font is called and the array CHARARRAY contains the string ABC, the first character typed will be the one whose GROATS number corresponds to the internal code of the letter A, that is no. 33, ∟, the medial form of *alif* will be typed. Similarly for B, the character with GROATS no. 34, ــ, the medial form of *be* is typed and for C, no. 35, the medial form of *chim* ـجـ. It follows that only the first 64 characters or table 2(1) of a GROATS font can be accessed directly. To overcome this difficulty, GROATS has a facility to allow certain characters to be defined as 'shift' characters or 'setting characters' as they are known. To access the other three tables, three sets of shift characters are required. We decided to use:

+ −   for table 2(2)—final forms
⟨ ⟩   for table 2(3)—initial forms
, .   for table 2(4)—independent forms

Thus to type a character from the second table, it is necessary to precede the input for that character by + and follow it with −. The effect of the + is to add 64 to the GROATS number of all following input characters until − is encountered which removes it again. To type the final form of F, the array CHARARRAY would contain the string +F−. This would type only one character ـف. Similarly the effect of ⟨ is to add 128 to the GROATS number of the input character and type the initial form, for example, ⟨E⟩ would type ع. The independent forms are accessed by adding 192 to the number of the input character. ,Y. would type ی.

A 'setting character' of a different kind was required to type *shadda* over the letter to which it belongs rather than after it as it is input. By this time all available characters in the first table had been used and the setting character itself had to be put into another table and surrounded by shift characters. GROATS character 146 was chosen and the input required for this was the character with the internal code 18 (that is, 146-128), which is the number 2. The setting character itself was therefore represented by $\langle 2 \rangle$. When this character is encountered in the string, one blank is typed in the opposite direction to the normal typing. As the typing position is advanced immediately after typing a character and before the next character is read, this setting character merely restored the position for the previous character. The next character is thus typed on top of the previous one. A different form of *shadda* was typed if it fell on K or L, as the one suitable for the other letters overlapped these two tall letters. This character was made GROATS number 148 to be accessed and typed by $\langle 24 \rangle$.

From all this it would appear that to type the simple word شکّر which we have transliterated $K:R, an elaborate input of $\langle \$ \rangle K \langle 24 \rangle + R-$ is required. However, it will be shown later that the computer can be used to simulate rules of Arabic orthography.

In the course of developing the typing program, experiments were made in character size and spacing and distance between lines. Before beginning to type in GROATS it is necessary first to set the starting position. The SC 4020 screen can be divided into whatever units are desired. A call of:

> **limits** (0, 0, 10, 21);

will divide it into 10 units horizontally and 21 units vertically. A call of:

> **movetypeto** (9.5, 20);

will set the typing position to a suitable place to start a frame of Persian, that is, the top right of the screen, slightly inset. Character size is controlled by the program and the characters can be typed any size. A call of:

> **characterfactor** (1.2);

was found most suitable for typing Persian. A negative character space was used to type a line from right to left and considerable experimentation was necessary to find the best spacing for joining the letters. A call of:

> **characterspace** ($-1.58*$widthchar);

was found most suitable.

CONCORDANCE RUNS

When the correction of the text was complete, the word-count was run again. This showed that the total number of words was 71,304 and the size of vocabulary 5,396. These totals included the prefixes and suffixes which were to be omitted but still left us to expect about 80,000 lines of output including blank lines and keywords. The present version of the COCOA program does not allow words to be omitted when the concordance is run only on part of the alphabet. As it was out of the question to generate 80,000 lines of output in one run, we had to include the words which were to be omitted and remove them later. A concordance for each letter of the alphabet was written up separately to magnetic tape. The text was accessed from the multi-access files by a batch job using the facility available in COMPILER FILES. A typical job, one to run the letter J, is listed below.

```
JOB I0187 SUSAN HOCKEY HAFIZ J TO TAPE
COMPUTING 5 MINUTES
EXECUTION 8 MINUTES
OUTPUT 0 LINEPRINTER 500 LINES
OUTPUT 1 TAPE 730/LINEPRINTER 10000 LINES
NO246 DIVAN 1
DISC COMMON 21/500
DISC COMMON 22/500
DISC COMMON 23/500
DISC COMMON 24/500
DISC 1 R016 COCOA
DISC 2 R000SYSTEM DISC
OUTPUT 2 ANY 120 BLOCKS
COMPILER FILES
INPUT 1 HAFIZ
OUTPUT 2
USE SPECIAL
COCOA
0 ⟨ – ⟩
1 ⟨:?|,⟩
3 ⟨.ABPT = JCHXD*RZ)S$IαV&EUFQKGLMNW(O + Y'⟩
W 0 20
Q ⟨N0V1⟩ [⟨0⟩⟨1⟩⟨2⟩⟨3⟩⟨4⟩⟨5⟩⟨6⟩⟨7⟩⟨8⟩⟨9⟩] ⟨ZZZZZ⟩ 1000000
C ⟨N3 V2⟩ 100/10 [J J'''/1 10000]
```

In the COCOA program itself the character - is a word separator, that is, type 0. The characters of type 1 are padding letters, that is, they are shown in the context but do not affect the sorting. The characters of type 3 are the alphabet in the order required for sorting . W indicates a maximum word length of 20 characters. The line beginning with Q selects every reference in the text which is introduced by N or V. An ordinary concordance, type C, was used and a line width of 100 characters selected. This was wide enough to avoid any wrap-around in the context. This particular example will generate a concordance of all words in the alphabetic range J to J''' occurring between 1 and 10,000 times and write it to the tape N0246 DIVAN 1 beginning at block 730.

The longest of these runs, that for the letter B, took less than five minutes to generate 8,960 lines of output on tape. The shortest, that for), generated only 12 lines in just over two minutes. As (cannot be the first letter of a word in Persian and the only two entries for ' were suffixes to be omitted, these two letters were omitted from the final run as, naturally, were the letters + and . which we had inserted into the alphabet.

When all these runs were complete, we were left with a tape containing the complete concordance in sections, one for each letter, but also containing entries for prefixes, infixes, and suffixes which we wanted to omit. The other problem we met at this stage was that COCOA does not print characters of type 1 (our :?|,) on the keywords which appear at the head of the entries for each word. Although words containing these characters are correctly listed under the same headings as words without them, for example, NUM?O listed together with NUMO, in certain cases, notably all words beginning with |A, the keyword should also be written with the padding letter. The only way to find these was to examine the concordance listings and note all the keywords that needed to be altered. The incorrect and correct forms of each of these keywords were punched, one pair to a card. A short FORTRAN program with machine code input / output was written to copy the concordance to a second tape substituting the correct forms for the incorrect forms using the punched cards as data. The same program removed the entries for the words that were to be omitted (table 3 shows a list of these). It was not necessary to run this program on the concordance for every letter. There were no keywords to be altered or words to be omitted for the letters =,), α and w. The concordance for these letters was copied straight to the second tape. The longest of the other 28 runs, that for the letter B, took less than twenty seconds on Atlas.

EDITING OF CONCORDANCE

The next stage in the project was to insert the shift and other characters which would enable the concordance to be printed in Persian script on the SC4020. The first problem encountered here was the question of numerals in the line references and frequency counts of keywords. Although the Arabic script is written from right to left, the numerals are written in the same direction as ours, for example, 1972 is written ۱۹۷۲. Our concordance at this stage read from left to right and it was intended simply to type it backwards starting at the right-hand side of the page. This meant that all the numerals had to be reversed. It was decided to remove all the leading zeroes from the references and type the poem number followed by the verse number leaving three spaces before the context or two when the verse number consisted of two digits. The frequency count for each keyword was also reversed and placed after the keyword so that in effect these were the same way round as in the left to right concordance.

-AT	L-
-A$	-M,M-
AL-	MY-
-AM	-N
-AND	-ND
-A+Y-	NMY-
-AYM	-O
B.-	-OA
-T	OMY-
-TAN	-Y
-RA	-YM
-$	-'Y
-$AN	-'YM
F-	

Table 3. List of prefixes, infixes and suffixes which were omitted.

The concordance still contained the letters we had inserted + and . , and the hyphens used as word separators. These were next removed. As some of the characters in our Persian alphabet could not be accessed directly by GROATS, these had also to be changed. : was altered to ? and α to / to correspond with the Persian font table (table 2). At this stage of the program the ? after A and W at the end of a word was changed to Y and the ? before O changed to ' removing the O. It will be seen that two different letters are represented by ' in the Persian font table, but no overlap will be found as ﻞ and ﻪ are final and independent forms and ﺴ is a medial form. The other character to be altered at this stage was | which was altered to 1. The preposition B which we had prepared as a separate word so that it could be listed in the concordance is in fact joined on to the following word. Thus we had to remove the space after B.

The concordance was now ready to be re-aligned. In the output from COCOA the keywords in each line of context are aligned in the middle of the page. While this is useful for most languages, it is not very suitable for Persian where several of the keywords are in fact only half a written word. It would also mean that the context width would be too great to fit on the SC4020 screen. We therefore aligned the context lines down the left-hand side of the normal output, that is, to the right-hand side when printed in Persian.

All that remained for the editing program was to insert the shift characters to determine what form of each letter was to be typed. The rules for writing Arabic script were used as a basis for this part of the program, namely:

1. Every letter in a word joins on to the next one except for A, D, *, R, z,), w, (, and *alif madde* which is now 1. In effect, the medial forms of these letters are followed by the initial form of the succeeding letter (or the independent form if that letter is the last of the word).

2. The first letter of a word is always the initial form.

3. The last letter in a word is the final form (or the independent form under the first rule above).

4. The independent form is also used for a word consisting of a single letter.

Several refinements to these rules were necessary. The setting character $\langle 2 \rangle$ was inserted before *shadda*, which is now represented by ?. This part of the program also inserted the setting character and the different representation of *shadda* which we found necessary for ﺯ and L. The correct form was inserted for the O in the middle of compound words marked by a comma. As it is in an initial position, the 1 representing *alif madde* would automatically be put in the third table in the font so that ﺍ would be typed instead of the numeral ١ which it represents in the first table.

This editing program was originally written in FORTRAN with machine code input/output. It simply read a line of the concordance from one tape, processed it once to alter the characters to fit the GROATS Persian font table, re-aligned it, processed it a second time to insert the shift characters and wrote it up to another tape. Atlas FORTRAN has a variable type TEXT and variables declared as such may be compared using FORTRAN logical IF statements. As only one line of text was being processed at a time, it was read in in such a way that only one character was in each element of an array. This meant that no unpacking or packing was necessary. Once a working version was obtained, all the logical IF statements and most of the assignment statements were re-written in machine code, using the facility in FORTRAN V to insert machine code statements in the middle of a FORTRAN routine with FORTRAN labels and the names of FORTRAN variables as addresses. The speed of the program was improved in this way and it took just over five minutes using 19 blocks of store to process the 8,500 lines of letter A (which was now the longest after the large number of omissions from B).

PRINTING OF CONCORDANCE ON THE SC 4020

Only a short ALGOL program was required to generate a half-inch magnetic tape to drive the SC 4020. This program merely read the output from the previous program line by line with the procedure **readstring** and turned it into SC 4020 plotting orders using the procedure **typestring**. Twenty lines were written for each frame of output using the character size and spacing previously decided upon. Once again individual runs were done for each letter and two runs were necessary for D, K, and M, and three for A and B to avoid very long jobs. The time taken to generate the plotting orders was about 5 frames or 100 lines per minute using 57 blocks of store on Atlas. When all the tapes had been generated, a few test runs were done on the SC 4020 to find a suitable aperture setting for the camera. The tapes were then run on the SC 4020 at a speed of about 10 frames or 200 lines per minute. As two cameras can be used in the same run, we were able to obtain two copies of the concordance, one on 35 mm film and one on photo-recording paper or hardcopy. Examples of the final output are shown in figures 1 and 2.

This project has been something of the nature of an experiment and our main aim was to produce a readable text. Until now the lack of any suitable output facilities has been a serious drawback to any Orientalist wishing to make use of a computer in his research. Whilst it is relatively simple to devise a suitable input method as we did for Persian, to produce output which could be read by anyone not familiar with the transliteration scheme required the purchase of an expensive print-chain. Only very large amounts of work in the same script would justify such an expense. The use of a microfilm recorder brings computer facilities within the reach of any scholar whose work involves languages written in non-Roman scripts. At the Atlas Laboratory a project to output Greek in a similar manner but with variable width typing is almost complete and

۱ ۲۱۰	بگشا بند قبا تا بگشاید دل من
۱ ۲۱۱	تا کجا باز دل غمزدهٔ سوخته بود
۳ ۲۱۳	از صبا پرس که مارا همه شب تا دم صبح
۱ ۲۱۶	سر تا قدمش چون پری از عیب بری بود
۳ ۲۱۶	تا بود فلک شیویه او پرده‌دری بود
۷ ۲۱۷	مرا تا عشق تعلیم سخن کرد
۱ ۲۱۸	تا ابد جام مرادش همدم جانی بود
۳ ۲۲۳	تا ابد سر نکشد و ز سر پیمان نرود
۸ ۲۲۶	بس نکته غیر حسن بباید که تا کسی
۱ ۲۲۷	تا ریا ورزد و سالوس مسلمان نشود
۷ ۲۲۷	تا دگر خاطر ما از تو پریشان نشود
۸ ۲۲۷	ذرّها را تا نبود همّت عالی حافظ
۱ ۲۲۸	تا از آنم چه بپیش آید ازینم چه هود
۷ ۲۳۱	گفتا مگوی با کس تا وقت آن در آید
۱ ۲۳۲	تا که قبول افتد و که در نظر آید
۱ ۲۳۳	دست از طلب ندارم تا کام من بر آید
۳ ۲۳۱	از خدا میطلبم تا بسرم باز آید
۸ ۲۳۱	همّتی تا بسلامت ز درم باز آید
۳ ۲۳۷	قد بلند ترا تا ببر نمیگیرم
۳ ۲۴۹	تا معطر کنم از لطف نسیم تو مشام

Figure 1

٤ ٢٦٢   هر که چون لاله کاسه گردان شد

کاش ٣

٢ ٤٢٦   دهقان جهان کاش که این تخم نکشتی
١ ٤٤٥   ز پرده کاش برون آمدی چو قطرهٔ اشک

کاشانه ٤

١ ١٧   آتشی بود درین خانه که کاشانه بسوخت
١ ١٧   یا رب این شمع دلفروز ز کاشانهٔ کیست
٥ ٢٢٦   گر بکاشانهٔ رندان قدمی خواهی زد
٧ ٢٦٠   سرخوش از میکده با دوست بکاشانه روم

کاشت ١

١ ٤٢١   هر کو نکاشت مهر و ز خوبی گلی نچید

Figure 2

U

we have experimented with Hebrew, Egyptian hieroglyphs, Akkadian cuneiform, and Armenian on the SC4020. We are also able to display Japanese and Chinese characters on a VT-15 display linked to a PDP-15 computer using a tape obtained from Professor Kuno at Harvard. A new method of defining characters using a light pen and the VT-15 display has recently been introduced and new software linking this to the GROATS system on the Atlas Laboratory's 1906A computer should greatly facilitate the definition of additional character fonts. It is to be hoped that more Oriental scholars will avail themselves of these facilities and take advantage of the speed of an electronic computer.

Acknowledgements
This project was initiated by Mr Alan Jones, Vice-Master of St Cross College, Oxford, and I am grateful for his encouragement and valuable suggestions. The text was prepared, checked and corrected in Oxford by Mrs Inger Milburn of St Hilda's College. I would also like to record my thanks to F. R. A. Hopgood of the Atlas Laboratory for adding new procedures to the GROATS package to facilitate the definition of character fonts.

REFERENCES
Churchhouse, R. F. & Hockey, S. (1971) The use of an SC4020 for output of a concordance program. *The Computer in Literary and Linguistic Research*, pp. 221-30 (ed. Wisbey, R. A.). Cambridge: University Press.
Hopgood, F. R. A. (1971) *Algol GROATS Manual*. Chilton: Atlas Computer Laboratory.
Russell, D. B. (1967) *COCOA Manual*. Chilton: Atlas Computer Laboratory.

Programming for literary research

Developing a machine-independent
concordance program for a variety of languages

This paper describes a new version of the concordance and word-count program based upon the ideas of COCOA developed at the Chilton Atlas Computer Laboratory by D. B. Russell in 1967. This new version is being implemented on the ICL 1906A which is to replace the Atlas computer. The program—written in a form of USASI FORTRAN—is intended to be to a large extent machine-independent and is currently also being tested on the ICL System 4/70 at University College, Cardiff. It is also intended to implement it on an IBM 370/195. At the Atlas Laboratory there exists, moreover, a facility (described by R. F. Churchhouse and S. Hockey 1971) for processing the output of a concordance in a non-Roman alphabet on the Stromberg Carlson SC4020 to obtain a graphic representation of the characters. The progress to date of this graphical output project is reported by Susan Hockey elsewhere in this volume.

The new program embodies substantially the same features as COCOA. In addition, it incorporates some of the new facilities provided by CONCORD—the Edinburgh Regional Computing Centre version by N. Hamilton-Smith (1970)—as well as some further features introduced as a result of the valuable criticism and suggestions of users of the COCOA version with the intention to make the program even more versatile in dealing with a great variety of languages. Both the COCOA and CONCORD programs have been extensively described by N. Hamilton-Smith (1971) at the Cambridge conference on computers in literary and linguistic research. The facilities offered by these programs need hence only be briefly summarized here.

FEATURES OF COCOA

A word-count produced by COCOA consists of a frequency profile and three tables containing the words in frequency, dictionary and 'graphic rhyming' order. A concordance outputs keywords in context, sorted either on the reference or on the context to the left-hand or the right-hand side of the keyword. It is possible to limit the output by frequency restrictions, alphabet range and in- or exclusion lists.

The most outstanding feature of COCOA is the facility offered to the user of specifying his own alphabet and collating sequence as well as the 'type' of each character declared. There are six relevant types of letters. *Word separators* will normally be the usual punctuation marks and 'space'. *Padding letters* may be such characters as the hyphen and apostrophe if the user does not wish them to be treated as word separators (e.g. *time-table* and *mother's* to be considered as single items). *Normal letters* would generally include the majority of alphabetic characters. *Guide letters* are included in the sort of the keyword only but do not appear in the context. If one wanted, for example, to distinguish 'row' (propel a boat) from 'row' (line of objects) and from 'row' (heated argument), the first might be punched simply as ROW, the second as ROW£ and the third as ROW$. The three words would thus be listed separately (consecutively if required) but all three would appear as ROW in the context. *Root letters* are set aside for a preliminary sort but do not appear in the output. A possible use for this type is the sorting together of variants of the same 'lemmatic form'. If one wished, for example, to list together all forms of the verb 'be' this could be achieved by prefixing every form by some character such as * or π which is otherwise unused in the text. (Or, if the data is prepared on paper tape, by underlined BE.) However, as will be mentioned later, the new version incorporates facilities for grouping items under the same lemma which do not require any pre-editing.

Finally, *strong letters* are similar to 'root letters' except that they do appear in the output. This particular type enables the user to sort on characters featuring in the middle of words—essential when dealing with such languages as Arabic. Other, more generally applicable suggestions for the use of 'strong letters' are: concordances of all hyphenated words, of all one-syllable words containing the vowel 'a', etc. . . . With some ingenuity, a user interested in stylistics may apply this facility in studying metrical patterns, vowel alliterations, and so on.

ADDITIONAL FEATURES OF CONCORD

The most interesting new facilities of CONCORD are the possibility of sorting together pairs of collocating items or variants of a particular form, and of specifying a concordance request of words ending in particular suffixes. It is hence possible to look for set phrases, for example COMMON SENSE, rather than having to look under the keywords COMMON or SENSE. Furthermore, by specifying the maximum number of words which may intervene between the two collocating items one would obtain idiomatic expressions consisting of more than two words (e.g. HOUSE OF COMMONS). Or, even, if the user were, for example, a 'socio-linguist', he might deem it relevant to group together all co-occurrences of, say, LANGUAGE and CULTURE.

All variants of a particular form considered as the 'lemma' can be sorted together by the user's simply listing all such variants in his program. If a user is interested in grammar, he may request a concordance of all items ending in, say, '-ed', '-es', '-ing'; whereas with COCOA only one suffix at a time can be concordanced.

SOME NEW FEATURES

One feature of the new COCOA which is likely to be of the greatest assistance to linguists dealing with languages other than English is the facility to declare up to three characters as a single unit in the sorting sequence. The relevance of this facility, in conjunction with the type declarations already described, can be best illustrated by means of a number of examples of sorting problems posed by specific languages, which will be discussed in the next section. It should be pointed out that this facility is not subjected to the restriction—imposed by both COCOA and CONCORD—that every character be declared only once, but the same character (including 'punctuation marks') may be used in several combinations of characters. This new feature has the additional advantage of greatly increasing the limit of the character set-size imposed on the user. In the previous version of COCOA the alphabet was restricted to a maximum of 44 characters. The new version allows theoretically a maximum of 256 different characters for the '1 character' and up to 85 for the '3 character' option. The possibility of using the same character in different combinations to a large extent overcomes the limitations of the standard keyboards. This facility is not only extremely useful when dealing with non-English alphabets but it may also prove to be a valuable tool in stylistics, for it enables the stylistician to search for particular clusters occurring medially as well as initially and finally.

A further facility implemented for those users requiring only a straight-forward concordance of a continuous text is the provision of a 'standard concordance request', which assumes the English alphabet and the standard punctuation marks, thus obviating the necessity to study the manual. Other envisaged extensions of the new program include a more sophisticated statistical word-count package and the production of sets of collocating items.

SORTING PROBLEMS IN A VARIETY OF LANGUAGES

Very few of the languages employing the Roman alphabet use it in pre-cisely the same way as does English; they tend especially to expand its resources by the addition of diacritics to certain characters, as in French and Czech; the invention of extra, non-Roman characters, as in Icelandic and Faeroese; or the combination of two or more characters to form a separate letter, as in Spanish and Welsh. The various new facilities incorporated in the program permit more satisfactory concordancing of such languages than has previously been possible.

Of languages which make frequent use of diacritics, French is un-doubtedly the most widely known, and it is therefore to French that we shall turn for examples. This language uses five diacritics: the acute and grave accents, the circumflex, the cedilla, and the diaeresis. The custom is to represent these by a number immediately following the letter in conjunction with which they occur; for example, E1 for 'é', E2 for 'è', E3 for 'ê', C4 for 'ç', and E5 for 'ë'. The disadvantage of this has been that the usual type of concordancing program separates a word including a diacritic thus represented from other words not including the diacritic but otherwise spelt similarly. Thus 'à' is listed after 'azur', whereas in a dictionary it heads the words beginning with 'a'. One of the facilities in our program will allow '1', '2', '3', '4', and '5' to be declared as a special type of character, to be ignored in an initial sort, but subsequently used to differentiate words spelt with these characters (i.e. with diacritics) from those without them which are otherwise spelt similarly. Thus 'à' will be separated from 'a' *only after both have been separated from all other words and allotted the alphabetic position appropriate to 'a'*. This will result in concordancing by approximately normal dictionary order. If the inclusion of so many numbers as diacritics is thought to interfere too severely with the readability of the output, one could perhaps make use of the facility on the Stromberg Carlson s c4020, treating French as if it were written with a non-Roman instead of an adapted Roman alphabet. The advantages of this latter procedure in French are marginal; they become greater in Czech, for example, where the incidence of diacritics is much higher.

The same facilities would go a long way towards alleviating problems arising from the idiosyncrasies of the Icelandic alphabet, which also contains diacritics. Here we find in addition two purely non-Roman letters, 'þ' and 'ð'. Normally one would be obliged to represent these by non-alphabetic characters which would not at first sight suggest the correct pronunciation. By exploiting the new facility of declaring two or more characters to represent a single letter, we can now replace 'ð' by DH, the latter being a conventional method of writing the sound represented by 'ð'. It would be very satisfactory if we could similarly use TH for 'þ', but since 'th' is a possible sequence in Icelandic in its own right, we must employ some such representation as T&H, using three characters per letter but giving a very fair indication of the pronunciation required. If these devices, coupled with the large number of diacritics represented as numerals, are thought to impinge too severely upon the readability of the text, recourse to the s c4020 facility could always be considered.

Where a language itself uses two or more Roman characters to form an extra distinct letter of the alphabet, this means that the ordering of words in that language may be greatly affected. For instance, Spanish includes in its alphabet the letters 'c', 'h', and 'l', but it also regards 'ch' as a separate letter in its own right, following 'c' in the alphabet, and 'll' as another separate letter, following 'l'. Thus in a Spanish dictionary 'churro' comes after 'cobarde', and 'llano' after 'luz'. In addition, whereas an accent on a letter does not affect word order, 'n' with a *tilde*, i.e. 'ñ', is held to constitute a separate letter, coming after 'n'. By declaring two characters (of which one may be blank) to represent one item, we can arrange the alphabet as follows: /A, B, C, CH, D, . . . L, LL, M, N, N2, O, . . ./.

Greater problems arise with a language such as Welsh, which regards

'ch', 'dd', 'ff', 'ng', 'll', 'ph', 'rh', and 'th' as individual letters, with
the added complications that 'ng' must follow 'g', not 'n', and that 'ng'
may in certain cases be the two separate letters 'n' and 'g'. Fortunately
the words in which 'n' and 'g' occur together as separate letters are fairly
few and well known; the most familiar are 'Bangor' (the town in North
Wales) and 'dangos' ('to show'). If some form of pre-edition is used in
these cases, we can declare the Welsh alphabet as: /A, B, C, CH, D, DD, E,
F, FF, G, NG, H, I, J, K, L, LL, M, N, O, P, PH, Q, R, RH, S, T, TH, U, V, W, X, Y,
Z/. Several of the normal Latin letters, for example, 'k', 'x', and 'z', are
not used in Welsh, but it is wisest to include them in the alphabet in
case the text to be concordanced contains foreign words spelt with these
letters.

A more serious difficulty, which can be seen at its most acute in Welsh
and other Celtic languages, particularly Breton, is the occurrence of
grammatical changes which result in variants of the same root being
concordanced far apart in the output. A change in the ending of a word
is not serious, since all the morphological variants will still be listed
close together by virtue of their having the same letters at the beginning.
But Celtic languages possess the quality known as 'mutation', by which
the *initial* letters of words may alter. In Welsh, initial 'c' may become 'g',
'ngh', or 'ch'; 'g' may become 'ng' or disappear altogether; 't' becomes
'd', 'nh', or 'th'; 'd' becomes 'dd' or 'n'; 'm' becomes 'f'; 'p' becomes
'b', 'mh', or 'ph'; 'b' becomes 'f' or 'm'; 'll' becomes 'l'; 'rh' becomes
'r'; and words beginning with a vowel may acquire an initial 'h'. As a
result, in normal concordancing a word such as 'cadair' (chair) will be
listed in four different places, depending on whether it occurs as 'cadair',
'gadair', 'nghadair', or 'chadair'. These mutations are in fact regular
and predictable, but any attempt to insert a subroutine for mechanical
re-ordering of mutated variants under their root-forms will run into
difficulties through the tendency for the mutated form of one word to
form a homograph with the unmutated root-form of another. For
example, 'teg' (fair) mutates to 'deg'; but 'deg' is also a root-form
meaning 'ten', and can itself mutate to 'ddeg'. Moreover, since both 'b'
and 'm' mutate to 'f', 'fodd' could be the soft mutation of either 'bodd'
(consent) or 'modd' (manner). Pre-edition could be resorted to, but it
would be a formidable undertaking. We could improve the output somewhat by declaring three characters per item, and establishing the alphabet
as follows: /A, B, C, NGH, CH, D, DD, . . . etc./, inserting NH after T and
MH after P; but this would not go very far towards grouping all forms
under one heading, since the mutated forms which cannot be so rearranged are precisely those most commonly encountered. In any case,
'cadair' would still be separated from 'nghadair' by all the remaining
words beginning with 'c', so that very little would be gained.

The problem is not a particularly urgent one, since speakers of initial-
mutating languages are well used to complications of this kind; for

instance, a mutated word in a text must be looked for in a dictionary under its root form. But similar difficulties arise with regard to 'augments' in Ancient Greek (where a verb may add an initial vowel or change an existing one) and radical-changing verbs in Spanish ('volver' conjugates as 'vuelve', 'cegar' as 'ciegan', and so on). Therefore we must assume that a demand will arise for some more satisfactory solution to this problem, and it will be for computational linguists versed in the relevant languages to provide that solution, assuming that any is possible.

IMPLEMENTATION OF THE PROGRAM

Although it is intended to implement the program on a number of machines, including an IBM 370/195 and possibly a CDC 7600, we shall only report here our experience with the ICL 1906A and System 4. As COCOA was written in a specific machine restricted language—namely ABL—ATLAS BASIC LANGUAGE—it was decided to write the new version in FORTRAN, a language which is implemented on the majority of computers. The actual language used is so-called 'PIDGIN FORTRAN', a FORTRAN IV subset developed—among others—by J. C. Baldwin of the Atlas Computer Laboratory. Although there exists already a well-defined standard FORTRAN, namely USASI FORTRAN, experience has shown that the various FORTRAN compilers are not quite compatible in the USASI statement they will accept. For the sake of simplicity, PIDGIN FORTRAN may be considered as an even more restrictive version of USASI FORTRAN. Restrictions comprise exclusion of type 'logical' and of any relational (e.g. .LT. or .EQ.) and logical expressions (e.g. .OR., .AND.). Arithmetic 'IF' statements are to replace all logical 'IF' statements and multiple subscripts are avoided.

As character manipulation is reputedly tricky in FORTRAN, and particularly on the 1906A (character comparison is apt to cause the 'overflow register' to be set), the safest course is to adopt a numerical coding system for the characters. In both machines, characters are stored in the most significant position of the word, the remaining position(s) being filled with spaces. The internal representations of characters are obviously entirely machine-dependent. Colin A. Day (1971) defines a function ('KRUSH') which stores a character modulo 514:

$$\text{KRUSH (INT)} = \text{INT} - (\text{INT}/257) * 257 + 257$$

The effect of this function is to reduce any character read under A1 format uniquely on most machines to an integer lying between 1 and 513. On the 1906A 'A' becomes represented by 146, 'B' by 150, 'C' by 154. . . . On the System 4 (owing to its different internal character representation) 'A' becomes 127, 'B' 126, 'C' 125. . . .

However, the character set declared will be considerably smaller than 513. This number may be reduced further by introducing a table look-up. A vector of length 513 is used. For a character set of, say, length 60, the numbers 1 to 60 are placed in the vector at positions corresponding to the 'krushed' values of the characters. When the characters have thus been reduced to small integers, several may be packed into one word by means of multiplication. The number of characters held in one cell is dependent on (a) the size of the character set and (b) the bit configuration of the computer. The packing strategy is hence perforce machine-dependent but it is possible to read it in as a parameter in the general program. The limiting size of the character set was stated earlier as 256. In the case of the 1906A—having a 24 bit word—up to 4 integers (treated as digits to the base 2^6) can be packed into one integer word, if the character set is less than 64. If the character set is 64 or larger, only 3 integers (treated as digits to the base 2^8) can be thus packed. In the case of the System 4—having a 32 bit word—the packing density will be 4 for any size character set within the limit, 2^8 being the multiplication factor. The cells containing packed integers may now be compared arithmetically when sorting the items according to the collating sequence specified by the user.

As the text is read in, every 'graphic word' is tested for keyword status against the user's specifications. If wanted, a message of fixed length is set up containing the sortkey, reference and as much of the context as is requested. When the buffer containing these fixed size records is full, the messages are sorted and then written to two magnetic tapes as fixed size contiguous blocks. When the entire text has been processed, the sorted blocks are merged. At the moment, a 'magnetic tape' merge (simulated on the filestore of the 1906A) is used to ensure greater machine transferability. Two more magnetic tapes are used for the merge. A block is read down from each of the first two work tapes and merged into a single string. The merged strings are written forward alternately to the two new tapes. With each pass, the number of strings is halved. Simultaneously with the last pass, the merged items are counted and sent to the appropriate output channel.

Saving of core store can be effected by using 'half word' (16 bit) integers on the System 4, wherever appropriate; on the 1906A, the declaration 'Compress integer and logical' has the effect of cutting by half the storage required for integers (which normally take up two 24 bit words, the second word being unused). Effectiveness can be further increased by replacing certain FORTRAN routines—particularly the packing and sorting routines—by their respective machine code routines.

REFERENCES

Churchhouse, R. F. & Hockey, S. (1971) The use of an sc4020 for output of a concordance program. *The Computer in Literary and Linguistic Research*, pp. 221-37 (ed. Wisbey, R. A.). Cambridge: University Press.

Day, A. C. (1971) FORTRAN as a language for linguists. *The Computer in Literary and Linguistic Research*, pp. 245-58 (ed. Wisbey, R. A.). Cambridge: University Press.

Hamilton-Smith, N. (1970) *CONCORD. User's Specification*. Edinburgh Regional Computing Centre.

Hamilton-Smith, N. (1971) A versatile concordance program for a textual archive. *The Computer in Literary and Linguistic Research*, pp. 235-44 (ed. Wisbey, R.A.) Cambridge: University Press.
Russell, D.B. (1967) *COCOA Manual*. Atlas Computer Laboratory.

The interactive interrogation of text and concordance files

Over the past five years I have produced, for myself, a large number of computer-generated concordances: conventional ones, where keywords are sorted on order of occurrence in the text, and possibly less conventional ones sorted alphabetically on the word following or preceding the keyword, these latter being used, hopefully, to isolate peculiar stylistic mannerisms. For instance, 'to say the truth' and 'hurry of spirits' appear to be distinctive phrases in Henry Fielding's acknowledged writings, and such phrases stand out in concordances alphabetically sorted around the keyword. One result of producing so much concordance material is a large quantity of computer line-printer output which, besides being bulky and heavy, presents acute storage problems. How much of this output is actually used? The majority of the concorded words are most probably looked at once only, and a word frequency list would probably be just as useful for this purpose, whilst a small proportion of the concorded words are examined in detail together with their contexts. If such a small proportion only of concordances is actually used, is there really much point in producing a complete concordance, unless for publication? Maybe the outputting of a complete concordance on microfilm (Churchhouse and Hockey 1971) is more realistic than using line-printer paper.

When using a concordance, I find that, having looked at a particular word, the surrounding context often suggests other words of like theme, mood or subject, which are then followed up; or else certain pairs of words occurring close together (separated by up to four words, say) may appear to be distinctive. This type of use made me wish for a smaller and more flexible concordance, and as I hope to show later in this paper, I believe that I have, to a certain extent, achieved this.

In order to describe how this is done I will first briefly explain my concordance program written in Pop-2. Firstly, the words in a text are sorted alphabetically and, associated with each word-type, a list of textual references is kept, each reference pointing to the occurrence of the word in the text (Farringdon 1971). Each word-type and its frequency is stored in a *pair* and the references, page and line, say, to each occurrence of a word, are stored in *records*, these records being held in a *list*. A sorted word list will look like this:

$$[('ALL', 1) [\langle 132\ 5 \rangle] ('ARE', 3) [\langle 132\ 4 \rangle \langle 132\ 4 \rangle \langle 132\ 5 \rangle]$$
$$('AS', 2) [\langle 132\ 3 \rangle \langle 132\ 7 \rangle]].$$

The lists of references are then used to output the keywords with as much context as is desired.

Although my texts are semi-permanently stored on magnetic tape and disc, the word lists with their references were lost once the concordance had been printed. For the past few years I have been able to use POP-2 only in batch-processing mode. However, since it became available in on-line mode at Swansea University College in the Summer of 1971, I have been using POP-2 programs to interrogate my text files from an on-line consol. To do this effectively, the word lists and their references had to be constructed in such a way that they could be searched quickly and stored conveniently on disc files. Taking a new text, it is stored on disc, one page of text per file, and in a batch-mode run the words of the text are sorted by a conventional binary tree sorting procedure with twenty-seven trees being constructed, one for each letter of the alphabet, words being initially sorted by their first letter into *A*, *B*, *C*, etc., trees, the twenty-seventh tree being used for words such as *3rdly* and *&c.* Each node of the tree structures is a POP-2 record containing the word-type and its associated information together with left and right pointers to succeeding nodes; a record class NODE may be defined

recordfns ('NODE', [00000])→RIGHT→REFLIST→FREQ→WORD→
    LEFT→DESTNODE→CONSNODE;

A function ADDTOTREE which, given a word-token, the text references to the word, and the tree on to which the word is to be added, either adds a new node to the tree if the word is a new type, or updates the frequency and list of references if the word is already represented in the tree. Assuming a function COMPARE compares two word strings, then the function ADDTOTREE may be defined as

```
function ADDTOTREE TOKEN REFS TREE;
vars LORR COMPARISON TOKENLGTH;
datalength (TOKEN)→TOKENLGTH;
L1: COMPARE (TOKEN, TOKENLGTH, WORD(TREE))→COMPARISON;
if COMPARISON =0 then REFLIST(TREE)<>REFS→REFLIST(TREE) ;
                    FREQ(TREE)+1→FREQ(TREE);
     else if COMPARISON = −1 then LEFT→LORR
                              else RIGHT→LORR
        close;
        if LORR(TREE) =nil then
           CONSNODE(nil, TOKEN, 1, REFS, nil)→LORR(TREE);
           else LORR(TREE)→TREE;
              goto L1
        close
     close
end;
```

When the text has been completely alphabetized into the tree structures, these trees are stored on disc files for later use. A word frequency list or an index to the text may be produced by 'flattening' the trees into lists described above. This 'flattening' process is achieved by a function

TREETOLIST which 'walks' through the tree structure and produces a list structure.

The function TREETOLIST may be defined as

function TREETOLIST TREE;
if LEFT(TREE) = *nil* **then** *nil* **else** TREETOLIST(LEFT(TREE)) **close**
⟨⟩[%*conspair* (WORD(TREE), FREQ(TREE)), REFLIST(TREE)%]⟨⟩
if RIGHT(TREE) =*nil* **then** *nil* **else** TREETOLIST(RIGHT(TREE))
                                                                    close
end;

After the batch run, the tree structures are available, together with the text, on disc files and ready for interrogation from an on-line consol. The decision to use tree structures to hold the sorted words was taken because searching a tree for a particular word is very quick, and much faster, on our implementation of POP-2, than using such techniques as hashing. Binary search trees, such as these, have long been recognized as efficient for searching large files (Sussenguth 1963; Salton 1968). The shape of the trees depends on the order of the words when input, so that a natural language text will produce randomly growing trees and the resultant structures are order dependent. The efficiency of the searching could be improved by restructuring the trees so that each was balanced (Landauer 1963).

A small package of POP-2 programs has been written so that by typing a command on a consol, such as

        INDEX (*list of words*)

each word in the list, its frequency of occurrence and all textual references to it are printed. Similarly, the command

        CONCORD (*list of words*)

gives each occurrence of each word in a line of context, together with its references. These commands copy the appropriate tree structures for the words concerned into the core store, search the trees for the wanted words and, depending on the command, print the list of references found, or use the references to read and then print the lines of text from the text files. More complex commands using concepts of Boolean algebra are available, for example, INDEX(*word*/AND/*word*) outputs both words, the number of times they occur within *one line* of each other and their references. This is an example of logical intersection, $A \cap B$, A and B. Other Boolean concepts which are implemented, but which I have rarely used, are logical union, $A \cup B$, A or B, and logical negation $A \cap \bar{B}$, A but not B. These logical functions enable quite complex commands to be made. Words in the command list may be terminated with a ?, so that

        CONCORD (HEAR?)

will retrieve all words beginning with the root *hear*, such as *hear*, *heard*, *hears*, *hearing* together with such words as *hearts* and *hearty* as an unexpected bonus.

Of course, one does not need a conversational language to write program packages for use from a consol. However, as soon as the user's needs deviate from the program package, programming on-line in POP-2 enables the user to interrogate his files, text or concordance, in as flexible a manner as he might wish.

The varied functions of retrieval languages and the relationships of structure to function are very fully discussed by Vickery (1971) and anyone proposing to write a retrieval package would be well advised to read Vickery's paper.

To illustrate the way in which text and concordance files may be interrogated, I have attempted some content analysis on the lines of the General Inquirer system (Stone, Dunphy, Smith and Ogilvie 1966), using D. H. Lawrence's *St Mawr* (1971) as my text. As Ellis and Favat (1966) remark

> Especially promising to the literary scholar is the General Inquirer's application to the novel and, more generally, to criticism.
>
> The literary critic, consciously or not, usually gathers . . . evidence by analyzing the content of the text, seeking out patterns, categorizing them, finding their conjunctions, and the like. Content analysis, then, seems to be one part of the process of literary criticism, a process that moves from reading to analysis to evaluation.

St Mawr is, as Dr Leavis (1964) remarks in his book on Lawrence, a long short-story or a 'novella', and therefore a less complex work than a normal-length novel, so perhaps for this reason less likely to yield the kind of results which would *fully* justify automatic content analysis. Nevertheless, for practical as well as literary reasons, this fairly short work was chosen in the hope that it would provide useful pointers.

The enquiry was, therefore, a modest one, and centred on an analysis of themes of the book. The main general theme was taken to be the familiar Lawrentian one of death-in-life in modern civilization, the relation— or non-relation—between human consciousness, will, mental processes, civilized mind, and the creative sources of life beyond mental knowledge. The particular sub-theme chosen for the enquiry was that of 'art' and the 'idea of the artist'. Since Dr Leavis points to the presence of the creative intelligence of Lawrence as author fulfilling the abstract ideas postulated by Lou in the book, and to *St Mawr* as itself a work of art justifying the propositions contained in this theme, it seemed an interesting investigation to examine the figure of Rico, who 'was being an artist', and the references in the text to the artistic process. The whole text was used for this interrogation, and I compiled an *Art* tag for an initial retrieval. The words suggested by this theme included:

(1) ART (also ARTIFICIAL, ARTIFICIALLY, ARTIST, ARTISTICALLY)
(2) BEAUTY (also BEAUTIFUL)
(3) EYE
(4) SEE
(5) BLIND

(6) PICTURE
(7) PAINT(also PAINTER, PAINTING)
(8) ILLUSION

I found that (1) had twenty-one occurrences, and that the idea of 'the artist', mainly in the person of Rico, was continually associated with drifting, being uprooted, with unreality, with posing, with the non-genuine:

Narrative

They were the drifting artist sort . . . (p.14)

Rico

'Don't you think the man is rather fascinating, too?' he said, nursing his chin artistically . . . (p.24)

Narrative

. . . an artist . . . he was trying to become staid and to persuade himself that English village life with squire and dean in the background, humble artist in the middle and labourer in the common foreground was genuine life. (p.60)

Lou

'How tremendously his [Rico's] career as an artist, a popular artist matters to him.' (p.121)

Correspondingly, 'artificially' in its only two occurrences was used in a pejorative sense, as an adverse comment on modern civilization:

Narrative

It was all so queer: so crude, so rough, so easy, so artificially-civilised, and so meaningless. (p.137)

Narrative

. . . walking his horse alongside in the shadow of the woods-edge, the darkness of the old Pan, that kept our artificially-lit world at bay. (p.110)

The idea of the artist, particularly as 'painter', necessarily implies 'vision', a way of *seeing*, or apprehending through the eye, which in turn connects with the aesthetic notion of 'the beautiful'. The special importance of the relation between the artist and the *eye* is explicit in the following references from the first retrieval on the *Art* tag:

Narrative

. . . And all Rico could do was to gaze with *the artist's eye* at the horse, with a glance at the groom. (p.24)

Lou (to Phoenix)

'And, you know, *as an artist*, it's terrible if anything happens to his eye-sight' — (p.49)

The 'eye' references included EYE (30 times), EYES (119 times), EYELIDS (twice), EYEBROWS (8 times), EYESIGHT (twice), and EYED (4 times). This would seem an unusually large total for a short work, and could well be significantly related to the theme of 'the artist'. Reactions of characters were continually described, I found, in terms of expressions

X

of the eyes, and characters were continually related to each other through eye-contact. In addition, there is the very long episode where the ability to 'see' the 'hidden mystery' of life is described at length in terms of 'the third eye' (which can be equated with the true artistic or creative vision):

> 'He was Pan. All: what you see when you see in full. In the day-time you see the thing. But if your third eye is open, which sees only the things that can't be seen, you may see Pan within the thing, hidden: you may see with your third eye, which is darkness.' (p.62)

In *St Mawr*, the eye is both that organ which perceives and expresses, and the organ which reveals the truth of the inner life:

> *Narrative*
> At the middle of his [Rico's] eyes was a central powerlessness that left him anxious . . .
> . . . but now since she had seen the full, dark passionate blaze of power and of different life in the eyes of the thwarted horse the anxious powerlessness of the man drove her mad . . . that black, fiery flow in the eyes of the horse was not 'attitude'. (p.23)

It is this contrast between Rico and St Mawr that is of central importance to the theme of the modern artist, his 'attitudinizing' and his lack of creative power, a contrast paralleled in the repeated references to each of them in terms of ideas of 'beauty'.

The first retrieval on the *Art* tag produced 21 occurrences for BEAUTY and 23 for BEAUTIFUL. These included explicit conjecturing on the abstract notion of 'beauty', which supports its significance as a central idea:

> *Narrative*
> Beauty! What was beauty, she asked herself? The Oriental exquisiteness seemed to her all like dead flowers whose hour had come, to be thrown away. (p.126)

The retrieval revealed repeated contrast between two different ideas of beauty in the book—the 'artificial', symbolized by Rico and his way of art, and the 'natural', symbolized by the horse St Mawr. Both Rico and St Mawr are often described as 'beautiful':

> *Lou (to Rico)*
> 'Why not, dear boy? You'd look so beautiful.' Rico was divided. He had a certain uneasy feeling about horses. At the same time he would like to cut a handsome figure in the park.
> *Rico (of St Mawr)*
> 'Yes, dear, he certainly *is* beautiful: such a marvellous colour . . . He'd be marvellous in a Composition. That colour!' and all Rico could do was to gaze with the artist's eye at the horse . . . (p.20)

The 'idea of the beautiful' here is clearly connected with achieving pre-conceived effects, with the picturesque, with turning spontaneous life into dead art-objects for admiration. Rico can only 'see' with the modern

'artist's eye'. But the 'idea of the beautiful' of which St Mawr is a symbol
is that finally found by Lou in the desert of Arizona:

> ... there was beauty for the spirit to soar in ... Ah, that was beauty!
> —perhaps the most beautiful thing in the world. It was pure beauty,
> *absolute* beauty! There! That was it ... (p. 153)
>
> It was always beauty, always! It was always great and splendid and
> for some reason, natural. It was never grandiose or theatrical. ...
> And if it had been a question simply of living through the eyes, into
> the *distance*, then this would have been Paradise, and the little New
> England woman on her ranch would have found what she was always
> looking for, the earthly paradise of the spirit. The New England
> woman had fought to make the nearness as perfect as the distance:
> for the distance was absolute beauty ... (p. 155)

Here, in this long passage, 'beauty' is clearly associated with the natural,
the anti-theatrical, and with perfect vision.

This brief consideration of the theme of the artist in *St Mawr* has
shown that automatic content analysis can lead to consideration of certain
aspects of a work not obviously apparent: for instance, a side result has
been a noting of the large number of references to classical or mythological
figures—Adonis, Anthony, Cleopatra, Apollo, Argus, Pan, Caesar,
Cassandra, Iphigenia, nymphs, dryads (and it is interesting that some of
these are traditional symbols of beauty). Thus the whole weight of the
classical tradition of art makes its presence felt in the book, along with
descriptions or episodes that seem like tableaux of classical paintings, for
example, the description of Rico with his head on a plate like St John the
Baptist, as in the famous painting, or as an invalid posing as Adonis and
ministered to by Flora. Again, this interrogation suggested the strong
visual element appropriate to a work with the theme of art: it led to noting
the profuse references to colour (e.g. COLOUR 19, BLUE 38, BLACK 42,
etc.).

Finally, the initial retrieval on PAINTING and PICTURE led to noticing
their association with *apple* and a consequent retrieval on this word shows
the extraordinary cohesion of the symbolism throughout *St Mawr*:

> *Narrative*
>
> He saw Lou sitting in her slim white frock on the coloured swing
> bed, under the trees with their hard green apples. 'Good morning,
> Lady Carrington. If I may say so, what a picture you make—a
> beautiful picture—' (p. 47)
>
> *Narrative*
>
> The very apples on the trees looked so shut in, it was impossible to
> imagine any speck of 'Knowledge' lurking inside them. Good to eat,
> good even for show. But the wild sap of untameable and inexhaust-
> ible knowledge—no! Bred out of them. Geldings, even the apples.
> (p. 98)

Mrs Witt (of Rico)

He would go round the orchard painting life-like apples on the trees, and inviting nymphs to come and eat them. *Why, Sir Prippy, what stunningly naughty apples!*. There's nothing so artificial as sinning nowadays. I suppose it once was real. (p. 118)

Narrative

Every new stroke of civilization has cost the lives of countless brave men, who have fallen defeated by the 'dragon', in their efforts to win the apples of the Hesperides, or the fleece of gold. (p. 160)

She saw the fallen apples on the ground . . . with indifference. (p. 161)

The use of *apple* as a symbol has of course a special significance in a work whose theme is the death-in-life of Western civilization and of modern Christian culture.

This has been an illuminating experiment, and has been able to generate useful lines of enquiry into a literary text. Its main virtue is the ready accessibility of textual material for critical enquiry and its ability to suggest new ideas.

I wish to acknowledge the use of a number of disc routines written by David Cooper; for help and inspiration in the use of content analysis on *St Mawr*, my grateful thanks to Jill Farringdon.

REFERENCES

Churchhouse, R. F. & Hockey, S. (1971) The use of an sc4020 for output of a concordance program. *The Computer in Literary and Linguistic Research*, pp. 221-31 (ed. Wisbey, R.). Cambridge: University Press.

Ellis, A. B. & Favat, F. A. (1966) From computer to criticism: an application of automatic content analysis to the study of literature. *The General Inquirer: A Computer Approach to Content Analysis*, pp. 628-38 (eds Stone, P. J., Dunphy, D. C., Smith, M. S., Ogilvie, D. M.). Cambridge, Mass.: M.I.T. Press.

Farringdon, M. G. (1971) POP-2 as a programming language for literary research. *The Computer in Literary and Linguistic Research*, pp. 271-9 (ed. Wisbey, R.). Cambridge: University Press.

Landauer, W. I. (1963) The balanced tree and its utilization in information retrieval. *I.E.E.E. Trans. electronic Comput.*, **12**, 863-71.

Lawrence, D. H. (1971) *St Mawr* and *The Virgin and the Gipsy*. Harmondsworth: Penguin.

Leavis, F. R. (1964) *D. H. Lawrence: Novelist*. Harmondsworth: Penguin.

Salton, G. (1968) *Automatic Information Organization and Retrieval*. New York: McGraw-Hill.

Stone, P. J., Dunphy, D. C., Smith, M. S. & Ogilvie, D. M. (1966) *The General Inquirer: A Computer Approach to Content Analysis*. Cambridge, Mass.: M.I.T. Press.

Sussenguth, E. H. (1963) Use of tree structures for processing files. *Communs Ass. comput. Mach.*, **6**, 272-9.

Vickery, B. C. (1971) Structure and function in retrieval languages. *J. Docum.*, **27**, 69-82.

A programming system for
literary (or linguistic) experimental use

The system described here is being developed in order to fulfil a need for a text-processing facility that is both fast, in the sense of consuming minimum processor time, and easy to use, particularly for the non-specialist. No such system exists yet. The fastest programs of course are those that are written at the level of assembly code, which can take advantage of any machine-dependent features that happen to be suitable for speeding up text-processing operations. But machine-code programming is something that no non-specialist should be expected to do. Moreover what is gained from fast program execution is lost several times over in the time it takes to develop a working production program in assembly code.

EXISTING SYSTEMS

Most text processing at present is done in existing high-level languages — particularly FORTRAN, ALGOL, PL/1, and SNOBOL. FORTRAN and ALGOL 60 were originally designed for numerical work, and their use for textual material is, to say the least, a little unnatural. Nevertheless, they are usable, program-development time is not intolerably long for the sort of job we are considering, and execution time, though substantially longer than for a hand-coded program, is still quite acceptable. ALGOL, being less system-dependent, is generally regarded as easier to use than FORTRAN (though some would dispute this); on the other hand ALGOL provides many facilities that are absent in FORTRAN, though several of these are little or no help in text processing, and therefore represent an unnecessary overhead cost in compiling and running time. Some rough measurements by the author have indicated that on text-processing work ALGOL 60 is from 1·5 to 3 times slower than FORTRAN IV, depending on the implementation. On the whole, ALGOL tends to come off better on British machines than American. Recent years have seen the development of a number of 'ALGOL-like' languages, some of which have much better text-processing facilities than ALGOL 60; but no timing comparisons appear to have been made yet on text-processing work.

PL/1 was intended from the start to be all things to all men. It has not lived up to this aim in every field; but for processing text it does seem to be fairly successful. This is because it provides intrinsically certain string-processing facilities such as catenation and substring definition. Further rough measurements have indicated that PL/1 is not so very much slower than FORTRAN in executing text-processing jobs, though execution time does appear to be very sensitive to the type of work carried out. This would appear to be a feature of the data structure and algorithm underlying the language. The author's measurements indicate about twice the compilation time of FORTRAN and two to three times the execution time on a 360-series machine for programs doing the same job. In view of its convenience and wide availability, PL/1 is likely to become the preferred language for the processing of text in the near future.

SNOBOL was developed for symbol manipulation, which is not quite the same thing as text processing. It has built into it certain recursive features which make it an extremely powerful tool; but these are not needed in the majority of straightforward text-processing applications. Symbol-manipulation algorithms require pattern definitions to be dynamic, that is, to be variable at execution time; and this is normally achieved by executing programs interpretively. Now the interpretive mode of execution is necessarily slow; and measurements indicate that SNOBOL programs for text processing run five to ten times slower than FORTRAN programs doing the same jobs. By contrast, SNOBOL is easy to use: a program involving a few simple pattern-matching and output operations can be written and checked out in two or three runs, in contrast to the ten or more runs that would be necessary with FORTRAN or ALGOL.

There is thus a need for a language for processing text that is at least as well job-oriented as SNOBOL but gives rise to a program that will run as fast as if it had been written in FORTRAN. Job orientation in this case means the ability to define static patterns and consequential actions, which in the first instance consist of either counting or the output of substrings. Although all the languages we have been discussing are procedural, there is nothing inherent in the pattern-matching process that demands a procedural approach. Consequently the system described here has been made non-procedural, though an option will be left open for the introduction of procedural features later on should they be found to be desirable.

PATTERN DEFINITION

Several schemes have been devised for defining classes of patterns in strings of text. Probably the best known is the transformational grammar, in which a class of patterns is defined by a set of permissible transformations that can be applied in any sequence starting with a single base item. Another approach to pattern definition is to recognize the fact that a pattern class can be represented as a graph, and to use the graph-theoretic concepts of 'node' and 'edge' to provide a description of the graph, and hence of the pattern class. A third is a state table, in which successive pattern elements represent state transformations; the final state, given a standard starting state, is then indicative of a particular sequence of pattern elements. The technique we shall use here, which is similar to that used in SNOBOL, represents pattern classes as modified regular expressions.

The algebra of regular expressions consists of a set of variables together with the three operators of catenation (for which we use no symbol), set inclusion (for which we use an oblique, /), and closure, or indefinite repetition (for which we use a star, *, placed after the item to be operated on). The normal operator precedence is closure, catenation, inclusion; but parentheses can be used to change the order of application of operators just as in arithmetic expressions. Thus the expression

a* / b c*

will match the strings a, aa, aaaaaaa, b, bc, bcccccc and so on, as well as the null string, whereas the expression

((a* / b) c)*

matches the null string and any string made up of successive elements of any of the forms, c, bc, ac, aac, aaac, and so on.

To allow us to define succinctly patterns involving a finite number of repetitions of an element, the element to be repeated is followed by either one or two integers in parentheses. One integer indicates a fixed number of repetitions: two indicate the limits for a variable number. Thus a b (3) matches only abbb, while a b (0, 3) matches a, ab, abb, and abbb.

Patterns are constructed from spaces, a set of letters, a set of digits, and a set of punctuation marks. For default purposes the 'letters' comprise the upper-case English alphabet together with the hyphen and the apostrophe. The default punctuation marks include a set of arithmetic symbols as well as the normal punctuation symbols.

A pattern definition is written as an equality, the left-hand side of which consists of the dollar symbol followed by an integer identifying the pattern. The right-hand side consists of a regular expression followed by a new line. Pattern elements may be literals, in which case they are enclosed in string quotes, variable strings (identified by alphabetic names), or pattern identifiers (dollar sign followed by an integer). For example, the pattern defined as

$11 = 'THE`A'OF`

would match the strings

THE KING OF

THE ULTIMATE EXPRESSION OF

THE FIRST FINE CARELESS RAPTURE OF

and so on, assigning the values KING, ULTIMATE EXPRESSION, and FIRST FINE CARELESS RAPTURE respectively to the variable A.

Pattern identifiers $1 to $10 are reserved for intrinsic patterns. Of these, the first four are

$1 = '1` / '2` / .... / '9` / '0`

$2 = 'A` / 'B` / .... / 'Z` / '-` / '''

$3 = '.` / ',` / ';` / ':` / '?` / '(` / ')` /
    `/ '+` / '—` / '/` / '*` / '=`

$4 = ('' / $3) $2* ('' / $3)

The last of these has the additional property that its leading space or delimiter may be the closing space or delimiter of a preceding pattern, and thus corresponds to the normal concept of a word or an alphabetic identifier. The values given here for the first four patterns are default values, and can be altered by the user.

In the example given above, pattern $11 assigned a value to A without any constraints. If we wish A to conform to a particular pattern, we can make it do so by attaching the pattern to it by means of a dot operator. Thus in

$$\$11 = {\rm 'THE`} \ \$4\,(1,3)\,.\,{\rm A'OF`}$$

variable A could take the values KING and ULTIMATE EXPRESSION, but not FIRST FINE CARELESS RAPTURE, and the third of the four phrases would not therefore be matched.

In the preamble we said that one of the aims was to produce a system that was easy to use. It may seem from what has just been said that this aim is not being achieved. Unfortunately the complexity lies in the nature of the problem. Pattern definition is a complicated business, and there is nothing at all that we can do about that. Moreover, pattern definition is the *only* complexity in the present system, and the whole of the time consumed in program development should be associated with getting the definitions right. It is contended that the approach to pattern definition using modified regular expressions is the simplest that has been devised to date.

PROGRAMS

A program consists of two parts: a set of pattern definitions, and a set of consequential statements. A consequential statement comprises a pattern identifier followed by one or more actions, followed by a full stop. An action consists either of the word PRINT with a string identifier or the word COUNT with an integer identifier. The only actions we are providing at the moment are printing and counting; these however do go a good way towards providing for the needs of formatting, lexicometry, and stylistic analysis.

As an example, let us suppose that we wish to count the number of relative clauses in a piece of text. In a simple-minded way we might define a relative clause as one not coming at the beginning of a sentence, introduced by WHO, WHOM, WHICH, or THAT, and terminated by a punctuation mark. We might additionally require the THAT clauses to be printed so that we can eliminate by inspection those in which the word is used demonstratively instead of relatively. The program would be

```
$11 = 'THAT` X $3
$12 = ('WHO` / 'WHOM` / 'WHICH`) Y $3
$13 = '` $4 * ( $11 / $12)
$13 = COUNT REL $11 PRINT 'THAT` X.
$0 = PRINT REL.
```

Pattern 0 is a notional pattern that is matched only by the end of the data. Notice that, as the program is written here, patterns 11 and 12 are detected only when they match substrings of pattern 13.

THE ALGORITHM

The system is intended to be used with a body of text too long to hold in immediate-access storage, and which must consequently be scanned through a moving 'window' that can be thought to travel along the text in jumps as long as the data unit of the device on which the text is submitted. The window size together with the jump length determines the longest pattern that can be recognized fully, though an indication will be given if a possible pattern is limited by the characteristics of the system. Both window size and jump length are to some extent under the control of the user. For default purposes, a jump length of one card (80 characters) and a window size of four cards are being used.

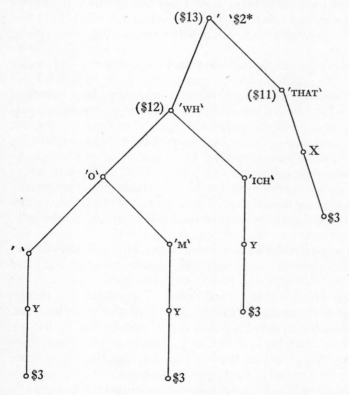

Figure 1

In the current version, a straightforward character-by-character match is being used to find patterns. Later it may be possible to use short-cut hashing techniques. Any set of patterns can be partitioned into subsets such that each subset consists entirely of patterns starting with the same pattern elements; and each subset matched by more than one string can be partitioned likewise. If the partitioning is such that the subsets are maximal, that is, if no two subsets can be combined into one by choosing a shorter initial subpattern, then the subsets form a tree. For example, figure 1 shows the tree corresponding to the patterns in the example we have just given. The nodes correspond here either to separate pattern elements or else to segments of pattern elements that serve to associate or distinguish pattern classes.

The algorithm operates in the normal manner of a heuristic tree search, attempting by pattern matching to find a path from the root of the tree to one of the terminal nodes, trying each branch in order from left to right. As each node is matched, its position in the data is marked by pointers, so that the search can return to it if the next line of exploration proves fruitless. Pointers are used too to mark those nodes that appear at the beginning or end of a named substring, such as the nodes marked ($12) and X in figure 1. Subsequent print operations then refer simply to the corresponding markers.

Each symbol in the buffer is used in turn as a starting point for a possible pattern match. If a match is found, a further attempt is made to achieve another match starting at the same character but using a later branch of the tree. As a result, there is no restriction whatever on overlapped patterns. This is probably what is wanted during program development; but for production work some user-definable control over pattern overlapping is desirable, and some sort of masking device will eventually have to be provided. Overlapping subpatterns, that is, adjacent subpatterns where the tail of the first is intended to be also the head of the second, can usually be handled by treating the overlapped position as a separate pattern element; but it may turn out to be more efficient to use some other approach.

IMPLEMENTATION

The system is being developed initially on an ICL 4100 series machine in NEAT, the 4100 assembly code, using the macro-processor ML/1 to perform the compilation. Later it is intended to make FORTRAN the target language, which will give some degree of transferability, though even then only on to machines that have ML/1. At this stage, however, it should be possible to get a measure of the efficiency of FORTRAN compared with an assembly code for the processing of text. One consequence of using ML/1 is that the language requires the use of more delimiters than are implied in the foregoing description.

The eventual aim will be to incorporate such features into the language as will make it possible to write a macro-generator in the language itself. At that stage it will be possible to 'bootstrap' the system on to any machine one wishes. The main features that will make this possible will be the storage and retrieval of named strings, together with some means of doing this at execution time.

REPLIES TO QUESTIONS

1. Two questions dealt with the closure operator and the fact that this can give rise to alternative pattern matches over the same string of text.

Reply. At present we are treating the closure operator in effect like a node with an infinite number of branches. This means that we get not only the shortest and the longest match but also every possible match in between. I agree that the user will sometimes want the shortest match and sometimes the longest; and so we shall have to provide him with the means to specify this. In fact this is a special case of the general problem of overlapped patterns, which, as I have said in the paper, is something we have not tackled yet.

2. Two questioners asked about the relationship of the proposed system to SNOBOL and in particular whether it would have any advantage over a SNOBOL compiler such as the one currently being written at Bristol.

Reply. I should have to know a lot more about the proposed SNOBOL compiler before I can answer this question properly. Of course a compiled SNOBOL is bound to run faster than present interpretive SNOBOL systems; but the language has so many dynamic features that I cannot help feeling even a compiled system must involve a great deal of interpretive activity. Because our system is inherently designed to do a simpler job, it should operate faster than any form of SNOBOL compiled or interpreted.

I think our system should be easier to use than SNOBOL, too. What we have tried to do is put the basic default data handling, that is reading individual cards or file blocks and making up print lines, behind the scenes. The user of SNOBOL has to be conscious all the time of the structure of his peripheral data; and he has to perform the operation of sticking data segments together into a continuous stream himself.

A literary computing centre

Research carried out at the
Centre de Traitement Electronique des Documents
of the Catholic University of Louvain

The Centre for the electronic processing of documents (CETEDOC) was established in 1968 with the basic function of developing automation in the field of the study of documents. The word 'document' suggests the essential preoccupation of the Centre: the processing of alphanumerical documentation (texts, archives, registers, etc.).

The Centre functions

1. as a centre of research for the constitution and perfecting of computer programs for the study of documents;

2. as a service which puts its programs at the disposition of researchers, and produces new programs to meet the needs of proposed research;

3. as a centre for testing programs and applying them to a given domain. The members of the Centre themselves are concerned particularly with the automation of the study of literary texts, especially texts of the Latin Middle Ages. (Medieval Latin, it should be said, is a complex linguistic phenomenon, and therefore provides a particularly interesting testing-area);

4. as a training centre for the application of computing science to the human sciences. This training should be secured at all levels; all the researchers must have a minimum of training in computing science, in order to implement the new possibilities offered by modern techniques. Some of them should receive a specialized training, so that they can apply new methods of resolving the processing problems peculiar to their own field of research.

CETEDOC is situated in the wider framework of the Centre pour l'Informatique en Sciences Humaines (Centre for Computerisation in the Human Sciences), whose task is to coordinate all research in the field of the application of computing science to the human sciences. At the moment it comprises three sections: a statistical section, constituted by the Belgian Archives for Social Sciences (BASS), a simulation section, and the documents section, namely CETEDOC.

In this paper I propose to outline the research already completed, as well as that currently in progress, and I shall split up my description into four sections: research in applied computing science, the applications carried out at the Centre itself, the applications carried out at CETEDOC in collaboration with other centres, and finally the applications made by various researchers who have availed themselves of the scientific and technical collaboration of the Centre.

RESEARCH IN APPLIED COMPUTING SCIENCE

The Centre works on the analysis, recording, and perfecting of computer programs facilitating the processing of documents. The language currently used is COBOL. The majority of our processes are characterized by the control of a particularly heavy input and output. Accordingly, our problems are similar to the problems of administration.

Up to the present, we have used the disk operating system, working with an IBM 360/40 computer, with a memory of 128 K. This year, one of our essential concerns is the changeover to an operating system based on an IBM 370/155 with a memory of 1024 K. The principal operational procedures allow us to effect the following functions:

The storing of documents on magnetic tapes. (Where we still use punched cards, it is solely as an intermediate support between the original document and the magnetic tape.)

Automatic referencing. (This provides the precise reference of each item stored, of each record, or, in the case of a literary text, of each word, e.g. book, chapter, paragraph, page, number in the line or verse, number in the sentence and in the work.)

The constitution of indices, multiple concordances, and statistical abstracts.

The updating of established information-banks.

The enumeration of various types of analysis.

The compilation of tables for the statistical distribution of various phenomena.

The preparation of different types of indices, concordances, frequency lists, etc., with a view to printing by offset.

We might comment on each of these procedures in some detail, but let us simply say that these programs as a whole enable us to store multiple analyses in successive phases of increasing complexity, and to exploit all the analyses made. These procedures can be applied to documents of various kinds and in various languages. All the documents processed to date have been in latin characters (the Latin-Arabic lexicon which we compiled is, likewise, in latin characters). This year we will be able to process Greek texts, using a printer which provides for all the characteristics of the Greek alphabet. Another project is concentrating on the processing of Armenian documents, and the perfecting of a printing drum with Armenian characters.

Among the computer procedures now being completed, I shall single out:

The automatic comparison of coded data. (The comparison of manuscript traditions is one application of this which I shall mention later.)

The automatic analysis of texts. (One realizes the complexity of this problem, and recognizes that, in most cases, analyses made by the computer must be controlled and minutely revised by the researcher. For instance, there is no truly automatic analysis for a Latin text, and there probably never will be one, because the degree of ambiguity is so high; so the whole problem is to develop the most dependable system to provide the optimum balance between the amount of information which the computer can provide and the extent to which the researcher must intervene.)

The processing of co-occurrences. (The construction of our concordances, notably the 'optimalised' concordance for which the computer chooses the context of each word to the best effect within the sentence, already permits the study of syntagmata, groups of words; we are particularly concerned to perfect the possibilities of studying groups of words.)

New kinds of updating. (Everyone knows that the constitution of multiple programs of updating plays a very large part in the problems of processing information; these programs condition the whole flexibility of the system. In principle, we compile magnetic tapes in such a way that they can continually be submitted to new types of analysis. The documentation is compiled once and for all; various researchers with different interests can then enrich this documentation by the results of their own analysis.)

RESEARCH CARRIED OUT AT CETEDOC

Advanced philological research in the field of Medieval Latin. This research aims at perfecting a method of philological analysis, coding, processing by computer, and exploitation of the results of the processing, in order to permit an advanced philological study of Middle Latin works. (In addition, the Centre possesses a collection of works containing the published results of certain studies: *Indizes, Konkordanzen, statitische Studien zur Mittellateinischen Philologie* edited by Georg Olms, Hildesheim.)

Obviously in many cases this method can be applied as it stands to the study of works written in another language; in other cases it can easily be adapted, provided one has clearly defined its principles.

The texts chosen for this research are of a literary, historical, philosophical and theological nature:

The *Chronique de Saint-Hubert*, called *Cantatorium* (12th century).
The *Gesta abbatum Trudonensium* of Raoul and Gislebert de Saint-Trond (12th century).
The work of Sigebert de Gembloux (+1112).
The *De rationibus fidei* and *De substantiis separatis* of St Thomas Aquinas. These last are studied in the cadre of a study of scholastic Latin.

A particularly interesting contribution to this study is the corpus of philosophical texts carried out at the CETEDOC, which I shall mention further on.

These works are submitted to exhaustive lexicographical, morphological, syntactic, and stylistic analyses.

Y

For all this research, a comparison between individual works is of paramount importance. This enables us to discern the characteristics proper to a work, an author, a literary genre, or to a period.

The comparative study of related texts. This is so important as to constitute a specific field of research, in our case the successive rewritings of *vitae sanctorum*. Thus we are currently studying the successive versions of the *Vitae Ursmari*, and carrying out a lexicographical, morphological, syntactic, and stylistic comparison of the various versions. The essential phases of this research are the establishment of a single concordance for the works in question, the paralleling of the various analyses, and the comparative statistical evaluation. In many cases, we have to begin by establishing a new edition of the text. Naturally, the problems of manuscript variants claim close attention, and the same holds for the study of sources. These various elements necessitate the introduction of special codes on our recordings.

The comparative study of manuscript traditions. The problem here is one of analysing and coding the variant readings presented by different manuscripts of the same text in order to establish by computer how these manuscripts are inter-related as regards copying, and in order to indicate, or reconstruct by computer, the text which is closest to the original.

The method used here comprises the following stages:

1. *Stage of storing*: we create as many records as there are variant readings presented by the different manuscripts. The manuscripts and the different characters peculiar to each reading are then coded and stored on magnetic tape.

2. *Stage of automatic comparison*: the computer employs these various elements to determine the groups of manuscripts which are in full or partial agreement or disagreement.

3. *Stage of analysis*: the results of this comparison are then submitted to an analysis which should permit the establishment of the relation between the manuscripts and the designation of the most primitive models preserved. At this point, one can formulate the instructions to be given to the computer for the construction of the hypothesis of a primitive text.

The problem of the automation of textual criticism is extremely complex. At present, we have already realized a series of programs which permit the comparison of manuscripts. But a major problem is that of computer time, in view of the huge number of comparisons the computer must carry out for each variant reading.

CETEDOC IN COLLABORATION WITH OTHER CENTRES

Preparation of a Belgian dictionary of Medieval Latin. The Belgian National Committee for the Dictionary of Medieval Latin, and the Belgian Centre of Studies of Medieval Latinity have asked the Centre to develop and carry out the electronic processing of Belgian Middle Latin texts anterior to 1200, as part of a programme of research under the auspices of the *Fonds National de la Recherche Scientifique* of Belgium. All our texts are thus catalogued, coded, put on magnetic tapes, analysed, and processed. In the immediate future we will be engaged in providing lemmatized concordances and frequency-lists to all the works written in Belgium during the Middle Ages. The processing of ninth-century texts is completed as of now, as is the storing and analysis of the majority of tenth-century texts.

Study of the medieval oecumenical councils (12th-15th centuries). This research, pursued in collaboration with the Seminar of Medieval History at the Sorbonne (director: Professor Michel Mollat), aims at the construction of a series of research-tools for studying the oecumenical councils of Middle Ages from Lateran I to Lateran V. As in most comparable cases, the method consists of the integral storing of texts, philological analysis (here reduced, for the moment, to the lexicographical and morphological stages), the study of sources, and the exploitation of the information provided. An initial stage, dealing with the councils from Lateran I to Lateran IV is in the process of completion: this will constitute the subject matter of a first volume.

APPLICATIONS MADE BY VARIOUS RESEARCHERS

Miss J. Hamesse describes below the studies carried out in the philosophical domain: the *Auctoritates Aristotelis*, the *Thesaurus Bonaventurianus*, and the lexicon of Avicenna's *De Anima*; I myself have already referred to the researches concerning scholastic Latin. Here I shall limit myself to mentioning the other projects of electronic processing completed or in progress:

Processing of the Old Testament pseudepigrapha (A. Denis). Work executed: lemmatized concordance of the *Book of Jubilees*.

The *De paenitentia* of St Ambrose (R. Gryson). Compilation of a concordance, frequency-lists, and an index verborum (published in the collection *Sources Chrétiennes*, Paris, 1971).

The canonical collections anterior to the Decree of Gratian (G. Fransen and E. Van Balberghe). Analysis in progress.

The *Legenda de origine ordinis fratrum servorum Virginis Mariae* (A. Dal Pino). Concordance and lists of frequency compiled.

The *Proces de Jeanne d'Arc* (J. Fraikin). Analysis in progress.

The official texts of the *Second Vatican Council* (Ph. Delhaye). Storing completed. Lexicographical analysis in progress.

Some minor items have also been stored, notably certain French and Spanish documents; similarly, we have stored information gleaned from civil and parochial registers. There are several other projects under consideration, particularly as regards texts in Greek.

One of our fundamental concerns must be to develop dynamic working methods. I consider it important, therefore, to establish stores of data

Y*

which can be enriched, following new analyses. Traditional manual methods involve a considerable waste of time and energy; and recourse to the computer assures, in addition, the capacity to process large masses of material in an exhaustive manner.

One important advantage of the application of data-processing methods lies in a complete analysis of the problems. The necessity of applying rigorous logic to all the stages of a study, of breaking down each stage into many simple elements, gives paramount importance to the methodological approach to our problems. The computer forces us to master our problems as perfectly as possible; otherwise we run the risk of being furnished with deceptive output, and of having our principal questions left unanswered.

**Automatic processing of philosophical works
at the Catholic University of Louvain**

Research carried out at the Centre for the Electronic Processing of
Documents (CETEDOC) at the Catholic University of Louvain, directed
by Professor Paul Tombeur (see the preceding paper), and the computer
programs developed there, facilitate the elaboration of a whole new range
of research-aids. Since 1969, these methods have been applied to several
philosophical texts.

THE 'AUCTORITATES ARISTOTELIS'
The first text processed in this way was a medieval florilegium of Aristotle,
containing some 3,000 quotations and about 30,000 words (Hamesse
1970). In their study of medieval texts, scholars are continually meeting
citations from the Stagirite, whose source they can trace only at the cost
of prolonged research. Since the identifications which I made of quotations from Aristotle could be of use to these medieval scholars, it was
important to furnish them with an instrument of research which they
could readily use for the rapid identification of whatever quotations are
attributed to Aristotle in a given work.
   The method followed can be schematized as follows:
The text of the edition which we have established is stored *in continu*.
Each word of the text is referenced according to the order of the books of
   Aristotle within the florilegium, the order of the quotations within each
   book, and the order of the word in the quotation and in the florilegium.
Lexicographical and morphological analysis of each word.
Automatic compilation of a concordance where each word is accompanied
   by its lemma, preceded by the frequency of usage in the work. Because
   of the kind of context constructed by the computer, this concordance
   permits the immediate recovery of the integral text of the quotation in
   which the word or notion in question occurs.
Storing of the identifications of quotations.
Compilation of various indexes of identifications.
Printing, by offset, of computer output, of a concordance of content
   words, an index of function words, and identification-tables of quotations (Tombeur and Stainier 1968–1970).
   The essential characteristic of this work is to furnish researchers with
an automatically compiled instrument of research which permits an
immediate recovery of the exact source of each quotation. Thus, when
one consults, for example, the concordance for the lemma *causa*, one finds
the following quotation:

1,124   *Causa et effectus debent esse proportionata.*

We can immediately determine the source of this extract by consulting the index of identification classified in the order of the text. The identifications of the 3,000 citations were stored on magnetic tape, and the computer automatically compiled an index which provides, opposite each quotation, the reference of the florilegium as well as the real identification with a precise reference.

In the present case, the author of the florilegium deems 1,124 to be a quotation from the fifth book of Aristotle's Metaphysics. In actual fact, it is an extract from St Thomas in the Commentary on the Physics, ii, lect. 6, n. 197.

It can be established immediately, from these tables, that the supposed author of a quotation is not always the real author. A considerable number of extracts which the author of the florilegium attributes to Aristotle are in fact taken from the works of other writers, particularly from the commentaries of Thomas Aquinas. These findings highlight the whole problem of false attribution in the Middle Ages.

The researching of sources by traditional means was clearly the bulk of the work in this present instance. But on the basis of this information, and given that we now have a first thesaurus of medieval philosophical quotations at our disposal, we can envisage further possibilities of automatic research.

This work will be the next one to be published (Hamesse 1972a). The same methods will be applied to other florilegia.

THE 'THESAURUS BONAVENTURIANUS'

A project to establish an automatic concordance of the whole corpus of St Bonaventure, with the help of the computer, was launched early in 1971 at the Catholic University of Louvain. The project is under the direction of Monsieur Christian Wenin, Professor at the Institut Supérieur de Philosophie and Secretary of the Société Internationale pour l'Etude de la Philosophie Médiévale; I am responsible for carrying out the work at CETEDOC.

The Bonaventure corpus is enormous: the nine-volume Quaracchi edition contains some 3,000,000 words. To establish a general concordance for the whole work is a task that will take several years to carry out, and the resources of electronics are indispensable for its completion.

The method for the *Thesaurus Bonaventurianus* is exactly the same as that outlined for the *Auctoritates*, and the principal outcome will be the publication of a series of instruments of research. The first volume of the *Thesaurus* will comprise concordances for the *Itinerarium mentis in Deum* and the *De reductione artium ad theologiam*. The processing of these two works is already completed, and this volume will be published during the course of the year (Hamesse 1972b). The *Breviloquium* is being studied at the moment, and after that we will tackle the three series of *Collationes*. We hope to have the concordances for these works completed for 1974, the 700th anniversary of the death of St Bonaventure.

For each work of St Bonaventure we will provide a concordance of content words, an index of function words, and frequency lists. In addition we are including for this author a list of his quotations from others, because these sources have an important bearing on St Bonaventure's thought and because we deemed it of interest to distinguish the vocabulary peculiar to Bonaventure from that which he takes over from other writers. Faced with the diversity of quotations, some literal, others very different from the original text, we thought it better to distinguish between quotation proper and simple reminiscence. We considered as quotations only texts that were literal reproductions of the source quoted —accepting, of course, all unimportant variants. (As it turned out, there were few real quotations and a great many reminiscences, which is not surprising when one considers the manner in which the medievals treated quotation.) All the words belonging either to a quotation or to a reminiscence were assigned a special code to facilitate their precise identification (Aristotle, Antiquity other than Aristotle, Old Testament, New Testament, St Augustine, Arabic texts, Liturgy, Middle Ages up to the twelfth century, Middle Ages from the twelfth century onwards, Fathers of the Church). This code appears beside each form in the concordance. In the same way, we have decided to use a letter-code to distinguish the titles, for we are not always certain of their authenticity.

These various elements of analysis appear in the lists of vocabulary established automatically for each work. The first list is in alphabetical order. The computer gives, for each lemma, the number of times it occurs in the work, the usages peculiar to St Bonaventure, as well as the usages taken from quotations, titles or reminiscences. We consider these distinctions highly important for a more profound study of the writer: the data assembled here will make it possible to evaluate the importance of the influence of Aristotle, St Augustine and others on Bonaventure. And one might go on from here to an automatic comparison of the vocabulary in the different works of Bonaventure.

A second list classifies the vocabulary according to decreasing frequency of occurrence. When we have completed the concordances for several works, it will then be possible to study in depth the content of various concepts. At that stage, analyses of a new type can be applied, and 'complete phrase' contexts established for a given concept.

In addition, a table, in alphabetical order, of all the authors quoted in the work will appear at the end of each volume. This table, constituted by computer, will provide the point of departure for a more exhaustive study of the sources used by St Bonaventure.

THE 'DE RATIONIBUS FIDEI' AND THE 'DE SUBSTANTIIS SEPARATIS' OF ST THOMAS AQUINAS

Father A. Stainier, a member of the Leonine Commission and an assistant at CETEDOC, is at present working on these two texts of St Thomas, analysing in depth the morphology, syntax and style of the author. His analyses will provide the basis for a wider study of the linguistic structure of theological and philosophical discourse; and this research will itself fit into the pattern of a projected more general study of Scholastic Latin. Ultimately it should be possible to compare the language of St Bonaventure and that of St Thomas. It is also hoped to employ automatic processing to study the permanent structures in the linguistic expression of their thought, the arguments they use in dealing with a particular question, the stereotyped schemata they follow in their argumentation by question and answer.

THE 'DE ANIMA' OF AVICENNA

Mademoiselle Simone Van Riet, Professor at the Catholic University of Louvain, has employed the resources of CETEDOC in establishing a Latin-Arabic and Arabic-Latin index of the first three books of Avicenna's *De anima*. The work will be processed as a whole at a later stage. In its present state, the index provides a parallel of the Latin forms with the corresponding Arabic (the root or, for function words, the vocalized Arabic word).

This index has helped towards the establishment of the critical edition of the text. Besides its inherent interest for the study of Arabic translations, it is a work which provides a basis for the comparative study of two documents, a text and its translation.

We consider the establishment of such instruments of research to be a fundamental necessity. Of course, this is only the beginning. The interest of these techniques lies not only in the fact that they furnish us with exhaustive documentation, but also in that they enable us to make further analyses, which will underpin a more profound study of these texts.

REFERENCES

Hamesse J. (1970) Les 'Auctoritates Aristotelis'. Histoire de la tradition imprimée, édition, identification des citations, concordance. A dissertation presented for the degree of doctor of philosophy and letters. Louvain, 4 vol.

Hamesse, J. (1972a) *Auctoritates Aristotelis, Senecae, Boethii, Platonis, Apulei et quorundam aliorum.* Concordance, Index, Tables d'identifications. Louvain: CETEDOC.

Hamesse, J. (1972b) *Itinerarium mentis in Deum. De reductione artium ad theologiam.* Concordance, Index, Relevés statistiques. Louvain: CETEDOC.

Tombeur, P. and Stainier, A. (1968–1970) Les méthodes et les travaux du Centre de Traitement Electronique des Documents. *Bulletin de Philosophie Médiévale*, **10-12**, 141-74.

Armstrong, Christine, M.R.C. Speech & Communication Unit, University
   of Edinburgh, 31 Buccleuch Place, Edinburgh
Bailey, R.W., Department of English, University of Michigan, Ann Arbor,
   Michigan 48104
Bender, T.K., Department of English, University of Wisconsin, Madison,
   Wisconsin 53711
Berry-Rogghe, Godelieve L.M., Atlas Computer Laboratory, Chilton,
   Didcot, Berks
Bromwich, J. I., 48a Selwyn Road, Cambridge
Crawford, T.D., Arts Building, University College, Cardiff
Dilligan, R.J., Department of English, University of Southern California,
   Los Angeles, California 90007
Emery, G., Department of Computer Science, University College of Wales,
   Penglais, Aberystwyth, SY23 3BZ
Farringdon, M.G., Department of Computer Science, University College
   of Swansea, Singleton Park, Swansea, Glamorgan SA2 8PP
Fortier, P.A., Department of Romance Languages and Literatures,
   University of Manitoba, Winnipeg, Manitoba R3T 2N2
Frautschi, R.L., Department of French, S 404 Burrowes, Pennsylvania
   State University, University Park, Pennsylvania 16802
Geffroy, Annie, Centre de Recherche de Lexicologie Politique, Ecole
   Normale Supérieure de Saint-Cloud, 2 Avenue du Palais, 92 Saint
   Cloud, Paris
Hamesse, Jacqueline, Institut Supérieure de Philosophie, Université
   Catholique de Louvain, Burgemeesterstraat 1, B-3000 Louvain
Hockey, Susan M., Atlas Computer Laboratory, Chilton, Didcot, Berks
Kiss, G.R., M.R.C. Speech & Communication Unit, University of
   Edinburgh, 31 Buccleuch Place, Edinburgh
Kliman, Bernice, Department of English, Queens College, City University
   of New York, Flushing, New York 11367
Lafon, P., Centre de Recherche de Lexicologie Politique, Ecole Normale
   Supérieure de Saint-Cloud, 2 Avenue du Palais, 92 Saint Cloud, Paris
Martin, W., Institute of Applied Linguistics, University of Louvain,
   Vesaliusstraat 2, Louvain
McConnell, J. C., Department of Computer Science, University of Manitoba,
   Winnipeg, Manitoba R3T 2N2
Michaelson, S., Department of Computer Science, University of Edinburgh,
   The King's Buildings, Mayfield Road, Edinburgh
Milroy, R., M.R.C. Speech & Communication Unit, University of Edinburgh,
   31 Buccleuch Place, Edinburgh
Morton, A.Q., Department of Computer Science, University of Edinburgh,
   The King's Buildings, Mayfield Road, Edinburgh
Ott, W., Zentrum fur Datenverarbeitung der Universitat, Kollestrasse 1,
   7400 Tubingen
Pêcheux, M., Centre National de la Recherche Scientifique, Laboratoire
   de Psychologie Sociale de l'Université, Paris VII
Piper, J., M.R.C. Speech & Communication Unit, University of Edinburgh,
   31 Buccleuch Place, Edinburgh
Robinson, J. L., Department of English, University of Michigan, Ann Arbor,
   Michigan 48104

Ross, D., Department of English, University of Minnesota, Minneapolis,
    Minnesota 55455
Seidel, Gill, 19 Broadhurst Avenue, Edgware, Middlesex
Schneider, Jr, B.R., Department of English, Lawrence University, Appleton,
    Wisconsin 54911
Tallentire, D.R., Literary & Linguistic Computing Centre, University of
    Cambridge, Cambridge
Tollenaere, F. de, Institut voor Nederlandse Lexicologie, afd Thesaurus,
    Stationsweg 39a, Leiden
Tombeur, P., Centre de Traitement Electronique des Documents,
    156 Tiensevest, B-3000 Louvain
Tournier, M., Centre de Recherche de Lexicologie Politique, Ecole
    Normale Supérieure de Saint-Cloud, 2 Avenue du Palais, 92 Saint
    Cloud, Paris
Waite, S.V.F., Kiewit Computation Center, Dartmouth College, Hanover,
    New Hampshire 03755
Wesselius, Jacqueline, 191 rue Belliard, 75018 Paris
Zarri, G.P., Via Ausonio 26, 20123 Milano

Editors:
Aitken, A.J., Dictionary of the Older Scottish Tongue, 27 George Square,
    Edinburgh
Bailey, R.W., Department of English, University of Michigan, Ann Arbor,
    Michigan 48104
Hamilton-Smith, N., Edinburgh Regional Computing Centre, The King's
    Buildings, Mayfield Road, Edinburgh

concordance in Persian characters,
  291-306
  alphabet transliterating Persian
    characters, 291, 292
  conventions for transliteration,
    291-3
  editing, 301-3
  input and correction of text, 293-6
  preparation of text, 291-3
  printing of, 303-6
  printout of, 304-5
  re-aligning, 302
  runs, 299-301
  spellings, 293
concordances
  absence of full frequencies, 39
  amount of context in, 48
  beyond the, 85-99
  collection of statistical data from,
    42-3
  computer-generated context, 26
  Cornell Yeats, 42, 43-6
  duplication of effort in, 39
  effort put into production of, 98
  for each letter of the alphabet, 300
  forward, 255
  grammatical, 170
  keyword, 168
  KWOC, 248
  machine-readable, 168, 242
  method of providing statistical
    data in, 42
  multiple, 336
  need for statistical data in, 39-40
  numerical indicator, 86
  of titles, 184
  optimalized, 337
  parsed, 41
  phase of prosodical analysis, 242
  pre-editing of text for, 85
  pre-empting the market, 39
  program, machine-independent,
    309-15
  proliferation of machine-made, 39
  request, 310, 311
  reverse, 255
  specialized, 167
  to establish a norm, 40-1
  to the poems of Hafiz, 291-306
  traditional uses of, 40
  treatment of 'non-significant'
    words, 48-9
  use in computation of collocations,
    105

words as the basic units of, 41
concurrence
  in conservation, 226, 227
  in innovation, 226
conditions of production, 137
conjunctions
  anisotropic distribution of, 81-2
  as function words, 87
  frequency of occurrence, 75
  in dialogue and prose, 76
  kai, 75-7, 78, 81-2
  positional distribution of, 76-7
  position of, in Greek texts, 74
connectives, 73
connex graphs, 138
connexions
  branching trees, 123-9
  connecting marks, 137-8
  from co-occurrences to, 115-16,
    132
  from text to, 113-15
content
  analysis, automatic, 323
  words, 87, 96
contest of words
  arrangement by, 21
  limits of period of conflict, 16,
    18-19
  place of conflict, 19
context
  abridging, 32
  amount of, in concordances, 48
  automatic flexible, 25
  based on rigid typographic units,
    26-8
  based on syntactic units, 27-8
  flexibility of computer-made, 25,
    34
  for poetry, 26-7, 28, 33
  for prose, 27-8, 33
  hand-made, 26
  in computer-aided lexicography,
    25-34
  in monolingual dictionaries, 25
  line-overlapping, 26-8
  mini-contexts, 28
  need for flexible, 26
  non-pre-edited texts, 28-33, 34
  number of lines, 26-7
  preceding the keyword, 27
  pre-editing method, 28
  program focussed on formal pro-
    perties of text, 28-9
  punctuation, 28-9

z

metrical—*contd.*
  research on Plautus, 253-62
  studies, use of computers in, 253
metricality, 245
Metzger, B.M., 71
Michaelson, S., 79, 82, 83
Michigan Early Modern English
    Materials (MEMEM)
  augmentation of collection, 9
  composition of, 8-9
  dissemination by magnetic tape,
    8, 10, 11
  dissemination by microfiche, 8-9, 13
  distribution of entries, 8
  file-management system, 9
  future program, 9
  line-overlapping principle used
    in, 28
  maximizing value of quotations, 10
  modal auxiliaries used, 8, 9, 10
  multiple use of citations, 9-10
  participation in, 11, 12-13
  secondary index, 10, 11
  selectivity, problem of, 9
microfiche
  computer-generated, 11-12
  costs, 9
  dissemination by, 8, 11, 13
  participation through dissemina-
    tion, 11
  readers, 8, 11
  usefulness of, 8-9, 13
microfilm
  associative thesaurus on, 157, 161
  concordances on, 317
  in lexicography, 3-13
micro-units of speech, 117
Middle English Dictionary (MED)
  quality of excerpting, 15
  production of, 3, 21
  resources devoted to, 3
  use of paragraphs for tagging, 17,
    21
  value for loan-words, 21
Milburn, Inger, 306
Miles, J., 50-1
Milic, L.T., 50, 88
Milroy, R., 157
Miron, M.S., 41
mobile words, 73-4, 76-7
modal auxiliaries, 8, 9, 10
Modern Language Association of
    America, 9
Mollat, M., 339

morphological
  markers, 97
  variants, 188, 313
morpho-syntactic categories, 138
Morton, A.Q., 76, 78, 79, 82, 83
Mouvement du 22 Mars
  characteristics of, 137
  context of 'lutte', 135-51
  crucial element, 146, 148-9
  exteriority problem, 148, 150
  immediate action, 150
  lexicometric analysis of tracts,
    113-33
  long-term political goals, 142-3,
    150, 151
  reference to workers' struggle, 142
  solidarity question, 148-9
  view of organization, 137, 146
  view of students, 143
MTST, *see* Magnetic Tape Selectric
    Typewriter
Muller, C., 65
multi-access files, 293, 295, 300
multidimensional spacing, 154
'multifides' *stemmata*, 225
multiple analysis, 336
multivariate analysis, 69
Murison, D., 3
mutation, 313
Mylne, Vivienne, 183

nationality of words
  codifying, 19
  sorting and printout, 21
  tagging, 16
national origin of phrased calques, 16
negative exponential distribution, 82
new vocabulary in EMNE period, 5, 6
  see also incoming words
new words
  concept of, 61-2
  distinguished from neologisms, 62
  distribution of, in Dutch poem,
    61-4
  distribution pattern and expecta-
    tion, 62-4
  formula for determining, 62-3
  in poetry, 62
  non-stationary distribution, 64
  quantitative aspects of, 62
  stationary distribution, 62-3
Nicolau, E., 225
node(s)
  analysis, 116

LITERATURE STUDY
IN THE HIGH SCHOOLS

LITERATURE STUDY
IN THE HIGH SCHOOLS

THIRD EDITION

DWIGHT L. BURTON

Florida State University

HOLT, RINEHART AND WINSTON, INC.

New York   Chicago   San Francisco   Atlanta   Dallas
Montreal   Toronto   London   Sydney

LIBRARY
University of Texas
At San Antonio

PREFACE

To bring onto today's whirling scene of educational change a book on as broad a subject as literature study in the high schools requires a certain brashness; the subject so obviously presents a wide range of problems. This third edition is dedicated to the same general proposition as that of the first two editions: that literature should occupy the place of centrality in secondary school English in order to maintain a humanistic orientation in the curriculum. I do not mean to imply that composition, oral and written, language study, and the nonprint media are not valuable components of the curriculum and may not also be "humanistic." I simply want to reassert my belief that literature should occupy the place of greatest prominence, and restate what I consider are the major rewards to the student of literature.

Part of this brashness results from my attempt to make this text serve as a one-volume handbook for teachers and prospective teachers in courses in English or literature instruction for adolescents. I have tried to consider the relationship of literature in the secondary school to new trends and problems, but I am aware that some highly important matters need more intensive, specialized treatment than I have been able to give. Literature for culturally deprived students, for example, or literature and the nonprint media are subjects that deserve volumes of their own.

Part One, new in this edition, presents an analysis of the position of literature in the secondary English curriculum, and is meant as a general lead-in to the specifics discussed later in the book. I hope that the opening chapters will lead to intensive investigation of the various topics briefly outlined. Part Two is a combination of new material and material from the previous two editions. Gladys Veidemanis has revised her chapter on teaching drama. In Part Three, I have consolidated material on literature for adolescents, added to it, and updated the sample bibliographies. I retain my conviction that literature written specifically for adolescents has an important function in the literature program of the school and in the literary education of young people.

It would not be possible to acknowledge each and all of the individuals who have commented on the earlier editions and made suggestions for this one. The discussion, constructive criticism, and encouragement involved in the preparation of this book since the original edition appeared in 1959 have enriched my life personally and professionally.

D.L.B.

Tallahassee, Florida
December 1969

CONTENTS

part one

THE LITERATURE CURRICULUM IN THE JUNIOR AND SENIOR HIGH SCHOOL: BASIC CONSIDERATIONS

1
Why Teach Literature?

The answer to the question "why teach literature?" which is asked in this first chapter has not changed for the author since his preparation of the first edition; and most teachers and prospective teachers can give the ready answer, because love of literature was probably the major reason they chose the career of teaching English. But a number of things have changed in the school situation, including student attitudes, since publication of the revised edition. Movements to define the content and structure of English and to establish bases for sequences, to find more effective ways of bringing students and teachers together, and to create new materials for study have swept the country in the past few years. One of the objectives of the present edition is to relate the study of literature in the secondary school to changing conditions and to promote the humane orientation of the English curriculum.

To open a book with such a purpose on a negative note may seem unfortunate. But there is a reality which teachers of literature must face. At the time this edition was completed, it was obvious that the literature program of most high schools lacked relevance and virility for many students. Except perhaps for some girls in the upper and middle class, students tended to view the literature course as a garden not populated with real toads. Evidence of the relevance gap for many young people was found in the kind of paraliterature program that students had established for themselves outside of school, a program in which shockers such as *Last Exit to Brooklyn, In Cold Blood,* and *Giovanni's Room* carried more impact than the books studied in the

3

classroom; in which motion pictures such as *The Graduate* and *Guess Who's Coming to Dinner?* were major happenings; in which *Eye* magazine claimed a wide following; in which Simon and Garfunkel were more important than Wordsworth and Frost.

These specifics will be replaced by the time this edition appears in print, but the relevance gap may even have widened. A first approach to the problem is that teachers individually must identify basic rewards of literature study for their students, rewards in which each teacher can truly believe. Traditionally, the profession seems loath to be specific and hardnosed about the objectives of literature study.

The English-teaching community seems to have passed through three general prevailing attitudes toward the study of literature in the past three decades. In the late 1930s and early 1940s, as the country emerged from an economic depression and entered World War II, teachers of literature displayed a marked inferiority complex, covertly admitting that literature was not, after all, very important in the school program. Practicality and immediacy dominated high school curricula. Literature did not contribute much to the aims of secondary education as then identified. Writers of textbooks on education assigned to literature a vague place in the esthetic development of the student, or viewed it as a kind of recreational dessert capping the solid nutriment of the really important components of the curriculum. Literature study as such disappeared in many junior high schools, and in some senior high schools. "Core" programs or "common learnings" became widespread, and in the resulting "bloc," literature appeared only when ingenious teachers could drag it into units on "Modern Transportation" or "Home and Family Problems."

The era of the inferiority complex was succeeded by an era characterized by a lofty, rather precious attitude toward the values of literary study. Literature, many teachers felt, offered a moral guide to life. There was a preoccupation with theme and idea. Slogans were legion. "Literature as Equipment for Living" was a phrase used by the eminent critic and scholar Kenneth Burke. The author of the present book wrote an article entitled "Literature and the Heightened Mind." The slogans were titillating, but the sour fact was that in many classrooms literature study was not equipping students for living nor heightening their minds.

A period of reaction naturally followed, representing a delayed response in the high schools to the influence of the "New Criticism."

Now literature was made a discipline and there was much emphasis on "close reading" of individual works. The function of literature was to be true to itself—whatever that meant to individual teachers. To be specific about the rewards of literature was to be somehow unsophisticated. The distinguished Commission on Literature of the National Council of Teachers of English had great difficulty agreeing on a statement of the purposes of literary study. Fear of "going outside the text" frequently resulted in overconcern with technique and often students groaned under the process of meticulously picking selections apart.

The profession at present seems to be in a period of synthesis and rapprochement in which the favorite word attached to literature study is "engagement." Reporting on the Anglo-American Conference on the Teaching of English held at Dartmouth College in September 1966, Herbert J. Muller wrote that a favorite theme at the conference was: "The immediate object of the teacher should be to get the child actively 'involved' or 'engaged'. . . . In simpler terms, the teacher should make or keep literature alive, as it naturally is for little children." [1] Obviously, there is concern with getting students involved, intellectually and emotionally, with a work on its own terms so that a full literary experience will ensue.[2] Although most teachers feel the obligation to help students learn to deal with selections in sophisticated terms—allowing the final rewards to be the student's private business—there is a feeling that there should be some sureness in the teacher's mind as to what the ultimate rewards might be. These ultimate rewards, to this writer's mind, are discussed in the rest of this chapter.

LITERATURE AS LIBERATION

Literature is liberating in the sense that it helps to free us from the inherent shackles fastened upon us by our society. Crucial in the

---

[1] *The Uses of English* (New York: Holt, Rinehart and Winston, 1967), 79.

[2] Two important publications relating to students' involvement with literature appeared as this manuscript was in preparation: The revised edition of Louise Rosenblatt's *Literature As Exploration* (New York: Noble, 1968), and *Response to Literature,* edited by James R. Squire (Champaign, Ill.: NCTE, 1968), one of the Dartmouth Seminar monographs.

quest for identity, as opposed to a deadening relating to the crowd, is the ability to shake off, when necessary, the emotional censors of society. One can accomplish this in the literary experience and therein lies the great enduring value of literature. Northrop Frye says something similar when he distinguishes among three levels of the mind which also represent three levels on which words are used: (1) The level of ordinary experience and necessary public self-expression. (2) The level on which language is used in the practical world to convey knowledge and information, the level on which language is used, that is, in organized bodies of knowledge and doctrine—philosophy, history, religion, and so on. (3) The level of the imagination represented by the use of language in literature. These uses of language represent, to Frye, the dual categories of living, "what you have to do and what you want to do—in other words, necessity and freedom." The imaginative use of language, he says, allows a person to construct a "vision or model in your mind of what you want to construct." [3]

It is a mistake therefore to view involvement in a literary selection as merely a momentary escape from reality. Experience with literature enables the reader to build a level of imaginative living which is real in itself, lying somewhere between dead-level literalness and hallucination. Even in so-called escape reading, for example, one comes to terms with experience while escaping from it at the same time. There is particular significance, for instance, in the adolescent boy's zest for stories of physical adventure—whether they are laid in the northern forest, in the Old West, at sea, or on the battlefield. All these settings represent freedom from the complexities of social machinery. Men survive here through individual strength and resourcefulness. Through projection into these stories, the young reader tests himself vicariously, as he must inevitably do in reality. A major ingredient in growing up is the haunting trepidation about one's adequacy to play an adult role, to handle adult problems and experience. A lifetime is a long time to wait to find out what life is like. Thomas Bailey Aldrich notes at one point in *The Story of a Bad Boy* that "I certainly would have committed suicide if I could have done so without killing myself." And Tom Sawyer, at a low point in his romance with Becky, rues the fact that he can't die *temporarily*.

[3] *The Educated Imagination* (Bloomington: Indiana University Press, 1964), pp. 17–21.

If I could only know what it is *like* to be in crucial situations, the young person agonizes, before I get into such situations! G. Robert Carlsen focuses on this problem when he says that young people "come to a semi-integrated picture of themselves in many kinds of roles that it is possible for a human being to play. . . . He (the adolescent) wants to know what it would feel like to be a murderer, even though he is not planning to be one. He wants to know what it feels like to give one's life to religion, to be corrupt in politics." [4] In a real sense, he can find out through literature. One reason why imaginative literature is so important in the quest for the "I," for identity, is that it serves as pre-experience on the imaginative level. Thus the thirteen-year-old girl may enjoy reading a novel about a seventeen-year-old girl's first serious love affair more than would an actual seventeen-year-old. And the teen-aged boy's interest in war stories does not necessarily indicate a morbid zest for blood and violence but affords him a vicarious tryout in the most crucial of all human situations—facing death.

It seems appropriate to note here that there is, in general, a need for greater permissiveness and flexibility in school libraries and classrooms. Teachers and librarians are sometimes too concerned with the quality of books made available to students. By all means young people should be introduced to works of high literary quality, but it is important to realize, too, that there is a vital developmental dimension in enthusiasm for reading.[5] Studies show that adults who are enthusiastic readers of mature works almost invariably went through an undiscriminating, voracious state in their own reading during which they devoured tons of frequently trashy and juvenile pages of the vintage, for example, of the Bobbsey Twins, Nancy Drew, Tom Swift, or the Joseph Altsheler books.

It has become clear that many of the restrictions on the kinds of books and other reading materials to be placed in libraries and classrooms have crippling effects on reading interest. Sometimes there is an invidious, and often unconscious, censorship imposed on reading at the very points where restrictions of the right to read should be resisted most vigorously. This censorship is inflicted by teachers who in-

[4] "Behind Reading Interests," *English Journal*, XLIII (January 1954), 10.
[5] Daniel Fader's *Hooked on Books* (Berkeley: University of California Press, 1966) furnishes an object lesson.

sist that students should read only "great" books, that is, literary masterpieces; and by school librarians who will not stock certain kinds of books nor permit some books to be in general circulation. One must, however, be sympathetically aware of the complexities surrounding such policies. But frequently adults underestimate the potential of young people to cope with the powerful emotions engendered by what they read.

The general point being made is that literature is a liberating force. For young people, especially, it liberates first through helping to free them from the emotional and intellectual blockings that result from inadequate knowledge of human nature. A book, a story, a play, or a poem may help to ease what James Street called "just the damn hurt of youth, which I contend is not a happy time, but a rather terrifying time of doubts."

Growing up involves, fundamentally, a developing understanding of human nature; and a principal touchstone of maturity is the awareness of its complexity. Characters in good literature exemplify the complexity of human motivation. The mysteries of personality are explored in literature, beginning with the child's first exposure to it. Even the characters in nursery rhymes, for the most part, are people of fault as well as of virtue. Commentaries on the human species, its nobility and its foibles, come early in the experience of some children who may read in the elementary school years, books such as Kenneth Grahame's memorable *Wind in the Willows*.

It is no wonder that *Huckleberry Finn* has been translated into virtually every language known to man. For Huck represents universal adolescence as he discovers the complexity of his own motivations in his battle with his conscience about whether to turn Jim over to the authorities. His tortured conclusion, "All right, I'll go to hell!" echoes every adolescent's painful conviction regarding his own dark and lonely thoughts.

In literature the young person comes to grips with the most pervasive of all themes in human experience—the struggle between good and evil. In *Tom Sawyer,* Mark Twain was concerned both with this struggle and with the rendezvous with evil—the inevitable destiny of the person growing up. Tom's rendezvous is traumatic—the stabbing scene in the graveyard—as was Mark Twain's own, since he himself had witnessed a real stabbing near his home in Hannibal, Missouri, an event that gave him nightmares for many weeks. This rendezvous with evil is dramatized impressively, too, in contemporary novels for adolescents. For example, in Paul Annixter's *Swiftwater,* a boy fights and finally kills a wolverine he encounters on his father's trapline. The wolverine here symbolizes evil, and it waits inescapably along the boy's path of responsibility.

Awareness of the complexity of human personality is gained partly, too, through reflection on the factors in the greatest moments in the human drama, no matter what the individual's station in life. Courage, for example, is one of these factors. It is of great concern to the adolescent who realizes that he must plumb the depths of his own courage in coming to terms with himself, his environment, his fellows, his universe, his god. This inward reaching is exhibited by the hero of Armstrong Sperry's *Call It Courage,* who has to prove his courage to himself and others; by the protagonist who has to make his separate peace with life in John Knowles's *A Separate Peace;* by Anne Frank who, as revealed in her diary, had to accept a martyr's role she never wanted.

Young people are becoming aware, sometimes bewilderingly, of the clash of values among men. Literature, as a humanistic study, is necessarily concerned with human values. Underlying its study are such eternal questions as these: What is the good life? What do men do with their lives? What do men live by and for?

Selections of literature, from Chaucer's *Canterbury Tales* to James Michener's *The Bridges at Toko-Ri* and Archibald MacLeish's *J.B.,* dramatize what men live, and perhaps die, for. Biography plays an important part here. Careers as diverse as those of Albert Schweitzer, Jane Addams, Lord Nelson, Mary of Scotland, and Louis Armstrong illustrate what real people have made of life under varying conditions.

Literature reveals, too, the revolt of men against some of the prevailing values of their culture. With regard to revolt, traditionally associated with youth, the adolescent is in a paradoxical position. On the one hand, he is a rebel against adult authority and certain adult values; on the other, he is a slavish conformist within his own peer culture. In truth, the timeless conflict between conformity and individuality is a genuine concern. This conflict furnishes the theme for many selections of literature, past and present.

Another awareness, too, is important in the struggle to come to terms with experience. Major problems, whether of an individual or a society, lie in the reaches that stretch between man and man. Our comfort is prey to John Donne's seventeenth-century admonition, "No man is an island." Literature plays an important part in developing awareness of the commonness of the human drama. What an impact a work has when the reader finds in it a fellow sufferer, one who obviously knows "what it is like"!

Of course no one, least of all young people, seeks to be depressed. Yet a feeling for the tragic elements in experience provides a needed tempering of the spirit, an attuning to the "still, sad music of humanity" that Wordsworth heard, and it is all to the good for adolescents to feel, for example, the slash of the sleety New England wind in *Ethan Frome*. Tragedy, after all, makes suffering bearable by making it understandable, and understanding of tragedy should be an aim of the senior high school literature program. Students may often finish their reading of *Macbeth* without really understanding why it is a tragedy when good triumphs at the end. Certainly, an understanding can be developed of the difference between tragic and "sad" in the Hollywood connotation. Students can learn rather quickly that the "weepy" story is not necessarily the tragic one.

Another criterion of the mature mind is the ability to perceive significance and beauty in the humdrum. Overwhelmingly, the television and movie screens, the radio, and the popular magazines feature one limited kind of experience—the exotic, melodramatic aspects in which few people can share directly. Prose and poetry that treat of everyday sights and sounds and people, and through which everyday experience can be evaluated, are the leavener in all this. A novel such as James Street's *Goodbye, My Lady* can do for young adolescents what any good literature can do—illuminate beauty. And the adolescent is more likely to associate beauty with a dog and the natural sounds of the swamp than with, for example, a field of daffodils; but the beauty of the daffodils or a Grecian urn or a stand of birch trees or a brickyard by moonlight may later become real, through the chemistry of experience and verbal symbol.

The chemistry of experience and verbal symbol bears repeating, not for any lyrical value it may have, but because it is probably the key to the ultimate function of literature. Literature brings insights into human experience because of the properties of its subject matter. Certain other disciplines, however—psychology, sociology, ethics, for example—share some of these properties and also furnish certain insights. But the unique kind of knowledge to which literature leads—call this "felt knowledge"—arises from the particular functions of *language* in imaginative literature and the particular interplay of language and content.

It is the particular power of serious literature to produce lyric thinking that helps us, as Wallace Stevens phrased it, "not to fear to step barefoot into reality." Language, lyrically ordered, gives us the metaphors before which our most toxic fears dissolve. Each person, consciously or unconsciously, feels at his back "Time's wingèd chariot hurrying near." Fear of death is a human legacy. It is impossible for most people to think of death in any but a metaphorical way, religious or otherwise. Browning in the poem "Prospice" finds his metaphors: "the snows begin and the blasts denote I am nearing the place . . . the press of the night . . . the fog in my throat . . . the mist in my face." Tennyson chose other metaphors: "Sunset and evening star, and one clear call for me."

To identify metaphorically the fears that obsess one is to experience the power of tragedy "in which all man's knowledge, wisdom, joy, sorrow, triumph, despair—and even the awareness of death's inevitable hour—may come together in a pattern of rhythm, imagery, reason, and emotion." [6] Tragedy as represented in the total metaphor of a *Moby Dick* or a *King Lear,* for example, is the realistic conquering of evil, for evil is represented by the debilitating fears and temptations that beset one.

But one need not talk only about high tragedy in this connection. There are lesser fears and confusions against which the power of metaphoric language is a major defense. Thomas Wolfe, in his archetypal wanderings in the dead of the Brooklyn night or through the dream-laden streets of his boyhood town, concluded in the last words he wrote for publication: "I believe that we are lost here in America, but I believe we shall be found . . . A wind is rising and the rivers flow." [7] In the symbolism of rivers and winds, with their timelessness and inexorable movement, Wolfe expressed the stay of anguish so es-

[6] Albert Upton, *Design for Thinking* (Palo Alto: Stanford University Press, 1961), p. 219.

[7] *You Can't Go Home Again* (New York: Dell, 1960), pp. 669, 671.

sential in the separate peace everyone must negotiate. And Archibald MacLeish, knowing that he could not grasp, as Omar Khayyam put it, "this sorry scheme of things entire," wrote during the confusions and inchoate yearnings of his expatriate years, "America is West and the wind blowing. America is alone and the gulls calling."

It is sometimes through the ironic metaphor that one finds comfort as did Toulouse-Lautrec when he declared sourly that "Marriage is a dull meal with the dessert at the beginning," or as did the children in Harper Lee's *To Kill a Mockingbird* when they viewed their not-too-welcome aunt: "Like Mt. Everest, she was cold and she was there."

This relationship of imaginative language to the preoccupations that lie below the threshold of expression is a particularly important one to young people, for whom the emotional conflicts of adulthood are still amorphous. To look over the brink into the abysses of life and to return unafraid is the catharsis literature provides.

People often mourn the emphasis on the sordid, the unhappy, and the perverted which they find so frequently in present-day literature. But works which present in artistic language the sordid and distorted, the dark sides of experience, represent highly moral art to which students at appropriate levels of development should be led, not protected from. Attempts at blind protection or suppression, characteristic of some segments of the lay public and even of the literary profession, arise from ignorance, not morality. Many Americans, sophisticated in technology and informed on space science, are at the same time ignorant of the function of the literary or esthetic experience.

The serious literature of today is morally, rather frequently religiously, oriented. It is no vagary of literary history that the two predominant forces in contemporary American fiction, for example, are the southern writers and the northern Jewish writers. The Jews have a sense of mythology and a broad and saving conception of irony born of a tradition of suffering. Bernard Malamud's novel *The Assistant* has its share of the sordid—there is a rape scene, for example—but his major theme is the meaning, morally and spiritually, of being a Jew—to what extent are all men Jews? The southerners have their knowledge of the Bible and a sense of history plus a laid-on guilt complex stemming from the days of slavery. The overall theme of the late Carson McCullers, a major Southern writer whose works contain many grotesque elements, is that of love without reciprocation, and the late Flannery O'Connor's principal theme is redemption through suffering. The latter's purpose was to make people aware of evil and to reveal the nature of redemption.

Probably the ultimate power of liberation in literature is to lead from the narrower limits of thinking and feeling—political ideology, sociological theory, sexual mores—to broader systems of belief, the identification of central myths in our culture.

The literary experience conjures up, in the words of C. C. Jung, the racial memories or emotional memories out of which we recognize the significance of archetypes and myths, those generalizations, latent within us, to which we can relate all the trivia of experience. This fact has given imaginative literature its staying power over the centuries, for we are at once the victims and the beneficiaries of the myths and archetypes of our tradition, and our dreams and aspirations are the products of these myths and archetypes. Each person needs before him a vision of human life, an archetype, that will give meaning and order to existence. It is through the reading of literature that many young people may frame their conceptions of the archetype, a vital part of the search for the "I." It is essentially the vision which literature may give that accords it a place in the curriculum equal in importance to that of mathematics or science.

SELECTED BIBLIOGRAPHY

Farmer, Paul, "Literature Goals: Myth or Reality?" *English Journal,* LVI (March 1967), 456–460.
Suggests approaches which might make the goals of "delight" and "human understanding" more attainable and more self-evident to students.

Frye, Northrop, *The Educated Imagination* (Bloomington: Indiana University Press, 1964).
A profound statement of the importance of literature to today's students.

——, "Criticism, Visible and Invisible," *College English,* XXVI (October 1964), 3–12.
A serious argument for the position that we can never really "teach literature," but can only teach criticism, the reading of literature.

Hipple, Ted, "Through Literature to Freedom," *English Journal,* LV (February 1966), 189–191.

Argues for the use of literature to develop in students a broader sense of their own "humanness," especially with regard to racial issues.

Irmscher, William F., "An Apology for Literature," *English Journal,* LII (April 1963), 252–256.

Argues that the humanistic and liberal apologies are inadequate, that we can and should defend the teaching of literature for its contribution to other language skills, especially composition.

Knights, L. C., "The Place of English Literature in a Liberal Education," in Brian Jackson and Denys Thompson (Eds.), *English in Education* (London: Chatto & Windus, 1964), pp. 214–227.

Justifies literature study for its "skills" values, its value in educating the imagination, and for its relation to important aspects of civilization.

Miller, James E., "Literature in the Revitalized Curriculum," *NASSP Bulletin,* LI (April 1967), 25–38.

Argues for the centrality of literature in the English curriculum and for a more virile program.

Rosenblatt, Louise M., *Literature as Exploration,* rev. ed. (New York: Noble, 1968).

An important book on the totality of the literary experience.

Shoben, Edward Joseph, "Texts and Values: The Irrelevance of Literary Education," *Liberal Education,* LII (May 1967), 244–251.

Discusses the significant contribution of literature to the development of personality, emphasizing the distinction between "literary scholarship" and "direct literary experience."

Squire, James R. (Ed.), *Response to Literature* (Champaign, Ill.: NCTE, 1968).

A summary of the Dartmouth discussions on the subject with selected individual essays.

Stafford, William, *Friends to This Ground* (Champaign, Ill.: NCTE, 1967).

A statement by the Commission on Literature of the NCTE on objectives and issues in the teaching of literature.

Sutcliffe, Denham, "The Heart Needs a Language," *Teachers College Record,* LXV (January 1964), 318–323.

Briefly takes issue with the arguments against literature as an "impractical" subject, and develops an eloquent argument for literature as a "language of the heart."

White, Helen C., "New Perspectives on Teaching Literature," *College English,* XXIII (March 1962), 433–436.

A statement to English teachers of objectives in teaching literature which was subsequently reflected in many NDEA summer institutes.

Wilhelms, Fred T., "Using the Curriculum To Build Personal Strength," *NASSP Bulletin*, XLVIII (January 1964), 90–115.

The author uses literature to demonstrate how a subject may accentuate the individual and his "growth in power of personality" while maintaining "a deep and necessary commitment to knowledge."

2

The Shape of the Literature Curriculum

section I
THE STRUCTURE OF LITERATURE

The word "structure" has been a key word in education since the publication of Jerome Bruner's now famous book, *The Process of Education*.[1] Bruner's thesis is that there are certain key principles in every discipline which can furnish the basis for a "spiral" sequence. These key principles, Bruner says, can be taught and understood at all grade levels with the materials and examples becoming more mature as the pupil moves upward in school.

Curriculum planners in English have paid due homage to Bruner's theory, but views of the nature of structure in literature take various shadings, and judgments differ as to the practical usefulness of Bruner's theory in planning literature programs. Purported discussions of structure in literature frequently eventuate in discussions of the structure of individual selections rather than in consideration of the basic principles in the "discipline" of literature. Such discussions are helpful, generally, but arguments such as whether the overall structure of a work must be grasped before the component parts are considered, for example, are largely irrelevant in the planning of literature programs.

A succinct and inclusive discussion of varying approaches to the structure of literary selections is that by Walker, who lists nine points

[1] Cambridge: Harvard University Press, 1960.

16

of agreement among teachers who advocate these various approaches.[2]

1. The study of literature should include a careful analysis of the work itself to see what structural relationships exist.
2. The investigation of structure should be inductive. All advocates of structure proceed by discovering particular relationships to make later generalizations.
3. The structure of literature is what gives it unity or enables it to have a unifying effect.
4. Structure is the overall pattern of relationships that holds the parts together.
5. The study of structure involves the study of form and content.
6. The study of structure should begin with a view of the whole.
7. The study of structure facilitates understanding and interpretation of literature.
8. The understanding of structure broadens the base of literary appreciation by enabling the reader to appreciate literature not only for its appeal or meaning to them, but also for the craftsmanship involved in its creation.
9. The study of structure facilitates transfer of general principles pertinent to literature, composition, and the process of investigation. An understanding of the relationships found in a piece of literature should hasten the understanding of a similar work. An understanding of how writers combine parts to produce wholes should help students improve their own writing. The systematic process of investigation involved in the study of structure can be used in other studies.

Walker and Evans find particular advantages in one view of structure, namely, "that structure exists in the interaction between a reader and the work of literature, in the literary experience."[3] These authors go on to say that "The significance of this view of structure for the student is that it makes him a collaborator in the work of art and frees him from having to account for everything in the work. He need account only for what he attends to."[4]

[2] Jerry L. Walker, "The Structure of Literature," *English Journal,* LV (March 1966), 305–315.
[3] William H. Evans and Jerry L. Walker, *New Trends in the Teaching of English in Secondary Schools* (Chicago: Rand McNally, 1966), p. 42.
[4] Evans and Walker, p. 43.

One must, of course, accept the importance of the interrelationship of reader and selection, an interrelationship that often can be guessed at but never predicted with sureness for individual students. Yet such acceptance is not very useful in planning a sequence in literature. Teachers need to know what they are teaching in literature and what are the valid components of literature. Then they are in a position to decide how to make their teaching and the sequence in their school bear on these components.

As efforts to lay a basis for sequence in literature accelerate, through the Curriculum Study Centers funded by the U.S. Office of Education, among others, a skepticism has grown toward Bruner's theory as applied to literature. Frank Whitehead, the British educator, asks, "Can the concept of structure, however, be applied to the 'subject' of English in anything more than a loose metaphorical sense?" [5] Stoddard Malarkey, associated with the Curriculum Study Center at the University of Oregon, says: "Agreement as to what constitute the 'great and simple structuring ideas' of literature seems impossible of achievement." [6] Referring to Bruner's concept of a spiral curriculum, the authors of a pamphlet produced in the Oregon center say: "This is fine in theory, but how is it to be applied to a literary work in which no single aspect—imagery, form, structure, point of view—is an island unto itself in the totality of the esthetic effect?" [7]

The Oregon writers, in fact, avoid the term "structure" and proceed to say that the study of literature subdivides under "three main headings—subject, form, and point of view." These three aspects of literature are considered directly in grades 7–9 in the Oregon curriculum with more sophisticated aspects and implications left to the upper grades.

The work of the Oregon authors was of value to this writer in identifying the structure or subdivisions in literature which can serve as a basis for planning a sequence. Teaching literature must involve three aspects: substance, mode, and form.

In considering substance, the teacher will lead students to a percep-

---

[5] From an unpublished "working paper" written for the Anglo-American Conference on the Teaching of English, September 1966.

[6] "Sequence and Literature: Some Considerations," *English Journal,* LVI (March 1967), 395.

[7] *A Curriculum in English, Grades 7–12* (Eugene: Oregon Curriculum Center, University of Oregon), pp. 3–4.

tion of what the selection is really about, not only on the surface, but in terms of the themes and ideas that are developed or dramatized about human experience. All literature is concerned with four major relationships: man and deity; man and other men; man and the natural world; man and himself. A great variety of specific themes may be developed from these four relationships, but a balanced literature program will introduce works representing different periods and forms which deal with each of the four major relationships.

Mode refers to the general point of view on life experience which the selection represents. Since each work is by an individual, that individual's vantage point on life is often evident, though many selections cannot be classified neatly as to mode. The modal approach has been given especial vitality through the work of Northrop Frye who identifies four modes—romantic, comic, tragic, and ironic—and holds that the romantic and comic modes are more easily comprehended and therefore should be stressed in the early school years with later emphasis on the tragic and ironic modes.[8] The author, finding support from a number of other sources, adds a fifth mode—satiric. Frye, in his book, *Fables of Identity,*[9] identifies basic modes in terms of the human condition which they frame: the nature and predicament of the hero or protagonist. If the hero is superior in *degree* to other men and to his environment, we have the typical romance and its literary affiliates, the legend and folktale. If the protagonist is superior in degree to other men and is a leader but is not superior to his natural environment, we have the hero of most tragedy and epic. If the hero is superior neither to other men nor to his environment, we have the comic mode. If he is inferior in power or intelligence to ourselves so that we have a sense of looking down on a scene of frustration or absurdity, the protagonist belongs to the ironic mode. Frye also identifies the typical subordinate characters that go with these modes and links the modes with basic archetypal patterns related to solar movement. Romance and comedy are linked with birth, dawn, and spring, and with marriage, triumph, zenith, and summer; while tragedy and irony relate to death, sunset, autumn, and to dissolution, darkness, and winter.

Form, of course, refers to the various genres and sub-genres of lit-

[8] *Design for Learning* (Toronto: University of Toronto Press, 1962), p. 10.
[9] New York: Harcourt, 1963, p. 16.

erature as well as to certain elements of structure—point of view, setting, dialogue, and the like—and certain devices—metaphor and symbol, for instance—which are common to more than one genre.

section II
AN ILLUSTRATIVE SEQUENCE

A definition of the structure of literature, such as that just presented, should serve the practical purpose of providing a basis for sequence. It has been suggested earlier that not everything can be sequential and incremental in a literature program. There is still room for necessary opportunism on the part of individual teachers and for application of the threadbare slogan, "Take them where they are," regardless of the neat course of study that may exist. Yet it is necessary for school faculties to develop some kind of overall sequence. The specific nature of the sequence must depend on the view English faculties have of the structure of literature and on the characteristics of students in given schools.

The illustrative sequence that follows, based on the analysis of structure of literature in Section I of this chapter, was developed in part through the work of the Curriculum Study Center at the Florida State University * and in part through the writer's work with curriculum committees in Miami and Pensacola, Florida.

SEVENTH GRADE

Substance

Two thematic units designed to show how literature is concerned with the problems of everyday living:

1. "Man against Nature"—short selections showing facets of man's struggle with natural elements and his attempts to control the natural environment, culminating in study of the novel, *Third Man on the Mountain* by James R. Ullman. (Other approaches

---

* The work of the Center in junior high school English, which featured test programs in six Florida schools, was completed in June 1968.

to the novel are featured also. See "Mode" and "Form" below.)
2. "The Hero"—short selections in prose and poetry showing qualities of heroism in everyday life. Students should frame some tentative answers to the question, "What are the qualities of the present-day hero?" (This unit follows the one on myth, legend, and folklore.)

Mode

Concern with the romantic mode is incorporated in the study of *Third Man on the Mountain*. General characteristics of romantic literature provide the focus.

Form

1. Myth, legend, and folklore—the extensiveness of the unit depends on the background a class has developed in the elementary school.
2. Introduction to the major imaginative genres with certain emphases.
   a. Short story—attention to elementary symbolism in fiction.
   b. Poetry—narrative verse, especially ballads; simple lyrics about aspects of everyday life.
   c. Novel—consideration of the genre in connection with *Third Man on the Mountain*. An alternative, if teachers wish to form a separate unit around another novel, is study of *Shane* by Jack Schaefer.
   d. One-act play.

EIGHTH GRADE

Substance

Two thematic units designed to show how events become ideas or abstractions in literature.

1. "Courage"—use of the Scholastic Literature Unit, *Courage*, or a similar one designed to show illustrations of the various guises of courage in everday life. Short selections.
2. "The Frontier Spirit"—short selections illustrating qualities of life and character on the Western frontier. Some concern with how

historical events and backgrounds are used in imaginative literature.

Mode

Comic mode—centered around *The Matchmaker* by Thornton Wilder. Use of some old silent comic films. Some emphasis on the difference between "comic" and "funny."

Form

1. Novel—the idea of allegory illustrated by *The Pearl* by John Steinbeck or *Call of the Wild* by Jack London.
2. Short story—emphasis on characterization in fiction. Consideration of point of view.
3. Poetry—relatively simple lyric poems that express ideas or abstractions. Consideration of the "three voices of poetry."
4. Full-length comic drama—*The Matchmaker*.
5. TV drama—study of *Visit to a Small Planet* by Gore Vidal.

NINTH GRADE

Substance

Two thematic units emphasizing human conflicts:

1. "Individualism versus Conformity"—short selections, a key one of which is "Paul's Case" by Willa Cather.
2. "The Quest"—the central selection is Hemingway's *The Old Man and the Sea*. Introduction of the idea of archetype with the quest as example.

Mode

1. Satire—short selections with the unit culminating in either Orwell's *Animal Farm* or Leonard Wibberleys' *The Mouse that Roared*.
2. Introduction to tragedy—*Antigone* and, for more able classes, *Romeo and Juliet*.

2. "The Carpe Diem Theme"—some stress on the Cavalier Poets with comparison to more modern selections.
3. "The Search for Identity"—with more able groups, study of Conrad's *The Secret Sharer*. Short selections with less able groups. Further concern with the idea of archetype.

Mode

1. Shakespearean tragedy—*Macbeth* or *Othello*.
2. Cosmic irony—Hardy's *The Mayor of Casterbridge* (to be omitted in less able groups.)

Form

1. Short story—ambiguity as method in the short story.
2. Novel—the novel as allegory; use of symbol.
3. Poetry—the dramatic monologue; the sonnet; the nature of metaphysical poetry.
4. Drama—Shakespearean drama.
5. The novel as allegory (if *The Secret Sharer* is studied).

Any specific sequence in literature will not be feasible for all schools. It is not *the* sequence that is important, but rather *a* sequence. A literature program in the junior and senior high school is more than just six years of reading selections of literature; it should be six years of considering literature in some significant pattern. The sequence outlined in this chapter is an illustration of one attempt to fashion such a pattern.

SELECTED BIBLIOGRAPHY

Booth, Wayne C., *The Rhetoric of Fiction* (Chicago: The University of Chicago Press, 1961).
A brilliant analysis of the relationship of author to audience, examining most structural aspects of the novel in light of their rhetorical significance.
———, "The Use of Criticism in the Teaching of Literature," *College English*, XXVII (October 1965), 1–13.
Questioning Frye's premise of a unified structure of literature, Booth

suggests that teachers shift their attention from abstract structures to the students' reactions to the literature.

Cottrell, Beekman W. and Lois S. Josephs, "A Genuine Accumulation," *English Journal,* LIV (February 1965), 91–94.

An examination of the Carnegie Institute's Curriculum Center courses for Grades 11 and 12, illustrating the use of theme as a basis for sequential ordering of the program.

Dunning, Stephen, "Sequence and Literature: Some Teaching Facts," *The High School Journal,* XLVII (October 1963), 2–12.

Suggests six basic concerns based on the principle of students' and teachers' individual differences which must be considered in planning for sequence in the literature program.

Guth, Hans P., "Approaches to Literary Study," and "The Meaning of Literature," in *English Today and Tomorrow* (Englewood Cliffs, N.J.: Prentice-Hall, 1964), pp. 220–252.

Guth discusses the promise and many of the teaching problems raised by the structural approaches to literature.

Hillocks, George Jr., "Approaches to Meaning: A Basis for a Literature Curriculum," *English Journal,* LIII (September 1964), 413–421.

Outlines a literature program based on three basic but relatively accessible structural areas: man in his environment, levels of meaning, and genre.

Lansu, Helvi, "The Shape of Literature," *English Journal,* LIV (September 1965), 520–524.

Demonstrates approaches to teaching an understanding of literary structure on three levels: plot, theme, and tone.

Malarkey, Stoddard, "Sequence and Literature: Some Considerations," *English Journal,* LVI (March 1967), 395–401.

Miles, Josephine, "Reading Poems," *English Journal,* LII (March 1963), 157–164.

In her discussion of the "literal" and "metrical" aspects of poetry, Professor Miles illustrates an important use of the structural approaches to literature.

Ojala, William T., "Thematic Categories as an Approach to Sequence," *English Journal,* LII (March 1963), 178–185.

Outlines a curriculum for Grades 7–12 based on thematic units.

Scribner, Duane C., "Learning Hierarchies and Literary Sequence," *English Journal,* LVI (March 1967), 385–393.

Relates recent developments in learning theory to determination of sequence in the teaching of literature.

Walker, Jerry L., "The Structure of Literature," *English Journal,* LV (March 1966), 305–315.

An excellent brief summary of three dominating points of view on what constitutes the "structure of literature."

3

Approaches to Literature: Old and New

The title of this chapter may seem presumptuous since entire books have been written that could bear the same title, and a number of possible approaches to a work of literature will not be identified. But the chapter itself is meant only to touch briefly on certain approaches to a work of literature that may be appropriate in the high school classroom. No matter what definition of the structure of literature or what design for sequence a teacher may adopt, he comes inevitably to choices of approach and strategy in teaching individual selections. Each teacher may have his prejudices concerning approaches to works of literature, but it is obvious that students should be introduced to the variety of ways in which a selection of literature may be considered.

"Close reading" of individual selections has been considered in recent years as a new development. Hans P. Guth, for example, refers to "the close reading of the text itself" as one of four major movements affecting the teaching of English in the past few decades.[1] Intensive (one could say laborious) reading of texts is nothing new in the classroom. But the almost word-for-word reading of *Silas Marner* or *Macbeth* or some other canonized work that in the past (and in the present, to some extent) was featured in high school classrooms is not the close reading being discussed today. "Close reading" now most often refers to a formalistic or intrinsic approach promoted by what for a number of years has been called the New Criticism.

Though the intrinsic approach is valuable, there is some tendency

[1] *English Today and Tomorrow* (Englewood Cliffs, N.J.: Prentice-Hall, 1964), p. 18.

28

among teachers to view it as the only avenue to close reading of the text. This chapter identifies several approaches to a work, all of which may require close reading. (A later section deals with classroom procedures in leading discussion of individual selections no matter what the specific approach.) The first part is devoted to older, established approaches; the second part to newer ones.

TRADITIONAL APPROACHES

Moral Approach

The label "moral" as an approach to literature may make some teachers shudder as they recall the dogged search for "the moral" in literary selections that marked an earlier era. But "moral" taken in a broad sense—"humanistic" might be a synonym—is a most valuable and interesting approach with young people. In their book *Teaching Language and Literature,* Loban, Ryan, and Squire make an essential point: "Literature cannot be taught apart from the morality of humanity. . . . To view literature as a formula for moral action is to mistake its nature and miss its rewards. However, because it can enlarge our awareness of values and refine our discrimination among values, literature is a force of tremendous potential for education." [2]

It is difficult to keep a class, especially one composed of younger students, from veering away from the text in a discussion of values or human conduct which may be touched off by a selection of literature. The immature reader is inclined to judge human acts and motivations in actual life situations which he knows about rather than in the situation developed in the work. Yet the study and discussion of literature furnishes the young student with one of his major opportunities for reflection on values. In works built around ethical or moral ideas or assumptions, the moral approach is obviously the path to what is central in the work, though matters of form need not be neglected.

Psychological Approach

Mention of a psychological approach to literature may cause some negative reactions, too, if one thinks of forced Freudian interpreta-

[2] New York: Harcourt, 1961, p. 602.

tions or dubious deductions about the personal lives of authors as a way of illuminating their works. But the psychological approach is of long standing, and one of the monuments of criticism is probably Ernest Jones' interpretation of Hamlet's dilemma in the light of the oedipus complex.[3]

Facts about an author's life may sometimes help to interpret his work, but much time has been wasted in having students learn insignificant personal facts about writers. Far more important is another dimension of the psychological approach, that in which motivations and actions of characters are analyzed. In modern literature, especially in fiction and drama, the psychological element is very strong whether one thinks of Proust, Mann, and Joyce or Salinger, Malamud, and Bellow, or writers of junior novels. The principal preoccupation of modern fiction is with the relationship of man and his inner self. The modern short story often represents an "epiphany," a label attached by Joyce to the story in which a character achieves some flash of insight after which he is never the same again. Careful reading is required if the student is to comprehend what really has happened to the character.

Directing students to analysis of the motivations and the mental and emotional states of characters need not mean turning the literature class into a psychology class if teachers make sure that the students work within the context of the text itself.

Sociopolitical Approach

High school students have as natural an affinity for the sociopolitical approach as they have for the moral, though literary scholars have fumed over making literature study into bastardized sociology, and one can think of the excesses of Marxist criticism. Yet literature may be an examination of group living, and it is not difficult to document Harry Levin's statement that ". . . the relations between literature and society are reciprocal. Literature is not only the effect of social causes; it is also the cause of social effects." [4] In modern literature, again, the sociological and geographical contexts are important. Saul Bellow cannot be read without regard for the large northern cities in

---

[3] "The Oedipus Complex as an Explanation of Hamlet's Mystery," *The American Journal of Psychology*, XXI (1910).

[4] "Literature as an Institution," *Accent* VI (Spring 1946), 164.

which most of his novels are set, and the small southern town is a vital element in the fiction of Carson McCullers, to cite two examples among major contemporary writers.

Literature with sociopolitical themes, especially satire, is appealing to older adolescents in whom social and moral idealism often tends to clash with a certain mood of cynicism. Social protest has been traditionally an important element in literature, and students need to be made aware of how imaginative literature can illuminate social and political problems.

Modal Approach

The definition of structure of literature presented in the preceding chapter makes clear the author's belief that a modal approach to selections of literature is a useful one in the secondary school. Clearly there are limitations to this approach, as most teachers of literature are aware. There are selections that do not fit one of the modal pigeon holes, and bootless arguments have taken place over whether Hemingway, for example, was or was not a romantic. But there is value in the student's perceiving that literature tends to cluster in modes which represent various interpretations of the human condition. An excellent foundation for the modal approach is furnished by Northrop Frye's celebrated work. Frye identifies four basic modes (romantic, comic, tragic, and ironic) in terms of the human condition as they frame it, in terms of the nature and predicament of the protagonist. A brief summary of Frye's theory was given in the preceding chapter. It seems legitimate to add a fifth mode, the satiric.

Mere classification of selections will defeat the aim of the modal approach, but well-directed analyses of selections as examples of basic modes may enrich literature study.

Mythic or Archetypal Approach

The mythic or archetypal approach, sometimes termed the anthropological or totemic approach, is much in the forefront in recent literary criticism, but little application of this approach has been made in the secondary school. "Myth" and "archetype" are not synonymous, and both terms are put to many uses as Willard Thorp points out in the opening chapter of the monograph, *The Teacher and American*

Literature.[5] Yet the two words may be combined appropriately in ti-tling an approach in the high schools. The mythic approach has cap-tured the imagination of young people as John Gerber testifies: "The mythical approach . . . is the one that most immediately engages the student and causes him to see the literary work as an expression of life. Nothing seems to excite our students so much about a poem or novel as the discovery of a reformulation of a primitive myth. They pounce upon it as a personal treasure that is inside them—as indeed it is—as well as inside the poem or novel." [6] Gerber cautions, however, that "The difficulty is holding the students under control. They are willing to see the reenactment or the Fall of Man every time the nonhero gets dead drunk and drops to the floor." [7]

There are probably four dimensions which the mythic approach may assume in the high school. (1) Concern with specific mythic figures such as Job in MacLeish's *J.B.* or Faust in John Hersey's *Too Far To Walk.* (2) Identification of archetypal symbols such as cer-tain animals—the lamb or the eagle, for instance—and certain flowers—the red rose and the lily. (3) Identification of archetypal themes such as the edenic or the fall, the quest, and initiation. (4) Perception of the basic kinds of myths as Northrop Frye outlines them in terms of the predicament of the hero: (a) Birth of the hero, triumph over the powers of evil, with father and mother as subordi-nate characters. (b) Marriage and success of the hero; his entry into paradise or perfect happiness; the bride and the companion are subor-dinate heroes. (c) Isolation of the hero and his death or downfall, often violent death; traitors and sirens are subordinate characters. (d) Defeat of the hero or leader and the triumph of the powers of dark-ness; often there are great physical calamities such as fires, floods, or eruptions; ogres and witches are the subordinate characters.[8]

Probably the key to the value of the mythic approach is to be found in Erich Fromm's statement that a myth is "a message from ourselves to ourselves, a secret language which enables us to treat inner as if outer event." [9]

[5] Champaign, Ill.: NCTE, 1965.

[6] John Gerber, "Literature—Our Untamable Discipline," *College English,* XXVIII (February 1967), 357–358.

[7] Gerber, p. 358.

[8] Northrop Frye, *Fables of Identity* (New York: Harcourt, 1963), p. 16.

[9] As summarized by W. Y. Tindall in *Forces in Modern British Literature* (New York: Vintage Books, 1956), p. 311.

As suggested in the opening chapter, development of the archetypal approach may be a major breakthrough in literature in the high schools.

Formalistic or Intrinsic Approach

Form and structural elements in a work of literature will never be lost sight of no matter what the approach, for, as stated earlier, consideration of form keeps literature from becoming ethics, psychology, sociology, or something else. The major cautions are that teachers not do too much too early with form and structure and that consideration of form not become a high and dry concern.

A formalistic approach, under the direction of a competent teacher, will become a full-bodied thing in which concern with the generic characteristics of story, novel, poem, or play or with literary devices such as foreshadowing, symbolism, or metrical patterns will not prevent parallel concern with the historical and biographical context of the work nor with its ideas, meanings or effects. As Harold Osborne writes:

> The form of a poem, the prosodic structure, the rhythmic interplay, the characteristic idiom, are nothing any more when abstracted from the content of meaning; for language is not language but noise except in so far as it expresses meaning. So, too, the content without the form is an unreal abstraction without concrete existence, for when it is expressed in different language it is something different that is being expressed. The poem must be perceived as a whole to be perceived at all. There can be no conflict between form and content . . . for neither has existence without the other and abstraction is murder to both.[10]

NEWER APPROACHES

A certain restlessness with traditional ways of approaching literature is a part of the present scene in the teaching of English, and a brief review of several newer concepts concerning study of literature seems appropriate, although the author can claim only rudimentary acquaintance with each one.

[10] *Aesthetics and Criticism* (New York: Philosophical Library, 1955), p. 289.

Field Theory

It is inevitable that science would have an impact on the teaching of literature as it has had on practically everything else in the past few years. The field theory of the physical sciences as applicable to literature has gained momentum. William Holtz [11] and Edward Fagan [12] have written lucidly on the subject. The basic tenet of field theory as applied to literature is that a selection of literature or an integral part of it is perceived as an element of an organized whole. Holtz writes:

> Any given thing participates in many larger systems (fields) which always include the observer himself, and in which all elements interact in a complex, dynamic balance. [13]

And Fagan holds that a work of art occurs in the reader's mind only to the extent that a fusion or unity occurs between the ideas of the author and those of the reader.

These writers find in literature an analogy to the *particle* and *wave* which in physics are the ultimate units. The particle is a unit isolated from its context while a wave is a unit perceived within a continuum, merging with the adjacent units. Both particles and waves are parts of space or fields. Holtz points out that in a poem images may correspond to particles and lines to waves.

Holtz illustrates how field theory can be applied to the reading of *Tristram Shandy*. The work, Holtz maintains, is a problem of field or space apprehension where the field is that of Tristram's consciousness. The reader has to put discrete particles together as mental property of a self like himself. Similarly, Fagan illustrates application of field theory to George R. Stewart's *Storm*, in which, Fagan believes, the reader needs to see that the people in the work are symbols—and symbols as areas of meaning in motion correspond to waves—representing a composite man who "is fearless because he is confident, in his flexibility, that he can meet any emergency."

[11] "Field Theory and Literature," *Rhetoric: Theories for Application* (Champaign, Ill.: NCTE, 1967), pp. 52–65.

[12] *Field: A Process for Teaching Literature* (University Park: Pennsylvania State University Press, 1964).

[13] Holtz, "Field Theory and Literature," *Rhetoric: Theories for Application*, p. 54.

Cognitive Psychology

The interest in the work of Jerome Bruner and other cognitive psychologists has been noted earlier in discussion of structure and sequence of literature. Some applications of cognitive psychology are also pertinent to method in choosing and approaching individual works. The most direct application of which the writer is aware is that of Herbert Karl [14] who draws on the work of Jean Piaget. Karl shows how the "thought matrix" of Piaget—involving the processes of identity, inversion, reciprocity, and correlation—might form the basis for approaches to works of literature. The student often must form "identities" to understand a selection of literature. If, for example, someone named Bonnie is referred to in a poem, the reader must identify her as a person, a girl. Identity is the process necessary generally in getting the plain sense of the work—basic plots, meanings of terms, and so on.

Inversion, the second process, implies negation or elimination. "When a learner conceives a structural relationship in terms of inversion," Karl writes, "meaning is achieved by recognition of the effect of opposing elements." Inverse relationships underlie such literary matters as irony, satire, paradox, contrast, and others. The third process, reciprocity, connotes symmetry or analogy, and analogical relationships result from sets of details that are similar in some way. Obviously, reciprocity underlies such matters as metaphor, simile, personification, and allegory.

The fourth process, correlation, is that of structuring relationships between two separate contexts. Within a selection of literature, for instance, the student might need for purposes of interpretation to relate the title of a poem to an image within the poem. Or beyond the context of the selection itself a reader may need to correlate his own experience with that in the work if he is to enter imaginatively into the work. Finally, Karl says, the process of correlation is the basis for relating works of literature, or elements within them, to other media such as art or music.

[14] "An Approach to Literature through Cognitive Processes," *English Journal,* LVII (February 1968), 181–187.

Rhetorical Approach

Both the rhetorical approach and the linguistic approach discussed below are really variations on the intrinsic or formalistic approach. The recent revival of interest in rhetorical studies has brought attention to the possibilities of rhetoric as an approach to literature. In his preface to *The Rhetoric of Fiction*,[15] Wayne C. Booth makes the point that a selection of literature, as a work of art, must communicate itself if it is successful. Therefore, there is a rhetorical dimension, obvious or otherwise, in any selection. Booth's approach is to examine "the rhetorical resources available to the writer of epic, novel, or short story as he tries, consciously or unconsciously, to impose his fictional world upon the reader."

Specific lines of inquiry in the rhetorical approach can be illustrated from an essay by Sam Meyer.[16] Meyer is interested in exploring the relationships of the poet to his subject. Using the "Concord Hymn" as an example, he lists questions that might serve as basis for examination of the poem:

Is concentration on the present paramount in the "Concord Hymn"? What is the speaker's attitude toward time?

What seems to be the speaker's mode—dramatic, oratory, ritualistic? What is the rhetorical level—colloquial, formal, or something else?

Does assigning the title "Concord Hymn" require the poet to have a perspective different from the one needed to project the *person* who speaks in the poem?

Who seems to be the speaker's immediate audience? Is there a removed or fictive audience as well? Is the address to the spirit at the end really a "turning aside," in the literal meaning of the word *apostrophe?* [17]

Linguistic Approach

The attempt to relate linguistic analysis to literature is one part of the general burgeoning of ramifications of linguistics during recent years.

[15] Chicago: University of Chicago Press, 1961.

[16] "Teaching the Rhetorical Approach to the Poem," *Rhetoric: Theories for Application* (Champaign, Ill.: NCTE, 1967), pp. 82–89.

[17] "Teaching the Rhetorical Approach to the Poem," p. 89.

The aim of linguistic analysis of literature is descriptive and analytical, not evaluative, as Seymour Chatman points out.[18] Linguistic analysis, of course, is concerned with the phonological and structural aspects of a work of literature. In the essay alluded to above, Chatman says that the job of phonemic analysis in poetry is to furnish a description of how esthetic effects are achieved from sources involving patterns and clusters of phonemes, and that such effects are achieved mainly through unusual frequency and unusual patterning of phonemes. Dell Hymes, for example, has made a phonological analysis of a sampling of English sonnets.[19] Chatman has shown, too, how linguistic analysis can serve oral interpretation of literature.[20]

W. Nelson Francis demonstrates the analysis of syntax in poetry, using the first sonnet from "Alterwise by Owl-light" by Dylan Thomas.[21] Francis states that the major contribution of syntactic analysis is to resolve syntactic ambiguities in poetry, but he cautions that such analysis will not "lead us to a lucid interpretation of the poem. But it will supply the framework which such an explication, if one is possible, must follow, and set the bounds beyond which it must not venture." [22]

This very cursory review of newer approaches to literary study is meant only to indicate trends and to provide bibliography for those readers who may wish to pursue a specific approach in greater depth.

The point implied throughout this chapter is that eclecticism is the key to approaching literature for high school students. Some students will become intrigued with a particular approach. But all students should develop a repertoire of approaches if literature study is to achieve its vital and rich potential. John Gerber makes the case for eclecticism cogently:

[18] "Linguistics, Poetics, and Interpretation: The Phonemic Dimension," *Quarterly Journal of Speech,* LXIII (October 1957), 239–256.

[19] "Phonological Aspects of Style: Some English Sonnets," *Style in Language,* Thomas Sebeok (Ed.) (Cambridge: Massachusetts Institute of Technology, 1960), pp. 109–131.

[20] "Linguistic Analysis: A Study of James Mason's Interpretation of 'The Bishop Orders His Tomb,' " *The Oral Study of Literature* (New York: Random House, 1966), pp. 94–130.

[21] "Syntax and Literary Interpretation," *Applied English Linguistics,* Harold B. Allen (Ed.) (New York: Appleton, 2nd ed., 1964), pp. 515–522.

[22] Allen, p. 518.

The kind of eclecticism I think I see ahead will require the most astute teaching. We have developed great facility in teaching those matters requiring detachment: we have been chary of those which demand the student's engagement. And well we might be. For in engaging the student's belief or disbelief we must steer between the Scylla of indoctrination and the Charybdis of an undiscriminating relativism. Yet this is the course we *must* steer if the literary work is to engage the student's whole mind. We must learn how to raise issues of belief as adroitly as we have learned how to raise issues of form and content. In the process we may come to feel that our discipline is less tamable than ever. But we must make the attempt if we would successfully exploit our subject matter and if we could meet the deep psychic needs of our students.[23]

SELECTED BIBLIOGRAPHY

Bodkin, Maud, *Archetypal Patterns in Poetry: Psychological Studies of Imagination* (London: Oxford University Press, 1963).
One of the major references on archetypal criticism.

Booth, Wayne C., *The Rhetoric of Fiction* (Chicago: University of Chicago Press, 1961).
The major work on the rhetorical approach to literature. Illustrates with much discussion of specific selections.

Daiches, David, *Critical Approaches to Literature* (Englewood Cliffs, N.J.: Prentice-Hall, 1956).
A readable and useful standard reference.

Fagan, Edward R., *Field: A Process for Teaching Literature* (University Park: Pennsylvania State University Press, 1964).
Defines the field approach, suggests its uses and applications, and advocates training teachers to use the approach.

Fraiber, Louis, *Psychoanalysis and American Literary Criticism* (Detroit: Wayne State University Press, 1960).
A depth treatment of the influence of psychoanalysis on criticism.

Frye, Northrop, *Anatomy of Criticism: Four Essays* (Princeton, N.J.: Princeton University Press, 1957).
This celebrated work contains these essays:
(1) "Historical Criticism: Theory of Modes"
(2) "Ethical Criticism: Theory of Symbols"
(3) "Archetypal Criticism: Theory of Myths"
(4) "Rhetorical Criticism: Theory of Genres"

[23] Allen, p. 358.

Gerber, John C., "Literature—Our Untamable Discipline," *College English,* XXVIII (February 1967), 351–358.
A thoughtful statement on how to involve students with literature most profitably.

Guerin, Wilfred L., and others, *A Handbook of Critical Approaches to Literature* (New York: Harper & Row, 1966).
A very useful discussion and illustration of a number of approaches to literature.

Holtz, William, "Field Theory and Literature," *Rhetoric: Theories for Application* (Champaign, Ill.: NCTE, 1967), pp. 52–65.
Succinct discussion of the basis of field theory as an approach to literature.

Hook, J. N., "Multiple Approach in Teaching Literature," *English Journal,* XXXVII (April 1948), 188–92.
Discusses the possibilities of six approaches—historical, sociopsychological, emotive, didactic, paraphrastic, analytical—in heightening interest in literature.

Karl, Herbert, "An Approach to Literature through Cognitive Processes," *English Journal,* LVII (February 1968), 181–187.
Discusses the use of cognitive process—including identity, inversion, reciprocity, and correlation—in studying literature.

Lucas, F. L., *Literature and Psychology* (Ann Arbor Paperbacks: The University of Michigan Press, 1962).
Divided into "The Interpretation of Literature" and "The Judgment of Literature"; presents various interpretations of works of literature along with corresponding case studies in psychology.

Ohmann, Richard, "Literature as Sentences," *College English,* XXVII (January 1966), 261–267.
Argues that "at the level of sentences, the distinction between form and content comes clear, and that the intuition of style has its formal equivalent."

Pike, Kenneth L., "Language—Where Science and Poetry Meet," *College English,* XXVI (January 1965), 283–293.
The author explains the application of tagmemic theory to the teaching of poetry.

Pingry, Lillian S., "Some Approaches to the Teaching of Literature in the High School," *Peabody Journal of Education,* XXXI (January 1954), 227–239.
Various approaches are cited along with illustrative selections, but always the approaches are derived from interest in the student and his development.

Richards, I. A., *Principles of Literary Criticism* (New York: Harcourt, 1926).

A landmark work, still helpful.

Scott, Wilbur, *Five Approaches of Literary Criticism* (New York: Crowell-Collier-Macmillan, 1962).

A collection of modern essays illustrating the moral, psychological, sociological, formalistic, and archetypal approaches to literature.

Sebeok, Thomas A. (Ed.), *Style in Language* (Cambridge: Massachusetts Institute of Technology, 1960).

A series of essays illustrating linguistic analyses of style.

4

The Relationship of Literature Study
to Composition and Language Study

The basic question—What is English?—that has been vexing the profession for years still has no one final answer. There is agreement, of course, that literature, language, and written and oral composition are the major components of the curriculum and that teaching should relate them when possible and desirable. But there is still lack of agreement on the nucleus or integrating center of the subject.

This author, for reasons stated or implied in chapter 1, believes that the nucleus of the English curriculum is literature. By this statement I mean simply that literature should occupy the position of greatest prominence in the curriculum. I do not imply that all other study should or can grow out of literature study. However, literature study can be related profitably to composition and language study at a number of points. The purpose of this chapter is to identify some of these points.

LITERATURE STUDY AND ORAL
AND WRITTEN COMPOSITION

Spoken language, surprisingly long neglected in English classrooms, is today for the first time getting serious attention by the profession. Most of this impetus comes from England. The following statement by Andrew Wilkinson represents the current mood:

> The spoken language in England has been shamefully neglected. There are many reasons for this. One, certainly, is that teachers and educa-

tionists have not considered it important. Of the oral skills, reading aloud (which few people are ever called upon to use) has had some attention in the classroom, usually for the wrong reasons. But the ability to put one word of one's own text to another of one's own in speech, to create rather than to repeat, a skill which everybody is exercising most of the time, has not been regarded as worthy of serious attention.[1]

The recognition of the need for greater attention to spoken language in general has accelerated attempts to integrate oral language activities with literature study. The two major types of such activities are oral reading of literature and dramatic exercises.

Oral reading of literature.   When Andrew Wilkinson, in the statement cited above, spoke of oral reading getting attention "usually for the wrong reasons," he probably was thinking of such practices as having students take turns reading aloud a selection of literature as a substitute for prepared teaching of the selection or of the word-by-word oral reading of Shakespeare or some other author the class has had difficulty reading silently. Despite such deadly procedures as these, reading aloud is an important concomitant of literature study. But if it is to be profitable, two rather obvious conditions must obtain: the reading should be prepared and it should have a valid purpose. Impromptu reading often results in the student stumbling through a selection to the agony of himself and his class, and is a sure antidote for enjoyment of literature. One can think of occasions when impromptu reading might be appropriate—citing passages to support points in discussion, for example—but any extended reading should be prepared in advance. It is not avuncular to say that this admonition applies as well to the teacher who is planning to read something for the first time.

Oral reading by the teacher is an important ingredient in the literature classroom. Some teachers spend too much time reading aloud, to the detriment of their students' developing individual silent reading abilities. But again and again, studies of the characteristics which make English teachers popular with students show that oral reading by the teacher is remembered with pleasure. The teacher who is a skilled oral

[1] National Association for the Teaching of English, *Some Aspects of Oracy,* II (Summer 1965), 3.

reader and interpreter of literature has a real advantage, and there is some tendency in teacher education to include, or at least encourage prospective teachers of English to get, some training in oral interpretation.

What is "a valid purpose," which was posited as the second condition necessary for effective use of oral reading of literature, may be variously interpreted by different teachers. It seems however that there are two major purposes: the esthetic one of providing another dimension of experience with literature and the practical one of helping students gain further comprehension and appreciation of selections.

As I have said already, it is important to give students the opportunity to hear skillful oral reading of prose and poetry. The reading need not come only from students and teachers since there are rich opportunities to hear professional readers and literary artists themselves on recordings. The National Council of Teachers of English and various commercial agencies have available a great array of recorded readings from which every English department should have a well-selected stock.

Discussion of literature accompanied by oral reading can often increase comprehension and enrich appreciation. For example, it is sometimes helpful for students to hear a recorded reading of a selection while they follow the printed text. This method may be especially beneficial to students of lesser ability.

Oral reading of whole selections or even of selected passages also will often increase students' awareness of the effect of literary devices. Certain poems, for instance, must be read aloud if some students are to sense the effect of particular types of rhyme or meter or understand such devices as onomatopoeia. The significance of the choice of certain patterns of syntax in prose may become clearer too when passages are read aloud.

Consideration of the contribution oral reading may make is an essential part of the planning of any lesson in literature.

Dramatic activities.   Dramatic activities of various kinds long have been prominent in elementary schools but have had little place in English programs at the secondary level. Some educators, particularly in England, are now demanding that great emphasis be put on dramatic activities at all levels, both related and unrelated to literature that is studied. Several purposes are cited: to provide imaginative experience; to promote fluency and skill of expression; to provide therapy for the student; and to aid in personality development, comprehension, and preparation for literature that is to be read. Concerning these last two purposes, J. W. Patrick Creber writes:

> It must be clear that many novels offer situations that lend themselves to dramatic treatment, but it is worth noting that this is essentially a two-way process, for the acting out of such situations may be expected to modify and deepen the actors' comprehension of the novel whence they were taken. Furthermore the children's receptivity to a particular play may sometimes be notably improved by dramatic improvisation on some of the situations, themes, and characters it contains, before the play itself is read. It is possible also to act scenes that are not in the play, but which are taken for granted or referred to. Occasionally the understanding of the bias of the play may be helped by enacting a scene on the same lines as one actually in it, but concentrating upon the feelings of characters who achieve no such prominence in the original. Devices such as these are particularly helpful when working on plays where the language constitutes an initial barrier that is often never effectively overcome when the text is studied *in vacuo*.[2]

Another Englishman, Frank Whitehead, asserts that there is strong reason for "giving dramatic work a place of honour near the very centre of the curriculum" and he has treated dramatic activities in detail in his book, *The Disappearing Dais*.[3] Whitehead believes that the main value of dramatization of literature in the classroom is that it is a "fulfilling" experience, "a vital imaginative experience," and an "outlet for wish fulfillment." Whitehead believes, as Creber does, that mime is an essential activity in preparing for dramatization with speech, and dramatization to him is central to the study of literature. In his book, Whitehead gives many specific suggestions on the handling of dramatization in the classroom.

Closely paralleling the views of Whitehead are those of James Moffett. In his monograph, *Drama: What Is Happening,* Moffett argues that "drama and speech are central to a language curriculum, not peripheral," and he discusses several types of speech and dramatic activi-

---

[2] *Sense and Sensitivity* (University of London Press, 1965), p. 93.
[3] London: Chatto & Windus, 1966.

ties, two of which are closely related to study of literature—dramatic improvisation and performing of scripts.[4]

In dramatic improvisation, students create and act out an original drama based on a selection of literature or a part of it. Moffett assigns various values to this activity, but its specific contributions to literature study he expresses as follows:

> Before a child can enjoy drama in script form—play reading—he can do so by creating the imitative actions of which scripts are a blueprint. Later, his power to bring a script alive in his mind is constantly recharged by his continued experience in inventing dramas. For narrative, improvisation renders a special service: it translates *what happened* back to *what is happening*. . . . For older students, converting narrative to drama demonstrates the relationship of the two: plays specify what narrative summarizes, and narrative, unlike drama, is told by someone addressing us.
>
> And, finally, improvisation can be used as an entree into a literary work soon to be read: the teacher abstracts key situations—say, Cassius' efforts to persuade Brutus to join the conspiracy—and assigns this as a situation to improvise before students read the work, so that when they do read it they already have an understanding of what is happening and of how differently the characters *might* have behaved. This kind of prelude also involves students more with the text.[5]

Performing of scripts, Moffett says, may involve dramatizing short plays written either by the students themselves or by professionals. As indicated in the passage above, he shares the view of Creber and Whitehead that dramatizing is a necessary prelude to reading plays silently.

Writing about Literature

Much of the writing program, though not necessarily all of it, can grow out of the study of literature. There seem to be three basic kinds of writing related to literature study: (1) Noncritical writing for which ideas or literary elements in a selection serve as springboards; (2) Interpretative and critical writing; (3) Imitative writing.

[4] Champaign, Ill.: NCTE, 1967.
[5] Moffett, pp. 27–28.

Ideas or literary elements as springboards.   Writing that stems from ideas or meanings in a work is common in English classrooms; writing triggered by literary elements much less so. The following is a fairly typical example of writing activity of the first type, devised by the author for a tenth-grade class:

> This unit is entitled "Conflict in Allegiances." The kind of conflict symbolized in *Antigone* is a universal human problem. Perhaps this problem of conflict of allegiances is an especially crucial one for young people. For example, a high school student often may be caught in a situation in which his friends put pressure on him to do one thing, and his parents, to do another. Write a paper in which you identify some of the kinds of conflicts of allegiances in which high school students may become involved. Give examples of specific conflicts. You need not write about yourself, but rather write about high school students generally.

In this type of writing literature serves as motivation and furnishes preparation. Writing and literature can be brought together in a more reciprocal relationship when writing activities are designed to clarify or reinforce understanding of literary structure and technique. The difference between this kind of writing and critical and interpretative writing may not be apparent immediately, but the following example of a writing activity designed by the author may show that there is a difference:

> (After a reading of Pierre Boulle's *Face of a Hero*)
>
> Irony is evident, as we have noted, in *Face of a Hero* from the title through the final scene. There are various uses of the term "irony," but in literature irony, in general, involves a discrepancy between surface reality and actual reality in what is said or in what happens. Irony, humorous or otherwise, is very common, of course, in everyday experience. There are many stock situations in popular movies, television programs, and comic strips, for example, based on humorous irony. Johnny's father wonders why Johnny suddenly is treating him with elaborate consideration. Johnny replies that he has decided his father is "a great old pop." But Johnny and the reader know that Johnny is about to get a bad report card. Or Maisie, the glamorous blonde, meets her rival and treats her with dripping sweetness, but we know that she has the urge to kill. Write a brief paper in which you describe a scene or event

or relate an incident which was ironic. The paper may be humorous or serious, and what you write may be based on your actual experience or may be imagined.

An interesting and different way of developing this basic relationship between literature and writing is illustrated by Rev. William J. O'Malley, S. J.[6] In teaching poetry, for example, Father O'Malley has students read a poem like Masters' "Levy Silver" in which there are the lines: "Why did I sell you plated silver? . . . The question at stake is why did you buy?" Then he asks the students to write "brief, concrete pictures of the faces and clothes and actions of a couple buying imitation jewelry in a pawn shop."

Father O'Malley's premise for his techniques is that "Writing exercises should be geared to elicit student reduplication of the elements of the poem." He illustrates his method, also, with traditional devices of poetry. He gives students statements or phrases with blanks where key words or groups of words are to be filled in. Some examples follow. (The italicized words are those filled in by the students.)

Simile: "The old man's eyes looked like *freshly opened oysters.*"

Personification: "Poverty is a *child with a runny nose.*"

Onomatopoeia: "the *whump* of motar shells."

Interpretation and criticism.   Interpretation and criticism of literature continues to be, as in the past, the most frequent type of writing about literature in English classes. Such writing can take many forms but the overall objective of any particular form used in the high school is to deepen student understanding and appreciation of literature.

The major criterion, to the author, for student assignments in interpretative and critical writing is that they be addressed to specific points about a work. Overall commentary on a selection often is of little value to the student in sharpening his perception. Among the most appropriate *foci* for critical and interpretative writing in the high school are these: analysis of actions of characters; discussion of the ways character is developed in a work; interpretation of specific passages, events, or symbols; comparison of works on specific points; dis-

---

[6] "Literary Craftsmanship: The Integration of Literature and Composition," *English Journal,* LII (April 1963), 247–252.

cussion of the ways theme is developed in a work; criticism of specific techniques; support or refutation of given generalizations about a work. Edgar V. Roberts' book, *Writing Themes about Literature,* treats and illustrates fifteen kinds of interpretative and critical writing.[7] Though designed for college freshmen, the book is a useful resource for high school teachers.

Imitative writing.   A stock-in-trade of the English class earlier in the century, imitative writing apparently is the object of a minor revival today. The specific values of imitative writing long have been debated. The basic argument for it has been based on analogies: for example, one will watch a bowling contest with greater enjoyment and understanding if he has tried his hand at bowling. Yet it is difficult to establish objective evidence in this area; consequently there is no basis for believing that imitative writing contributes to greater ability in reading literature.

Aside from its possible contribution to literature study, imitative writing may have inherent values, of course, in providing another kind of imaginative experience and in injecting variety into the classroom. Certainly students should be given a chance to try their hands at imaginative forms from fable to *haiku,* though rarely should students be assigned imaginative writing that is to be graded by the teacher.

Imitating stylistic and syntactic models apparently is the major direction of imitative writing today. Such exercises usually connect writing and factual or nonfictional prose with which this chapter has not been concerned. Imitation of these models has more to do with skill in writing than with literature study. However, James F. McCampbell illustrates a broader use of imitating models. He has students read a descriptive passage from Kipling, for example. They analyze the patterns of the passage, then invent their own substance to fit the patterns. Maintaining that "The structural conventions of our language are a key to understanding literature as well as improving composition,[8] McCampbell urges inductive analysis of the models by the entire class, then small-group writing, and finally individual writing.

---

[7] Englewood Cliffs, N.J.: Prentice-Hall, 1964.
[8] "Using Models for Improving Composition," *English Journal,* LV (September 1966), 772–776.

LITERATURE AND LANGUAGE STUDY

Broadening of language study has been a key trend in the secondary English curriculum in recent years. More excitement, in fact, has been generated by the "new linguistics" than by any other aspect of English study. Until the last few years language study in the junior and senior high school English curriculum meant traditional grammar, "correction" of usage, vocabulary development and use of the dictionary, and mechanics of language. This range may still exist in some school programs, but in many others the language program is now concerned with such additional aspects as nature of language, semantics, phonology, dialects, lexicography, history of the language, and transformational grammar.

The general explosion of activity and knowledge in linguistics has quickened interest in linguistic analysis of literature, as noted in the preceding chapter. Some scholars, including James McCampbell, maintain that understanding of language structure furthers comprehension of literature, and no one would deny the probability of such a general relationship. However, no specific evidence yet exists as to how study of language structure can aid comprehension in reading. Literature is language used in certain ways and in certain forms, so in the basic sense, study of literature *is* study of language. Recognizing this, the staff of the Curriculum Study Center in English at the University of Minnesota has built a secondary English curriculum on certain basic concepts about language which are illustrated and reinforced at each of the grades. Literature becomes a part of the study of these concepts.

Whether or not one agrees that such an approach will allow literature study to assume its full dimensions, one can agree that literature can become involved in any aspect of language study from history of the language to phonology. How to develop approaches that will exploit relationships for the benefit of both language study and literature study is frontier work that needs doing.

One such relationship with mutual rewards for language and literature study is in the field of dialects where students can study the use of dialects in literature. Illustrating possible activities in this connection is the following from *Discovering American Dialects* by Roger W. Shuy:

1. Compare a dialogue sequence in *The Yearling* or *Hie to the Hunters* with one in *The Catcher in the Rye* or *It's All Right, Cat!* Note the differences between back country and urban spoken language. Are the vocabulary differences related to different times, different needs, and different environments?

2. Discover some of the influences of Norwegian or American English by reading John Van Druten's play, *I Remember Mama*. You may do the same thing with Ole Rolvaag's *Giants in the Earth* and *Peder Victorious* as well as Martha Ostenso's *The Mad Carews*. Look up the Norwegianisms in a Norwegian-English dictionary.

3. Make a list of Pennsylvania Dutch words and phrases (especially in word order) found in Elsie Singmaster's short story "The Belsnickel" and in Patterson Greene's play *Papa Is All*.

4. Note the Nebraska vocabulary found in the novels of Willa Cather (*O Pioneers!* and *My Antónia,* for example). On the basis of the word lists given in chapter 2 would you call Nebraska a Northern or Midland dialect area?

5. Observe the influences of Yiddish on American English in the short stories of Arthur Kober ("That Man Is Here Again" and "Bella, Bella Kissed a Fella," for example) and in the novels of Leo Rosten (*The Education of Hyman Kaplan*), Bernard Malamud (*The Natural*), and Saul Bellow (*Seize the Day; Herzog*).

6. Collect examples of Chicago Irishisms in the novels of Finley P. Dunne (*Mr. Dooley Says* and other "Mr. Dooley" novels) and James T. Farrell (*Studs Lonigan*).

7. Note east Tennessee vocabulary and syntax in the novels of Mary Murfree (*In the Tennessee Mountains* and *The Prophet of the Great Smoky Mountains*) and in the collections of short stories by Mildred Haun (*That Hawk's Done Gone*).

8. Observe the different dialects found in Mark Twain's *Huckleberry Finn*. Do Huck and Jim speak a prestige dialect? Does the fact that Twain realistically describes the speech of Negro slaves affect his argument against slavery and racial discrimination?

9. Note the grammatical structure and vocabulary of Quaker speech as you observe it in the short stories of Jessamyn West ("The Battle of Finney's Ford") and Mabel Hunt ("Little Girl with Seven Names"). Pay particular attention to the second person personal pronouns and third person singular present tense verb forms. In Albert C. Baugh's *A History of the English Language,*

look up the history of these forms, noting especially the influence of George Fox and the Quaker movement.

10. Examine Irene Hunt's short story "Across Five Aprils" for its use of eye-dialect. Assuming that the author wants us to note the maturity of Jethro and the simple-minded weakness of Eb, how does her use of eye-dialect contribute to this purpose? Note especially the words fer (for), git (get), comfert (comfort), jest (just), fergit (forget), yore (your), stummick (stomach), ner (nor), kin (can). Who uses them? Who does not? Should an author have only the "bad guys" use dialect? [9]

Underlying what has been said in this chapter is the author's fear that the rather wide acceptance of a "tricomponent" curriculum in English of language, literature, and composition may lead to compartmentalization of these components and a resultant dehumanization of the curriculum in which language study smacks of the scientific and composition seems solely skill oriented. All of the components can represent humanistic study in themselves, but when they are related at appropriate points the sum is greater than the study of each part in isolation can produce.

THE MASS MEDIA IN THE ENGLISH CLASS *

One of the most obvious principles of teaching is that the clearer the presentation of a lesson or an idea, the more it will be remembered by students. The obligation to be clear, to ask unambiguous questions, to delineate the limits of a particular subject, to lead students through an orderly series of lessons, is clearly an obligation which is accepted unquestioningly by any teacher worthy of the name. It is also an obligation accepted by school administrators, who spend a great deal of time and effort in designing student schedules so that the school day will be—from the students' point of view—highly organized, full of precise injunctions about where the student should be and when he should be there. To do otherwise would be to invite chaos. Yet it is precisely this constant striving for order and pattern and sequence which brings the *school* (considered as an environment) into direct

* Written by Daniel A. Lindley, Jr., Yale University.
[9] Champaign, Ill.: NCTE, 1967, pp. 61–62.

and sometimes irreconcilable conflict with the *world*. Insofar as the world itself is ambiguous and puzzling, the clarity of the school world seems unrealistic and over-simple. The school is, in fact, in conflict with what Marshall McLuhan has called the "electric age," and the student, who has been exposed from infancy to the "cool" and involving medium of television, is quite likely to be put off by the "hot" and linear patterns of school. The terms "hot" and "cool" are used here in the way McLuhan uses them, and will be discussed further below.

This conflict between the world of school and the world as experienced by the student is a central problem for the teacher who wishes to teach the mass media. For if we assume, with McLuhan, that the student is already more involved with television and his own music than he is with what is going on in the English class, then the teacher, by bringing these media into the classroom, appears to be doing so merely to capitalize on the student's involvement; in other words, the teacher runs the risk of appearing to try to "con" the student into being interested in English-in-general. Furthermore, the teacher's way of understanding and analyzing media may be far removed from the student's way of understanding the same items. For example, it is easy to imagine a poetry lesson based on George Harrison's lyrics to the Beatles' song, "Within You, Without You"—the theme of which is surely similar to that of "The Love Song of J. Alfred Prufrock" or Emily Dickinson's "I Cannot Live With You," or even—stretching the point a little—"Richard Cory." And having gotten to "Richard Cory," the teacher could bring in Simon and Garfunkel's version of that poem, and so on. But this method, which appears so logical and appealing, may appear to the student as essentially phony, an attempt on the part of the teacher to buy his attention and his loyalty. And this problem must be overcome in teaching the mass media. For what the student finds in "Within You, Without You" may have nothing to do with the associations the teacher finds in it. In general, the teacher's problem is not to "relate" the mass media to the existing curriculum in English, because that would merely aggravate an already existing conflict between the world and the school.

The solution to this problem is to involve students in the actual production of materials which use the technologies of the media. This means the making of films, videotapes, speech essays, and taped "expansions" of poems, news stories, and the like.

Most teachers—perhaps especially English teachers—are naturally somewhat intimidated by the prospect of having to master various machines, such as movie cameras or tape recorders. But in many schools, the advent of the electronically amplified guitar and the re-recorded lyric has brought with it a legion of technologically sophisticated students who would be delighted to run the machines needed.

Let us consider first the making of a film. What follows is an account of an actual project undertaken by a teacher who had never before made a film. The project was undertaken with the basic objective of teaching the concepts of unity, coherence and purpose in writing, and the idea was to use the making of a film to demonstrate what these principles actually mean in a concrete situation: after all, a film must have these qualities for the same reasons that apply to a piece of writing. Another idea, that of point of view, is also implicit in the production of a film.

The first step was to look at several short films, mostly with the idea of learning together some elementary principles of camera use. During this phase of work, several books were a considerable help with terminology. The effects of fades, dissolves, and various kinds of cuts became increasingly obvious when attention was paid to them. The motion of the camera (in panning and dollying) turned out to have profound effects on how the viewer came to understand what was going on. Students began to notice many details of filming which they had taken for granted. For example, in the film *Shane,* students saw that if an actor is supposed to be walking (or riding) from the farm to the town, he must always be photographed from the same side, so that he will move in the same direction throughout the sequence. They noticed also that a person moving from left to right on the screen seems to be going *toward* something, while a person moving from right to left seems to be *going away.*

The next step was the making of an actual film. The football coach kindly loaned the 16-millimeter camera used to make game movies. Economics dictated that the film be short—film and processing are expensive items. The students, working in small committees, came up with several plots. Some were too elaborate and had to be rejected. The one finally agreed upon by the class (the teacher scrupulously stayed out of the decision-making process) was a simple enough story: a teacher becomes so carried away with his irrelevant lesson

that he does not notice that his students are sneaking out of his class
—all but one, who stays because he has fallen asleep. After a number
of scenes showing the teacher teaching (frantic and oblivious) and the
students sneaking out, the movie ends with a close-up of the sleeping
student. Although the whole film is only four minutes long, there are
eighteen different scenes in it. A tape recording of a honky-tonk piano
is used as backgroud music, which underlines the silent film style in
which the picture was made.

A project such as this one has several desirable outcomes. In the
first place, the necessity for careful planning and script writing becomes apparent. Many students who are "reluctant writers" will write
a great deal of material for such a project when they understand that
the success of the finished product really does depend on the care with
which it is planned. But just as important is the fact that students see
that they are involved with basic issues in communication: the film
must make sense to *anyone* who may see it. It cannot have a private
meaning for one particular group of students, or for just one teacher,
as most student writing does. Communicating to an unknown audience is a rigorous discipline by comparison.

All the above remarks about film apply with equal force to the
making of videotapes by students. There is, however, a trap for the
unwary teacher in this medium. Videotape, unlike film, makes it possible to see results immediately. But if mistakes are made, there is no
expense involved in re-shooting, as there is with film. The comparative ease with which videotapes may be made is all too likely to tempt
teachers to make videotapes of what are really stage productions: students acting out scenes from plays, and the like. This is in no sense a
use of the *medium,* which should be treated in the same way that film
is, with the same considerations of camera use, scene continuity, and
so on. In addition and especially if a portable camera is available—
students can put together news and feature programs involving people
and events in the school and the community. Here again, intelligent
choices must be made: what is important to show and why? how
much time should each segment of the show receive? Once again, the
old issues of unity, coherence, and emphasis reappear in this use of
the medium. Note however—and the point cannot be made too
strongly—that it would be a gross error for the teacher to call attention to these issues *as such,* for that would be to behave as a teacher is

expected to behave: that is, he would be making serious intellectual efforts designed to take all the fun out. The concepts will inevitably assert themselves in the planning and the execution phases just described. If the teacher hangs official labels on these principles, the time to do it is when the product—tape or film—is finished.

It is true that both film and videotape imply a certain amount of technical skill on *someone's* part. On the other hand, the speech essay involves nothing more intricate than a tape recorder and a record player. Basically, in this exercise an extended statement of a single idea is recorded (usually a statement made "off the cuff" by some reasonably articulate person); the original tape is edited, and relevant material is added to give it more coherence and force. Tapes of radio or television broadcasts may be altered and augmented in the same way. The simplest technique for this exercise is to use a stereophonic tape recorder, putting the speech on one track and the added material on the other. An example of the effectiveness of this technique is provided by Simon and Garfunkel's *The Seven O'Clock News*. This recording consists of short news items on topical events such as: "Richard Speck, accused slayer of eight student nurses . . . Nixon predicts the Vietnam war could last five more years . . ." and similar fragments—*and,* playing simultaneously, a sentimental rendering of *Silent Night* in the background. The bitterly ironic contrast is obvious but extremely powerful. It is this sort of juxtaposition which is central to the technique of the speech essay. And again, the material to be added, and the editing of the original speech, are matters which students must decide in the process of planning and executing such a production. By way of a demonstration it is helpful to have prepared in advance an example of the speech essay. The script of a portion of one such essay is provided here merely as a suggestive example. (Note: if a stereophonic tape recorder is not available, similar effects may be obtained by reading the speech part of the material into a microphone while records or other material is added simultaneously—by other people speaking at the same time, for example. Note also that, if a record player is used, it is possible to vary its volume appropriately as the speech segment proceeds. The more the speech elements are obscured —within limits—by other sounds, the more involved the audience will be in attempting to understand what is happeninng. Intense audience involvement is an essential principle of all mass media, and we will re-

turn to it in the general discussion which closes this chapter.) Here is
a transcript of a portion of a speech essay:

Narrator's Voice
Tallahassee Democrat, Florida's Capital Newspaper
Sunday Morning, May 26, 1968 — Twenty Cents
Partly cloudy—rain
High 88 low 70

A Poor Vigil Held at Capitol
They came bearing signs. They sat in a one-hour silent vigil on the steps
of the Capitol. They prayed together and departed. Florida State University Graduate School of Social Welfare showed up in force. A graduate student said, "We support the proposals for bettering the plight of
the poor overwhelmingly . . ."
Pompidou Suspends Right of Assembly
Paris' Latin Quarter was calm last night after three days of rioting . . .
Students linked arms and helped police . . .
You can't see or touch integrity . . . but it's one of our most valuable
assets . . . that's why we're proud to carry Kuppenheimer suits. Come
in and see why. Alford Brothers, 212 South Monroe.

New FSU Phase Seen . . . (AP) A student leader says that the protest
movement at FSU has entered a new phase with demonstrators more
discouraged than they were and wary of a stall by the administration.
The president of the 15,200-member student body said that the committee focused the issues involved when it recommended that the FSU
president be insulated from student publications.
Bob is twenty years old . . . a Junior at Florida State University, majoring in English. He will leave for Florence shortly to spend a year
abroad. I asked him over the other night . . . to talk about education.

Bob's Voice:
So much of college is removed from life in the outside world, outside
the community of scholars . . . one thing I would do would make it
necessary—I would have a three-hour course in ghetto studies, poor-people studies, right here in Tallahassee. On three sides of the campus
you've got ghettoes. So many of the kids go all the way through college
and don't know what's there. Anyone who gets a four-year degree and
doesn't know what's across the street. Just what kind of people are
there? I think it's an aspect you don't get on campus. // * The whole
* Double slashes indicate places where tape has been edited.

idea of this course is that you're not going to read your damn sociological studies. You're not going to read statistics. You're not going to read graphs. You're not going to talk to a PhD sitting in Classroom Building "A" talking about black people. You're gonna be talking *to* black people—who don't understand the complexity of their problems, they just know they have them. // Let's do the same thing with people in Appalachia. // You see, all we're getting is a view of what the upper 10 percent think. All we know is what the PhD's think. // We sit in front of a textbook and when we're through we get a sheet of paper that says we have a degree. // I think we need more firsthand information and less secondhand information. // To get on to another question that puzzles a lot of people today, and that is, what the hell is going on with young people, what do they think, what do they want? What are they doing, what are they trying to do? Well, first of all, it's not a homogeneous group, but I think the majority of them is increasingly questioning the values that have been handed to us, spoon-fed to us for so many years, and all of a sudden we find that they don't hold up; they just don't hold up, they just don't work // they don't hold up // they don't hold up, they just don't work // they don't hold up, they just don't work //

We don't have a set of values, of dictums, that we can rely on, to show us the way //

> Beatles—"It's Getting Better All the Time" brought up in volume as the following proceeds:

We're moving so fast now, and I think that education has to change, to keep up with it; we have to take a more total approach //

Narrator's Voice:

McLuhan talks about the "information overload."
He says, "the young student today grows up in an electrically configured world. It is a world not of wheels but of circuits, not of fragments but of integral patterns. The student today lives mythically and in depth . . ." //

> Beatles—"It's Getting Better All the Time"

Bob's Voice:

// Things move so fast we can't keep up with them. And now education has to change. It has to be—the leader of the change, it has to be on the vanguard. I think the textbook is fading because I think we have other media that are taking over. Simon and Garfunkel are college graduates; they are spokesmen, they are, as accurately as anyone, reflecting what is happening. By the same token, we've got a hell of a lot of conservative //

Narrator's Voice (quoting McLuhan):
Technologies begin to perform the functions of art, in making us aware of the psychic and social consequences of technology. Art as antienvironment becomes more than ever a means of training perception and judgment. Art offered as a consumer commodity rather than as a means of training perception is as ludicrous and snobbish as always. //

Narrator's Voice (quoting newspaper):
Remember your graduate with the most significant gift of all:
Magnavox Solid State Stereo // 1968 Zenith Color TV. We'll take a trade to make you an even better deal // A Mercury outboard is designed to catch fish, not weeds // 1968 Zenith Color TV // Magnavox // Play it cool with an ARA Auto air conditioner // (*Bob's Voice:*) If all of a sudden they know that they can prevent hookworm / Financing available, Capitol Lincoln-Mercury // *Bob's Voice:* . . . that's something. What . . . the hell is going on with young people. The majority of them are increasingly questioning the values that have been handed to us . . . they don't hold up. They just don't work. // They don't hold up. They just don't work. //

Simon and Garfunkel's *Sound of Silence:* volume brought slowly up then volume is dropped until the tape runs on in silence.

It can readily be seen that the basis for the foregoing speech essay is to be found in the remarks of "Bob," the college student, and that the thesis of his remarks provides the theme for the essay as a whole. There are, however, other possible starting points besides informal speech. One particularly promising technique is that of the "expansion" of a poem. In this use of the medium of tape, a poem (preferably as read by the poet) is used as the starting point for associations which are added to the poem as it proceeds. For example, in "The Love Song of J. Alfred Prufrock" there is this line, "There will be time to murder and create." In making a tape of the poem, the reading was interrupted at that line, and the voice of Chief Justice Earl Warren reading the oath of office to President Kennedy was added. The effect is both poignant and startling. Another line in the poem, "They will say/How his hair is growing thin," is recorded just as the poet reads it, but the lyrics of the Beatles' "When I'm Sixty-Four" can be heard in the background. Again, after the line "I have measured out my life with coffee spoons," the words "coffee spoons" are made to echo in the following lines. The final product is certainly more than a simple recording of a reading of the poem. Rather, it represents the poem and some possible associations by a sensitive reader.

There are two hazards in working with poetry in this way. The first is that the technique puts a premium on random, rather than on disciplined, associations with the poem. In other words, there is some possibility that students may get the idea that they are quite free to find anything they can think of in any poem under consideration, because anything may seem to "fit" with the poem as the tape is being made. The teacher, on the other hand, may quite reasonably object to this treatment of the poem as a source for any and all associations, however wild. A poem, after all, is not a Rorschach inkblot, and there is discipline and orderly method involved in working through to the meaning of a good poem. The need for discipline indeed is in conflict with the freewheeling spontaneity which should be operating when students are thinking up material to add to the recording of the "straight" poem. The anxiety on the part of the teacher that the poem itself may disappear under a cacophony of speeches and songs is entirely understandable; and for this reason the making of such tapes is probably best done as a means of entry into the study of poetry, not as the entire study. To use this technique in this way is entirely appropriate, not only because it produces all sorts of excitement and curiosity, but—more importantly—because it demonstrates that the teacher recognizes that any person reading a good poem for the first time *ought* to think of all sorts of things, *some* of which may turn out to be irrelevant, but *many* of which will continue to enrich the poem for any reader. Much of the teaching of poetry carried on since the development of the "new criticism" has represented an overrational search for *the* meaning of the poem, with a consequent denial of what the student may be developing as *his* meaning of it. The tapes recognize and reward whatever associations students may bring to a poem. Thus the students feel more free to get into the poem, and the teacher learns something about the students' ways of thinking. After all, the tape is made from what the students bring to the poem.

What the students bring.   Throughout this section on the media, the emphasis has been on student production and student creativity. Thus these exercises in the media have not been plans to teach *about* them (except in incidental ways) but rather to involve students in the media themselves. The distinction is a crucial one because, as I pointed out at the beginning of this chapter, it is very important that work on those techniques which touch the lives of students so intimately in the "electric age" does *not* appear to them as just another part of the school routine. McLuhan says,

> The young student today grows up in an electrically configured world. It is a world not of wheels but of circuits, not of fragments but of integral patterns. The student today *lives* mythically and in depth. At school, however, he encounters a situation organized by means of classified information. The subjects are unrelated. They are visually conceived in terms of a blueprint. The student can find no possible means of involvement for himself, nor can he discover how the educational scene relates to the "mythic" world of electronically processed data and experience that he takes for granted. As one IBM executive puts it, "My children had lived several lifetimes compared to their grandparents when they began Grade One.[10]

Unless, in short, students are involved with the media, there is no way to teach anything about them. Students presumably know everything about the media except how it feels to create in them. So the teacher's task is simply one of providing that chance.

SELECTED BIBLIOGRAPHY

Barnes, Douglas (Ed.), *Drama in the Classroom* (Champaign, Ill.: NCTE, 1968).
A summary of the discussions of the subject at the Dartmouth Seminar, including a drama syllabus for the secondary school.
Cannon, Garland, "Linguistics and Literature," *College English,* XXI (February 1960), 255–260.
Considers possibilities for relating linguistics to the teaching of literature.
Cohen, B. Bernard, *Writing about Literature* (Glenview, Ill.: Scott, Foresman, 1963).

[10] Marshall McLuhan, *Understanding Media: The Extension of Man* (New York: McGraw-Hill, 1964), p. 9.

Reviews various principles of writing and analysis and focuses on the practical problems encountered in writing about literature.

Creber, J. W. Patrick, *Sense and Sensitivity* (London: University of London Press, 1965), pp. 85–108.
A discussion of the values of dramatic activity and its relation to the teaching of literature.

Evertts, Eldonna L., "Composition through Literature," *Instructor,* LXXV (March 1966), 105.
Praises the teaching units from the Nebraska Curriculum Center which stress the teaching of composition through literature.

Farrell, Edmund J., *English, Education, and the Electronic Revolution* (Champaign, Ill.: NCTE, 1967).
A comprehensive discussion of the implications for the classroom of the electronic age, with a chapter on the specific place of various media in the English classroom and an extensive bibliography.

Judy, Stephen, "Style and the Teaching of Literature and Composition," *English Journal,* LVI (February 1967), 281–285.
Argues that teaching style as "effects" or connotations created by language and manipulated by writers, the teacher helps the student to understand style in literature and supplies him with more concrete advice and instruction in writing.

Marckwardt, Albert H., "Linguistics and the Study of Literature," *Linguistics and the Teaching of English* (Bloomington: Indiana University Press, 1966), pp. 100–121.
Holds that linguists offer ordered, systematic procedures dealing with the language of literature.

McCampbell, James F., "Using Models for Improving Composition," *English Journal,* LV (September 1966), 772–776.
Describes a plan for teaching composition through imitation of models.

Media and Methods. Published monthly, September through May. Publishing office: 134 North 13th Street, Philadelphia, Pa. 19107.
A highly useful periodical with helpful articles on a wide range of topics relating to the media and the classroom.

Moffett, James, *Drama: What Is Happening?* (Champaign, Ill.: NCTE, 1967).
A plea for greater stress on oral language and discussion of the nature and function of dramatic activities in the classroom.

O'Malley, William J., S.J., "Literary Craftsmanship: The Integration of Literature and Composition," *English Journal,* LII (April 1963), 247–252.
Specific description of how literature and writing can be related.

Postman, Neil and Charles Weingartner, "Linguistics and Reading," in *Linguistics: A Revolution in Teaching* (New York: Delacorte Press, 1966), pp. 176–196.

Treats the two kinds of problems involved in reading: "cracking the code" and analyzing and evaluating the language. Attention is given to different responses to passages, according to the meaning of meaning.

Roberts, Edgar V., *Writing Themes about Literature* (Englewood Cliffs, N.J.: Prentice-Hall, 1964).

Identifies and illustrates a number of types of writing about literature.

Tacey, W. C., "Cooperative Activities for English and Speech Teachers," *Education,* LXXX (April 1960), 463–467.

Suggests plans for unifying the study of literature and speech.

Vanderlain, Aldona S., "Dramatic Approach in Teaching Literature," *Baltimore Bulletin of Education,* XXVII (March 1960), 28–30.

Suggests dramatizing literature as a way of interpreting it. *Treasure Island* is the example.

Whitehead, Frank, *The Disappearing Dais* (London: Chatto & Windus, 1966), pp. 122–151.

Goes into detail on how to organize and conduct dramatic activities in the classroom.

part two
TEACHING PROBLEMS

The student's involvement in the literature program in the junior and senior high school may take various forms. He will discuss selections of literature in the total class and in small groups. He will read individually. He will write about what he reads and he will participate in oral activities based on what he reads. He will be introduced to various approaches to a work of literature, and he will be involved in units of study organized in various ways. But underlying all his activities is the need to learn to read the several genres of literature as maturely as his potential will permit.

Alan C. Purves and Victoria Rippere, from an analysis of students' written responses to literature, have identified four basic categories of response: *Engagement-involvement*—". . . the various ways by which the writer indicates his surrender to the literary work, by which he informs his reader of the ways in which he has experienced the work or its various aspects." *Perception*—the reader's perception of structure, technique and craftsmanship, the "ways in which a person looks at the work as an object distinct from himself." *Interpretation* —the reader's attempts to find meaning, to generalize, to draw inferences, to relate a work to the universe. *Evaluation*—the reader's judgments of the goodness or badness of the work.[1]

This classification of responses is useful as a paradigm for the teaching of reading skills. The teacher cannot teach responses, but he can

[1] *Elements of Writing about a Literary Work,* Research Report No. 9 (Champaign, Ill.: NCTE, 1968).

help his students develop skills that will enable them to become sophisticated in each of the four dimensions of response. The net result should be a continually deepening experience with literature. The power of imaginative entry into a work of literature is the basis for engagement or involvement. Again, the teacher cannot teach imaginative entry but he can promote it and help set the stage for it; and he can help students to overcome the obstacles to imaginative entry that the various genres may present. Underlying the power of perception is the understanding of conventions and devices and the ability to relate them to the whole of a work of literature. Of course, interpretation and judgment of the artistic and personal significance of a work of literature will depend on everything the student has learned about reading and on his ability to relate his own experience to the work.

The following four chapters, though not organized identically, are all concerned with the ways in which students can be helped to develop and refine the skills and understandings identified above.

5
Fiction in the Literature Program

The decline of fiction since World War II has been noted by many observers in the literary world. In contemporary publishing, nonfiction titles far outnumber those of fiction, and magazines devote much less space to fiction than they did some years ago. But if the post-World War II era may be a golden age of nonfiction, fiction nevertheless is far from moribund. The novel flourishes today and may be the characteristic form of our time as, for example. the epic and verse drama were in certain earlier periods.

In fact, it is quite possible that there has been no real "decline" in the popularity of fiction, only less reason on the part of the general public to seek fictionalized experience in printed form. Television is now the chief medium for popular fiction, satisfying mass taste better than does the printed page. The popular magazine story has lost its patrons to the television screen. For the high school teacher, television can be a stimulant as well as a depressant in teaching literature. Television provides a handy, interesting (to most students) avenue through which to approach the world of fictionalized experience, offering examples and comparisons on which understanding can be built and discrimination heightened, not only in televiewing but in reading fiction. It comes as something of a revelation to the adolescent that fiction, that is, stories, are all around him in everyday life—in television, radio, motion pictures, newspapers, conversation, and jukebox ballads—not just entombed in his anthology or in books in the library. A discussion beamed to this revelation is a good way to introduce a unit on fiction for younger students.

Because of this prevalence of fictionalized experience and because the pupil enters the junior high school with some natural interest in stories, fiction probably will be the keystone of the literature program in the secondary school, although students should certainly have broad experiences with the several literary genres. It is in the high school that many adolescents, naturally inclined to action and concerned with happenings, should realize, paraphrasing the philosopher Santayana, that one of the chief functions of literature is to turn events into ideas. It is only then that the student will be able to derive, in his own experience, the real rewards of literature discussed in the opening chapter of this book. Sterile teaching and poor choice of selections are the surest ways of guaranteeing that students will remain at the television level of fiction. And this curtailed development is unfortunate, because the highest rewards of fiction come from that written by the serious artist and read by the serious reader. Through studying how to read fiction, in constant interplay with wide experiences in reading the novel and short story, many students will develop the ability to read serious fiction well.

TEACHING THE SKILLS OF READING FICTION

The short story and the novel, like other forms of literature, pose special problems for the reader. Although there has been, in the past thirty years, a vast number of publications about the skills involved in reading—and although reading-skill programs are now features of many high school textbook-anthologies—there is a paucity of specific suggestions for the teachers to follow in helping students develop skill in reading fiction or other literary forms. There appear to be two major explanations for this lack of detailed instruction. First, skill in reading fiction simply may involve the application of those much-discussed skills in vocabulary, "word-attack," [1] and comprehension. Second, the process by which the mature reader reads a significant novel or story may defy analysis, making it impossible to enumerate

---

[1] "Word-attack" refers to the methods a student uses in trying to handle a word unknown to him which he meets in his reading. It may be of three kinds: phonetic analysis, structural analysis (as of prefixes, suffixes, roots), and guessing from context clues.

the specific skills involved. Attempting the full description of such a process would be as impossible, perhaps, as delineating the process by which a music lover "got that way."

The relation of skill in reading literature to the broader objective of appreciation is a knotty problem that cannot be examined in any detail here. Obviously, critical skill in reading fiction—knowledge of criteria for judging value and ability to apply these criteria—does not guarantee that the reader will enjoy a book or a story, or be moved by it. A technically masterful novel or story may leave even some highly intelligent readers "cold." Undoubtedly certain factors enter in—type of personality, point of view of the selection, the total context in which the selection is experienced, and a host of others. Many writers have attempted to define "appreciation" in literature or to identify the factors in appreciation. For example, Robert C. Pooley writes: "Appreciation, then, I shall define as the emotional responses which arise from basic recognition, enhanced by apprehension of the means by which they are aroused." [2] James R. Squire, in a study of adolescents' responses to four selected short stories, identifies several factors that commonly obstruct mature response: (1) *Failure to grasp the meaning.* Obviously readers must comprehend the narration in stories. Squire found that there were three common difficulties in grasping the "essential intention" of the author: (a) Failure to understand key words; (b) Failure to grasp the implications of details; (c) Incorrect inferences. This difficulty frequently took the form of failure to keep details suspended in memory and to relate them to later details in the story. (2) *Reliance on stock responses.* Some students tend to rely on stereotyped patterns of thinking as they interpret situations in literature. Squire identified five general stereotypes in ninth graders' responses to the four stories ("All the Years of Her Life" by Morley Callaghan; "Prelude" by Lucille Vaughan Payne; "Reverdy" by Jessamyn West; and "The Man in the Shadow" by Richard Child): (a) Adolescents are not responsible for their own actions; (b) A boy or girl in trouble does not have a very healthy home life; (c) Wealth and happiness are incompatible; (d) When adults and adolescents are in conflict, the adults are almost always wrong; (e) Punishment for adolescent wrongdoing accomplishes little and should be avoided. (3)

[2] "Measuring the Appreciation of Literature," *English Journal*, XXIV (October 1935), 628.

Happiness binding. Some students "continually assume, infer, and hope for the best. They are 'happiness bound' both in their demand for fairy tale solutions and in their frequent unwillingness to face the realities of unpleasant interpretation." (4) *Critical predispositions.* Some readers bring to fiction critical yardsticks which they attempt to apply to any story—whether it is "true to life" or includes "good description," for example. (5) *Irrelevant associations.* Random associations from memories of personal experience tend, in some students, to get in the way of a unified view of the work. (6) *The search for certainty.* Some readers insist on clarity and definiteness in interpretation even when a story gives no definite basic for a single interpretation.[3] Squire's findings make clear that the junior or senior high school teacher of literature needs to identify the skills important in reading fiction and to provide direction and practice in those skills. It is vital, first, that the student be made aware of the things that are important to think about when one reads fiction. Then, naturally, the student must be given much practice—criticized practice—in applying these processes of thought to fiction appropriate to his level of experience, since the constant relation of one's experience to the printed page is essential in any true comprehension. These processes of thought, which lead to skill in reading fiction, seem to divide into two general categories: those necessary to comprehend form and therefore to determine the significance of a short story or novel, and those necessary to apprehend a variety of implied meanings inherent in fiction.

Reading To Comprehend Form

Because the novel or the short story is a particular way of reconstructing experience, the special way in which the author has used the form may be important for the meaning or significance of the selection. Many students (and adults, for that matter) read only for "the story," for the literal sequence of events. They tend to read all stories in the same way, and if the given story does not jibe with their way of thinking about what a story should be, as Squire's findings show, they are likely to complain that they "don't get it." Yet the same student who

[3] *The Responses of Adolescents While Reading Four Short Stories.* Research Report No. 2 (Champaign, Ill.: NCTE, 1964), pp. 37–49.

is impatient with form as a factor in understanding the selection may be the boy who would never be content with knowing only the amount of yardage gained on an around-end play in a football game; he would want to know how the play was executed and from what formation it was run, for this awareness would add to his enjoyment. Or the impatient student may be a girl who is sophisticated in music—at least in the form popular at the moment. She would never be satisfied merely to recognize the melody; she also would be a keen critic of the artistry of the musicians and arranger. Analogies such as these, presented in class, may help students to see the importance of form in literature—at the least, they may break down some antagonisms.

High school students are frequently baffled by certain modern fiction of the highly symbolic or elliptical variety. For example, this author has been most unsuccessful in teaching a favorite short story, Hemingway's "The Killers," to senior high school classes. Merely following the events of the story, the students come out blank and virtually snarling with frustration. On the surface the story seems stupid (a favorite word in the adolescent's vocabulary of literary criticism). Two sinister-appearing men turn up in a diner in a small town. They carry on a rather pointless conversation with the counterman in the diner. Finally they produce guns, holding the countermen and the cook prisoner, waiting apparently to kill one Ole Andreson, who usually eats at the diner. Ole doesn't come and the men give up and go away. Nick Adams, one of the waiters at the diner, goes to warn Ole, who seems resigned to his fate. The baffled young waiter goes back to the diner, where he exclaims to his partner. "It's too damned awful." The partner's reply is the last line of the story: "Well, you better not think about it."

Furiously, the students want to know why the men are out to kill Ole Andreson. And they want to know how the story *ends*—does Ole get killed or doesn't he? The impasse results from their failure to take into account the role played by the form of the story in expressing its meaning—a failure certainly excusable in the average adolescent, though not in the able student. The mature reader realizes, perhaps from a previous reading of Hemingway, that the author is pointing to the pervasiveness of evil in the world, and it does not matter at all, for instance, whether or not Ole Andreson actually gets killed nor why the men want to kill him. The psychological plot of the story involves Nick Adam's traumatic rendezvous with evil, and in terms of that plot the end is just right. Such understanding comes, of course, from sustained experience in reading fiction under the guidance of a skilled teacher.

Studying Plot

What is the starting point in developing the overall skill of organizing a selection of fiction in terms of its form and content? In the junior high school the students can learn the various purposes that fiction may have: simply to entertain through a funny, exciting, or unusual story; to present some serious idea about life; to satirize or burlesque something; to create some kind of effect or impression; to portray or dramatize an emotion; to present an insight into a person's character. In the senior high school the student should learn the way in which traditions of romanticism, realism, and naturalism have affected fiction, and he should have some experiences with historical, sociological, and psychological fiction. More specific ways of dealing with these matters are suggested in the following sections.

Since students enter the junior high school naturally interested in "the story" in a piece of fiction, work with plot and its role in the art of fiction may be stressed in the early years, although in classroom work the various elements of fiction should never be isolated one from another. Students will need practice with various methods of plot construction. As the writer has stated elsewhere:

> Most will have little trouble with the plot which presents a straight chronological sequence of events, but they will need training in following the story which starts with a problem, regresses in time to tell how it arose, and moves forward in time to tell how it was solved; or the one which starts at the end, goes back to the beginning, and runs on to meet the starting point, the end of the person's life. In their early acquaintance with plots of this type, it may help students to draw jagged time lines to show the chronology of the story. In the novel, particularly the long nineteenth-century novels, students have the problem of following several plots involving various groups of characters through hundreds of pages. Simple charts showing the various plot strands and the characters involved may help, although the need for too many charts and dia-

grams may indicate that the novel is too difficult for the level of ability of the readers.[4]

The study of plot will involve students in important discrimination in reading fiction. The mature reader rejects improbability and too much coincidence in what he reads, recognizing the fact that in good fiction, as in the experience it reconstructs, there is a basis of cause and effect in the happenings. A good study question for students is: "Was there any preparation for this happening, any reason for it in what has gone before, or did this happen purely by chance or coincidence?" The literary matter of "foreshadowing" is the point. After reading a "surprise-ending" story, such as those by O. Henry, students may enjoy looking back over the story to see whether the writer purposely led them astray in order to trick them at the end, or whether the surprise ending could grow logically out of the story.

Judging Character

Teachers are fond of asking students to "characterize" so and so after reading a selection. This task, too, will be difficult for the student who has not learned to work with a variety of clues. Discussion of ways to use such clues might be introduced by asking, "How do we arrive at our judgments of people in real life?" Students will usually answer this question with such responses as: "By the way they act." "By what they do." "By what other people say about them." "By the way they talk." "By the way they dress." "By the kinds of things they like to do." Then the teacher can point out that in fiction one arrives at estimation of character through the same kinds of clues, perhaps listing for the class "The nine basic methods of revealing a character," as identified by J. N. Hook:

1. Telling what kind of person he is.
2. Describing the person, his clothing, and his environment.
3. Showing his actions.
4. Letting him talk.
5. Relating his thoughts.
6. Showing how other people talk to him.

[4] "Developing Competence in Reading," in Angela M. Broening (Ed.), *The English Language Arts in the Secondary School* (New York: Appleton-Century, 1956), p. 185.

7. Showing what other people say about him.
8. Showing how other people react because of him.
9. Showing how he reacts to others.[5]

It is important for the teacher to point out the close relationship of characters and events in mature fiction. That is, a character is often revealed by his reactions in the crisis that provides a climax for a story. And in artistic fiction certain traits of certain characters lead to events. It is a mark of immature, formula fiction that this close relationship of characters and events is lacking, as, for example, when characters do highly improbable and unpredictable things merely for the sake of the plot.

Using Clues to Setting

Often the setting in fiction is obvious. Yet occasionally, especially in maturely written short stories, the reader has to infer the time or place, and it may be most important that he do this. Simple stories of the Far North, the desert, and the tropics, for example, in which there are obvious clues to setting, will provide training for junior high school pupils in making this type of inference. This training will make it easier for them to handle more subtle clues later, when it may be important for them to understand that a story about a pepper-eating contest is taking place in Mexico, or a certain Christmas story is set in Wales. Consideration of the geographical setting is important, too, in the local-color stories of American literature. Occasionally, the inference of time from clues is also important. Certain excellent but "dated" stories of the World War II period would be bewildering to the student who had not determined the setting in time. Or a story such as Faulkner's "Race at Morning" would lose its impact if the reader did not determine from rather scanty clues that it took place many years ago.

Reading for Implied Meanings

A readiness to draw inferences, to read between the lines, is essential to successful reading beyond the literal story level. A typical response

[5] *The Teaching of High School English* (New York: Ronald, 1965), pp. 174–75.

of adolescents to a teacher's or a classmate's interpretation is an astonished "Where'd you get that out of it?" To the highly trained but inexperienced teacher in literature, it sometimes seems inconceivable that a student does not recognize an elementary matter of symbolism. Yet to many youngsters beginning junior high school English, the whole matter of symbolism in literature is foreign, and it never occurs to them to look beneath the surface of happenings for implied ideas. They are often loud in their protest against the writer who doesn't "come right out and say what he means." The process of learning to think with literary material develops gradually through the junior and senior high school years—but it can develop.

Using Details To Determine or Illuminate Theme

Not all fiction is concerned with any definite theme—to cite an extreme example, the stories of Poe. However, it is important that students develop the ability to handle theme in mature fiction. Certainly there is no pat outline of devices by which this ability could be developed since the factors involved in dealing with an author's theme are so complicated. Yet, after students have an understanding of what theme in fiction is, they can be made aware of the way in which understanding the use of details can aid them to perceive it. Often there will be statements of the theme by the author or by his characters. This is the case, for instance, in James Michener's novel of the Korean war, *The Bridges at Toko-Ri,* in which the theme—why American men had to fight and die in a strange, little-known country—is rather clearly stated near the end of the book. This statement of theme was overlooked by the girl who complained that she did not like the book because "it had such a sad ending." In view of the theme, there could be no other ending!

In order to deal with theme, and the general significance of a selection, high school students need to learn to judge details in terms of the author's attitude toward his material. These attitudes lie on a continuum between symbolism and naturalism. Of course, the problem of interpreting symbolism underlies the entire study of literature and is as important to the reading of fiction as to the reading of poetry or any other form of literature. To the symbolist, such as James Joyce or D. H. Lawrence, details are likely to be unimportant, or even meaningless, at the literal level, and this makes reading their work extremely difficult. Only a few high school students will be able to comprehend Joyce or Lawrence, for example, but a general acquaintance with symbolism and a habit of looking below the surface of details can begin in the junior high school. Seventh-graders may discuss the significance of the blue willow plate in Doris Gates's *Blue Willow,* and eighth- or ninth-graders may consider the symbolic value of the black coffee in James Street's *Goodbye, My Lady.* Naturalistic writing, in which the author presents a stark cross section, or "slice," of life, may be as baffling to adolescents as the highly symbolistic. It helps them to know the purpose of naturalistic writing. In the senior high school, students should learn something of the continuum of authors' attitudes toward their material. Preparation for reading the major writers of fiction includes placing them on this continuum.

An author's central meaning or theme in a piece of fiction may be dependent upon such devices as irony, satire, and allegory. In addition to explaining these devices, the teacher needs to provide practice in reading selections in which they are used, selections appropriate to the students' level of awareness. If there is careful preparation, the junior high school is not too early for introduction of these matters.

APPROACHES TO THE NOVEL

At all grades in the junior and senior high school, the novel has been important in the literature program, but because of the amount of time that must be invested in study of the novel, teachers have encountered some particular difficulties, both practical and philosophical. The practical problems center on the availability of material for class use. Library facilities vary widely from school to school. Some teachers have one copy per student of several novels and multiple copies of many others at their disposal, whereas some teachers are virtually restricted to the selections in the anthology—and sometimes there is a shortage of anthologies! Editors and publishers have been loath to include full-length novels in anthologies because so much space is required and because no matter what novel is included, many teachers often are dissatisfied with the choice. Only in the books for the ninth and the tenth grades have full-length novels commonly been included. However, a great boon has come to the teacher—the phenomenon of paperbound books. Use of paperbacks in the classroom and their inclusion in school and public libraries have become commonplace in the last decade.

Other problems in teaching the novel are philosophical ones. For a long time there has been among teachers a rather widespread suspicion of selections that are popular and that students find easy to read. Teachers have insisted upon choosing for common reading novels that really give them something to teach. However, the commendable zeal to provide challenging experiences has resulted frequently in the choice of novels that are appropriate only for the upper third or fourth of the class, and only frustrating to the rest. It is probable, for example, that *Silas Marner* and *A Tale of Two Cities* are more appropriate for the twelfth grade, if they are to be taught, than to the tenth, where they—*Silas Marner,* at least—are practically canonized items. However, many teachers have ignored the nature of a student's growth toward maturity in reading fiction. This gradual type of growth makes it necessary for a girl to learn to read, say, *Seventeenth Summer* well before she can read *Wuthering Heights* well. To some extent a rather widespread burden of contempt for the "juvenile" and the contemporary has crippled teaching of the novel.

A major philosophical problem in teaching the novel, or any other form of literature, for that matter, involves the teacher's view of his point of departure—does he consider more important the novel itself, or the experience in reading it he wants the students to have? To those teachers who accept a certain novel, or group of novels, as their point of departure, their problem becomes one of getting the selection "across" to students, of making it meaningful and, if possible, interesting. Articles in the *English Journal* and other professional magazines have shown the ingenuity and resourcefulness that teachers have mustered to meet this problem. Commitment to this point of departure in literature has resulted in production of "simplified classics," abridged or rewritten versions of famous selections. Though these books may have some uses in the general reading program, the disadvantages of using them outweigh the advantages. It is questionable, for one thing, whether a really fine piece of literature can be simplified or even abridged without creating something entirely different. There is a danger that many students may get the idea that they are really experiencing *Les Misérables,* for instance, when they read a simplified edition. (There are even comic-book versions of this and other masterpieces!) Some students who might ultimately read a selection in the original may be discouraged from doing so through the early reading of the simplified version. It seems legitimate to reason that if students are not prepared to read a certain selection in its original form, they should read another selection that, though of lesser merit or complexity, preserves its unity and integrity as a work of art.

Many other teachers, especially in recent years, have maintained that the point of departure should not be any one novel or group of novels but rather the kind of intellectual and emotional experience that students should have. For these teachers the problem is to determine what experiences a certain class of students should have, and then to find the novels most likely to provide those experiences.

No doubt this basic cleavage concerning point of departure in the literature program will continue to exist among teachers and others concerned with the reading and literary experiences of young people. Yet the research and experimentation of the past several decades lend support to the viewpoint that the point of departure in teaching the novel should be determination by the teacher of the type of experience he desires his students to have, and then selection of the novels most likely to induce that experience. Considering the entire literary tradition, it is difficult to defend the position that any two or three novels are the *sina qua non* of the literary education during adolescence. It is quite obvious that, no matter what may be a teacher's opinion of a particular novel and no matter what position the book has held in literary history, it will be rewarding to a student only in terms of *his* reactions to it and of the value *he* perceives in his experience of reading it. It is unfortunately apparent that the majority of high school graduates look back on their tenth-grade experience with *Silas Marner,* for example, as relatively unpleasant, though the novel has a secure reputation in the literary tradition. As noted in the opening chapter of this book, a greater permissiveness must characterize choice of selections for classroom use. Canonized selections may need to be thrown out, with works such as Golding's *Lord of the Flies* and Baldwin's *Go Tell It on the Mountain* replacing *Silas Marner* and *Great Expectations.*

Novels for Reading in Common

Regardless of many differences of opinion, there seems to be one unanimous point of agreement among teachers of literature: there should be *some* reading in common. Exactly what that common reading should be at each grade and how much of it there should be may be controversial, but the value of occasional experiences in having a class all reading the same novel at the same time is universally acknowledged. At least one novel should be read in common in each grade, seven through twelve, although, as this author frequently has stated, there is no pat formula to prescribe which selections should be read in a particular class. Probably each novel chosen for reading in common should meet three general criteria:

1. Any novel chosen should furnish a profitable experience for a typical class, heterogeneous in its intellectual and esthetic potential. It should provide appropriate opportunities for the able without being either completely incomprehensible or unrewarding to those at the lower ranges of ability.
2. The work chosen should pose reading problems and demands that are, in large part, common to many other novels. That is, the unique or greatly experimental work might legitimately be ruled out for total class study. Among commonly taught novels, *Huckleberry Finn* is such a book. To be sure, many students should read *Huckleberry Finn,* but the work is so much in a class by itself that it may lack real value for in-common study. Of particular value is the book that has a concrete, literal line of progression and at the same time a possible continual allegorical or symbolic progression, for example, *The Old Man and the Sea, The Secret Sharer,* and *The Pearl.*
3. The novel must have some natural affinity with youth, with adolescence. There is, of course, no sure way by which this amorphous quality of "affinity" can be judged, but it seems important that teachers consider it with as much insight as they can muster. For adolescents, however bright intellectually or mature socially and physically, are different, in general, from adults. There are certain themes, attitudes, mind-sets that are naturally more acceptable or

comprehensible than others to young people. A work must be appraised carefully in terms of the resources of a given class for entering imaginatively into it and responding to it.

In order to give some practical help to teachers in choosing novels for common reading at the various grade levels, the author surveyed articles on the teaching of the novel appearing in the *English Journal*, recent syllabuses and courses of study, and a number of reading lists published by the National Council of Teachers of English, the American Library Association, and other organizations. He also talked personally and corresponded with teachers from various parts of the country. The following list of suggested novels for reading in common is the result. Several somewhat obvious things should be pointed out about the list. First, there is nothing "objective" about the placement of the selections in the various grades; this placement was determined both in terms of common practice across the country and in terms of the writer's opinions about appropriateness. For example, *Great Expectations* appears in the twelfth-grade list, although a cut version that appears in a widely used anthology is commonly taught in the ninth grade. On the other hand, *Old Yeller* could be read before the ninth grade by many students. Second, it is obvious that some of the selections would be useful only for certain groups—*Shane* for students of lesser ability and *The Dead* for highly able readers, for example. One of the real problems of selecting novels for reading in common by seventh- and eighth-graders is that boys and girls at those levels have such markedly different interests. Therefore, in the main, the selections for those grades have been suggested because of their appeal for both boys and girls.

In the list that follows, those books available in paperback edition when this volume went to press are marked with an asterisk.[6]

Seventh Grade

Buck, Pearl, *The Big Wave*. A typhoon destroys a Japanese village.
Knight, Eric, *Lassie Come-Home*. The original story of the famous fictional collie.

---

[6] Teachers should check in the most recent edition of *Paperbound Books in Print* (New York: Bowker).

Shotwell, Louise, *Roosevelt Grady*. Story of family life among migrant Negro workers.

Sperry, Armstrong, *Call It Courage*. A South Sea island boy proves his courage in a lonely ordeal.

Ullman, James Ramsey, *Third Man on the Mountain*. A boy conquers a great mountain on which his father met death.

Eighth Grade

L'Engle, Madeleine, *A Wrinkle in Time*. A fantasy of travel through time, with a strong ethical theme.

London, Jack, *Call of the Wild*. One of the great dog-and-man stories.

Steinbeck, John, *The Pearl*. Short allegory of the curse of a great pearl.

Stevenson, Robert, *Treasure Island*.

Street, James, *Goodbye, My Lady*. A boy and an unusual dog in the Mississippi swamp country.

Wojciechowska, Maia, *Shadow of a Bull*. The son of a great Spanish bullfighter feels impelled to follow in his father's footsteps at the same time that he feels he is not suited to be a bullfighter.

Ninth Grade

Barrett, William E., *The Lilies of the Field*. Unusual story of a young Negro who helps a group of German refugee nuns build a chapel.

Forbes, Esther, *Johnny Tremain*. A young silversmith's part in the turbulent pre-Revolutionary War days in Boston.

Gipson, Fred, *Old Yeller*. Family life and an incorrigible yellow dog in pioneer days in Texas.

Neville, Emily, *It's Like This, Cat*. Episodic story of a year in the life of a New York City boy and his pet cat.

Richter, Conrad, *Light in the Forest*. A white boy is returned to his parents' civilization after years of captivity by the Indians.

Schaefer, Jack, *Shane*. A quality western.

Wibberley, Leonard, *The Mouse that Roared*. A lighthearted satire of the tiny Grand Duchy of Fenwick's "war" on the United States.

Tenth Grade

Annixter, Paul, *Swiftwater. A Maine woods boy, his ambitions, his family, and the girl in his life.

Boulle, Pierre, *Face of a Hero. An ironic story of a prosecuting attorney who sends an innocent man to his death.

Hemingway, Ernest, The Old Man and the Sea.

Hilton, James, *Lost Horizon.

Wilder, Thornton, *The Bridge of San Luis Rey. The patterns of the lives of five people who are killed when a Peruvian bridge collapses.

Eleventh Grade

Baldwin, James, *Go Tell It on the Mountain. Hard-hitting novel about Harlem Negroes who try to find meaning in religion.

Borland, Hal, *When the Legends Die. A Ute Indian boy becomes a successful broncobuster in the white man's world, but returns to his people.

Clark, Walter Van Tilburg, *The Ox-Bow Incident. Psychological story of the lynching of innocent men in early Nevada.

Crane, Stephen, *Red Badge of Courage.

Faulkner, William, *The Bear.

Hawthorne, Nathaniel, *The Scarlet Letter.

Knowles, John, *A Separate Peace. An outstanding prep school story with an "initiation" theme.

Lewis, Sinclair, *Babbitt. An attack on the philistinism and hypocrisy of middle-class business culture in the 1920s.

McCullers, Carson, *The Heart Is a Lonely Hunter. Strangely assorted personalities come together in a Southern town.

Melville, Herman, *Billy Budd.

Wharton, Edith, *Ethan Frome.

Twelfth Grade

Boulle, Pierre, *The Bridge Over the River Kwai. An ironic tale of World War II soldiers and their Japanese captors.

Bronte, Emily, Wuthering Heights.

Conrad, Joseph, *Heart of Darkness and The Secret Sharer.
Dickens, Charles, *Great Expectations and *A Tale of Two Cities.
Golding, William, *Lord of the Flies. A group of boys, marooned on
an island, regress to savagery.
Hardy, Thomas, *The Mayor of Casterbridge and *The Return of
the Native.
Joyce, James, *The Dead.
Paton, Alan, *Cry, the Beloved Country. Lyrical novel of race rela-
tions in South Africa.

Intensive Study of the Novel

The student's ability to read fiction will develop gradually through the
junior and senior high school years. But his experiences in intensive
class study of the novel are crucial because these experiences—and
there is time for but few of them—will be the milestones toward perceptive reading of the mature novel.

Three kinds of abilities need attention in intensive study of the
novel:

Those needed for imaginative entry into the novel

Those needed for perception of meaning or central purpose in the
novel

Those needed for perception of artistic unity and significance

Imaginative Entry

Imaginative entry or empathy is the first essential, otherwise the
reader is barred from an esthetic experience; he is not *reading* literature. Unless he can enter imaginatively into the work, he cannot determine for himself the meaning or purpose, though he may take someone else's word for it. And if he has not experienced literature deeply
enough to perceive its meaning or purpose, he has no business judging
its artistic unity or significance. It is our common failing that we demand judgment of literature by students before they know what the
literary experience is, and we have the sterile tradition of class periods
in which students criticize the plot, the style, the imagery, the characterization before they know how any of these relate to meaning or
central effect.

We know, of course, that some students are more imaginative than others, more ready to suspend disbelief. But regardless of quickness of imagination or inherent flair for the nonliteral, all students are capable of imaginative entry into vicarious experience merely because they *are* human and because they have had many experiences. The problem is to relate the experience recreated in the work to their own experience, and the answer lies in the identification of correlative experience. Just as the novelist expresses emotion indirectly through his work, so the reader must cull up experiences in the *general* field of emotion represented, for only occasionally can the reader's actual experience closely match that reproduced in the work. Our student reads a novel in which a man is killed, and he must empathize with the killer. He has not ever killed anyone—we hope—but perhaps he has seen someone killed. Or perhaps he has killed an animal or seen someone else do so. The reader of *Huckleberry Finn* has not traveled down the Mississippi on a raft with a runaway slave and tussled with his conscience over knowledge of law versus feeling of personal loyalty, but he probably has been in some situation which involved a conflict between his relations with an individual and his relations with society or a group. The reader of *The Old Man and The Sea* has not spent a day and night upon the ocean fighting and finally subduing a giant marlin, vainly fighting off sharks, bringing to shore, in complete exhaustion, only a great skeleton, but perhaps he *has* realized the hollowness of a victory or carried on a lonely struggle that no one has understood.

But the student must learn to *use* his experience, to examine it constantly for its relevance to the work of literature. This is not easy for, by and large, in his early years he has read in the escape tradition. Reading of literature, from the fairy tales forward, has represented escape from his experience. In general, he has learned to approach literature as something divorced from his own life, and therein, in fact, has been its appeal. His experience with television further fortifies his approach. The happenings in the horse opera or space opera or blood-and-thunder piece are related only to an unreal world to which he likes to escape occasionally. Escape is, of course a legitimate function of literature, but a minor one.

The secret of the success of juvenile fiction, the junior novel, is that it often is read literally, requiring only literal identification, with no search for correlative experience. Perhaps this is as it should be in early adolescence. Mary or Joe reads a novel about a school like theirs, a family much like their own, people like those they know, problems similar to those they are encountering. The work then has true meaning since they can find themselves in it so easily.

Abstract identification or entry, through the avenue of correlative experience, is quite another matter, but it is not beyond most high school students. What is the teacher's role? Perhaps we cannot really *teach* imaginative entry but certainly we can *promote* it. We can help, first, by selecting for study those novels which offer a legitimate chance for the student to use his experiences as the touchstone for imaginative entry; second, by helping him to think about his experiences in connection with those recreated in the work.

There is one question teachers must live with: what basis does the student have for entering into the emotional experience of this novel through plumbing of correlative experience? Most seventeen-year-olds could not be expected to identify with Jake Barnes in his frustration over the impossibility of consummating his love for Brett in *The Sun Also Rises*. Nor can most adolescents understand why the attractive and wealthy Tom and Daisy Buchanan always seem so tired and bored in *The Great Gatsby*. But even the younger student can identify with Bucky Calloway, who in Annixter's *Swiftwater* meets the dreaded wolverine on his father's trap line, because most high school students already have had to face evil in obvious form and make decisions about it. And though *A Tale of Two Cities* presents a number of difficulties, its Sidney Carton is a natural for adolescent identification. His final grand sacrifice is the stuff of adolescent dreams. Identification with Sidney Carton induces pseudo emotions, central in the esthetic experience. These pseudo emotions are not less powerful than "real" emotions, but they are more satisfying, as Aristotle said so long ago. The essential problem is to propel students from the launching pad of literal identification into the rewarding process of abstract identification. The teacher must make students aware that their experiences to date are the key to imaginative entry into a novel of whatever time, place, problem, or situation.

Thomas Hardy once wrote that the "writer's problem is how to strike the balance between the uncommon and the ordinary so as on the one hand to give interest, on the other to give reality." The student's problem is parallel: how to immerse himself in the experience of the work and yet retain his esthetic distance so as to organize the work for the perception of meaning or purpose. The word "easy" (a most slippery term when used in connection with literature) can best be applied to those novels in which very little organization for perception of meaning is required—the traditional romance, for example, in which the experience represented in the novel is exempt from the conditions that we know are usually found in reality. *The Prisoner of Zenda* is a good example.

Perception of Meaning

The second emphasis therefore should be on helping the student build those skills by which to perceive meaning or purpose in a novel, on acquainting him with the devices involved in the constant interplay of form and content. It is possible here to cite only a few examples of things students must learn if they are to perceive meaning in a novel.

In general what is required might be called the method of hypothesis in reading a novel. That is, from the very first, the reader constantly has to hypothesize about what happens, what is said, what objects or scenes are introduced. The reading becomes a matter of continually positing and testing hypotheses. Some of these hypotheses will receive sufficient test in a few pages; others, not until the book is finished and the reader has reflected on it. For example, the hypothesis that Zeena's feigning of illness is used as a weapon to control Ethan Frome cannot be finally accepted or rejected until the end of the book. This is not to suggest that any two readers necessarily will come to the same conclusions or even raise the same hypotheses, but it is the process that is important. Student interpretations will be judged, then, mainly in terms of the process the student has used in arriving at his interpretation.

It is easy and natural for the immature reader to flow along with the plot of the story, going from episode to episode, without any real consideration of the value or use of the individual episode. Such a reading makes *The Red Badge of Courage,* for example, a rather flat tale of a farm boy at war. Episodes or scenes may be used for various purposes—to reveal character, to heighten effects, to provide meaning through allegory or satire, simply to satisfy the reader's curiosity about what happened to someone or what happened as aftermath to some event. The reader, then, must be willing to hypothesize about each scene. For example, the scene from *Swiftwater* in which a boy fights and kills a wolverine, is generally symbolic of the meeting with evil and of the coming to terms with it. This is a key scene in developing the theme of a boy's growing up. In *Huckleberry Finn,* to take a far different example, individual scenes assume key importance. For instance, the scene in which Colonel Sherburn shoots Boggs and then faces down and disperses the mob that follows him to his house has broad meaning of itself in Mark Twain's view of the world. This meaning can be interpreted without reference to other things in the novel.

But, of course, individual scenes or episodes usually cannot be interpreted without reference to all the rest of the work, and the student must be willing to hypothesize not only about immediate meanings but also about the possibility of total allegorical or symbolic framework in a novel. Such hypothesis seems necessary for a sophisticated reading of *The Old Man and the Sea* or Walter Van Tilburg Clark's *The Ox-Bow Incident,* to cite two novels rather commonly taught in high school, although students might profitably read these books at lesser levels of perception.

Interpretation of symbolism especially requires use of the method of hypothesis. Yet at the mention of the word "symbolism" cautions may flicker across teachers' minds since occasionally the bright and well-meaning student "gets hot" on symbolism and mires himself in a bog of symbols. However, the reader of *The Great Gatsby* who, early in the book does not set up hypotheses concerning the use and meaning of the valley of ashes, the great dumping ground outside New York City, or of the billboard with the eyes of T. J. Eckleburg, cannot accomplish a full reading. The same is true of Conrad's *Heart of Darkness.* Here the ivory is a basic symbol. It accounts for the ruin of Kurtz and it symbolizes what may account for the ruin of mankind. Much is lost if the reader does not perceive this meaning. It may be well in this instance to direct students' reading by telling them in advance that ivory is the basic symbol. Where they go from there will be up to them.

Hypothesis is important, too, in considering point of view. How much the narrator can be expected to know is a crucial question for the student to keep in mind if he is to read discriminately. But, more important, meaning in the novel may be definitely tied up with the nature of the narrator. Why did Mark Twain force himself to see the world through the eyes of Huck Finn, Stephen Crane through the eyes of Henry Flemming, Scott Fitzgerald through the eyes of Nick Carraway, Herman Melville through the eyes of Ishmael? Though final answers may differ, unless these questions are asked, the student is not on the track of important meaning.

A not insignificant function of hypothesis may be that it is often a student's means of avoiding boredom and keeping his interest alive through dull parts of otherwise rewarding books. The author has always found it necessary to warn students about the openings of *The Secret Sharer* and *Heart of Darkness:* it takes patience to become engaged with a Conrad novel. It takes patience, too, to wade through the middle of *A Tale of Two Cities* in order to discover what it has to do with the end. In this context, the method of hypothesis may improve the student's morale if not his interpretation!

Perception of Artistic Unity and Significance

It is the rare high school teacher of literature who has not been confronted many times with the time-honored questions, "Why is this supposed to be so good?" or "What's so great about this?" These questions may only reflect the student's rebellion at being told, implicitly or explicitly, that he should appreciate this selection because it is great literature. Or, more hopefully, the questions may signal a genuine quest for insight into the literary experience. Whatever the genesis of the questions, satisfying answers to them can come only as the individual is able to perceive the artistic unity and, beyond that, the artistic significance of the novel.

I mentioned earlier the possibility of falling into the fallacy of forcing students to judge a work of art before they have made sufficient progress in the skills leading to imaginative entry and perception of meaning or purpose. The experience of too many students in studying a selection of literature is limited to reading of the piece followed by discussion in which the selection is criticized or dissected. Is it true to life?—whatever that may mean. Were the characters real? Was the plot improbable? Was the author skillful in description? These are germane questions for the classroom, but until the student has become aware of the central meaning or purpose of the work—this awareness in turn dependent upon imaginative entry—he is in no position to answer such questions sincerely.

For example, what about this much-used phrase, "true to life"? It is important to make students understand that it is verisimilitude, the appearance of truth or reality, that we are talking about, not reality itself. Literature is not life, and verisimilitude in a selection has to be judged not only by the reader's experience with life, but by life as presented in the work. Is the coincidence that brings Stephen Kumalo and Jarvis together toward the end of *Cry, The Beloved Country* contrived, if we consider all that has gone before? What about the reality of characters? It is all to the good that we have worked hard to make students aware of stereotypes of character. Yet it seems important, too, at the level of judging artistic unity and significance, to make a distinction between stereotypes and archetypes. Archetypes are a part of our mythology. Representing a type of man the archetype may be greatly individual as is Joe, who, in *Great Expectations,* is a representative of the poetic approach to life. The stereotyped character, on the other hand, lacks individuality and is based not on racial experience but on oversimplification and half-truth.

The student who is to judge the artistic unity of a work of literature must be able to recognize any discordancies: the irrelevant details and descriptions that clutter bad fiction; the forced rhymes and stale metaphors with which bad poetry is studded. The perfectly unified selection is like the equation in mathematics—everything in balance, nothing unessential. The result is a truth that is truer than real life itself.

Beyond consideration of the unity of a work of literature lies judgment of significance. Laurence Perrine poses as the ultimate test of significance in literature: "How many and how diverse are the materials which are unified in the work?" When the student reaches a level at which he can deal with this question, he will be able to assign a proper niche to the story of plot, no matter how ingenious, and he will be beyond asking, "Why can't we read this just to enjoy the story?"

THE SHORT STORY IN THE LITERATURE PROGRAM

Junior and senior high school English teachers universally find the short story a most successful form of literature with adolescents. Stories are eminently "teachable" partly because they are inherently appealing. Everyone from three to threescore years likes a story, whether in printed or visual form. Also, the magazine, the television screen, and the school anthology make the short story the most available form of literature. Furthermore, the form is especially suited for reading in common. Simply in terms of time investment, the story far above (or below) the level of individual students does not carry the same amount of penalty that the novel or drama or epic poem does; reading the short story gives the poorer reader a sense of accomplishment impossible for him to have from reading these longer forms. Most short stories can be read and discussed within one class period, and using a group of stories gives the teacher a chance to cover a great deal of ground in teaching the skills of reading fiction.

Despite the ease with which it can be used in the classroom, however, the short story should not be overstressed at the expense of the novel, for it lacks the power of the novel. Although it has been pointed out that the short story is to literature what the microscope is to science,[7] giving us otherwise impossible glimpses of experience, it cannot give the same opportunity for identification, for insight into human motivation that the novel affords. The short story's scope is "moral revelation"; the novel's, "moral evolution." [8]

Though the short story has been a major literary form since early in the nineteenth century, the last three decades have brought wide variety and experimentation in the genre, and high school students need definite training if they are to deal intelligently with many serious stories. It may be profitable to discuss with them, and illustrate by specific stories, the four "amalgamations" discussed by Mark Schorer: story method, character portrayal, attitude toward material, and style.[9]

The "older" story is narrative in method, like the older novel, proceeding, by and large, in chronological sequence with a tightly knit plot leading to a definite climax, denouement, and conclusion. In the modern period the short story has often been dramatic rather than narrative in technique, presenting a single scene, often featuring a seemingly abrupt ending, as if the curtain fell while the characters were still in full action. The contrast between a Hawthorne tale and a *New Yorker* story shows the evolution in story method. In character

[7] Ray B. West, "The Modern Short Story and the Highest Forms of Art," *English Journal*, XLVI (December 1957), 531–539.

[8] Mark Schorer, *The Story: A Critical Anthology* (Englewood Cliffs, N.J.: Prentice-Hall, 1950), p. 433.

[9] Schorer, p. 431.

portrayal the range is from the highly subjective to the highly objective. Short-story writers of the nineteenth century, particularly, furnished much direct background material about the characters, whereas in the modern story, as has been pointed out earlier, the author often forces the reader to infer the background from scanty clues to character. Dickens and Hemingway might illustrate the contrast of these extremes in character portrayal.

The author's attitude toward his material, ranging from naturalistic to symbolistic, has been discussed earlier in this chapter. The fourth "amalgamation" which Schorer identifies is that in style, from "low" to "high." Hemingway, again, illustrates clearly the "low" style. That is, his stories are written in the language his characters speak. Part of Hemingway's effectiveness lies in his ability to reproduce the speech patterns and idioms of the kinds of people he writes about. O. Henry, perhaps, is a good example of the "high" style. Though he may write about a New York City tramp, as he does in "The Cop and the Anthem," the speech patterns and vocabulary are still O. Henry's.

Classroom Illustrations

Because units on short stories and aids to teaching individual stories are widely available to teachers in the many anthologies on the market, a detailed discussion of classroom approaches to the short story seems unnecessary here. However, a few techniques that have proved effective in actual teaching situations are suggested below.

Study of magazine fiction.   Although the amount of space given to fiction in magazines has been decreasing in favor of the nonfiction article, still, because of the wide distribution of magazines in the United States, the short story is virtually at everyone's fingertips:

> More short stories are bought and read today than any other form of literature. In fact, when historians write about the twentieth century they may well decide that the short story is the typical and representative literary form of this age, just as the drama has been the great literary form in some periods and the poem in others.[10]

Study of magazines, valuable in itself in high school classes, can be tied in profitably with the study of short stories as students build crite-

---

[10] Wilbur Schramm, *Great Short Stories* (New York: Harcourt, Brace & World, 1950), p. 2.

ria for themselves by which to distinguish poor, mediocre, and superior fiction. A senior high school class might be divided into three groups, each group to study the fiction in a certain class of magazines. Group I might consider such periodicals as the *New Yorker,* the *Atlantic Monthly,* and *Harper's,* and possibly even some of the literary magazines. Group II could study such middle-grade "slicks" as *McCall's* and *Redbook,* while Group III would consider low-grade "slicks" and even the pulps. Each group would work out a descriptive "profile" of the fiction appearing in its group of magazines, with generalizations concerning plot, characters, theme, and style. Each group could then make a report to the class, and the profiles would be compared. General differences in the fiction in the various groups of magazines will become apparent, although students should be given to understand, naturally, that occasionally a truly outstanding story appears in *McCall's,* for example, while a bad story may turn up even in one of the literary magazines.

This device helps students at least to see the differences between commercial-formula and serious fiction. The reports by the groups of students probably will bring out points of difference such as those listed below, which were established by the writer's own analysis of large numbers of short stories from magazines generally considered to be "high quality" or "low quality."

1. The "low quality" stories not only have very definite plot structure but rely on several stereotyped plot patterns. Plots deal more frequently with romantic love, crime, and violent adventure than with any other subjects.

    Stories from "quality" magazines tend to have looser plots and much greater variety of subject matter.

2. Stories from "low quality" sources tend to resolve problems very conclusively and definitely. Endings are satisfyingly final. (Of course, marriage is the usual ending for the love story.)

    The stories from more literary sources frequently present no definite solutions to problems. (To the immature reader, endings often seem abrupt and mystifying.)

3. Coincidence and improbability often characterize the stories from "low quality" sources, though they are usually cast in a realistic framework.

4. Physical action is paramount in the "low quality" stories. The stories from "quality" sources often rely on psychological action.
5. The "low quality" stories rely on character stereotypes.

Plot summary device.   The author has found that the material reproduced below is useful in promoting discussion and in illustrating important points of difference between the mature and the immature short story. The material may be used, too, as an evaluating device at the end of a unit on short stories. Each item below summarizes a story up to a certain point; then three possible completing summaries are given. The student rates these three in order. The ranking of the completing summaries in each item was agreed upon unanimously by twenty college and high school teachers of English. This ranking is given in parentheses after each summary ("best" is 1; "poorest," 3).

PLOT SUMMARY EXERCISE [11]

Directions to students.   After each Roman numeral below is a summary of a short story. The summary of the story stops at a certain point. Then three summaries—lettered A, B, C—are given of how the story could be developed from that point. Decide which of these three versions would be the best development of the story—that is, which most probably would give the best quality story. Then decide which would be second best and which poorest. Rank the summaries by putting a number before each letter—1 for best, and so on. Be ready to defend your choices.

I. At Midwestern University, fraternity and sorority initiation week for freshman pledges was coming to an end. Jerry Barnes was thankful that this was his last evening of initiation. He had been doing zany stunts all week. Now he had been assigned his last stunt. He was to go to the streetcar stop, stop the streetcar as if he wanted to get on, and then put his foot on the step, tie his shoe, and thank the streetcar operator for the use of the car. So Jerry, following instructions, stopped the first streetcar. He calmly put his shoe on the step and began to tie it, but the irate operator, accustomed to college pranks, saw what Jerry was doing and kicked his foot.

[11] Teachers have permission from the publisher to reproduce the following exercise for use in individual schools.

A. Jerry sprawled backward into the street. As he scrambled to his feet, he realized that a pretty girl who had just gotten off the car was laughing. She asked if he was being initiated. He explained as they started down the street, and he told her the worst one was having to go in and ask silly questions of old "Frozen Face" McDougal, history professor. He told her what a pill "Frozen Face" was. She accepted his invitation to have a coke, and after they sat down in the drugstore, he asked her what her name was. "Helen McDougal," she answered, smiling. " 'Old Frozen Face' is my dad!" Jerry, completely embarrassed, apologized heartily. The girl laughed gaily and invited Jerry to her house "to see how Dad really is." Jerry found that Professor McDougal was very human, and he left that evening having made a date for Saturday with Helen. (2)

B. Jerry sprawled backward into the street. Hearing someone laugh, he looked up to see a pretty girl on the curb. "Are you being initiated?" she asked. Jerry told her about the initiation and they walked down the street together. He told her of all the stunts he had had to do, and she accepted his invitation to have a coke. After the coke, she invited him to her sorority house. When they reached the house, she said, "I'm afraid you'll have to go now. We're having a meeting. I'm sorry, but you'll understand. I'm being initiated, too, and I had to pick up a boy and get him to walk home with me!" (1)

C. Jerry lost his balance, slipped, and fell, his legs going under under the car, which had already started. He lost consciousness as the wheels passed over him. As Jerry recovered in the hospital, something happened to his thinking. When he finally left the hospital with an artificial leg, he knew what his purpose was. He returned to school and started a one-man campaign against the initiation week. He was determined to save others from being victims of silly and dangerous stunts. At first, he made himself very unpopular. A fraternity group threatened him. But gradually he turned sentiment to his side. Finally, through his efforts, the university outlawed the initiation week, and at a convocation, Jerry was commended personally by the president of the university. (3)

II. Old Mr. Farnsworth, millionaire, wasn't given too long to live. He had no particular illness, the doctors said, but his mind was slipping badly. The old man had no important reason for living longer. He had a million dollars with nothing in particular to spend it for. His wife had divorced him many years before. His niece and her husband, with whom Mr. Farnsworth lived, were engrossed with their own concerns. They were instructed not to let the old man out of the house alone. But one stormy night, Mr. Farnsworth was taken with the desire to go out. About midnight he managed to slip out of the house. An hour later he was hopelessly lost and half frozen in the swirling snow. A youngish woman, probably a waitress on her way home, encountered the old man groping along the deserted street. He was unable to tell her where he lived, so the woman took him to her little apartment. She installed him near a warm radiator and made coffee.

A. Meanwhile, Mr. Farnsworth's absence had been detected and the distraught niece and her husband had the police start a thorough search. Early the next morning the old man was found walking happily along a street some distance away. He told the amazed officers a strange story about a young woman who had taken him in and given him coffee. He had stolen away after she had gone to sleep in a chair. He couldn't remember where she lived now, but he insisted that his niece advertise for the woman and offer a $10,000 reward. A few months later when the old man died, the reward was still unclaimed as his disgusted niece had told her friends it would be. (1)

B. In a few minutes the old man went to sleep. Unable to find any identification in the clothes he wore, the puzzled young woman made him comfortable on the couch and dropped to sleep herself in a big chair. In the morning the old man's mind was clear. He was humbly grateful and gave the young woman his niece's telephone number. While they waited for the niece's husband to come, the young woman made breakfast and they talked. She told him about her job at the restaurant. When the old man was safely home again, he sent for his lawyer with more animation than he had shown in months. Within two days, Mr. Farnsworth had bought an attractive restaurant and installed the young woman as manager. With great enthusiasm, he went to the restaurant often and watched from a private little booth. The doctors changed their predictions. (2)

C. After talking happily for a few minutes, Mr. Farnsworth dropped to sleep. The puzzled young woman went through his pockets for identification. She found his wallet and a little diary the old man was fond of writing in. As she looked through the diary, she grew pale and trembled, and she began to shake with sobs. Now she knew who her father was, whom her mother had always refused to discuss! Here he was, in her apartment, and he was a millionaire! She put back the diary and wallet and made the old man comfortable on the couch. As she regarded him, she thought bitterly of her own life, her job in the disreputable cafe. She did not sleep. In the morning the old man's mind was clear. He was very grateful and began to thank the young woman. In tears, she told him who she was. The old man became very angry at what he thought was a trick by an unscrupulous woman. He stamped out, throwing a little money on a table as he went. He told the woman it would have been more if it had not been for her shabby trick. (3)

III. Victims of bad train connections, James F. Webster and his two business associates, Hal Russell and Winston Crane, found themselves faced with a five-hour stopover in the little town of Hutchins, sixty miles away from their home city. This loss of time was a great irritation to James F. Webster who had never lost any time in his life. It was his ability to make every minute count that had made him president of the company at thirty-six. He hadn't even taken time to marry any of the attractive young women who had come into his life. The three men decided to take a hotel room and clean up. There was only one room left vacant at the town's one hotel, not a very good room, but they took it, resignedly. Mr. Webster took a bottle of expensive liquor from his suitcase and suggested a drink. There was no room service, so Mr. Crane volunteered to go for some soda. The other two sprawled in chairs. Mr. Russell reached down and picked up a crumpled piece of paper lying on the floor. He smoothed it out and examined it lazily. Then with a smile he handed it to Mr. Webster. On the paper was scrawled "Cash on hand . . . 17.60." Then there was a column:

Jimmy's doctor bill	163.50
Back rent	52.00
Owe Thompson	15.00
Grocery	17.00
Need	246.00

Then there followed some aimless doodling. Then the notation, "Try to borrow from Mr. Hadkins."

A. Mr. Webster looked at the paper with boredom and tossed it on the table as Mr. Crane arrived with the soda. As they sipped their drinks, Mr. Webster grunted, "What a place to spend five hours!" He picked up the paper again and toyed with it idly. He noticed that the calculations had been made on the back of an envelope. On the other side was the address:

J. A. Manley
Hopkins Falls
Illinois

Mr. Webster, grinning, called the desk and asked to have a call put through to J. A. Manley in Hopkins Falls. When the call came through, Mr. Webster asked an amazed Mr. Manley if he had gotten the loan from Mr. Hadkins. When the answer was that he had not, Mr. Webster said, "Well, you will," and hung up. Handing Mr. Crane the paper, he took a coin from his pocket. "A little game of chance," he grinned. "Loser sends Mr. Manley the money he needs." Groaning, the others agreed. Mr. Webster was the loser. "First time I've lost on a coin in a long time," he complained as he reached for his checkbook. (2)

B. Mr. Webster read the note with boredom. He noticed that it was written on the back of an envelope. On the other side was the address:

J. A. Manley
Hopkins Falls
Illinois

He knew the town. It was a suburb of his home city. Suddenly he picked up the phone receiver and sent a telegram to J. A. Manley, Hopkins Falls, Illinois: "COME OFFICE J. F. WEBSTER ILLINOIS PRODUCTS CORP. TOMORROW STOP HAVE OFFER FOR YOU" The next day, a pretty but puzzled young woman was presented to Mr. Webster, who asked if she had gotten the loan from Mr. Hadkins. More amazed than ever, the woman said that she hadn't. Mr. Webster explained everything and offered her a position which the delighted young woman accepted. A few months later, the newspapers carried the news of Mr. James F. Webster's engagement to Miss Jane Manley. (3)

C. Mr. Webster read the paper. "Well, do you think the guy got the money from Mr. Hadkins?" he asked Mr. Russell with a smile.

"Naw," yawned Mr. Russell, "Mr. Hadkins probably told

him he was sorry, but times weren't good and he had expenses
of his own."

"You're too pessimistic," Mr. Webster answered. "Hadkins
probably gave him the money interest-free."

"Nuts," rejoined Mr. Russell. "The old skinflint probably has
a mortgage on the house." Just then Mr. Crane came back.
"We'll leave it up to Win to decide," Mr. Russell grinned. He
handed the paper to Mr. Crane, who looked at it blankly and
said, "I don't get it." The others laughed and Mr. Crane looked
at the paper again. Then he said, "Oh, I see. It's added up
wrong!"

Mr. Russell snatched the paper. "By Gad, it *is* added
wrong!"

As the other two men roared with laughter, Mr. Crane said,
"I still don't get it." (1)

IV. I had been seeing Sorenson at lunch for several weeks before our
conversation got beyond the point of exchanging pleasantries. He
and I usually sat next to each other at lunch. I eat at the Capitol
Cafe, which is the kind of place that has a steady lunch clientele
of clerks and bookkeepers like myself who have to live economically. We eat at large tables and everyone gets used to sitting at
the same place each day. I had been interested in Sorenson from
the beginning. He invariably ordered the cheapest thing on the
menu. He never had a desert or a cigar. He always seemed quite
preoccupied. Our conversation became more familiar at each lunch
time. I found out what firm he worked for. One evening he invited me to his home for dinner, where I met his wife, a plain,
quiet little woman. One hot day he told me his secret. For years he
had been saving, skimping on every penny, to buy a little piece
of land on which there was a supply of marble about which only
he knew. Enough marble, he said with his cheeks flushed, to make
him a small fortune. With shining eyes, he confided that in a few
weeks he would have the necessary money. An insurance policy
was to come due and it would enable him to buy the property.
After that, we often talked about it. And as the day grew near
when he would buy the property, I began to envy him and share
his excitement. Through the years, I had often dreamed of a stroke
of luck that would take me out of my humdrum existence.

A. One day, near the appointed time, he came to lunch, his face
strained and grey. He told me that the property had gone up

in price, and that he would lack $2000 of being able to pay the price. A loan was impossible; he had no security. He dared take no one into his confidence, he said. Suddenly a thought stabbed through my mind. I had a little over $3000 in savings. Hesitantly, I suggested that he accept me as a partner. He stared at me and then, as tears came to his eyes, he said, "Of course! I should have thought of you! But I had no idea. . . ." So I turned over the money to him and we signed the agreement. The next day I wanted to discuss some details with him, but he didn't appear at lunch, so I decided to go to his home that evening. He looked startled when he saw me. I noticed that he and his wife were packing. Suddenly I became suspicious. But he drew a pistol and forced me into a room which he locked. When I finally got free and reported to the police, I found that I was only one of a number of victims. The police had been looking for him for months. (2)

B. One day he didn't appear at lunch, nor the next. Curious, I called at the offices of his firm and inquired about him of a young man at a desk. "Oh, Old Marble is sick," the young man said.

" 'Old Marble'!"

"Yeah," the young man grinned. "Hasn't he ever told you about that marble that he's going to get rich on?"

"Well, yes, he has. . . ."

"I thought so," the young man laughed. "He's been telling that for twenty years. That insurance policy is always about to come due. He's told that so much he believes it himself. I think that's what keeps him going." (1)

C. A few days before Sorenson was to have his money, my firm sent me out of town on a business errand. I thought of him, envying him after I arrived home and he no longer appeared for lunch at the Capitol. I heard from him a month and a half later. He called one night, jubilant. He had allowed quarry operations to begin on his land; there was already a handsome profit. I couldn't help being chilly in my response. His success made me despair even more of my own lot. A year passed. One morning as I was reading the *Inquirer* hurriedly, some lines of print leaped out at me. ". . . week-end death toll was brought to twenty-four when F. J. Sorenson, president of Sorenson Marble Company, and his wife were killed when their car was struck by a train at. . . ." Two days later, a lawyer called at my office. Sorenson had no relatives. In his will I was the only beneficiary after his wife. I now owned the controlling interest in the Sorenson Marble Company! In later days I thought often of those lunches at the Capitol. I named my summer mountain retreat "Sorenson Lodge." (3)

RELATED ACTIVITIES

Various assignments in writing and other activities may be developed profitably from study of short stories. Susan Jacoby and Richard J. LaVigne offer the following suggestions, for example, from experience in their own classes in the John Read Middle School, West Redding, Connecticut.

1. Pass out the story without the title. Ask the class to read the story and upon its conclusion write an appropriate title. This exercise is a good way to determine whether a student is aware of the impact and content of the story.
2. Give the students mimeographed copies of a suspense story minus the crucial ending. Ask them to write an appropriate ending. Here they must be able to carry out an author's style as well as infer his intent.
3. Phrase an old problem in modern terms. With Anton Chekhov's "The Bet," for example, you might make this assignment: Take the same situation (a wager), the same people (a greedy banker, an ambitious lawyer), the same title ("The Bet") and write a conversation between these two making a wager today. (The students might base their version of "The Bet" on such issues as: the space race, segregation, and Vietnam.)
4. Emphasize the various aspects of press reporting with a variety of assignments. A story of controversy might be editorialized while one of human interest might be written for the feature page. The story itself might be reviewed either from a present perspective or by past standards if it is not contemporary.
5. Some stories leave the reader with questions to ponder. Allow students to explore these situations through composition. What came out—the lady or the tiger? The lawyer in "The Bet" is seen fifteen years after his confinement. Where is he seen and why is he seen there?
6. Have the students rewrite an incident in a short story from

another viewpoint. In Truman Capote's "A Christmas Memory" we see everything through the child's eyes. How would things look through the eyes of the reader? of the elderly cousin?

7. Take a universal theme in a story and discuss the students' attitude toward it. If it is failure, success, or greed, for example, how do the students react to these things? Have them prepare a poem, a stream of consciousness essay, or dramatic dialogue illustrating their point of view.

8. If the element of suspense pervades the plot, assign a "How would you handle it if you were—an F.B.I. agent, Sherlock Holmes, James Bond, Perry Mason, Mike Hammer, and so on?"

9. Though characterization is not a strong point of the short story, many authors have done a superb job. How can one forget Fortunato, General Zaroff, or Professor Herbert? Students can be asked to write stream of consciousness essays about character (for example, Fortunato—thoughts of a man as he sits chained behind a brick wall approaching death).

10. (a) In schools where it is possible, and especially in the junior high school, make the short story a unit in the interrelated disciplines. With the aid of the music department, find suitable music for the background of short story dramatizations. Find the same themes appearing in literature in musical composition.

    (b) In art have the students illustrate the story theme through photomontage. The following are some specific correlated art/ English projects we've developed for the stories listed:
    1. "The Bet"—metal sculpture—to create a three-dimensional piece of work based on some human conflict.
    2. "The Cask of Amontillado"—clay *en bas relief*—to explore the innate potential and deficiencies of a particular medium.
    3. "To Build a Fire"—paper construction—to construct a model house for an extreme climate exploring the varied use of paper.

11. In some instances these short stories are available as movies. Read the story. Discuss ideas which would be pertinent to the production of a motion picture—impact, selectivity, color versus black and white, closeups, cinemascope, and so on. Then view the motion picture and compare the judgments of the class. This method also provides an adequate opportunity to explore the visual media available to see how literature can be adapted from the written form for sight and sound.

12. Often these stories are available on records. Read the story; then

play the recording. Cyril Ritchard reading "The Open Window" (Saki) or Basil Rathbone reading Poe might add some new light to the story. This is a very effective technique with the slow reader.[12]

TEACHING SUGGESTIONS
FOR SELECTED MODERN NOVELS

Shane by Jack Schaefer (eighth or ninth grade)

I. *The Novel*

    A. Outline the novel by arranging the following plot incidents in the order in which they occurred.
1. Ledyard tries to overcharge for the cultivator.
2. Shane fights Chris and breaks his arm.
3. Fletcher and Wilson come to the ranch and threaten Joe.
4. Shane and Joe fight Morgan and Curly.
5. Shane knocks out Joe, straps on his gun, and goes to town.
6. Fletcher returns with the gunslinger Stark Wilson.
7. Shane meets Chris and walks off with cherry soda pop.
8. Shane arrives at the Starrett ranch.
9. Shane's gunfights with Stark Wilson and Fletcher.
10. Bob discovers Shane's gun kept in his blanket.
11. Chris comes back to the Starretts to take Shane's place.
12. Shane and Joe cooperate in removing the stump.
13. Shane shows Bob how to use a gun.

    B. Choose one of these as the turning point of the book. Be able to justify your statement. Is the turning point the same as the climax of this novel?

    C. Describe the following characters in two or three sentences each. What is the relationship of the characters to each other?
1. Marian Starrett
2. Joe Starrett
3. Red Marlin
4. Chris
5. Stark Wilson
6. Henry Fletcher

[12] From "The Super Short Story," *English Journal*, LVI (September 1967), 856–857. Used by permission of the authors and the National Council of Teachers of English.

D. What do you think Shane's past life had been? What was Shane running away from? Cite evidence in the book for your answer.

E. After reviewing the concept of a "symbol," consider Shane as a symbol. What does he represent? Do any of the other characters represent an idea or a human quality?

F. List several ways in which Shane changed the lives of the Starretts and the homesteaders in general.

G. What do you think happened to Shane after the end of the book?

II. *Collateral Work*

A. Describe in an essay how the novel might have been written from a point of view other than that of a young boy.

B. Compare the hero Shane with one of the following characters. You should tell how Shane is similar to and different from one of these heroes:
1. Matt Dillon (or a similar TV hero)
2. Robin Hood
3. Davy Crockett

A Separate Peace by John Knowles (tenth or eleventh grade)

I. *The Novel*

A. Who is the main character or protagonist? Is this a study of Finny or of Gene?

B. Do we really get to know Gene? Is he left shadowy purposely? What is his motivation in pushing Finny off the tree? What mistake does he make about his relationship with Finny? Does he ever understand Finny?

C. Consider the "roundness" of other characters such as Leper and Brinker. What do they represent?

D. What is the significance of Leper's going to war? Discuss the meaning of the later meeting of Leper and Gene.

E. What is the theme of the book? What is the significance of the title? What "separate peace" is negotiated? What symbolic moment is tied to the theme? Cite passages that further the theme.

II. *Collateral Work*

A. Write an essay discussing the novel in relation to a theme of conflict between innocence and reality.

B. Any of the following is suitable for small-group reading and oral presentation in its relation to *A Separate Peace:*
1. Joseph Conrad, *The Secret Sharer.*

       2. Herman Melville, *Billy Budd.*

       3. J. D. Salinger, *The Catcher in the Rye.*

    C. Other related novels for group reading or for individual reading, with oral or written reports, include:

       1. Dorothy Baker, *Young Man with a Horn.*

       2. Henry Fielding, *Tom Jones.*

       3. Rumer Godden, *Greengage Summer.*

       4. James Joyce, *Portrait of the Artist as a Young Man.*

       5. Conrad Richter, *A Light in the Forest.*

       6. Betty Smith, *A Tree Grows in Brooklyn.*

       7. John Steinbeck, *East of Eden.*

The Old Man and the Sea by Ernest Hemingway (tenth or eleventh grade)

  I. *The Novel*

    A. Is this a tragic novel? In what sense is the novel tragic? Consider Aristotle's definition, for example.

    B. Is this work a novel of affirmation? in what sense?

    C. Is Santiago a hero? a tragic hero? an epic hero? In what ways is he an extraordinary man? Does he differ from other Hemingway heroes, or in what ways is he like them?

    D. Is there allegory here? Is there a theme?

    E. What is the significance of Santiago's experience to others?

    F. What is the relationship between the boy and the old man?

    G. What does the novel say about the relationship between man and nature?

    H. Is there religious symbolism pervading the novel?

    I. Discuss the possible meanings of the sharks, the skeleton of the great fish, the lions in Santiago's dream.

    J. Find specific examples of the following aspects of Hemingway's unique style in the novel:

       1. Use of simple and compound sentences

       2. Naturalistic concern for authenticity of detail

       3. Sparse, objective, masculine tone and over-all style

  II. *Collateral Work*

Write an essay in which you consider the novel in relation to the following: The honorable, honest man is scarred and battered by the forces of existence. He realizes the futility but struggles only to lose. In the struggle, however, is the only meaning of life, and in the struggle, man reveals his stature and dignity. Is Hemingway's final theme dealing with the dignity of man in the face of the adversity of life?

The Ox-Bow Incident by Walter Van Tilburg Clark (eleventh grade)

I. *The Novel*

    A. Relate the time and place of the novel to the conflict with the character or characters. Would the theme of the book be meaningless if the time or the place were changed?

    B. What is the nature of the characters that brings them into conflict? Is there a main character or a protagonist? Are the characters representative of a minority group? What characters specifically represent groups and which characters are more representative of all man?

    C. Is the conflict with other men as individuals—as groups—or with intangible attitudes and institutions within the society?

    D. What is the outcome of the conflict? To what extent does the character control the outcome? To what extent does "fate" or destiny control the outcome?

    E. How does the author feel about man as indicated by this work?

    F. How does the author present the ideas? Does he give the situation without comment? Does he interpret the actions and situations of the character?

    G. Is the conflict in the novel a contemporary problem? Is the conflict also one that has always been present?

II. *Collateral Work*

Accept the hypothesis that this novel is an allegory of humanity approaching the democratic life. In an essay choose three of the following characters and defend or reject them as representing the characteristics listed below.

    Art: Everyman.

    Gil: The good-natured, simple but emotional type.

    Farnley: Meanness and viciousness.

    Canby: Vested neutrality.

    Davies: The ineffectual, liberal, intellectual reformer.

    Osgood: The ineffectual representative of religion.

    Smith: The status-seeker.

    Gabe: The completely stupid follower.

    Mapes: Organized religion that has become corrupt.

    Tetley: The fascist.

The Bridge of San Luis Rey by Thorton Wilder (tenth or eleventh grade)

I. *The Novel*

    A. The setting is significant in that it is remote in time and place, thus indicating perhaps a romantic outlook. The idea of universality is implied so that the reader looks for meaning in terms of pervasive ideas rather than specific commentary on a certain period in history.

    B. The inner life and the outer life of the characters are narrated with objectivity. The author makes no didactic commentary.

    C. The concept of truth presented is that of an absolute or divine truth.

    D. The universe is viewed as having a plan or an ordering by a divine being. Each character, having reached a kind of climax in his life, had to die. Love is regarded not as an entity in itself but as a link—love links the living and the dead through memory. The love as a link is enough; it acts as a kind of end by being a means.

    E. Man is viewed as having relatively little free will and control of his destiny. The view is not pessimistic, however, but positive, since love is central in the order of the universe.

    F. Art and the imagination and the "poetic view of experience" enter into the characters of Uncle Pio, who has a need to create; Perichole, the actress; and to some extent into the literary letter writing of Dona Maria. Implied in the work are ideas on the function of the arts and the beauty of the imagination.

    G. Generally the novel discusses manifest forms of love—love that is not completed—but the existence of the love is enough. Thus, the idea of unfulfilled love as good in itself would place Wilder generally in the romantic mode.

II. *Collateral Work*

    A. Speculate on what would have been the fate of a character had the bridge fallen. Remain faithful to the character as portrayed in the novel.

    B. Discuss the symbolism of the bridge in these terms:

        1. Its calamity brought forth a revelation of love among men. These five accident victims are raised to a "universal" level through their means of proving this love in Juniper's investigation.

2. The bridge not only brings together suffering humanity but closes the gap between this world and the next.

The Bridge over the River Kwai by Pierre Boulle (twelfth grade)

I. *The Novel*

A. Consider the novel in the tragic-ironic mode. Is Colonel Nicholson a tragic hero? Consider these four typical situations of the tragic hero in relation to Colonel Nicholson:
   1. The hero's role is basically but not solely a guilty one.
   2. While above the average man, the hero is not completely good and just.
   3. The hero is destroyed through fate or external evil, but he is not overcome with this evil.
   4. From one point of view the hero's action is guilty. From another point of view his action is innocent.

B. Consider the symbolism of the bridge. For each of the separate characters, the bridge takes on a personal meaning. The construction of the bridge may be in a larger sense considered as a means of artistic expression or as creativity. Relate each of the following statements about art to the individual perceptions of the bridge in the novel.
   1. Art is an expression of the reality of the spirit.
   2. Art is a social sharing of man's best experiences.
   3. Art is the language of emotional attitude.
   4. Art is the imaginative expression of a wish.
   5. Art is a secondhand copy of reality.
   6. Art is the play of the man.

C. Consider the novel in a unit dealing with war in literature.
   1. Discuss the setting historically and geographically and its significance.
   2. Discuss the effect of war on an individual character and/or a particular group.
   3. Discuss the conflict or conflicts in the novel. Is there resolution?
   4. Does man have a choice as to his fate in this novel? Can the characters change their destinies?
   5. What seems to be the author's point of view toward the issue of war?
   6. How is the story told? Who tells it? Is it told in chronological order, by flashback technique, or the like?
   7. Discuss the author's use of symbolism and of figurative language.

8. Can you see any relation of the structure or form of the novel to its effectiveness in communicating the theme?

II. *Collateral Work*

Consider the novel's presentation of man in relationship to the universe. In an essay discuss one of the following concepts in connection with the novel.

A. "Men are continually in competition for honor and dignity"—Thomas Hobbes

B. "Man is wholly and throughout but patch and motley"—Michel de Montaigne

C. "Man in nature is the mean between nothing and everything"—Blaise Pascal

D. "All events are interdependent and necessary"—Benedict Spinoza

E. "Perceptions are according to the measure of the universe"—Francis Bacon

F. "Struggle is an indispensable accompaniment of progress"—Immanuel Kant

G. "Man functions as an harmoniously operating 'divine machine' in a 'best of all possible worlds' "—Wilhelm Leibnitz

H. "Things are good or evil only in reference to pleasure or pain"—John Locke

I. "A cause contains as much reality as its effect"—René Descartes

J. "Good is obtained by harmonizing ideals and natural objects"—Plato

Cry, the Beloved Country by Alan Paton (twelfth grade)

I. *The Novel*

In this particular novel there seem to be nine characters—two main characters and seven very important minor characters, who should be considered separately and individually. The following questions could be asked in general about each:

A. What kind of person is he or she?

B. Describe this person, in particular the clothing and the environment.

C. Briefly give his importance in the novel.

D. Show the interrelationship among these characters.

    1. Stephen Kumalo

       Is he kind or unkind, patient or short-tempered, generous or selfish? Back up your opinion with examples. Did you feel sympathetic toward him? Would you say he is the main character—why?

2. James Jarvis

   What do you learn about James Jarvis in Chapters 18 and 19? Does he know his son? What sort of man does he portray? What do you think he felt upon learning of his son's death? Is there a great change in his attitude? Could this man be typical of the white man in Africa?

3. Arthur Jarvis

   Did we meet or read of this character? Could he be considered a living character or one we meet through the eyes of other characters? Why was he important? What was his contribution?

4. Msimangu

   Would you say this character was interesting? What do you think he means when he says, "I am a weak and sinful man, but God put His hands on me, that is all"? Why was he kind to Kumalo? What does this show about his character?

5. Absalom

   How do we know this character? What do we learn about him from the interview at the prison? during the trial? before he dies? What does this character contribute to the novel?

6. Gertrude

   What is your opinion of this character? Did she really repent or not? When she left, did you believe that she was going to become a nun? Why or why not?

7. The young white man at the prison

   Why is this man important? Is he honestly helpful or does he want to keep from failing or having the sense of failure in this case? What is his attitude in general?

8. John Kumalo

   What sort of person is he? Why was he cruel to his brother? What was his general attitude? What happened in the last meeting between the two brothers? What was your opinion of this event?

9. Stephen's wife

   Though this character is mentioned in only two places, why should she be considered a very important minor character? What is Paton saying about her when he writes, "Then she sat down at his table, and put her head on it, and was silent, with the patient suffering of black women, with the suffering of oxen, with the suffering of any that are mute"? What more do we learn about her in Book III?

II. *Collateral Work*

A. Discuss the thread of fear that runs throughout the novel.

B. In an essay discuss the paradoxical statements that are made in the novel:

1. In Chapter 6, Msimangu's statement: "I am not a man for segregation, but it is a pity that we are not apart."

2. In Chapter 22, the paradox concerning the law, justice, and being just.

3. When Jarvis, in Chapter 32, learns that there is to be no mercy, he says: "I do not understand these matters, but otherwise I understand completely."

Lord of the Flies by William Golding (twelfth grade)

I. *Preparation*

A. Discuss the possibility and plausibility that the events told in the story could actually occur in this nuclear age.

B. Instruct the students to read the novel so they can visualize the problem and the actions and decisions made to overcome it, evaluate these actions, and offer alternatives based on their own viewpoint and experience.

C. Define the British expressions that might present problems in reading and understanding the novel.

II. *The Novel*

Class discussion of the book, either chapter by chapter or on the basis of three identifiable areas of the book: the world of the game; the world of fear; and the world of reality or destruction and evil. The following are representative questions from the chapters:

A. Chapter 1

1. How is the glamour of the situation and the island conveyed to the reader?

2. What suggestions are there that this glamour may be an illusion?

3. How successful is the beginning government likely to be, and why?

B. Chapter 2

1. How secure are the rules of government and on what are they based?

2. Why do the characters feel that the other side of the island is unfriendly?

3. Where does the blame for the child's death lie?

C. Chapter 3

1. How would you describe the nature of the conflict between Jack and Ralph?

2. What is the nature of Simon's experience and feeling?

D. Chapter 4

Can degrees of seriousness and danger be distinguished?

E. Chapter 5

1. What are the expressed attitudes toward the "beast" and what attitudes to life as a whole do they imply?

2. What does "man's essential illness" mean to Simon?

F. Chapter 6

1. What is happening to the importance of the rescue?

2. What does the sign from the adult world mean?

G. Chapter 7

1. What is the difference in Ralph's view of themselves and of the sea? Why does it produce such strain?

2. Why is the ritual dance in this chapter different from other ritual dances?

3. What is the effect of schoolboy language at this point?

H. Chapter 8

In what ways can we now see that this novel is more than a boy's adventure story?

I. Chapter 9

What on the mountain is a sign of man's inhumanity to man?

J. Chapter 10

Why do none of the children fully recognize what they have done and its significance?

K. Chapter 11

1. What is the full symbolic meaning of the conch?

2. What power and desire have finally been liberated in the children?

L. Chapter 12

Is the conclusion just a trick to make a happy ending, or does it serve deeper purposes?

III. *Collateral Work*

Relate one of the following statements to the novel. Accept or reject the statement, using specific illustrations from the novel as evidence for your conclusion.

    A. A democratic society must be mutually organized for the survival of all the members.

    B. Each member must contribute to the general welfare of all.

    C. Leadership in a democratic organization entails a responsibility to all members.

    D. The more capable members must assume the guidance and control of the less experienced or less capable members.

    E. Cooperation in a democratic society must be maintained or chaos will result.

USEFUL COLLECTIONS OF SHORT STORIES

Animal Stories, Nell Murphy (Ed.) (New York: Dell, 1965).
    Twenty-two stories, some for younger readers, some sophisticated.

Best Short Stories by Negro Writers, Langston Hughes (Ed.) (Boston: Little, Brown, 1967).
    A distinguished collection of twentieth-century selections.

Beyond Belief, Richard J. Hurley (Ed.) (New York: Scholastic Book Services, 1966).
    Eight science fiction tales.

Big Woods (New York: Random House, 1955).
    The hunting stories of William Faulkner. Contains "The Bear," "The Old People," "A Bear Hunt," "Race at Morning." Excellent for use in the eleventh and twelfth grades.

Hit Parade of Sports Stories, Dick Friendlich (Ed.) (New York: Scholastic Book Services, 1966).
    Varied sports are represented, with both female and male protagonists.

The Hunting Horn, Paul Annixter (Ed.) (New York: Hill & Wang, 1957).
    A fine collection of dog stories.

Out West, Jack Schaefer (Ed.) (Boston: Houghton Mifflin, 1955).
    An unusual and varied collection of quality western stories, edited by the author of *Shane.*

Pioneers West, Don Ward (Ed.) (New York: Dell, 1966).
    Fourteen frontier stories, mostly by name writers.

Point of Departure, Robert S. Gold (Ed.) (New York: Dell, 1967).
    Nineteen stories of "youth and discovery" by modern name writers.

Stories, Frank G. Jennings and Charles J. Calitri (Eds.) (New York: Harcourt, Brace & World, 1957).

A splendid collection, highly varied in form, theme, and difficulty, with a good teacher's edition.

Stories for the Dead of Night, Don Congdon (Ed.) (New York: Dell, 1957).

A collection of horror suspense by modern writers.

Stories for Youth, A. H. Lass and Arnold Horowitz (Eds.) (New York: McGraw-Hill, 1950).

The stress is on human values—one of the best anthologies for teenagers.

The Story: A Critical Anthology, Mark Schorer (Ed.) (Englewood Cliffs, N.J.: Prentice-Hall, 1950).

A resource for the teacher. Furnishes insight into the art of the short story and contains some directly teachable material.

Tales Out of School, M. Jerry Weiss (Ed.) (New York: Dell, 1967).
Humorous school stories.

Tomorrow the Stars, Robert Heinlein (Ed.) (New York: Doubleday, 1952).

Fourteen good science fiction stories.

Treasury of Great Ghost Stories, Ira Peck (Ed.) (New York: Popular Library, 1965).

Classic stories of dark fantasy.

Twenty Grand, Ernestine Taggard (Ed.) (New York: Bantam Books, 1962).

A group of stories with great range in subtlety and variety. Several involve teenagers.

Young Love, Marvin E. Karp (Ed.) (New York: Popular Library, 1965).

Ten stories of first experiences with love, featuring John Updike, Eudora Welty, Jessamyn West, and others.

Youth, Youth, Youth, A. B. Tibbets (Ed.) (New York: Franklin Watts, 1955).

A brilliant collection of stories dealing with the problems of adolescence.

6
Teaching Poetry

Most teachers of high school English seem to agree that the study of poetry should occupy an important place in the English curriculum. At least, English teachers spend long, and often unrewarding, hours at the task of "covering" with their students the poems included in the anthologies to which so many teachers are bound. Whether this practice stems from the training and convictions of the English teacher or simply from the whims of the anthology publishers, the instinct that places special emphasis on the study of poetry is very sound.

It is a truism that there is poetry inherent in the human spirit. But, as the teacher of adolescents knows, it profits little to tell this to students. In poetry, perhaps more than in any other phase of the teaching of literature, lie the shoals of frustration, especially for the young or inexperienced teacher. Love of literature, and especially of poetry, is the characteristic bond among all teachers of English. But poetry is not popular with the majority of adolescents or of adults. In this fact of the culture lurks disillusionment for the teacher. Sam, the young college undergraduate preparing to teach English, probably has an unbounded enthusiasm for poetry. Perhaps he even strolls under the campus elms with a thin volume of verse. But then he reaches his senior year and, as a student teacher, meets his adolescent charges. Perhaps he will teach ninth graders who, redolent from the gym class the preceding hour, are not in any mood to "dig" his starry-eyed approach to all that poetry stuff. So, if Sam is truly devoted to teaching, he recovers, learns the facts of life and adolescent culture, and adjusts thereto. If not, he may get out of secondary school teaching, or stay in it and become more and more bitter toward his students and more and more unhappy within himself.

There *is* poetry in everyone; deep down beneath, where everyone really lives, lies poetry. For poetry represents one way of ordering experience and thereby of making it manageable. It may be interesting to adolescent boys to compare a poem with a formula or an equation in mathematics. Both represent a great compressing of experience into a small set of symbols. Both (if the mathematics is correct and the poem good) have nothing extraneous. Both are important ways of communicating experience. As a way of communicating and managing experience, poetry in one form or another is pervasive in modern living. One has only to look at television for a half hour to note the importance of jingles and various types of word play in advertising. And all around us are mottoes and slogans, helping to remind us who we are and what we are and supposedly helping to keep us oriented to whatever values we hold. Of course, as the semanticists remind us, there is the danger that our slogans may lead us to form tight categories—those of overgeneralization, of confusing words with the things they stand for. Yet mottoes and slogans are one form of poetry. So are proverbs, which, according to some anthropologists, started with primitive, nomadic peoples and represented a rudimentary system of laws when there were no statute books.

Poetry is not, however, only a means of communication; it has an esthetic function as well, and in this sense it reaches everyone, though not necessarily through the poems most often taught in high school and college courses in literature. There is a fundamental human need for rhythm which poetry serves, even though for some people the rhythm may be at the level of the barroom phonograph. In fact the current hits can be very useful in teaching poetry. Their use of the refrain and other devices of balladry, for example, can be compared to that in the old ballads found in almost any literature anthology.

For most people, the nursery rhyme is the first formal contact with poetry. And it is an important contact indeed. It is the rare child who does not like nursery rhymes. The child is very responsive, in general, to the esthetic possibilities of language. He likes to chant words even when he has no idea what they mean.

The seeming decline of the natural zest for poetry is the phenomenon that leaves many a secondary school teacher gloomy. What is the explanation for this decline? Probably, the answer lies partly in the nature of human growth. Poetry is emotional, and as one grows older, the emotions retreat further and further below the surface. Adolescence is particularly a time of inhibition.

But the explanation may lie partly, too, in the traditions of teaching and in the procedures used by many teachers. Two traditions in the teaching of literature, and especially of poetry, are relevant: the "academic" tradition and the "sentimental" tradition. The academic tradition implants the idea that poetry is a discipline, a rigorous vehicle for developing the mind, sharpening the powers of abstraction, and enlarging the vocabulary. Poetry can induce these accomplishments, but an emphasis on this tradition in the high school often results in painful dissection of poetry, in scansion of lines, analysis of rhyme schemes, and drill on figures of speech. Often there is compulsory memorizing and laborious, monotonous paraphrasing. Again, these elements may be important at times; certainly there are skills of reading poetry to be developed. Yet an overemphasis on poetry as discipline has undoubtedly been a factor in developing distaste for it.

On the other hand, the sentimental tradition features the sighing, rhapsodic approach, the idea that poetry is a precious form of experience reserved for the esoteric few. In this approach, normal adolescent boys may be expected to trip through the daffodils with Wordsworth when they should be reading Kipling's "Danny Deever" or Karl Shapiro's "Auto Wreck." Emoting *through* poetry is one thing; emoting *about* it, another.

How finally *do* we justify the claims we have made for the importance of poetry? Why, after all, do we say that poetry, particularly the intensive reading of poetry, should have an important place in the English program? John A. Myers, Jr., in the revised edition of this book, gave at least three reasons.[1] First of all, poetry can provide intense enjoyment, can add a rich dimension of delight in the language that is our heritage, can make us more responsive to the verbal world in which we do so much of our living. And because of this increased verbal awareness, students can find much more in and take much more from all their other reading, all their other experiences with language.

---

[1] Part of the material which John A. Myers, Jr. wrote on the teaching of poetry for the revised edition has been incorporated, with his permission, in this chapter.

Second, the close reading of poetry provides us with a kind of verbal or semantic safeguard and censor. It makes us more discriminating in our own use of language and more exacting in the standards of verbal honesty and precision we demand from others. It makes us less willing to tolerate language that is cheap and slovenly and fraudulent, less likely to fall victims to those who would manipulate us to their own ends, be they the political or merely the commercial persuaders. It is poetry, after all, that keeps the language alive and vital, that saves it from the ravages of time and hard use.

Finally, poetry extends the territory of our perceptions, enlarges and deepens and refines our emotional sensibilities, our capacity to feel—and by so doing makes us more sensitive, more responsive, more sympathetic human beings. This, indeed, may be its most important contribution to our lives. For it may well be that the crucial danger of our times is the terrible separation of thought and *feeling,* and the attendant atrophy of the imagination. Archibald MacLeish reminds us powerfully of this last and greatest contribution of poetry:

> Great poems are instruments of knowledge—a knowledge carried alive into the heart by passion . . . knowledge without feeling is not knowledge and can lead to public irresponsibility and indifference, and conceivably to ruin. . . . We are deluged with facts, but we have lost, or are losing, our human ability to feel them. . . . Slavery begins when men give up the human need to know *with the whole heart.* . . . The real defense of freedom is imagination, that *feeling* life of the mind which actually knows because it involves itself in its knowing, puts itself in the place where its thought goes, walks in the body of the little Negro girl who feels the spittle dribbling on her cheek. . . . The man who knows with his heart knows himself to be a man, feels as himself, cannot be silenced.[2]

CHOOSING POEMS

Junior and senior high school teachers and librarians are all painfully aware of the objections which students raise to poetry. Elizabeth Rose's summary of some of the complaints of junior high school pupils is still an apt one:

[2] "The Poet and The Press," *Atlantic,* CCIII (March 1959), 44–46, and elsewhere.

When the teacher has disproved the idea that all poets are strange-looking, weak creatures, he has another misconception to straighten out with the young: that poetry is written about sissy things, about sentimental love, pink and blue skies, and hosts of yellow daffodils, or about death and the serious realities of life, about sad, unhappy, far-off things and places long ago. Youth needs to be shown that all poetry is not sentimental or whimsical, moralistic or rhetorical.[3]

A first principle, therefore, in teaching poetry in either the junior or senior high school is that selections must be chosen which show the wide variety and virility of poetry and which are linked to student concerns.

To choose poems that will show the true range of poetry and its connection with everyday life, the teacher may have to go outside the ordinary classroom anthology, which tends to include traditional poems —many of which may not be appropriate for a given class at a given time. The copy machine will be an important asset here; so will the school librarian if she is willing to stock a variety of poetry anthologies. By working together, the teacher and the librarian can assemble at least an adequate collection for use in the classroom. (See the suggested list at the end of the chapter.)

In introducing students to the range of poetry and its connection with everyday experience, teachers will find the following categories of poems rewarding:

Animals and the Outdoors—"Catalogue" by Rosalie Moore; "Crows" by David McCord; "Seal" by William Jay Smith; "Giraffes," by Sy Kahn.

Machines and Technology—"Buick" by Karl Shapiro; "Steam Shovel" by Charles Malam; "Transcontinent" by Donald Hall; "Crossing" by Philip Booth; "Southbound on the Freeway" by May Swenson; "Fifteen" by William Stafford.

Sports—"The Base Stealer" by Robert Francis; "Foul Shot" by Edwin Hoey; "The Pheasant" by Robert P. Tristram Coffin.

Unusual Slants on Everyday Experience—"The Term" by William Carlos Williams; "Gamesters All" by DuBose Heyward; "Reflections Dental" by Phyllis McGinley; "On a Squirrel Crossing the Road in Autumn, in New England," by Richard Eberhart.

[3] "Teaching Poetry in the Junior High School," *English Journal*, XLVI (December 1957), 541.

Humor—The verse of Richard Armour, Phyllis McGinley, Ogden Nash.

By the time students reach senior high school, they should be growing aware of the variety of poetry, both in form and content. One might start an interesting discussion by asking a class what poetry is usually about. The answers probably will be stock ones mainly: poetry is about nature, love, death, "deep things." Then the teacher may add that poetry can be about dumping garbage and prove it with the following poem, "From This the Strength," by Fred Lape: [4]

The fog had made a twilight on the water.
The shore rocks rose, ugly and aged teeth
Of earth, discoloured at their bases where
The tide had ebbed. Upon their tops the gulls
Stood silently facing the hidden sea.

Two boys with garbage came to the land's edge.
The gulls rose in the mist, circling the boys,
Crying about their heads, gliding down air.
The boys leaned out and slung their load of waste
Over the rocks. Shrieking the gulls swept down.

Their bodies wove together by the cliff.
The strongest found the food. The others swung
In circles waiting turn, or poised on water,
Beating their wings like butterflies, or clinging
To the wet rocks, let the slow roll of surf
Surge under lifted wings. One gull flew out
With red meat in his bill. The fog received
Him in its arms; only the white tail shone,
A comet curving down the sphere of mist.
Two gulls settled upon the cliff again.
They stretched and shook their wings, and folded them
Feather by feather to their sides, like old
Housewives storing their linen into drawers.

The boys went back. The gulls had cleaned the waste
And one by one soared off into the fog.
The ugly was consumed, gone to the bone,
The sinew, feather, wing, to the sure grace
Of flight, the strength to beat against the air
And take the strong wide currents of the sky.

[4] Reprinted by permission of Fred Lape.

After reading the poem and discussing its content, the teacher should point out that this is an example of blank verse.

Or one might introduce a class to Wilfred Owen's "Dulce et Decorum Est" with its "ugly" lines:

If in some smothering dreams, you too could pace
Behind the wagon that we flung him in,
And watch the white eyes writhing in his face,
His hanging face, like a devil's sick of sin;
If you could hear, at every jolt, the blood
Come gargling from the froth-corrupted lungs,
Bitter as the cud
Of vile, incurable sores on innocent tongues,
My friend, you would not tell with such high zest
To children ardent for some desperate glory,
The old Lie: Dulce et decorum est
Pro patria mori.[5]

It may come as a healthy surprise to both boys and girls that such "unattractive" subject matter as the physical effects on soldiers of a gas attack in World War I can be the legitimate material for a poem. More important will be their realization (if it is clarified by the teacher) that when they respond with pleasure to such lines, they are responding to something infinitely more subtle and complex than the subject matter. What they are responding to, of course, is the *language* of the poem and the way in which the poet has *ordered* the various resources of language so as to give us a pleasing *esthetic* whole. The teacher can show that by his art the poet has resolved individually ugly items in the poem into an *experience of the poem* that is anything but ugly, an experience that gives not only pleasure but a kind of knowledge.

By skillful reading and then by careful questioning, the teacher can make the student aware that his response to the poem was both emotional and intellectual. Emotionally the student will have responded, albeit unconsciously, to such sound effects as the combination of alliteration and assonance in "watch the white eyes writhing" and "devil's sick of sin." Nor does the teacher have to use these technical terms to point out the onomatopoetic effect of such words as "gargling" and "froth-corrupted."

Intellectually, as well as emotionally, the student can be made to respond to the "drama" of these lines, to the bitter irony with which the speaker regards Horace's "old Lie"—"It is sweet and becoming to die for one's country," an irony that is emphasized by the rhyming of *glory* and *mori, zest* and *est*. It can be pointed out that even the most innocent tongues, deceived by dreams of glory, can be corrupted in war and that both *innocent* and *corrupted* have double meanings here. The teacher might ask if there is a connection between the "devil" simile and the idea of "froth-*corrupted* lungs." Students love word play, and they can easily be made to understand that the poet has dramatized—through his imagery, his sound effects, his tonal irony—how really *desperate* such glory can become.

Finally, young students can learn from this poem (there are three other stanzas) that it is the legitimate business of poets to use descriptive details, sometimes with no direct commentary on these details, to convey a deeply felt *attitude* toward some institution such as war.

CLASSROOM ACTIVITIES

The principal reason for including this rather vaguely and briefly titled subsection is to allow the author to make the point that enjoyment as well as understanding is an objective of teaching poetry to adolescents. Overseriousness about poetry and monotony of approach are two major pitfalls. The teacher with a great love of poetry and a feeling of mission, which it is hoped all teachers have, easily can become overserious. Monotony of approach is a particular by-product of the recent emphasis on "close reading." Reading of individual poems followed by explication is a valuable procedure, but when it drags on period after period, it can become deadly.

J. N. Hook succinctly puts the case for enjoyment:

The solution [to helping students enjoy poetry] seems to lie in doing many things with poetry—not just one thing again and again. . . . Teachers and class can (1) read aloud, (2) dramatize, (3) present choral readings of, (4) sing, (5) discuss, (6) compare, (7) write about, (8) emulate or imitate, (9) illustrate with words, (10) illustrate with pictures, (11) listen to recordings of, (12) laugh about, (13) memorize (voluntarily), (14) collect favorite poems or passages, and (15) with modern poetry, serve as co-creator.[6]

Poetry sometimes may have its closest connection with important aspects of adolescent experience, its greatest impact in the search for the "I," when it is read without being discussed or "worked with" in any way. Every person, and especially the adolescent, remains, to an extent, a bundle of inchoate thoughts, of poignant but formless feelings which lie far below the surface. Self-revelation is furthered when we find words to express these feelings and thereby give them form.

Adolescents are basically very serious people, much given to broad and vague semiconcepts which they are struggling to bring over the threshold of intellectualization. Some poems, which they may be loath to discuss, serve them well in this effort—poems, for example, of doubt and pessimism, such as those of A. E. Housman, the less sentimental poems of love, and poems of protest. One tenth-grade teacher organized a successful poetry unit around the theme "Private Moods."

It would be very easy to become wishy-washy in applying the obvious principle of having fun with poetry. The "Isn't this fun approach!" in teaching is highly suspect among adolescents. However, poetry study certainly can be a means for having fun occasionally. First, there is humorous poetry. Arthur Guiterman's "Pershing at the Front," for example, is almost sure to draw a laugh. The verse of Ogden Nash, W. S. Gilbert, Richard Armour, Phyllis McGinley, and Franklin P. Adams, among others, appeals to various senses of humor. With younger students, limericks might be a starting point in humorous verse.

Choral and group reading is another avenue toward students' pleasure in studying poetry. The teacher need not worry about turning out the kind of polished performance that might be wanted for an assembly or PTA program. The more experimental the attempts at choral reading in the regular classroom are, the better. Poems by Kipling, Poe, Service, James Weldon Johnson, and many others are appropriate for choral experimentation. Students should be encouraged to work out and suggest groupings to achieve certain effects. A simple

[6] *The Teaching of High School English,* 3rd ed. (New York: Ronald, 1965), p. 200.

arrangement for choral reading of Poe's "The Bells" is a good starting point.

Parodies are often enjoyable for adolescents, too, and can serve as a leavener even in units on serious poetry. Of course, students may write original parodies on well-known poems, or they may enjoy reading or hearing read the parodies that successful poets themselves have written. In a twelfth-grade class which has been studying English literature, for example, the reading of Yeat's "Lake Isle of Innisfree" could be followed by Ogden Nash's delightful "Mr. Fortague's Disappointment."

TEACHING STUDENTS TO READ POETRY

Enjoyment and skill go together in reading poetry just as they do in most other activities. The more interested a student becomes, the more he develops skill in reading; and the more skillful he becomes, the more interested in reading he gets. Establishing positive attitudes and arousing interest come first in teaching poetry to adolescents. But the student's friendship with poetry is likely to be short-lived unless he develops some skills and understandings important to reading mature verse.

There are many entire volumes on how to read poetry, and it is not the purpose here to attempt any comprehensive analysis of all the possible factors that might enter into mature reading of verse. Rather, the purpose of this section is to identify some elementary skills and understandings which are of legitimate concern in any high school classroom.

Students need to be made aware, first of all, that there are different kinds of poems; that poems, like short stories or novels, may have different purposes; that the form and technique of the poem, as well as the content, are designed to accomplish that purpose; and that different kinds of poems have to be read in different ways. In a narrative poem, the reader must be able to follow the plot just as he must in reading fiction. A didactic poem must be read slowly and reflectively, and paraphrased, to get the meaning. On the other hand, the poem which seeks merely to create a word picture or sensory impression—Sandburg's "Fog," for instance—cannot be paraphrased. Essential to reading most poetry is the ability and willingness to let the imagination be completely free to make what it can of the lines. Students need to discover, through group reading and discussion, that it is often worthwhile to reread a poem a number of times.

The mere mechanics of poetry may cause difficulty to some students—especially in the junior high school—who have a tendency to read line by line, letting their voices fall on the right margin, whether or not there is any punctuation to mark a stop or pause. Naturally, this kind of reading, oral or silent, can make comprehension impossible. Students have to be taught to observe punctuation in poetry as in prose. Again, oral reading by the teacher and group reading by the class can help.

Inversion in word order, characteristic of poetry, poses another difficulty for many students who might read through the following lines with no idea of the subject-predicate relationship:

> Full many a gem of purest ray serene,
>   the dark unfathomed caves of ocean bear

Ellipsis, also common in poetry, is a related difficulty in lines such as:

> Stone walls do not a prison make,
> Nor iron bars a cage

These difficulties are especially prominent in poetry of earlier periods with which senior high school students must deal in their anthologies. It is not unusual for the student to reach twelfth grade without a good orientation to the peculiar syntactic devices of poetry. In short, a starting point is to teach the student that in reading poetry, as in reading anything, he must be clear on the syntax.

The author has found it helpful to introduce students to the basic "pattern" of much lyric poetry. Many lyric poems fall basically into three parts. The first part is an expression of the experience that triggered the poem; the second, an immediate reaction to the experience, possibly just the expression of a mood or image; the third, some kind of universal application of the experience or broader reflection on its meaning or effect. In Karl Shapiro's "Auto Wreck"—a fine selection for teaching in high school—we have first the image of the ambulance, pulsing red light, racing to the scene of the accident where the mangled bodies are put aboard; then we have the immediate reaction, the stunned feelings of those who witnessed the accident, their banal remarks; finally, we have the reflection, a wonderment at the senselessness of this kind of death. If someone were to count all the lyrics in the language, he might find more that do not fit this pattern than do, but enough do fit to make the approach helpful.

Most artistic poetry can be interpreted at various levels of meaning. Robert Frost's much-explicated little poem, "Stopping By Woods on a Snowy Evening," for example, can be interpreted quite legitimately on at least three levels. First, it may be a poem about a man who stops to enjoy the beauty of a snowfall in the woods at night, but who can't stay long because he must get home. Second, it may be a poem about a man whose need to hurry on from a scene of beauty reminds him of the general way of life, the need for allegiance to responsibility. Finally, it may be an expression of the death wish, with the dark woods symbolizing death. Students should be encouraged to start with the simplest interpretation they can support and to branch out from there. Frequently students, especially bright ones, feel that if they cannot come up with an esoteric, far-out interpretation they have not done well. Other students, awed in the presence of serious poetry, feel that there is one official interpretation of a poem which can be unlocked by those who somehow have been admitted into the mysterious inner circle.

ANALYSIS OF POETRY

Since poetry embodies certain formal characteristics that distinguish it from other forms of literature and that figure prominently in its discussion and analysis, sooner or later the student will have to become familiar with certain technical terms used to identify these characteristics. Just as the study of grammar, usage, and rhetoric provides the teacher and the student with a common vocabulary for discussing writing problems, so poetry has its own "grammar," which can help to expedite and sharpen any discussion of a poem. Much as we desire the student's experience of the poem to be a felt synthesis of all its elements, we cannot teach a poem without being able to converse intelligently about its separable parts: its diction, its imagery, its figures of speech, its controlling metaphors, its sound effects, its tone, its dramatic structure, its rhythmical movement, even its punctuation and its grammar. The terms used to identify and describe these elements and their functioning should be kept to the very barest minimum, at least until the tenth grade; but there is no reason why the average student, in the upper two or three grades, should not be able to recognize and use such concepts as connotation and denotation, imagery, metaphor, symbol, and allusion. On the other hand, much more important than being able to distinguish between metaphor, simile, metonymy, synecdoche, and personification is the understanding of the *principle* of metaphor in its broadest sense, which is the analogical or comparative principle fundamental to poetry. As one writer reminds us, metaphor in its largest sense "is not, as we were taught at school, a figure of speech. In language it is the means by which we extend our awareness of experience into new realms. Poetry is a part of this process of giving apparent order to the flux of experience." [7]

As the student matures and gains more experience with language analysis, he should be able to recognize and manipulate the more intellectual terms related to *tone* in poetry: irony, understatement, overstatement, paradox. He should gradually become acquainted with the terms by means of which we describe the *sounds* of poetry: alliteration, assonance, consonance, onomatopoeia, and rhyme schemes.

Most difficult and perhaps least important in the student's equipment for reading poetry is the whole area of prosody and the various line and stanza forms. There is nothing intrinsically difficult about learning and recognizing the five basic feet in English poetry (iambic, trochaic, anapestic, dactylic, and spondaic) and the names for the number of feet per line (tetrameter, pentameter, and so on), and there is no particular reason for avoiding these terms; but nothing is more futile than having the student indulge in scansion *for its own sake*. If advanced students can be taught to relate meter and metrical variation (along with various sound effects) to the *sense* of the poem, if they can learn to view these aspects functionally and see their contribution to the *total meaning* of the poem, there is no reason for the teacher to hold back on them. But this is a subtle business, difficult for even the most experienced English teachers, and more time has

[7] David Holbrook, *English for Maturity* (New York: Cambridge, 1961), p. 69.

probably been wasted in the classroom on prosody than on any other aspect of the teaching of poetry.

Poetry analysis can be an exciting and enormously profitable intellectual experience for young students, but the teacher must remember that analysis should always be followed by synthesis or there has been no real response to the *whole* poem, which is always greater than and different from the sum of its parts. The terminology of poetry can easily become abstract and meaningless for the student, and a teacher's preoccupation with it can leave a student feeling that poetry is nothing more than an elaborate and boring system of jargon.

If, however, there are many traps for the teacher to avoid in teaching poetry, there are a number of tried and proven paths by which he can safely lead the student into the poem. It is not within the scope of this chapter to describe in detail the process of poetic analysis. Besides, there are so many excellent critical anthologies available today in inexpensive editions, and so many exegeses of individual poems, that no English teacher need remain uninstructed in these techniques. But it may be helpful to list some questions which teachers can ask, and train their students to ask, about any poem. The order in which these questions are asked and the different emphasis that each is given will depend upon the individual poem.

Who is the *speaker* of the poem (for all poems have a speaker, who is either a projection of one of the "selves" of the poet or a character created by the poet for a particular occasion and purpose) and what can you tell about him from his diction and his tone of voice? Whom is the speaker *addressing* and what is the *occasion* for this particular utterance? What is the *setting* in time and place? What is the purpose of the poem? What is its *theme* or underlying idea or main concern? Can you paraphrase the poem? How does the poem's *diction* and *imagery* contribute to its *tone*? What examples of figurative language do you find in the poem and what do these contribute to the overall effect? Do they seem appropriate? Is there a *pattern* to the imagery? the figures of speech? What evidence is there of *progression* in the *structure* of the poem? Are all the steps in the "logic" of the poem provided? Does the poem contain any words that can be regarded as *symbols*? Can the whole poem be regarded as an allegory? If so, what is the allegorical meaning? Are there any *allusions* and why has the poet used them? Do you find examples of *understatement, overstatement, irony, paradox?* What is their function? What striking devices of sound and meter do you find? How is the sound "an echo to the sense"? Do you understand the *syntactical structure* of each of the poem's sentences?

Grouping Poems for Study

Most experienced teachers agree that sustained units of poetry are usually unsuccessful. Poetry is too rich and concentrated for large dosages at one time; normal reading of poetry by mature adults does not proceed ordinarily in a systematic, day-after-day pattern. Of course, class study cannot be organized to fit the vagaries of individual mood, but it seems wiser to intersperse poetry with the reading of other types of literature than to concentrate it in long units.

Nevertheless, it is valuable occasionally to group poems in some logical fashion. Many of the literature anthologies which are organized chronologically or by literary types may tend to obscure the natural grouping which can be made for class study. Simple themes or topics may often provide the unity for a one- or two-day unit of poetry. For example, the teacher may choose the following poems on death: Seeger's "I Have a Rendezvous with Death," Arnold's "The Last Word," Browning's "Prospice," Tennyson's "Crossing the Bar," Landor's "Finis," and Stevenson's "Requiem." Then he may ask the students to match the poems with the following statements:

I have a meeting by appointment with death. (Seeger)
Death is rest. (Stevenson)
Death is the final defeat. (Arnold)
Death is an embarking. (Tennyson)
Death is a looking forward. (Browning)
Death is the end. (Landor)

In thematic organization of literature, the teacher might frequently introduce poems to reinforce and clarify the themes studied through prose. In one anthology of short stories, a story is often followed by a poem which treats a similar theme; thus Willa Cather's "Paul's Case" is followed by Robinson's "Richard Cory," and Roald Dahl's "The Great Automatic Grammatisator" (in which a machine is built which writes fiction) is followed by Stephen Vincent Benet's "Nightmare Number Three."

With twelfth-grade classes, the author found successful a unit on love, in which poetry and a few prose selections were used. The teacher opened the unit by commenting that probably more poems had been written about love than about any other subject, and that these poems, spanning centuries, reflected certain attitudes toward love. A group of light or cynical poems was read first: Housman's "When I Was One and Twenty," Thomas Moore's "The Time I've Lost in Wooing," Edward Vere's "A Renunciation," Suckling's "The Constant Lover" and "Why So Pale and Wan?" Herrick's "To Virgins, To Make Much of Time." Then Thomas Hardy's humorous short story, "Tony Kytes, the Arch-Deceiver," was read. After this, the class made a collection of the lyrics of the hit tunes of the moment, and compared them with some of the poems they had already read. A certain amount of hilarity went with learning at this point.

Next, a group of short poems, more serious in tone, all addressed to a particular lover, was considered: Herrick's "To Althea Who May Command Him Anything," Jonson's "To Celia," Burns's "A Red, Red Rose," Wordsworth's "She Dwelt Among the Untrodden Ways," Byron's "She Walks in Beauty," Shelley's "The Desire of the Moth," Conrad Aiken's "Music I Heard With You," and Witter Bynner's "Voices." The unit concluded with the reading of several short stories dealing with love, and a one-act play, "The Will," by James Barrie.

"People in poetry" is a subject that furnishes a good entree with adolescents who, like adults, are fundamentally interested in people. Treatment of this subject might form the basis for a unit, or might be incorporated in a unit of biography. Whatever the approach, there are many good poems about people, character studies in verse, from Chaucer to the present. Roger Hyndman describes an approach in which Robinson's "Richard Cory" is the first poem studied in eleventh-grade American literature:

> To prepare my pupils for a reading of the poems, I tell them that we are about to meet an outstanding inhabitant of an imaginary town. On the board they see written *Tilbury Town* and beneath it is a list of such notable names as Richard Cory, Miniver Cheevy, Bewick Finzer, Reuben Bright, Aaron Stark, Annandale, Cliff Klingenhagen, Uncle Anan-

ias, Flammonde. (Copies of these poems are available in the classroom library.) Richard Cory and his follow citizens, I explain, are the creations of Edwin Arlington Robinson, a writer reared in a small Maine community.[8]

Theme, of course, is not the only basis for grouping poems, as Stephen Dunning points out in his excellent treatment:

> Clusters can be arranged in many ways; the grouping principle need be valid only for a particular purpose. . . . One handful of poems represents a particular poet; variations on a given theme or subject; poems alike (or dramatically dissimilar) in form make up other sets; poems may be grouped for study of similar metaphors, for their uses of irony, and for similar narrative techniques. Ideally, groups of poems should show a progression toward difficulty and from emphases that are readily understood to emphases that are substantially demanding.[9]

Not all students—indeed, only a few—will leave the English classroom as avid readers of poetry. But the realization by many, through their experiences while in the classroom, that poetry speaks out of the depths of human need gives an important dimension to the task of the teacher of literature.

SELECTED BIBLIOGRAPHY

Collections of Poetry

A Journey of Poems, Richard F. Niebling (Ed.) (New York: Dell, 1964).
A paperback collection of poems for young people by selected British and American poets.

Story Poems New and Old, William Cole (Ed.) (Cleveland: World, 1951).
A paperback narrative collection especially appropriate for younger adolescents.

Cavalcade of Poems, George Bennett and Paul Molloy (Ed.) (New York: Scholastic, 1967).
A paperback collection of poems selected by high school students and the editors. Groupings are highly appropriate to adolescent interests.

---

[8] "The First Poem," *English Journal,* XLVI (March 1957), 158.
[9] *Teaching Literature To Adolescents: Poetry* (Glenview, Ill.: Scott, Foresman, 1966), pp. 75–76.

Poems for Seasons and Celebrations, William Cole (Ed.) (Cleveland: World, 1961).
Poems for all the major holidays and seasons.

New Negro Poets: U.S.A., Langston Hughes (Ed.) (Bloomington: Indiana University Press, 1964).
Poetry written by young Negro poets on a wide range of themes.

Sprints and Distances, Lilian Morrison (Ed.) (New York: Crowell, 1965).
A valuable book of poetry about sports.

Imagination's Other Places, Helen Plotz (Ed.) (New York: Crowell, 1955).
An unusual collection of poetry related to the sciences and mathematics.

Poems for Pleasure, Herman Ward (Ed.) (New York: Hill & Wang, 1963).
Poems selected by the editor's senior high school classes.

Immortal Poems of the English Language, Oscar Williams (Ed.) (New York: Simon and Schuster).
A paperback anthology covering the whole range of British and American poetry.

Stories in Verse, Max T. Hohn (Ed.) (New York: Odyssey, 1961).
An excellent collection of narrative poetry, with reading directions for students.

Story Poems, Louis Untermeyer (Ed.) (New York: Pocket Books, 1961).
Narrative verse—serious, fantastic, and humorous.

The Magic Circle, Louis Untermeyer (Ed.) (New York: Harcourt, 1952).
For young readers—narrative and dramatic poems.

A Gift of Watermelon Pickle and Other Modern Verse, Stephen Dunning, Edward Leuders, and Hugh Smith (Eds.) (Glenview, Ill.: Scott Foresman, 1967).
A beautiful volume of contemporary poetry brilliantly geared to adolescent concerns.

Poems for Young Readers (Champaign, Ill.: NCTE, 1967).
Selections from their own writings by poets who attended the Houston Festival of Contemporary Poetry, 1966, with commentaries by the poets. An accompanying record of the readings of the poems by the poets available from the NCTE.

The Teaching and Reading of Poetry

Brooks, Cleanth, and Robert Penn Warren. *Understanding Poetry* (New York: Holt, Rinehart, and Winston, 1960).

Holbrook, David, *English for Maturity*. *2nd* ed. (New York: Cambridge, 1967). Ch. 5.

Perrine, Laurence, *Sound and Sense: An Introduction to Poetry* (New York: Harcourt, 1963).

Dunning, Stephen, *Teaching Literature to Adolescents: Poetry* (Glenview, Ill.: Scott, Foresman, 1966).

College Entrance Examination Board, *12,000 Students and Their English Teachers,* "Poetry."

7
Drama in the Literature Program[*]

Despite the very notable increase in publication of plays in paperback or special anthologies, drama still must be regarded as the Cinderella of the secondary classroom, a kind of stepchild relegated to fourth position after short stories, novels, and poetry. True, probably more plays are being taught in American high schools today than in any preceding decades. Such standard Shakespearean choices as *The Merchant of Venice, Julius Caesar,* and *Macbeth* have been supplemented by *Our Town, The Miracle Worker, The Glass Menagerie,* and frequently *Oedipus Rex* and *Antigone.* O'Neill is also likely to be represented by an inoffensive one-act and a biographical sketch, while the widely anthologized *Pygmalion* and *Arms and the Man* guarantee a painless showing for Shaw. Some communities, such as Providence, Rhode Island; New Orleans; and Los Angeles, are especially fortunate to have specially established resident companies, created and supported by government agencies to produce high-caliber drama for high school students and to stimulate wide-spread interest and involvement in drama, music, and art. The fact remains, however, that for far too many teachers drama continues to constitute a kind of pleasant interlude between the seemingly more serious concerns of the curriculum, a pleasant diversion inserted to make the daily routine more palatable.

This situation is not surprising when we consider both the problems of the contemporary theater and the limited drama background of most classroom teachers. Modern drama is clearly in a period of tran-

* Written by Gladys Veidemanis, Oshkosh High School, Oshkosh, Wisc.

sition, struggling to define new forms and even its place in American life. And along with the other performing arts, the theater is in serious financial trouble. As attested by the continually dwindling output of new plays each year, the Broadway theater is steadily losing in the struggle against spiraling production costs, outmoded theater buildings, and off-Broadway competition. Further, the theater is failing to attract the kind of adventurous, tolerant audience it needs if it is to progress—a dedicated following willing to support new plays and playwrights, not just sure "hits" and name-star musicals. Unfortunately, as the Rockefeller Report on the Performing Arts so candidly asserts: "As a nation we have traditionally possessed no great thirst for music, dance, drama; if anything, we have inherited a suspicion that the practice of these arts is unmanly and superfluous and that support of them is of no vital importance to our national well-being." [1] For most Americans, "live drama" still means a junior or senior class play or possibly attendance at a community theater production once or twice a year.

How necessary it becomes then to reassert drama's rightful position in the curriculum and the English teacher's responsibility to develop in students interest in and support of quality drama in all its forms. What emphasis drama should be given can best be demonstrated by a discussion of why it should be taught, what should be taught, and how.

DRAMA—A MIRROR OF LIFE AND OURSELVES

Why teach drama? Perhaps the most important reason is to discover more about what it is to be a human being, for man, in all his complexity and conflicts, constitutes the central subject matter of drama. Drama not only mirrors the environment, but helps us to surmount it, to grow in sympathy, imagination, and understanding. The very root of the term "drama"—the Greek *dràu,* to act, to do—suggests its possibilities: it is perhaps our most effective and direct means for depicting and working out social conflicts, moral dilemmas, and personal problems without suffering the specific consequences of our actions.

[1] Rockefeller Brothers Fund, *The Performing Arts: Problems and Prospects* (New York: McGraw-Hill, 1965), p. 184.

The dramatist compels us to empathize with the play's protagonist, to feel his emotions, and to experience his conflicts, yet spares us the actual suffering or indignity his characters must endure. Through tragedy, we are enabled with little pain to learn what life could so painfully teach and are provided a vision of man's endurance and nobility to admire and emulate. Through comedy we can enjoy the purging of laughter, the revelation of "human beings for what they are in contrast to what they profess to be." [2] Well-wrought melodrama, fantasy, or farce can dispel our skepticism, enlarge our imaginations, and take us temporarily out of ourselves. It is not surprising, therefore, that drama has become a recognized tool for therapy. Psychiatrists, for example, frequently utilize psychodrama as an effective means of enabling patients to gain insight into their past experiences and to prepare them in advance for "roles" they will have to resume in normal life. Sociodramas have been found to perform a similar function for small groups, enabling participants to assume fictional identities while working out conflicts that face them in family and community living.

Drama, then, must be viewed as an essential humanizer, a spur to imagination, to insight, to reflection, and, hopefully, to self-knowledge. Appraising the importance of the dramatic arts, business executive Fletcher B. Coleman, speaking at the dedication of the dramatic arts building at Illinois Wesleyan University, so eloquently commented:

> Are the dramatic arts important? Do they serve the welfare of a free society? I think they do for these reasons.
>
> They hold up the mirror in which society can see itself. They give life, impact, form and substance to the printed word. They stimulate popular support for noble goals; they prick pomposity. They bring light and color and sound and movement to great ideas. They resurrect history and remind us of its lessons.
>
> The dramatic arts rephrase and refreshen a society's ideals and aspirations and remind it of its failure. They help man see himself in an infinite variety of contexts. They bring to life experiences and situations remote in time or distance—they let us share the cultures of other peoples and give us new insight into the many worlds in which we live.

[2] Louis Krononberger, "Some Prefatory Words on Comedy," in Marvin Felheim (Ed.), *Comedy: Plays, Theory, and Criticism* (New York: Harcourt, 1962), p. 195.

They can probe as no other medium can into man's mind, his societies, his institutions. . . .

Yes, we are in a race with Russia, but we are locked in a larger combat . . . This is man's unending war with himself, his higher nature against the base animal, his age-old wavering choice between the bright stars and the black abyss, between his visions and venality.

From Aristophanes and Sophocles to O'Neill and Williams, this is the battle to which the dramatic arts have always been committed.[3]

The dramatic arts are actually the most direct link we have between literature and life.

DRAMA REDEFINED FOR THE TWENTIETH CENTURY

What drama should we teach? To consider only those works performed on the legitimate stage as "drama" would be tantamount to turning our backs on the mass media revolution that has permanently altered the character of American life and education. But to consider only television and movies as the theater of today betrays an equally limited perspective. We need, therefore, a broadened definition of drama that encompasses its various contemporary manifestations— living theater, television, and motion pictures—and which recognizes each as fulfilling valuable and complementary functions. That these media compete for attention is surely true, but to assume that one form need eclipse another, as some critics insist, is to overlook the distinctive features of each. Their very differences suggest a starting point for the teacher of English, who could profitably utilize a comparative approach to convey to students the rich possibilities of each medium.

Class discussion might be opened, for example, with the problem of what happens to Wouk's *The Caine Mutiny* when transferred from the stage to the movie lot to the television studio. As Father John Culkin first noted, the emphasis in this work has been shifted in every medium in which it has been presented.[4] In the novel, Willy Keith, the immature sailor who advances to self-knowledge, is the indisputable hero. The U.S. Navy dominates the film version, very likely because

[3] As cited in *The Milwaukee Journal* (Nov. 5, 1962), p. 22.
[4] Father John M. Culkin, S.J., "Of Media Study and Male Alligators," speech presented at NCTE Convention, Miami, Florida, Nov. 24, 1962.

of its more elaborate sets and sweeping camera eye. In the stage production, Greenwald, the intellectual, emerges as the commanding figure, while in the televised cutting, Captain Queeg preempts attention. Other works could be similarly analyzed. What happens to a *Pygmalion* when transformed into *My Fair Lady,* or to an *Advise and Consent* that moves from the massive novel to the stage, then to film? Or to *Romeo and Juliet* updated as *West Side Story?* And what transmutations can be traced in the Arthurian legends as they have come down to us through Tennyson, T. H. White, and *Camelot,* on stage and screen? By means of such comparisons, teachers can very effectively lead students to discover that one medium need not replace or imitate another but rather enhance, complement, and extend it more fully and richly.

In widening our definition of drama to include television and film, we must also emphasize the need for attention to drama of all periods. Without in any way undermining the value and appropriateness of the Shakespearean perennials, we would have to argue that one-sided attention to a few plays from a single historical period does injustice to the tradition from which they arose and which they helped to perpetuate. Students need to experience not only Elizabethan tragedy, but also the comedy of manners, farce, melodrama, and fantasy, and to discern for themselves the recurring themes, dilemmas, and human needs reflected in drama of every age. They should have the opportunity to discover that an Antigone joins hands across the centuries with a John Proctor of *The Crucible,* choosing personal integrity and death rather than life with dishonor; that a Medea shares the agony of jealousy with a passionately tormented Othello; that a fervid Lavinia in O'Neill's *Mourning Becomes Electra* emulates the vindictiveness and persuasiveness of her Greek counterpart, if not her enduring nobility.

Most important, we can not afford to exclude from the classroom representative drama since World War II. Young people who have personally witnessed on their television screens such events as the murder of a President's assassin, rioters plunging through the streets of Watts and Detroit, and daily views of American soldiers in ugly combat in Vietnam are not likely to be shocked by the recurrent themes of cynicism, violence, and alienation in contemporary drama. It is to be hoped that the experience of such works as Ionesco's *The Bald Soprano,* Albee's *The Zoo Story,* Sartre's *No Exit,* even Tom Stoppard's

Rosencrantz and Guildenstern Are Dead can underscore the need for genuine communication and love in a world that seems otherwise illogical and meaningless. *The Diary of Anne Frank,* Bolt's *A Man for All Seasons,* and Duerrenmatt's *The Visit* portray not only the evil of which man is capable, but also the nobility and endurance of the human spirit in the face of oppression. We indeed owe our students the critical and enlightening view of their own world that contemporary drama can uniquely provide.

OBJECTIVES FOR DRAMA TEACHING

Having broadened the definition of drama and affirmed its values in the English program, we need to formulate specific objectives that can, in turn, determine the nature and amount of drama emphasis at a particular level. These objectives should of course be defined within the larger context of the overall goals for the course and should include emphasis on the development of the skills of thinking and communication for which the total English program assumes major responsibility. The following set of objectives suggests goals that could be reasonably attempted in a four-year high school drama program:

Develop pleasure and skill in reading and interpreting drama, and acquaint students with some significant dramatic works and lists of plays for future reading. On the whole, the difficulties entailed in reading plays have probably been overstressed. Most students genuinely enjoy reading plays; and while they have to learn to interpret stage directions and to visualize scenes for themselves, they are rewarded by getting a lot in a short time, by fewer vocabulary problems than often face them in novels or short stories, and by peaks of action in every act. We would have to agree with Maynard Mack that "drama is by far the easiest of all the literary forms to make exciting in the classroom . . . and it is also the most effective introduction to the pleasure of reading literature and the skills involved in enjoying it." [5] We would also have to agree that unless a person learns to enjoy *reading* plays, he will never discover most of the great dramatic works

[5] Maynard Mack, "Teaching Drama: *Julius Caesar,*" in Edward J. Gordon and Edward S. Noyes (Eds.), *Essays on the Teaching of English* (New York: Appleton-Century, 1960), p. 320.

of the past, which are so rarely performed in our theaters. For that matter, he will know very little about contemporary drama, since only "smash hits" stay on Broadway and most community theaters cautiously limit their production choices to a few well-known and proven works.

Acquaint students with the dramatic tradition, the role of drama in the history of man. Since drama is so integral a part of our literary and cultural heritage, the study of its rich and varied history is warranted for its own sake as well as for its value as background against which to appraise the theater of our own day. The program of study, however, should concentrate less on the surface history of drama, more on the causes for the emergence of particular dramatic forms and theaters during different historical periods. For example, students better perceive the intentions of tragedy once they realize that it has been the product not of disillusioned, depressed cultures, but of societies, such as those during the times of Sophocles and Shakespeare, that most prized individual resourcefulness, personal freedom, and human happiness. As William Van O'Connor suggests: "The Greeks' joyful consciousness of life sharpened their awareness of death. . . . When life lost its zest for the Greeks the tragic muse departed." [6] Similarly, the comedy of manners or satirical drama should be seen in the context of the Restoration Period, broken loose from a decade of Puritan austerity, or of the eighteenth century, with its surface proprieties, material concerns, and inflexible class distinctions inviting the playwright's mocking or witty scrutiny.

Students should also be led to analyze the ways in which audience expectation and the actual shape of the theater building have affected the form and content of drama. Recent developments in the American theater are illustrative: The present movement away from realism is being accompanied by a parallel movement away from formal staging, confining sets, explicit stage directions. We would not be exaggerating to suggest that probably the most significant—and precedent-setting—dramatic event of our century was the erection of the Stratford, Ontario, theater building, which discards the proscenium arch and the box seat, with their rigid frame around life, and brings the audience back again into more immediate contact with the play.

[6] William Van O'Connor, *Climates of Tragedy* (Baton Rouge: Louisiana State University Press, 1943), pp. 21–22.

Develop critical standards and taste in drama, film, and television.
In a memorable and still pertinent editorial in the *Saturday Review*
for Nov. 21, 1959, Norman Cousins accused television of perpetrating
a massive fraud—not that publicized by quiz show scandals, but the
incessant exploitation of crime and the glamorizing of violence. He
condemned, in particular, the excessive brutality on many programs,
their obvious indifference to the fragility and value of human life.
These objections have even more basis when applied to the majority
of present-day film and stage offerings, whose "adult entertainment"
formula or "subterranean nihilism" (so characterized by drama critic
Robert Brustin)[7] makes them increasingly questionable for immature audiences. As Mr. Cousins originally suggested, what is really
most disturbing is not the candid treatment of sex, crime, and abnormal behavior nor, indeed, the total moral revolution reflected in our
mass media, but rather the possibility that young people may gradually be losing the capacity to be shocked, moved, or delighted by
what they experience. Like their parents, today's generation is discovering only too quickly that unprecedented affluence, personal freedom, and uninhibited opportunities for leisure are no guarantee of joy
in art or in living.

Good taste and genuine pleasure in the arts can never be forcefully
imposed but they *can* be nurtured in classrooms which maintain lively
exposure to and dialogue about the dramatic arts. One of the first
tasks the teacher should undertake is to help students become more
articulate about the films and plays they see, less ready to make monosyllabic or cliché responses. Students also need to discover publications with provocative discussions and evaluations of the mass media
and should be asked to apply their own critical standards to current
television productions, films, and plays. They must also be taught to
evaluate drama both as art and as craft, as a medium demanding integrity, self-control, significance of theme and language, discipline of
body and voice, fusion of spectacle, technique, and idea. Through
such experiences, they should gradually learn to distinguish the artistic
and original production from the tawdry or imitative, to be able to
enjoy such phenomena as "multimedia happenings," yet be able to
place them in a larger cultural context than the transitory present.

[7] Robert Brustein, *Seasons of Discontent* (New York: Simon and Schuster,
1965), p. 310.

Encourage interest in playgoing and the support of community ventures in drama. Playwright Marc Connelly once commented that the United States is the only country that seems not to recognize the importance of theater to "national health." [8] He was, of course, implying a need for subsidies to the arts, especially in these times when production costs have become so prohibitive. His remarks remind us, however, that unless the school stimulates interest in playgoing, both through planned theater trips and regular publicizing of worthwhile community productions, the majority of our students will probably never shift from exclusive patronage of motion pictures and television, the less expensive and more accessible media. In addition, we must do more to encourage young people to support not only the tested and established drama, but the new—and on faith. Professor Ronald Mitchell advises:

> Let us be theatregoers, but not just "fashionable" theatregoers, seeing only those plays "everyone sees." This type of person is proud to wait for his tickets, pay double, and lord it over the person who is still waiting. Everyone then having seen the same thing—there is nothing to talk about! [9]

We need to educate students to determine hits for themselves and to resist the blinding power of the critic, whose judgment is surely fallible.

Increase students' understanding of the importance of drama as a source of insight into personal and social problems. As their tastes refine, young people should also grow in understanding of others and of themselves through the study of drama. George Jean Nathan said that great drama speaks to man "in solitude and in crowds"—and we know what he meant. We have all been lonely; and thus we can understand Frankie when she says in *Member of the Wedding,* "All people belong to a 'we' except me." And we know that feeling of inadequacy that Biff in *Death of a Salesman* suggests when he exclaims, "I'm a dime a dozen!" Or reading such plays as Elmer Rice's *Adding Machine,* or Capek's *R.U.R.,* or seeing such films as *La Dolce Vita* and *Judgment at Nuremberg,* we can recognize the forces in our own

[8] Marc Connelly, lecture at the University of Wisconsin, Milwaukee, July 23, 1962.
[9] Ronald Mitchell, "Learn by Theatregoing," lecture at the Winter Workshop of the English Association of Greater Milwaukee, Feb. 10, 1962.

society that threaten to destroy individuality, thwart creativity, induce disaster. Clearly, the experience of drama compels us to penetrating self-examination, to enlargement of sympathy and tolerance, to awareness of what it is to be a human being.

A SEQUENTIAL FOUR-YEAR PLAN
FOR THE TEACHING OF DRAMA

If these objectives are to be realized, drama must find its place in the total curriculum and be planned for and structured so that skills can be developed in sequence and constant overlapping avoided. One common shortcoming of our present procedures is that we often end up doing practically the same things with a dramatic work on every level and ignoring what the student has done before. There is surely room in our curriculum for handling drama by several methods—as a type or within thematic or chronological units—but surely it should not be handled as a type on all four levels, nor should the history of drama or the Shakespearean theater be discussed in detail every time students start a drama unit. By whatever method of organization, drama should be taught both as literature and as theater, not exclusively as one or the other. A play is language, rhythm, spectacle; and we do it injustice to act as though it were either permanently entombed on its pages or just as ephemeral as the life of a single production.

The study of drama, of course, must directly contribute to the development of the basic communication skills with which the English program is most concerned. The following outline of a four-year program attempts to take into account the kinds of skills needed to read and evaluate drama and to suggest kinds of assignments that simultaneously meet the objectives of the drama program as well as those of the over-all course. Starred (*) activities are recommended for able groups primarily or as optional assignments.

    I. English 9 and 10—Introduction to the Play as a Literary Type and as a Work for the Stage

        A. English 9

           1. Type: One-act plays primarily; three-act with capable groups

2. Skills to be developed
   a. Visualizing setting, character
   b. Interpreting characters from dialogue, action
   c. Detecting foreshadowing, plot unfolding, climax
   d. Identifying theme
   e. Supplying missing segments
   f. Recognizing stage directions
   g. Demonstrating clear, meaningful oral reading
   h. Distinguishing differences in techniques of TV, film, theatrical presentations
   i. Applying criteria for evaluating effective TV programs
3. Concepts
   a. Understanding why the author chose the dramatic form
   b. Being aware that plays reflect human life and experience
   c. Recognizing that a play can provide reading pleasure
   d. Being aware that playgoing is both enjoyable and worthwhile
4. Suggested activities
   a. Discussion
      (1) Give out a sheet of selected dialogue passages and have students make references about character traits, personal problems, social class, and so on. Such an exercise well illustrates what dialogue is used to reveal in a play.
      (2) Take a short story and discuss what changes would have to be made to transform it into a play. Emphasize the importance of dialogue to convey characterization and conflict. Identify ways of creating mood by means other than author description.
      (3) Inductively arrive at criteria for evaluating TV programs by starting with the question, "What is there to say about a TV program besides 'I liked it' or 'It bored me' "? Try to lead students to an awareness of the three "I's" with which to view and evaluate:
         Determine: Intention—purpose, theme (if any)
                    Invention—originality of plot treatment, quality of dialogue, use of setting, special effects
                    Impact—power to move, convince, apply to our own lives

(4) Plan varied experiences to develop skills in oral reading by having students undertake such activities as these:

    (a) Select passages to read that introduce a major character and reveal his dominant traits.

    (b) Pick out and read only the climax scene and state why you consider it the turning point of the play.

    (c) Pick out the *funniest* passage of a play and justify your choice by getting the class to laugh.

    (d) Choose passages that appeal to a specific emotion —grief, terror, hate, jealousy, and so forth—try to convey that emotion through skillful reading.

b. Composition

(1) Assign various topics for expository writing, 1 to 3 paragraphs in length:

    (a) Why I *didn't* like a specific TV program

    (b) Reaction to a school play or dramatic assembly

    (c) The purpose for a minor character

    *(d) Proving why a specific judgment of a character is or is not false (In advance, distribute a sheet of quotations appraising a dramatic character. Have students find proof in the play to support the particular stand they are defending.)

    (e) Tracing clues that give away the ending (requires recognition of foreshadowing)

(2) Encourage occasional narrative/descriptive writing:

    *(a) Dramatize a short ballad or one scene from a longer narrative poem.

    (b) Describe the most memorable movie "minute" in your film-viewing experience.

    (c) Describe an episode in your life that could well provide the basis for a dramatization.

*c. Individual/Small-group projects

(1) Do a collage that suggests the different moods of a play you have read or seen.

(2) Read additional one-act plays to discuss individually with the teacher. Possibly prepare an interesting report on one you would like to persuade others in the class to read.

(3) Report on a community play you have seen and that you considered particularly effective.

(4) Actually dramatize a short episode out of your own life or that of a person you have known closely.

B. English 10
1. Type: Three-act plays primarily; introduction to Shakespeare
2. Skills to be developed
   a. Review of skills from English 9
   b. Identifying mood and tone
   c. Reading a Shakespearean play
      (1) Reading blank verse
      (2) Adjusting to Elizabethan theater conventions: soliloquies, asides, absence of stage directions, archaic expressions, allusions, metaphor
   d. Discussing criteria for evaluating effective films
   e. Evaluating view of life in some current TV or movie productions (especially view of family)
3. Concepts
   a. Review of concepts from English 9
   b. Awareness of historical development of drama from Age of Sophocles to Age of Elizabeth
   c. Discovering universality of Shakespeare, pertinence of ideas to our own lives
4. Suggested activities
   a. Discussion
      (1) Provide and discuss a list of vocabulary words that suggest character traits, e.g., diabolical, furtive, pert, impudent, and so on. Then apply to various characters, having students justify their judgments with textual proofs. A list of verbs could be used similarly and applied to character actions.
      (2) Do occasional paraphrasing to check on meaning of selected passages—and not only from Shakespearean plays.
      (3) Discuss popular "family," western, or nature programs on TV. Identify common characteristics in these programs and evaluate to what extent they represent realistic life situations.[10]
      (4) Present Shakespeare within the context of his times. Find out what students already know and work from there. Discuss ways in which the stage and audience

---

[10] *See* Neil Postman, *Television and the Teaching of English* (New York: Appleton, 1961), pp. 105–107.

would affect the kind of play that could be presented. Identify some major differences in English language usage in Shakespeare's time and ours and different theatrical conventions. Discuss the term "Renaissance" and how Shakespeare fits into the movement.

(5) Drawing particularly from *Julius Caesar,* identify ideas that continue to have pertinence for our time, such as the difficulty of balancing personal and public loyalties, feeling and reason, practical goals with ideals.[11]

b. Composition

(1) Have students describe an idea for a TV show that they think would attract a large audience, but that, to their knowledge, has never been tried.

(2) Analyze:

    (a) Nature of conflict in a play—inward, outward

    (b) What the play has to say to us today

  *(c) Effect of a particular theater building and audience expectation on dramatic structure and content

(3) Compare two characters within the same play, emphasizing a dominant trait they share in common. Use proofs from the text to support your comparison.

*(4) Creative writing:

    (a) Write dialogues revealing character traits or attitudes (for example, arrogance, uncertainty, jealousy). Punctuate and paragraph conversation accurately and work for creating convincing and natural dialogue.

    (b) Rewrite the ending of a play to fit another logical interpretation.

    (c) Dramatize an episode that will arouse our indignation.

    (d) Write stage directions for a play that lacks them (especially Shakespearean).

*c. Individual/Small-group projects

(1) Prepare bulletin boards on such subjects as these: drama of different periods; worthwhile current movies and TV productions; ideas suggested by *Scholastic*

---

[11] *See* Mack, pp. 320–336, and Robert Ornstein, *Shakespeare in the Classroom* (Urbana, Ill.: Educational Illustrators, 1960).

or *Literary Cavalcade* material on personalities that have dominated the stage, and so on.

(2) Prepare tape recordings of significant episodes from plays studied.

(3) Design a model set or prepare a series of set sketches for a play studied in class or read individually. Adhere closely to directions given in the play and try to capture the essential mood and period.

(4) Present original oral-topics on aspects of dramatic history such as, A Visit to the Annual Festival of Dionysus, The Revival of Drama in the Middle Ages, The Debate over Shakespeare's Identity. Avoid the flat encyclopedia recital!

II. English 11 and 12—Evaluation and extended reading of drama
   A. English 11
      1. Type: Three-act plays primarily: American drama, Shakespeare
      2. Skills to be developed
         a. Understanding irony, symbolism, and implication
         b. Justification of outcomes
         c. Independent interpretation of plays
         d. Relating drama to larger themes, Puritanism, individualism, and so forth
         e. Applying criteria to the evaluation of a play, movie, or TV production
         f. Revealing drama as an exposition of significant ideas
      3. Concepts
         a. Insight about the place of drama in American life and literature
         b. Familiarity with major American playwrights and significant developments in American drama
         c. Introduction to idea of tragedy
         d. Evaluation of the view of American life commonly represented on TV and in films
         e. Developing empathy with characters
      4. Suggested activities
         a. Discussion
            (1) Acquaint students with major American dramatists, both by studying them individually and by using reading lists. Have students as a class compile their own annotated list of recommended plays.

(2) Discuss the impression that American films and TV convey to others, especially people abroad. To what extent is this view of American life convincing, real, precise? Identify productions that have given a valid or a deceptive view.

(3) Try role playing, in which students assume the roles of characters in a play and speak in justification of some action or conduct in the play.

(4) Have students select a TV program, film, or play and discuss how creative thinking could give it more richness, meaning, significance.

(5) Discuss how ideas in drama apply to contemporary situations. Explore such issues, for example, as what *Inherit the Wind* has to say about freedom of thought in a democracy, how *The Crucible* reflects on twentieth-century "witch-hunting," what *Point of No Return* suggests about the role of the individual in big business, and so on.

(6) Debate the responsibility of the protagonist for his actions: Is Macbeth a free agent or merely a pawn of fate? Is Captain de Vere justified in applying the death penalty to Billy Budd? Is Joe Keller of *All My Sons* to be condemned for thinking first of his family's well-being?

(7) Do oral paraphrases of difficult or especially significant passages.

b. Composition

(1) Analysis:

(a) Consistency and logic of ending, fate of protagonist

(b) Characters as types, representations

(c) Playwright's method of developing his theme

(d) Some aspect of style: symbolism, irony, and so forth

(e) Critical analysis of play read independently

(2) Evaluate a movie, play, or TV production according to given criteria.

(3) Compare handling of theme, character, or conflict in two different plays.

*(4) Creative writing:

     (a) Dramatize a short story or scene from a novel or biography.

     (b) Attempt a parody of a selected scene. Study the style of the original carefully.

     (c) Attempt an original scene suggested by a play and in the style of the original.

  *c. Individual/Small-group activities

     (1) Present a well-planned floor talk on a major American play.

     (2) Organize a panel discussion on a significant TV production, such as a Hallmark Theater special.

     (3) Attend special after-school sessions to hear special play recordings or tapes which cannot be fitted into the regular class program.

B. English 12

  1. Type: Three-act plays primarily: Greek, Shakespearean, modern

  2. Skills to be developed

    a. Review of techniques for evaluating plays, movies, TV productions

    b. Evaluating reviews of mass media in periodicals; distinguishing responsible and irresponsible reviewing

   *c. Recognizing specific dramatic genres—comedy of manners, tragedy, melodrama, satire.

   *d. Comparing drama of different historical periods, for example, Greek, Shakespearean, modern tragedy.

  3. Concepts

    a. Acquaintance with some key theatrical personalities of past and present times

    b. Awareness of major English and world dramatists to explore for future reading

    c. Enlightenment on recent developments in drama in the local community

   *d. Insight into the place of drama, TV, film in contemporary life and recent developments in each media

   *e. Deepened insight into the concepts of tragedy, its origins and development to modern times

   *f. Knowledge of key periodicals dealing with evaluation, discussion of mass media, theater

  4. Suggested activities

a. Discussion
   (1) Hold roundtable talks on plays that students have read individually. These could be structured around a theme, for example, "Facing Reality"—or else each student could be asked to discuss a play he has most enjoyed, pointedly commenting on (a) the play's central conflict, (b) theme(s) the author has directly expressed or suggested, (c) key characters and the change in them throughout the play, (d) a key scene, in which the central character most reveals himself, (e) an estimate of whether the play provides a significant dramatic experience.
   (2) Have occasional preplanned ten- to fifteen-minute discussions on "What's New on Broadway." Encourage students to bring in newspaper and magazine articles on dramatic personalities and writers. Also use "What's New in TV, in Films."
   (3) Discuss characteristics of effective reviews as well as of irresponsible, destructive reviewing. Encourage comparison of reviews from several sources as well as confidence in one's own judgment.
   (4) Discuss imaginative and unimaginative TV productions. Encourage a discussion about whether TV, movies, or theater is living up to its public responsibility. Stimulate thinking about the problems of the script writer today and the sponsor's potentially stifling power.
   (5) Use various essays and articles that discuss modern drama and mass media. Identify some of the problems faced by drama today—the plight of Broadway, the subsidiary position of drama in American culture.
   (6) Have panel presentations on important books on theatrical personalities or historical developments, *Act One, Prince of Players, Gertude Lawrence as Mrs. A,* and so on.
b. Composition
   (1) Analyze:
       (a) Use of minor characters as foils, contrast, "lenses"
       (b) Moral dilemmas or themes, integrity, love, social protest, illusion/reality

      (c) Play's significance for revealing the values and norms of an age

      (d) The contributions of an individual to the theater —or price of success as revealed in a significant biography

      (e) The role of drama in our own community, in American life

    (2) Compare/contrast:

      (a) Author's handling of the same theme in two different plays

      (b) Dramatic techniques and conventions of different periods

     *(c) Play "Twins," for example, *Electra, Mourning Becomes Electra; Hamlet, Winterset*

     *(d) Play with its film or TV counterpart

     *(e) Various reviews of the same play

    (3) Evaluate:

      (a) A play's unity, integrity, effectiveness

      (b) A play as dramatic experience: staging, impact, actors' response to challenge of the role

     *(c) Extent to which a particular play fulfills intentions of its type: satire, tragedy, comedy, and so on

  *(4) Creative writing

      (a) Write an original scene suggested by a play, Ophelia's soliloquy, Saint Joan in prison, and so forth, in style of original.

      (b) Write a dramatic sketch suggested by a news story, choosing one with definite conflict.

  c. Individual/Small-group projects

    (1) Keep journals of individual play-reading, especially noting theme and resolution of conflict.

    (2) Report on major theatrical personalities, books revealing them.

   *(3) Explore some developments in the avant-garde or European theater, the theater of the "absurd," Bertolt Brecht Company in East Germany.

III. Activities for all levels

  A. Encourage attendance at and follow-up discussion of school plays.

  B. Plan occasional field trips to community plays. Publicize and discuss plays that students could get to; take advantage of the many opportunities for student rates.

C. Expand filmstrip library, such as those on the Shakespearean theater. Allocate important films to various levels and keep a department file on worthwhile films, records, filmstrips, tapes.

D. Use recorded scenes of plays not directly studied, but which illustrate emphasized concepts.

E. Try to have at least one drama-oriented bulletin board display during the year.

SPECIAL PROBLEMS IN DRAMA TEACHING

Unless a teacher plans wisely, drama study can easily become overextended and tedious. Nothing can be more depressing for both teacher and students than belaboring a play week after week until it has lost all vitality or appeal. Avoidance of both superficiality and surfeit thus requires a skillful varying of approaches and emphases.

Method of Discussion

Should a play be discussed in its entirety or piece by piece? Perhaps the best answer is a compromise: suit the method to the play. A Shakespearean drama, by virtue of length and complexity, usually requires a section-by-section approach. Students first starting to read three-act plays probably also need to be assigned individual scenes or acts one at a time. Yet in both instances the sections must ultimately be put together more meaningfully to illuminate the whole. When studying modern plays, students in the junior and senior years should generally be required to have read the entire work prior to initial discussion, then to go back for a second and, it is hoped, a third rereading and careful analysis of selected sections. This method has the advantage of putting greater responsibility on the student for drawing his own conclusions and seeing the play as an artistic unit; and it avoids the problem of holding all students to specific page limits. Rather than straining to make a single play yield all of its riches, the high school teacher will wisely distribute emphasis, letting one play reveal the possibilities of dialogue, another the force of ideas, yet another the use of irony, contrast, or symbolism. Ultimately the skills emphasized in one should transfer to and illuminate the reading of other plays. Above all, students must be encouraged to read widely, even at the expense of some detail, if teachers are to expect them to acquire an interest and skill in an area in which they usually have far too few experiences.

Oral Reading or Dramatizing of Play Scenes

We all know what happens when parts are assigned and deadpan Jane runs monotone through every passage, despite pre-preparation. We also know how tedious it is to hear a scene that students have carefully read first on their own massacred by poor classroom readers, then played on record, and finally dissected endlessly in class until it has lost all appeal. Here again a compromise must be made so that students have opportunities to cultivate skills in oral reading without killing all pleasure for the others in the class. The best solution is to make specific assignments in oral reading: students could be asked to select and read key scenes, passages revealing character, or moments of climax—all of which require careful selection, yet which are brief enough to retain classroom interest. Also, rather than stressing the same scenes again and again, teachers should use recordings for plays beyond the capacity of student readers but not duplicate what has already been sufficiently stressed in class.

The Best Use of Audio-Visual Aids

Audio-visual aids should fulfill the promise of their name—to serve as aids and enrichment rather than replacements for the original work. Too often records, films, and filmstrips totally supplant rather than supplement the dramatic experience or else constitute nothing more than time-fillers or incidental recreation. These media should be used instead to motivate study, to suggest an approach for reading, possibly to present a different interpretation. In addition, teachers need to make better classroom use of records of plays that have not been directly studied, thus enabling students to transfer skills acquired in the study of one work to the interpretation of another. More time should also be given to class evaluation of film and record interpretations—to appraising characterization, ensemble work, total effectiveness. And within the coming decade, no self-respecting school is likely to be without a well-equipped Materials Center, stocked with extensive film, record, and filmstrip resources for use by individuals and small groups. The multimedia revolution should really mean that the coming generation will have more opportunities to read, see, and hear drama than ever before.

Special Techniques in Teaching a Shakespearean Play

Enobarbus' words in praise of Cleopatra—"Age cannot wither her, nor custom stale her infinite variety"—apply to Shakespeare's works as well. W. H. Auden has noted that every one of Shakespeare's works is unique so that the reader must experience them all to get a proper idea of the Shakespearean world. However, he also comments that "no one is less a writer for the young, for persons, that is, under the age of thirty." [12] Difficult, mature, demanding—Shakespearean drama calls upon the full resources of a teacher's creativity, persuasiveness, and careful planning. In particular, the classroom teacher must overcome the problems of attention, of verse, of emphasis.

The problem of attention. While Shakespeare fills his plays with considerable attractions for the "groundlings"—murders, quarrels, suicides, duelings, insanity, slapstick comedy, patriotic fervor, and spectacle—his essential appeal is to the ear, to the mind, to refined perception. The problem of attention, then, is basically that of luring students to come to grips with a literature requiring mature thought, concentration, and insight. "Well digested in the scenes, set down with as much modesty as cunning," his plays call for an ear attuned to subtlety, paradox, ambiguity. In the first place, students must learn that a play can be enjoyable even when the plot is known in advance. Like more sophisticated members of the Greek or Elizabethan audience, they must learn to anticipate and enjoy the unique treatment of a previously worked subject and to let language more than spectacle and action work upon their imaginations and emotions. Robert Ornstein has well observed that "the relatively bare Elizabethan stage was perfectly suited to the drama of great personalities which Shakespeare created," for his heroic characters dwarfed their background and

---

12 W. H. Auden, "Three Memoranda on the New Arden Shakespeare," *The Mid-Century,* No. 21 (January 1961), 3.

shaped their worlds and their own destinies.[13] The focus of attention must thus be upon the inner conflicts with which his characters struggle and the consequences of their actions—and especially upon the language they use to define these conflicts. Thus viewed, Shakespeare's characters take on universal significance, for they wrestle with and clarify problems men of all periods have struggled to resolve.

The problem of verse. Besides demonstrating maturity and sensitivity, students reading Shakespeare must develop specific skills for handling poetic drama. T. S. Eliot, in "The Three Voices of Poetry," reminds us that the poetic line in drama bears the weight of three responsibilities: conveying plot and character while retaining its poetic form.[14] Students must thus acquire a series of reading skills that work together. First they must learn to read blank verse without halting at the end of each line or being trapped by occasional archaic expressions or extended figures of speech. Then they must learn to see how specific passages reflect the character traits of the speaker. For example, they should come to detect how Polonius' mishandling of language reflects his mismanagement of human affairs, or how Laertes betrays a strain of superficiality by indulging in florid bombast. They should also become skilled enough to discern how Hamlet's shifts from introspection and depression to passionate anger with himself and the world are precisely reflected by the variety of his speech, the flavor of his rhetoric. Unless they see language as mirroring essential character traits, they will miss much of the impact of the Shakespearean line.

Students must also discover how richly Shakespeare uses imagery to enforce mood and idea. For example, how repeatedly throughout the history plays he apostrophizes sleep and thereby emphasizes the wearying responsibility of a king upon whose head "uneasy" lies the crown. Using the images of disease, plague, disruption, insanity, and revolt in *Julius Caesar, Hamlet,* and *Lear,* Shakespeare succeeds in conveying the very atmosphere of states whose social organization has suffered violent change and upheaval. John Ciardi also reminds us that Shakespeare's verse needs to be studied for its own sake as poe-

---

[13] Ornstein, *Shakespeare in the Classroom,* pp. 5–6.
[14] T. S. Eliot, *On Poetry and Poets* (New York: Farrar, Straus, 1957), pp. 96–112.

try, particularly for its precise word choice, skillfully suggestive over-tones, and unified construction.[15] Rather than wearying every line with exhausting interpretation, however, we need to vary discussion procedures, letting one passage, for example, serve as a reflection of an inner state of mind, another as revealing specific character traits, yet another to show contrast and irony. Often it may be necessary to concentrate on plot events alone, for verse analysis must never become so laborious that students feel they are making no headway in the play.

The problem of emphasis. Those who have taught Shakespeare over a period of years recognize how rewarding recurrent experiences have proven to be, for each rereading with different classes brings new insights and values. On the other hand, how dangerous it is to assume that every student will gain as much from a first contact! The solution, then, is to suggest, not exhaust, the possibilities of a Shakespearean play, to make it rewarding enough that a student will want of his own accord to return to it for rereading or to go out of his way to attend an actual performance. Most teachers spend perhaps too much time on a single play and do too much for the students, who thus fail to ac-quire the skills necessary for independent exploration in other Shakes-pearean works. Three to four weeks is ample time for most works used in high school and is actually all that can be reasonably afforded in the already overcrowded English program. However, since the ma-jor themes of Shakespeare's plays recur in literature of all periods, the teacher has the opportunity frequently to refer back to the works stud-ied earlier and thus revive their significance and applicability. Not without warrant has it been said Shakespeare's plays were "for all time."

THE DRAMA OF SOCIAL DISSENT

In an era in which protest has become almost a way of life and dissen-sion a gospel, English teachers will make little headway by serving up

[15] John Ciardi, *How Does a Poem Mean?* (Boston: Houghton Mifflin, 1959), p. 785.

pleasant plays with tidy conflicts and prudent themes. But today's adolescent can be strongly "turned on" by the drama of social dissent— the experience of plays in which outstanding individuals of different historical periods demonstrate that the actions of one person can still make a difference in reversing the course of injustice, civic complacency, and mass hysteria. A unit on the drama of social dissent invariably turns the secondary classroom into an arena of truly significant dialogue and demonstrates that the genuine heroes of history are also "men for all seasons," as relevant today as in their own times.

Selection of appropriate works for a unit on social dissent should not be difficult. Though technically not a drama, Plato's *Phaedo,* through its use of dramatic dialogue, actually provides an archetypal "drama of dissent," starring the most admirable protestor of all time —Socrates. One might profitably begin with the *Phaedo* and portions of the *Apology,* then move to Anderson's *Barefoot in Athens,* a most readable and discussable contemporary treatment of Socrates, which humanizes the man while combining humor and dignity in the re-creation of his unavoidable martyrdom. Immortal Joan is also available in several worthwhile works, most notably the plays of Anouilh and Shaw. Becket, the worldly saint, can be approached through Eliot's stylized treatment of the Archbishop rejecting his temptors in *Murder in the Cathedral* or through Anouilh's *Becket,* a portrait of the profligate playboy, compelled ultimately to defend the "honor of God," even at the expense of his long friendship with King Henry II and the price of his life. Sophocles' Antigone; Sir Thomas More, a true "man of all seasons"; tactless but admirable Thomas Stockmann of *An Enemy of the People* and John Proctor of *The Crucible* are obvious nominees to the select rank of dissentors whose actions can be said to have affected the course of human events, if only to stir the consciences of reasonable and moral men.

The three study guides which follow are intended to serve as aids in the development of a meaningful unit on the theme of social dissent. Under no circumstances should they be considered a definitive selection. But each has literary and dramatic merit; and each demonstrates, in action, an individual who dared act as a "majority of one," despite personal sacrifice, family pressures, and political considerations. Each is also highly discussible and likely to stimulate keen interest, lively discussion, and meaningful composition.

THE CRUCIBLE
Arthur Miller

I. Introductory Activities

A. As with all plays in this unit, try to get the students directly into the first act of the play, then through a complete first reading. Important scenes can later be re-created by means of class dramatizations and recordings. (Arthur Miller has recorded a very moving reading of Act II.)

B. Possibly precede introduction of this play by reading and discussing selections which reveal Puritan attitudes and values. Portions of Perry Miller's *The American Puritans,* selected short stories of Hawthorne (especially "The Maypole of Merry Mount," "The Minister's Black Veil," and "My Kinsman Major Molineaux"), and even Shirley Jackson's "The Lottery" would give students insight into the Puritan preoccupation with sin, the concept of a theocracy, and the concern with the dual nature of man which Puritans so fully dramatized.

II. Analyzing the Play

A. As history

1. Ask students to study the facts of the 1692 witch trials in Salem, then determine how faithfully Miller has reflected actual people and real happenings in the play. Two indispensable references for this purpose are Marion Starkey's *The Devil in Massachusetts* (New York: Dolphin Paperbooks, n.d.) and David Levin's *What Happened in Salem?* (New York: Harcourt, Brace & World, 1960). Students should conclude that, except for the fabricated adultery theme and emphasis on marital conflict in the Proctor household, the play very precisely re-creates real characters and conflicts of the period.

2. Examine the basis for belief in witchcraft, especially in a Puritan community, raising such questions as: Who qualified as a witch? According to common belief, what supernatural powers did witches acquire and what kinds of evil were they known to inflict? How could their evil influence be exorcized? (Students would be fascinated by the information in a delightful pamphlet on "Witchcraft in Olde Salem," available upon request from the Pilgrim Motel, 40 Bridge Street, Salem, Mass.)

3. Because *The Crucible* had its first public performance in 1953, shortly after Miller had been personally indicted for contempt of Congress because of his refusal to reveal information about the activities of some of his acquaintances, the play inevitably forces comparison with the guilt-by-association and smear tactics of the McCarthy hearings. It is clear that Miller intended his play to constitute a denunciation of witch-hunting not only in Salem, but in any era; and it is also clear that he was most bold and courageous in writing and presenting a work that could further enflame his critics. Students should be asked to ponder just why this play, which has been so enthusiastically acclaimed abroad and brilliantly revived in recent years, received such a relatively cool reception when it was first produced. Why did it suffer rather than become enhanced by comparison with this appalling episode in modern American history? Hopefully, students will recognize that a truly great play must have universal significance and must also do more than serve as a political pamphlet or dramatized polemic. Now that time has blurred its topical stand, *The Crucible* can be evaluated on its own merits. Some critics have now come to consider this play Miller's best achievement, his most successful fusion of historical drama and personal tragedy.

B. As a view of—and attack upon—Puritan values and practices.

1. In several inserted prose segments in Act I, Miller comments at length on social, economic, and psychological causes of the Salem witch trials. Since these portions are highly sophisticated and abstract, they should really be read aloud and analyzed in class, with students listing both strengths and shortcomings in the Puritan way of life and system of values.

a. Strengths: Students should note such admirable qualities as the Puritans' belief in self-denial and self-discipline; their insistence on purposefulness in daily occupations, avoidance of vanity and luxury, and the application of stern justice in cases requiring court judgment. They should also recognize how strongly Puritans were guided by the conviction that man is basically corrupt, that he could be saved only by "election," and that eternal happiness could be guaranteed only by visible demonstration of virtue and absence of hypocrisy, sensuality, self-preoccupation, and greed.

b. Shortcomings: Students should easily identify such limiting aspects of Puritanism as: repression of children and youth activities; excessive self-denial and austerity; stultifying social insulation; open interference in the personal lives of individuals and minority groups; intolerance; hyperemphasis on surface appearances and public opinion; adherence to a single system of belief and conduct.

2. Ask students to determine which aspects of Puritanism are most under attack in the play (hypocrisy, emotional repression, inflexibility, and breakdown of communication, among others). But also point out that "tolerance" was a relatively new concept for Puritans, to many an "abomination," because it threatened the stability and permanence of the Puritan theocracy. Also stress Miller's idea, set forth in Act I, of the difficulty in any society of maintaining the balance between freedom and order. Ask students to analyze in what ways this balance was being threatened in the Salem community of 1692.

3. Discuss to what extent John Proctor actually qualifies as the best Christian of all the Salemites, even though he has committed adultery, failed to attend church regularly, and stumbled in his recitation of the commandments before Rev. Hale.

C. As an illumination of human problems and moral issues of universal significance.

1. Have students identify and discuss underlying sources of conflict in the play which have universal application, such as:

a. The breakdown of communication, especially between husband and wife, priest and parishioner.

b. The practice of determining "guilt by association," leading to unjust and brutal character defamation.

c. Oppressive regimentation, disregarding individual rights and differences.

d. The absence of sanctioned outlets for emotion or violence, contributing to periodic outbreaks of witch hunting and scapegoating.

e. The power of fear, superstition, and irrationality to engender mass hysteria and injustice.

2. Examine the social and psychological conditions which Miller suggests are likely to lead to outbreaks of public hysteria and irrationality.

3. Determine the major themes and psychological truths which the play conveys, among them the following:

   a. Evil begets evil.

   b. Injustice and mass hysteria are common consequences of repression and bigotry.

   c. Breeches of the moral code can have far-reaching consequences.

   d. A man cannot live without self-respect. Preservation of one's honor and integrity are necessary if life is to have meaning.

   e. Any social system must maintain a balance between freedom and discipline, reason and emotion, in the conduct of human affairs.

   f. One honest man can turn the tide, can constitute a "majority of one."

D. As a psychological revelation of the hidden motives behind the actions of real people.

1. For several characters in the play, a mask of virtue and Christian ardor conceals the true motives for vicious, destructive behavior. Have students examine, in particular, the personal history and character traits that might account for the destructive actions of each of the following: Abigail, Betty Parris, Mr. and Mrs. Putnam, Mary Warren, Rev. Parris, and Rev. Hathorne.

2. The play is filled with moral dilemmas, forcing characters into decisions where neither alternative is really desirable. Examine closely what decisions each of the following characters is forced to make, determining why they decide as they do: Rev. Parris, Mary Warren, John and Elizabeth Proctor, Rev. Hale, Rev. Danforth, and Giles Corey.

3. Several characters really change greatly throughout the play. Which are strengthened? Which deteriorate?

E. As a work of art, having both literary and theatrical merit.

1. Is there any discernible organizing pattern, besides chronology, to unify the play?

   a. Students should discover on their own that the total action of the play is based on a series of *trials,* public and private. Each act portrays people undergoing rigorous interrogation to explain or defend their actions and beliefs. In Act I, Parris cross-examines the hysterical children with ruthless persistence and is succeeded by an equally persevering Rev. Hale. In Act II, Elizabeth Proctor's frigid reproaches goad her husband to exclaim, "I cannot speak but I am doubted, every moment judged for lies, as though I come into a court when I come into this house!" Later in the same act John bears down upon the timorous Mary Warren, then is himself cornered by Rev. Hale and the delegation that come to take Elizabeth to jail. In Act III Proctor's efforts to impugn Abigail and terminate the trials end only in his public degradation, Elizabeth's public lie, and Mary Warren's failure to overcome her personal fears when she has the opportunity to tell the truth. Act IV is Proctor's Gethsemane, his night of agony, when he must weigh the cost of a lie against the loss of his life. Like Saint Joan, he signs the fraudulent confession, then rips it to pieces, recognizing that, for him, a life without honor is unthinkable. His death coincides with the rising of the sun, symbolic of his spiritual victory and the promise of a return to rationality and justice in Salem.

b. Note the balanced organization of the play, the alternation of episodes of public frenzy with calmer views of private life. Acts I and III are high-pitched group scenes, each ending with the children in an active state of hysteria. Acts II and IV examine the effects of the trials on private life and focus on the tormenting decisions individuals are forced to make once their privacy is totally invaded.

2. Discuss various ways in which the title applies to the events and themes of the play. It suggests, of course, that Salem has become a "heated kettle" in which emotions have reached the boiling point. It further symbolizes the severe trials which take place and the many trials and testings which individuals and the entire town must endure.

3. Discuss the play as a work for the stage, raising such questions as:

a. Some directors have emphasized the social themes, others the personal tragedies of individuals in the play. How,

dramatically, could these different emphases be conveyed?
- b. Can the characters emerge as credible human beings once the detailed commentary of the written version has been removed? It has also been charged that the characters are unconvincing, more symbolic than real. Is such a judgment warranted?
- c. In an early review of *The Crucible,* one critic charged that the play exercises only the mind, not the heart. Do the students agree?
- d. What are the key scenes and speeches? Dramatize a few, especially the final confrontation of John and Elizabeth Proctor in Act IV.

III. Possible Composition Topics
- A. Why has Miller named the play *The Crucible?* Analyze the various ways in which the title applies to events and themes of the play.
- B. Discuss: *The Crucible* is not so much a dramatization of "witch hunting" as it is an illumination of human weakness, hypocrisy, and vindictiveness.
- C. What could a psychologist learn about human behavior from a close analysis of *The Crucible?* For example, what insights could he gain about the effects of emotional repression, the bases of marital conflict, the sources of fear and irrationality, devices for avoiding reality, etc.?
- D. In what ways does *The Crucible* not only attack the weaknesses of Puritanism, yet also illuminate some of its finest strengths and values in the lives of individual characters?
- E. The play uses the "trial" situation as a dominant metaphor for the action of the entire play. Discuss various "trials" dramatized in the play, noting the appropriateness of this metaphor to the overall work.
- F. Just why are the children believed and the wise adults ignored? Reexamine the play to determine why irrationality and hysteria dominate the life of an entire community for more than half a year.
- G. Compare Abigail of *The Crucible* and Hester Prynne of *The Scarlet Letter,* both guilty of adultery, yet greatly differing in their response to public interference in their private lives and to their personal suffering.

A MAN FOR ALL SEASONS

Robert Bolt *

I. *Introduction and background*

A. Distribute a short summary of More's life, highlighting his many accomplishments in religion, literature, and public life. Stress his ambivalent relationship with Henry VIII—first as his religious spokesman, then as adversary—particularly as represented in the following events:

1518   More's first year in Henry's service

1521   "Ghost writer" of Henry's defense of the Pope and attack on Luther

1529   Wolsey's replacement as Chancellor—the first layman in English history to hold the office

1531   "Submission of Clergy"—religious officials accede to Henry's limitations of their power

1534   Act of Supremacy, acknowledging Henry VIII as supreme authority of the Church of England; occasion of More's first arrest

1535   July 7—the execution of Sir Thomas More on a charge of treason

B. Review the history of the Tudors and their accession to the throne, stressing the role of the Wars of the Roses in bringing Henry VIII to power.

C. Anticipate and clarify potentially difficult references:

1. "And . . . who recommended you to read Signor *Machiavelli?*"

2. "Since you seem to be violently opposed to *the Latin dispatch,* I thought you'd like to look it over."

3. "D'you think *two Tudors* is sufficient?"

4. "Do you remember *the Yorkist Wars?*"

5. "He sounds like *Moloch.*"

6. "May I not come simply, to pay my respects to *the English Socrates*—as I see your angelic friend *Erasmus* calls you."

7. Other terms: *farrier   advocate   pragmatist   bracken*

II. *Reading and analysis of the play itself*

A. With fast groups, assign pre-reading of the entire play. With

* From Gladys Veidemanis, "A Play for All Seasons," *English Journal,* LV (November 1966), 1006–1015. Used by permission of the author and the National Council of Teachers of English. Quotations from *A Man for All Seasons* used by permission of Random House, Inc., as publishers. (Robert Bolt, *A Man for All Seasons.* Copyright © 1962 by Robert Bolt.)

less able groups, take each act individually, perhaps reading the first scene aloud to clarify difficult references and introduce characters. Ask students to outline the sequence of events in each act, dating them according to the information given by the Common Man.

B. Discuss the extent to which the play parallels actual history, noting the individuals who played a comparable role in actual life. On this question Bolt, in program notes for a presentation of the play in Milwaukee in 1963, said:

"I will claim (diffidently) that all the events essential to the action of his life during the period covered are present in the play, and (confidently) that none of the events essential to the action of the play is entirely my own invention. That is, none of the events as they relate to More himself; the other characters have been combined and collapsed so as to keep the play to a tolerable length.

"He was a pivot of English life at a time when England was negotiating the sharpest corner in her spiritual history, and to have brought into the play even a fair sample of his acquaintances would have swamped it in a pageant of great names."

Students should, of course, recognize the historical accuracy of the following portraits:

Wolsey—a man of fantastic power and ignominious decline

Roper—More's son-in-law and later biographer

Henry VIII—a versatile, vibrant monarch, ruthless in securing his own will

Rich—a sycophant, willing to betray a friend to the highest bidder; a "lucky" traitor

Cromwell—a shrewd opportunist but ultimate victim of Henry's power politics

Norfolk—More's friend, who places personal safety above friendship and principles

C. Clarify any confusions about plot and action raised by students after a first reading of the play. (Some will surely be unclear about Roper's many philosophies, Wolsey's sudden disappearance, and Chapuys' strange behavior at the end of the play.) Other key questions:

At what point does More find it necessary to resign his office as Lord Chancellor?

On what charge is he placed in prison?

What major legal device does he use to avoid—temporarily —the death sentence?

How is More's death finally "engineered"?

Despite his death penalty, how does More really get the better of his accusers?

D. Explore possible reasons for the division of the play into two acts, leading to the awareness that Act I could be sub-titled "The Man, His Age, and His Dilemma," Act II, "The Hour of Testing and Decision."

E. Review with the class various techniques playwrights use to reveal character and identify the particular methods used in this play to illuminate More's many-faceted personality. Re-explore the text through such questions as these:

1. What personal qualities does More reveal through his conversation and actions with friends and family? (They should discern that he is witty, sophisticated, generous, practical, wordly [to the extent that he likes wine, good company, music], independent, resourceful, and intellectually brilliant.) How does he show himself throughout to be a man who truly understands human nature?

Does he fit the qualifications of a saint as defined by the Common Man early in Act I?

Does he change in any way throughout the course of the play?

2. What clues in Act I foreshadow More's coming resistance to Henry's divorce? (Students should note such passages as:

Wolsey: "If you could just see facts flat on, without that moral squint; with just a little common sense, you could have been a statesman."

Common Man as Steward: "My master Thomas More would give anything to anyone. Some say that's good and some say that's bad, but I say he can't help it—and that's bad . . . because some day someone's going to ask him for something he wants to keep and he'll be out of practice."

More: ". . . I believe, when statesmen forsake their own private consciences for the sake of their public duties . . . they lead their country by a short route to chaos."

"I neither could nor would rule my King. But there's a little . . . little area . . . where I must rule myself. It's very little—less to him than a tennis court.")

F. Have students define the central moral dilemma of the play (whether to obey conscience and God or the dictates of a temporal ruler) and explain why Henry forces More to take a public stand. Why *must* Henry insist upon More's support or his death? (Students should not miss More's conversation with Henry in Act I:

> More: "Then why does Your Grace need my poor support?"
> Henry: "Because you are honest. What's more to the purpose, you're known to be honest . . ."

Or Cromwell's comment to Rich in Act II:

> "The King's a man of conscience and he wants either Sir Thomas More to bless his marriage or Sir Thomas More destroyed. Either will do . . . If the King destroys a man, that's proof to the King that it must have been a bad man, the kind of man a man of conscience *ought* to destroy— and of course a bad man's blessing's not worth having. So either will do.")

G. King Henry, in his conversation with More, lists four major kinds of followers: "There are those like Norfolk who follow me because I wear the crown, and there are those like Master Cromwell who follow me because they are jackals with sharp teeth and I am their lion, and there is a mass that follows me because it follows anything that moves—and there is you." Explore these various character types, and others, in the play and various stands on Henry's divorce proceedings:

1. Henry himself
   a. What elements of Henry's personality are revealed directly and indirectly in the play? (Students should note his sensual zest for living, his impulsive behavior, his pride in his own achievements and artistic talents, his domineering, ruthless nature, his great skill in rationalization.)
   b. How does Henry try to justify his controversial divorce action? (Note that he cites the Bible (Leviticus) as long as it supports his case but rejects those portions in Deuteronomy on marriage to a brother's wife as "ambiguous." He considers his strongest argument the necessity of acquiring a male heir.)
2. Norfolk
   a. How does he demonstrate, throughout the entire play, that he always means well and yearns to remain More's friend, but doesn't dare to risk his status or security?

b. What is the basis for the quarrel between More and Norfolk in Act II? Why does More initiate it in the first place? What is the purpose of More's references to water spaniels and his exhortation—"Is there no single sinew in the midst of this that serves no appetite of Norfolk's but is, just, Norfolk? There is! Give *that* some exercise, my lord!"?

3. The "Jackals"—Cromwell, Rich, Chapuys
   a. Cromwell
      (1) Does Cromwell have any admirable qualities? (Students should note that this son of a farrier has risen high by virtue of his legal ability and shrewdness. He is a hard-nosed realist who never masks his actions behind a layer of pretty words or rationalizations.) But where does he most fully reveal his ruthlessness, even a sadistic streak? (Note actions at end of Act I.)
      (2) What is Cromwell's doctrine of "political convenience" as defined in his conversation with Rich in the last scene of Act I? Is Cromwell correct in his assumption that "The situation rolls forward in any case," making the efforts of *"upright, steadfast* men" useless and ill-advised?
      (3) Why does Cromwell say, "And if I bring about More's death—I plant my own, I think"? (Note that he is realistic enough to know that Henry's tender conscience, which demands More's execution, will probably also require a scapegoat upon which later to transfer blame for More's death.)
   b. Rich
      (1) How does Rich demonstrate from his first line in the play—"But every man has his price!"—that he can be very easily bought? What are his major values? How does Cromwell manipulate him? How is he treated by the Common Man?
      (2) In how many ways does Rich betray More—and his own soul—and what is his "price" each time? Is Rich a true convert "to the doctrines of Machiavelli"?
   c. Chapuys
      (1) In what ways does Chapuys demonstrate that he functions for the King of Spain in the same capacity as Cromwell for the King of England? What

causes Chapuys to say of More, whom he earlier admired, "The man's utterly unreliable!"?

(2) Why are Cromwell and Chapuys, officials of opposing powers, shown leaving the stage together at the end of the play, arms linked, smiles conspiratorial? (Note that for these exponents of political convenience, More has become extremely *in*convenient and troublesome. As Chapuys learns in the letter episode, More's loyalty to England is unswerving. His conflict with Henry is essentially moral rather than political.)

4. The representative of the "mass that follows"—The Common Man
   a. Identify and discuss the three major functions of the Common Man in this play:
      (1) A one-man Greek chorus and stage manager to provide transition, background, commentary.
      (2) A means of introducing comic relief into a serious play.
      (3) A personality in his own right, involving the audience in the play by being its most direct representative and indicting by his own actions those people of any age who set self-interest above all other values.
   b. How far is the Comman Man willing to compromise himself? Where does he draw the line? How does he reveal himself to be a crafty opportunist, but a moral coward?
5. Other characters to note:
   a. Wolsey
      (1) What is the subject of the communication Wolsey shows More? Why does he ask him to read it? (Note that he is very much aware of More's "moral squint"!)
      (2) What reasons does Wolsey give for personally helping Henry secure a divorce? (Note especially his reference to the Yorkist wars.)
      (3) What are Wolsey's criticisms of More's character? What traits does he himself possess which he would like to find in More?
   b. Roper
      (1) Though courageous and outspoken, how does Roper reveal himself as immature and somewhat superficial? What qualities of More are lacking in Roper? (Roper is surely humorless and not a little obtuse!)
      (2) Why does More forbid Meg's marriage to Roper at

first, then later allow it? Altogether, what is Roper's major function in the play?

c. Alice

(1) In what ways does Alice make More's continued quarrel with Henry more painful? How do we know that family solidarity and well-being are her highest values? (Note her outburst when More removes his chain of office: ". . . Sun and moon, Master More, you're taken for a wise man! Is this wisdom—to betray your ability, abandon practice, forget your station and your duty to your kin and behave like a printed book!")

(2) Why is Alice at first so cool and aloof when she visits More in prison? What causes More later in that scene to exclaim, "Why it's a lion I married! A lion! A lion!"?

d. Meg

(1) Meg is a remarkable young woman, almost *too* bright for a woman of her age. What exceptional abilities does she exhibit before King Henry during his surprise visit? What indications do we have that More dotes on his daughter? (Note that Alice is somewhat hurt when More speaks of "hiding" his daughter but makes no specific reference to shielding her.)

(2) Why is Meg a most potent "Eve" to tempt her father after his year in prison? What four arguments does she present to try to persuade her father to swear to the Act of Succession? Are his responses convincing? How do her appeals compare with those of the four tempters in T. S. Eliot's *Murder in the Cathedral?*

6. More's personal stand and legal strategy

a. How many different kinds of pressures must More resist to maintain his stand? (Note the hardships imposed on his family, Chapuys' letter from the King of Spain, the tempting offer of money from the bishops, the endless inquisitions, the miserable conditions in jail, the painful entreaties of his loved ones.)

b. Why does More maintain his stand, even though he knows Henry will ultimately have his way anyhow? Note that his various comments indicate that his decision hinges on

personal integrity: "Well, as a spaniel is to water, so

is a man to his own self. I will not give in because I oppose it— *I* do—not my pride, not my spleen, nor any other of my appetites but *I* do—*I!*"

religious conviction: "In matters of conscience, the loyal subject is more bounded to be loyal to his conscience than to any other thing."

concern for public morality: "Can I help my King by giving him lies when he asks for truth? Will you help England by populating her with liars?"

c. Study carefully the passage in which More declares to his family that he will utilize every possible means to escape martyrdom:

"God made the *angels* to show him splendor—as he made animals for innocence and plants for their simplicity. But Man he made to serve him wittily, in the tangle of his mind! If he suffers us to fall to such a case that there is no escaping, then we may stand to our tackle as best we can, and yes, Will, then we will clamor like champions . . . if we have the spittle for it. And no doubt it delights God to see splendor where he only looked for complexity. But it's God's part, not our own, to bring ourselves to that extremity! Our natural business lies in escaping—so let's get home and study this Bill."

Discuss ways in which More succeeds in living up to this philosophy.

H. Ask students whether they have noted any dominant pattern of imagery throughout the play. Hopefully they will have detected the many references to hunting, fishing, and snaring and to animals and animalistic behavior, such as these:

"But in the thickets of the law, oh there I'm a forester."

"Sir Thomas is going to be a slippery fish, Richard; we need a net with finer mesh."

"Better a live rat than a dead lion."

". . . they are jackals with sharp teeth and I am their lion. . . ."

More is hunted down and "mounted." Unfortunately, as the play implies, there are always too many "rats," too few "lions."

III. *Culminating activities*

A. Evaluate the appropriateness of the title. According to Bolt's program notes for the play: "The title of the play is taken from a passage which was composed by Robert Whittinton for Tudor schoolboys to put into Latin: "More is a man of angel's wit and singular learning; I know not his fellow. For where is the man of that gentleness, lowliness, and affability? And as time requireth, a man of marvelous mirth and pastimes; and sometimes of as sad a gravity; 'a man for all seasons.' "

B. Extract and discuss some of the moral issues in the play, such as those below, with which men of all ages have had to wrestle:

1. How much can any one man affect the course of public events and remedy obvious evils? Should he even try?
2. What comes first—loyalty to family, self, or principles?
3. Do the ends justify the means?
4. Can a man say one thing and believe another without betraying his principles?
5. Is the Common Man right—"Better a live rat than a dead lion"?

C. Relate themes of the play to other important literary works and to life situations:

1. Students could very profitably go on to read other works dealing with individuals facing comparable moral dilemmas, e.g.: Plato's *Apology*, Sophocles' *Antigone*, Shaw's *St. Joan*, Anouilh's *Becket*, Eliot's *Murder in the Cathedral*, Ibsen's *Enemy of the People*, Miller's *All My Sons*, and others.

2. Ask students to write on one of the following topics:

a. The Common Man states, "I'm a plain simple man and just want to keep out of trouble." To what extent has his philosophy of "no involvement" permeated modern life and in what ways has it proven—and can it prove—highly detrimental to public life?

b. More has been called "the English Socrates." In what ways is the designation appropriate?

c. Persuade us that More was or was not justified in his stand.

d. How does the play present More as a figure deserving the designation "A Man for All Seasons"?

e. Bolt wrote also that "The action of this play ends in 1535, but the play was written in 1960, and if in production one date must obscure the other, it is 1960 which I wish clearly to occupy the stage. The 'Life' of a man like Thomas More proffers a number of caps which in this or any other century we may try on for size." Analyze what makes the play relevant to our times and what "caps" we are offered to try on for size.

3. Dramatize key scenes, such as Henry's visit, More's quarrel with Norfolk, and More's last meeting with his family.

AN ENEMY OF THE PEOPLE
Henrik Ibsen

I. *Introducing the play*

A. Assign complete reading of the play prior to discussion, but first present specific aspects of background information that have bearing on the play and its construction:

Ibsen's role in developing the realistic theater; his concern with social problems and controversial issues.

Ibsen's influence on other dramatists, especially men like Shaw and Miller, who shared his concern about social problems and moral issues.

Ibsen's personal experiences, which classified him as a kind of Thomas Stockmann, ready to assume the role of a "majority of one" who must inevitably pay a severe price for standing up for the truth.

B. Overcome student skepticism about the actual possibility of polluted baths by describing the happenings in Zermatt, Switzerland, in February, 1963, as described in *The Saturday Evening Post,* May 25, 1963. Elicit discussion about other situations in which the actual facts of a situation have been withheld from the public in order to assure community profits and continued stability.

C. On what should major classroom emphasis be placed?

1. Crucial moral issues raised in the play:

What price integrity?

What role should the individual seek to play in public affairs?

What form of government is really best?

What comes first—loyalty to family, to principles, to the larger community?

2. Considerations of logic and persuasion in the action and rhetoric of the play:

Where do we find instances of faulty reasoning? irrationality?

What different tactics of persuasion are attempted in the play and for what reasons? How effective do these tactics ultimately prove to be?

Are all of Dr. Stockmann's "discoveries" tenable, particularly those propounded in Acts IV and V?

3. Attention to structure, tone, characterization, and dominant symbols.

What does each act contribute to the total action of the play?

How does Ibsen want us to regard Dr. Stockmann and the plight into which he and his family are plunged?

What does Dr. S. learn as a result of this total experience that he did not know when he first exposed the pollution of the baths?

Is his learning complete?

How does Dr. S. contrast with his brother in character and motivation?

Are the other characters "round" or "flat"? For what purpose has each been introduced?

What elements in the play take on symbolic significance?

II. *Analyzing the play*

A. Clarify possible confusions about plot events by administering a factual quiz, covering such questions as these:

1. Short answers:

a. Why is Captain Horster dismissed from his ship command?

b. Following the town meeting, why does Marton Kiil buy up all the shares in the baths?

c. What reason does Hovstad give Petra for supporting her father?

d. What causes Dr. Stockmann to tell Aslaksen and Hovstad to jump out of the window?

e. What role has Dr. S. played originally in the development of the baths? What earlier advice that he had given was, unfortunately, ignored by the town officials?

f. Dr. S. is not perfect. Give one example that shows he also has personal faults.

g. If you had the opportunity, which character in the play would you nominate as *really* the worst "enemy of the people"? Why?

h. State one or two ideas which Dr. S. expresses at the town meeting which particularly frighten the townspeople and turn them against him.

2. Name the character who states each of the following convictions:

a. "There is so much falsehood both at home and at school.

At home one must not speak, and at school we have to stand and tell lies to the children."

b. "The whole town! Well, it wouldn't be a bad thing. It would just serve them right, and teach them a lesson. They think themselves so much cleverer than we old fellows. . . . Now they shall pay for it. You pull their legs, too, Thomas!"

c. "We shall proceed with the greatest moderation, Doctor. Moderation is always my aim; it is the greatest virtue in a citizen—at least, I think so."

d. ". . . and in my opinion a journalist incurs a heavy responsibility if he neglects a favorable opportunity of emancipating the masses—the humble and oppressed. I know well enough that in exalted circles I shall be called an agitator, and all that sort of thing; but they may call me what they like. If only my conscience doesn't reproach me, then."

e. "Oh yes, right—right. What is the use of having right on your side if you have not might? . . . good heavens, one has to put up with so much injustice in this world. . . . There are the boys. . . ."

f. "And then, when you have had six months to think things over, if, after mature consideration, you can persuade yourself to write a few words of regret, acknowledging your error . . ."

g. "I intend to be free to express my opinion on any subject under the sun."

B. Outline with the class ways in which each act contributes functionally to the overall development and effect of the play.

Act   I: Introduces all characters, provides inciting action (the letter), sets up *personal conflict* between the brothers, and presents Stockmann as idealistic, but highly naive about life and people.

Act II: *Rising action*

Hovstad, Aslaksen, and Billing agree to support Dr. S., but for purely selfish personal reasons.

Peter introduces the *political conflict* (power versus right) and arouses Dr. S. to passionate adherence to his original position, despite pressures from his wife.

Act III: *"Technical climax."*

Hovstad, Aslaksen, and Billing bandy brave words

and convictions until Peter apprises them of a few material facts.

Dr. S. appropriates the mayor's hat and stick a few minutes, until bluntly informed that the other three men have withdrawn their support.

The *reversal* begins, even though Dr. S. only partially recognizes what has happened.

Overcoming fears for her family, Mrs. S. nobly sides with her husband.

Act IV: The *reversal* is complete.

Stockmann forces the conflict to an *ethical* level and is branded an "enemy of the people" for his denunciatory and unconventional philosophy.

This act is essentially essential for Dr. S.'s personal enlightenment, but also reveals that he still has much to learn about "how to win friends and influence people."

Act V: Dr. S.'s convictions are put to the test and he is not found wanting. He vigorously resists three temptations to back down from his position and finally makes the decision to stay where he is and fight back.

Dr. S. is also further enlightened about the degree of corruption in other men and about the power of the independent man. His personal education and enlightenment are, however, far from complete.

C. Ask students to diagram the organization of the play, noting the inverse relationship of Dr. S.'s attempts to enlighten the community and his own personal growth in knowledge and insight.

Dr. S.'s path to enlightenment

Dr. S.'s practical efforts to clean the baths

D. If one of the important patterns in the play is Dr. Stockmann's movement from ignorance and naiveté to greater enlightenment, students need to identify the idealistic beliefs he holds in the beginning of the play and which he is forced to abandon as the action unfolds:

1. He believes scientific facts carry weight and speak for themselves; he is unaware of the force of sociological/economic/political factors.

2. He believes individuals operate out of disinterested motives; only later does he realize that most men pay "lip service" to social ideals ("support stops where the pocketbook begins").

3. He assumes credit will go where credit is due and is unaware of the multiple interpretations that can be applied to human actions.

4. He believes that society ("the compact majority") honors reason and truth—and also honors the men who attempt to spread the truth—and has yet to realize the full extent of hypocrisy and rationalization in human life.

5. He believes that free men have the right to say anything they wish in public, regardless of who is offended or what is attacked; he has yet to learn that independent opinion can be strangled, censored, misinterpreted, ignored—*particularly* by the "liberal-minded independent press."

(Students must, of course, identify various experiences in the play which cause Dr. S. to alter these beliefs. They should also note elements of his background experience, such as his long isolation in a northern Norwegian rural community, that could account for his extreme naiveté. They should, in addition, note instances where Stockmann displays excessive pride and self-satisfaction, character traits that could limit his personal influence and effectiveness.)

E. Are all of Dr. S.'s new ideas ("discoveries") tenable? Which are half-truths? Students should critically examine such contentions as these:

1. Are leading men "like billy-goats in a young plantation; they do mischief everywhere. They stand in a free man's way whichever way he turns. . . ."?

2. "The majority *never* has right on its side. The minority is always in the right."

3. "These 'majority truths' are like last year's cured meat—

like rancid, tainted ham; and they are the origin of the moral scurvy that is rampant in our communities."

4. Can we agree with Stockmann that "isolated, intellectually superior personalities have a greater right "to pronounce judgment and to approve, to direct and to govern"?

5. Do we agree "that the strongest man in the world is he who stands most alone"?

In what ways is Dr. S.'s "learning" still incomplete? What does he need to learn about methods of changing the attitudes and behavior of others?

F. The entire play is really a series of discussions and debates, in which several characters display very faulty thinking or use ineffective tactics of persuasion. Have students point out some of these instances in the play and possibly read selected scenes as illustrations.

G. Even though Dr. S. has his faults, he is still a highly admirable man, especially when we compare him with the others in the play.

1. How does he contrast with his brother—in habits of living, family life, political beliefs, integrity? (It is hard to believe they have the same mother!)

2. What are Stockmann's motives for wanting to expose the pollution of the baths? Do the other men support him for the same reasons? (Students will quickly perceive that Dr. S.'s supposed supporters have only selfish motives:

Kiil—wants revenge for past slights, a chance to gloat over his critics.

Billing—is out for "kicks"; note his brave talk about dynamite and revolution.

Aslaksen—sees a means of dramatizing (inoffensively!) the unity and strength of the small tradesman.

Hovstad—sees an opportunity for self-important target practice on "authorities."

3. In what ways are Dr. S.'s former supporters revealed as moral cowards and true enemies of the people? Students should evaluate both their conduct and rhetoric:

Kiil guards his reputation at all costs; he is totally egocentric, unfeeling, blustery, and illogical, appropriately labeled "the Badger."

Billing is "a many-sided man" who talks big but risks nothing; he is an arm-chair hero and pseudo-non-conformist who runs from every real battle.

Aslaksen is a kind of Uriah Heep, always "moderate" and repulsively cautious, a total conformist and mealy-mouthed hypocrite.

Hovstad is really the vilest hypocrite of the group, as betrayed in his conversation with Petra about her translation, his belief that all men can be bought, and his glib declaration that "every animal must fight for its own livelihood" as justification for corrupt behavior.

4. What is the function of these minor characters: Mrs. Stockmann; Petra; Captain Horster; the drunkard at the meeting?

H. What is the *tone* of the play? How are we supposed to feel about the plight of Dr. S. and his family? (Proceed into a discussion of the mixture of humor, satire, and irony in the play; also note irony of the title.) Has Ibsen weakened the impact of the play by making the hero somewhat ridiculous and extreme?

I. What elements take on symbolic significance in the play? (Note especially the use of the baths to represent both physical and moral pollution; the mayor's hat and stick which Dr. S. briefly borrows in Act III just before the reversal occurs; the detailed use of animal imagery in Acts IV and V, especially the distinction between "cur men" and "poodle men."

J. Identify some of the major themes of the play:

1. Society has far too few Stockmanns—men who dare translate ideals into action and act independent of groups or political parties.

2. Paradoxically, self-interest is ultimately best served by placing the welfare of the total community ahead of selfish personal and family concerns.

3. Social change is a gradual process, best achieved through education and skillful persuasion.

4. Democratic society moves forward only because of the courage, vision, and the example of an enlightened minority, ready to discard what is outmoded or corrupt. In contrast, the unrestrained majority is only too ready to limit individual liberty, free thought, and needed change.

K. Identify some of Dr. S.'s declarations that all men of integrity should support, for example:

"I mean to have the right to look my sons in the face when they are grown men."

"A matter of such great importance—the welfare of the town at stake—it is no time to shirk trouble."

"All the men in this town are old women—like you; they all

think of nothing but their families, and never of the community."

III. *Possible composition topics*

A. Trace the repetitive use of such key words as *truth, public opinion, majority, poison, self-government* throughout the play and then come to some conclusion on this question: Does Ibsen believe in democratic government?

B. Present your nomination of "Enemy of the People No. 1" in this play. Support your case adequately by reference to specific scenes and actions.

C. What does Dr. Stockmann learn about man and society that he did not comprehend before? In what ways is his education still far from complete?

D. Analyze the various devices used by characters in the play to justify inaction, unethical conduct, and hypocritical behavior.

E. One critic has stated: "A careful reading of Ibsen's play with the orientation of modern psychology may lead one to conclude that Stockmann suffers from an acute persecution complex, that he actually seeks his own destruction. At times he seems in a frenzy to develop hostility against himself, and we feel that all of his aims might have been accomplished if he had only been somewhat less hysterical." [16] To what extent do you agree or disagree with this interpretation?

The responsibility for developing a rich and meaningful drama program falls, of course, on already overburdened English teachers, who may also have to overcome the handicap of poor background preparation. Taking more courses in drama is surely only a partial solution, for the love of drama can be transmitted only by teachers who genuinely value reading plays, regularly attending theatrical productions, reading periodicals dealing with the dramatic arts, seeing effective TV and film productions, and following the development of drama in all its forms within our American culture and in other countries of the world. Only through such enthusiastic and dedicated persons can drama be withdrawn from the wings and restored to the center of the classroom stage, to share a leading role with the other dominant forms of our literary tradition.

[16] Edwin Sauer, *English in the Secondary School* (New York: Holt, Rinehart and Winston, 1961), pp. 192–193.

SELECTED BIBLIOGRAPHY (*Outstanding)

Bentley, Eric, *In Search of Theater* (New York: Vintage Books, 1954).
———, *The Playwright as Thinker* (New York: Meridian, 1955).
Bradley, A. C., *Shakespearean Tragedy* (New York: St. Martin's, 1904).
*Brustein, Robert, *Seasons of Discontent* (New York: Simon and Schuster, 1965).
———, *The Theatre of Revolt* (Boston: Little, Brown, 1964).
*Downer, Alan S. (Ed.), *American Drama and Its Critics* (Chicago: University of Chicago Press, 1967).
———, *Fifty Years of American Drama* (Chicago: Regnery, 1951).
*Esslin, Martin, *The Theatre of the Absurd* (New York: Doubleday, 1961).
Fergusson, Francis, *The Idea of a Theater* (New York: Doubleday, 1955).
Freedley, George, and John A. Reeves, *A History of the Theatre* (New York: Crown, 1943).
*Frenz, Horst, *American Playwrights on Drama* (New York: Hill & Wang, 1965).
*Gassner, John, *Directions in Modern Theatre and Drama* (New York: Holt, Rinehart and Winston, 1965).
———, *Producing the Play* (New York: Holt, Rinehart and Winston, 1942).
Goodman, Randolph, *Drama on Stage* (New York: Holt, Rinehart and Winston, 1961).
Gould, Jean, *Modern American Playwrights* (New York: Dodd, Mead, 1966).
*Granville-Barker, Harley, *Prefaces to Shakespeare* (2 vols.; Princeton, N.J.: Princeton University Press, 1926–1946).
Harbage, Alfred, *Shakespeare's Audience* (New York: Columbia University Press, 1941).
Harbrace Drama Sourcebooks (New York: Harcourt):
  Felheim, Marvin (Ed.), *Comedy: Plays, Theory, and Criticism,* 1961.
  Harrison, G. B., *Julius Caesar in Shakespeare, Shaw and the Ancients,* 1961.
  Kernan, Alvin B., *Modern Satire,* 1962.
  Levin, Richard (Ed.), *Tragedy: Plays, Theory, and Criticism,* 1961.
Knight, Arthur, *The Liveliest Art: A Panoramic History of the Movies* (New York: Crowell-Collier-Macmillan, 1956).
*Lerner, Max, "The Arts and Popular Culture" in *America as a Civilization* (New York: Simon and Schuster, 1957), Ch. 2.

*McCarthy, Mary, "Realism in the American Theater," *Harper's,* July 1961, pp. 45–62.

————, "General Macbeth," *Harper's,* June 1962, pp. 35–39.

*MacIver, R. M. (Ed.), *Great Moral Dilemmas in Literature: Past and Present* (New York: Harper & Row, 1956).

*McLuhan, Marshall, *Understanding Media* (New York: McGraw-Hill, 1964).

Roberts, Vera Mowry, *On Stage: A History of Theater* (New York: Harper & Row, 1962).

Rockefeller Brothers Fund, *The Performing Arts* (New York: McGraw-Hill, 1965).

Schramm, Wilbur and others, *Television in the Lives of Our Children* (Palo Alto, Calif.: Stanford University Press, 1961).

*Sewall, Richard B., *The Vision of Tragedy* (New Haven, Conn.: Yale University Press, 1959).

Sontag, Susan, *Against Interpretation* (New York: Farrar, Straus & Giroux, 1966).

Wilson, John Dover, *Life in Shakespeare's England* (Baltimore: Penguin, 1959).

SOURCES PERTAINING TO TEACHING OF DRAMA

*Benedict, Stewart H. (Ed.), *A Teacher's Guide to Modern Drama* (New York: Dell, 1967).

Boutwell, William D., *Using Mass Media in the Schools* (New York: Appleton, 1962).

Dunning, Stephen and Henry W. Sams (Eds.), *Scholarly Appraisals of Literary Works Taught in High Schools* (Champaign, Ill.: NCTE, 1965).

Evans, Bertrand, *Teaching Shakespeare in the High School* (New York: Crowell-Collier-Macmillan, 1966).

Lambert, Robert G., "An Enemy of the People: A Friend of the Teacher," *English Journal,* 54 (October 1965), pp. 626–628.

Loban, Walter, Margaret Ryan, and James R. Squire, "Literature: Drama and Poetry" in *Teaching Language and Literature* (New York: Harcourt, 1961), Ch. 7.

*Mack, Maynard, "Teaching Drama: *Julius Caesar*" in Edward J. Gordon and Edward S. Noyes (Eds.), *Essays on the Teaching of English* (New York: Appleton, 1960), Ch. 17.

NCTE Studies in the Mass Media, 508 South Sixth St., Champaign, Ill. Eight issues a year.

*Ornstein, Robert, *Shakespeare in the Classroom* (Urbana, Ill.: Educational Illustrators, 1960). NCTE publication.

Postman, Neil, *Television and the Teaching of English* (New York: Appleton, 1961). NCTE publication.

Rosenheim, Edward W., Jr., *What Happens in Literature* (Chicago: The University of Chicago Press, 1963).

*Sheridan, Marion C. and others, *The Motion Picture and the Teaching of English* (New York: Appleton, 1965).

The Teachers Guide to Media and Methods (Media and Methods Institute, Inc., 124 East 40th Street, New York 10016). Nine issues per year.

SELECTED MODERN PLAYS FOR CLASSROOM USE

Grade 9

One-act plays

The Valiant, Holworthy Hall and Robert Middlemas

A Shipment of Mute Fate, Les Crutchfield

Trifles, Susan Glaspell

The Devil and Daniel Webster, Stephen Vincent Benét

The Will, James M. Barrie

Two Crooks and a Lady, Eugene Pillot

Beauty and the Jacobin, Booth Tarkington

The Apollo of Bellac, Jean Giraudoux

A Night at an Inn, Lord Dunsany

The Mother, Paddy Chayevsky

TV and radio plays

The Weans, Robert Nathan

Invasion from Mars, H. G. Wells

Visit from a Small Planet, Gore Vidal

Out of Control, William Bruckner

Three-act plays

I Remember Mama, John Van Druten

The Barretts of Wimpole Street, Rudolf Besier

Life with Father, Howard Lindsay and Russell Crouse

The King and I, Richard Rodgers and Oscar Hammerstein II

West Side Story, Arthur Laurents, Leonard Bernstein, and Stephen Sondheim

The Hasty Heart, John Patrick

Abe Lincoln in Illinois, Robert Sherwood

The Late Christopher Bean, Sidney Howard

Antigone, Sophocles

Grade 10

The Miracle Worker, William Gibson

The Desperate Hours, Joseph Hayes

Sunrise at Campobello, Dore Schary

The Diary of Anne Frank, France Goodrich and Albert Hackett
Yellow Jack, Sidney Howard
The Admirable Crichton, James M. Barrie
Journey's End, R. C. Sherriff
The Winslow Boy, Terence Rattigan
Ah, Wilderness!, Eugene O'Neill
Teahouse of the August Moon, John Patrick and Vern Sneider

Ten Little Indians, Agatha Christie
A Majority of One, Leonard Spigelgass
Watch on the Rhine, Lillian Hellman
Romanov and Juliet, Peter Ustinov
Twelve Angry Men, Reginald Rose
Pygmalion; Arms and the Man, George Bernard Shaw
She Stoops to Conquer, Oliver Goldsmith

Grade 11

The Emperor Jones, Eugene O'Neill
The Adding Machine, Street Scene, Elmer Rice
Inherit the Wind, Lawrence and Lee
The Glass Menagerie, Tennessee Williams
The Green Pastures, Marc Connelly
The Little Foxes, Lillian Hellman
A Raisin in the Sun, Lorraine Hansberry
The Silver Cord, Sidney Howard
Death Takes a Holiday, Walter Ferris
A Bell for Adano, Paul Osborn
Our Town; Skin of our Teeth, Thornton Wilder

All My Sons; The Crucible, Arthur Miller
Of Mice and Men, John Steinbeck
The Time of Your Life, William Saroyan
What Price Glory?, Maxwell Anderson and Laurence Stallings
Billy Budd, Louis Coxe and Robert Chapman
The Andersonville Trial, Saul Levitt
The Caine Mutiny Court Martial, Herman Wouk
Member of the Wedding, Carson McCullers
Home of the Brave, Arthur Laurents
The Scarecrow, Percy MacKaye

Grade 12

Victoria Regina, Laurence Housman
Cyrano de Bergerac, Edmond Rostand
A Doll's House, The Wild Duck, An Enemy of the People, Henrik Ibsen

Caesar and Cleopatra, Saint Joan, Major Barbara, G. B. Shaw
The Cherry Orchard, Anton Chekhov
The Corn Is Green, Emlyn Williams

Death of a Salesman, Arthur Miller

Medea, Robinson Jeffers

Darkness at Noon, Sidney Kingsley

Winterset, Elizabeth the Queen, Mary of Scotland, Maxwell Anderson

A Man for All Seasons, Robert Bolt

The Mad Woman of Chaillot, Jean Giraudoux

The Importance of Being Earnest, Oscar Wilde

R. U. R., Karel Capek

Murder in the Cathedral, T. S. Eliot

Becket, Jean Anouilh

Blood Wedding, Frederico Garcia Lorca

Beyond the Horizon, The Hairy Ape, Mourning Becomes Electra, Eugene O'Neill

The Circle, Somerset Maugham

J.B., Archibald MacLeish

The Visit, Friedrich Duerrenmatt

Dear Brutus, J. M. Barrie

Rosencrantz and Guildenstern Are Dead, Tom Stoppard

The Bald Soprano, The Chairs, Eugene Ionesco

No Exit, Jean Paul Sartre

The Royal Hunt of the Sun, Peter Shaffer

The School for Scandal, The Rivals, Richard Sheridan

Oedipus the King, Sophocles

Tartuffe, Molière

The Zoo Story, Edward Albee

8
Biography and Essay
in the Literature Program

Biography, unlike fiction, is not an inherently popular form of literature. The general public *is* interested in people, but the popular taste in recent years has run to the personal narrative of adventure, which often has true literary merit, and to autobiographical confessions of the "I was a Communist" or "I was an alcoholic" variety, which have nothing of literary artistry about them. An occasional biography of high quality—such as Moss Hart's *Act One* or Catherine Drinker Bowen's *The Lion and The Throne*—catches the public fancy, but in general the reading of serious biography is limited to the intelligentsia and the specialists.

Compared with the novel, short story, poem, or play, biography is a minor form of literature, although school anthologies determinedly include selections from biographies, past and current, and teachers dutifully present the form in their classes. There is justice in this, for biography, which is actually more popular among adolescents than among adults, presents some important possibilities and advantages as well as some problems when it is used in the high school literature program.

BIOGRAPHY IN THE LITERATURE PROGRAM:
PROBLEMS AND OPPORTUNITIES

Foremost among the problems posed by teaching biography as a literary genre is the fact that between excellent mature biography and most junior biography there is a wide hiatus, much wider even than that between the better junior novels and mature novels of superior caliber. The best of adult biography, at least since World War II, is in the tradition of the scholar and the historian. The result is that it is often difficult reading—requiring analysis and reflection. By stating this face I do not argue for the exclusion of mature biography from the high school, but suggest that it often may not be feasible for the average and below-average readers.

The best biographies not only are often weighty in style and formidable in organization; they tend naturally to deal with mature phases of life and the conflicts and emotions that accompany these phases. Almost always the person of eminence, about whom a biography is likely to be written, has attained his eminence and made his greatest contributions in later life. Even in Bill Severn's *Adlai Stevenson: Citizen of the World,* for example, a biography for the teen-age audience, the mature phases of Stevenson's career have to be stressed, not his boyhood and youth. Biography often offers little inherent appeal to adolescents or chance for identification by them.

Then, too, the mature biography of the statesman, or scientist, or specialist in any area may demand a background of knowledge beyond that of the average adolescent. For that reason, biographies are especially difficult to use for reading in common. Also, for the adolescent reader, the adult biography, often organized in expository rather than narrative fashion, may be an unnatural kind of reading, far from the tradition of the well-constructed plot or the happy ending. Biography may well be a more valuable adjunct to the social studies or some other class than it is to the English class. Of course, the nature of adult biography points out clearly one responsibility of the senior high school English teacher: to teach students to read it as a distinct form of literature for purposes that may serve more than simple enjoyment.

Yet biography used in the high school program offers some advantages in widening reading horizons. For some adolescents, biography or autobiography has greater impact than fiction because the people and events are, presumably, real. The literal-minded student who has not yet developed a clear perception of why good fiction gets at the truth of human experience may be more impressed by the biography than by the novel. This is particularly true of adolescents who have a certain handicap, especially a physical one. To such students, the inspiration of a story like that of Helen Keller or of Glenn Cunningham, as told in David Boynick's *Champions by Setback,* or that of the girl who loses a limb in Louise Baker's *Out on a Limb* may be nothing short of phenomenal. The reality of the biography may make identification easier for some readers.

Biography, particularly that written for the juvenile audience, often features the kind of heroism, idealism, and martyrdom that the essentially romantic mind of the adolescent especially admires. The person who fights for what he believes in against great odds is a hero to many adolescents—probably to many adults, too, for that matter—and this theme frequently is present in biography such as John F. Kennedy's popular *Profiles in Courage.*

Certainly, biography offers an opportunity to meet students' differing individual interests in various fields. Madelene Goss for example, has written some excellent biographies of great musicians. There are many biographies of sports heroes. No matter what his interest, the adolescent can find it represented in biography. For this reason, biography is valuable in enriching study of science, social studies, and other subjects.

Reading and study of biography can also provide natural motivation for writing about personal experience. Both literature and writing contribute to the student's awareness of the significance of his own everyday experience, and the two come together naturally in connection with biography or autobiography. After reading autobiography students may be better prepared to write thoughtfully about aspects of their own personal experience, and writing an autobiography might be the culminating activity in a class unit on biography and autobiography.

APPROACHES IN TEACHING BIOGRAPHY

The problem of the transition from fiction to biography, in the junior high school, is one which best can be approached through biographies that are fictionalized or that use the techniques of fiction. Biography for the early junior high school should have the same qualities as fiction for that level—action and excitement, human daring and courage, humor and human interest. Fictionalized biographies such as those of Sitting Bull, Kit Carson, and Buffalo Bill by Doris Shannon

Garst are especially appropriate. Not only the content but the style must be considered in choosing "transition" biographies. Some relatively mature biographies utilize the techniques of fiction. For example, compare the passages below, which open biographies of Garibaldi and Leonardo da Vinci, respectively:

> A chill autumn rain was falling; the bitter wind swept it in gusts against his face as he turned into the quiet shabby street. He had left the noisy, lighted wineshops of the harbor quarter behind him. . . .
> The young sailor paused for a moment beneath a flickering gas light, examining the superscription of a letter.[1]

> When you go to Florence, Italy, and look at the city and the rocky, hilly country around it, you may think that all of this has changed very little since the great palaces and bridges were first built.[2]

There is little doubt that the first, which opens like a novel, is more effective in engaging the young reader's interest.

Though a sample unit on biography is outlined later in this chapter, the direct "biography" unit is not the only vehicle for teaching or introducing the genre. Often biographies and autobiographies can be included in thematic units that involve the various types of literature. Biographies of heroes in sports and other fields might be included in an eighth-grade unit on "Heroes Past and Present"; a tenth-grade unit on "To Dare Greatly" might be organized with autobiographical or biographical accounts of mountain climbing, undersea exploration, aviation, and so forth; and "Men of Destiny" in the twelfth grade might include drama and fiction as well as mature biography.

Reading Biography

No matter what the plan of organization for introducing and teaching biography, however, one responsibility is clear: students need to be taught how to read the form, just as they must be taught how to read the other genres of literature. Mature reading of biography demands two major skills: skill in following various patterns of organization, and skill in critical evaluation.

Biographies may be either narrative or expository in organization.

[1] Nina Brown Baker, *Garibaldi* (New York: Vanguard, 1944), p. 11.
[2] Emily Hahn, *Leonardo da Vinci* (New York: Random House, 1956), p. 1.

In the junior high school, of course, narrative biography will be the staple, forming the natural bridge from fiction. Senior high school students, though, should be introduced to biographies that are organized in a variety of expository patterns. For example, the biographer may choose to interpret the character and assess the stature of his subject through analysis of a number of key episodes in his life. This is true, for instance, of Benjamin Thomas' fine one-volume biography of Lincoln.[3] Or the biographer may analyze the various influences on the life and work of the subject. This is often done in biographies of literary figures. A familiarity with various expository forms of organization in biography is especially important for the able student in the senior high school.

Critical evaluation in reading biography, of course, as in reading other forms of literature, is vital. One useful method is for the teacher and the class to draw up a check list that can be used for critically judging biography, whether read individually or by the class in common. Such a check list might be based on two major points.

Authenticity.   It is often hard, without doing research on the subject, to make a judgment about the authenticity of a biography when the subject is relatively obscure or the events are remote. A first distinction that students need to make, with the help of the teacher, is that between biography and biographical fiction, such as the popular stories of Presidents' wives written by Irving Stone or the novels based on biography. Usually, simple examination of the book makes this clear, and permits one to expect that a writer assumed the responsibilities of either the biographer or the novelist.

Having determined that he is dealing with biography, how can the student arrive at some conclusions about authenticity? First, he can look to see whether any bibliography, or list of sources, is given. One or the other often appears even in the better junior biography. He can then consider the adequacy of those sources. Thus, he might be suspicious of one biography of the great Filipino, Carlos Romulo, that is based almost entirely on the speeches and writings of Romulo himself.

One difficulty in trying to assess authenticity is that even in the best of biography certain techniques of fiction might be used. Dialogue may be manufactured, events guessed at, and sequence occasionally

[3] Benjamin Thomas, *Abraham Lincoln* (New York: Knopf, 1952).

based on hypothesis. Lytton Strachey, who is represented frequently in high school anthologies, and who was the most influential biographer in the world during the early twentieth century, introduced the school of readable biography that "broke away from documentation and the rigid bonds of fact," [4] and paved the way for other biographers to exploit its innovations to the fullest. John Garraty writes:

> Some of them ventured daringly beyond the sources; they invented dialogue, described minute actions that *might* have occurred, and presumed to record the thoughts as well as the words and deeds of their subjects. Of course this practice was as old as biography itself—Xenophon could never have remembered Socrates' conversations in the detail with which he recorded them in the *Memorabilia*. Plutarch was a master of this technique as of most others, and even the conscientious Boswell was not above elaborating on his notes.[5]

However, even in the junior high school the pupils can begin to practice identifying obviously fictitious incidents and conversations in biography and those that might have been based on actual documentation. For example, in Garst's *Sitting Bull* there are some things that could have been verified by United States government records, others that could have come from no source but the imagination of the author.

Biographer's relationship to the subject.   The significance and worth of a biography may depend much on the relationship of the biographer to his subject, and appraisal of this relationship is important to discriminating reading of the work. Most good biographies grow out of a biographer's natural affinity for his subject—not true of the authors of the potboilers relatively prevalent among junior biographies. Many junior (and adult) biographies are produced to fill a gap in the market, and the adolescent, after some experience in reading the form, can usually tell when a book "is the product of a harmonious mixture of writer, subject, and surrounding circumstance" [6]—and when it is not.

Garraty complains that "too many biographers drift to their sub-

4 John A. Garraty, *The Nature of Biography* (New York: Knopf, 1957), p. 122.

5 Garraty, pp. 126–127.

6 Garraty, p. 155.

jects haphazardly, depending upon chance alone for a happy combination. They have not weighed their interests and capabilities against the requirements of their selected tasks." Furthermore, Garraty points out that "Many biographies are the result of mutual interest. A specialist in some field, whose work has made him aware of the contribution of one of his predecessors, decides to expand his knowledge and ends in writing a biography." [7] The high school reader of biography, then, can ask, "What qualifications does this biographer have for writing this biography?"

An intimate knowledge of the subject does not necessarily ensure good biography, of course. Quite frequently, the biographer may be a member of the subject's family—a wife or husband, son or daughter. Usually, when that is true, the work is designed as a monument, and the reader needs to separate this from the more objective type of biography. On the other hand, the high school reader should become familiar, too, with the "debunking" tradition in biography. Again, the biographer's background almost always will furnish the clues to this information; and one may guess, for example, that the lifelong conservative is not likely to write anything but a debunking biography of Franklin Delano Roosevelt.

The biographer, then, will be criticized on the grounds of his use of and access to authentic information about his subject, his relationship to the subject and his qualifications for writing the biography, and his literary artistry. The perfect combination of these will result in the biography that presents with vividness a human being and the significance of his achievement.

OUTLINE OF SEQUENCE FOR A UNIT
ON BIOGRAPHY (NINTH GRADE)

PEOPLE IN PRINT [8]

    I. The teacher leads a discussion of well-known contemporary persons who, in the class members' opinions, are leading interesting lives. Then the discussion switches to which well-known, contemporary people are making the greatest contribution to the welfare of the country or civilization as a whole.

[7] Garraty, p. 155.
[8] This unit was taught by the author in classes at East High School, Superior, Wisconsin, and at University High School, Minneapolis, Minnesota.

II. A teacher-prepared quiz is given in which the students are asked to identify a number of famous people in various areas—sports and entertainment, military, general adventure, science, education, the arts, politics, and so on. (Invariably, the students are able to identify more people in the sports-entertainment area than in any other. The teacher may do a bit of good-natured baiting at this point!)

III. The teacher leads a discussion of biographies and autobiographies that class members have already read, jotting various titles on the board. Discussion includes which ones were liked or disliked and why; then proceeds to the purposes and values of reading biography and autobiography.

IV. The teacher distributes a list, appropriate to the range of ability and interest in the class, of biographies and autobiographies available in the school or public library or locally in paperback form. The assignment is that each student must read one book.

V. The teacher and class draw up a check list for judging and evaluating biographies. (The teacher has this reproduced, and distributes it to the class.)

VI. For two or three days, while the class members are choosing books and beginning reading, the class as a whole reads and discusses the several short selections of biography and autobiography included in the class anthology. Reference is made to the check list drawn up earlier.

VII. While the individual reading is progressing, the class studies a series of poems about people, character sketches in verse, which are included in the class anthology, or which the teacher reads aloud or has reproduced from other sources.

VIII. Several subgroups are formed within the class, according to the types of biographies being read. For example, there may be groups of students reading about scientists, sports figures, adventurers, political figures, and so forth. Assignments of group and individual reports are made:

A. Group report: Each group prepares a report of a type such as the following:

1. A panel discussion on the field (science, politics, or others), its opportunities and obstacles, as revealed in the books read in the group.

2. A "This Is Your Life" program based on the career of one of the people read about in the group.

3. A series of interviews in which group members play the roles of people read about.

    4. A "Guess Who" quiz in which a series of clues are given until someone in the class can guess each of the subjects of the biographies read.

  B. Individual reports: All students must write an evaluation of their books, using the check list drawn up earlier.

  C. As enrichment activities, individual students may:

    1. Read another biography of the same person and compare the two treatments.

    2. Do library research on the person, using factual sources, and discuss the biography in view of this research.

 IX. While individual reading is being completed and group reports are being prepared, the class members write character sketches of people they admire in real life. Class time is given to criticism and correction of the papers, as with any set of themes.

  X. Group and individual reports are made.

THE ESSAY

The essential difficulty today in dealing with the teaching of the essay lies in defining "essay." The student in the junior and senior high school assuredly should deal with a wide range of nonfictional prose, other than the biography. But how much of this can be labeled "essay"? For example, are magazine articles essays? And what about editorials or letters? These types of writing—articles, editorials, informative and argumentative prose generally—are the province of all teachers, not only English teachers, just as the development of general reading ability is an all-school rather than an English-class responsibility.

Examination of courses of study in literature and commonly used textbook-anthologies shows that although the essay is a vaguely defined literary genre it enjoys a secure place in the school program. One popular textbook-anthology for the ninth grade, for example, includes eight different essays and articles, ranging from a humorous sketch by James Thurber to a deductively organized discussion of the habits and characteristics of Britons. But experienced teachers are aware of the general unpopularity of essays of the formal type. The major reason for this unpopularity of course is the inherent difficulty of the formal essay. In his very early book on the teaching of high school English, Charles Swain Thomas recognized this difficulty:

Our taste for story is innate, melody and rhyme delight us in our juvenile years, we are early won by the concreteness of the drama; but a liking for the essay has, in most cases, to be carefully developed. This is particularly true if a writer deals primarily with abstract subjects.[9]

Reed Smith has pointed out that the formal essay, such as that written by Bacon, Emerson, Macaulay, Huxley, or Newman, "is the product of an adult mind, written for other adult, trained minds."[10] Of course, even the much anthologized informal or personal essays of Addison, Lamb, and Stevenson, for example, are adult and urbane reflections and meditations.

Many students enjoy such light, humorous essays as those by James Thurber, Stephen Leacock, Robert Benchley, and Art Buchwald. The skills required in reading such essays are essentially the same as the skills required in reading fiction. Indeed, it is difficult to draw the line, for instance, between a Thurber essay and a Thurber short story.

The skills necessary to read the formal essay are the same as those needed to read general formal or analytical discourse—textbooks, for example. Many of the essays commonly included in anthologies for the eleventh and twelfth grades are extremely difficult and abstract. Naturally, it is all to the good for the able student to tackle Bacon or Emerson or Huxley. But it is futile to expect students of less than average ability to read essays by these writers. Essentially, the reading problem, of course, is one of organization. Reed Smith suggested in his book many years ago that teachers furnish the students with outlines of difficult essays. Yet perhaps the process is too often reversed; the teacher asks students to outline essays they are not ready to read. Reading the formal essay requires logical thinking and recognition of patterns of organization in expository discourse. Improvement in these abilities is as gradual as it is in other aspects of literary education. Though essay reading should not be the vehicle for grueling exercises in outlining, it may be extremely valuable as a springboard for student writing. This is true especially of the personal essay that deals with the seeming trivialities, the small awarenesses of living. Currently, this form of writing is largely relegated to newspaper and magazine columns and "departments." It is the mark of the immature ado-

[9] Charles S. Thomas, *The Teaching of English in the Secondary School* (Boston: Houghton Mifflin, 1917).

[10] Reed Smith, *The Teaching of Literature in the High School* (New York: American Book, 1935).

lescent to think that he has nothing worth writing about unless he has undergone harrowing adventure. His reading of informal essays may cause him to reflect, and thus to be prepared to write, on the everyday details of his own existence. And in this lies one pathway to maturity.

The Case for the Essay

Jerome Carlin, former head of the English Department in the Fort Hamilton High School of Brooklyn, presents a lively case for the teaching of the modern essay. A portion of Dr. Carlin's article follows:

> The case against the essay includes these charges: (1) It's dull. There's no story line. Kids won't be interested. (2) It's difficult. Since nothing *happens* and since so much is on an abstract level, those lower-I.Q. boys and girls especially won't stay afloat in an essay unit. (3) It's archaic. Addison and Steele haven't much to say to the generation of Lerner and Loewe. (4) Its form is hard to analyze. Plot, setting, climax, blank verse, rhyme scheme—terms like those, which are such handy labels in lessons on other works, are not to readily available for the essay. Let's look at these charges.

Appeal of the Essay

Dull is it? Young people do take interest in dating, automobiles, flying, sports, comics, money, parents, vacation, college, and even high school. These are the topics of essays in today's textbooks.

"Malinda didn't look as though she knew I was alive after we arrived at the dance . . . She didn't speak to me except to talk about other boys. . . . I found out among other things that she liked 'muscle goons.' I am definitely not athletic. . . . I ended up by walking home alone on my first date." One would be ashamed to accept his monthly check if he failed to draw fire from a class with those lines in the story essay "My Last Date." Written by a fourteen-year-old high school freshman, Philip Thompson, and published originally in *Boy's Life,* the essay appears in a recently published textbook. There is no need to analyze its fascination.

There is no need to puzzle, either, over the appeal of a story essay which appears at the beginning of another textbook collection, the essay "Father Opens My Mail" by Clarence Day. The rights and responsibilities of children and parents give rise to fighting talk even in a drowsy nine o'clock class. A few staunch supporters of respect for parents are bound to speak for patience and filial submission to Father's foibles. Some others will argue, perhaps with careful impersonality, "Yes, many parents are like that—but shouldn't be." With that lead the man behind the desk has a chance to say, "When you become a parent, how will you avoid the failings that you find in Father in this essay?"

For shock effect bring a class face to face with Art Buchwald's statement in "Don't Be a Pal to Your Son": ". . . we should give American children something they desperately need and crave for—brutality. We must make them feel neglected, insecure, unwanted and unloved. . . . They'll be so eager to be wanted that they'll do everything in the world to please us." Come on in, kids. The water is cold—but bracing.

Another kind of interest is aroused by Ruth Sawyer's poignant essay "Crippled: An Appeal to Motorists." "John Paul," says Mrs. Sawyer, "is four years old. He will never get up again—that is, never as a whole, free, exultant little boy. He will never throw back the covers of his cot, shoot across his room and ours, and drop like a plummet, stomach down, on our bed, shouting, "Here I come—Daddy and Mum!" Farther along, the author describes the youth who had been driving a borrowed car without a license, who still doesn't know what he has done—the boy who is restless, nervous, shallow; the boy who says "straightforwardly to the police: 'I was going fifty—late for a date.' " When he visits the hospital and learns that the crippled child is out of danger, this boy is "relieved of all responsibility. 'Gee, I'm glad. If he'd died now—I'd felt awful.' " Even if a student has never sat behind the wheel of a moving car, he is a potential driver. Many a one is eagerly awaiting the day when Dad and the law will allow him to unhitch the Chevrolet and gallop gallantly down the road. Once when I asked a wholesome class of average juniors—no intellectuals—what makes drivers like the one described in the essay so dangerous, I heard wonderful talk of the reckless use of the motor car as a prop to the weak ego, as a display of powers that the driver relates to himself, and as a status symbol of maturity falsely assumed by the immature.

Once drawn in by the lure of essays with such direct appeal to youthful interests, boys and girls won't flinch at tackling subjects of greater depth. In no other type of literature are the opportunities so great to deal directly with values. By the time a student has reached sixteen, the beginning of the middle age of youth, he is ripe for a look at Big Questions. If the groundwork is properly laid, he will react seriously and searchingly to the excerpt from Thoreau's *Walden* "Where I Lived, and What I Lived For." He will read critically Fosdick's "Six Ways to Tell Right from Wrong," and he will single out those of the six which seem most useful in everyday moral decisions. He will come to grips with problems of human relationships and justice in Neuberger's "Their Brothers' Keepers"; of economic relationships in Johnston's "A Warning to Labor and Management"; of governmental and political relationships in Russell's "How to Beat Communism."

So much of the time, the English teacher is a poor Don Quixote leveling his spindly red pencil against errors. If there were a Hippocratic Oath for those entering the profession of English teaching, surely it would declare, "You will exercise your art for the spiritual enrichment of your charges, and you will not spend all of your powers in the cure or prevention of material ills alone." The splendor of literature teaching is its illumination of life. With the essay, particularly, teacher and student can probe at the ideas about life and society that thoughtful writers have deliberately exposed to view. Other literary forms may have other aims. There is no ambiguity about the serious essayist's intention to put ideas before the reader.

What Is the Essay?

Some of the titles already mentioned provide evidence that the essay is a flourishing part of contemporary literature. What has become almost archaic in commercial usage is only the word *essay* itself. The form is as up-to-date as this morning's newspaper or this week's magazine. The current issue (when this was written) of the *Saturday Evening Post* includes in its contents: an article on social attitudes toward the physically disabled, "They Think We Have the Evil Eye," by Bentz Plagemann; a discussion of "Why I Deprive My Children" by Katharine Britton Mishler; and an analysis of economic thinking, pro and con, in "The Great Tariff Battle" by Joe Alex Morris. The current *Harper's* parallels the *Post* with articles on subjects attuned to the interests of its own readers: attitudes of the public toward contemporary art, proposals for a better way to teach deaf children, and the pros and cons of foreign policy regarding Africa, Asia, and the Western Alliance. Examples from local newspapers of the past week include an analysis of the problem of twin children whose capacities are not equal, an exposé and a slashing attack on abuses of mental hospitals, and a dance critique concluding that, in Jacques d'Amboise, America has at last produced a great male ballet dancer. If any of these examples seem too elevated for average readers in or out of high school, a few glances through the pages of teen and movie magazines will reveal the equivalents on another level. There is something for every taste and interest in the modern essay, which in newspaper and magazine goes by the name of article, feature, department, or column.

By the same token every level of reading difficulty exists among essays in commericial publications and has its counterpart in high school textbooks. Where your students tend to take their stand on the normal curve of reading ability should determine your choice of essays for their study. Whether you depend on the essay section of a general anthology or whether you have at hand a textbook collection solely devoted to the essay, you can command materials with a level of reading difficulty ranging from that of *Boys' Life* to that of *Atlantic*.

Neither from the student's point of view nor from the teacher's, need the essay be the psychological hazard that it sometimes becomes. True, if our teaching approach stresses form more than substance, it will prove to be bad magic, drying up that sea of hands around us.

Matters of form need not, should not, be overlooked. Labels enough are ready for application: formal, informal, personal, familiar, descriptive, reflective, philosophic, critical, abstract, factual. But these are mechanical matters of classification—too much like cataloguing books in a library instead of taking them home to read and enjoy.

Keep that shiny enthusiasm undulled. Bring the reader to any essays with the promise that it will reveal something worth considering about a live topic. "What do you think of the practice followed by many colleges in giving valuable scholarships to inferior students who are good athletes?". . . "How do *you* decide whether a particular action is right or wrong?" By such questions arouse interest in the topic; then study the essay for what it has to say on that subject; and only afterwards turn to the matter of form. "Now that we've considered what the author has to say, let's see *how* he said it . . . How did he organize his ideas? . . . What are the characteristics of his style? . . . What examples can you find of statements that are especially appealing or forceful in style? . . . What does this author do that you can put into practice in your own writing?" For the student there is much more excitement, as well as much more to be gained, in first dealing with the substance and in then briefly studying the technical processes by which that content is conveyed.[11]

The brevity of this chapter as contrasted with the chapters on teaching fiction, poetry, and drama is indicative of the author's belief that biography and essay should have a comparatively minor place in

---

[11] Jerome Carlin, "This I Believe—about the Essay," *English Journal,* LI (September 1962), 403–411.

the literature program. But he hopes, however, that the chapter has given ample reasons why they should not be ignored.

SELECTED BIBLIOGRAPHY

Carlsen, G. Robert, "Biography—The Bridge between Fact and Fiction," *Books and the Teen-age Reader* (New York: Bantam, 1967). Ch. 11. Commentary on a number of biographies, junior and adult.

Cook, Don L., "On Teaching Essays." In *On Teaching Literature* (Bloomington, Ind.: Indiana University Press, 1967), pp. 135–150. Identifies benefits in studying essays and discusses teaching approaches with Emerson's "Self-Reliance" and Orwell's "Shooting an Elephant" as illustrations.

Curwen, Henry Darcy, *Teaching Biography in the Secondary School* (Princeton, N.J.: College Entrance Examination Board, Publications Office, 1965). A kinescript which discusses teaching approaches to Moss Hart's *Act One,* Maugham's *The Summing Up,* and Catherine Drinker Bowen's *A Yankee from Olympus.*

Garraty, John A., *The Nature of Biography* (New York: Knopf, 1957).

Kendall, Paul Murray, *The Art of Biography* (New York: W. W. Norton, 1965). Two illuminating discussions of the genre.

Peet, C. Donald, "On Teaching Biography." In *On Teaching Literature* (Bloomington, Ind.: Indiana University Press, 1967), pp. 151–182. A useful discussion ending in a suggestion for a major writing activity growing out of study of biography.

9
Organizing and Planning the Program in Literature

PATTERNS OF ORGANIZATION

Organizing instruction in the secondary school literature program is a perennial problem. English-teaching conferences and workshops have resounded for years with arguments about whether to teach certain "classics"; about whether to organize the literature program by types, by themes or topics, or by chronological survey. There is no magic inherent in any plan of organization; none can offer a sixty-day guaranty of success. The important outcomes discussed in the first chapter of this book can be sought quite successfully through various plans of organization, and the most successful junior and senior high school literature programs probably are eclectic in their basis. Each of the major plans has advantages and disadvantages, some of which are discussed below.

Organization through a Set of Specified Selections

A plan of organization popular several decades ago was based on specific selections. In those days it was customary to see, in senior high school classes at least, sets of thin volumes of individual works—*The Courtship of Miles Standish, The House of the Seven Gables,* and *A Tale of Two Cities.* Certain selections were allocated to each grade level, and entire classes studied them in common. However, this neat and uniform, and rather deadly, method of organizing the year's literature program disappeared, largely because of the appearance of the "omnibus" anthology for each grade, and the majority of teachers used the anthology to teach their grade, whatever the plan of organization of the book.

The wide distribution of paperbound books has brought a revival of the use of sets of novels, biographies, plays, and books of nonfiction. Many junior high school teachers, especially, have taken advantage of the facilities of the Teen-Age Book Club,[1] which offers a convenient monthly plan for buying paperbound books. Some teachers in both junior and senior high school have used sets of paperbound books both for reading by entire classes and for reading in small groups. Paperbacks have been widely used, too, as the basis for classroom libraries. A number of publishers have made available inexpensive editions of full-length works with study guides and teaching aids.

The absence of an overall pattern for the literature program may indicate in some schools that literature study is haphazard and aimless, with no meaningful context, a series of assignments or lessons that add up to nothing in the mind of the student. Some teachers, on the other hand, maintain that an overall pattern of themes, topics, or chronology is unduly restricting and distorting; that each selection of literature should be approached as a thing in itself, an individual work of art. Organization by individual selections is probably most effective in advanced senior high school classes in which the students already have developed rich backgrounds and sophisticated insights and are ready to progress through a series of major works.

Organization by Genres

One of the oldest and best-known ways of organizing the literature program is through study of the genre of literature—novel, short story, poetry, drama, biography, and essay. This plan is especially prevalent at the ninth and tenth-grade levels, and most of the textbook-anthologies for use in those grades are organized by literary types.

There are important advantages in this method. It is neat, orderly, easy to plan and administer, and easily understood by the students. Furthermore, it provides an obvious context in which to teach the skills necessary for reading the various forms of literature.

[1] 50 West 44th Street, New York 10036, N.Y.

There are some serious drawbacks, however, in this plan of organization. First, it is easy for the teacher to become preoccupied with technique, with literary craftsmanship—with verse forms and meter, plot construction, dramatic structure, and so forth. Of course these things have importance, but they should not be stressed at the expense of interest and broader interpretation. Skillful teachers can avoid this pitfall in the genre plan of organization as they can in any other.

Then, too, some of the literary genres do not lend themselves readily to the genre approach. This is true of the longer forms—novel, epic, drama, and biography. It is virtually impossible for a class to read more than one of these types during one unit of work. Therefore the comparing and contrasting essential in the genre approach cannot be done except over a long period of time. Teachers—and anthologies —often resort to excerpts from long works, although as material for genre study excerpts have obvious failings, since they do not represent artistic wholes. Another drawback is that poetry does not fit well into the genre approach. A diet of poetry, sustained over several weeks, is too concentrated for many high school students. Even the most mature readers rarely read poetry that way.

Organization by Chronology

The chronological approach to literature is ordinarily limited to courses in the eleventh and twelfth grades, but there it is widespread. Tradition has placed American literature in the eleventh grade, English literature in the twelfth. In recent years there has been a trend toward other patterns of organization at these grade levels, but probably the majority of eleventh- and twelfth-grade teachers, and certainly the great majority of anthologies for the two grades, still follow the chronological plan. The principal advantage of the chronological survey lies in the perspective it can give to the origin and development of forms of literature and to the growth of the literary tradition as it is related to the development of English and American culture in general. Again, this plan is orderly, logical, and satisfying to the teacher who thinks it important to teach adolescents the historical development of literature.

A trenchant summary of the disadvantages of the chronological approach was made by Robert C. Pooley, in an article published more than three decades ago:

The grave danger of chronology in literature is the tendency to teach the history of literature rather than the literature itself. Facts, dates, and details of biography are stressed. Often relatively unimportant literature is dragged in to complete the historical picture, or student interest is sacrificed to scholarly thoroughness. The early periods in English and American literature are difficult and rarely interesting to more than a few students, yet they come at the beginning of the course when interest is hard to arouse. Furthermore, the chronological plan is exceedingly difficult to tie up with the normal voluntary reading of students. Only exceptional students will read voluntarily literature prior to 1800 with genuine enjoyment and profit.[2]

What is done within the framework of chronology may differ greatly from teacher to teacher. There is no doubt that in terms of student experiences, the chronological survey in many classrooms is deadly. Many teachers are unable to avoid the "factual error" in teaching literature, as defined by Thomas Clark Pollock:

. . . the history of a work of literature is not the work of literature. Facts about a poem are not the poem. They may help a student to understand the poem. To the degree that they do, they are important to the teacher; but it is the literary experience itself in which the teacher should be primarily interested. Our literary heritage lies in the *actual,* if in one sense vicarious, *experiences* which literature can communicate. It is still true that the letter killeth, while the spirit giveth life; and we cannot make our literary heritage real to the youth of America through the letter of factualism.[3]

Yet some teachers, even within the context of the chronological survey, are able to avoid this as well as other pitfalls. One description of an enlightened approach to the survey of English literature is given in an article by Dorothy Bratton.[4] Within recent years, many schools have experimented with modest modifications of the traditional surveys. For example, such American writers as Herman Melville, Mark Twain, Thomas Wolfe, Ernest Hemingway, and William Faulkner are

---

[2] Robert C. Pooley, "Varied Patterns of Approach in the Teaching of Literature," *English Journal,* XXVIII (May 1939), 345.

[3] Thomas Clark Pollock, "Transmitting Our Literary Heritage," *English Journal,* XXXI (March 1942), 204.

[4] Dorothy Bratton, "English Literature for the Non-College-Bound," *English Journal,* XLV (February 1956), 84–91.

often studied in the twelfth grade. Many senior courses have also introduced "world literature," involving mainly selections from European writers but occasionally from Oriental, Latin American, or other literature. A few twelfth-grade teachers are even experimenting with chronology in reverse—starting with the present and working backward, rather than vice versa. Certainly, there is merit in this if the aim is to make literature of the past relevant to the concerns of youth today.

Organization by Themes

Organization of the literature program by themes has been, since the late 1930s, a popular, though continually controversial, pattern. Definition of the thematic plan cannot be as clearcut as that of any of the patterns discussed so far, for thematic organization may suggest anything from reading of a group of selections having something to do with a broad topic to close tracing of an archetype through a series of works.

Simple classification of selections under a topic supposedly of interest to students—The World of Sports, The Animal Kingdom, Suspense, Danger and Daring—has been common in textbook-anthologies for the junior high school for a number of years. In such organization, the topic provides a convenient way of dividing up the selections to be read, and the main stress is on the individual selections with little real concern for the topic itself.

In some units of teaching, on the other hand, the major stress is on a theme of significance to adolescents as it is illuminated by a series of selections, although there is usually concern with genre and form. A junior high school group studied, for example, "The Many Faces of Courage," to discover how different kinds of courage were exhibited in a group of selections of prose and poetry. A class of seniors studied attitudes toward nature, as expressed in literature, in a unit entitled "Every Common Sight." A series of themes may provide the framework for the entire program in literature. In the Curriculum Study Center in English at the Florida State University, a junior high school literature program was built on six "thematic categories," with one unit in each category introduced in each grade, according to the following chart.

Thematic Category	Seventh Grade	Eighth Grade	Ninth Grade
The Unknown	Qualities of Folk Heroes	Deeds and Qualities of Men of Myth	Concern for the Unexplained
Frontiers and Horizons	Faraway Places	The Village	Frontiers in Space
Decisions	Courage	Responsibility	Justice
Teamwork	Team Leaders	The Family	The Team and the Individual
Man in Action	Man and Nature	Man among Enemies	Man Alone
Relationships	Images of Adolescents	Close Adolescent Relationships	Mirrors (relation with self)

One great advantage of the thematic unit, no matter which of the three varieties of those just discussed it may represent, is that it permits the teacher to start with aspects of experience that students themselves recognize as important. There is an inherently better chance of interesting students by introducing a theme or topic—sportsmanship, qualities of success, attitudes toward love—than by announcing a unit on poetry or one on the next forty pages in the anthology. Most students are interested in ideas, and a skillfully chosen idea, stated as a theme for study, may serve as a real spark to student motivation.

The appeal to students' vital interests of a well-developed thematic unit furnishes built-in motivation and preparation for oral and written composition. A related advantage is that thematic organization makes for a natural and profitable relating of literature to other arts such as painting and music and to other media such as motion picture and television.

Another major advantage is that thematic organization provides an excellent opportunity to adjust the necessarily group process of teaching to a room full of individuals often startlingly disparate in their potentialities for emotional and intellectual adventure. Unable to deal profitably with the same selection or series of authors, they still may deal on a feasible level with the same theme or problem.

There are pitfalls to be avoided in the thematic plan of organization as in any other. The first of these pitfalls may lie in the selection of the theme. Is the theme significant to the intellectual and esthetic development of the students at a given grade level? This is a key question. Many thematic units probably dwell on fulsome platitudes or on ideas that may be bewitching to the teacher but completely baffling to the students. Though the teacher may have proudly produced a term paper on "The *Carpe Diem* Theme in Elizabethan Lyrics" in one of his graduate courses, the subject may not be appropriate for high school classes. On the other hand, student interest is not a completely reliable criterion either. Motorcycles may seem a vital subject to many adolescents but they will not provide a sound basis for a teaching unit.

Another pitfall lies in the selection of material to be read in a certain unit. Once the theme is selected, the teacher's next step is to choose selections of literature that are relevant in developing the theme and appropriate both to the students and to important aims in teaching literature. All these conditions are important; it is not enough that the selections represent a useful kind of propaganda—that they merely "have something to say" about the theme. They must fit into the teacher's broader purposes in teaching literature to a particular group of students.

Attempts to find selections that "fit" a certain theme have sometimes involved teachers in the ludicrous. Teaching Shelley's "To a Skylark" in a unit on "Living in an Air Age" seems farfetched. The problem of finding material appropriate to the theme may sometimes lead teachers to settle for inferior selections that give no real chance to teach literature or to lead students to higher levels of awareness. Doggerel about going swimming, for example, may be relevant to a unit on sports, but may not be useful in achieving the purposes of teaching poetry to a group of junior high school students.

The thematic unit also is rather easily prey to aimlessness or lack of direction. The teacher has to work constantly to keep the program of reading directed somewhere. Younger students, especially, may quickly lose sight of the theme unless the teacher keeps it constantly before them. Discussion of literature in a unit in which not everyone has read the same selections may wander into a directionless, though possibly interesting, morass unless the teacher carefully prepares and structures the discussions. Some teachers have found it helpful to prepare for and assign a discussion a day before it is actually to be held, rather than launch into it impromptu. Some years ago Bertha Handlan wrote an article on guiding a discussion of reading in a class where students had read different selections, and it remains a helpful reference on the topic.[5]

The most common criticism of thematic organization is that student attention is diverted from literature to social issues and matters of ethics and morals. This is not necessarily a valid criticism for it may be all to the good that literature study sometimes leads to such concerns, and these broader concerns and concern with literary art need not be thought of as a dichotomy. Yet it is important that student attention be focused essentially on literary matters.

Combination of Approaches

As noted at the opening of this chapter, an eclectic approach to organization is evident in many literature programs, and patterns often merge in well-conceived units of teaching. The illustrative sequence outlined in chapter 2, for example, combines three patterns of organization—by theme, by literary mode, and by genre. A course in world literature offered at the Jackson High School, Miami, Florida, includes the following major units:

The Middle Ages (including common reading of the *Iliad* and of excerpts from several national epics)

The Literary Hero (including common reading of Ciardi's translation of the *Inferno* and of Chaucer's *Prologue*)

Satire and Man's Search for Utopia (including reading of sections of *Gulliver's Travels,* More's *Utopia,* Plato's *Republic,* Voltaire's *Candide*)

Man Looks at the Devil (including reading of Part I of *Faust* and all or parts of other works; the Faust legend in music)

The Development of the Novel (including reading of Joyce's *The Dead,* Gogol's *The Overcoat,* Faulkner's *The Bear*)

Youth: The Search for Understanding (including group reading of John Knowles' *A Separate Peace*)

[5] Bertha Handlan, "Group Discussion of Individual Reading," *English Journal,* XXXII (February 1943), 67–74.

One genre frequently may be studied in relation to a theme, as illustrated in the grouping of poems suggested in chapter 6. Sometimes individual "classics" may be studied in thematic units—one class studied *Macbeth* as the climax of a unit entitled "Trial by Conscience." It is also quite possible to utilize chronological organization at some points in a year's course without casting the entire program in that mold. A class might study the neoclassical and romantic periods and then examine the contemporary influences of those periods, and at other times study genre or thematic units.

The trend toward de-emphasis of grades and toward module scheduling opens new possibilities for organization of the literature program. Some senior high schools have moved away from "tenth-grade English," "eleventh-grade English," and so on in favor of one-semester, or shorter, specialized courses—modern literature, growth in literature, Negro literature, and so forth, in which students from more than one grade may be enrolled. One form of module scheduling, such as that followed at the Florida High School, Tallahassee, Florida, features units of several weeks length in literature (and other aspects of English) focused on themes, modes, genres, or elements of technique in which students from various grades may be enrolled.

The Extensive Phase of the Program

The literature program should include intensive experiences that come from class study and analysis of selections of literature and extensive experiences that come from individual reading. The in-class literature program that does not lead to voluntary out-of-class reading by many of the students may well be suspect. But the choice of whether to carry on individual reading cannot be left to the adolescent. All students, it is hoped, will have some time and inclination to read for pure recreation, no matter whether their choices of material are or are not related to school subjects. Individual reading, as distinct from purely recreational reading (though the twain should often meet!), should be an integral part of the literature program. Individual and extensive reading grows very naturally out of the topical or thematic pattern in which students first consider together selections related to the topic or theme and then go individually, or in small groups, to other selections suited to their tastes and abilities but still relevant to the topic or theme. But whatever the plan of organization individual reading is essential in promoting reading interests and in providing for individual tastes and capacities. The individual reading program cannot be something separate, something divorced from the in-class study of literature. The fairly widespread requirement of "outside" reading—usually involving a written or oral book report every six or eight weeks—profits little if the outside reading program is not planned and individualized. The Tuesday book report session and the mimeographed reporting forms are remembered with distaste by the majority of high school graduates.

The extensive individual reading phase should be as carefully planned as the in-class, intensive phase of the literature program. There are two main general ways in which a planned out-of-class program may be set up. First, the teacher may outline several alternatives for independent reading in each of the literature units during the year, alternatives appropriate, of course, to the range of interests and capacities in the class. The literature units distributed, for example, by the Scholastic Book Services are organized usually in three phases, proceeding from total class activities, in the first phase, through small-group activity in the second, to individual reading relating to the theme or topic of the unit in the third phase.

Second, the teacher may set up with each student an individual reading design that will appropriately supplement and enrich the in-class literature study for the term and will reflect each student's interests and abilities. Stephen Dunning outlines a five-step plan for individual reading designs:

1. The teacher talks individually with students about possible reading programs that will fit their interests. Suggestions appropriate to the different capacities of students are made.
2. The student writes out his plan and perhaps includes a tentative bibliography.
3. The teacher discusses the plans with each student, giving further suggestions.
4. The student then submits a final plan or "contract."
5. The teacher keeps informal contact with the students as the plans are carried out and probably provides some kind of feedback for the class from some or all of the projects, which may range from

something as broad as "Literature of Pre–Civil War America" to something as specific as "Wives of Three Presidents." [6]

Some feedback to the class from the individual reading, as just suggested, often may be beneficial to the individual student or the class. Certainly the stereotyped book report on the standardized form is outmoded, and certainly the student should not be required to report formally on everything he reads. At times a general, informal class discussion on a certain category of books—current novels, for example—will serve in lieu of individual reports. The teacher-student conference, when feasible, may cover a lot of ground. Yet the individual report will occasionally be needed. Jerome Carlin describes a number of possibilities for the book report:

Analysis by a man of the future. In a time capsule or in the ruins on the planet Earth some man of the future finds the book and writes a paper on what it reveals of life of the earlier time.

The diary of a major character. At least three crucial days in the life of the character are dealt with as if they were being summarized in that person's diary.

A letter written in the role of a book character.

Written analysis from a specific standpoint.

Formal book review. The superior student can clip a book review from a newspaper and use it as a model for a review of the book which he has read.

The scholarly critical paper. Honors classes may combine research on "what the critics and authorities think of the author" with critical opinion on "what I think about those of his books which I have read." A separate section on the latter is a wise requirement, to encourage original thinking.

Round-table discussion under a student chairman.

Conversation. Students are paired for conversation about a book.

Oral reading and discussion of brief excerpts.

Significant incident or anecdote. Each student is a speaker on a TV program about good books. He must interest the audience by telling only one incident or anecdote from his book—comic, tragic, suspenseful, or otherwise possessed of human interest.

[6] "Sequence and Literature: Some Teaching Facts," *High School Journal,* XLVII (October 1963), 2–12.

Dramatization. A committee prepares and presents a scene in radio-script fashion.

Reporter at the scene. While it's happening, a crucial scene from the book is described on the spot by a TV or radio reporter.

The trail of a major character. Defendant, prosecuting attorney, defense attorney, and witnesses may participate in the case. The charge should preferably be one of acting unethically, unfairly, or even unwisely, rather than one of breaking a law.

Interview. A character in the book is interviewed by a reporter or by a TV interviewer.

The author meets the critics. Three, four, or five students may form a group. Thus Charles Dickens may defend his *A Tale of Two Cities* against two critics, as they ask: "Why didn't you save Carton by some plot twist, giving the book a happy ending? . . ."

Monologue or dialogue. A pupil takes the role of the major character and in a process of "thinking out loud" talks about the critical situation or problem he is facing at the high point of the story. This may be varied by using two students in a dialogue.

Sales talk. The student represents himself as a salesman endeavoring to sell the book to the class by means of a talk on its good points.

Presentation to a publisher. The class is the selection committee for a publisher or for one of the publishing book clubs. The student presents his report on a book from the standpoint of whether it should be published or of whether it should be offered to the book club membership.

Discussion of proposed production conducted by a "playwright" and a "producer."

Outline of a TV or motion-picture version.

Art and other creative work. Book jackets, advertising blurbs, maps, scenes from the story, pictures of characters, posters, and the like are generally useful as supplements, but they do not always serve the purpose of requiring thoughtful consideration of the book. An accompanying analytical talk or paper is desirable if the creative work is intended to serve as a book report.[7]

The teacher scarcely can expect the students to read extensively and to share reading in various kinds of reports if he himself does not show an enthusiasm for reading and for sharing his reading experiences with his classes. The teacher's comments on the books he is

[7] Jerome Carlin, "Your Next Book Report . . . ," *English Journal,* L (January 1961), 16–22.

reading or has read are a rich source of motivation for students. Not only is the well-prepared teacher of literature thoroughly grounded in the literary tradition; he also makes an effort to keep abreast of the current scene through active reading of new books and of magazines such as the *Saturday Review,* which presents reviews and a coverage of the literary world.

THE DIMENSION OF STUDENT POTENTIAL

Teachers in most situations will meet roomfuls of students with varied, sometimes startlingly so, potentials for experiencing literature. Though "individual differences" was a common refrain in the prospective teacher's professional courses, the encounter with the problem in the flesh often is a shock and it remains with the teacher at every turn in planning and organizing the literature program.

The problem of heterogeneity in potential probably is more acute in English, at least in the senior high school, than in other subjects since in most schools all students are required to take English in each grade. Students do not ordinarily enter classes in physics or chemistry, or in advanced algebra, geometry, or trigonometry, for example, unless they have shown some proficiency in earlier courses in mathematics or science. The major approach to the problem in schools with the traditional grade levels is homogeneous grouping or "tracking," in which the students within each grade are grouped, according to certain criteria, at three or four levels of ability. Controversy surrounds the system of ability grouping and its effectiveness has never been fully established or refuted. Many teachers are uneasy with the obvious fact that ability grouping in English turns out to be, by and large, also grouping according to socioeconomic status. Teachers of high-ability groups are usually pleased with the plan; teachers of low-ability groups are much less enthusiastic and, in fact, are often in despair. Discipline problems tend to pile up in the low-ability groups, and such groups lack the inspiration or leavening influence which the brighter students can give. In general, success with ability grouping in English seems to depend upon two conditions:

1. *The grouping is actually effective in separating students according to their ability in literature or in other aspects of the English*

course. Sometimes, groups may be real only on paper. Problems of scheduling individual students, carelessness, or lack of guidance may result in many students being out of place. Potential and actual achievement have to be balanced in grouping students. For example, a student with a very high IQ may be basically uninterested and unmotivated in English and may therefore not belong in the highest ability group. A combination of past achievement in English, a high IQ, and reading ability seems to be the most effective basis on which to group students for work in English.

2. *Once the students are efficiently grouped, the program must be differentiated in each group.* It is futile to group students at three or four levels and then to offer the same English program at each level, or to differentiate only in quantity of work or in the pace with which ground is covered. Yet this is what is done in many schools, accounting for many of the problems, disciplinary and otherwise, in lower-ability sections.

Homogeneous grouping, or tracking, is not the only, or necessarily the best, answer to the problem of a range of capacities. In smaller schools, track systems may not be feasible administratively. The development of ungraded programs, team teaching, modular scheduling, the replacement of year-long, grade-level courses with shorter-term, specialized electives, and other innovations in bringing students and teachers together may already have made the traditional ability grouping passé. Difference in potential for experiencing literature will remain no matter what scheme is used to bring a group together, and no matter what the scheme, the teaching of literature can be adjusted effectively to the range in potential through a combination of three basic approaches:

1. *Differentiation in the discussion or in the activities based on a selection read in common.* Reading of the same selection by all the members of a class does not rule out possibilities of adjusting to different levels of ability. In setting up guide questions for the reading, or in phrasing questions for discussion following the reading, the teacher can keep in mind the various categories of students in his class. Some questions should be beamed to the lowest ability level, some to the highest, some in between. (This is a matter treated more fully in the next section of this chapter.) Other kinds of oral or written activities which may be based on a selection read in common may be planned, too, to make greater or lesser demands on the student.

2. *Grouping within the class.* For many years, teachers in the elementary school have grouped classes for work in reading and other phases of the program. Often, a high school English class, too, may be divided into several groups to read certain selections or sets of selections. This method is common to the Scholastic Literature Units, referred to earlier in this chapter, and the technique is described in detail in an article by James Squire.[8]

3. *Individualization of reading.* At times good programs in literature will feature complete individualization in selections assigned or read. It was pointed out earlier that the thematic or topical unit is especially helpful in providing a core of unity for widely differentiated individual reading. The extensive phase of the program which may feature individual reading designs, as discussed earlier, offers obvious possibilities for each student to perform at his level of potential.

Planning for Groups with Specific Characteristics

What has been said so far in this chapter is directed to the inevitable problem of differing potential for approaching literature that any group of individuals represents, no matter what the basis for assembling the group. Plans for ability grouping and scheduling and sociological accidents which account for certain schools being located in certain areas, however, result in students of certain characteristics appearing in given classes and given schools. The last decade and a half has seen almost frenetic efforts to develop programs adapted to students with certain kinds of intellectual, cultural, and emotional characteristics. The remainder of this chapter attempts to identify and illustrate the characteristics of programs in literature for the superior, the untalented, and the disadvantaged student.

The Superior Student

Several years ago when the author was preparing the revised edition of this book there was a tremendous concern with English programs for gifted students. It seemed impossible to keep up with the publications on the subject. Now, at this writing, concern with the gifted

---

[8] James Squire, "Individualizing the Teaching of Literature," *English Journal,* XLV (September 1956), 314–319.

seems to have all but vanished if one is to judge by current publications. Today the major concern seems to be with English for the disadvantaged student. No criticism is implied in these remarks. Programs for the gifted are now probably well established whereas those for the disadvantaged are not, and the gifted student seldom is a teaching problem once his abilities are recognized and taken account of in planning. There has been a recognition possibly, too, that many of the best traditional curricula and materials in literature, offered to all students, actually are suitable only for the superior. In literature, the needs of superior students have been met by various applications of the basic procedures for differentiating instruction just discussed. A survey of actual practices of various schools throughout the country shows that the following are the principal ways of providing for superior students in literature:

Ability grouping.   In English classes where only students of highest ability are enrolled, teachers can go far beyond the familiar boundaries of the high school course. Yet in these classes, the plans of organization and methodology tend to be similar to those in the heterogeneous classes. The most successful programs for high-ability students seem to be marked by wide reading of works too mature and difficult for the general run of students, by close analysis of individual works, and by exploration of themes or topics too advanced for average students. In the Portland, Oregon, public schools, superior students are allowed to enroll in "seminars" which carry the following kinds of projects:

> A sophomore project in one school presented the literature of certain high points in the development of Western civilization. The period of the Greeks, for example, students read *The Iliad,* Euripides' *Trojan Women,* Plato's *Apology,* and supplementary readings in Sophocles, Aeschylus, and Xenephon. . . . In a junior English seminar, students studied contrasts in the philosophies of American writers—for example, the pragmatic approach to life's problems as exemplified by Samuel Sewall and Benjamin Franklin in contrast with the theological approach of Jonathan Edwards; and the idealism of Whitman and Emerson in contrast with the critical realism of Sinclair Lewis. A senior seminar, aiming to deepen understanding of certain English masterpieces, made a comparative study of similar genres from other periods or countries: for example, in connection with study of *The Canterbury Tales,* stu-

dents also read *Tristram and Iseult* and *Aucassin and Nicolette,* and *Connecticut Yankee in King Arthur's Court,* and in comparison with *Macbeth,* certain Greek tragedies, and plays by Ibsen, Molière, and George Bernard Shaw.[9]

The Curriculum Study Center in English at the Carnegie-Mellon University developed a senior high school English curriculum for "able college-bound students." The outline of the literature program follows:

WORLD LITERATURE
UNIVERSAL CONCERNS OF MAN
Grade 10

Introductory Unit

"Old Milon," Guy de Maupassant
"The Stranger's Note," Lin Yutang
"The Stream of Days," Tāhā Hussein
"The Bet," Anton Chekhov

Unit One:
Social Concerns

A Tale of Two Cities, Charles Dickens
"Biryuk," Ivan Turgenev
"Rashōmon," Ryūnosuke Akutagawa
"Chastity," Lin Yutang
"Golden Bells," Po Chü-i
"Remembering Golden Bells," Po Chü-i
"My Lord, the Baby," Rabindranath Tagore
"Return: Two Poems," Abioseh Nicol

"Tell Freedom," Peter Abrahams
An Enemy of the People, Henrik Ibsen
"The Prisoner," Po Chü-i
"The Dwarf Trees," Seami Motokiyo
All Quiet on the Western Front, Erich Maria Remarque
A Child's Christmas in Wales, Dylan Thomas

Unit Two:
Love

The Cradle Song, G. and M. Martínez Sierra
"Love: Three Pages from a Sportsman's Book," Guy de Maupassant
"Chienniang," Lin Yutang
"Half a Sheet of Paper," August Strindberg

[9] Reported by Marian Zollinger, Supervisor of Language Arts, Portland Public Schools, in a talk at the convention of the NCTE, Minneapolis, Minn., Nov. 29, 1957.

"Our Lady's Juggler," Anatole France

The Book of Ruth, Psalms (selected)

"Hymn of Love to God," Rabindranath Tagore

"Song of Praise to the Creator," G. H. Franz

I Corinthians, Chapter 13

"Tāj Mahal," Rabindranath Tagore

Carmen, Prosper Mérimée

Cyrano de Bergerac, Edmond Rostand

Unit Three:
Reality and Illusion

"War," Luigi Pirandello

"A Character is Distress," Luigi Pirandello

"Maya," Vera Inber

"In a Grove," Ryunosuke Akutagawa

The General's Ring, Selma Lagerlöf

Unit Four:
Heroism

The Iliad of Homer, I. A. Richards (Trans.)

Exodus, Deuteronomy, The Story of Moses

Beowulf from *The Medieval Myths*, N. L. Goodrich (Ed.)

The Song of Roland from *The Medieval Myths*, N. L. Goodrich (Ed.)

The Cid from *The Medieval Myths*, N. L. Goodrich (Ed.)

Julius Ceasar, William Shakespeare

Plutarch's Lives (Caesar; Brutus)

"Mateo Falcone," Prosper Mérimée

Master and Man, Leo Tolstoy

Unit Five:
Human Weakness

"Christ in Flanders," Honoré de Balzac

"The Queen of Spades," Alexander Pushkin

"A Coup d'État," Guy de Maupassant

"My Uncle Jules," Guy de Maupassant

"A Piece of String," Guy de Maupassant

The Miser, Molière

"How Much Land Does a Man Need?" Leo Tolstoy

"The Father," Björnstjerne Björnson

"As the Night, the Day," Abioseh Nicol

Unit Six:
The Search for Wisdom

"The Story of a Story," Selma Lagerlöf

"Sotho Boyhood," A. S. Legodi

"Rammone Returns to the Kalahari," M. O. M Seboni

Memoirs of Childhood and Youth, Albert Schweitzer

Wind, Sand and Stars, Antoine de Saint-Exupéry

The Plague, Albert Camus

"Chu-ch'ēn Village," Po Chü-i

"Watching the Reapers," Po Chü-i

"Passing T'ien-mēn Street," Po Chü-i

Haiku poetry (selected)

"Flute Players," Jean-Joseph Rabéarivelo
Ecclesiastes (selections)
"On This Tiny Raft," Rabindranath Tagore

The Parables of Jesus (selected)
"What Men Live By," Leo Tolstoy
The Apology of Socrates, Plato
The Death of Socrates (from *Phaedo*), Plato

AMERICAN LITERATURE
MODIFICATION BY CULTURE PATTERN
Grade 11

Unit One:
The American Puritan Attitude

The Crucible, Arthur Miller
The Scarlet Letter, Nathaniel Hawthorne
"Observations of the Bewitched Child," Cotton Mather
"An Arrow Against Profane and Promiscuous Dancing," Increase Mather
"The Simple Cobbler of Aggawam," Nathaniel Ward
"Thomas Shepard's Autobiography" (selections)
"A Narrative of the Captivity," Mary Rowlandson
"The Day of Doom," Michael Wigglesworth
"Young Goodman Brown," Nathaniel Hawthorne
Ethan Fromme, Edith Wharton
"New England," Edward Arlington Robinson

Unit Two:
The American Desire for Success

The Autobiography (selections), Benjamin Franklin
The Rise of Silas Lapham, William Dean Howells

All My Sons, Arthur Miller
The Great Gatsby, F. Scott Fitzgerald

Unit Three:
The American Idealism

"The American Scholar," Ralph Waldo Emerson
"Self-Reliance," Ralph Waldo Emerson
Walden, Henry David Thoreau
"To a Waterfowl," William Cullen Bryant
"Thanatopsis," William Cullen Bryant
"The Chambered Nautilus," Oliver Wendell Holmes
"Days," Ralph Waldo Emerson
"Nature," Henry Wadsworth Longfellow
"Gettysburg Address," Abraham Lincoln
"Second Inaugural Address," Abraham Lincoln
"Song of Myself," Walt Whitman
O Pioneers!, Willa Cather
Selected Poems, Emily Dickinson
"Love Is Not All," Edna St. Vincent Millay
"Renascence," Edna St. Vincent Millay

"Chicago," Carl Sandburg

"The People Will Live On," Carl Sandburg

"Skyscraper," Carl Sandburg

"Mending Wall," Robert Frost

"Two Tramps in Mud Time," Robert Frost

"Stopping by Woods on a Snowy Evening," Robert Frost

"The Tuft of Flowers," Robert Frost

"all ignorance tobaggans into know," e. e. cummings

"what if a much of a which of a wind," e. e. cummings

Our Town, Thornton Wilder

Unit Four:
The American Darker Spirit

"The Fall of the House of Usher," Edgar Allan Poe

"The Masque of the Red Death," Edgar Allan Poe

"The Cask of Amontillado," Edgar Allan Poe

"The Boarded Window," Ambrose Bierce

"The Lottery," Shirley Jackson

"Wash," William Faulkner

"Flight," John Steinbeck

The Emperor Jones, Eugene O'Neill

Moby Dick, Herman Melville

"The Raven," Edgar Allan Poe

"Annabel Lee," Edgar Allan Poe

"To Helen," Edgar Allan Poe

"Ulalume," Edgar Allan Poe

"Margrave," Robinson Jeffers

The Glass Menagerie, Tennessee Williams

Unit Five:
The American Social Conscience

The Jungle, Upton Sinclair

The Adventures of Huckleberry Finn, Mark Twain

Winterset, Maxwell Anderson

"The Man with the Hoe," Edwin Markham

"The End of the World," Archibald MacLeish

"Factory Windows," Vachel Lindsay

"next to of course god america i," e. e. cummings

"pity this busy monster, manunkind," e. e. cummings

Babbitt, Sinclair Lewis

Unit Six:
The Modern American Quest for Identity

The Hairy Ape, Eugene O'Neill

The Red Badge of Courage, Stephen Crane

"The Day of the Last Rock Fight," Joseph Whitehill

"In Greenwich There are Many Gravelled Walks," Hortense Calisher

"Cyclists' Raid," Frank Rooney

"The Four Lost Men," Thomas Wolfe

"The Rich Boy," F. Scott Fitzgerald

"Birches," Robert Frost

"The Road Not Taken," Robert Frost

"To Earthward," Robert Frost

The Unvanquished, William Faulkner

ENGLISH LITERATURE
LITERARY ART FORMS, GENRES, TECHNIQUES
Grade 12

Unit One:
The Tale

The Decameron (selected tales), Boccaccio
Sir Gawain and the Green Knight, Brian Stone (Trans.)
The Canterbury Tales (selected tales), Geoffrey Chaucer
"The Prisoner of Chillon," George Gordon, Lord Byron
The Secret Sharer, Joseph Conrad
Introduction to *Tellers of Tales,* W. Somerset Maugham (Ed.)

Unit Two:
Tragedy

King Oedipus, Sophocles
Macbeth, William Shakespeare
Wuthering Heights, Emily Brontë
"The Substance of Shakespearean Tragedy" from *Shakespearean Tragedy,* A. C. Bradley

Unit Three:
Lyric Poetry I

"Out Upon It!", Sir John Suckling
"Let Me Not to the Marriage . . ." William Shakespeare
"Gather Ye Rosebuds," Robert Herrick
"On His Blindness," John Milton
"Edward," Anon.
"Since There's No Help . . . ," Michael Drayton
"That Time of Year Thou Mayst in me Behold," William Shakespeare

"To His Coy Mistress," Andrew Marvell
"Fear No More," William Shakespeare
"A Valediction: Forbidding Mourning," John Donne
"Song to Celia," Ben Jonson
"My Mistress' Eyes . . . ," William Shakespeare
"When in Disgrace . . . ," William Shakespeare
"Death, Be not Proud," John Donne

Unit Four:
The Epic

Beowulf, Edwin Morgan (trans.)
Paradise Lost, John Milton
from *A Preface to Paradise Lost,* C. S. Lewis

Unit Five:
Satire

Arms and the Man, George Bernard Shaw
Gulliver's Travels, Jonathan Swift
Don Juan, Canto I, George Gordon, Lord Byron
"The Nature of Satire" from *English Satire,* James Sutherland

Unit Six:
Lyric Poetry II

"Ah, Are You Digging on My Grave?", Thomas Hardy

"La Belle Dame sans Merci," John Keats

"My Last Duchess," Robert Browning

"Ulysses," Alfred, Lord Tennyson

"Journey of the Magi," T. S. Eliot

"The Lamb," William Blake

"The Tiger," William Blake

"Lines Composed a Few Miles Above Tintern Abbey," William Wordsworth

"Dover Beach," Matthew Arnold

"Ode on a Grecian Urn," John Keats

"Ode to the West Wind," Percy Shelley

"Neutral Tones," Thomas Hardy

"I Wake and Feel the Fell of Dark," Gerard Hopkins

"The World Is Too Much with Us," William Wordsworth

"Ozymandias," Percy Shelley

Unit Seven:
The Novel

Great Expectations, Charles Dickens

Far From the Madding Crowd, Thomas Hardy

"As They Look to the Reader" from *Early Victorian Novelists,* Lord David Cecil

The Horse's Mouth, Joyce Cary

The Heart of the Matter, Graham Greene

Unit Eight:
Social Drama

The Admirable Crichton, James M. Barrie

The Cocktail Party, T. S. Eliot

Man and Superman, George Bernard Shaw

from *A Treasury of the Theatre,* John Gassner (Ed.)

Elective courses. In those schools in which the English curriculum is organized in short-term, specialized courses, particular courses such as Shakespeare, modern poetry and world masterpieces can be organized for the most able students. Some schools which generally follow the traditional pattern of year-long, grade-level courses, provide specialized courses which superior students can substitute for the general courses.

Special group or individual projects within regular classes. Some teachers require special advanced work of superior students, either as a substitute for or in addition to the regular class work. Socrates Lagios describes a project in which four superior students in his senior class at the Concord, Massachusetts, High School read eighteen novels, one a week, starting with *Moll Flanders* and ending with *The Old Man and the Sea.*[10] These students were excused from some of the

[10] Socrates Lagios, "Challenging the Gifted," *English Journal,* XLVI (November 1957), 501–503.

regular class work. Phyllis Peacock reported that in her senior classes able students carried on independent projects which culminated in "lecturettes" or productions in which other interested students and parents were invited to attend.[11]

"Honors" work.   A few high schools have experimented with plans in which superior students are exempt from a part of the curriculum in order to work independently. The English teacher, of course, directs projects in literature.

Literary clubs and special seminars.   Well-guided clubs, functioning as extracurricular activities, have provided rich experiences for able and interested students in some schools. Some teachers have arranged special voluntary seminars in the evening or on Saturdays in which students discuss works of their choice or hear guest lecturers.

Literature study for gifted students needs to be carefully planned to avoid two common pitfalls. Superior students should certainly be concerned with structure and form, and they are able to deal with technique in a way impossible in the regular class. Yet they are not a breed apart so far as interests and rewards sought in reading are concerned. It is quite possible for bright students to present glib technical analyses of selections without necessarily developing any expanded interests or any really mature understanding of literature as reconstruction of experience.

There is another closely related danger. In some high-ability classes a number of classics may be "covered"—given a surface reading, without any real understanding or appreciation resulting. Depth rather than coverage should be the goal in classes for superior students.

The Untalented Student

"Untalented student" is a weasel term to an extent. At least the untalented student is harder to characterize than the superior student, especially when one plans to discuss the "disadvantaged student" in a separate section. As used here, the term "untalented" refers to the student who has marked intellectual and linguistic handicaps short of the mental retardation which would prevent participation in the regu-

[11] "Highlights of Senior English for the Superior Students," *High School Journal,* XLIII (November 1959), 71–74.

lar program of the public schools. Such students frequently come from disadvantaged cultural and social backgrounds, but the two sets of criteria—linguistic-intellectual on the one hand and social-cultural on the other—should be kept separate. This is the reason for differentiating in this chapter between the "untalented" and the "disadvantaged." Students often may legitimately fit both categories but, in many instances, culturally deprived students may not be linguistically or intellectually handicapped and students from the higher social-cultural mileus may be.

Students who are not necessarily culturally deprived but who are intellectually and linguistically handicapped (short of mental retardation) tend to fall into two major groups: (1) the student who has a specific disability in reading—the "retarded reader"—whose problem may be solved if he obtains remedial help. It is not, however, within the scope of this text (nor is it necessary, because a large amount of professional information exists on the subject) to deal with the problems of the retarded reader; (2) the "slow learner" who has low intellectual and linguistic potential. His reading level will be low, too, but within a range expected in view of his potential.

In planning literature study for slow learners, teachers will have to ignore traditional patterns. Much of the difficulty teachers have with low-ability groups comes from attempting to impose literature programs designed for average and above-average students. The problem of appropriate materials is a pressing one. Certainly the standard textbook-anthologies are hardly useful with low-ability groups. Realizing this, some teachers have, in desperation, virtually given up the teaching of literature to slow groups, and instead, stress exercises in reading manuals and workbooks. This type of activity is important, but literature study need not be abandoned in low-ability groups. The teacher should realize however that traditional literature patterns—chronological survey, reading of "classics," and analysis of types—will be of little avail. Short and very simple topical units—such as "Adventure at Sea" and "Brave People"—may be the most fruitful approach. In such units, junior novels and biographies can be used as well as such special series as the Landmark Books of Random House and the Teen-Age Tales of D. C. Heath and Company.

A ninth-grade program in literature for less able students might be organized around the following units:

Stories People Talk About—retelling of famous myths, legends, American folk tales. Much use of recordings, films, pictures, and oral reading by the teacher and invited guests.

People Who Were Different—short, simple biography and nonfiction featuring individualism, idiosyncrasy, people who have overcome handicaps.

Strange Things Happen—the weird and the grotesque in poetry, short stories, and nonfiction.

Western Days—reading of short selections and common reading of Jack Schaefer's *Shane*.

Slow learners will always find the printed page an obstacle. Obviously, rich experiences in literature should be provided through the nonprint media—recordings, screen, photography, and oral experiences should be stressed in any program in literature for slow learners. Short selections will be used most of the time, of course. One-act plays and TV plays are especially valuable in classes of slow learners. Though a certain amount of daily routine may give security in such classes, variety of activities is essential, and flexibility and improvization should be the teacher's slogans.

The Disadvantaged Student

The disadvantaged student—the child with a background of economic poverty and squalor and cultural deprivation and alienation—has become, at long last, a major concern of education in recent years. As noted earlier, the disadvantaged student often may be deficient in linguistic skill—at least from the traditional middle-class view—and handicapped intellectually; but his over-riding problem is one of morale, motivation, and self-image. He stands alienated from the cultural values underlying the school program, and his slogan often is "What's the use?"

The teacher of literature faces a formidable, but vital and often greatly rewarding, task with the disadvantaged student. Important with all students, the problems of relating life to literature and of providing immediate rewards in experiences with literature become the vitally important objectives with disadvantaged students. But development of skills and literary insights, though definitely secondary in importance, need not be lost sight of altogether with the disadvantaged. One of the most important projects on English for disadvantaged students is that carried out in the Hunter College Curriculum Study Center resulting in the Gateway English Program for grades seven, eight, and nine.[12] The following excerpts from an essay by the director of the Hunter project, Marjorie B. Smiley, points up the philosophy and principles generally basic in most work in English for the disadvantaged:

> Certainly students whose score on standardized reading tests are substantially below grade, who do not respond to traditional English curricula, who reject and are rejected by their schools and many of their teachers, require a different kind of English curriculum. But the differences introduced to meet retarded reading skills, to arouse latent interests, and to exploit particular experiences, and to build self-regard and self-confidence need not and should not subvert the special contributions which literature and the language arts can make in the education of all children. If it is true, as Muriel Rukeyser declared, that poverty "makes thin the imagination and the bone," poor children need all the riches literature can supply . . . To begin with, the curriculum is thematically organized. In each grade, three of the four units are developed around themes selected for their relevance to the personal and social concerns of adolescents; the literature core in each of these units consists of short works or excerpts from longer works in fiction, biography, other nonfiction, drama, and poetry. A fourth unit in each grade explores comparable themes but in this instance entirely through poetry.
>
> The seventh-grade units have these titles: *A Family Is a Way of Feeling, Stories in Song and Verse, Who Am I?,* and *Coping.* Eighth grade units are *Striving, A Westerner Sampler, Creatures in Verse,* and *Two Roads to Greatness.* Ninth grade units are *Rebels and Regulars, People in Poetry, Something Strange,* and a still untitled unit on *justice.* As their titles suggest, the themes for the seventh grade relate closely to the student himself; the literature presents familiar, personal, and relatively concrete situations in which mostly youthful protagonists cope with human relations in family, school, and peer group. In the eighth grade the themes are explored in literature in which the milieu is larger in scope and less immediately related to the students' own experience. In two of the eighth grade units the literature centers on life and historic figures in the American past. *A Westerner Sampler* introduces, through

---

[12] Published by Crowell-Collier-Macmillan, New York, N.Y.

literature about the American Indian the concepts of cultural identity and culture conflict; it also examines, through the American Western as a print and film genre, stereotyped versus more realistic presentations of character and solutions to social dilemmas. *Two Roads to Greatness,* an anthology of biography, drama, verse, and fiction, presents as parallel models of struggle, despair, and achievement the lives of Abraham Lincoln and Frederick Douglass. In the ninth grade, *People in Poetry* explores the relatively sophisticated concept of individuality in its inward and outward manifestations. *Rebels and Regulars* deals with the personally and socially important issue of conformity and nonconformity; *Something Strange,* through fantasy and science fiction, is concerned with such questions as what is man? what is human society? what is real? what is illusory?

Within this context students learn such reading skills as these: to follow a variety of narrative sequences—chronological, flashback, the story within a story; to locate details used in characterization; to read for explicit and for extended meanings; and to recognize clues to mood, tone, and foreshadowing to derive word meanings from context. These relatively sophisticated critical reading skills are achieved by previously slow and reluctant readers partly because the literature has extremely high interest for them, but also, we believe, because of the teaching approach employed in the program.

We have taken seriously characterizations of lower class children as more responsive to physically active than to merely verbal learning. Stories and poems are read aloud to and by the children. Role-playing of comparable situations is frequently used to introduce a selection. Incidents in stories are dramatized; choral readings of poems are planned and taped by students. Indeed, Louise Rosenblatt's description of good reading as a "performing art" even when silent, is particularly suggestive to those of us concerned with improving the reading of underprivileged and underachieving students. These children especially, though all children ideally, need to *live themselves* into what they read.

We have found students welcome opportunities to tape their reading —as well as their dramatic improvisations, and we have found, too, that such experiences lead to spontaneous self and peer "corrections" in reading. Since all the verse "read" in the Gateway English is on tapes or records, students hear a good oral reading of each poem before or as they read it themselves. Students' oral reading of these poems often reveals a very close approximation to the professional reader's intonations, stress, and rhyme emphases.

Students respond actively to the literature they read in the Gateway program by drawing scenes and characters. In the ninth-grade unit on *People in Poetry* students draw or construct masks to reflect the inner and outer qualities of characters in poems like Richard Cory. Here it is, of course, not the quality of the art product but the students' engagement with visualizing the author's intent which lays the graphic base for the student's eventual verbal formulation of the meaning of the poem. Photographs and reproductions of art works presented to students with the challenge that they associate them individually with individual stories, poems, and characters enable them to demonstrate understanding of mood and tone. Such active, involving, graphic experiences are steps on the road toward perceptive reading.[13]

Two other reports of English projects for the disadvantaged student amplify the points made by Professor Smiley. In *Hooked on Books,*[14] Daniel N. Fader and Morton H. Shaevitz report on the English program developed at the W. J. Maxey Training School, Whitmore Lake, Michigan, a penal institution for adolescent boys. Teachers in the school were successful in getting the boys to read a great variety of books through making them easily available and through permissiveness in what could be read, with an avoidance of traditional taboos on what adolescents should encounter in print. The report stresses the psychological advantage of paperbound books with disadvantaged students. Hardbacks, especially textbooks, of course, are symbols of defeat to such students. A report of an institute on urban education conducted by Princeton University and the Trenton, New Jersey, public schools emphasizes the importance of nonprint media with disadvantaged students. In the volume, David A. Sohn describes a film-based course and proves again that viewing of film stimulates reading of the works on which the films are based. The reports agree that in classes of disadvantaged students literature and social studies can be profitably integrated.[15]

Teaching materials oriented to the disadvantaged student are becoming increasingly available. In addition to the Gateway English pro-

---

[13] "Gateway English—A Literature Program for Educationally Disadvantaged Students," *Ivory, Apes, and Peacocks: The Literature Point of View* (International Reading Association, 1968), pp. 86, 88–92.

[14] New York: Berkley Medallion Books, 1966.

[15] Kontos, Peter G. and James J. Murphy (Eds.), *Teaching Urban Youth: A Source Book for Urban Education* (New York: John Wiley, 1967).

gram cited above, several others seem valuable to the author: *The Way It Is* program published by Xerox; the *Impact* program published by Holt, Rinehart and Winston; and the *What's the Name of the Game* program published by New Dimensions in Education. These programs, of the package type, are basically similar and feature paperback reading materials and related audio-visual materials of various types.

Some Summary Principles

Experienced teachers reading through the preceding pages in this section will become aware probably that certain perennial principles, stated or implied, underlie the planning of literature programs whether for superior, average, untalented, or disadvantaged students. It may serve some purpose to summarize some of these.

1. *Books should be made easily available.* Physical availability is an important factor in developing a reading habit. Classroom libraries help, and a good stock of paperbound books is important. Teachers of other subjects should be enlisted in the effort to promote reading.

2. *Literature study should bring immediate rewards, not just deferred ones.* Students need to become actively involved in the literature class and not merely watch the teacher perform with a selection. Varied types of oral and dramatic activities in connection with the literature are enjoyable to most students. Nonprint media—recordings, films, and so on—and other art forms—painting, music, photography—should be featured.

3. *Selections appropriate to the students' actual concerns and needs should be chosen.* A great degree of permissiveness in individual reading should be allowed.

4. *The extent to which the orientation of the program will be literary rather than personal and social will depend on the characteristics of given classes.* Matters literary may be the major focus for superior students but the orientation for untalented and disadvantaged students will be largely personal-social.

5. *The literature program should challenge students but not always.* It is possible to challenge able students to the point of encouraging superficiality and untalented and disadvantaged students to the

point of developing frustration. Many of the experiences of the litera-tre class should be comfortable in terms of linguistic and intellectual demand.

6. *The student's potential for literary experience should be re-spected, whatever it may be.* His interests and values should be taken into account and his viewpoints and reactions considered seriously and respectfully.

DISCUSSING THE INDIVIDUAL WORK

Perhaps the most frequent type of planning, and among the most cru-cial, which the teacher of literature carries on, is preparation for dis-cussion of a selection read by the class in common. This is the point in the literature program at which the actual teaching process is most acutely brought to bear. So often teachers just "have discussion" of selections with no real planning, no real objectives for the discussion. Much of the editorial paraphernalia that commonly follows selections in the standard textbook-anthologies is unconnected, often trivial, leading nowhere. Unstructured give-and-take about books occasion-ally may be enjoyable and profitable in a class, but group discussion of a work, in which teacher questioning is vital, should have two gen-eral objectives: (1) to illuminate the student's reading of the work and to increase his involvement with it; and (2) to increase his ability to deal with the particular genre which the work represents.

Teacher questioning about a selection read in common is not meant necessarily to lead to particular conclusions (though no teacher should feel hesitant at expressing his own conclusions in the course of discussion) but rather is aimed at helping the student with a process appropriate to examining the given work. Individual responses, how-ever far out to the teacher, should be considered with respect, but, of course, students should become aware that some responses to given questions are more defensible than others. Questioning, too, as indi-cated earlier in this chapter, can be an important way of taking into account differences in student potential. Careful choice of questions which make varying demands on the students can be a means for in-volving all students with the work at appropriate levels of sophistica-tion.

In a useful essay, Royal A. Gettman suggests that the teacher has a choice of three possible areas in which questions can be asked about a selection of literature: (1) Author—how did the work come into existence? (2) Reader—what does the work do to the reader? (3) Work—what is the work? How is it to be described? Gettman suggests that the *first* question always concern the work, that it should not lead away from the work and should not provoke argument.[16]

Attention to a hierarchy of types of questions, as suggested by Edward J. Gordon, may be very helpful to teachers not only in planning effective discussions but also in involving students of different levels of ability.[17] Gordon's hierarchy of five levels of questions is based on the degree of abstraction demanded by each level, as follows (material in parentheses is the author's, not Gordon's):

1. Questions requiring the student to remember a fact in a selection
   (What objects did the poet refer to?
   What happened in the story immediately after the storm?)
2. Questions that require the student to prove or disprove a generalization someone else has made
   (One critic has said that _____. Can you cite any examples from the novel to substantiate this?)
   (Or the teacher may pose an hypothesis for the students to prove or disprove:
   This story is an attack upon_____.)
3. Questions that require the student to derive his own generalizations
   (What relationship do the coffee drinking scenes in the novel have to the central theme?
   How does the poet make use of flower symbols?
   If there is little or no response to the question, the teacher needs to go back to simpler levels and build up to this level again: Where is a red rose referred to in the poem? Can you find any support for this interpretation: The rose symbolizes _____. Now what other flower symbols do you find?)
4. Questions that require the student to generalize about the relation of the total work to human experience
   (What is the universal human problem dramatized in _____?)

[16] "Asking the First Question," *College English,* XXVIII (May 1967), 591–595.
[17] "Levels of Teaching and Testing," *English Journal,* XLIV (September 1955), 330–334.

5. Questions that require the student to carry generalizations derived from the work into his own life

(Is the kind of experience which this poem glorifies one that your friends value?)

Discussion of given selections does not always require that questions be asked at each of these levels, but it is true that teachers do not make sufficient use of questions at the lower levels of abstraction. Often when the question is answered after discussion begins at level 4 in the Gordon hiearchy, many students file the "school solution" away in their minds and are kept from learning how to examine a selection which discussion of it would afford.

Daniel A. Lindley, Jr., of Yale University, has developed a hierarchy of questioning in literature based on the kinds of thinking identified by J. P. Guilford. The following is an excerpt from an unpublished paper read by Mr. Lindley at the 1965 convention of the National Council of Teachers of English:

Let us start by considering some questions which might be asked in an English class discussing Shakespeare's *Julius Caesar*. Suppose that the class has reached Act III, scene 1—the scene in which Antony gets Brutus' permission to "speak in Caesar's funeral." This permission is, of course, crucial to the events which follow, and considerable attention to what happens is certainly justified. Here is the sequence of questions which the teacher uses to lead the discussion:

1. Where has Antony come from as he approaches Brutus?
   (Answer: from his house; he left the scene of the assassination and then returned.)
2. Why might this be important for what will happen next?
   (Antony has had time to think, alone, about what he might do.)
3. We know what Antony does do. What are some other ways in which he might have accomplished his goals?
   (Kill Brutus. Organize a counter-conspiracy. Get the army on his side.)
4. Antony says, after the conspirators have left him:

   "Woe to the hand that shed this costly blood.
   Over these wounds now do I prophesy . . .
   A curse shall light upon the limbs of men;
   Domestic fury and fierce civil strife
   Shall cumber all the parts of Italy;
   Blood and destruction shall be so in use

And dreadful objects so familiar
That mothers shall but smile when they behold
Their infants quartered with the hands of war . . ."

Is it right for Antony to start the very fury and strife which he seems to know will follow his speech to the "mob?"

The problem now is to go back over each question and analyze the kind of thinking involved for the student. In the first question, what must the student know? He must at least have *read the play*. Not only this, but he must have read with some care. In III, 1, we have this insignificant interchange:

Cassius: Where is Antony?
Trebonius: Fled to his house amazed.

Not much of a conversation, but there it is, and it is the answer to the question. Of course the student may not *remember* this; he may, when he hears the question, thumb back over his text and find it. In either event, however, familiarity with the text is the sole requirement for answering the question. It matters little how that familiarity was gained. This is, in other words, a *memory* task, and the mental activity involved is an operation called *cognitive memory* (adapted from Guilford).

The second question begins with the word *why*. This alone is usually sufficient evidence for the assertion that more than memory will be involved as the student gets down to work on the question. In the first place, the student must begin to put some elements together in his head before he can even speak. He must consider the answer which has been given to the previous question. Then he must consider what will in fact happen in the rest of the play. So far these are cognitive memory activities. But, having put these two pieces of his knowledge side by side in his head, so to speak, he must then *make a connection* between these two sets of data. It is this making of connections which is forced on the student by the word *why*. The student must fill in a missing piece; he must imagine Antony leaving and coming back, and he must infer that Antony has been using this time to sort things out and decide on a course of action. The more the student knows of Antony, the more logical this inference becomes; that is, the more the student sees Antony as a carefully calculating politician, the more he will infer careful calculation. In any case, all this inferring must take place within the framework supplied by the play. This is important. Guilford calls this kind of thinking *convergent*. To quote Guilford:

The second large group of thinking factors has to do with the production of some end result. After one has comprehended the situation, or the significant aspects of it at the moment, usually something needs to be done to it or about it . . . In convergent thinking, there is usually one conclusion or answer that is regarded as unique, and thinking is channeled or controlled in the direction of that answer. . . .[18]

It is particularly important to note that the 'channeling' or 'controlling' of the thinking is being done by the structure of the play under discussion. The thinking must "converge" on the play. If the student gratuitously leaves the play for some easier or more attractive (to him!) area, then the teacher may quite rightly chastize him for "not answering the question." For example, if the student begins his answer by saying, "Well, if *I* were Antony . . ." the teacher is surely within her rights to interrupt and point out that the question is about the *play*, not about the student.

The third question involves still another, and extremely important, kind of thinking. The key part of the question is "some other way"— ways, in other words, that the student must *make up*, or *imagine*. These ways will have some relationship to the play, of course, but the best answers will reflect much more about the students who provide them than about the play. For example, Antony might have killed Brutus then and there. Or he might have attempted to work for political power through the Senate. Or—as a student once suggested to me—he might have gotten so scared at the idea of running the country that he might have travelled north to join the Gauls. Guilford calls this sort of thinking "divergent." It is thinking that does 'diverge' from the subject at hand, but this is not to say that it therefore has no value. The suggestion of alternatives for the play helps to make clear why the play is in fact put together the way it is. But far more important is the idea that divergent thinking *involves the student with himself. His* inventions are being solicited and, ideally, rewarded by the teacher.

The problems of what the teacher rewards, and how much reward she hands out, in class, are better handled by the Flanders system. But in connection with divergent thinking, it is important to find out what the teacher intends to reward as an answer to a divergent question. Theoretically, I suppose, if the teacher knows she has asked such a question she should accept and praise *any* answer, however bizarre it may be—and she should be intolerant only of commonplace or obvious ideas. I suspect that whether a teacher actually will reward *any* answer is dependent on the amount of tolerance she has for different ideas. Once a teacher is made aware of the potential for student creativity in

[18] J. P. Guilford, "The Structure of Intellect," *Psychological Bulletin,* LIII, 1956, 267–293.

such questions, her tolerance of wild answers can, in my experience, be easily increased.

The final question asks for a *moral* judgment. We, as adults, are sophisticated enough to wonder what "right" means. "Right" for a Machiavelli? In the case of an adolescent, I imagine that his answer is more likely to be based on some intuition about his own value system, along with an educated guess about what he thinks the teacher wants to hear. In any event, the problem is to make a moral judgment. This sort of thinking Guilford terms "evaluative." Aesthetic judgments are also included here—thus the question, "Is this a good play?" will also produce evaluative thinking.

Thus we have four kinds of questions, and four kinds of thinking: memory, convergent, divergent, evaluative. The first step for teachers is to recognize the four kinds of questions involved as they come up in normal class discussion. I have already mentioned the depressing conclusion of one piece of research—that given teachers tend to use only certain kinds of questions, and thus make no allowances for the ability levels of the classes they teach and few allowances for different kinds of thinking.

SELECTED BIBLIOGRAPHY

Albright, Daniel, "An Organic Curriculum for English," *English Journal,* LII (January 1963), 16–21.

Applies the "techniques of literary criticism" to curriculum construction and proposes the elimination of in-class literature teaching in favor of a "free-reading program" and a series of short "courses" which students may elect.

Barosko, Sam, "Teaching the Novel to Slow Learners," *Wisconsin Journal of Education,* LXXXXIX (December 1966), 20–22.

Presents a plan for helping slow learners sense achievement in reading the novel.

Burke, Etta M., "Project for Slow Learners," *English Journal,* LV (September 1966), 784–85.

Describes a project in newspaper and novel reading carried on in twelfth-grade classes.

Carlin, Jerome, "A Pattern for Teaching Literature," *English Journal,* LV (March 1966), 291–297.

Discusses various responsibilities of the classroom teacher in planning the literature program.

College Entrance Examination Board, *Freedom and Discipline in English* (New York: 1965), pp. 42–79.

A very influential report suggesting a works-centered curriculum for the college-bound student.

Damon, Grace E., "Teaching the Slow Learner, Up the West Staircase, With Apologies to B. K.," *English Journal,* LV (September 1966), 777–783.

Suggests various activities and methods in literature successful with slow learners in the junior high school.

Evans, William H., and Jerry L. Walker, "Literature and the New Method," in *New Trends in the Teaching of English in Secondary Schools* (Chicago: Rand McNally, 1966), pp. 37–50.

A lucid discussion of current trends in literature programs as influenced by the structure and subject emphasis of the "new method."

Frye, Northrop, "Elementary Teaching and Elemental Scholarship," *PMLA,* LXXIX (May 1964), 11–18.

Argues for a new theoretical conception of literature which places poetry at the center of the literature program.

Henry, George H., "The Idea of Coverage in the Teaching of Literature," *English Journal,* LIV (September 1965), 475–482.

A well-conceived argument that the development of concepts and not an attempt at "coverage" should and can guide the development of the literature program.

Herbert, Phil, ". . . That's the Question," *English Journal,* LVI (November 1967), 1195–1196.

Another insightful discussion of the art of questioning about a work of literature.

Hillocks, George, Jr., "Literature and Composition for Average Students in Grades Seven to Nine," *NASSP Bulletin,* XLVIII (February 1964), 62–75.

Discusses the program developed at a Project English Demonstration Center which integrates the "content" and "skills points of view into a viable literature program for junior high school.

Johnson, Frances, "A Unifying Theme for the Year," *English Journal,* LII (February 1963), 97–101.

Describes a program unified by the pursuit of one major theme throughout the year's work.

Keller, Charles R., "Humanities in the High School," *English Journal,* LIV (March 1965), 171–190.

Several articles discussing the possibilities of teaching literature within the framework of humanities courses and programs.

Largmann, Malcolm G., "The Novel and Bright Students: An Answer to Cynicism," *High Points* XLIX (May 1966), 25–32.

Noting that most of our brighter students are unprepared emotionally and by experience to deal with the cynicism of such authors as Joyce, Dostoevsky, and Lawrence, Largmann suggests that works stressing positive values are more effective and, surprisingly, are better received by bright students.

Lin, San-Su C., "Disadvantaged Student? or Disadvantaged Teacher?," *English Journal,* LVI (May 1967), 751–756.

A discussion of the functions of literature for disadvantaged students.

Mersand, Joseph, "Teaching the Slow Learner in English," *High Points,* XLVIII (May 1966), 38–52.

A specific discussion of ways to adapt the English program for slow learners.

Norvell, George W., "Watchman, What of Literature in Our Schools?," *English Journal,* LII (September 1963), 434–437.

Restates his earlier thesis that student interest is the crucial concern in selecting literature for study in high school English classes.

Sauer, Edwin H., "The High School Literature Program Reconsidered," *English in the Secondary School* (New York: Holt, Rinehart and Winston, 1961), pp. 141–158.

A provocative discussion of considerations in choosing literature for the secondary school program.

Simpson, Ray H., and Anthony Soares, "Best- and Least-Liked Short Stories in Junior High School," *English Journal,* LIV (February 1965), 108–111.

Report of a study assessing the reading preferences of junior high school students; presents several guide lines for selecting stories to teach.

Tincher, Ethel, "Helping Slow Learners Achieve Success," *English Journal,* LIV (April 1965), 289–294.

Specific discussion of the content of a literature program for slow learners.

Wertenbaker, Thomas J., Jr., "A Surfeit of Surveys: Thoughts on Chronology and Theme in American Literature," *English Journal,* LII (January 1963), 9–15.

Argues that unity of ideas and critical thinking are central considerations in construction of a literature course.

part three
THE FUNCTION
AND NATURE OF LITERATURE
FOR ADOLESCENTS

The term "literature for adolescents" may be a rather amorphous one for many people, even teachers. Unlike "children's books," a term which evokes a relatively standard image of appearance and content, "literature for adolescents" may suggest anything from the subliterary series book to the "classics" most often offered in secondary school English classes. This sweeping definition is a proper one if by the term one means anything that adolescents like to read—provided one also includes comic books and a number of other kinds of reading material. As used in this section, "literature for adolescents" refers, first, to the rather substantial and highly important body of literature produced by predominantly serious writers specifically for the audience aged from about twelve to about seventeen, in other words principally junior and senior high school students. Second, it refers to that adult literature which has particular relevance to the adolescent and particular significance to the aims of literature teaching in the secondary school.

The purpose of Part Three therefore is to discuss the function and nature of this body of literature. The discussions of the literature written expressly for adolescents or for adults and the suggested bibliographies are delimited by the author's convictions about what literature in either category is of concern to the teacher in the junior and senior high school. A number of varieties of nonfiction, both for the adolescent and the adult, that may be of interest to teachers of other subjects are not discussed. Neither is poetry nor drama discussed, since the earlier chapters on these genres incorporate concern with works written for or of special significance to adolescents.

10
The Function of Literature
Written for Adolescents

Literature for adolescents is written with an eye to the interests and concerns of teenagers which have remained relatively stable despite the great cultural changes of the past several decades. Satisfaction of interests, though important, is not the major aim of the literature program. The major function of literature written expressly for adolescents is to provide a vital transition in the literary education.

The point has been made earlier that the literary education represents the same kind of continuum as education in mathematics, science, or any other field of knowledge. The junior high school student cannot jump instantly from the experiences of children's literature to the adult masterpiece. Books for adolescents serve the transition function in two ways. First, in a broad sense, they prepare the young reader to comprehend mature works in later years, induct him into the processes of becoming involved with a work of literature. The student who can read the junior novel well, for example, probably will develop the ability to read the serious adult novel well. If in the junior high school the pupil is able to discern the simple symbolic treatment of the theme of good versus evil in something like Annixter's *Swiftwater*—in one exciting scene a boy fights with a wolverine—he is making important preparation for reading later, say, the novels of Thomas Hardy, or Nathaniel Hawthorne. Second, books for adolescents provide satisfying experiences in themselves at the stage of development represented by early and middle adolescence when many adult works do not provide such experiences.

"Start where they are," though an educational cliché, is still a viable motto for the teacher of literature. But where *is* the pupil in his potential for experience with literature when he enters the junior high school and encounters, in many cases, his first real study of literature? The answer will vary greatly from one individual to another, but some pertinent generalizations can be drawn about these young human beings who flock into seventh- and eighth-grade classrooms.

Most important, young students are not averse, in general, to reading and are eager for vicarious experience. In fact, voluntary reading may be more important to the seventh-grader than it ever was before or ever will be again. But much of this reading may be of the kind that chills the blood of the English teacher—comic books, for example. Although circulation of comic books has declined somewhat in the last few years, partly because of attempts to suppress objectionable ones and partly because of the influence of television, the comic book still remains near the top of the reading interest list for junior high school students and bulks fairly large even in the reading of senior high school students. A survey conducted by the author in several schools while this revision was being written showed that 75 percent of students in grades seven to nine and 53 percent in grades ten to twelve read comic books.

Today, though, the student's principal source of vicarious experience and entertainment, as well as the adult's, is the television screen. Junior high students spend nearly as many hours watching television each week as they spend in school (approximately the same number as their parents!) and senior high students spend about half as much time televiewing as they do in attending classes. (Both groups also spend a substantial amount of time listening to recorded music.)

BASIC APPEALS OF POPULAR SCREEN AND PAGE

The vicarious experiences most popular with the junior high school pupil—whether of television or the comic book—have certain common patterns of appeal. Examination of these patterns is important for the teacher of literature. One obvious appeal of the comic book and the television program is that they require little effort, much less effort than is required by the ordinary book. Although the vocabulary in many comic books is not particularly easy, the actual text need not be read at all. Looking at the pictures and reading a few words here and there are enough. Capable readers may read as many comic books as poor readers, but the less able reader may be especially attracted to the comics if the required reading in class is continually beyond him. Little imaginative effort is needed in looking at a TV show or in reading a comic book. There is no need to conjure up images in the mind's eye. The situations and characters, complete with bulging biceps, golden tresses, or evil visages, are there already. Because of these facts, there is a danger that these media may be a deterrent to real play of the imagination. It should be clear, of course, that the author is not implying that television is necessarily inferior to print. Some television programs do indeed stimulate and demand a real play of the imagination and may represent a valuable adjunct to the literature program.

The characteristics of the most popular comic books and of many popular television programs among early adolescents are very similar. Among girls, in the survey conducted by the author, the favorite comic-book subject matter was love, romance, and humor, while the content of the favorite television programs was love, romance, humor, and space adventure. Among boys, the favorite comic books feature superheroes, space adventure, humor, and the fantastic, while the favorite TV programs were in the same categories with the addition of westerns and violent adventure of the "Mannix" variety.

The content of such popular comic books and television programs is highly compatible with the nature of early adolescents. Common to them are the ingredients of adventure, violence, romantic love, humor, and the fantastic. The characters in the chosen programs are either superheroes—physically attractive and socially adept people who represent a kind of ideal fulfillment—or buffoons to whom the reader can feel superior. The adolescent, sensitive about his own finesse and acceptability, delights in the antics of Archie and his girl friends.

The appeal of the comic-book, popular-television level of experience is rooted, too, in the fact that its picture of life and the assumptions underlying it are naturally acceptable to the immature mind of the reader or viewer. Life is an exciting physical adventure or should be; heroism and courage are measured in physical daring—this is one assumption. Another assumption is that people are either good or bad. Often one can tell the difference by physical appearance alone. It is obvious that clean-cut Marshal Dillon is a "good guy," while his un-shaven adversary is a crook. The villains in various comic strips usually have revolting physical characteristics and mannerisms.

Another assumption underlining this type of representation of ex-perience is that romantic love and money lie at the heart of life's problems; a familiar twist ranges the affluent on the side of evil. Ro-mantic campaigning is waged pretty much on the "cave-man" level. Another assumption is that the end justifies the means. Though triumph of good over evil is a common theme, it matters not that the hero kills a few people and destroys countless dollars' worth of prop-erty so long as ostensibly he is on the side of righteousness.

A familiar assumption, too, is that people in authority—statesmen, teachers, civic leaders, and often parents—are misguided in their deci-sions and values, and their humiliation is appealing to the early ado-lescent who is under the thumb of adult authority and beginning to chafe from it. The rebellion against established authority, whether of the melodramatic or humorous variety, furnishes a very real lure. Sheer availability is an obvious advantage of the television and com-ic-book experience. Most American families now own television sets, and comic books and other popular magazines are on sale at any drugstore or supermarket.

GENERAL CHARACTERISTICS
OF TRANSITION LITERATURE

Generalizations such as those just made about dominant patterns in the comic-book reading and televiewing of early adolescents always need qualification. Though these patterns fit a great number of young people, it is true that individuals exhibit widely varying tastes. Some pupils, for example, enter the seventh grade already well beyond the road block of superheroes and the romantic writings of the comics. (Perhaps they never stopped there in the first place.) There are also young people who never develop the interests of the majority. For many pupils, however, the early junior high school may be a crucial period of transition from enthusiasm for comic books and certain tele-vision programs to liking for reading and viewing fare in which human experience is reconstructed in more mature modes. It is important for the literature program in the seventh and eighth grades to make available selections that can facilitate this transition. The nature of the basic appeals of popular reading and viewing fare furnishes the key to characteristics of such transition selections, which have similar basic appeals but which provide them in more artful form.

Transition literature will be easy to read.   Much work-reading must be done at any level of school, and a rigorous concern with reading skills is necessary in the junior or senior high school. However, a student's difficulty in recognizing more than one word in a hundred will quickly kill his pleasure in reading, and pleasure is basic to appreciation. Mature readers may enjoy the struggle with a profound and difficult selection, but the junior high school student, just embarking on his literary education, is often far from this point. Although the difficulty level is low, a selection may be artful and esthetically satisfying, as writers such as Eleanor Estes, Doris Gates, and Stephen Meader have demonstrated.

Transition literature will reflect experience compatible with the nature of the reader.   Identification with characters and situations in a selection is a keystone of appreciation. Many selections in the junior high school literature program should feature adolescent characters and exciting or familiar kinds of experiences with which the early adolescent wants to identify.

Transition literature will not grossly distort experience.   As teachers we may be willing that the experience represented be simplified, since life for most early adolescents is still relatively uncomplicated. Action still may occur mostly on the physical plane, but the plots will avoid the wild coincidence and improbability of the comic-book level of fiction. Often in these transition selections, it is true, the young protagonists may do surpassing things in a world curiously detached from adult control. Yet such "unreal" episodes may be acceptable at this stage of the pupil's literary education. Traumatic experiences involving macabre violence and the sordid should not be featured.

Transition literature will have action, suspense, danger, romance.   Pupils should not get the idea that the required or recommended selections are more likely to be dull than interesting.

Such selections will be easily available.   Classroom libraries, book exhibits and bazaars, and bulletin board displays of book jackets will help. PTA's and other groups that are disturbed by the nature of some popular television programs and with the comic-book "menace" should concern themselves with making other materials more plentiful and available.

LITERATURE FOR ADOLESCENTS AND PERSONAL CONCERNS

Books written expressly for adolescents are valuable not only in paving the way for perceptive reading of adult works in the future, but also provide immediately satisfying experiences at a certain stage, just as fairy tales, for example, provide satisfying experiences at an earlier stage.

Books for adolescents reflect various interests and concerns of young readers, but they have their greatest impact, probably, because of their connection with the personal problems of adolescents, and they afford the young reader a chance to stand off and view the seeming turmoil of his life in perspective, to reflect on things that are of the greatest moment to him, whether or not they may seem trivial to adults. Personal problems, inherent in the lifelong struggle toward self-realization and the search for identity, are not unique to adolescents. But the in-between period that is adolescence is a particular time of stress—a no man's land of questioning and doubting and fearing and aspiring. The happy vagueness of the "when I grow up" in the childhood period has given way to the sharp realization that the growing up is nearly complete and that, in the senior high school period at least, there must be a coming to terms with personal shortcomings and a facing of the question: How do I measure up to a role in the adult world? The high school period is frequently marked by a heightening of conflicts between adolescents and parents, as the teenager strives to advance toward independence and adult status faster than his parents think he should. And yet, despite his striving, the fact is—psychologically if not physiologically—that the adolescent is *not* adult. The adolescent culture has its own unique and rigid code, in which a type of conformity is at a premium, and the teenager who would have reasonably satisfactory status with his peers (and which one would not!) can only pretend to be adult within the boundaries of the peer culture and the rules enforced by adults. Around the stresses of the adolescent period a large body of literature has developed, particularly fiction, which has high popularity with adolescents. Most of the personal problems of adolescents cluster in the categories identified below with which much of the literature discussed in the following two chapters relates.

Coming to terms with self. Most adolescents are actively taking stock of themselves, even though for some the process may be carried on under a veneer of irresponsibility and devil may care. The student who has been struggling to maintain a "C" average realizes that MIT and a career in engineering are not for him. The plain girl with the unenticing figure faces the fact that the coming years probably will bring no increase in glamour. And the introverted, retiring boy decides, reluctantly or otherwise, that he will never be the center of "the gang." Though most adolescents tend to be realistic in their stocktaking, all need to establish a favorable personal image, though all do not succeed.

Problems of relations with peers. Popularity, which may be tempered ultimately to acceptance, is a major goal of adolescents. The pull to live up to peer-group or gang-set standards, to conform, may involve the teenager in conflicts with his parents, his teachers, and his convictions. For example, the intellectually gifted student may have to play down his ability in order to avoid being labeled "a brain." Of course, the whole web of boy-girl relations presents major issues of social know-how, of going steady, and of sexual morality. Senior high school students are much more serious about love than their parents or teachers frequently realize. A few students marry before completing high school, and many think seriously about marriage and their future roles as homemakers. The problem of dating is more serious to the girl, who is an outcast if she doesn't date, than to the boy, who may be merely labeled a "woman-hater."

Family problems. Although the adolescent tends to pull away from domination and control by his parents, he greatly needs their advice and guidance. Countless minor tensions are created by the adolescent in the household. Occasionally, his problems may be deep-seated. It is not unusual for the adolescent to feel ashamed of his home or of some member of his family.

Preparation for the future adult role.   His role as a marriage partner is not the only aspect of his future with which the adolescent is concerned. He also has the problem of deciding if he should or should not go to college, and of choosing a career or an occupation. Boys may be preoccupied with their military obligations.

Moral and philosophical problems and issues.   Few adolescents would admit openly to an interest in "philosophy of life." Yet teenagers are keenly concerned with values, with the things that people live for, and with the motives that impel men. The "Omar Khayyam" period has long been associated with the adolescent experience, and *weltschmerz,* sometimes serving as a defense mechanism, is a hallmark of the teen years. Often the adolescent has to carry on a lonely tussle with concepts of right and wrong. Typically, adolescence is a time of outward cynicism and inward idealism. Today there is much discussion of the generation gap as young people around the world are rebelling against the adult culture. The "hippie" and "beat" movements are part of this rebellion. Because of the cultural ferment, adolescents, in general, are interested in and concerned with social and political issues at earlier ages than they were until recently, and extremism, both of the left and the right, is more common today among teenagers.

Search for "kicks."   Partly related to the sharpened conflict between youth and adulthood is the fact that young people's search for "kicks" has intensified and taken more extreme forms such as experimentation with drugs.

The mere fact that the publication of books for adolescents increases each year is evidence that this body of literature has a secure place in the lives of teenagers. The school program can take good advantage of the appeal of these books directed to young people. It is the task of the school and of the teacher to identify the most significant and artistic in the outpouring of books for adolescents and make them serve the important purposes which they have the potential to serve.

11
Fiction for Adolescents

section I
THE JUNIOR NOVEL

THE ANATOMY OF THE JUNIOR NOVEL

The term "junior novel" apparently came into use in the 1930s at the outset of the great surge of books written expressly for adolescents. Some critics have attacked the quality of the junior novel, dismissing it as a "subliterary" genre, and it is quite true that the majority of these novels are slight, mediocre at best, and wanting greatly in literary quality. The same thing, though, can be said of fiction for the general audience: the majority of adult novels also are unworthy of serious attention. Good, mediocre, and wretched work is to be found both in literature for adolescents and in that for adults.

Though the great majority of junior novels are ephemeral, the genre cannot be dismissed lightly. Its value in the school program was cited in the preceding chapter and, as a literary form, the junior novel has established its respectability because of the achievement of some of its writers. The dividing line between the junior and adult novel sometimes may be tenuous. Some novelists have written for both audiences—Leonard Wibberley, James Ramsey Ullman, and Farley Mowatt among others. The junior novel is not merely "easier" or less mature than the adult novel, although in the main it is shorter and easier to read than its adult counterpart. Its general themes and categories of content are indicated by the divisions of this section. Its uniqueness, for better or worse, however, is born of some rather rigid conventions of form and content.

The taboos imposed upon writers of books for adolescents have called forth severe criticism of the overinnocuous quality of junior fiction. One scathing analysis concluded:

> The adolescent's world is fraught with change; its charms "are wound up," its horizons are pulsing with expectancies and actualities. His most heartfelt cry is, as Sherwood Anderson warned us long ago, "I want to know why!" The pastel, gum-drop fiction that has been wrought for him avoids both question and answer.[1]

The taboos of the junior novel are the same as those rigorously enforced as a rule by publishers of literature anthologies for the junior and senior high school. The "seamy" side of life is generally avoided; erotic drives are ignored; smoking and drinking are seldom alluded to (adolescents, of course, never drink in the books); swearing and bad grammar are avoided—these are some of the most obvious taboos. It can be argued, therefore, that in much junior fiction basic realism is avoided, and that a rounded view of life is not given. Insistence upon a too-narrow concept of "wholesomeness" may tend to cripple the junior novel as a true form of literature, but avoidance or violation of taboos such as those just cited has little to do with the quality of a work. Good taste as well as verisimilitude is important to adolescent and adult fiction alike. Criticism has centered mainly on the fact that in many junior novels there is slick superficiality, a failure to plunge below the surface into the deeper and more complex human emotions and motivations. In discussing junior novels in which the focus is on the problems of teen-agers, Richard S. Alm writes:

> . . . most novelists present a sugar-puff story of what adolescents should do and should believe rather than what adolescents may or will do and believe. Such stories reveal the novelists' lack of knowledge or insight into adolescent behavior as well as a lack of writing ability.

[1] Frank G. Jennings, "Literature for Adolescents—Pap or Protein?" *English Journal*, XLV (December 1956), 526–531.

These writers do not penetrate beneath the surface of the situation they create. Their stories are superficial, often distorted, sometimes completely false representations of adolescence.[2]

Superficiality obviously is not a unique shortcoming of fiction for teen-agers. There is patterned, formula writing for both the adult and the adolescent markets, and there is the serious writing for both audiences. Even some talented writers for adolescents, however, apparently feel impelled to "write down," and their failure to probe deeply is intentional. With adolescents, as with adults, the superficial formula story may be popular, but it is important that teachers and librarians stock the fiction shelves and make up book lists from books that represent art rather than artifice.

Despite what has been said so far about the nature of the junior novel (substantially the same things said in the previous edition of this book), it is apparent that in the last few years there has been a relaxing of conventions and taboos and more significant substance in the better junior novels. There is less fluff of the beach party and prom date variety and a greater concern with the problems that can bring real unhappiness and emotional disaster to young people. While Henry Felsen's *Two and the Town,* the story of a forced teen-age marriage, brought a storm of controversy a few years ago, Jeanette Eyerly's *A Girl Like Me,* also about teen-age, out-of-wedlock pregnancy, raised few eyebrows in 1966. There is also increased concern with the non-middle class, less-fortunate levels of living, for example, S. E. Hinton's *The Outsiders,* dealing with the gang fights in New York City's East Side, and Louisa Shotwell's story of migrant Negro workers, *Roosevelt Grady.* Dialogue has become more real, and dialects more often are rendered with validity. Even some mild profanity appears, and we have occasional passages such as this from Carol Brink's fine *Snow in the River* which show a loosening of taboos:

A thin girl with untidy hair and a pair of sailor's boots on her feet sat in a corner opposite and looked at him with calculating eyes. He avoided her gaze, and when she followed him into the street, he had no patience with her. He shook her plucking fingers off his sleeve.

"Nay, lass, ye're too easy," he said, "I like to pick my own."

[2] Richard S. Alm, "The Glitter and the Gold," *English Journal,* XLIV (September 1955), 315–322.

The junior novel remains greatly didactic, frequently obtrusively so to the mature reader, partly because its sale depends largely on the favorable judgments of teachers and librarians who are much interested in the power of fiction to "teach" and to dramatize values. Though didactic, the junior novelist seldom attempts to be "inspirational" in the venerable success-story tradition; there is little of the Horatio Alger influence. Within the boundaries of its conventions, the junior novel is realistic, pointing toward adjustment and featuring the minor triumphs that are the best most people can hope for.

Accordingly, the adolescent reader finds himself mirrored, sometimes penetratingly, sometimes only in a vague blur with few of his own ideas or feelings. The young super-hero of a few decades ago is uncommon now. The adolescent finds it easy to identify with the characters of the junior novel, but only infrequently has he a desire to change places with them, to drop into the middle of the book, as one girl reading *Little Women* wished to do. He observes the people in the run-of-the-mill story with interest, but it is only in the extraordinary selection that he can identify with protagonists to the point of pain or exhilaration. The junior novel shares with contemporary adult fiction an oft-bewailed failing—memorable characters are hard to find.

In structure and technique, the junior novel tends to be quite rigidly patterned, though the past few years again have brought greater flexibility and maturity. The length of the junior novel is standardized at slightly more than half the length of the average adult novel. The time span of the action is usually short, almost never more than a year, often a summer or a school year. Generally, plots are straightforward and on a single plane, building to a climax near the end of the book and giving a very brief wrap-up, though variations such as the flashback are noticeable in recent junior novels. Style is plain and uncomplicated, an inevitability in works read mostly by twelve- to fifteen-year-olds. Traditionally, the junior novel has featured almost exclusively the omniscient point of view (with a few exceptions such as Maureen Daly's celebrated *Seventeenth Summer*) but there are interesting experiments with point of view in recent books. Hila Colman's *Classmates by Request,* for instance, alternates between the point of view of a Negro girl and a white girl in a school desegregation crisis.

VARIETIES OF THE JUNIOR NOVEL

Animal Stories

An analysis is not necessary here of the human psychology involving animals and pets to which the early adolescent's interest in animals is linked. The appeal of the vastly popular animal story probably lies partly in the flattering devotion of the dog or horse to the young master which is almost invariably stressed. Since adolescence is likely to be so much a time of doubts and fears and insecurities, the unswerving loyalty and faith and courage that the horse or dog often exhibits are qualities the young adolescent especially values. In the animal story that takes place in the wilds, from Jack London's *Call of the Wild* to the many basically similar contemporary selections, there is an added appeal. In such stories the animal survives and prospers according to his individual cunning and strength. This is the survival-of-the-fittest code that the young adolescent respects, as he demonstrates on the playground and in his neighborhood gathering places.

Learnings through class discussion. It is no problem, at any rate, to motivate most junior high pupils to read animal fiction. But where does such reading fit into the continuum of the literature program? By skillfully recommending books that will provide important comparisons and contrasts and by carefully planning discussions of them the teacher can lead a class to important learnings.

CREDIBILITY OF PLOT. The junior high school pupil should develop a healthy wariness of the fraud of undue coincidence and improbability in poor quality fiction. For example, the far-fetched plot of Farley's *The Black Stallion* can be contrasted with the down-to-earth, yet suspenseful sequence of events in Gipson's splendid *Old Yeller.* Foreshadowing is definitely evident in this book, and in, say, Street's *Goodbye, My Lady,* but is obviously lacking in the Farley story.

AWARENESS OF THEME. Even the juvenile animal story can say something significant about human experience, and the pupil must develop an awareness of theme at this level if he is to deal with it in more mature books. Most junior high school pupils will be able to recognize the theme, the boy's growing up, so sensitively handled in

Goodbye, My Lady. And they will be able to see by contrast that Lippincott's *The Wahoo Bobcat,* though it is excellent in some ways, has no recognizable theme to give the book unity.

A very common theme in animal fiction is that of faith justified; the faith, perhaps, of the young master that the animal will become a successful hunting dog or racing horse, despite the doubts of others. This theme can be handled skillfully, or clumsily and sentimentally. For example, James Kjelgaard develops this theme well in the popular *Big Red,* the story of a boy and his Irish setter. Oversentimentality is one of the most common faults of animal fiction, and junior high school pupils are sensitive to "mushiness" in anything. On this point alone, it is possible for them to recognize the adequacy of Thomas Hinkle's stories and the excellence of *Old Yeller* and *Goodbye, My Lady.*

CHARACTERIZATION. The young people in animal fiction are monotonously similar from author to author. Often, there is no real attempt to bring them truly alive. As pupils discuss books they have read, describing and contrasting main characters, it may become apparent which authors have developed multidimensioned characters, such as those Eric Knight creates in *Lassie Come-Home.*

DIFFERENCES IN QUALITIES OF STYLE. The best authors can communicate unobtrusively the wonder of wild places and the amazing rhythm of nature in locales where man does not usually penetrate—the deep swamps and thickets and high peaks. Joseph Lippincott, for example, suceeds in doing this in *The Wahoo Bobcat,* set in the Florida swamp land. Reading aloud by the students and teacher will be helpful in illustrating this point. Few pupils fail to respond to a passage like the following:

> Uncle Jesse slouched in his chair and puffed his pipe and took in the beauty of the words he did not understand, the words about marvels that only his fancy could picture; the prairies so different from the swamp and so far away. The hard dry gulches, the brave men, the brave land—the never-felt land of his own boyhood dreams.
>
> Out there the winds sang high and free. Thus the words said. Here in his world the winds hummed and sobbed, crying for something that had no answer—like something never seen but only felt and this something touching the strings to the heart of an unlettered old man who could not speak the things he felt and who felt them all the more because he could not speak them: the aching hurt of being old and the happy sor-

row of watching a boy grow up and knowing that he, too, must wear a symbol around his neck, that he, like all men, must carry some foul thing forever, some weakness—and also knowing that some day the swamp winds, the home sounds so long remembered, would feel for the strings to the boy's heart and bring forth only the echo of the melody of what used to be—the beauty of the sprouting years, the hope of longing, then the misery of loving something that must grow old; all this the mystery that the old man felt and could not say, this miracle of man's life on God's earth.[3]

"READING BETWEEN THE LINES." *Goodbye, My Lady,* again an example, is rich in symbolism. In this book, the obvious but satisfying symbolism of the coffee and its value in the theme of growing up is worth discussing. For this and other reasons already implied, Street's book is excellent for group reading in the seventh or eighth grade.

One of the well-known Scholastic Literature Units, entitled *Animals,*[4] represents a skillfully built unit for seventh-graders. The interest generated in reading from the unit anthology a series of short selections of fiction and nonfiction about animals leads into work in oral and written composition and small-group and individual reading of full-length books.

REPRESENTATIVE BOOKS *

Appell, David, *Comanche,* Harcourt.
  The horse which survived the Custer massacre tells the story. (E)
Balch, Glenn, *The Midnight Colt,* Crowell-Collier-Macmillan.
  Two young people and a spoiled, temperamental race horse.
Ball, Zachary, *Bristleface,* Holiday.
  The growing up a little of a boy and his dog some decades ago. (E)
Chipperfield, Joseph, *Storm of Dancerwood,* McKay.
  The theme of the part-wolf dog who returns to the world of man.
Corbin, William, *Golden Mare,* Coward-McCann.
  A ranch boy has to part with a wonderful horse. (E)

* In this and the other lists that follow, books discussed in the text are marked with an asterisk (*) and are not annotated. "E" means that the book is especially easy.
  [3] James Street, *Goodbye, My Lady* (Philadelphia: J. B. Lippincott, 1954), pp. 137–138. By permission of the publishers.
  [4] Stanley B. Kegler, *Animals,* a Scholastic Literature Unit (New York: Scholastic Book Services, 1962).

Gipson, Fred, *Old Yeller,* Harper & Row.
   A boy and an incorrigible yellow dog in the Texas hill country of the 1860s. (Also *Savage Sam,* featuring the son of Old Yeller.)
Grew, David, *Beyond Rope and Fence,* Grosset & Dunlap.
   The career of Queen, a buckskin horse.
Henry, Marguerite, *King of the Wind,* Rand McNally.
   An Arabian boy and the ancestor of the great race horse, Man o'War. (E)
*Kjelgaard, James, *Big Red,* Cadmus Books. (E)
————, *Haunt Fox,* Holiday.
   An unusual fox and the boy who hunted him. (E)
————, *Stormy,* Holiday.
   Unusual story of a boy left alone with his dog in a lake cabin when his father is sent to prison. (E)
*Knight, Eric, *Lassie Come-Home,* Holt, Rinehart and Winston.
   The moving story of the great collie and her long trek back to her real home.
*Lippincott, Joseph, *The Wahoo Bobcat,* Lippincott.
   A boy and a magnificent bobcat in the Florida swamp country.
Lyons, Dorothy, *Dark Sunshine,* Harcourt.
   A teen-aged polio victim finds new life in training her horse.
Montgomery, Rutherford, *The Golden Stallion and the Wolf Dog,* Little, Brown.
   A mystery and a great white stallion that challenges the golden stallion —a series book. (Also, *Crazy Kill Range,* World. Another fine horse story.)
Powell, Miriam, *Jareb,* Crowell-Collier-Macmillan.
   A Georgia pine country boy and his "no account" hound dog.
*Street, James, *Goodbye, My Lady,* Lippincott.

Sports Stories

The interest in sports fiction grows naturally out of the preoccupation with athletics in most junior and senior high schools. The thrill of the clash on gridiron or diamond or court is a part of the experience of almost every student, whether participant or spectator. Adolescents in the junior high school, especially boys, are likely to admire physical prowess more than almost anything else, and of course sports heroes are legion. A continuing spate of sports fiction is directed at this interest. These books, whether wretched or excellent, are guaranteed an audience. The minority of good books present credible, well-knit plots, solid characterization, authentic play-by-play action, and occasionally a theme of some significance.

Learnings through class discussion.   Like animal stories, sports fiction has a place in the junior high school literature program, exciting the interest of some pupils who are likely to be classified as naturally "unliterary." From the soil of sports fiction can sprout some discriminating reactions to literature. In a seventh- or eighth-grade unit on "Sports and Sportsmanship" or "Heroes, Past and Present," for example, the class, or a group within the class, may consider sports fiction. The following questions discussed in class may lead the students in the direction of appreciating some of the elements of good writing.

DO THE ATHLETES AND THE COACHES IN YOUR BOOKS SEEM REAL?   Does their conversation sound natural? The boys who are athletes themselves and who are working with coaches are in a good position to discuss these questions. Use of stereotypes or creation of real characters is a literary matter worth discussing here. In sports fiction, coaches, for instance, are likely to fall into two stock categories: dark villains who exploit their players or impossible bundles of omniscience who are concerned much more with building character than with winning games. In these books, dialogue is often badly handled. Scenes are common in which coaches deliver pompous orations in locker rooms between halves and thus send forth rejuvenated teams that sweep all opposition away before them. Pupils quickly catch the falseness of this. And they can recognize the ridiculousness in this statement by the gangling seventeen-year-old southpaw who has just been offered an athletic scholarship: "I appreciate the offer more than I can tell you, sir. But it isn't a real business proposition. I mean you are offering to lend us considerably more money than we can offer security for, are you not?" They can see the superiority of characterization in, say, John Tunis' *Keystone Kids,* in which the main characters chew tobacco and talk as many major league baseball players really do.

HOW DO THE SPORTS HEROES IN YOUR BOOKS GAIN SUCCESS, SOLVE THEIR PROBLEMS?   What sorts of obstacles do they encounter? In the better sports fiction, success is not won easily; sacrifice and dedication, involving training and learning, are usually featured. The southpaw does not often move from the sandlot to the big league and strike out the "murderers' row" in his first appearance on the mound. And the junior high school boy, yearning for the athletic peak himself, is able to recognize the truth of experience. The most common theme in sports fiction is that of an individual coming to terms with himself, finding confidence or throwing off some immature pattern of reaction. Such themes are valid in sports stories—they can be mawkishly handled, featuring perhaps a sudden "coming to realize" twist; or well handled, in which the gridiron or the diamond becomes the proving ground that it can be for certain traits of character. Some writers have even injected social themes into sports fiction. One of John Tunis' books, for example, features a Jewish baseball player, another, a Negro football player. His two least popular books, *Yea! Wildcats!* and *A City for Lincoln,* are frankly political. Bill Carol's *Full-Court Pirate* is built around a sociological theme in that a high school basketball hopeful is convinced that his living in the "wrong" neighborhood jeopardizes his chance for success. Consideration of theme, then, is not out of place even in discussion of sports fiction.

HOW MUCH ACTUAL GAME ACTION DO YOUR BOOKS HAVE?   Does the author really reproduce the excitement of the game? Are there any lines in your books in which the action of a game is especially well described? Again, the junior high school pupil is in good position to judge these matters from his own experience. Although the adult reader might be appalled at the seemingly endless round of games and "tight spots," it is the amount and quality of game action that makes or breaks the book for the adolescent. Among the writers who usually can produce taut play-by-play are John Tunis, C. Paul Jackson, Dick Friendlich, and Curtis Bishop.

In the junior high school, sports fiction may open new avenues in reading and in thought. The nonbookish boy may be led from fiction to biographies of sports heroes or into other areas of fiction and nonfiction involving courage and prowess. Units such as "Sports and Sportsmanship" and "Heroes, Past and Present" may extend the conception of fair play and of heroism.

REPRESENTATIVE BOOKS

Bishop, Curtis, *Rebound,* Lippincott.
  Solid basketball action and a touch of romance.

Bowen, Robert, *The Big Inning,* Lothrop.
A big league baseball player overcomes an injury that forces him to give up baseball.
*Carol, Bill S., *Full-Court Pirate,* Steck-Vaughn.
Carse, Robert, *The Winner,* Scribner.
From high school competition to professional tennis.
Decker, Duane, *Long Ball to Left Field,* Morrow.
A hard-hitting young pitcher is reluctant to switch to the outfield.
Douglas, Gilbert, *Hard to Tackle,* Crowell.
An exciting football story with a racial theme. (Also, *The Bulldog Attitude,* basketball.)
Flood, Richard T., *Penalty Shot,* Houghton Mifflin.
Another Radford Academy story. Hockey action from page 1 to the end.
Friendlich, Dick, *Baron of the Bull Pen,* Westminster.
A relief pitcher and a feud between two young players—the self-confidence theme.
Jackson, C. Paul, *Rose Bowl All-American,* Crowell-Collier-Macmillan.
Exciting football with the "finding confidence" theme. (Also *All-Conference Tackle* and *Tournament Forward.*)
Jackson, C. Paul, and O. B. Jackson, *Puck Grabber,* Whittlesey.
Unattenuated hockey excitement—high school competition.
Meader, Stephen, *Sparkplug of the Hornets,* Harcourt.
A "shorty" makes the grade in high school basketball.
Tunis, John, *All-American,* Harcourt.
A high school football story with a well-handled racial theme.
*———, *Keystone Kids,* Harcourt.
A brother combination in major league baseball.
———, *Schoolboy Johnson,* Morrow.
A temperamental rookie pitcher becomes a winner and a man.
Waldman, Frank, *The Challenger,* Harcourt.
A hard-working athlete wins the heavyweight boxing title.

Stories of Physical Adventure and Ordeal

Though the literature of adventure belongs to no particular age group, it has special appeals to the adolescent, and a large body of adventure fiction has been written for young people. Whit Burnett describes adventure as "a climate of the mind." In the introduction to his anthology, *The Spirit of Adventure,* he says: "Adventure is an atmosphere and essence. . . . It is the man, plus the place and event; a man out of the ordinary in daring, endurance, and vision, and a place out of our common ken, even perhaps out of the world." [5]

Everyone likes to imagine that if circumstances demanded he would prove to be out of the ordinary in daring, endurance, and resourcefulness. During the pall of routine one keeps an inner vision of himself, and it is fascinating to hold this up to comparison with those who have met peril surpassingly. This is especially true of the adolescent, who feels a pressing need for private opportunities to test himself, vicariously as well as actually.

Hazardous undertakings, out-of-the-ordinary characters, and places "out of our common ken" have been the essentials of the traditional adventure story, and remain so in the junior novel of adventure. The popularity of science fiction, treated separately in this chapter, attests to the taste for the "out of this world." The more significant of the adventure novels retain these essentials but rise to a level at which the hero's understandings—and perhaps those of the reader—are enlarged and his attitudes modified as a result of his experiences.

Though the junior novel of adventure, like its adult counterpart, presents a broad spectrum of experiences, the major categories feature outdoor adventure and the sea and make their greatest appeal to boys. Adventure and peril may be at the heart, too, of other categories of novels treated in this chapter—such as stories of earlier times and of the adolescent culture. War is a prime interest of boys, but little has been done with the topic in the junior novel. Exceptions are John Tunis's *Silence Over Dunkerque,* featuring a peerless British sergeant in the great disaster of World War II, and Frank Bonham's *War Beneath the Sea,* which tells of a young sailor's experiences on the submarine *USS Mako.*

The theme of survival or man against nature is a most common one in the novels of outdoor adventure. Outstanding in this category is James Ramsey Ullman's *Banner in the Sky* (reprinted in paperback as *Third Man on the Mountain*), the story of a Swiss boy's battle to conquer the mountain on which his father had lost his life. The mountain is the obvious symbol of the boy's aspiration. This novel is a worthwhile one for group study in the early junior high school. Notable, too, is Armstrong Sperry's lyrically written little novel, *Call It Courage,* about a Polynesian boy's attempt to prove his courage through an

[5] New York: Holt, Rinehart and Winston, 1955, pp. 12–13.

ordeal on a deserted island. Other appropriate examples are Kerry Wood's *Wild Winter,* the account of a young writer's excruciating winter in a log cabin in northern Canada, and Kenneth Gilbert's story of the hazardous adventures of an Eskimo boy and an American boy in the far north, *Arctic Adventure.*

Another common theme in these books is the joy and therapy of wild places coupled with a strong didacticism concerning conservation of natural resources and wild life. James Kjelgaard and Montgomery Atwater are perhaps the major examples in this category. Both write highly masculine stories of adventure in the woods. Atwater is best known for his youthful forest ranger Hank Winton, and Hank's associates in the forest service. Kjelgaard's characters are generally inveterate hunters, and he usually injects some sort of mystery into his stories. Both authors are skillful in constructing credible, straightforward plots. Neither's style is distinguished and neither makes any attempt at real characterization.

The seas, covering a large proportion of the earth, have been a traditional setting for adventure fiction, from the blood and thunder tales of piracy to the profound allegory of *Moby Dick.* Byron's famous lines beginning, "Roll on, thou deep and dark blue ocean, roll!" express the eternal fascination with the power and vastness and inscrutability of the sea. The midwestern farm boy who has never seen an ocean is as interested in sea fiction as the boy who has spent his life on the seacoast.

Shipwreck, another variation of the survival theme, is prominent in adolescent fiction of the sea. Two suspenseful tales by Richard Armstrong are good examples. *Cold Hazard* recounts the perils of a small group of people set adrift when an iceberg collides with their ship. In *The Big Sea* a young sailor is left alone on board a sinking freighter, and the action is both physical and psychological. The traditional search-for-treasure theme, represented most prominently by *Treasure Island,* is a minor one in recent junior novels, though Frank Crisp and Harry Rieseberg have written appealing stories of modern treasure hunting. Perhaps the most talented writer of sea adventure for young readers is Ireland's Eilis Dillon. Into her thoroughly romantic stories —such as *The Lost Island,* in which a boy finds his long-shipwrecked father and a strange treasure on a lost island, and *The San Sebastian,* the mystery of an abandoned vessel on the Irish coast—she has injected an effect of mood and a sensitivity of style rare in the writer of junior novels. Though basically realistic, her stories are shot through with Irish legend, folklore, and superstition, and there is a fullness of characterization lacking in many writers of adventure tales.

Diving and underwater adventure is a common theme in recent adventure fiction for adolescents. A good example is Philip Harkins' *Where the Shark Waits,* the story of a sixteen-year-old boy's perilous adventures in diving.

These novels of adventure and ordeal usually feature characters of adolescent age, most often boys, who are placed more or less on their own in precarious situations. Although adults often play important parts, parents usually are conveniently absent for one reason or another. Almost never is there a love plot.

REPRESENTATIVE BOOKS

*Armstrong, Richard, *Cold Hazard,* Houghton Mifflin.
   (Also *The Big Sea,* McKay.)
*Atwater, Montgomery, *Hank Winton: Smokechaser,* Random House.
   A young forest ranger's adventures, underlain by a message on forest conservation.
*Bonham, Frank, *War Beneath the Sea,* Crowell-Collier-Macmillan. (E)
Crisp, Frank, *The Treasure of Barby Swin,* Coward-McCann. (E)
   Life in a whaler and a strange treasure story with a well-wrought villain.
Dietz, Lew, *Full Fathom Five,* Little, Brown.
   Three college boys become involved in a summer vacation mystery.
*Dillon, Eilis, *The Lost Island,* Funk & Wagnalls.
   (Also, *The San Sebastian.*)
Gates, Doris, *North Fork,* Viking.
   A summer in a logging camp toughens an aristocratic tenderfoot. (Also, *River Ranch.*)
*Gilbert, Kenneth, *Arctic Adventure,* Holt, Rinehart and Winston.
   (Also, *Triple-Threat Patrol.*)
   Adolescent boys solve a summer vacation mystery involving timber thieves in Puget Sound.)
Haig-Brown, Roderick, *Mounted Police Patrol,* Morrow.
   An exciting story of the Canadian Mounted Police.
*Harkins, Philip, *Where the Shark Waits,* Morrow.
Hoffman, Peggy, *Shift to High!* Westminster.
   Three boys take a trip in a rebuilt car—disaster in a humorous context all along the way.

Janes, Edward C., *Wilderness Warden*, McKay.
  A young game warden's battle against poachers in northern Maine.
Kjelgaard, James, *Hidden Trail*, Holiday.
  Outdoor winter fiction involving a young conservation department cameraman who solves the mystery of a lost elk herd.
  (Also *A Nose for Trouble*. Exciting forest adventure and mystery.)
Lathrop, West, *Northern Trail Adventure*, Random House.
  More Canadian Mounted Police adventure in the far North.
Mays, Victor, *Fast Iron*, Houghton Mifflin. (E)
  (Also *Action Starboard*.)
Rieseberg, Harry, *My Compass Points to Treasure*, Holt, Rinehart and Winston. (E)
  Searching for lost treasure ships in the Caribbean.
*Sperry, Armstrong, *Call It Courage*, Macmillan. (E)
Stanford, Don, *Crash Landing*, Funk & Wagnalls.
  The son of a policeman is involved in a well-written adventure and mystery involving airplanes.
*Tunis, John R., *Silence over Dunkerque*, Morrow.
*Ullman, James R., *Banner in the Sky*, Lippincott.
Whitney, Phyllis, *A Mystery of the Angry Idol*, Westminster.
  A girl's stay with her grandmother is taken up with a strange mystery.
*Wood, Kerry, *Wild Winter*, Houghton Mifflin.

Stories of Earlier Times

A quick survey of the shelves of any library or of publishers' lists is sufficient to illustrate the vogue for historical fiction, or at least for the historical romance in the adolescent as well as the adult novel. The reasons for the recurring popularity of historical fiction can be traced to the functions of literature, the rewards sought in reading, which are discussed in earlier chapters. There is, certainly, an inherent fascination in looking backward as well as in looking forward. Just as the science-fiction piece is an escape into the future, so the historical novel is an escape into the past. The past, in general, induces a special kind of nostalgia on the part of most readers, and "the good old days" are still very much revered. Since the past has been lived through, it always seems more orderly, and seems to present less complexity than "the fast pace of nowadays." And subconsciously, too, the reader may feel a certain satisfying superiority as he or the author compares the past with the present.

The kind of people and the events that tend to be emphasized in the typical historical romance are exactly of the type that appeals to the adolescent mind. The characters are people of action—the man of great physical prowess, the woman of surpassing courage. To the average adolescent, the exciting events of the past are physical, stressing action and daring, melodrama and spectacle. Frequently the role of the martyr or of the person who is willing to fight for his cause against great odds is accentuated. These are roles much admired by the adolescent.

So far as teachers and parents are concerned, historical fiction may seem to possess advantages that some other types of literature do not. Even in entertainment many teachers and parents are much concerned with what is "educational," and the supposed opportunities to learn history may make historical fiction seem more "worthwhile" than contemporary romance.

Perhaps, too, part of the appeal of historical fiction may be found in the fact that it stresses certain broad themes or ideas that find sympathetic response among most readers. Underlying the fiction of the American past, for instance, is the "American dream," its extension and implementation, and the triumph of individual liberty over tyranny is the basic theme in many a historical novel. The worth and dignity of the individual is at the heart of American historical fiction.

Then, too, the typical historical romance affords a comfortable type of excitement, akin to that of viewing the Friday night boxing match on television. Because the story is removed in time and because events already fully resolved are likely to receive more careful attention than are people, there is less likelihood of intense, and therefore possibly painful, identification than with some other genres. As John T. Frederick points out, " 'Spectacle' is the word that expresses the essence of traditional historical romance: spectacle as distinguished from drama." [6] The reader therefore is more likely to play the role of observer than of participant. As Frederick goes on to say, "In the best of historical romance the spectacle has meaning; in its totality it achieves grasp of an age, illustration of a general truth of human nature." [7]

If students are to approach historical fiction seriously, they must be made aware of a problem that lies at the heart of skillful reading, of

[6] "Costain and Company: The Historical Novel Today," *English Journal,* XLIII (April 1954), 173.
[7] Frederick, p. 80.

discrimination in the genre—the relationship between history, or historical facts, and fiction. Novelist John Hersey has commented cogently on this relationship:

> Palpable facts are mortal. Like certain moths and flying ants, they lay their eggs and die overnight. The important flashes and bulletins are already forgotten by the time yesterday morning's newspaper is used to line the trash can to receive today's coffee grounds. The things we remember for longer periods are emotions and impressions and illusions and images and characters: the elements of fiction.[8]

Hersey is implying that historical fiction *is* fiction, not history or journalism; its responsibilities are to fiction. Further, he implies that good historical fiction is timeless rather than timely, and its essential concern is not for events but for people, for the truth of human character, which is unchanging—the constant in human experience.

It is important to remember, too, that the function of historical fiction, as of any fiction, is not necessarily to set forth the literal truth, but rather only an impression of it. In good historical fiction, the major facts of a period must be adhered to, of course, but specific details and events may be secondary in the novel which, as James T. Farrell puts it, "re-creates the consciousness and the conscience of a period. It tells us what has happened to man, what could have happened to him, what man has imagined might happen to him." [9] Errors in minor historical details are unimportant. The difference might accurately be defined as that between fiction and journalism, a problem apparent in many war novels. Jessamyn West has explained the failure of many war novels—and of popular taste—in terms of this difference:

> . . . the reader's love of the "true story" is no help to the novelist. The wars produced more violence and cruelty, courage and devotion than the novelists of the world can equal. First-hand accounts satisfy the reader's hankering for facts and convince him that reality is what happened at a named place on a specific day. So the novels he reads in quantity tend to be either nostalgic retreat from "the facts," or them "the facts" are made even more irresistible by being attached to a narra-

---

[8] John Hersey, "The Novel of Contemporary History," *Atlantic Monthly,* CLXXXIV (November 1949), 80.

[9] James T. Farrell, "Literature and Ideology," *English Journal,* XXXL (April 1942), 269.

tive hook of a romantic-sexual nature which sinks deeply into frail flesh.[10]

The basic difference between the journalistic novel and that which rises above it lies probably in the complexity of characters and in the presence of an idea (or ideas) that gives unity to events. What a soldier did in a war is less important than why he did it, and in the great novel he becomes a symbol of humanity. The run-of-the-mill historical novel allows us to witness history; the truly good novel, to live it.

Another distinction is important in the relationship of historical facts and fiction: fiction, unlike history, may be highly selective, pretending to no rounded view. In a historical novel, some specific phase of history may be viewed through the eyes of an individual character, and the reader therefore sees and understands only what the character sees and understands. In fiction, the final impression of an actual historical personage may be quite at variance with the scholarly consensus. For example, Gertrude Finney's *Muskets along the Chickahominy,* a competent historical novel for adolescents, views Bacon's Rebellion, and the character of Nathaniel Bacon, through the eyes of a young indentured servant who much admires Bacon.

It goes almost without saying, too, that in historical fiction there still is need for the imaginative creation of comic and heroic and tragic events. The story woven through whatever facts of history is more important than the facts themselves.

Because of certain relationships it has to the school curriculum and to the reading development of adolescents, historical fiction can have considerable value in the high school program. Often in schools there is an attempt to correlate the content of social studies and English, and historical fiction, of course, is a particularly appropriate type of material for such programs.

In the field of social studies, especially in history, historical fiction can be a valuable means, not only of enriching the program generally, but of sharpening and deepening pupils' concepts of time, thus adding an important dimension to their study of the past. To many students, even after considerable exposure to American history, the American Revolution remains a rather remote and hazy mélange of tea in Bos-

---

[10] Jessamyn West, "Secret of the Masters," *Saturday Review* (September 21, 1957), 14.

ton Harbor, a midnight ride of Paul Revere, and patriots whose feet were frozen at Valley Forge. A novel like Esther Forbes's *Johnny Tremain* provides a moving close-up of that momentous time from the point of view of a realistic adolescent; understanding of the time and its issues as they entered the lives of people, which no history text can supply, is apparent in the imaginative work.

Through its stress on people and their reactions and emotions, thereby putting flesh on the skeleton of history, historical fiction, if it is good, can help develop an ability to see the past in perspective. Large movements and trends, momentous events, and great personages are, of necessity, the major stuff of history. It is for fiction to furnish the human element, the vision of the ordinary, historically insignificant individual. In Stephen Meader's well-written junior novel, *A Blow for Liberty,* the main character is a "bound" boy of Revolutionary times who longs for a life at sea. He is allowed to sign aboard a privateer and furnishes the reader with a personalized account of the perils and excitement of privateering as the issues of the war become real to him.

It is easy, however, to overstate the case for historical fiction, and mentioning certain limitations of the genre and cautions in using it is in order. One must remember that historical fiction *is* fiction. Though valuable as a supplement to the study of history, it can never be a substitute for history, though many teachers and laymen have been impressed by its apparent possibilities as a painless "backdoor" approach to the subject. Furthermore, many historical novels, even though set in the past, do not really have anything to do with the facts of history or with interpreting a period.

American backgrounds are predominant in the junior novel of earlier times, though non-American backgrounds have been featured more frequently in recent years. The settings and events of the American background stories most frequently feature the wars, the adventures and perils of frontier life, and the "Old West."

One authentic historical novel for adolescents stands alone in its conception and literary quality—*Johnny Tremain* by Esther Forbes. Out of her research on the pre-Revolutionary War years, the author, who won a Pulitzer Prize for her biography of Paul Revere, has wrought the authentic background for her story of a young Boston silversmith's apprentice who became involved in patriotic activities, including the Boston Tea Party, just prior to the outbreak of hostilities. Famous figures such as Paul Revere and Samuel Adams play important parts in the story.

Johnny Tremain, however, which is in rather wide use as common reading in grades eight to ten, is not a popularized history text. It is a genuine novel of exciting events and character. Tenn-age Johnny is one of the most interesting characters in junior fiction. At the outset of the story he is the completely vain and cocksure young bully. An injury to his hand ends his career as a silversmith's apprentice, completely changes his life, and involves him ultimately in the revolutionary movement. Johnny's personal tribulations are the major subject of the story, but the adolescent reader is able to live with Johnny through the stirring pre-Bunker Hill times in a manner that marks the best in historical fiction.

Several of Stephen Meader's long list of junior novels have historical settings. *A Blow for Liberty,* about a boy's experiences in privateering during the Revolution, was cited earlier. Meader also has written a sort of junior version of *The Red Badge of Courage* in *The Muddy Road to Glory,* in which a farm boy enlists in the Army of the Potomac which pursues and finally corners Lee at Gettysburg. The plots of both books are lusty and taut and there is some attempt at characterization in depth.

Two of the best of the recent stories of frontier life and pioneering are *Snow in the River* by Carol Brink and *The Far-Off Land* by Rebecca Caudill, both authors long established as writers for adolescents. *Snow in the River* is the story of two very different brothers who go to northwestern America from Scotland in the early nineteenth century. The story is narrated by the niece of one of the brothers who recounts memories from childhood—an unusual technique in the junior novel. There is tragedy and realism in the work along with touches of humor and a uniqueness of style. In *The Far-Off Land,* a seventeen-year-old Moravian girl travels with her brother and his family to a settlement in the Tennessee wilderness. A major theme is the protagonist's struggle to maintain her ideals in the face of the warring of Indians and whites.

The Old West of gunfighters and fearless marshals and women of beauty and courage, of stampedes and stage coach robberies seems invulnerable in appeal. The hour-long western romance is a staple of television fiction and accounts for some decline in the output of western novels.

Interestingly, the junior western, of which there are not many, seems of better quality, in general, than its adult counterpart. Perhaps the western best known among young readers is Jack Schaefer's *Shane*. Its plot is traditional horse opera: a lean, mysterious stranger appears at the Starrett farm, takes part in a war between the ranchers and the small farmers, and disappears, much to the chagrin of Bob Starrett, the young adolescent who tells the story. But the characterization of Shane comes through, even though that of the adolescent does not. Fortunately, the incipient love triangle involving Shane and Bob's mother and father never really develops, and there is no other love angle. A sense of values, unusual in western fiction, pervades the story.

A fifteen-year-old boy, son of an Army officer at Fort Dodge, is the principal character in Val Gendron's *Powder and Hides,* suitable for reading in the junior or senior high school. Accompanying two veterans, the boy goes on the last great buffalo hunt in 1873. Gendron's characterization is adequate and her style terse. A strong feeling for the passing of an epoch is threaded through the unmelodramatic story.

Much of the better western fiction has ignored the hackneyed cattle-rustling intrigues and sundown gun duels and has concentrated on the historically significant conflict with the Indians inherent in the westward movement. Elliott Arnold, for example, has been preoccupied with the relations between the Army and the Apaches. In writing a simplified version of his long *Blood Brother,* he has produced a worthy book for adolescents, *Broken Arrow,* dealing with the last stand of Cochise and his strange friendship with the white man, Tom Jeffords.

The Cheyenne Indians, whom she presents with insight, are the interest of Mari Sandoz. Though her style is in general undistinguished, she has a flair for detail in characterization and description and creates an admirable unity of plot. *The Horsecatcher* sensitively traces a Cheyenne boy's struggle for acceptance and prestige in his family and tribe. Younger adolescents may find much to discuss in the Indian boy's rejection of the role of warrior for the more pedestrian one of horsecatcher.

The theme of Eastern tenderfoot "making it" in the West is a familiar one in western fiction. An appropriate example of a reworking of the theme among recent junior novels is Lee McGiffin's *The Mustangers,* in which a New York boy goes to Texas and eventually becomes a first-rate mustanger, capturing his own special horse. The simple but picturesque story gives a real feeling for the Texas of the 1870's.

REPRESENTATIVE BOOKS

Allen, Merritt P., *The Wilderness Way,* McKay. (E)
A capture-by-Indians-torture-and-escape plot featuring an eighteen-year-old who accompanies LaSalle on his ill-fated attempt to reach the mouth of the Mississippi.
*Arnold, Elliott, *Broken Arrow,* Little, Brown.
Brink, Carol, *Snow in the River,* Macmillan.
(Also, *Caddie Woodlawn.* A girl and her family on a Wisconsin farm in Civil War days.)
Butters, Dorothy, *The Bells of Freedom,* Macrae.
A young adolescent boy is caught in a conflict between loyalty to a friend and his patriotism during the siege of Boston during the American Revolution.
Carr, Harriet H., *Gravel Gold,* Farrar, Straus. (E)
A sixteen-year-old prospects for gold in Colorado in the 1850s with moderate success and much adventure.
*Caudill, Rebecca, *The Far-Off Land,* Viking.
Cawley, Winifred, *Down the Long Stairs,* Holt, Rinehart and Winston.
An adolescent boy, his life complicated by his father's death in the Royalist cause in the English Civil War and his mother's decision to marry a Roundhead, runs away to join Royalist recruits.
Chute, Marchette, *The Innocent Wayfaring,* Dutton.
The adventures and romance of a boy and girl who run away from home and meet on the road to London—Chaucer's time. (Also *The Wonderful Winter.* A young man runs away to London and spends the winter acting in Shakespeare's company.)
*Finney, Gertrude, *Muskets along the Chickahominy,* McKay.
*Forbes, Esther, *Johnny Tremain,* Houghton Mifflin.
*Gendron, Val, *Powder and Hides,* McKay. (E)
Lane, Rose W., *Let the Hurricane Roar,* McKay. (E)
A young wife's excruciating winter on a Dakota homestead.
Maddock, Reginald, *The Last Horizon,* Nelson.
A talented South African writer of novels for adolescents tells the story of a young man who led his fellow Bushmen against the Boers.
Malvern, Gladys, *Behold Your Queen,* McKay.

Based on the life of Queen Esther of Persia. (Also *The Foreigner.* The biblical story of Ruth and Naomi.)

*McGiffin, Lee, *The Mustangers,* Dutton.

*Meader, Stephen, *A Blow for Liberty,* Harcourt. (Also *The Muddy Road to Glory.*)

Norton, Andre, *Stand to Horse,* Harcourt. (E)
  A young cavalry recruit fights the Apaches in 1859.

Patterson, Emma, *The World Turned Upside Down,* McKay.
  War and romance become real problems to a New York farm boy at the outbreak of the Revolution.

Richter, Conrad, *Light in the Forest,* Knopf.
  A white boy, reared among the Indians and returned to his parents, goes back to his Indian home and to divided loyalties.

*Sandoz, Mari, *The Horsecatcher,* Westminster. (E)

*Schaefer, Jack, *Shane,* Houghton Mifflin.

Sutcliff, Rosemary, *The Lantern Bearers,* Walck.
  A tale of Britain after the Roman withdrawal—battle and romance. More complicated and challenging than most novels for the adolescent.

Vocational Stories

Concern with his future role as an adult is a major preoccupation of the adolescent, especially when he reaches the senior high school. From this concern has come the "vocational story," which presents in fictional form information about professions and occupations. These books, though rather widely read, have little significance for the literature program. Most of them could quite fairly be called "subliterary," and many of them have doubtful value as sources of information. The senior high school student who is seriously considering a vocation is inclined—and should be urged—to consult authentic sources of information that lie outside the area of literature.

The vocational novel for adolescents probably had its beginning with the publication of Helen D. Boylston's first Sue Barton story in 1936. The subsequent series that takes Sue Barton through the various stages of her training to become a nurse and subsequent professional life has been extremely popular with girls in their mid-adolescence. For some reason—probably the romantic tradition surrounding the profession—stories of nursing have been a staple in this genre of writing for young people. Another popular series about nursing, somewhat better in quality than Boylston's, is that by Dorothy Deming. Mary Stolz, however, has contributed the best stories of nursing in her *Organdy Cupcakes* and *Hospital Zone*. Though these books lack the introspection and lyricism of other Stolz novels, and the "writing down" in them is evident, they are definitely a cut above most of the others in this genre.

Teaching is another of the professions most commonly treated in the vocational stories. All of them feature young women who encounter tribulations in teaching but who eventually win the devotion of their students. Often, of course, a romance is involved, and the profession is depicted as relatively attractive. One of the best of the more recent junior novels on teaching is Mary Dalim's *Miss Mac,* a supple, witty story of a young teacher's trying moments in the classroom and her romance with the assistant coach.

The better vocational novels, of course, are able to present authentic, unglamorized information in the context of a well-told story. Adele de Leeuw has accomplished this in some of her many vocational stories, the best known of which is probably *With a High Heart,* dealing with rural library work. Also unusually well done is Phyllis Whitney's *A Window for Julie,* in which the heroine starts as a salesgirl in a department store and finally becomes a window-display designer.

Another unusual book that fits loosely into the vocational category is Nancy Hartwell's *Dusty Cloak,* in which the tribulations of getting a start in the professional world of acting are delineated. The heroine experiences disappointment without disillusionment, and a deftly handled love plot is woven skillfully into the well-written story.

It is obvious from this discussion that most of the vocational stories are written for girls, though some of the boys' books, not principally vocational, include details about occupations and professions. The talented Nat Hentoff's fine story, *Jazz Country,* might conceivably be called a vocational novel. It is the story of a white boy's struggle to break into jazz music in Harlem.

Science Fiction

The teacher of adolescents is keenly aware of the modern vogue of science fiction, which is likely to envelop boys in about the ninth or

tenth grade. Developing rapidly since the mid-1920's, science fiction
was given tremendous impetus, as was science nonfiction, by the ex-
ploding of the atomic bomb—which ushered in a era possibly more
fantastic than the science fiction writers had ever imagined. In his illuminating book, *Inquiry into Science Fiction,* Basil Davenport identifies the basic appeal of science fiction:

> . . . That man is a creature with awesome potentialities for achieve-
> ment and for self-destruction, and that the inhabitants of Earth are not
> the only powers in the universe—these are truths that men have never
> been able to forget for more than a generation or two. It is science fic-
> tion which is telling them to us now." [11]

Science fiction reflects man's eternal curiosity about the unknown
and his fascination with predicting the future. The fantastic imaginings
of one day, the prophecies of science fiction, become the commonplace realities of another. The reader of science fiction asks himself,
"How long before this will come true?" In March 1944, barely a year
before the dropping of the first atomic bomb, *Astounding Science Fiction* magazine carried a story entitled "Deadline," about atomic weapons and how they were made. The story prompted an FBI investigation because the government was convinced there was a "leak" from
the research laboratories!

Basil Davenport points out that science fiction, although in its present form dating from the founding of *Amazing Stories* in 1926, has
forerunners that extend back across centuries. Francis Bacon's *The
New Atlantis* in 1627, for example, predicted submarines, airplanes,
refrigeration, and the conveying of sound over long distances. Of
course, a specially important ancestor of science fiction is Jules
Verne's *Twenty Thousand Leagues under the Sea,* still relatively popular with adolescents. In the early twentieth century H. G. Wells's fiction predicted atomic energy, rockets, and helicopters, among other
things.

Like the western story and other popular forms of fiction, space
adventure is widely associated with the comic book and the juvenile
movie and television programs. Yet science fiction covers a broad
range of subjects other than space travel, from radioactive mosquitoes

[11] Basil Davenport, *Inquiry into Science Fiction* (New York: McKay,
1955), p. 81.

to extrasensory perception, and some of its writers have risen to a rank of respectability in contemporary literature. Significantly, selections of science fiction have begun to appear in junior and senior high school literature anthologies.

Basil Davenport and other critics have identified several kinds of science fiction: the "space opera," the story based on scientific hypotheses, the gadget piece, the speculative story, and the fantasy. The space opera is that story in which the wild profusion of events just happens to occur in outer space instead of in the jungle, on the cattle range, or in the New York City underworld. It is the typical pulp-magazine adventure story in which the only requirement is action.

The gadget story, apparently in decline now, and the story based on scientific hypotheses both utilize scientific material. Based usually on some curious scientific fact, the gadget story is focused on a device. Some writers of science fiction, like Isaac Asimov who is a scientist himself, have utilized known information to develop and extend a hypothesis through a process of logical reasoning. Excellence or the lack of it in this type of story, dear to the original science fiction fan, who is at least an amateur scientist, may be lost on the ordinary reader—who may not be able to tell a ridiculous "scientific" hypothesis from a sound one. For example, as Davenport points out, many stories have included man fighting insects as large as man himself. The impossibility of this is not evident to the person who does not realize that because of the difference in circulation between mammal and insect, an insect cannot be much bigger than a tarantula or a mammal much smaller than a shrewmouse.

All science fiction is based essentially on the projection into the future of present trends or tendencies. The speculative story, however, is likely to be based on trends outside the natural sciences. From the nineteenth century, Edward Bellamy's *Looking Backward,* uncannily accurate at points, is still fascinating. It is interesting that contemporary authors of the speculative story usually foresee a grim future in which man, through his own distorted values, is again living in caves or in abject slavery.

Discussion of science fiction in class might lead into a writing assignment to which adolescents usually respond with interest—projecting into the future a trend they discern in the present. Or, conversely,

VARIETIES OF THE JUNIOR NOVEL 273

the writing assignment may lead into discussion of science fiction. The main value of science fiction in the high school literature program lies not in any back door to scientific information that it might open nor in any light it might throw on eternal themes in human experience— though it may possibly have both these values. For some students, science fiction will provide another type of vicarious adventure, helping to satisfy the appetite for the unusual. Perhaps for even more students, science fiction is a respectable form of fantasy, the usual varieties of which are not popular in the adolescent culture, where the need for occasional fantasy is kept well camouflaged. "Fairy" tales, magic carpets, and jinns are not for the adolescent. But their counterparts, space ships and time machines and otherworld creatures, may be because they are tied, implausibly or not, to something called science. The main value of science fiction in the high school literature program lies in the fact that interest in the better-level science fiction may lead to a taste for other explorations of the unknown and unworldly in prose and poetry.

Science fiction is popular with adults as well as adolescents, and many of the science fiction novels popular with adolescent readers were written for the general reading public. The two principal writers who have concerned themselves with books specifically for adolescents are Robert Heinlein and Lester Del Rey. Heinlein's work is less unworldly than most science fiction. His concerns are family life and human problems, and experiences similar to those of today, in future settings. His books are also more lighthearted than most other science fiction novels. *Citizen of the Galaxy,* for example, is the story of a young businessman's problems with his family's interplanetary interests. *The Rolling Stones* recounts the interplanetary vacation of a family that buys a used rocket. In *Farmer in the Sky,* a group of colonists settle on one of Jupiter's moons and struggle to survive in an inhospitable climate. Lester Del Rey turns out well-plotted, absorbing stories with youthful protagonists. One of his better recent books is *The Runaway Robot,* in which a sixteen-year-old and his robot escape from a rocket ship and experience an assortment of adventures throughout the solar system.

In the list that follows some of the better adult science fiction novels are listed along with those written for adolescents.

REPRESENTATIVE BOOKS

Asimov, Isaac, *Caves of Steel*, Doubleday.
  A robot teams with a human detective in solving a mystery in the New York City of the future.
Bonham, Frank, *The Loud, Resounding Sea*, Crowell-Collier-Macmillan.
  An adolescent's adventures with a dolphin that talks.
Bradbury, Ray, *The Martian Chronicles*, Doubleday.
  An earth group visits Mars in the twenty-first century.
Brown, Fredric, *Martians, Go Home*, Dutton.
  The funniest science fiction episode results when the Martians—two and a half feet tall, green, and with very unpleasant personalities—invade Earth.
Del Rey, Lester, *Outpost of Jupiter*, Holt, Rinehart and Winston.
  A plague threatens to wipe out the settlers on Ganymede until the Jupiter creatures assist them. (Also *The Runaway Robot*, Westminster.)
Heinlein, Robert, *Citizen of the Galaxy*, Scribner. (E)
  (Also *Tunnel in the Sky, The Red Planet, Rocket Ship Galileo, Space Cadet, *The Rolling Stones, *Farmer in the Sky.*)
Leinster, Murray, *The Last Space Ship*, Frederick Fell.
  A strong social theme underlies this prophecy of future despotism; "matter transmitters" are featured.
L'Engle, Madeleine, *A Wrinkle in Time*, Farrar, Straus.
  A highly unusual story of three young people's search through a fifth-dimensional world for a missing physicist and their encounter with an evil being who threatens the freedom of the universe.
Norton, Andre, *Star Rangers*, Harcourt.
  Adventures of a space patrol in A.D. 8054. "Mind control" plays a dominant part.
Shute, Nevil, *On the Beach*, Morrow.
  The few survivors of a cobalt war find they are doomed from radiation.

NOVELS OF SOCIAL PROBLEMS

The tradition of social significance and of social protest has been a major one in the literature of the world. In 1956 the New American Library published a paperbound edition of the book by Robert B.

Downs entitled *Books That Changed the World.* On the cover is a reference to the fact that the books discussed "caused people to revolt against oppression, started wars, and revolutionized man's ideas about the universe and himself." Many of the books discussed in this particular volume do not belong in the sphere of imaginative literature; yet the novel has been a powerful shaper and inciter of public opinion on social issues and conditions. In the nineteenth century, Victor Hugo, with *Les Misérables,* and Charles Dickens, with books like *Oliver Twist,* centered attention on social injustice in France and England. One of the most incendiary books in American history is Harriet Beecher Stowe's *Uncle Tom's Cabin.* It is generally conceded that Upton Sinclair's powerful *The Jungle,* which revealed conditions in the Chicago stockyards at the turn of the century, was influential in bringing the passage of the pure food and drug laws. Sinclair Lewis' widely read novels savagely attacked America's small-town business culture. Later in the century John Steinbeck dramatized the plight of the migrant worker in *The Grapes of Wrath;* Richard Wright, in his *Native Son,* protested angrily against the condition of the Negro; Laura Hobson attacked anti-Semitism in *Gentlemen's Agreement;* Willard Motley pointed to the relationship between delinquency and living conditions in *Knock on Any Door;* Irwin Shaw etched the dilemma of the American liberal, caught between communism and extreme reaction, in *The Troubled Air.* The fundamental protest against conditions that diminish man and his spirit is reflected in the literature of all periods.

Teachers have realized for a long time, apparently, that literature which deals with social or group problems can aid in improving human relations and in developing a rational approach to social problems, an approach based upon an awareness of alternatives in our group life. First, literature can help to relieve group tensions by stressing the universals, the basic similarities in life as it is lived at many different levels and under many different conditions in our American society and in our world. Although we have in our society a number of economic levels, people in these varying groups are faced with the same basic need for finding some measure of success and happiness.

The basic problem of finding his or her place, of harmonizing the various forces playing upon him or her, is the same for the Seminole

Indian boy in Zachary Ball's *Swamp Chief,* the young Negro boy in
Louisa Shotwell's *Roosevelt Grady,* and the older adolescent boy in S.
E. Hinton's *The Outsiders,* although the three are of different nationalities and races, live in different parts of the country and are the
products of vastly different cultures and environments. The dramatization of what different people have made of life under different conditions helps to make literature the integrating force it always has been
in men's lives.

This integrating function can be applied, too, to literature dealing
with the various minority groups. Books about Negro life and problems not only portray the unique problems of people of the Negro
race, although these are important, but also serve the function of helping Negro children to find satisfaction in life, its beauty and humor as
well as its squalor and pathos—as Langston Hughes suggests in *Not
Without Laughter,* the story of a Negro boy's struggle to get an education.

The second of the dual purposes which literature serves in human
relations is to develop a sensitivity to the problems of people living
under conditions different from one's own and to reveal the stake each
of us has in the plight of other groups. Most readers come away from
Richard Wright's *Native Son,* for example, not only with a depressed
feeling about the tragic and sordid net of circumstances in which Bigger Thomas is entrapped but also with an awareness of the importance for all of us of Bigger's experience. Wright's novel is meant to
pose a problem, stir action. The same is true of Motley's *Knock on
Any Door* or Steinbeck's *The Grapes of Wrath.*

Closely allied to the function of literature in improving human relations is that of aiding students to become aware of alternative approaches to group problems. Such awareness is the touchstone of the
informed, individual conscience for which we can never substitute the
censorship of constituted authority.

The vicarious participation in different ways of life may have
a . . . broadly social liberating influence. The image of past civiliza-
tions or of past periods within our western civilization, as well as images of life in other countries today, can help the youth to realize that
our American society is only one of a great variety of possible social
structures. When this insight has been attained, the individual is able to
look at the society about him more rationally. He is better able to eval-

uate it, to judge what elements should be perpetuated and what elements should be modified or rejected.[12]

This "broadly social liberating influence" of which Dr. Rosenblatt speaks will not be manifest so much in terms of changed attitudes as in this awareness that alternative solutions to problems often exist. The whole matter of the relationship of a person's reading to his attitudes is a complex and controversial one, but research tends to indicate, for example, that the person who considers the Negro race anthropologically inferior to the white will not necessarily change his attitudes after reading Arna Bontemps' *We Have Tomorrow,* and may only deepen his prejudice by reading *Native Son,* although people with less entrenched predispositions may modify their attitudes considerably.

Intelligent reading in controversial literature makes for the informed conscience, the awareness of alternatives, which remains our best hope for finding solutions to group problems. One forte of literature is that it can translate the intangibles of experience—great abstractions such as equality, justice, freedom, and security—into the specific feelings and actions of human beings like ourselves.

Criteria for Judging Fiction Dealing with Group Problems

In judging and evaluating fiction that deals with a social problem, the reader has the formidable task of distinguishing his criticism of the selection as a piece of literature, a work of art, from his opinion of the importance of its theme or message. An ideology may favorably prejudice the reader's estimate of the literary worth of a selection, for when a book deals with values in which we believe deeply, which are interrelated with our security and by which we live, the matter of mere literary technique may become a minor one. On the other hand, a selection, wretched as an example of literary art, may receive serious attention because of the importance of the problem with which it deals. Most literary scholars agree that the importance of *Uncle Tom's Cabin* is historical rather than literary. *Gentleman's Agreement,* a well-known book in recent decades, can scarcely be defended as an

[12] Louise Rosenblatt, *Literature as Exploration* (New York: Appleton, 1938), p. 221.

example of mature technique in fiction, though the problem it emphasizes is vital.

It is important that teachers and librarians select fiction—and teach students to judge it—as fiction rather than as sociology, economics, political science, psychology, though fiction may have some elements in common with all these disciplines. Steinbeck's *The Grapes of Wrath,* or any other socially significant novel, must stand or fall on its merits as a novel and not on its importance sociologically. This is equally true of books written specifically for adolescents.

How do we distinguish between literary art and propaganda? What are some criteria that will help students to tell when the socially significant selection is literary art and when it is propaganda, either of the "good" or "bad" variety?

DOES THE SELECTION PLACE THE MAIN STRESS ON THE TIMELESS RATHER THAN THE TIMELY?   Because we can say "Yes" to this question about *Anna Karenina,* for example, the novel stands as one of the greatest of the world, though all the artifacts of life in nineteenth-century tsarist Russia have changed. The human problem of Anna and her decision remains timeless. Timeless elements are human emotions and problems and characteristics, though timely events and problems may have inspired many a timeless story. It is relatively unimportant that Dickens' *A Tale of Two Cities* has as its background the French Revolution; its memorable characters make the book live.

IS THE READER GIVEN ALTERNATIVES IN EMOTION OR ARE HIS FEELINGS RIGIDLY CHANNELED?   This question, like any other that might be posed in making a judgment of literature, brings different answers from readers of the same selection. A principal characteristic of propaganda, whether in fiction or in some other form, is the attempt to direct the emotions into a narrow channel. Objectivity, in the sense of impartiality, is not important. Little socially significant fiction is objective; much of it is impassioned. The essential difference again can be defined in terms of characterization: Does the author make us feel *with* the characters or only *about* them? When we feel *with* characters we become concerned with the "why" rather than the "what" of human acts; we are concerned with the basis of motivation. Thus, we are offered alternatives in feeling.

Richard Wright's *Native Son* illustrates the point clearly. Though it is an angry protest, the book offers the reader grounds for different ways of feeling about the final result. Bigger Thomas, a teen-age Negro, is the semihoodlum product of the Negro district in a large northern city. He gets an unusual "break," a job as chauffeur for a wealthy family. One evening the daughter of the family, whose parents think she is attending a concert, persuades Bigger to drive her and the man with whom she is having an affair on a round of night clubs. When they arrive home, the daughter, who has gotten drunk, makes advances to Bigger, who is terrified that the whole matter may be discovered. He gets her to her room, but in a desperate attempt to keep her quiet, accidentally suffocates her. Then in panic he takes the body to the basement and puts it into the furnace, finding it necessary to sever the head from the body. The rest of the story concerns the flight and capture of Bigger, his trial and execution.

Most readers feel sympathy with Bigger, though few would excuse his crime, made purposely horrible, and few would deny the justice of his execution. On the surface, the reader has every right to believe that Bigger got what he deserved. The propagandist melodrama would probably have had Bigger "framed" by a white man. Considering the "why" of Bigger's act, the thoughtful reader is led to a condemnation of certain elements in the social system. And, of course, this was Richard Wright's purpose. In short, the novel has a message but it rises above the level of propaganda. The same thing could be said, for example, of *Oliver Twist* or *Les Misérables*. The reader tends to hate Fagin in *Oliver Twist* and Javert, the relentless pursuer of Jean Valjean in *Les Misérables,* but he understands why they are as they are, how they "got that way." Novelist Jessamyn West makes this point in a memorable article:

> Openness, persisted in, destroys hate. The novelist may begin his writing with every intention of destroying what he hates. And since a novelist writes of persons, this means the destruction (through revelation) of an evil person. But in openness the writer becomes the evil person, does what the evil person does for his reasons and with his justifications. As this takes place, as the novelist opens himself to evil, a self-righteous hatred of evil is no longer possible. The evil which now exists is within; and one is self-righteous in relation to others, not to oneself. When the writer has himself assumed the aspect of evil and does not magisterially condemn from the outside, he can bring to his readers understanding and elicit from them compassion. This is why we do not, as readers,

hate the great villains of literature. Milton does not hate Satan; nor Thackeray, Becky; nor Shakespeare, Macbeth. For a time Milton *was* Satan; Thackeray, Becky; Shakespeare, Macbeth. And the openness of the novelist (together with his talent and his skill) permits us, his readers, though we know that Satan must be cast down and that Macbeth must die, to respond to them without narrowness—with compassion instead of hatred.[13]

WHATEVER PROBLEM IS DEALT WITH, DOES THE STORY REPRESENT THE TRUE ART OF THE STORYTELLER? The nature of the social problem on which the story centers, no matter how pressing it may be in contemporary society, has nothing to do with the worth of the selection as literature. The appeal of the original, well-constructed story must be there. Social significance cannot compensate for the absence of heroic or tragic or comic heroes and deeds, and of disciplined structure and artistic use of language.

These three are criteria that the high school student can learn to apply to all fiction, junior and adult.

RECENT JUNIOR NOVELS

In the revised edition of this book, the author noted the reluctance of junior novelists to treat social themes, a reluctance with certain obvious explanations: first, it is difficult to write a first-rate story of present-day social conflicts within the conventions, and especially the taboos, of the junior novel; second, adolescents, as a whole, for some years have not been greatly interested in social issues. The situation has changed somewhat, however, in very recent years. There has been a relaxing of taboos to some extent in the junior novel and a greater tendency on the part of writers to disregard traditional conventions. Too, young people of late have become much more concerned with social problems.

In the several years since the revised edition of this book was written, there has been a quickening of interest in certain social problems and a slackening of interest in others among writers of junior novels. The breakthrough in integration of the races in the schools and the

[13] Jessamyn West, "Secret of the Masters," *Saturday Review* (September 21, 1957), 13–14 and elsewhere.

heightened racial tension in the nation are reflected in the publication of junior fiction concerning Negro-white relations. Similarly, the increased recognition of the plight of the slum-dweller and disadvantaged generally has resulted in an increase of junior novels centered on young people in unfortunate social-economic situations. On the other hand, what was a flood of books a few years ago on the relations between ethnic and religious groups has abated greatly today.

Not only has the number of junior novels treating Negro-white relations increased, but the quality, in general, has improved in recent years. The mealy homilies which most of the earlier books represented have been replaced by at least a few junior novels which have reached a new depth of interest and feeling without obtrusive didacticism, though the taboos and happy endings are still there.

In her useful work, *Negro Literature for High School Students,* Barbara Dodd writes:

> In their dealing with race, junior novels tend to be optimistic. They usually relate specific incidents that high school students are likely to meet, like discrimination in athletics or student activities. Since they describe specific instances of discrimination rather than the cumulative psychological effects of prejudice, junior novels frequently have a happy ending. Those included here can be effective in helping white middle-class adolescents to understand Negro youths, for all show vividly the frustration and resentment of Negro youths when they are subjected to the common types of high school discrimination. Some of these novels may encourage white youths to stop discriminating; at least these books can help make white youths a little more sensitive to the feelings of their Negro classmates.
>
> Dealing as they do primarily with middle-class Negroes in integrated situations and often being written by white authors, junior novels do not reveal the explosive bitterness of the ghetto, the topic of many adult novels. Because junior novels generally hold to middle-class values and taboos—forbidding profane language, mention of sexual intercourse, or episodes of violence—they are unrealistic or too "nice," at times.[14]

Junior novels of Negro-white relationships continue to be set mostly outside of the South, despite the fact that problems of desegregation of the schools have been most severe in the South. Two earlier little novels by Jesse Jackson, a Negro writer, remain readable among

[14] NCTE, Champaign, Ill., 1968, p. 69.

the better stories which incorporate the race relations theme while retaining a lively plot line. In *Call Me Charley,* Charley Moss, a thirteen-year-old Negro, moves into a formerly white neighborhood, where he has a paper route, and becomes the first Negro to attend the junior high school in the area. Charley is subjected to some hazing, and he encounters prejudice on the part of both age mates and adults, but he finds that the majority of his acquaintances come to judge him as a person. The story is lively and supple, free of sentimentalism, with a social thesis made clear—that the hope of the Negro lies in *some* white people, provided the Negro is willing to make the best of himself under the existing conditions. *Anchor Man,* the sequel, finds Charley a senior, a member of the track team, and still the only Negro in the school. When other Negro students are transferred to the school, Charley is caught in an emotional no man's land, becoming the pivotal figure in the tense situation that develops. Jackson's books have a fair depth of characterization and the scenes of adolescent boys together are most skillful.

One of the best school stories with the theme of Negro-white relations is Hila Colman's *Classmates by Request.* This is the story of two families, one Negro and one white, and their involvement in school desegregation and racial tension in a northern town. The focus of plot and point of view shift back and forth from one to the other of the protagonists, the teen-age daughters in each family, who become friends when a few white students integrate a formerly all-Negro high school to support the demands of the Negro community for integration. However, when the white girl's father, who is appointed chairman of a commission to resolve racial problems, refuses to appoint the Negro girl's father to a position he expected, the two girls become estranged. They are brought together again in a demonstration against racial inequity which ends the book. Even though the novel falters on characterization and occasionally in plot, the writer's interest in matters literary as well as social is evident, and the book affords an insight into the complex web of racial tension.

Another competent school story of race relations is Catherine Marshall's *Julie's Heritage,* in which a Negro girl encounters prejudice in a predominantly white high school. Her problem—and the theme of the story—is how to stand up for her heritage as a Negro and still develop cordial relations with both Negroes and whites. Through the main character and three Negro friends, the author illustrates four different reactions to prejudice. Of course, in neither the Colman or Marshall novel is the love element lost sight of, though it is minor in both.

Among nonschool stories of Negro-white relations with girls as main characters, the best one the author has read is Catherine Blanton's *Hold Fast to Your Dreams* in which Emmy Lou Jefferson, whose main interest is ballet dancing, goes to Arizona to live with an aunt and to avoid the handicap of race prejudice in her Alabama town. However, she encounters prejudice in Arizona, too: her dancing teacher is forced to take a lead part in the school ballet away from Emmy, and there is an attempt to keep her out of the civic ballet in the town. However, Emmy Lou wins recognition and the book ends on a note of hope. Although the style is terse and the story well paced, there is little introspection or depth of character portrayal.

Of the recent books with boys as main characters, three stand out in the author's reading: the versatile Frank Bonham's *Durango Street* and Lorenz Graham's *South Town* and *North Town*. *Durango Street,* the story of a Negro delinquent, is hard-hitting for a junior novel. It begins when Rufus returns from a reform camp to the gang culture of his ghetto neighborhood. The major conflict is that between Rufus' desire to "go straight" and improve himself and the entrapping nature of his environment which makes him need the gang. The ending, which leaves Rufus's future uncertain, is less pat than that of most junior novels of this type.

Lorenz Graham's two books rise above the field both in social insight and literary quality. *South Town,* one of few junior novels of race relations set in the South, is the story of teen-age David Williams and his family's resistance to discrimination which ultimately leads to violence and to the Williams's decision to leave the South. In the sequel, *North Town,* David enters an integrated school and finds that his problems are not over. He has difficulty with both white and Negro students, and through a combination of circumstances is dropped from the football team. In the end, he succeeds in school and in football. Neither of Graham's books is distinguished by quality of writing, but both probe sincerely into reality and into the emotions of characters.

Nothing of particular note has been done recently in the junior novel with intercultural relations other than those of Negro and white, but a few of the earlier works remain readable and deserve continuing mention. Two simple, brief stories by Zachary Ball, *Joe Panther* and *Swamp Chief,* feature, in the context of exciting stories, the problems of a young teen-age Seminole Indian boy in the Florida Everglades country who has one foot in the primitive culture of his people and another in the cosmopolitan life of Miami.

The problems of Spanish-Americans in the United States have been the focus for a number of junior novels. In this category, Florence Means has made a notable contribution, especially in *Alicia,* in which a Denver girl of Mexican heritage rids herself, while attending the University of Mexico, of her feelings of inferiority about her background. As usual, Mrs. Means does not let her message interfere with a good story. In this same area, Lucille Mulcahy captures the spirit and the idiom of the Spanish-American people in the Rio Grande Valley of New Mexico in her book, *Pita.* The plot of the story is slight, centering on teen-age Pita's problems at school and at home. Pita's father is the most interesting character in this book. Definitely in the protest vein is Phyllis Whitney's *A Long Time Coming.* After her mother's death, Christie Allard goes to live with her Aunt Amelia in the town in which her father, who had been divorced from her mother, owns a canning plant. The plant depends upon imported Mexican labor, and the story is mainly about the attempts of Christie and her friends to secure better living and working conditions for the Mexicans and to counter the prejudices of people like Aunt Amelia who consider the Mexican inferior. Although the various attitudes toward the Mexican laborers are skillfully identified, there is little characterization and some of the scenes are overdone. Christie's somewhat pallid romance with a young newspaperman is not too successful in injecting added interest.

Among the recent books centering on the problems of the disadvantaged and slum dwellers, one is outstanding—S. E. Hinton's *The Outsiders.* This is the hard-hitting, violent story of three brothers, ranging in age from fourteen to nineteen, who live alone and are part of the gang life of a tough New York City neighborhood whose inhabitants are known to those outside it as "greasers." The teen-age greasers are at war with the teen-age "socs," equally gang-minded boys from more fortunate neighborhoods. Ponyboy, the fourteen-year-old first-person narrator, and a friend are attacked one night by a gang of socs, and Ponyboy's friend kills one of them. The two boys flee and hide outside the city in an abandoned church which, while they are away on one occasion, catches fire, trapping some children who are picnicking in the vicinity. Ponyboy and the friend rescue the children, but the friend is fatally injured. The story is climaxed with a great "rumble" between the greasers and socs, after which understanding is established between the two groups. The story ends with the social welfare authorities looking into the plight of Ponyboy and his brothers, a relatively happy ending but not a pat, rainbow wrap-up. Though the "coming to understand" theme involving the socs and greasers seems unreal and contrived, *The Outsiders* is a moving story of teenage crime and gang life, with a true insight into the effects of environment on a sensitive, intellectually inclined boy. The book is a definite contribution to the art of the junior novel.

A few of the older stories, too, of young people in unfortunate economic situations deserve continuing interest. The talented junior novelist Mary Stolz, in *Ready or Not* and *Pray Love, Remember,* deals in sequence with a New York City semi-tenement family in which the mother is dead. Though neither story conceivably could be called a protest, Stolz, through skillful use of detail, makes the reader feel keenly the protagonists' feelings toward their environment—the moments of dull hopelessness in which the griminess seems to close in, the moments of elation, and the yearning for better things.

Always preoccupied with social themes but always the conscious storyteller, prolific Florence Means has produced a commendable story in *Knock at the Door, Emmy.* Emmy is the teen-age daughter in an itinerant family living in a pickup truck that carries them from one work area to another. Eager for education, Emmy yearns to "settle down" somewhere, and she detects the same longing in her mother. The settling down is achieved in a story marked with a great sympathy, but not sentimentality, toward the characters—even the shiftless father—and a vibrant style. Despite her concern with the social theme, Means recognizes the need for incident, and there are exciting ones worked into the texture of the story, not dragged in. The rather coy and naïve love plot is the poorest feature of an essentially fine story.

REPRESENTATIVE BOOKS

Ball, Dorothy, *Hurricane,* Bobbs-Merril. (E)
Loosely-plotted, unpretentious but absorbing story of the friendship of a white and Negro boy in the Florida back country.

Ball, Zachary, **Joe Panther* and **Swamp Chief,* Holiday. (E)

Blanton, Catherine, **Hold Fast to Your Dreams,* Messner.

Bonham, Frank, **Durango Street,* Dutton.

Carson, John F., *The Twenty-third Street Crusaders,* Farrar, Straus.
A gang of teen-aged hoodlums is reconstructed through participation in a church basketball league and the help of the coach who is reconstructing his own life.

Colman, Hila, **Classmates by Request,* Morrow.

DeLeeuw, Adele, *The Barred Road,* Macmillan.
The story of a white high school girl's battle of conscience over belief in integration and interest in popularity.

Graham, Lorenz, **South Town,* Follett, and **North Town,* Crowell-Collier-Macmillan.

Hinton, S. E., **The Outsiders,* Viking.

Jackson, Jesse, **Call Me Charley* (E) and **Anchor Man* (E), Harper & Row.

Jacobs, Emma, *A Chance to Belong,* Holt, Rinehart and Winston.
A teen-age Czech boy in New York City is caught between American teen-age mores and his European family culture.

Marshall, Catherine, **Julie's Heritage,* McKay.

Means, Florence, **Alicia* and **Knock at the Door Emmy,* Houghton Mifflin.
(Also *Tolliver,* Houghton Mifflin.) A Negro girl, graduate of Fisk University, regains faith and romance through experience as a teacher and freedom rider.

Mulcahy, Lucille, **Pita,* Coward-McCann.

Stolz, Mary, **Ready or Not* and **Pray Love, Remember,* Harper & Row.

Tunis, John R., *The Catcher from Triple A,* Harcourt.
A Jewish catcher from the minors makes good on a major league baseball team.

NOVELS OF THE ADOLESCENT CULTURE

Books about the adolescent culture, the stresses and preoccupations and mores of the teen-age period, represent the bulk, as well as the highest achievement, of work in the junior novel. Most of the books in this category deal with the personal problems of individual adolescents in their family and peer culture.

Personal Problems and Literature

What significance do the personal problems of adolescents have for the junior and senior high school literature program? Certainly, it is not the burden of the literature program alone to help students solve their personal problems. Reading of books can never be the sole means of solving problems at any stage of life, and to the high school student the entire school curriculum, along with varied out-of-school influences, should offer help. The study of literature has other objectives, among them to contribute to the esthetic life of the individual and to acquaint each person with his cultural heritage.

Yet there are highly important connections between the personal problems of students and their study of literature. For one, the problems that vex students can motivate reading and can provide an opportunity to convince students that literature really is a reconstruction of experience, that it is related to things that are important and vital to them, not just something vaguely cultural and worthwhile, in the eyes of adults, upon which to spend leisure time.

It is important for the teacher to keep in mind the key role of identification in the literary experience. When the adolescent locates in fiction a kindred spirit, a fellow sufferer, the identification is acute and moving, and an important step has been taken in esthetic development.

Does this identification, the vicarious attack upon one's problems through identification with a fictional character, help one to solve his real problems? Research can give no definite answer to this, though many readers have vouched for the personal therapy of literature. It is safe, at least, to assume that the literary experience gives the adolescent a chance to approach his problems from the objective role of observer, to gain greater insight because of the creative writer's power to order experience, to identify the vital components, and to clear away the irrelevancies and ambiguities.

It seems important, however, for the teacher to avoid certain pitfalls in dealing with fiction that takes as its theme the personal problems of adolescents. First, one of the major contributions of literature lies in the understanding it gives of human experience. Thus the major insights into specific problems, whether those of adolescent or adult, will inevitably come through the broader comprehension of human problems that the study of literature affords. It is important for teacher and student to realize that not only the contemporary piece of fiction reflects contemporary problems. Not only the contemporary selection can be vitally related to students' problems. The erosion of time is in itself a criterion of the older book, giving it the power to wash away the irrelevancies and provide a steady view of existence. It is always good in the literature class to link past and present, gaining the rewarding perspective that results. Chaucer's Canterbury pilgrims, for example, live today because their problems are not far different from those of people who ride home on the bus with us each night. And the motivations of Malory's knights are not essentially different from those of the carbugs in our classes. Finally, it is important that the teacher judge—and teach students to judge—the contemporary novel about the adolescent culture on the basis of literary rather than psychological or social criteria alone.

In selecting and recommending novels of the adolescent culture, and in conducting student discussions of them, the teacher might direct attention to three major criteria:

The treatment of the problem.   Is the problem dealt with significantly? The nature of the problems that the book treats is unimportant. The run-of-the-mill book may deal with a serious problem, the estrangement of father and son, for example, and yet treat it superficially and patly with no real insight into its genesis or the motivations of the people involved. On the other hand, some junior novelists are prone to take a tongue-in-cheek attitude that assures the reader at the outset that the problem is really not important and that if he will be patient through 240 pages, all will be well.

By what means are problems solved or adjusted to? This is a key question by which the student often will be able to differentiate the valid from the formula piece. In the latter, solutions are often complete and phony, dependent upon external circumstance and coincidence rather than upon any development of the main character. For example, Jim's ambition is to make the football team, but he is woefully inept. His older brother takes him in hand for some private back-yard sessions, and Jimmy becomes a shifty tailback. Or Gretchen is the wallflower, aspiring to be part of the round of dates and picnics with "the gang." This comes to pass when a worldly-wise aunt shows her certain tricks of dress and mannerism. The better books often avoid any complete and final solution of a problem, emphasizing rather the inner change of the character as he gains greater maturity and understanding.

The viewpoint of adolescence. The most competent novels about the adolescent period—and usually the ones most popular with adolescent readers—are fundamentally serious, presenting characters who are complex people with dignity. Many of the personal-problem novels are actually written from the adult's point of view and turn into faintly camouflaged homilies. The formula book usually plays to the adult grandstand. It is easy, of course, for the adolescent reader to recognize the book that consistently presents the adolescent's point of view, and the student's effort to do so is a good exercise in literary discrimination. A certain tradition in writing about the adolescent, dating probably from Booth Tarkington's *Seventeen,* is still evident in the junior novel. In this, adolescence is a kind of madness, a period about which one will laugh later, and adolescent protagonists are caricatured rather than characterized. The tradition has been particularly evident in motion-picture and television treatments of adolescence, about which the real teen-ager can become indignantly vocal.

The storyteller's art. The point has already been made that the novel centering on personal problems—or any other kind of novel—must be judged finally on the basis of literary rather than psychological (or some other) criteria. In the good junior novel, the art of the story-teller is evident—the author's sensitivity to language, his power to build a compelling, suspenseful story from tragic, comic, or heroic events, the aura of verisimilitude with which he is able to surround the narrative. The realistic story, true to human experience, need not be pedestrian in style or plot.

Three trends are distinguishable in the past few years in junior novels of the adolescent culture. First, as indicated earlier, the books tend to be harder hitting, less frothy, dealing fairly frequently with such themes as broken homes, pregnancy out of wedlock, and delinquency.

Second, though the paucity of good books about the personal problems of teen-age boys still exists, there have been more noteworthy novels of this kind in recent years than formerly. Third, a number of junior novels by non-American writers about adolescents in other lands have appeared in translation.

Representative Junior Novelists

Because of the importance of books about the adolescent culture in the field of the junior novel, it seems appropriate at this point to attempt to evaluate further the achievement in the form with fuller discussions of a few major writers.

Anne Emery

Prolific Anne Emery has enjoyed a huge following among adolescent girls. In content and in structure, Emery's books epitomize the average in the junior novel, though her competency in using language is better than average. Scrupulously observing all the standard taboos, Emery presents a world largely purged of unpleasantness, in which the problems of teen-agers are real but highly manageable. "Wholesome" has frequently been applied to Emery's works, but the wholesomeness is rather frequently overwhelming, and "innocuous" probably is more apt.

Her third-person, single-track narratives proceed rapidly with only mild suspense to a very predictable ending, which lays a satisfactory basis for the sequel. There is lavish use of dialogue and little introspection on the part of the teen-age girls who are the main characters. Along the way there is a satisfying—to the girl reader—amount of detail concerning dates and dress and parties.

Probably part of the appeal of Emery's books lies in the fact that they dramatize the upper-middle-class norm—the secure, the average, the comfortable. The fathers in the stories are professional men, and the Burnaby family, on which centers a major series of Emery's books, lives, for example, on Juniper Lane. Hickory Hill is the name of the farm—and of the book that is a sequel of the 4-H story, *County Fair*—and through the farm runs Lazy Creek. Departures from the norm are rare among Emery characters and are rather severely frowned upon. This is evident most clearly in *High Note, Low Note,* one of the books in the Burnaby family series. Jean Burnaby becomes friendly with Kim Ballard, a new girl in school whose family is bohemian. Jean's parents view the friendship, and the Ballard family, with a very troubled eye, exhibiting, in the eyes of an adult reader, a rather amazing lack of sympathy for Kim. Finally, as the elder Burnabys had feared, Kim leads Jean astray, albeit not too seriously.

Characterization in *Emery,* in general, is limited to categories rather than individuals. There are five categories: fathers, mothers, adolescent girls, adolescent boys, and less-than-adolescent girls and boys. Within each category, characters are very much alike. Fathers are usually rather vague and preoccupied with their work, coming into the story mainly when money becomes an issue. Mothers are youthful, attractive, calmly philosophical, and intelligent. This description from *Campus Melody* is typical: "Mrs. Burnaby looked cool and fresh as she sipped her second cup of coffee while she wrote out 'Thing to Be Done Today.' "

The theme of "Mother (and occasionally Father) is right" is the most prevalent one, sometimes irritatingly so, in Emery's books. Early in *Going Steady,* Sally decides: "How could her mother be so wise?" And in *High Note, Low Note:* "But deep down underneath, try as she would to ignore it, Jean could not help wondering if her mother were not right." Perhaps the most irritating play for adult favor occurs at another point in *High Note, Low Note.* The morning after a minor tiff with her father over going to a party with Kim Ballard and some other friends, Jean Burnaby comes down the stairs to find at the bottom a paper on which is written: "X marks the spot where the world came to an end last night." And shortly after, Jean decides: "Oh, well . . . it's just as comfortable not to stay mad—especially when you can't win."

The adolescent boys in Emery's books—with the exception of *Vagabond Summer,* in which there are some rather well-developed characters, and the cad in *Campus Melody*—are almost indistinguishable from each other. Scotty, who appears in several books and epitomizes "the boy who lives next door," is exactly like Jeff, for example, who at one point is described thus: ". . . Jeff returned at 7:30, shining with soap and water." And Jean and Sally Burnaby, who share the major roles in the Burnaby series, are identical.

Though not her most popular book, *Vagabond Summer* may be Anne Emery's best, because of its originality and sounder characterization. The story's teen-age heroine goes on a summer hosteling tour with a group of other young people and makes some tentative decisions about her future. In this book, unlike most of Emery's others, there is an interesting group of well-drawn personalities. Of course, there is a radiantly happy ending with the quite typical final lines: "The world lay before them. All their bright young world."

Despite her shortcomings from a literary point of view, Anne Emery has captured the interest of a large number of adolescent girls, and in so doing she has made a contribution. She presents characters who experience, after all, the mundane kind of problems that are true, although not the whole truth, of adolescence. Identification with her characters furnishes no moving experience nor any depth of insight. But her readers find in her books what they are seeking there—entertainment and, to some extent, wish fulfillment.

James L. Summers

The books that James Summers has so far written, though of mediocre literary value, have helped to fill a long-existing gap—competent stories about teen-age problems for boys. The dearth of such books is partly explained by the fact that boys are less interested in the story that centers on teen-age romance and family problems than are girls, and partly because most of the writers of teen-age problem stories are women who choose to write of girls' problems.

Essentially, Summers is a humorist. His books are amusing, at points hilarious, and his over-all approach is light, though he evidences good insight into the adolescent culture. His approach is perilously near caricature, however, when his attempts to amuse sometimes get out of hand. Several reviewers of his books have noted that fathers might enjoy some of the passages more than their sons for whom the books are written. *Wild Buggy Jordan,* for example, the problem-frought story of a high school junior, is a burlesque of the adolescent culture, ranging from the adolescent's philosophy of life to his eating habits.

Like Anne Emery's heroines, Summers' heroes are virtually identical from book to book. Rodney Budlong of *Prom Trouble,* Don Morley of *Girl Trouble,* and Roger Holman of *Trouble on the Run* are all slightly-less-than-average boys who aspire, above all else, to be average. These characters are fit subjects for light treatment and provide easy identification for most readers, who can be genuinely amused at the protagonists' foibles.

Summers' plots are very similar: they involve his heroes, who cannot do anything too well, in two types of problems—love and school. The love plot usually involves the hero's pining for the wrong (as the end of the book shows) girl and a failing (until the end) to appreciate the right girl who was there all the time. The school problem involves the hero's being saddled with a responsibility for which he is not quite qualified. In *Prom Trouble,* Rodney Budlong is elected junior class president as a "gag," and has the task of directing plans for the prom. In *Trouble on the Run,* Roger Holman is put in charge of preparing a float. Both muddle through with moderate success. A variation in *Girl Trouble* has Don Morley having to drop football in order to work so that he can pay a traffic fine.

Like Emery, Summers relies largely on categories of characters and general impressions rather than on detailed delineation. His mother and father categories are similar to Emery's except that Summers' fathers are small businessmen. The Morleys in *Girl Trouble* are typical: "Both the elder Morleys were slim and faintly youthful." Perhaps because of his experience as a high school teacher, Summers is at his best in characterizing school administrators and teachers, whom he treats with kind humor and gentle irony. The details of school life in his books are authentic and genuine.

Summers consistently overwrites, as this passage from *Trouble on the Run* reveals:

> Glenn Harlan, on the other hand, was little and thin and a pretty fair hurdler who would be a neat guy if he could ever lay off math. His brain was water-logarithmed on the stuff and anything he couldn't find the square root of in one minute he regarded with suspicion and disdain. When Harlan was quiet, a person could almost hear his brain whirring around like Univac, feeding itself data about people, distance, and time, squishing the information around in the right tubes, and coming up with the perfect answer. If he hadn't been so boring with

math, he could have been one interesting guy. The way it was, everybody expected him to be blasted off in a Navy rocket in the interests
of national defense.[15]

And frequently Summers' dialogue, though usually amusing, is written
in a jargon and in patterns of speech that border on the grotesque.

Most of the statements made so far about Summers do not apply to
two of his books. One of his most unusual—though not necessarily his
best—is *Operation ABC*. Apparently, the author had become interested in the problem of retarded reading ability and had read the work
of Fernald or others who have used the "kinesthetic" approach to
remedial reading. The book tells an engrossing story of a senior boy
who is a retarded reader and very fearful that someone will find out.
He faces his problem realistically in an ending that is hopeful but semi-
tragic. Summers' most impressive novel, *The Limits of Love,* develops poignantly a theme highly unusual in teen-age fiction. The main
characters, a boy and girl just out of high school, face the problem of
controlling their passions. Deeply in love, they realize that immediate
marriage is impossible, and they agree to separate. The love scenes
are handled skillfully; in fact, in this novel Summers' style reaches a
level not found in any of his other books. These last two books are
proof that Summers can treat a serious theme competently.

Mary Stolz

Undoubtedly the most interesting and accomplished writer of junior
novels is Mary Stolz. Though she has produced a surprising number
of novels in a short time, the level of quality has remained consistently
high. Several of her books are definitely within the conventions of the
junior novel; several are iconoclastic.

Essentially, Stolz's books are love stories, though she injects minor
social themes in several. Her treatment of love in late adolescence is
far different from that of Emery, Summers, or even of Daly's *Seventeenth Summer*. Love, in the Stolz novels, is fraught with a tempes-
tuousness and an anguish that is foreign to most other novels for the
adolescent. This is true even of the books in the familiar junior novel

---

[15] From *Trouble on the Run* by James L. Summers. Copyright 1956, by
James L. Summers, the Westminster Press, Philadelphia. Used by permission.

pattern—*To Tell Your Love* and *The Sea Gulls Woke Me,* for example. Serious, intense Anne Armacost, of *To Tell Your Love,* suffers a bitter summer of putting on appearances, hoping, waiting for the telephone to ring, and of final hurt when her intenseness "scares off" the boy she loves. The ending, highly characteristic of Stolz, features quiet resignation on Anne's part. Though the members of the Armacost family—father, mother, younger brother—are akin to those in Anne Emery, they come to life to a much greater degree, and the portrait of Anne is a real triumph. As with all the Stolz protagonists, there is a pain in the identification with Anne; the Stolz novels are designed for a more mature and sensitive audience than those of Emery and many other junior novelists. Not at all in the lighthearted manner, the Stolz stories are overhung with a sense of the sadness of life, the possibilities of emotional disaster, and the *weltschmerz* that is highly characteristic of late adolescence.

Stolz has explored the problems of family life as it is lived at several economic levels. In *Ready or Not* and *The Day and the Way We Met,* sequel books, the family lives in a semitenement district in New York City and the father is a subway token seller. The first book concerns the problems of an adolescent girl in managing the household after her mother dies. In the second, the younger sister takes over when the elder marries. *The Day and the Way We Met* is a tender story that shows the typical lack of concern for plot and structure in the late Stolz books. Essentially, it is a well-done character study, but many adolescent readers would find the slow-moving narrative boring. The wonderfully conceived ending finds the heroine answering the phone, wondering—with the reader—which of three men is calling!

Characterization is especially splendid in *Pray Love, Remember.* The theme of this hard-hitting novel is prominent in Stolz—the estrangement of the adolescent heroine from her family. The conflict is particularly marked between Dody Jenks, the heroine, and her older brother, who appears even more loutish in her eyes than he really is. The younger sister is the "ugly duckling" and the contrast between her and Dody is effective. Dody is a highly unusual and interesting character, enigmatic even to herself. She is a great social success in her senior year in high school and much envied, though she is almost without friends. Her essential coldness, making her anything but endearing, is in marked contrast to the heroines of most of the other Stolz books.

All the Emery-Summers patterns of the father and mother and of the family situation are smashed here. The dialogue in general and the dinner table conversations in particular are superb. Graduating from high school, Dody finally escapes her family and the town by taking a position as governess with a wealthy family. Dody's love affair with a Jewish boy seems a rather artificial and tangential addition, and ends with the boy's death in a car accident and Dody's near collapse. However, the end finds her returning to her job as governess with a new sense of her identity.

The originality of *Rosemary* comes as a mild shock. The book begins in a fashion highly standard in teen-age fiction. Rosemary, who is working in a store rather than attending the college in her town, meets the dashing college boy and a date is set. But the boy, quite understandably misinterpreting Rosemary's rather tawdry behavior at a dance, makes a pass at her. This provides the opening trauma in the development of Rosemary's love interests and her relations with several people, including her none-too-appealing father.

Departing completely from the mold of the junior novel is the moving *Two by Two,* the only Stolz story in which a boy is the main character. The plot involves the conflict between Harry Lynch and his father, a wealthy lawyer, and Harry's love affair with Nan Gunning. Sex and the erotic impulses are thoroughly probed in the love plot, which is a far cry from the round of dates, picnics, and cool-lipped kisses of the Emery stories. In fact, Harry and Nan are discovered in her bedroom by her father. And in a scene in which Harry and a friend visit a night club, a waitress "hovered over them, muskily perfumed, in a dress deeply cut at the bodice, confident in a society where mammary worship came second only to mammon worship."

An air of doom hangs over the story; the reader may suspect that Harry will commit suicide. Instead, he kills someone else, a drunkard, accidentally when he drives away from the night club. Actually, the swift ending is happy—the reconciliation of Harry with his own and Nan's father. Like several of the other Stolz books, *Two by Two* is slow moving, full of the introspection, sometimes bordering stream of consciousness, typical of Stolz. The action is mainly psychological and, as in several of her other books, there are rambling lyrical passages at times slightly reminiscent of Thomas Wolfe.

Mary Stolz is a talented and original writer with a deep regard for the dignity of the adolescent. Done in richly subtle shades, rather than in pastels, her work bodes well for the future of the junior novel.

Henry Gregor Felsen [16]

A prolific as well as an extremely versatile author of junior novels is Henry Gregor Felsen. Probably best known for his novels involving cars, his writings also include such diverse subjects as war, humor, and conflict with society.

In his earlier novels, such as *Navy Diver,* the style is masculine, the plot is exciting, and the characters emerge as real with only a slight "willing suspension of disbelief" on the part of the reader. The total effect is a kind of cross between Howard Pease and Ernest Hemingway. However, there are overtones of meaningful issues. In *Navy Diver,* Jeff's best friend on the farm had been a Japanese. Felsen tersely illustrates his hero's conflict during the World War II crisis.

Contrasted with the dramatic conflict portrayed in *Navy Diver* is the slapstick comedy saturating the Bertie novels. The roly-poly protagonist of the series is Bertie Poddle, an overfed junior edition of Walter Mitty. The difference is that Bertie naïvely attempts to make his dreams materialize. His efforts inevitably backfire in hilariously ludicrous situations.

The chapters in the Bertie novels are rather episodic, unified by Bertie himself and his rather motley assortment of type-cast friends— handsome, intelligent Ted Dale and his equally remarkable sister, Marcia; Wiggins Hackenlooper, Heeble High School's powerful fullback; Wilbur Frost, the caustic agnostic who is finally humanized by Bertie's intensely candid efforts; and the female antithesis of Bertie also providing humor, Hyacinth O'Houlihan. Hyacinth, a wild redhead and as skinny as Bertie is phlegmatic, falls in love with Wiggins only because he can beat her at Indian wrestling. These characters are introduced in the initial book of the series, *Bertie Comes Through.*

Bertie provides more than just entertainment, however. Pervading the comic situations are significant ideas. In *Bertie Takes Care,* the hero is rejected as a camp counselor because of his overweight. Making the best of his misfortunes, Bertie herds together the town rejects,

[16] Commentary by Helen O'Hara Rosenblum, formerly of Florida State University.

organizes his own camp, and finally triumphs when beating the snobbish and egotistical baseball team from Camp Ijoboko. The Bertie novels are entertaining stories of achievement and good sportsmanship that especially appeal to younger boys.

Felsen's car novels, however, interest boys (and girls) in a range of junior high school through the late teens. There is no absolute upper interest limit for these stories of life adjustment, especially for the very popular *Street Rod* and *Hot Rod*. Both novels deal with boys in their late teens whose interest in cars is portrayed as a means of adjustment, a kind of compensation or escape from an indifferent culture. Bud Crayne in *Hot Rod* is without parents. School and other societal institutions apparently offer little for Bud. In a defiant gesture reminiscent of Holden Caulfield and Huck Finn, Bud wears an old fedora hat with the brim turned up in front and fastened to the crown with a giant safety pin. He makes his own rules until the guidance of Ted O'Day, a patrolman, and Mr. Cole, a shop teacher, demonstrates the real tragedy of an accident in which all but one of Bud's companions are killed. These characters, like Bud, have all sought refuge from a society where adolescents don't "belong." Felsen vividly conveys the problem of the search for identity. The funeral is, perhaps, a dramatic précis of the theme:

> Avondale buried its dead and their dreams.
> Ralph Osler was buried with his dream of a college career in sports. La Verne Shuler was buried with her dream of escape to Hollywood. Walt Thomas was buried with his dream of getting away from the farm. Marge Anderson was buried with her dream of being popular. And the others were buried with their dreams. There was no buying Ralph out of this scrape, no smiling her way out for La Verne, no blustering his way out for Walt.
> The victims of a careless moment were laid to rest.[17]

The "careless moment" is likewise important in *Street Rod*. Sixteen-year-old Ricky Madison attempts to set up the Dellville Timing Association so that the hot rodders may race without breaking speed laws. When the village council refuses to cooperate, Ricky and his friends operate outside the law. With the help of his girl friend Sharon, Ricky enters and wins an auto-design competition. On his way back from the competition, his careless immaturity results in death.

[17] From Henry Gregor Felsen, *Hot Rod* (New York: Dutton, 1950).

Impulsiveness is dealt with in more profound terms in what may be Felsen's most controversial novel, *Two and the Town*. Buff Cody, the senior football star, has reached his moment of heroic glory only to find it sour in the defeat of the big game. Elaine Truro, overly protected, quiet, and scholarly, gives the rejected Buff genuine sympathy, warm and tender feeling. In this moment of intensity, abstract feelings lose their meaning. With deep psychological insight Felsen describes the situation:

> . . . She became as furiously unrestrained as Buff himself, made one last, frightened effort to break away, and, in a situation where Carol would have laughed and saved herself, Elaine wept and was lost.

The remainder of the novel deals with the manifest problems inherent in a "forced" marriage. Felsen realistically portrays the problem in a specific setting, but the implications of the theme are more universal in scope. Because he deals with very human problems, Henry Gregor Felsen writes novels for young people that capably meet their needs and interests. His themes are communicated in a professional style that may provide an important step in the development of literary appreciation.

Madeleine L'Engle [18]

Madeleine L'Engle's books for young teenagers express a sense of the depth and seriousness of life usually found only in works for older adolescents. With an impressive variety of settings, plots, and interesting characters, she adapts and expands conventional story patterns to accommodate a serious treatment of the adolescent's confrontation with the uncertainties of the adult world. Time and again her protagonists echo the sentiments of John Austin in *Meet the Austins:*

> Why do things have to change and be different! . . . Why do people have to die, and people grow up and get married, and everybody grow away from each other? I wish we could just go on being exactly the way we are!

Because L'Engle's protagonists tend to be young (twelve to fifteen), intelligent and sensitive, and because the seriousness of their problems requires the treatment of serious themes, there is an ambiva-

[18] Commentary by Bryant Fillion, University of Illinois.

lence in several of the novels. The themes and the characters' concerns often seem intended for a more mature audience than the stories or the ages of the adolescent characters are likely to attract. *A Wrinkle in Time,* for instance, which won the 1962 Newbery award, is an interesting and beautifully told children's fantasy, but its complex structure, literary allusions, and chilling portrayal of evil forces in the universe all imply an older reader.

This same ambivalence is found, to some extent, in *Camilla,* best-written of L'Engle's adolescent romances and reminiscent of Maureen Daly's classic, *Seventeenth Summer. Camilla* is the story of fifteen-year-old Camilla Dickinson's first romance and her attempt to cope with the realities of her parents' marital difficulties. Camilla's relationship with Frank Rowan, the sensitive and intense older brother of her best friend, Louisa, helps her to face and understand her mother's illicit love affair and attempted suicide. The picture of upper middle-class life in New York City is well-drawn, the characterization of Camilla, her parents, and the Rowans is excellent, and the first-person narrative is flawless. Camilla's typically early adolescent and increasingly unsatisfactory relationship with Louisa, her relationship with her parents and with Frank, and her growing sense of the sadness and complexity of adulthood are skillfully and believably developed. Yet such concerns may demand more maturity than young teen-agers bring to a novel, and the heroine's age may discourage slightly older adolescents from reading the book, though they could enjoy it more.

In *Camilla,* and in most L'Engle novels, the protagonists' confrontation with the inequities of the adult world—infidelity, death, the confusion of appearance with reality, and social evils—results in a crisis of identity for the adolescent and a desire to return to the securities of childhood. A resolution and deeper awareness are achieved through unselfish love, or a commitment to another person or a cause. This symbolic initiation into the realities of adulthood is handled sympathetically and believably; most of the adolescent dialogues about questions of love, death, personal identity, and God seem remarkably true to the sensitive adolescent's concerns and conversation. The intelligent and sensitive characters who make such awareness and concern plausible are problematic, however. At times, the cultural facility and encyclopedic knowledge of the L'Engle children and adolescents become somewhat overwhelming.

In *And Both Were Young,* most conventional of the L'Engle books, artistic and sensitive Philippa (Flip) Hunter manages to achieve popularity in an exclusive girls' boarding school in Switzerland. The most interesting character in the book is Flip's boy friend, Paul Laurens, a war orphan whose concentration camp experiences have blocked out all memory of his past.

Meet the Austins is an episodic first-person account by Vicky Austin of her family's reactions to a series of events following the death of a close friend of the family, and the arrival of an orphaned ten-year-old girl to stay with them. Dr. Austin, his cultured wife, the four children, and several pets constitute an amusing and interesting household. The children's attempts to reinterpret their secure lives in rural Connecticut and to face the realities of death and change are perceptively portrayed. The sequel, *The Moon by Night,* is more completely Vicky's book, telling of a trip with her family, and her growing difficulties with her parents as she experiences her first serious relationship with a boy, Zachary, of whom her parents disapprove, and his rival, Andy.

In *The Arm of the Starfish,* a novel of mystery and adventure, sixteen-year-old Adam Eddington becomes involved in international intrigue and murder during his summer's work with a famous scientist, Dr. O'Keefe, off the coast of Portugal. The tale is exciting and well told, and there is a serious undertone in Adam's adjustment to adults' deception. Canon Tallis, a mysterious sleuthing priest, and the precocious Polyhymnia O'Keefe are particularly interesting characters. Dr. O'Keefe's statement about his daughter summarizes the "ideal" love in L'Engle novels:

> Poly's greatest talent is for loving. She loves in an extraordinary way for a twelve-year-old, a simple, pure outpouring, with no looking for anything in return. What she is too young to have learned yet is that love is too mighty a gift for some people to accept.

A far-fetched story, but a more serious undertaking, is *The Young Unicorns.* The portrayal of nameless sinister forces, the intense sense of frustration, betrayal, and overwhelming evil, and the building of suspense are skillfully achieved. The protagonist, Josiah Davidson (Dave), a reformed street-gang leader in New York City, looks after Emily Gregory, a blind musical prodigy. Dave, Emily, the Austin family—now living in the city—and Canon Tallis all become involved in a strange plot to take over the cathedral church and New York City. Despite its improbabilities, the story is exciting and notable for its brooding sense of evil and impending catastrophe.

The Love Letters, Madeleine L'Engle's adult novel, interweaves the story of a distraught twentieth-century woman with the story of Sister Mariana, a seventeenth-century Portuguese Nun, who was seduced and abandoned by a French army officer. Although it is technically interesting, the novel will probably appeal to few adolescent readers.

Because her books are well written and true to serious adolescent experience, Madeleine L'Engle's work represents an important achievement in the junior novel.

Other Writers

Betty Cavanna, who is as prolific and nearly as popular as Anne Emery, especially with younger girls, has dealt more convincingly with the adult culture than has Emery, and is more sensitive to the pain as well as the enchantment of the teen-age period. She has a particular gift for handling the scenes in which adolescents are together. One of her most notable books is *Going On Sixteen,* in which shy Julie Ferguson, who grows more confident in the course of the story, is the main character. *The Boy Next Door,* a competently written story, represents the typical admixture of school, love, and family problems in her novels. Her two most interesting variations occur in *Almost Like Sisters* and *A Time for Tenderness.* The former is the most unusual of the author's several mother-daughter stories. In this one, an awkward seventeen-year-old finds her boarding school life complicated when her young, attractive mother comes to live nearby. In *A Time for Tenderness,* a non-happy ending story, teen-age Peggy Jamison's family moves to Brazil where her romance with a Brazilian boy founders on the rocks of social misunderstanding and prejudice. Though her books are uneven and, on the whole, undistinguished, Betty Cavanna maintains a consistently realistic point of view toward the adolescent period. Her humorous, plotless, and episodic books, written under the name Elizabeth Headley, feature Diane Graham, and have been very popular. Though shallow in characterization, these books present effectively the jealousies and rivalries of middle-adolescent girls, and a few of the episodes are memorable—for example, the one in *A Date for Diane,* in which Diane, cringingly sensitive about the new braces on her teeth, discovers that the boy of her dreams has worn braces for months.

Very much in the mold of Anne Emery, and equally popular, in writing of the problems of boy friends and the light side of middle-class family life, is Rosamond Du Jardin. In *Class Ring,* Tobey Heydon, who is the main character in *Practically Seventeen* also, struggles with the problem of going steady and decides, in good didactic fashion, that one should not become too serious too soon. Written competently in the first person, *Class Ring* is light, frequently humorous, and deals with the typical round of boys, dates, and school affairs and with minor family conflicts, such as a crisis involving the length of Tobey's fingernails.

More original than most books of this genre are those by Laura Rendina. Her best book is *My Love for One,* a moving story of a girl's efforts—and her family's—to adjust to a new way of life after the death of the mother. Debbie Jones' quest for fulfillment has an adult depth, and her final satisfaction in love is far from the usual girl-gets-boy pattern. A more recent book, *Lolly Touchberry,* though undistinguished in style, is a better-than-average story of a fifteen-year-old Florida girl, her school, family, and dating affairs. A minor social theme, which finds Lolly thinking faintly that racial segregation is not right, is gingerly presented.

Beverly Cleary's stories, though essentially humorous, are not fluff or burlesque. *Fifteen* handles with unusual skill the theme of the adolescent girl's emergence from the awkward stage, the transition period in which she is learning to suffer in a girdle and turning ankles in high heels. Characterization of the adolescent girls and portrayal of their relations with parents are realistically done, though the dialogue is somewhat unrealistic. The woes of baby-sitting, so much a part of the modern adolescent's culture, are cleverly and convincingly portrayed. *The Luckiest Girl,* though somewhat less successful because of a strained setting—a sixteen-year-old girl rather unbelievably visits friends for a year—has the aura of real modern high school experience, in which grades *are* important, and a feel for the modes of adolescent life. *Sister of the Bride,* a kind of junior counterpart of *Member of the Wedding,* features the involvement of a teen-age girl in the wedding plans of her older sister. The psychological problems the situation brings to both girls are well handled.

Among the better writers for older girls is Zoa Sherburne whose books, though occasionally marred by a pedestrian style, flash occasionally to the dark sides of life and possess unusual originality. *Almost April* is the story of a girl's adjustment to her stepmother, an attractive young woman, and her friendship with a boy figuratively from the "other side of the tracks." *The High White Wall* features an older girl's break with family ties and her romance with a young poet, who is the most interesting character in the story. The mother in this story is well drawn, too. It is unfortunate that the heroine remains a vague character. A mother's return to her family after nine years in a mental hospital is the theme of *Stranger in the House*. The story is supple and moving.

Like Zoa Sherburne, Jeannette Eyerly is one of the writers responsible for putting more substance into the novel of adolescent problems. *The World of Ellen March* traces to a happy conclusion the trauma of a girl whose parents are divorced. *A Girl Like Me* features the theme of teen-age, out-of-wedlock pregnancy. With an unusual and more complicated plot structure than that of most junior novels, the story is narrated by a high school girl who avoids giving way to her passions but whose friend does not. The protagonist's view of the whole situation is altered when she discovers that she is an adopted child, born to an unmarried girl. The scenes in which the narrator visits the friend in the home for unmarried mothers are devastating, but the story ends with the boy marrying the girl.

Catering to the interests of boys is the car or hot rod story of which there are dozens. Chief among their authors are Henry Felsen, Philip Harkins, William Gault, Gene Olson, and Don Stanford. The plot lines and themes are varied, but the appeal remains the same in all of the books—details of car lore and the thrill of the race. The really unusual car story is *Car-Crazy Girl* by Hila Colman who ranges widely in the adolescent culture for her subject matter. The novel has an impact beyond that of the usual junior novel, though it has the unfinished quality of Colman's other books. A seventeen-year-old girl is given a car for her birthday by her upper middle-class surburban parents, who live in an unreal world of comfort and philistinism. Mixed-up Dina causes the death of a boy and receives a short jail sentence which is a catalytic factor for both her and her parents.

Junior novels that treat perceptively the problems of adolescent boys are not numerous, as noted earlier. Some, such as S. E. Hinton's *The Outsiders,* were discussed under other headings earlier in this chapter. One of the best remains the poignant *Swiftwater,* by Paul Annixter, in which lonely fifteen-year-old Bucky Calloway strives to establish a refuge for wild geese. The excellence of the book lies in the fine characterization of Bucky and his family and in the author's unusual flair for conveying the atmosphere of wild places. Noteworthy among more recent books is Emily Neville's story of New York City middle-class life, *It's Like This, Cat,* which delineates a fourteen-year-old boy's year of relationships with his cat, his family, his girl friend, and his various other friends. The novel is loose in plot, strong in characterization and in the treatment of the boy's relations with his parents and peers. Similar to the Neville book in its introspection in treating a young adolescent protagonist and in the father-son conflict is Joseph Krumgold's *Henry 3,* the highly original story of a precocious eighth-grader, I.Q. 154, in a New York City suburban community. Henry's association with a school outcast and his trauma in trying to understand the values of his father's business world are the two major threads in this well-written novel. Worthy of mention, too, is *The Hollow* by Thomas Liggett in which a tough boy is sentenced to a work camp for car theft but is given a new view of life by the understanding manager of the camp.

Publication of junior novels in translation of the adolescent culture in other countries is, in the main, a recent development. Margot Benary-Isbert's excellent books of post-World War II Germany, *The Ark* and *Rowan Farm,* are now, of course, dated and may have lost some of their interest, but they remain sensitive portrayals of family life in that period of devastation. The themes and techniques of the non-American novels are similar to those of their American counterparts, though translation poses a problem in appraising the authors' use of language. Paule Daveluy's *Summer in Villemarie,* for example, is a teen-age romance in the Emery-Cavanna tradition with a French Canadian setting. In Anne Marie Falk's *Who Is Erika?,* a fifteen-year-old Swedish girl faces the problems incident to her mother's remarriage and the family's move to a new town. A French boy's school problems and relations with his parents are the concerns in Michel-Aime Baudouy's *More than Courage*. Outstanding is the Newbery award winner *Shadow of a Bull* by Maia Wojciechowska, in which the son of a great Spanish bullfighter feels impelled to follow his father's career for which he has no taste.

REPRESENTATIVE BOOKS

Annixter, Paul, *Swiftwater*, Wyn.
Baudoy, Michel-Aimé, *More Than Courage*, Harcourt.
Benary-Isbert, Margot, *The Ark*, Harcourt.
  A German family, minus the father who is a Russian prisoner, tries to rebuild life in post-World War II devastation as they move into an abandoned railroad car. (Also *Rowan Farm*, the sequel in which the father returns and Margret is able to plan a trip to the United States.)
Cavanna, Betty, *A Time for Tenderness*, Morrow.
  (Also *Almost Like Sisters*, *Going on Sixteen* (E).)
Cleary, Beverly, *Sister of the Bride*, Morrow.
  (Also *Fifteen* (E) and *The Luckiest Girl*.)
Colman, Hila, *Mrs. Darling's Daughter*, Morrow.
  A realistic treatment of mother-daughter conflicts. (Also *Car-Crazy Girl*.)
Daly, Maureen, *Seventeenth Summer*, Dodd, Mead.
  A classic, though now dated, junior novel of first serious love and a memorable seventeenth summer for Angie Morrow.
Daveluy, Paule, *Summer in Villemarie*, Holt.
DuJardin, Rosamond, *Class Ring*, Lippincott.
  (Also *Practically Seventeen*.)
Emery, Anne, *Going Steady*, Westminster.
  Two high school seniors plan to be married but change their minds after thinking it through. (Also *Campus Melody*, *High Note, Low Note*, *Vagabond Summer*.)
Eyerly, Jeannette, *A Girl Like Me*, Lippincott.
  (Also *The World of Ellen Marsh*.)
Falk, Anne Marie, *Who Is Erika?*, Harcourt.
Felsen, Henry Gregor, *Bertie Comes Through*, Dutton. (E)
  Bertie, the fat boy, tries everything in school activities, but never quite makes the grade in anything by the affections of his classmates. (Also *Bertie Takes Care* (E), *Hot Rod*, *Street Rod*, *Two and the Town*.)

Gault, William C., *Dirt Track Summer,* Dutton.
Two brothers take to dirt track racing against the wishes of their father, himself in the racing game.

Harkins, Philip, *Road Race,* Crowell-Collier-Macmillan.
A boy builds a jalopy into a hot rod club winner.

Hartwell, Nancy, *My Little Sister,* Holt, Rinehart and Winston.
Two teen-age sisters find serious conflicts between their parents' ideas and those of their social crowd.

Headley, Elizabeth, *A Date for Diane,* Macrae. (E)

Krumgold, Joseph, *Henry 3,* Atheneum.

L'Engle, Madeleine, *The Arm of the Starfish,* Farrar, Straus.
(Also *Camilla,* *The Love Letters,* *A Wrinkle in Time,* *The Moon By Night,* *Meet the Austins,* *And Both Were Young,* *The Young Unicorns.*)

Liggett, Thomas, *The Hollow,* Holiday.

Neville, Emily, *It's Like This, Cat,* Harper & Row.

Nielsen, Jean, *Green Eyes,* Funk & Wagnalls.
Senior Jan Morgan's problems as high school newspaper editor and with her family.

Ogan, Margaret and George, *Pancake Special,* Funk & Wagnalls.
Teen-age love and auto racing are the fate of a high school graduate who is forced to give up an Air Force Academy appointment because of a physical disability.

Olson, Gene, *The Roaring Road,* Dodd, Mead.
A car-lore filled story of sports car racing and romance involving the son of a great racing mechanic.

Rendina, Laura, *My Love for One,* Little, Brown.
(Also *Lolly Touchberry.*)

Sherburne, Zoa, *Too Bad about the Haines Girl,* Morrow.
A realistic, undidactic story of out-of-wedlock pregnancy. (Also *Almost April,* *The High White Wall,* *Stranger in the House.*)

Stanford, Don, *The Red Car,* Funk & Wagnalls.
A sixteen-year-old rebuilds a wrecked car and enters it in the big race.

Stolz, Mary, *To Tell Your Love,* Harper & Row.
(Also *Two by Two,* *Rosemary.*)

Summers, James L., *The Shelter Trap,* Westminster.
The rather zany story of a teacher and a group of high school students trapped in a bomb shelter. (Also *The Limits of Love,* *Prom Trouble,* *Girl Trouble,* *Trouble on the Run,* *Operation ABC.*)

Wojciechowska, Maia, *Shadow of a Bull,* Atheneum.

section II
ADULT FICTION OF SPECIAL SIGNIFICANCE TO ADOLESCENTS

Literature from the entire world tradition should be available to the secondary school student as earlier chapters have indicated. For study of the novel, *War and Peace* might be appropriate here, *Third Man on the Mountain* there in the same school. A considerable amount of space has been given to the junior novel because of its important functions in the literature program, discussed in Chapter 10, and because teachers and prospective teachers have available to them little organized information and criticism on the genre. The purpose of this brief section is to call attention to certain categories and selections of the adult novel which the author's experience and study have indicated may have special significance to adolescents. The discussion is highly selective. Comment on many novels long familiar in school programs or on those prominently mentioned in some previous chapter is omitted.

ADVENTURE AND PERIL

The types of adult adventure novels most prominent in the reading interests of adolescents are the same as those in the junior novel—the sea, war, the western. As in the junior novels of the sea, the man-against-nature theme is prevalent in the adult story. Symbolic is Nicholas Monsarrat's title—*The Cruel Sea*—for his long, well-written book about a British ship on convoy duty during World War II. Definitely the best of Monsarrat's books, it is excellent for senior high school boys, and a long excerpt from it appears in the twelfth-grade anthology of one publisher. Alistair McLean's *HMS Ulysses,* another story of British naval experience in World War II, is also an admirable treatment of the struggle against a formidable sea. Of course, Nordhoff and Hall's earlier *Men against the Sea* is memorable.

A recurring variation of the man-against-nature theme is found in the tales of shipwreck, beginning with Defoe's celebrated *Robinson Crusoe;* perhaps most prominent among them is Johann Wyss's *Swiss Family Robinson,* an extraordinary story of courage and ingenuity.

Among the best of the recent books is Kenneth Roberts' *Boon Island,* based on an actual shipwreck off the Maine coast.

Kipling's clumsy but well-known *Captains Courageous* epitomizes another use of the sea in fiction—as a leveler and tester of men. In the Kipling story a wealthy mollycoddle is rescued from drowning by a fishing boat crew, and its harsh and exacting routine "makes a man" of him. Jack London, like many other writers, views the sea as an escape from the falseness and artificiality of social position and privilege, against which he protested in most of his works. The plot of *The Sea Wolf,* perhaps London's best novel, resembles that of *Captains Courageous.* A wealthy and prominent young man is rescued by a seal-hunting ship under the command of the ruthless and barbaric Wolf Larsen. The young man survives the voyage in complete ignominy, thoroughly beaten and cowed by Larsen. The plot, featuring a "shanghaiing" and the subsequent experiences of the novice on the sea, is generally popular.

With the outbreak of World War II, the sea story turned to the theme of heroism and leadership in naval combat. Before this, however, C. S. Forester had written his exciting, satisfying stories of Horatio Hornblower, an officer in the British navy that kept England safe from Napoleon. Hornblower, a full-dimensioned character with his quota of faults, represents the British navy's proud traditions of courage and discipline. Though the Hornblower books were written for the general audience, they have been highly popular with high school boys. Forester also produced one of the more interesting books of World War II naval combat, *The Good Shepherd,* with another indefatigable captain as the main character. A less admirable but more complex captain is found in the best-known sea story of World War II, Herman Wouk's *The Caine Mutiny.* Though marred by a somewhat maudlin ending, emphasizing Wouk's defense of authority, the novel is a fascinating study in divergent character, and the gripping plot is beautifully wrought. Strong, too, in characterization are Monsarrat's *The Cruel Sea* and Kenneth Dodson's *Away All Boats,* which traces the career of an American transport in the Pacific war.

With the sea as background, a few books, treating man's moral condition and his relationship with his universe, rise far above those so far mentioned. Perhaps the greatest is Melville's *Moby Dick,* which some high school students may read with profit. Excerpts from the book, in some of the high school anthologies, may be useful. Splendid for reading in high school is Ernest Hemingway's Nobel Prize winner, *The Old Man and the Sea,* the moving and tragic struggle of an old Cuban fisherman and a magnificent fish. The novel, most appropriate of Hemingway's books for high school use, will appeal to some students as a tale of action; more able students will be able to discern the symbolic and allegorical value so ably discussed in an essay by Leo Gurko.[19]

The sea as background for the examination of man's personality is most readily associated with Joseph Conrad. Though many of his books are too subtle for the majority of adolescents, *The Secret Sharer,* classed by critics as both short story and novel, seems especially appropriate for reading in high school and is included in several anthologies for the twelfth grade. Though the story is slow in starting, it builds into a compelling narrative that, like *The Old Man and the Sea,* can be read with profit at both a literal and symbolic level of awareness. At the literal level, it is a suspenseful tale of a fugitive helped to escape by a young sea captain who ultimately finds self-confidence. At the symbolic level, it is an exploration of Conrad's theme of the bond of the great human family and of the good and evil mixed in the human personality. The technical perfection of *The Secret Sharer* adds to its importance for class study.

THE WESTERN STORY

Most of the adult westerns, so prominent on the racks of paperbacks, are of the formula type, in the tradition of Zane Grey and Harold Bell Wright, and have slight appeal to adolescent readers. A few writers, while relying on familiar plot patterns and situations, have invested their novels with depth characterization, authentic atmosphere, and distinctive style. Conrad Richter's short, lyrical *The Sea of Grass,* with its theme of the breakdown of the great cattle empires, is among the best in this category. So, too, is Ross Santee's *Rusty* and Hal Borland's *When the Legends Die. Rusty* is the story of buffalo hunting and herd riding in the earlier West. Borland's novel of the later West

[19] Leo Gurko, "The Heroic Impulse in *The Old Man and the Sea,*" *English Journal,* XLIV (October 1955), 377–382.

is about a Ute Indian boy's induction into manhood, his career as a bronc rider, and his embitterment at his treatment in the white man's world.

A few westerns may appeal especially to girls. Mari Sandoz's *Miss Morissa* features a woman doctor on the Nebraska frontier of the 1870's. General Custer, Calamity Jane, and Buffalo Bill all appear in the book. Rose Wilder Lane's *Let the Hurricane Roar,* about a young couple on a Dakota homestead and the young wife's excruciatingly difficult winter, is popular with older girls. Somewhat similar, though more involved, is Loula Grace Erdman's *The Edge of Time,* about a young couple homesteading in Texas in 1885.

Probably the most important writer to use a western background is Walter Van Tilburg Clark. Although in its surface events it is a rather traditional western, his best novel, *The Ox-Bow Incident,* is a moving tragedy involving the psychology of mob action. Three men are lynched for a murder and then are found to have been innocent; the leader of the lynching posse and his son commit suicide. Critics have lauded the technical perfection of this novel.[20] *The Ox-Bow Incident* and another excellent novel by Clark, *The Track of the Cat,* are appropriate for reading in upper high school years. *The Track of the Cat,* too, is a psychological novel, about a Nevada family in the early 1900's. The plot is simple: three brothers, all different in personality, track a mountain lion that has killed some of their cattle. Two of the brothers are killed, one by the cat and one by his own fear. The plot is exciting on the physical level, and on the allegorical level it is clearly the struggle between good and evil. The black mountain lion of course represents evil.

WAR NOVELS

The theme of man in battle runs through the legends and myths and epics—through all literature—of all countries. Unfortunately, the war experience has loomed large in the human drama, and each of the great wars has harvested its crop of fiction, much of it ephemeral.

Battle, of course, presents one of the great testing grounds of

[20] Frederic I. Carpenter, "The West of Walter Van Tilburg Clark," *English Journal,* XLI (February 1952), 64–69.

human courage and stamina, and exploring the depths of human courage is one of the major themes in all literature of adventure. It seems ironic, perhaps, to classify war fiction as "adventure." Yet action and peril, which furnish the lure of adventure fiction, are inherent in the war story, which makes it popular with high school boys.

The older tales of war tended to stress its romance rather than its tragedy. Sometimes war was the pathway to escape from a tragic or distasteful civilian life. The French Foreign Legion, about which so many popular tales centered, became the symbol of the soldier fleeing from his past. One notable foreign legion story, Percival Wren's *Beau Geste,* is still read occasionally. Recent war fiction emphasizes the nightmare qualities of terror and hardship, in inescapably hair-raising narrative—and it is this fast-paced narrative to which the adolescent is most responsive. Yet many modern war novels present the terrible hardship of war as they also portray the exalted heroism of men who rise to the near impossible. James Michener's excellent story of aerial warfare in the Korean War, *The Bridges at Toko-Ri,* with its smashing ending, is a kind of memorial to the heroism that combat exacts, whereas Alistair McLean's *The Guns of Navarone* recounts the near-impossible mission of a small patrol in World War II. Among the most suspenseful novels of World War II is Pierre Boulle's *The Bridge on the River Kwai,* a tale of British soldiers forced to construct a railroad bridge for their Japanese captors. This novel is notable, too, for the quality of its writing and for its irony.

If these books, despite the authenticity of the events, come near to romanticism, there are others that are rock-ribbed in their realism, although they present occasional flashes of humor and even of sentimentality. Perhaps most unrelenting is Elleston Trevor's *The Big Pick-Up,* which deals with a squad of British soldiers at Dunkirk. In fact, in Trevor's spare novels is some of the most distinguished writing about World War II. His *The Killing Ground,* based on the terrible Falaise campaign in Normandy, contains one of the most gripping passages in war fiction. Its hero, Corporal Pike, in his heroism of resourcefulness as well as of necessity, represents the best of soldiers who went to war unwillingly.

Of course, the love element is not absent from war fiction. The theme of warrior and the lover who waits and fears is eternal and has been no more neglected in modern than in ancient tales. A tender, mature, and basically wholesome love story, told against the background of the planning and launching of the great invasion of Normandy in World War II, is the basis of Lionel Shapiro's *The Sixth of June.* Nevil Shute's love stories of World War II, *The Legacy* and *Pastoral,* are appealing to older girls.

Naturally, many of the most mature war novels are essentially protests. Horrified at barbaric events involving civilized peoples, authors have sought causes for these events. Norman Mailer's long, angry *The Naked and the Dead* places the blame on the capitalistic system. Irwin Shaw probes some of the neuroses of society through individual characters in *The Young Lions.* Such books as these suggest one of the major problems of teaching war fiction to classes of adolescents—the language used and the type of experience frequently portrayed. In *The Naked and the Dead, From Here to Eternity,* and some other war novels the language is extremely profane and gross. Occasionally there are detailed scenes involving sex. Even in James Gould Cozzens' Pulitzer Prize winning *Guard of Honor,* lauded by many critics as structurally the finest novel of World War II, there is a hotel bedroom scene that would make many high school teachers and librarians loath to recommend it.

Such books must be recommended and included in literature units with care. As suggested earlier, teachers and librarians frequently have been overprotective. It is as easy to underestimate the background and sophistication of adolescents as to overestimate it, and teachers have sometimes predicted shock at elements that did not bring even a lifted eyebrow from their students. Two criteria may guide selection: (1) Is the work excellent as an example of the art of fiction? (2) Is the theme likely to be comprehensible to adolescents? Certainly meeting the first test are such hard-hitting novels as *The Naked and the Dead, The Young Lions,* Heggen's *Mister Roberts,* Hemingway's *A Farewell to Arms,* along with a number of others with little objectionable material, such as *The Bridges at Toko-Ri* and Hersey's *A Bell for Adano.* Using the second criterion, however, Mailer's book and perhaps Hemingway's might be eliminated. But the presence of "dirty" language or erotic scenes is not reason enough alone for eliminating a book.

Adolescents must learn to judge details, sordid or not, in terms of their relevance to theme and purpose. In the spate of war fiction, the truly unified novel stands out because it interrelates events and characters in a significant whole, in the manner of Tolstoi's masterpiece *War and Peace*. Many of the ephemeral novels of World War II merely recount amazing events as their authors experienced them; of these the better-written ones are skillful journalistic pieces. But the battle arena affords a canvas for fascinating character portraits. In Tom Heggen's *Mr. Roberts* the young naval officer is one. He represents the effects of a certain aspect of war on sensitive, intelligent men, brought up in an atmosphere of culture, and when the reader identifies this theme, he recognizes the Rabelaisian touches in the book not as spicy sidelights but as essential details.

It is well for adolescent readers to perceive that the real heroes of war fiction (or nonfiction), past and present, are not the swashbuckling killers, but men of compassion for whom it is a tragedy, which we all share, that they must do what they do. The nature of the hero is a good point of departure for discussion of war fiction.

ADULT NOVELS OF ADOLESCENCE

The problems of adolescence, of course, have appeared not only in junior fiction. In fact, one critic remarks that "a few American novels about adolescence have embodied some of the most adult wisdom that America has produced." [21] The classic example, naturally, is *Huckleberry Finn,* which represents universal adolescence through Huck's struggle to come to terms with adult ways and to fathom the complexities of motivation.

Of course, there is the tradition in which adolescence is viewed as a temporary kind of insanity, the problems of which will dissolve in the stability and serenity of adulthood. In this type of book the adolescent is caricatured. But as Frederic Carpenter points out, "at his best the modern American novelist of adolescence describes the problems of his protagonists so that they become also the problems of our adolescent civilization, with both its mixed-up confusion and its splendid potentiality." [22]

[21] Frederic I. Carpenter, "The Adolescent in American Fiction," *English Journal,* XLVI (September 1957), 314.
[22] Carpenter, p. 319.

Probably the clearest illustration of the truth of Carpenter's observation is Thomas Wolfe. Wolfe's long, fervid novels can be read with profit by a minority of senior high school students, but they arouse a tremendous response in some of these students who find in this impassioned writer an echo of their own inner shouts. Carpenter's statement applies also to two of the novels by the late Carson McCullers. Her finest work, in the author's opinion, is *The Heart Is a Lonely Hunter,* the haunting story of the intertwined lives of six characters among whom a deaf-mute is a central, Christlike figure. The most prominent character is Mick Kelly, an imaginative girl whose yearnings are thwarted by her environment. The maturing of Frankie Addams through the events surrounding the marriage of her older brother is the theme of *Member of the Wedding,* cast in the comic mold unlike most of the author's work. Both books are appropriate for reading and teaching in the high school.

The most celebrated treatment of adolescent character in recent fiction is J. D. Salinger's *The Catcher in the Rye,* which, with seeming artlessness, touches the most tender and sensitive spots in the adolescent make-up. In the story, mixed-up Holden Caulfield views his world as "phony" and "crummy," searches for values, and suffers a nervous breakdown. Because of the language in some of the scenes, the book has been controversial as a selection for use in high school. But a number of students should not—and will not—miss it, though it is difficult to discuss in some class situations.

Strikingly similar to *The Catcher in the Rye* in accomplishment, though notably more positive in effect, is John Knowles' splendid *A Separate Peace,* set in a boys' preparatory school in New England during the early years of World War II. Gene Forrester, the protagonist, misunderstands the friendship of his roommate, Phineas. Torn between love and hate, he pushes Phineas from a tree and causes an injury that ultimately leads to Phineas's death. Through his relationship with Phineas and the events of his last year at school, Gene makes his "separate peace," in existential fashion, before he ever gets into the war. *A Separate Peace* is commonly assigned—and deserves to be—in high school classes. It is, to this writer, the most artful treatment of the archetypal initiation theme, central to all the novels discussed here, in contemporary fiction.

The Negro counterpart of Holden Caulfield is Duke, the teen-age protagonist of Warren Miller's *The Cool World,* a novel about the sordid gang life of boys in the Harlem slums. Duke ends in a reform school, but there is hope for better days to come. Dialect is well rendered, and the subject matter is grimly realistic.

A very different type of book, but one full of insight, is *Cress Delahanty* by Jessamyn West. Cress's adolescence is "normal" and usually happy. The book has its hilarious scenes as well as its poignant ones. Though highly appropriate for reading by adolescents and a highly valid treatment of adolescence, the book may have its greatest appeal to the younger adult looking back on the tribulations of that period in his life.

SIGNIFICANT CONTEMPORARY AMERICAN FICTION

A paradox has existed for some time in the teaching of literature in the high schools: the most important contemporary American writers virtually have been ignored, despite the major stress on American literature in most schools. The giants of the American novel in this century and in the very near past, Faulkner and Hemingway, have been given short shrift in the high school. An occasional short story by one of the two is studied; *The Old Man and the Sea* was welcomed with a gasp of relief. But very rarely has a novel by Faulkner or Hemingway been the focus of study in the high school classroom. And, of course, even more rarely has there been consideration of the work of present practicing fiction writers of stature in this country.

The situation cries out for an explanation. The most common one is that teachers have had little training in contemporary literature. There is some validity in this rationalization as any one can tell from an examination of the major requirements in literature for prospective teachers. But even in schools in which the English teachers are relatively sophisticated in contemporary American literature, the paradox remains, and its roots may go deeper than teacher preparation. Either the fiction writers of significance today are producing work which can be experienced profitably by only a very small minority of their fellow citizens, or the teachers of literature in the high schools have a distorted view of the potential of many of their students, or crippling taboos have been fastened upon the literature program in the high schools. It is the view of this writer that all three of these explanations have validity. The first, though, is of the least validity. Fiction of today *is* more esoteric than fiction, in general, used to be. But the reasons for its being esoteric lie as much in the presuppositions and assumptions of its reader as in its subject matter and technique. More crucial are the other two explanations. The writer has stated earlier that teachers (and parents and librarians) have a diminished view of the potentiality of adolescents for strong and virile literary experience, and though they are loosening, the taboos born of protectiveness, hypocrisy, and ignorance fastened upon the high school literature program have robbed it of its impact. If the teaching of American literature is to be truly viable, it must make a place for the serious writers of today and the recent past—Hemingway, Faulkner, Bellow, Malamud, Salinger, McCullers, O'Connor, Updike, and others.

One can only be sympathetic with the high school teacher in his problems of planning contact with Faulkner and Hemingway. Faulkner's convoluted style, intricacy of technique, and mythic framework, and Hemingway's central thesis that life is a losing battle in which the only significance is the quality of the battle constitute a formidable barrier between the authors and adolescents. But with an optimistic view of the potential of adolescent readers and a relaxed stance on taboos, the teacher, himself knowledgeable in the fiction of the two writers, can make a substantial bridgehead through use of the novellas of Faulkner—*The Bear* and *An Old Man*—and such Hemingway novels as (in addition to *The Old Man and the Sea*) *A Farewell to Arms* and *The Sun Also Rises*.

Consideration of such works, as well as those by other lesser but significant contemporary American fiction writers, in class groups is facilitated by the new types of teacher-student contact discussed earlier—short-term electives and module units—and by small-group techniques in traditional grade-level classes.

The remainder of this section of Chapter 11 is an attempt to sketch a brief context for contemporary fiction, with the hope that teachers will find it helpful in planning their courses and in selecting works for class study or individual reading.

Fiction of today tends to be literature of idea and mood predominantly. Though there is active experimenting with technique among fiction writers, there has been, as Ihab Hassan has pointed out in *Radi-*

cal Innocence, a tapering off in the quest for new forms and a trend back from the search for the ultimate in form represented, for example, in Joyce's *Finnegan's Wake,* in which the subject matter disappeared into the form or method and became virtually unrecognizable as such.

Most readers find in the serious fiction of today a general mood of unhappiness and anxiety which reflects this basically unhappy era, this *age* of anxiety. Despite the material opulence of the age, at least in this country, there is the intercultural strife, war, and the knowledge that man has concocted the weapons to destroy himself totally in a few minutes. Among writers, this underlying dissatisfaction with our world takes many shadings—melancholy, resignation, nostalgia, defiant shout, savage cynicism, ironic laughter. Yet present-day fiction is not a literature of despair; rather, our major writers seem to be working generally toward new reasons for hope.

What follows is an attempt to identify some of the major concepts and characteristics of significant contemporary American fiction. Perhaps the greatest emotional and intellectual force influencing fiction writers is existentialism, the variety formulated, largely, in the Paris underground of World War II. Its primary tenet is that existence precedes essence; man is born nothing but a blob of matter; what he becomes is entirely up to him as an individual. Corollary tenets have been expressed by the dean of contemporary existentialists, Jean-Paul Sartre:

> Man is nothing but what he makes of himself
> Man is anguish
> Man is condemned to be free

Existentialism is more of a mood than a philosophy; probably it is really an anti-philosophy. But its impact on fiction has produced, among others, two underlying hypotheses that explain much about contemporary fiction and why it has unsettled many readers. These hypotheses are explored by Ihab Hassan: [23]

> Chance and absurdity rule human action. The hero recognizes this, and knows that reality is but another name for chaos. . . . The pattern of fiction is therefore one that recognizes disorder . . .

[23] *Radical Innocence* (Princeton, New Jersey: Princeton University Press, 1961), p. 116.

Therefore, anguish is the state of life, and the task of Sisyphus in attempting to roll the boulder uphill is the central metaphor for many existentialists.

There are no accepted norms of feeling or conduct to which the hero may appeal. The eternal verities are either denied or affirmed in the spirit of irony.

A world without God, which is the existential world, creates an ethical vacuum. Holden Caulfield, for example, rejects the standards of the adult world as "phony" and "crummy," and only his fantasy of saving little children in the field of rye enables him to stave off madness. The individual is condemned to be "free" because there is no system or model which can chart his life.

The Beats in fiction clearly are offshoots of existentialism. *Big Sur* by Jack Kerouac, the king of the Beats in literature, provides a neat illustration of one facet of existential thinking. The existential philosopher Karl Jaspers found the embodiment of existential living in the meeting of "limit-situations," those high points of anguish or danger which life continually presents and in which the individual must assert his individuality or be lost. In *Big Sur,* the protagonist finds redemption in the survival of a limit-situation. After a typical Kerouac carnival of dissipation, the young man falls into an exhausted sleep fraught with terrible visions of death. He awakens to peace: "Just a golden wash of goodness has spread over all and my body and mind. . . . I will go back home across autumn America and it'll be like it was in the beginning—simple golden eternity blessing all."

Though the influence of existentialism is great in contemporary fiction, there are many works and writers that cannot be associated with it. There is still a considerable concern with values traditionally evolved in our culture. Bernard Malamud, certainly among the several most important figures in American fiction today, deals penetratingly, for example, with family values within the ironic mode of his work. Family unit and loyalty is a major theme of *The Assistant,* though disaster, emotional and material, is the fate of the little Jewish family featured in the book.

Middle-class and upper-class values and traditions, generally, have come in for some searching examination. John Steinbeck, in *Winter of Our Discontent,* takes a pained look at our excessive materialism.

John Cheever finds in suburbia a syndrome of boredom and philistinism, while corporation lawyer-novelist Louis Auchincloss nostalgically celebrates the virtues of the private schools as the embodiment of upper-class tradition.

Some writers, while tacitly ruling out God and group norms, nonetheless fill in some sustaining force for existence. The best and most cogent example is the late Carson McCullers. For her, love is the sustaining force, and her theory of love, consistently illustrated in her novels, is stated succinctly in *The Ballad of the Sad Café* and explains that strange novel as well as much of her other work:

> First of all, love is a joint experience between two persons—but the fact that it is a joint experience does not mean that it is a similar experience to the two people involved. There are the lover and the beloved, but these two come from different countries. Often the beloved is only a stimulus for all the stored up love which has lain quiet within the lover for a long time hitherto. And somehow every lover knows this. He feels in his soul that his love is a solitary thing. He comes to know a new strange loneliness and it is this knowledge that makes him suffer. . . . Let it be added that this lover . . . can be man, woman, child, or indeed any human creature on this earth.
>
> Now, the beloved can also be of any description. The most outlandish people can be the stimulus of love. . . . Therefore, the value and quality of any love is determined solely by the lover himself.
>
> It is for this reason that most of us would rather love than be loved. . . . And the curt truth is that, in a deep secret way, the state of being beloved is intolerable to many. The beloved fears and hates the lover. . . .

Another major characteristic of the contemporary American novel, one related to the influence of existentialism, is the changed concept and role of the hero. Frequently critics have bemoaned the lack of heroes in recent fiction, ending with the familiar question, "Who cares what happens to these people?" Just as Arthur Miller in drama has attempted to make the middle-class American a tragic figure, so have the novelists attempted to build their narratives around the jetsam of human existence, not the figures of stature. Hassan has pointed out that in fiction the hero-protagonist is usually a victim or a rebel, perhaps both at the same time, and he has identified a number of "faces" of the contemporary hero of fiction, of which the following examples seem to have especial affinity for the adolescent.[24]

"The lonely adolescent or youth, exposing the corrupt adult world . . ." —Salinger's *The Catcher in the Rye* or Purdy's *Malcolm*.

"The Negro in search of the eternal, elusive identity which white men refuse to grant him . . ."—Ralph Ellison's *Invisible Man* or James Baldwin's *Go Tell It on the Mountain*.

"The Jew engaged with Gentiles in a harrowing dialogue of reciprocal guilt and ironic self-betrayals . . ."—Saul Bellow's *The Victim* or Malamud's *The Assistant*.

"The grotesque, sometimes hell-bent seeker of godliness . . ."—Flannery O'Connor's *Wise Blood* and *The Violent Bear It Away*.

"The comic picaro, traveling through a crowded life with verve, and sustained by a gift of hope, but never finding for himself a home, except in the mythical territory ahead."—Bellow's *The Adventures of Augie March* and Capote's *Breakfast at Tiffany's*.

"The hipster, the holy-goof, in search of kicks and revelation . . ."— Kerouac's *On the Road*.

The writer would add one more to this catalog, the ineffectual, the person who is not "making it," professionally, maritally, or otherwise, as illustrated by the main characters in John Updike's *Rabbitt, Run* and *Of the Farm*.

With the prominence of such heroes in recent fiction, one is bound to find compassion for the transgressors of conventional middle-class mores, and this element has bothered a number of people. Homosexuality is prominent; perhaps the most searing example of its treatment is found in Baldwin's *Giovanni's Room*. Marital infidelity is rife; John O'Hara, for example, keeps retelling the story of Madame Bovary. Dope addiction and alcoholism are common, as in Nelson Algren's *The Man with the Golden Arm* and Updike's *Rabbitt, Run*. Yet the perceptive reader is aware that the sordid is often used for highly moral purposes—to create awareness of evil and the reasons for transgression—and can be the subject matter of artful and moving fiction.

Recent fiction is characterized, too, by a concern with the personal, private experience of its protagonists and with their essential isolation and alienation, with the general theme of man and his inner self rather

[24] "The Character of Post-War Fiction in America," *English Journal*, LI (January 1962), 5–6.

than of man and other men—the concern of past major novelists such as Sinclair Lewis, John Dos Passos, Upton Sinclair, Jack London, and Frank Norris. Social protest is little evident in recent novels, except in some of the war novels and in those with a theme of race relations, and most of the latter are narrated from specific points of view and are basically psychological rather than social. The big panoramic novel interpreting the American experience, for which we continue to yearn—the American counterpart, perhaps, to Tolstoi's *War and Peace*—has not appeared, though something like MacKinlay Kantor's *Spirit Lake* makes the attempt.

Obviously there is a lack of humor in contemporary fiction. There is indeed laughter at times. There is a Milton Berle-like unknown-identity scene in a cab, for example, in Salinger's *Raise High the Roof-beams, Carpenter*. But when there is laughter it is usually sad or ironic laughter. Mention of that existential product, the novel of the absurd, may be appropriate at this point. Borrowing the absurd from the tragic situation, the grotesque from the comic, the appearance of the novel of the absurd is close to farce, but the effect is close to tragedy. Perhaps the best example of the juxtaposing of horror and hilarity is Joseph Heller's *Catch 22*.

Some critics have seen in the years since World War II a progression through a kind of romanticism to a developing concern with myth and archetype. The gothic elements in Southern fiction, the grotesquerie of incident and character, contribute one kind of romantic element; the taking of man away from organized society to play out his lonely ordeals, as Hemingway did in much of his fiction and as Bellow did in *Henderson, the Rain King,* contributes another. Now there is some tendency to confront man and society through myth and archetype. The quest and the initiation are particularly prevalent archetypal themes in recent writing. In John Updike's *The Centaur,* all the characters in a Pennsylvania town and its high school have counterparts in classical mythology.

It is particularly the emergence of myth and archetype in contemporary fiction that indicates that the major writers of today, far from despairing, are seeking an order which science and reason cannot provide, a new premise for security of emotion, new subject matter for lyric thinking, and new possibilities for self-realization through the imaginative life.

For these reasons, contemporary fiction, no matter how repellent some readers may find it and no matter how many taboos of the high school program it violates, should have a place in the secondary school literature program. One particular possibility for its inclusion is the individual reading program discussed in Chapter 9. Mature students should be encouraged to develop reading designs in contemporary fiction. In the regular classes, small-group reading of contemporary novels may be the best approach generally rather than total class consideration, although there are various novels that lend themselves to total class study. Some suggestions for particular novels that may be especially appropriate are given in the list of representative books that follows.

REPRESENTATIVE BOOKS

Adventure and Peril

Aldrich, Bess S., *A Lantern in Her Hand,* Grossett & Dunlap.
The story of a young bride who goes to live in pioneer Nebraska.
Borland, Hal, *When the Legends Die,* Lippincott.
Boyd, James, *Drums,* Scribner.
A young man fights under the command of John Paul Jones.
Cather, Willa, *My Antónia,* Houghton Mifflin.
Antónia and her Bohemian peasant family in Nebraska's pioneer days.
Clark, Walter Van Tilburg, *The Ox-Bow Incident,* various publishers.
(Also *The Track of the Cat,* Random House.)
Conrad, Joseph, *Typhoon,* various publishers.
Captain McWhirr takes his ship through a furious storm. (Also *The Secret Sharer,* various publishers.)
Defoe, Daniel, *Robinson Crusoe,* various publishers.
Dodson, Kenneth, *Away All Boats,* Little, Brown.
Edmonds, Walter, *Drums along the Mohawk,* Little, Brown.
Warfare and life in the Mohawk Valley during the Revolutionary War.
(Also *Wilderness Clearing.*)
Erdman, Loula G., *The Edge of Time,* Dodd, Mead.
Forester, C. S., *The Good Shepherd,* Little, Brown.
Hartog, Jan de, *The Captain,* Atheneum.
Story of a courageous Dutch tugboat captain in the North Atlantic during World War II.
Heggen, Tom, *Mister Roberts,* Houghton Mifflin.

Hemingway, Ernest, *The Old Man and the Sea, Scribner.

Hersey, John, A Bell for Adano, Modern Library.

An American military government officer administers a small Italian town after the Italian surrender in World War II. (Also The War Lover, Knopf.)

Jones, James, Thin Red Line, Signet.

One of the best novels of island warfare in the Pacific during World War II.

Kipling, Rudyard, *Captains Courageous, Doubleday, and Grosset, & Dunlap.

Kuznetsor, Anatolli, Babi Yar, Dial Press.

A Ukrainian boy's involvement in the German occupation of Kiev in World War II and the Nazi atrocities against the Jews.

Lane, Rose W., *Let the Hurricane Roar, McKay.

London, Jack, *The Sea Wolf, various publishers.

McLean, Alistair, *HMS Ulysses, Doubleday.

(Also *The Guns of Navarone, Doubleday.)

Melville, Herman, Moby Dick, various publishers.

Michener, James, *The Bridges at Toko-Ri, Random House.

Monsarrat, Nicholas, *The Cruel Sea, Knopf.

Richter, Conrad, *Sea of Grass, Knopf.

Roberts, Kenneth, *Boon Island, Doubleday.

Sandoz, Mari, *The Horsecatcher, Westminster.

(Also *Miss Morissa, McGraw-Hill.)

Santee, Ross, *Rusty, Scribner.

Shapiro, Lionel, *The Sixth of June, Doubleday.

Shaw, Irwin, *The Young Lions, Random House.

Three soldiers, two Americans and one German, in World War II.

Shute, Nevil, Pastoral, Morrow.

A love story, in which the background is an RAF base in World War II. (Also The Legacy.)

Trevor, Elleston, *The Killing Ground, Macmillan.

(Also *The Big Pick-Up.)

Uris, Leon, Battle Cry, Bantam.

Marine combat action in World War II—one of the outstanding World War II novels.

White, Stewart E., The Long Rifle, Doubleday.

A Pennsylvania farm boy runs away to become a mountain man; a saga about the fur trappers and the role of the Kentucky rifle.

Wouk, Herman, *The Caine Mutiny, Doubleday.

Significant Recent American Novels

Baldwin, James, *Go Tell It On The Mountain,* Dell.
Harlem Negroes attempt to find direction in life through religion.
Bellow, Saul, *The Adventures of Augie March,* Viking.
Long, picaresque novel of a big city boy's quest in life.
Ellison, Ralph, *The Invisible Man,* Signet.
Frank, haunting story of a young Negro's struggle for identity.
Faulkner, William, *The Bear,* various editions.
The most celebrated of the author's "hunting stories."
Heller, Joseph, *Catch* 22, Dell.
World War II Air Force story, a major example of the novel of the absurd.
Hemingway, Ernest, *A Farewell to Arms,* Scribner.
An American serves with the Italian Army in World War I and has a tragic love affair with an English nurse. (Also *The Sun Also Rises.*)
Kantor, MacKinlay, *Spirit Lake,* Random House.
Panoramic novel of pioneering and Indian fighting in the upper Midwest.
Kaufmann, Myron, *Remember Me to God,* Lippincott.
Powerful story of Jewish family life in Boston and the love and Harvard experiences of the adolescent son.
Knowles, John, *A Separate Peace,* Macmillan.
Lee, Harper, *To Kill a Mockingbird,* Lippincott.
A story of childhood in a Southern town and a Negro's unjustified conviction of rape.
Malamud, Bernard, *The Assistant,* New American Library.
A young outcast attaches himself to a struggling grocer and finds salvation through ordeal.
McCullers, Carson, *The Heart Is a Lonely Hunter,* Bantam.
(Also *Member of the Wedding.*)
Miller, Warren, *The Cool World,* Fawcett.
O'Connor, Flannery, *Wise Blood,* Noonday.
Powerful, grotesque story of twisted lives in a Southern town.
Salinger, J. D., *The Catcher in the Rye,* New American Library.
(Also *Raise High the Roofbeams, Carpenter.*)
Steinbeck, John, *Winter of Our Discontent,* Bantam.
The unscrupulous attempt of a young man to rebuild his financial status ends in tragedy.
Styron, William, *The Confessions of Nat Turner,* Random House.

The story of the famous slave revolt told in the form of recollections of Turner while awaiting execution.

Updike, John, *Rabbitt, Run,* Crest.

A former high school basketball star encounters defeat and tragedy in the adult world. (Also *The Centaur.*)

West, Jessamyn, *Cress Delahanty,* Harcourt.

Wolfe, Thomas, *Look Homeward, Angel,* Scribner.

Eugene Gant's boyhood and adolescence, based on Wolfe's experiences in North Carolina.

12

Nonfictional Prose for Adolescents

JUNIOR BIOGRAPHY

Paralleling the rise of the junior novel is that of the junior biography. Though the line of demarcation between the junior and adult forms in biography is less distinct than in the novel, the history of the two junior forms has been similar. Both became distinct genres in the 1930's and have since developed rapidly. Both are popular with the adolescent audience. Achievement in each genre ranges from the completely patterned potboiler to the truly and distinctively artistic work. Didacticism, the passion to teach, has hamstrung junior biography even more than it has the junior novel. Many of the juvenile biographies are sketches of the lives of the great, held up as examples ("Lives of great men all remind us . . ."). Hero worship is rife in the junior biography. Often, too, junior biography has been excessively preoccupied with "human interest," with the "color angle," to the detriment of character interpretation and evaluation of deeds. Despite such inherently crippling tendencies, however, there are some remarkable achievements in the field of junior biography.

Athletes and Adventurers

The themes of sports and adventure are as popular in biography as in fiction. Still popular is Doris Shannon Garst with her fictionalized biographies of frontier heroes, Indian and white—Sitting Bull, Crazy Horse, Buffalo Bill, Kit Carson, and others. Using the techniques of the adventure novel, Garst's books stress action and spectacle and the capacity of the superhero for surpassing deeds. Few early adolescent readers can distinguish between fiction and the biographies by Garst and there is little need that they should.

Biographies of sports figures are almost as plentiful as novels about sports; in each case, distinguished books are few. Gene Schoor has risen above the run of the mill with his biographies of Jim Thorpe, the great Indian athlete, and of Casey Stengel, the baseball manager. Frank Graham's biography, *Lou Gehrig, A Quiet Hero,* tells with extraordinary skill the thrilling and poignant story of a great baseball player, and makes a real attempt to re-create a personality. Highly successful, too, though more for its subject than for its technique, is Bill Roeder's *Jackie Robinson,* an account of the career of the first Negro to enter big-league baseball.

A truly masterful junior biography, which towers above most of the others in the field, is Geoffrey Trease's *Sir Walter Raleigh.* Of course, the colorful Raleigh furnishes a natural subject for an exciting biography, and Trease takes full advantage of the intrigue-surrounded, up-by-the-bootstraps career of this great Elizabethan. Raleigh's struggle for success despite humble origins and his historic rivalry with Essex are both themes with great appeal to the adolescent. The authentic background of Queen Elizabeth's court and the passing references to literary figures of the time are bonuses in this biography, which reads like a superior romantic novel.

Nina Brown Baker, one of the leaders and pioneers in junior biography, also usually chooses colorful political figures as her subjects. Her biographies, though relatively mature, employ techniques of fiction that make them highly readable, and many students have come to know such figures as Garibaldi and Juárez more vividly through her books than through their study of history. More than most junior biographers, Nina Baker stresses the significance of her subjects' endeavors.

Scientists and Nurses

There have always been adolescents, especially boys, who have found their major literary experiences in biographies of scientists. This age of science has swelled their ranks, and even the standard anthologies give increasing space to the lives of scientists. The junior biographies of scientists have suffered from the problem of having to explain difficult material and of interpreting the subject in an abstruse context. Yet courageous, and in some cases successful, attempts have been made. One of the most notable of these is Rachel Baker's *Sigmund Freud*. Most adolescents—as well as many adults—connect Freud vaguely with sex dreams; Baker boldly presents the famous psychiatrist in a thoroughly acceptable way. Though the book is eminently readable, explaining in elementary terms the basis of Freud's theories, a curiously poetic strain runs through the pages, exemplified in a line such as: "Now the green years of growing come upon the boy. . . ."

Outstanding, too, is the achievement of Elma E. Levinger in her biographies of Galileo and Leonardo da Vinci. The story of Galileo is cast in dramatic fictional form as it builds up to the trial scene in which the suspense is acute. Unlike many junior biographies, it does not ignore earthy aspects of the subject's life—Galileo's refusal to marry his mistress, for example. Levinger's dialogue, rather exaggerated in the Galileo biography, is patently unreal, even for a Renaissance life; it is markedly better in her book on Da Vinci. Levinger is one of the few writers who have conquered the problem of making intellectual and artistic adventure interesting reading for adolescents.

J. Alvin Kugelmass assumed a formidable task in his biography, *J. Robert Oppenheimer and the Atomic Story*. Though, like Rachel Baker, Kugelmass is able to put in elementary terms some difficult principles of science, he never really brings his subject—a genius—to life, and the final effect of the work is awe rather than understanding. Kugelmass is far more successful in his biographies of Louis Braille, Ralph Bunche, and Roald Amundsen, whose careers lend themselves more readily to junior biography. The great Albert Schweitzer inspires awe, too, and a number of junior biographies of him have been attempted. The most successful is Joseph Gollomb's readable *Genius of the Jungle*. The famous Negro scientist, George Washington Carver, has also inspired a number of junior, as well as adult, biographers. The best biography of Carver for the senior high school reader is undoubtedly that by Rackham Holt.

Nursing also has been as popular a theme in biography as in the junior novel and, from a literary point of view, several of the biographies of nurses are far superior to most of the junior novels about nursing. Of course, the two most world-famous nurses are Florence Nightingale and Clara Barton. Jeannette Nolan, a well-known name in juvenile biography, has written books on both. These books feature the technique of the novelist, particularly in the lavish use of dialogue. Though *Florence Nightingale* evidences a good sense of scene and handling of incident, it is less mature in organization and style than *The Story of Clara Barton*. Among the best of the many junior biographies of Florence Nightingale is that by Cecil Woodham-Smith, a rewritten version of his adult piece. Clara Barton receives her best treatment, perhaps, in the work by Mildred Pace.

An extremely moving biography of a nurse is that by Juliette Elkon, *Edith Cavell, Heroic Nurse,* the story of the English nurse who was put to death by the Germans for her underground activities in Belgium during World War I. Like most successful junior biographies, this one is cast solidly in the pattern of the novel, with skillful use of dialogue and detail. The tragic ending is dramatic without being melodramatic. As in other good junior biographies, a bibliography of sources is appended. Striking, too, is Rachel Baker's *Angel of Mercy,* the biography of "America's Florence Nightingale," Dorothea Lynde Dix. However, this book is not so well written as most of the others by Rachel Baker, and is not so popular as her earlier *The First Woman Doctor,* concerning Elizabeth Blackwell.

Literary and Artistic Figures

Biographies of people renowned in literature and the arts usually are not widely read, either in the adult or the adolescent field. However, in the senior high school, especially, such biographies can be helpful in enriching the study of literature and in meeting highly individual interests. For the latter purpose, the biographies of musicians by Madeleine Goss and those of figures in drama and dance by Gladys Malvern, for example, are especially appropriate. One of the most unusual biographies in the field of the arts is that of Louis Armstrong, the great jazz musician, by Jeannette Eaton—*Trumpeter's Tale*. Although the book gives little insight into the nature of jazz, it is an unforgettable story of a true rags-to-riches career of the Negro boy born in the New Orleans slums, who learned to play his horn in a reform school and later played before the crowned heads of Europe and in concert halls and entertainment centers all over the world.

Entreé into the life of a painter is perhaps best represented among recent biographies by Howard Greenfield's *Marc Chagall,* which relates not only the career and associations of the famous artist, but his life as a Russian Jew early in this century.

Of literary biographies, Cornelia Meigs's *Invincible Louisa* is easily the most popular. Its appeal lies mainly in its engaging picture of the family life of Louisa May Alcott rather than in the story of her writing career. None of the few other junior biographies of literary figures has found more than a handful of readers. May Lamberton Becker, in her *Presenting Miss Jane Austen,* has written the kind of biography that teachers wish adolescents would read! Actually, some of the more mature and literate girls do read it, and for them it is rewarding. It is more in the tradition of scholarly adult biography than in the typical novel pattern of junior biography. To the girl who reads it, it furnishes considerable insight into the major novels of Jane Austen. In the field of general literary biography, Marchette Chute, with her books on Shakespeare, Chaucer, and Ben Jonson, is a leader. These are useful reference works for senior high school classes studying English literature.

Varied Fields

One of the most publicized books in recent times is the *Diary of a Young Girl* by Anne Frank. This autobiography of the Jewish girl who hid from the Nazis with her family in an Amsterdam retreat during World War II, was ultimately captured, and died in a concentration camp, is dated in its setting and events, but its amazing insight into the personality of an adolescent girl and the traumatic impact of its story will undoubtedly make its popularity endure.

Prolific Jeannette Eaton, already mentioned as the author of a junior biography of Louis Armstrong, has contributed some excellent biographies of people famous in public life. Among her best is *Gandhi, Fighter without a Sword,* the story of the great Indian patriot and pacifist. Many girls will find her biography of Eleanor Roosevelt interesting also.

Political figures, difficult to treat in junior biography, have been a greater focus of interest among writers in recent years than formerly. Probably the leader in this field among junior biographers is Bill Severn with his *Adlai Stevenson: Citizen of the World,* which gives considerable attention to this unique statesman's high school and college days, and his *Mr. Chief Justice: Earl Warren,* which features an unabashed admiration of the man as well as discussion of the political issues which furnish the backdrop for his career. In *A Dawn in the Trees* the talented and versatile Leonard Wibberley has produced a well-balanced portrait of Thomas Jefferson in the crucial years, 1776–1789, by presenting the multitalented Revolutionary from the varied viewpoints of those who surrounded him personally and politically. John D. Weaver's *Tad Lincoln* does as much for Abraham Lincoln as for Tad Lincoln, and adds importantly to the lore of Lincolnia in the junior field. No one has yet accomplished as much for the junior audience in writing about Franklin Delano Roosevelt as has Frances Cavanah in *Triumphant Adventure,* the story of FDR's personal and political triumphs and failures.

Though not aimed specifically at the junior audience, Ruth Painter Randall's books about the wives of famous men have attracted a following among adolescent girls. *I, Mary, I, Varina,* and *I, Elizabeth* are about, respectively, the wives of Lincoln, Jefferson Davis, and George Custer.

Shirley Graham has taken biographies of outstanding Negroes as her field, and from this effort has come one of the best junior biographies of Booker T. Washington, as well as some of lesser-known Negroes. Elizabeth Yates's Newbery prize-winning book on a Negro slave who purchased his freedom, *Amos Fortune, Free Man,* is appealing to pupils in the early junior high school, and her biography, *Prudence Crandall, Woman of Courage,* of a teacher who fought for the right of all to be educated, is of interest to older girls. Though Clara Ingram Judson's fine biographies are more appropriate for elementary school children than for adolescents, some of her books, such as *City Neighbor,* the story of Jane Addams, also are appropriate for the junior high school.

REPRESENTATIVE BOOKS

(Biographies discussed in the preceding chapter are marked with an asterisk [*]. Titles are annotated only if the nature of the content was not made clear in the chapter. [A] indicates adult biographies.)

Baker, Louise, *Out on a Limb*, McGraw-Hill. (A)
  A girl who loses a leg early in life learns to dance and swim and becomes a reporter.
Baker, Nina Brown, *Garibaldi*, Vanguard.
  Well-written story of the great Italian patriot. (Also *Juárez, Hero of Mexico*.)
Baker, Rachel, *The First Woman Doctor*, Messner.
  Elizabeth Blackwell overcame prejudice to enter the medical profession a century ago.
  (Also *Sigmund Freud*, Messner, and *Angel of Mercy*, about Dorothea Lynde Dix.)
Becker, May Lamberton, *Presenting Miss Jane Austen*, Dodd, Mead. (A)
Cavanah, Frances, *Triumphant Adventure*, Rand, McNally.
Chevigny, Hector, *My Eyes Have a Cold Nose*, Yale University Press. (A)
  Autobiographical account of conquering blindness with the help of a seeing-eye dog.
Curie, Eve, *Madame Curie*, Doubleday. (A)
  The amazing story of the discoverer of radium told by her daughter.
Davis, Sammy, Jr. and Boyar, Jane and Burt, *Yes I Can*, Farrar, Straus. (A)
  The struggles and beliefs of the Negro entertainer.
Eaton, Jeannette, *Trumpeter's Tale*, Morrow.
  (Also *Gandhi, Fighter without a Sword*.)
Elkon, Juliette, *Edith Cavell, Heroic Nurse*, Messner.
Frank, Anne, *Diary of a Young Girl*, Doubleday.
Garst, Doris Shannon, *Sitting Bull*, Messner.
  Exciting fictionalized story of the great Sioux chief. (Also *Buffalo Bill* and *Kit Carson*.)
Gollomb, Joseph, *Albert Schweitzer, Genius of the Jungle*, Vanguard.
Goss, Madeleine, *Beethoven, Master Musician*, Doubleday.
  The strange childhood and life of the great composer.
Graham, Frank, *Lou Gehrig, A Quiet Hero*, Putnam.
Graham, Shirley, and George Lipscomb, *Dr. George Washington Carver, Scientist*, Messner.

Greenfeld, Howard, *Marc Chagall, Follett.

Holt, Rackham, *George Washington Carver, Doubleday. (A)

Inouye, Daniel Ken, Journey to Washington, with Lawrence Elliot, Prentice-Hall. (A)

Autobiography of the first Japanese-American to become a U.S. Senator.

Judson, Clara I., *City Neighbor, Scribner.

Keller, Helen, Story of My Life, Doubleday. (A)

Famous story of Helen Keller and her teacher, Anne Sullivan Macy.

Kugelmass, J. Alvin, *Roald Amundsen, Messner.

(Also *Ralph J. Bunche: Fighter for Peace and *Louis Braille.)

Levinger, Elma E., *Galileo, Messner.

(Also *Leonardo daVinci.)

Malvern, Gladys, Curtain Going Up! Messner.

The career of Katherine Cornell to 1943.

Meigs, Cornelia, *Invincible Louisa, Little, Brown.

Miller, Floyd, The Electrical Genius of Liberty Hall: Charles Steinmetz, McGraw-Hill.

A readable treatment of Steinmetz' human and intellectual qualities.

Olsen, Jack, Black Is Best, Putnam. (A)

Subtitled The Riddle of Cassius Clay, the book describes the career of the controversial boxer and tells why he thinks "black is best."

Pace, Mildred, *Clara Barton, Scribner.

Randall, Ruth Painter, *I, Elizabeth, Little, Brown.

(Also *I, Mary and *I Varina.)

Russell, Bill as told to William McSweeney, Go Up to Glory, Coward-McCann. (A)

The great basketball star recounts the highlights of his career and comments on a variety of subjects including civil rights.

Severn, Bill, *Adlai Stevenson: Citizen of the World, McKay.

(Also *Mr. Chief Justice: Earl Warren.)

Strachey, Lytton, Elizabeth and Essex: A Tragic History, Harcourt. (A)

The dramatic story of Elizabeth I and Essex.

Syme, Ronald, African Traveler: The Story of Mary Kingsley, Morrow.

Miss Kingsley's unusual adventures in exploring Africa.

Trease, Geoffrey, *Sir Walter Raleigh, Vanguard. (A)

Warner, Oliver, Nelson and the Age of Fighting Sail, American Heritage.

A well-documented and readable narrative of the great British sea captain.

Weaver, John D., *Tad Lincoln, Dodd, Mead.

Wibberley, Leonard, *A Dawn in the Trees, Farrar, Straus.
Woodham-Smith, Cecil, *Lonely Crusader (Florence Nightingale), Mc-
  Graw-Hill.
Yates, Elizabeth, *Prudence Crandall, Woman of Courage, Dutton.

Collective Biography

Boynick, David, Champions by Setback, Crowell. (A)
  Inspiring short accounts of the careers of athletes who overcame ser-
  ious physical handicaps to become champions.
Briggs, Peter, Men in the Sea, Simon and Schuster.
  Biographies of nine pioneer workers in oceanography, with a chapter
  on the Alvin, the submarine that found the missing bomb in Spanish
  waters.
Gunther, John, Procession, Harper & Row. (A)
  Biographies of fifty world leaders of the past three decades.
Hirsch, Phil, Fighting Aces, Pyramid Books. (A)
  Twelve stories of famous combat airmen.
Porter, C. Fayne, Our Indian Heritage: Profiles of Twelve Great Leaders,
  Chilton. (A)
Rollins, Charlemae, They Showed the Way, Crowell.
  Sketches of the careers of forty outstanding Negroes.
Schaefer, Jack, Heroes without Glory, Houghton Mifflin. (A)
  The exploits of ten "good guys" of the Old West whose adventures
  are as exciting as the better known ones of the outlaws.
Shapiro, Milton, The Day They Made the Record Book, Messner.
  The exploits and records of Babe Ruth, Lou Gehrig, Don Larsen,
  Roger Maris, Maury Wills, Joe Dimaggio, and Sandy Koufax.

OTHER NONFICTIONAL PROSE

As noted earlier, the range of nonfictional prose is wide and has relevance to all areas of the school curriculum, not just to English or the
literature class. On a highly subjective basis the writer has decided to
include here discussion of two general categories of nonfictional prose
which he thinks especially appropriate for consideration in literature
programs—that concerned with personalized treatment of major historical events and that concerned with true adventure.

Personalized Views of Historical Events

The contributions in this category, though still highly limited and largely aimed to the general audience of readers, promise to form ultimately one of the more exciting genres of nonfiction for both junior and adult readers. A form of history, these books are also a form of personal, probably partly fictional, narrative as they bring to life from personal viewpoints the crucial moments of history. Their audience is largely the male one, adolescent and adult. Probably leading the way in this genre are Cornelius Ryan and Walter Lord, both treating major turning points of World War II.

Ryan's *The Longest Day* is an engrossing narrative of the first twenty-four hours of D-Day in Europe, told from the viewpoints of various Allied and German officers and soldiers, while his *The Last Battle* is a day-by-day chronicle based on eye-witness accounts of the twenty-one days prior to the fall of Berlin in 1945. Lord's *Day of Infamy* and *Incredible Victory* are similar approaches to, respectively, the Japanese attack on Pearl Harbor and the Battle of Midway, featuring both American and Japanese points of view.

What Lord does with the attack on Pearl Harbor, Carroll Glines does with the first bombing raid over Japan in *Doolittle's Tokyo Raiders* and Norman Polmar with the mysterious sinking of the atomic submarine *Thresher* in 1963 in *Death of the Thresher.*

The human interest approach to historical events is the basis also of a Messner series entitled *Milestones in History* which includes such titles as *Survival: Jamestown, After the Alamo, The Cloud over Hiroshima,* and *Disaster 1906: The San Francisco Earthquake and Fire.*

True Adventure

The period following World War II may well be cited in future literary history for the flowering of nonfictional prose. Certainly, the personal narrative of adventure, firmly rooted in the age-old longing to live dangerously, represents some of the finest in contemporary writing. The books of true adventure furnish a rich resource for the high school program in literature.

The true adventure narrative finds its earlier origins not only in the many adventure tales involving man against nature, but in such works as those by Izaak Walton and especially in *Walden* by Thoreau, works that explore the role of nature in the good life and its effects upon the personality of man.

Conquest of the sea, of the mountains, of the sky, or of remote and inaccessible places in general is the subject of a group of important true adventure books, beginning with Thor Heyerdahl's *Kon-Tiki* in 1950. Heyerdahl, a Danish anthropologist, and his associates made an amazing ocean voyage in a primitive craft to test a theory, and their exploit caught the public fancy. It is the underwater world, however, that has most challenged men's imaginations and ingenuity in recent years, and a number of books on undersea exploration have appeared. Jacques-Yves Cousteau and Frédéric Dumas, the authors of one of the finest of these, *The Silent World,* point out that since ancient times men have tried to penetrate the mysterious depths of the sea; even Leonardo da Vinci designed diving lungs—albeit they were somewhat impractical. Other superb books of undersea adventure are Philippe Diole's *The Undersea Adventure* and Hans Hass's *Diving to Adventure.*

The towering mountain peaks, long inaccessible to man, have always posed a challenge. Within very recent years the highest have finally been conquered. Probably the finest story of mountain climbing is Maurice Herzog's *Annapurna,* which describes the scaling of the giant Himalayan alp—at the time the highest peak ever climbed—a feat that permanently disabled Herzog. The feat, though not the book, was surpassed by an expedition commanded by Sir John Hunt, whose *The Conquest of Everest* records the ultimate victory in mountain climbing.

Adventure in remote places also has produced a long series of books. Of particular stature is Heinrich Harrer's *Seven Years in Tibet,* years in which the adventurer-writer became a sort of right-hand man to the fabulous Dalai Lama. Comparable is the account of a year spent among the Eskimos, *Kabloona* by Gontran de Poncias.

Superior books of personal adventure have certain elements in common with good fiction—exciting events, suspense, revelation of character, quality of style. Yet, as Gorham Munson points out, the fact that they are based on true experience gives them a stronger impact in disclosing man's great reserves of courage and resourcefulness, affording a catharsis to the reader even though the narratives of true adventure—unlike those of war—are romantic rather than tragic.[1]

What gives the true adventure narrative significance and what distinguishes the superior from the run of the mill? Why, in the first place, would a mature person want to climb a mountain when there is nothing but ice at the top, or plunge to the bottom of the ocean? Perhaps Maurice Herzog gives one of the most effective answers:

> Rocked in my stretcher, I meditated on our adventure now drawing to a close, and on our unexpected victory. One always talks of the ideal as a goal towards which one strives but which one never reaches. For every one of us, Annapurna was an ideal that had been realized. In our youth we had not been misled by fantasies, nor by the bloody battles of modern warfare which feed the imagination of the young. For us the mountains had been a natural field of activity where, playing on the frontiers of life and death, we had found the freedom for which we were blindly groping and which was as necessary to us as bread. The mountains had bestowed on us their beauties, and we adored them with a child's simplicity and revered them with a monk's veneration of the divine.
>
> Annapurna, to which we had gone emptyhanded, was a treasure on which we should live the rest of our days. With this realization we turn the page: a new life begins.
>
> There are other Annapurnas in the lives of men.[2]

In the books by Herzog, Cousteau, and Diole, for example, there is a nobility of motive, a symbolic value to their physical feats that invests them with significance, not just the thrill to be found, for instance, in the big-game hunting tales of Robert Ruark or Jim Corbett. The superior narrative of adventure makes clear the point of the experiences recounted, leading the reader to realize, with Herzog, that "events that seem to make no sense may sometimes have a deep significance of their own."

A maturity and sensitivity of style also distinguish the excellent adventure narratives. Again, Herzog, Diole, and Cousteau may be cited along with others such as Antoine de Saint-Exupèry and William O. Douglas. The following passage is an example:

[1] "High Up and Deep Down," *English Journal,* XLIII (December 1954), 481–487.

[2] Maurice Herzog, *Annapurna* (New York: Dutton, 1952), p. 311.

Like the sea, [the desert] reveals the depths of being within us. Through it, there is every chance of our arriving at a certain secret door within ourselves. From this threshold other inner landscapes appear before our eyes. When consciousness makes its way beyond this wall, it achieves the greatest of all transitions: the transplanting of the inner man.

It is here that the sea and the desert have an equal value, are one in their human significance. It is here that the spell of the Sahara and the spell of the ocean depths bring a richness and satisfaction to certain spirits that the charm of cities, the smiles of women, the sweetness of home cannot bestow. Is this the arrogance of choosing a bleak and naked destiny? The vanity of the hermit? I am not so sure of that. In these retreats into sparseness and solitude, these voluntary divestments of all that is extraneous, the same psychological alchemy is at work. There is always the question of a spiritual gain. The stake is the appropriation of the world by irrational means: a stake à la Rimbaud.

I have found again in the desert—or rather, I have brought to perfection there—the magic process by which, in the water, a diver is able to loose the ordinary bonds of time and space and bring life into consonance with an obscure inner poem: to bypass habit, language, memory. . . .[3]

Recent events have brought concern with adventures on social as well as physical frontiers. The Peace Corps, involving a great number of idealistic young people in educational missions in far-flung places, has resulted in at least two memorable books of interest for teenagers. In Earle and Rhoda Brooks' *The Barrios of Manta,* a young engineer and his teacher-wife describe their adventures among the poverty-stricken people of Manta, Ecuador. Leonard Levitt, a real individualist in the Peace Corps, tells in *An African Season* of his reception among the villagers of Tanganyika.

Books of true adventure can figure importantly in the high school program. The increasing prominence of nonfiction in contemporary literature makes it especially desirable to teach students to recognize excellence in this genre as well as in fiction. Selections of true adventure may be used along with fiction in units on the nonfiction of adventure by requesting permission from publishers to duplicate excerpts from such books, listed at the end of this chapter. Another

[3] Reprinted by permission of Julian Messner, Inc., from *Sahara Adventure* by Philippe Diole. Copyright September 27, 1956, by Julian Messner, Inc.

possibility is for all the students to read one of the true adventures together, using a paperback edition, and to read others from the library individually.

REPRESENTATIVE BOOKS

(All titles are of adult books. * Indicates those discussed in the text.)

Belfrage, Sally, *Freedom Summer*, Viking.
   The disturbing experiences of the author during a summer in Greenwood, Miss., as a SNCC worker.
Brooks, Earle and Rhoda, *The Barrios of Manta*, New American Library.
Conot, Robert, *Rivers of Blood, Years of Darkness*, Bantam.
   On-the-scene account of the events before, during, and after the 1965 Watts riots in Los Angeles.
Corbett, Jim, *Man-eaters of Kumaon*, Oxford.
   Hunting man-eating tigers in India.
*Cousteau, Jacques-Yves, and Frédéric Dumas, *The Silent World*, Harper & Row.
   Undersea exploration and salvage in the Mediterranean.
*DePoncins, Gontran, *Kabloona*, Reynal.
*Diole, Philippe, *Sahara Adventure*, Messner.
   Exploration by camel in the Sahara Desert. Poetic style. (Also, *The Undersea Adventure*, a classic of skin-diving, and *World Without Sun*, Harper, adventure in man's first underwater colony.)
DuFresne, Frank, *My Way Was North*, Holt, Rinehart and Winston.
   The twenty years of experiences in Alaska of a U.S. Biological Survey agent.
Glines, Carroll V., *Doolittle's Tokyo Raiders*, Van Nostrand.
*Harrer, Heinrich, *Seven Years in Tibet*, Dutton.
*Hass, Hans, *Diving to Adventure*, Doubleday.
Hersey, John, *The Algiers Motel Incident*, Bantam.
   Searing account of the incident in Detroit in which two young Negroes were shot by policemen.
*Herzog, Maurice, *Annapurna*, Dutton.
*Heyerdahl, Thor, *Kon-Tiki*, Rand McNally.
*Hunt, John, *The Conquest of Everest*, Dutton.
Levitt, Leonard, *An African Season*, Simon and Schuster.
Lord, Walter, *Incredible Victory*, Harper & Row.
   (Also *Day of Infamy*.)
Polmar, Norman, *Death of the Thresher*, Chilton.

Ryan, Cornelius, *The Last Battle, Simon and Schuster.
(Also *The Longest Day*.)
Saint-Exupéry, Antoine de, *Wind, Sand and Stars,* Harcourt.
Adventures of an aviator on three continents. Poetic and philosophical.
Scott, Robert, *Between the Elephant's Eyes,* Dodd, Mead.
A hunting story with a strange ending.
Tenzing, Norgay, and James Ramsey Ullman, *Tiger of the Snows,* Putnam.
The career of the Sherpa, Tenzing, who, with Edmund Hillary, reached the summit of Everest.
Wilkinson, Doug, *Land of the Long Day,* Holt, Rinehart and Winston.
Describes a year of living as an Eskimo.

INDEX

DATE DUE

MAY 23			
FEB 1 9			